W9-AYX-176

"From the depths of winter to the lushest summer day, there is always something fascinating for the New England naturalist to find. In *Naturally Curious*, Mary Holland takes the reader through a year in the Northeast, from the smallest insects and spring wildflowers to flocks of migrant birds, 'congresses' of breeding salamanders, and the natural antifreeze in a moose's feet—and it's all illustrated with her wonderful photographs. This book belongs on every woodswanderer's shelf."

—**Scott Weidensaul,** naturalist and author of *Of a Feather* and *Living on the Wind*

"The best way to learn about the natural world is to go outside and explore your own backyard, nearby woods and fields, and local streams and ponds. And it's even more fun when you can bring along an enthusiastic, experienced, and patient naturalist to show you all the wonderful organisms and phenomena you've been missing. *Naturally Curious* is like having Mary Holland with you on the best hike ever, in every month of the year. I wouldn't miss an opportunity like that!"

—**Lisa Purcell,** Director, Four Winds Nature Institute, and editor of *Hands-On Nature: Information and Activities for Exploring the Environment with Children*

"*Naturally Curious* is a delight to pore through. Rich in information and photographs, it gives readers a fascinating tour of many aspects of nature through a New England year. Mary Holland's book is one to refer to repeatedly."

—**Ernest H. Williams,** author of *The Nature Handbook* and the Christian A. Johnson Professor of Biology at Hamilton College

"The most curious aspect of *Naturally Curious*, is why no one has created this book before. Observing events in the natural world, and noting the dates of those occurrences, is a venerable pastime that is even more relevant in light of today's rapidly changing global climate. With clear text and superb photographs, Mary Holland gently guides students of nature to not only look at the natural world, but to actually see and document what is happening around us. This exquisite book engages us in a pleasurable pursuit that is also critical to documenting how human activity is transforming the dynamics of life on Earth."

—**Michael J. Caduto,** environmental educator, co-author of the popular *Keepers of the Earth® series,* and author of *Pond and Brook* (www.p-e-a-c-e.net)

"Mary Holland's journal is an inspiring window into New England's natural history. With great pictures and accessible narrative, *Naturally Curious* is a great read and an important home resource."

—**Ben Kilham,** naturalist and author of *Among the Bears*

"I love this book! *Naturally Curious* is the field guide to New England that I wish I'd been issued the moment I moved here. Now into my third decade exploring our fields, woods, and marshes, I found to my delight that Mary Holland has much to teach me. This is a wonderful, readable, fact-packed volume, full of stunning photos and dramatic stories. No nature library should be without it."

—**Sy Montgomery,** naturalist, documentary writer, and author of *Birdology; The Wild Out Your Window; and The Curious Naturalist*

NATURALLY CURIOUS

A Photographic Field Guide and Month-by-Month Journey
through the Fields, Woods, and Marshes of New England

MARY HOLLAND

Original Artwork by Chiho Kaneko

TRAFALGAR SQUARE
North Pomfret, Vermont

DEDICATION

To all who share my natural curiosity and lifelong sense of wonder.

First published in 2010 by
Trafalgar Square Books
North Pomfret, Vermont 05053

Printed in China

Library of Congress Cataloging-in-Publication Data

Holland, Mary, 1946-
  Naturally curious : a photographic field guide and month-by-month journey through the fields, woods, and marshes of New England / Mary Holland.
     p. cm.
  Includes bibliographical references and index.
  ISBN 978-1-57076-425-7
 1. Natural history--New England--Pictorial works. 2. Nature photography--New England. 3. New England--Description and travel. 4. Landscapes--New England--Pictorial works. I. Title.

  QH104.5.N4H65 2010
  508.74'0222--dc22

                    2010019919

All photos by Mary Holland *except:* pp. 40 *top left*, 42 *top middle*, 43, 78 *bottom left*, *right top and bottom*, 80 *right*, 81, 122, 123 *right top and bottom*, 129 *top left*, 161 *top right*, 162 *left top and bottom*, *middle and right bottom*, 164, 166 *left and right top*, 171 *left middle*, 198 *right top*, 199 *top left and top right*, 200 *bottom left*, *top right*, *and bottom right*, 202 *left*, 206 *top right*, 236 *top left and top right*, 237 *top left*, 238 *right*, 242 *bottom right*, 272 *left*, 278 *top left*, 311 *left*, 317, 333 *left bottom*, 365 *top middle and top right*, 375, 406 *left top and right top*, *right middle*, *right bottom*, 407 *right* (Mary Sue Henszey); pp. 38 *left*, 332 *top right*, 74 *bottom*, 117 *top left*, *bottom right*, 270 *right* (Jim Andrews); pp. 37, 304 *right*, 402 *top left* (Nicolas Arms); pp. 38 *right*, 158 *right*, 160, 234 *top right*, 235 *top right*, 271 *top left*, 332 *bottom right* (Kiley Briggs); pp. 39, 197 *left bottom* (Dan Foley); p. 184 *right* (Tom Wetmore); p. 416 (Susan Holland); p. 364 *top right* (B. Bond); p. 198 *left bottom* (J. Merrow).

Original artwork by Chiho Kaneko *except:* pp. 229 and 238 (Mary Holland).
Book design by Carrie Fradkin
Cover design by RM Didier
Typefaces: Scala Sans, ITC Century

10 9 8 7 6 5 4 3 2

Bear Tree

JENEPHER LINGELBACH

Blue sky and brutal cold,
We snowshoe trekked around and over ponds,
Looking, always looking,
For wildlife signs and finding
Tracks of different widths and depths.
From mouse with feet the size of apple seeds
That barely left a print,
To moose tracks so round and deep
Like stove pipes plunging in.

But it was a balsam tree
That held us mesmerized.
Shingles torn from bark,
Puncture wounds and gouges raked in lines,
Dried, curled splinters of wood
And then the hair.
One piece here, another there,
Caught by sunlight,
Seen only if you bent
And turned your head just right.

What does it matter that a bear has marked a tree?
It matters that there's more to life than you and me.

contents

✻Note: A colored ■ denotes a sidebar included here for quick reference.

Spring

Summer

JULY 157

AUGUST 195

SEPTEMBER 233

Fall

OCTOBER   269

NOVEMBER   303

DECEMBER   331

Winter

JANUARY   363

FEBRUARY 401

thoughts from a friend and fellow teacher

What does it take to be a fine writer, a superb photographer, and an excellent naturalist? It takes curiosity that may lead one beyond daylight, fatigue, and—some would say—safety. Since childhood Mary, with infinite patience and dogged determination, has followed, investigated, read about, and studied in depth, life in the natural world.

Mary is an ardent collector—bird nests, feathers, hornet nests, bones, skins, teeth, feet, tails, and scat. The shelves, walls, closets, and attic of her home are all mini-museums. To Mary, unlike most of the rest of us, a "road-kill" is a treasure, as it is an opportunity for study, or hopefully the source of a new skull for her collection.

Mary's adventures with wildlife are too many to mention, except, perhaps, for "The Bear." In Vermont, people lose bird feeders and suet to bears as a somewhat regular occurrence. In fall before hibernation, and in spring after emerging from hibernation, bears relish and often depend on the seeds and fat they steal. Mary had put up with days of empty, discarded feeders in the hopes of getting a glimpse of the hungry thief. When the bear brazenly came up onto the porch of her log cabin very early one morning and took off with a bird feeder in its mouth, Mary followed in hot pursuit, camera in hand. The result? Some remarkable photographs of the bear, asleep on pine branches, high above Mary's head.

Mary's interest is not limited to the extraordinary—she has spent hours photographing dragonflies emerging from their larval skins, cleaning skulls, studying differences between the hairs of different mammals, identifying bird songs, turning over logs in search of salamanders, examining the contents of scat from a variety of mammals, and looking for animal sign that provides information about the animal's life for those who may seek it.

There is nothing ordinary, however, about a walk in the woods with Mary. Trails you've walked a hundred times reveal their secrets. The invisible becomes visible. Mary's passion for and curiosity about the natural world knows no boundaries, and we are all the richer for it

JENEPHER LINGELBACH
Former Director of Education, Vermont Institute of Natural Science
Editor, Hands-On Nature: Information and Activities for Exploring the Environment with Children
Poet, Words like Leaves

NATURALLY CURIOUS

introduction

MOST PEOPLE LOOK SOMEWHAT ASKANCE at this passion of mine. There are beaver castor glands in my freezer, a fecal bear plug front and center in my prized living room cabinet, and a baculum (penis bone) collection right beside it. I have coexisted with snakes, lizards, a tarantula, turtles, frogs, toads, a skunk, orphaned mammals, birds, a hedgehog, and all types of insects at one point or another in my life. The natural world is an unending and constantly changing source of fascination for me—from the drip tips of a leaf to the barely audible cooing of a woodcock before it "peents." Every day of every season promises the potential of new discoveries. I am sharing some of those discoveries with you, between the pages of this book, in hopes that they will enrich your life as they have mine. *Naturally Curious* is compiled from firsthand observations, information gleaned from masters in the field, as well as from publications by biologists and naturalists more knowledgeable than I.

While the timing of seasonal phenomena—such as when wood frogs start singing, what month trilliums can be found carpeting the forest floor, or when the last ruby-throated hummingbird is likely to be seen at your feeder in the fall—isn't precisely the same every year, it is remarkably similar from year to year, often within a day or two of a given date in

any given location. Naturalists have been recording these types of observations for many years, and recently the study of the timing of these seasonally-occurring events, known as *phenology*, has received a great deal of attention, in part because it provides a window into the effects of global warming.

The exact timing of these natural phenomena varies in different locations due to climatic differences. Many factors affect an area's climate, including the temperature, amounts of precipitation, and day-length found at different latitudes and altitudes. On average, a given spring event, such as the migration of spotted salamanders to their breeding pools (see p. 3), occurs approximately one to four days later with each one-degree northward shift in latitude (about 70 miles), because of cooler temperatures. The reverse is true in the fall.

Altitude affects natural events in a similar manner; the flowering of specific plants sometimes occurs weeks later on top of a mountain than at its base. Temperatures can decrease as much as 3 to 5 degrees for every 1,000-foot increase in elevation; this is equivalent to a 200- to 300-mile northward change of latitude. While the temperature typically falls as the altitude increases, the amount of precipitation usually increases; as it rises and cools, air loses moisture. All of these factors affect the timing

Sample Weekly Natural History Calendar for Central Vermont
Latitude: 43.540N

These annual natural history events occur in central Vermont during the assigned calendar weeks. By comparing the relative latitude of any location within New England with that of this region, you can predict roughly when these events will occur in said location.

February Week 1	February Week 2	February Week 3	February Week 4	March Week 1	March Week 2	March Week 3	March Week 4
Red foxes breeding (listen for barking)	Black-capped chickadees singing spring song	Hairy woodpeckers drumming	Red-winged blackbirds and brown-headed cowbirds returning	Wood ducks returning	Brown creepers singing	Ruffed grouse drumming	Tree swallows, blue-winged teal returning
American black bears giving birth	Coyotes breeding (listen for howling)	Barred and great horned owls calling	Tufted titmice and mourning doves singing	Killdeer returning	Eastern screech-owls nesting	Belted kingfishers returning	American woodcocks displaying (aerial courtship)
Great horned owls nesting	American beavers breeding (peak)	Fishers leaving sign (due to approaching breeding season)	Ravens displaying (aerial courtship)	Male woodchucks emerging from hibernation	Waterfowl migrating (begins in earnest)	Eastern phoebes and great blue herons returning	Red-tailed hawks nesting
Eastern gray squirrels giving birth	Raccoons breeding	American beavers rambling on land (ice starting to melt)	Pileated woodpeckers drumming	Snow fleas appearing on warm days	Ermine molting white coat, growing in brown coat	Striped skunks breeding (peak)	American black bears emerging from hibernation
Stoneflies breeding	Northern flying squirrels breeding	Red squirrels breeding (peak)	Raccoons appearing during warm spells	Red-osier dogwood stems at their reddest	Eastern chipmunks coming aboveground	Sugar maple sap running	Pussy willows flowering

of the annual progression of natural phenomena throughout New England.

Data gleaned from scientific research such as bird banding, plant inventories, and state atlas projects documenting the dates and locations of reptile, amphibian, bird, insect, and plant sightings allow us to know the timing of many seasonal events in the Northeast. Records reveal that the occurrence of any given phenomenon may differ slightly from year to year, depending on a number of factors, but it is usually relatively predictable. Some events, such as the first call of a spring peeper (see p. 18), stretch over a period of days from southern to northern New England, but others, such as the return of the red-winged blackbird during the last week of February or first week of

This eastern newt (top) and spring peeper (bottom) are in a courtship embrace. The newt is delivering his pheromones to the peeper, in the misguided hope that mating will soon take place.

March (see p. 6), are surprisingly similar throughout the Northeast. The division of this book into monthly chapters allows for this discrepancy. Necessarily, there may be some overlap with the previous and following months of any given chapter, depending upon where the reader lives.

In the past, an awareness and understanding of nature's calendar was critical to human survival. Full moons afforded the opportunity for night hunting, the flowering and fruiting of plants provided much needed food at certain times of the year, the hatching of aquatic species of insects indicated the likelihood of successful fishing, and the migratory return of particular species of birds signaled that it was time to stop maple sugaring or start planting crops. While these events no longer play an integral part in the lives of most humans, awareness of them can provide a sense of connection with the earth that is unobtainable in any other way. The repetitive annual cycle of natural phenomena, such as the blooming of wildflowers, the singing of courting birds, and the emergence of hibernating

amphibians and reptiles, is one of the few things left in this ever-changing world that one can look forward to with any degree of certainty.

There is scientific proof, however, of the global impact of recent climate change on the phenology of plant and animal species. Analyses estimate an overall spring advancement of events such as butterfly, reptile, and amphibian emergence, as well as the return of migrating birds, of 2.8 days per decade across the Northern Hemisphere. However, the sequence, for the most part, remains the same, and an awareness of it affords everyone the opportunity to anticipate and enjoy these annual events. *Naturally Curious* attempts to provide their sequence, as well as their typical timing, and what I call "Nature Notes," charts, and short essays expand upon these phenomena, revealing how, where, and why they take place.

Hopefully this intimate look at the seasonal lives, activities, signs, and adaptations of plants and animals will foster a curiosity in, as well as a sense of stewardship of, the natural environment.

for the *Naturally Curious* reader

*In an effort to make the information contained in this book as accessible as possible to the reader, I've included the following User's Guide. The overriding intention of **Naturally Curious** is to familiarize the reader with the activities of different New England species as they are occurring over the course of a year, in the hopes that this information provides an incentive for, as well as guidance during, hikes and explorations out-of-doors. It is my greatest hope that this heightened awareness will promote a reverence for the earth and all its diversity.*

Why does *Naturally Curious* begin with the month of March?

Although our calendar year begins with January, the beginning of the progression of recurring natural phenomena over the course of a year seems to occur in March, when signs of life are becoming evident to even the casual observer.

What are "Nature Notes," and how and why were the subjects of the "Nature Notes" chosen?

A "Nature Note" is a brief summary of what a given species is doing at a particular time of year, or what animal sign you are likely to come across during the month in which it is written. There are six "Nature Note" categories in each month: *Amphibians, Reptiles, Birds, Mammals, Insects & Arachnids,* and *Plants & Fungi*. While every amphibian, reptile, and mammal found in New England (excluding marine life) has one or more "Nature Notes" written about it, there are "Nature Notes" about only some of the members of categories too large to cover in their entirety—birds, insects and arachnids, and plants and fungi. The selection of certain "Nature Note" subjects/species in a given month often has to do with the prevalence of the species and/or its activity that month. Occasionally, however, the selection is random, and has to do with my desire to cover each of the six categories every month, and as many of the animals in New England belonging to that category as possible.

Interspersed among the "Nature Notes" are charts, lists, and diagrams that provide quick-and-easy information regarding commonly asked natural history questions.

What happens in the section called "A Closer Look"?

While "Nature Notes" are brief summaries of one particular aspect of a given species or activity, each month also features "A Closer Look"—essays offering a broader and more in-depth examination of seasonally relevant subjects. This section includes an introduction to the topics of the month's essays, noted in bold with page references for ease of use. Each essay is accompanied by a list of pertinent "Fast Facts"—brief interesting nuggets of information about the subject that might be hard to find in other sources.

Why aren't species names capitalized?

Whether or not to capitalize the common names of species is not a hard-and-fast rule in the world of nature-writing. I chose not to do so within the text of *Naturally Curious* because it is a book to be read leisurely, as well as to be used as a field guide, and I feel this choice is less disruptive for the reader.

Why do some photographs appear to be out-of-season?

I took most of the photographs in this book—those I lacked but felt were essential were generously donated by the nature photographers listed on the copyright page (see p. iv). Occasionally photographs taken in one season are used to depict the species in another season, simply because a photograph of a species out of season is better than no photograph at all!

What's at the end of the book?

Rather than fill the main body of the book with hundreds of scientific names, I chose to (for the most part) list only common names in the "Nature Notes" and "A Closer Look" essays. On p. 435 you will find a complete list of all species included in this book, along with both their common and their scientific (genera and species) names.

In addition, along with a complete bibliography, you'll find a list of some of my favorite books and audio resources—these are the titles I've found helpful during my evolution as a naturalist. Now, I take the opportunity to recommend them to you.

"In order to capture the essence and beauty of nature, there must be an intimacy with it, not as an object, but as a process that is forever changing. The more you learn to see nature, to observe it with the quality of attention that is crucial to seeing, the more one is able to create works of art."

—FROM *WETLANDS: THE WEB OF LIFE* BY PAUL REZENDES

awakening

For several centuries the British parted ways with the Gregorian calendar and declared March 25 the first day of the New Year. This makes enormous sense to most natural historians, for March is the month of "awakenings," when the earth begins to thaw and life begins to stir after months of relative inactivity. Many hibernating mammals and amphibians resume their normal metabolism, mating seasons begin, a few flying insects appear, migrant birds return from their southern wintering grounds, sap flows in shrubs and trees, and the heat-generating skunk cabbage even blossoms. *March* is synonymous with *rebirth*—a new beginning for all living things.

nature notes

There are so many natural events taking place each month, it is difficult to choose a few to highlight. Nevertheless, here's a sampling of species that are emerging from hibernation, returning to breeding grounds, engaging in courtship, breeding, nesting, and flowering in March.

AMPHIBIANS

A wood frog calling (note his vocal sacs are inflated).

Wood Frog—*Breeding*
The wood frog, one of the earliest frogs to emerge from hibernation, digs itself up through the forest floor and migrates to a nearby temporary vernal pool where the male's duck-like courtship call can be heard reverberating through woodlands in the early spring. This process begins in March and usually peaks in April. Males, outnumbering females on an average of six to one, must compete aggressively for a mate. Soon after they arrive at the pool, they mate, often when there is still ice on the water. Males seek out females and grip them firmly around their abdomens from above. This mating clasp is referred to by biologists as *amplexus*. Occasionally you see several males attempting to grasp the same female, forming a "frog ball" with many extended legs.

The female wood frog lays up to 2,000 eggs in a clump, which she usually attaches to sticks or other vegetation under the water. Initially, this clump is roughly the size of a ping pong ball. The male, still clasping the female, then releases his sperm onto the eggs before letting her go. Within hours the "jelly" that encases each egg absorbs water and the cluster of eggs swells to the size of a grapefruit. After mating, the wood frogs return to the woods from which they came.

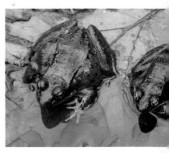
A female (left) and male (right) wood frog.

A "frog ball" of five males and one female.

■ Amphibians Breeding in March

Wood frog
Spring peeper
Spotted salamander
Blue-spotted salamander
Four-toed salamander
Jefferson salamander

Spotted Salamander—*Breeding*

The spotted salamander, along with the Jefferson, blue-spotted, and marbled salamanders, is a *mole salamander*. These salamanders live all their life under cover except for when they emerge to breed in temporary ponds early in the spring.

Spotted salamander.

Mating wood frogs and their eggs.

Many eggs must be laid in order for any to survive the next three weeks without being eaten by caddisfly larvae, eastern newts, leeches, or snapping turtles. Even though vernal pools, by definition, don't have fish inhabiting them, there are still many predators. Once tadpoles hatch, they spend the next two to four months eating algae and other vegetation until metamorphosing into four-legged, meat-eating adults. (Read about the adult wood frog in winter on p. 343.)

A vernal pool covered in wood frog eggs.

In the spring when the evening temperature reaches 45 to 50° F and rain continues from afternoon into the night, nocturnal spotted salamanders leave their subterranean environs and make their annual mass migration to the nearest temporary woodland pond or vernal pool. Pairs form and do a courtship "dance" in the water, after which the male deposits a packet of sperm called a *spermatophore* on the bottom of the pond. The female picks up the spermatophore with her *cloaca*, or reproductive cavity, and fertilization takes place. She then lays up to 250 eggs in up to 10 solid gelatinous masses before leaving the pond and resuming her life underground. (See sidebar, p. 4, and more about spotted salamanders on p. 20.)

Spotted salamander spermatophores.

Jefferson Salamander—*Breeding*

The Jefferson salamander is a relatively rare and elusive member of the mole-salamander family (which also includes spotted, blue-spotted, and marbled salamanders), and commonly hybridizes with blue-spotted salamanders. It can be found west of the Connecticut River in New England.

Jefferson salamander.

Jefferson salamanders hibernate on land—in upland forests often near the wetlands where they breed—either underground in burrows dug by other animals, or in rotting logs and stumps. Early in the spring, sometime between February and April (even before spotted salamanders—see p. 3), they crawl out of their hibernation sites and migrate—often over snow—to vernal pools and ponds, some of which are still partially covered with ice. Here they mate and lay their eggs. It is not uncommon to find cylindrical clumps of their eggs (usually about 30 per clump) attached to twigs or vegetation beneath the surface of the water.

Unlike spotted salamanders, which breed in large groups or "congresses," Jefferson salamanders mate in isolated pairs.

Blue-Spotted Salamander—*Breeding*

The blue-spotted and Jefferson salamanders resemble each other, both having relatively dark bodies speckled with tiny colored spots that are either light blue (blue-spotted) or white (Jefferson). These two species hybridize in New England (note: blue-spotted salamanders also hybridize with spotted salamanders in New England), making it necessary to check the color surrounding their respective *vent* (the reproductive/genital opening) in order to make a positive identification. The Jefferson salamander's vent is surrounded by gray, and the blue-spotted salamander's by black.

The blue-spotted salamander also stands apart

Blue-spotted salamander.

because of how it defends itself. When it senses danger, its tail lashes back and forth and produces a noxious secretion from two glands at its base. When the salamander's tail is grabbed, it "drops off" the salamander's body and continues wiggling, distracting the predator while the salamander escapes to safety. Eventually a new tail grows to replace the lost one.

■ How to Tell a Wood Frog Egg Mass from a Spotted Salamander Egg Mass

Wood Frog Egg Mass

Up to 2,000 eggs

Individual eggs smaller than those of spotted salamander

Entire egg mass not surrounded by layer of jelly (individual eggs are), giving egg mass a lumpy appearance

Spotted Salamander Egg Mass

Up to 250 eggs

Individual eggs larger than those of wood frog

Entire egg mass surrounded by thick, firm layer of jelly (as well as individual eggs)

REPTILES

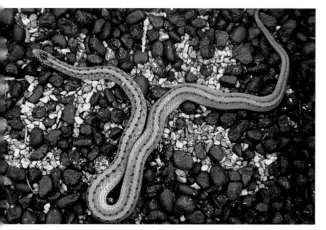

DeKay's brownsnake.

DeKay's Brownsnake—
Emerging from Hibernation and Breeding

The DeKay's brownsnake becomes active soon after the ground starts to thaw in late March or April. Because it is so cold-tolerant, it remains active until October or November, but you rarely see one. Not only is it well camouflaged (tan-colored) and only about a foot in length, it is also secretive and very good at hiding under flat rocks and logs. In addition, it is nocturnal and rarely out during the day.

Mating occurs from late March through May. The DeKay's brownsnake is *viviparous*—it can give birth to anywhere from 3 to 31 live young. Right after birth the 3½-inch-long young snakes stay close to their mother. At this age, they have a whitish-gray ring around their neck, which disappears by the time they're adults.

The DeKay's brownsnake is one of the few species of snake that thrives in heavily disturbed urban areas and is found in most major New England cities.

Wood Turtle—*Emerging from Hibernation, Breeding, and Laying Eggs*

The wood turtle is commonly considered strictly terrestrial, but research shows it is found as frequently in water as it is on land. It is often found basking on the banks of streams after it emerges from hibernation in March and April.

Wood turtles are surprisingly old when they begin to reproduce—well into their second decade of life. They breed from March through October (most frequently in May and June) in shallow areas of streams that have warmed up to 59°F or more. Wood turtles engage in fairly elaborate courtship behavior on land prior to mating in the water, with the male and female turtles approaching each other with neck extended, and then lowering their head and swinging it back and forth for up to two hours before breeding. Like all turtles, wood turtles seek sandy soil in which to bury an average of seven to eight eggs. However, the sex of wood turtle hatchlings is determined genetically, not by the temperature of the eggs as with some other turtle species (see p. 140).

Wood turtle.

BIRDS

MARCH

■ Birds Nesting in March

Bald eagle
Cooper's hawk
Rock pigeon
Barn owl
Eastern screech-owl
Barred owl
Long-eared owl
Gray jay

in late February and early March. His red and yellow *epaulets*, or shoulder feathers, are erected and prominently displayed as he hunches forward in song, claiming his territory and advertising for a mate. Males arrive first on their breeding grounds, establishing territories by the time the females appear in early April; breeding usually takes place in May. It is common for a male red-winged blackbird to mate with more than one female.

Turkey Vulture—*Returning Migrant*

Commonly referred to as the "buzzard," the turkey vulture gets its name from the red skin on its head and dark feathers on its body reminiscent of a turkey. The turkey vulture is well-adapted for its diet of decaying flesh, or *carrion*, in a number of ways. For example, while most birds have a poor sense of smell, the turkey vulture is a notable exception. The section of its brain responsible for process-

Turkey vulture.

Red-winged blackbird.

Red-Winged Blackbird—*Returning Migrant*

You know that spring is really on its way when the male red-winged blackbird's familiar "*konk-la-ree*" song bursts forth over marshes and open wetlands

ing odors is proportionately larger than that of other birds, enabling it to locate carrion with its keen sense of smell as well as its sight. In addition, the lack of many feathers on its head allows the turkey vulture to probe deep within the cavity of a decomposing animal. (See more about the turkey vulture on p. 283.)

American Woodcock—*Returning Migrant*

The American woodcock returns to New England in March, early in the month in southern New England, and toward the end of the month in the north. Look for it in wet areas where the soil has thawed and earthworms are available. It can grab hold of worms with its flexible-tipped beak. (Find out more about the woodcock on p. 60.)

American woodcock.

Killdeer—*Returning Migrant*

The most widespread and familiar American plover, the killdeer, is one of the earliest ground nest-

Killdeer.

ers to return to northern New England in the spring (it remains in southern New England throughout the year). Its call, *"kill-deer, kill-deer, kill-deer,"* is heard over open fields and pastures during March. While technically a shorebird, the killdeer has adapted well to humans and frequents parking lots and gravel rooftops as often as mudflats and gravel bars.

Tree Swallow—*Returning Migrant*

Like other members of its family, the tree swallow feeds on flying insects most of the year. Because it can subsist on fruit—particularly bayberry—when insects aren't available, it overwinters as far north as Long Island, New York—much farther north than any other swallow.

The tree swallow is the first swallow to appear on its breeding grounds in the spring. It is a cavity nester, using old woodpecker and other holes in

Tree swallow.

dead snags, as well as nest boxes provided by humans. Its nest usually contains feathers from other species of birds, including domestic chickens, which help keep the eggs warm.

The tree swallow is well known for its flocking behavior outside the breeding season; thousands may congregate in migratory flocks and at night roosts.

American Robin—*Returning Migrant*

The American robin, although considered a harbinger of spring in the Northeast, actually can be found throughout the year in much of its breeding range, including New England. But, because

American robin.

it is not searching for earthworms on front lawns in the winter, it is not as visible. Even in northern New England, some individual birds are permanent residents year-round, but these are the exception. In the spring, robins often return before the last of the snowstorms, and must rely on staghorn sumac berries and other fruits until the weather cooperates and it becomes possible to find earthworms. (See more about the American robin on p. 25.)

Eastern Screech-Owl—*Nesting*
The eastern screech-owl occasionally nests as early as March. It tends to nest in hollow trees but readily takes to nest boxes, adding little or no nesting material to the cavity.

Screech-owls are monogamous and mate for life. They engage in a fairly elaborate courtship display during which the male and female perch on a branch. The male bows, raises his wings, snaps his bill, and blinks at the female. He then brings her food, laying it on the branch near her as he hops and bows repeatedly. Pairs have been seen preening each other and have been heard calling together in a duet.

Screech-owls possess two common songs, neither of which is a "screech." One is a mournful, descending whistled "whinny," and the other a one-pitch whistled "trill," which often follows the whinny.

A gray-phase eastern screech-owl.

The eastern screech-owl can be one of two colors, *red* or *gray*, both of which can occur in the same brood.

Barred Owl—*Nesting*
One of the earliest species of birds to nest, the barred owl typically seeks out a tree cavity or an abandoned hawk nest, often that of a red-shouldered hawk, in which to lay its eggs. In fact, two nests found in different years contained incubated eggs of *both* barred owls and red-shouldered hawks *at the same time*. In one nest, barred owls were incubating, and in the other, a red-shouldered hawk was on the eggs.

Barred owl.

Barred owls often return to the same nest area year after year. In Massachusetts a set of barred owls, probably related, nested in the same pine woods for 34 years. (See more about the barred owl on p. 411.)

Ruffed Grouse—*Drumming*
The ruffed grouse is well known for the "drumming" sound (which somewhat resembles that of a lawn mower starting up in the distance) the male produces while standing on a fallen log, stone wall, or other raised surface. Although drumming occurs year round, it is most frequently heard in the spring, right after snow-melt (from March through May), when it is used to attract females and ward off other males. The drums are a series of progres-

Ruffed grouse.

peter—peter—peter," is repeated over and over, up to 11 times in succession, and begins to be heard with regularity in March. Occasionally female titmice sing; both male and female birds frequently utter fussy "scolding" notes.

The tufted titmouse mates until death or the disappearance of one pair member. It nests in May and June inside a natural tree cavity, an abandoned woodpecker hole, or occasionally in a man-made birdhouse. The cup nest frequently contains hair, fur, and the shed skin of a snake (see p. 318). Female titmice have been observed pulling hair for a nest from a live squirrel's tail, a woodchuck's back, and a man's head and beard.

Mourning Dove—*Nesting*

The mournful cooing of the mourning dove is a familiar sound in early spring, when territories are established and mates are sought. Although this bird was rare in New England at the turn of the century due to the pressure of extensive hunting, it is now a permanent resident throughout most of the region.

Mourning dove.

Nesting by these lifetime mates begins as early as March in some areas. During nest-building, the female stays at the nest and the male collects sticks. He returns and lands on the back of the female, then presents her with the material he has gathered, which she weaves into their rather flimsy nest. Once the two eggs are laid, the male usually incubates them from mid-morning until late afternoon; the female sits on them the rest of the day and night.

sively faster thumps created by air rushing to fill the vacuum the male creates under his wings when he rapidly flaps them in front of his body.

Tufted Titmouse—
Courtship Singing

Since the 1940s the tufted titmouse has expanded its range northward. Ornithologists attribute this range expansion to global warming, the

Tufted titmouse.

succession of fields into forests, and an increased number of bird feeders.

In the spring, paired titmice leave the mixed-species flocks in which they spend the winter and begin to defend their nesting territory. The titmouse's loud, clear, two-note whistle, "*peter—*

MAMMALS

■ **Mammals Emerging from Dormancy and Hibernation in March**

Striped skunk
Woodchuck
Eastern chipmunk

the delicacy of acorns and beechnuts. (See more on North American porcupines on p. 349.)

North American Porcupine—*Sign (Nip Twigs)*

A telltale sign of porcupines is a forest floor littered with the short tips of eastern hemlock branches. If you look closely at the cut end of the branch, you can see the marks made by the porcupine's inci-

Porcupine sign: hemlock nip twigs on the forest floor.

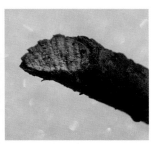

The end of the nip twig shows marks of porcupine incisors.

sors. Typically the porcupine, rather than risk falling by trying to reach the slender tips of branches where the choicest leaves, seeds, and nuts are found, remains on the more solid part of the branch, closer to the trunk. From this relatively safe spot it nips off the tip of the branch, consumes the edible parts, and drops the uneaten portion onto the ground.

In winter, hemlock leaves are considered choice. In the spring, red maple, red oak, and aspen buds are sought after. During the summer, porcupines may consume herbaceous ground plants, as well as leaves and buds in the canopy, while fall offers

Bobcat—*Sign (Tracks)*

Primarily nocturnal, solitary, and elusive, the bobcat deserves its reputation as "phantom of the forest." Although we rarely see a bobcat, its tracks can be found throughout the winter when it is active in

Bobcat.

the day as well as night. The overall shape of the front track of a member of the feline family is round (a canine's is more oval-shaped); its hind feet are oval and look more like those of a coyote. Although the bobcat has five toes on each front foot (four on the hind feet), only four usually register in its

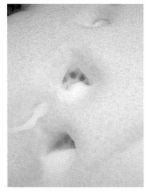

Bobcat tracks.

tracks, as the fifth is raised up on the leg. Its nails are retractable, and therefore often do not make an impression in the snow.

Look for signs such as tracks and scent posts during the months of February and March, when most bobcat breeding takes place and they are

MARCH

▪ Comparing Sign: White-Tailed Deer and Snowshoe Hare

Even if there are no tracks evident, it is quite easy to determine whether a white-tailed deer or snowshoe hare (or cottontail rabbit) has been eating the branches of a nipped shrub or tree. Due to its lack of upper front teeth, a deer grips the branch in its mouth and rips the tip off, leaving a messy, shredded end. The snowshoe hare, with its six incisors (two on the bottom jaw and four on the top, with two tiny incisors behind two larger ones) make a clean, 45-degree-angled cut. (See more about comparative animal sign on p. 420.)

Twig eaten by a white-tailed deer.

Twig eaten by a snowshoe hare.

especially active. You may even hear the shrill screams, harsh squalls, and deep-toned yowls that often accompany mating.

Red squirrel drinking sap tapped from a maple.

Red Squirrel— *Tree Tapping*

The red squirrel has a definite sweet tooth—in the spring, it commonly bites into sugar maples, allowing the sap, which is 2 percent sugar, to run. After it has dried, the squirrel returns to lick the dried sap, which—due to evaporation—is now 55 percent sugar.

Ermine and Long-Tailed Weasel—*Molting*

The replacement of the weasel's white winter coat begins in March, with only a few brown hairs appearing at first. Whereas in the fall the white hairs progress up its sides and then onto its back, the spring molt occurs in reverse, beginning on its back and then moving downward over its sides to its belly. By the end of April, weasels—both short- and long-tailed (short-tailed are also known as ermine)—have their full brown summer coat. (See more about molting, on p. 290.)

Eastern Chipmunk— *Breeding*

In early spring male chipmunks waken, emerge from their tunnels, and seek out a breeding partner. When a female in heat is located, males tend to congregate in her territory and indicate their readiness to mate by flicking their tail up and down. A frenzied chase

Eastern chipmunk.

ensues, accompanied by many vocalizations on the part of the males. When the dominant male catches up with the female, breeding takes place. Timing is everything, as the female is receptive for a total of only six-and-a-half hours. (See more about eastern chipmunks on p. 288.)

Woodchuck—*Breeding*

The woodchuck, or "whistle pig" as it is called because of the whistle it gives when alarmed, is the largest member of the squirrel family in New England. The woodchuck does not store food, nor does it waken periodically throughout the winter to eat. Rather, it is a "true hibernator," depending on the fat it puts on during the summer (up to a third of its body weight) to sustain it through the winter.

In late February or March, the male emerges from his woodland winter burrow and seeks out a female, who remains in her burrow. (Emergence dates vary and are about one

The entrance to a woodchuck burrow marked by a mound of dirt.

day later for each 10 miles of latitude, given comparable altitudes.) Look for dirt-laden paths leading from one tunnel to another in the snow.

Many species—including skunks, foxes, Virginia opossums, raccoons, cottontail rabbits, and mice—seek shelter in abandoned woodchuck burrows.

Striped Skunk—*Breeding*

The striped skunk wakes periodically throughout the winter, particularly during mild spells, but for the most part, it remains in a deep sleep, emerging in February or March to breed. At this time the males are out and about, searching for mates, and their tracks—and scent—are noticeable. Skunks are

Striped skunk.

polygamous, and while their breeding season lasts from mid-February through mid-April, the majority of mating takes place during the third week of March. Four to eight young are born in May or early June. The striped skunk possesses musk at birth, and can spray when it is eight days old.

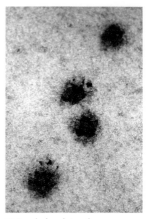

Striped skunk tracks.

American Mink—*Breeding*

The mink is considered one of the more robust members of the weasel family, appearing restless, curious, and bold to human observers. It is larger than both ermine and long-tailed weasels, and unlike them, it does not grow a white winter coat, but remains brown year-round.

A mink doesn't hesitate to prey upon animals that are much larger than itself. It is known to cache food and only eat it when the need arises—13 muskrats, two mallards, and an American coot were once discovered in a mink den 6 feet up in a hollow tree.

Mink breed from late February to early April, peaking in March. Males travel

American mink tracks.

great distances looking for mates, often along waterways, and have even been known to swim under the ice. During breeding both sexes have been heard making "chuckling" vocalizations.

Look for mink along streams, lakes, and marshes, where they prey on everything from fish and frogs to moles and muskrats. When pockets of water first open up in the spring, muddy mink tracks are often visible on nearby snow.

Gray Fox—*Breeding*

The gray fox has extended its range northward and is found throughout New England today, except for northern and eastern Maine. This range extension corresponds to the extension of the cottontail rabbit, a favored prey.

Gray fox.

The gray fox is distinguishable from the red fox (see p. 415) by the color of the tip of its tail— black on a gray fox and white on a red fox. The most unusual attribute of the gray fox is its agility in trees. When hunting prey or escaping enemies, it is common for this canid to shinny up the trunk of a tree to a limb, and ascend further by jumping from branch to branch.

Mating takes place between mid-January and May, peaking in March. From the breeding season through late summer, gray foxes live in family units, consisting of an adult male and female and their young.

North American River Otter—*Breeding*

River otters breed in March and April, soon after they give birth. Copulation usually takes place in the water, and the female can be quite noisy during coupling, caterwauling for all she's worth. She may mate several times over a period of several days. Delayed

North American river otter.

embryo implantation (it is present in her body, but is not immediately implanted in the uterus) is responsible for an 11-month gestation period.

The river otter is the most aquatic member of the weasel family and also the most social. When not busy catching and eating fish, frogs, crayfish, turtles, snakes, and birds, it can often be found engaging in playful antics with another otter, sliding down steep grass-, mud-, or snow-covered slopes. The 6- to 10-inch-wide grooves it creates when sliding on its stomach are unmistakable.

Fisher—*Breeding and Giving Birth*

The breeding season for fishers peaks in March, and there is a surge in male fisher activity at this time. Fisher sign is prevalent in the woods they inhabit

Fisher.

Fisher scat containing quills and foot pads of a North American porcupine.

Red Fox—*Giving Birth*

Young red foxes are born in March or April. Earlier in the year the mother locates and cleans several dens, eventually choosing one of them for giving birth to and raising her young. It is often situated on a wooded hillside in sandy, soft soil, close to an open area, and frequently there is a source of water within 300 feet. There are usually several entrances, the largest measuring no more than about 10 inches in diameter. Generations of foxes may use the same den for many years.

The female fox remains in the den for approximately 10 days, a few days before and several after giving birth, while her mate brings her food. During the time the female remains with her young (usually around five per litter) in the den, she wraps her body around them in order to keep them warm.

When red fox pups are born, the white tip of their tail can already be seen. By the time the pups' dark gray insulating coats grow in, their mother is already going on forays outside the den. At about five weeks of age her young will also venture outside. (For more about red foxes and the mating rituals of mammals, see pp. 26 and 415.)

this time of year. Look for their tracks, scat, and scent posts. Often the area all around the sapling chosen as a scent post is packed down (see p. 421).

March and April are extremely busy months for female fishers, for they give birth as well as mate. After a 10- to 11-month delay in embryo implantation (similar to the otter, the embryo is present but not immediately attached to the uterus), two or three young are born, often in a nest located in a cavity in a large, hollow tree. Roughly 10 days after giving birth, the mother leaves the den to mate. She returns and for the next five months, until they disperse, she raises her young by herself. (See more on fishers on p. 29.)

Red fox den.

INSECTS & ARACHNIDS

Mourning Cloak Butterfly—
Emerging from Hibernation

Mourning cloaks were so-named because of the velvety, crepe-like consistency of their dark purplish-brown wings, and their resemblance to clothes traditionally worn by mourners. Because they overwinter as adults, protectively hidden under loose tree bark, and because they have no metamorphosis to undergo, mourning cloaks are one of the first butterflies to be observed in the spring. They emerge from hibernation on the first warm days of March and can be observed drinking from injured tree branches, especially oaks, where they walk down the trunk of the tree to the sap and drink, head downward. They also feed on rotting fruit, and occasionally, flower nectar.

Mating takes place and the females lay their eggs on willow, cottonwood, elm, and birch trees,

Mourning cloak butterfly.

where their larvae, known as spiny elm caterpillars, have a readily available supply of food. These nomadic foragers typically line up side by side, with their heads aligned along the edge of the leaf as they eat. When disturbed, they all rear up on their back legs and shake.

Mourning cloaks have a lifespan of up to 10 months or more—a very long life for a butterfly.

PLANTS & FUNGI

■ Wildflowers Blooming in March

Skunk cabbage

Red-osier dogwood.

Red-Osier Dogwood—*Stems Changing Color*

Red-osier dogwood likes to keep its "feet" wet and is usually found growing in swamps, ditches, or on the edges of ponds and marshes. Its red stems and branches, as well as its "opposite" branching pattern (see sidebar, p. 16), help identify this shrub. In March, the branches of red-osier dog-

■ Flowering vs. Non-Flowering Plants

Flowering plants are referred to as *angiosperms*. They, as well as *gymnosperms* (conifers), are seed-producing plants. The characteristic feature of angiosperms is the flower. The purpose of a flower is to achieve pollinaton, so that a seed-containing fruit can develop.

Non-flowering plants, as their name implies, do not produce flowers, and consequently, do not produce fruit. They are some of the oldest plants on earth, and are generally simpler than flowering plants. Reproduction is achieved through spores.

Flowering Plants
Grasses
Maples
Oaks
Orchids

Non-Flowering Plants
Ferns
Horsetails
Liverworts
Mosses

LEAF/BRANCHING ARRANGEMENT

Trees and shrubs have three possible leaf and branching patterns: *alternate, opposite,* and *whorled.* By determining which pattern a tree has, you can narrow down the number of possible species it could be. The vast majority of deciduous trees have *alternate* leaf and branching arrangement, where one leaf or branch appears along a limb at any given spot, usually on alternate sides of the limb (oaks, birches, and hickories, for example). The leaves/branches of trees with *opposite* branching (such as maples, ashes, and dogwoods) appear opposite one another along a limb. Trees with *whorled* branching have three or more leaves/branches appearing at the same level on a limb (white pine is one example).

Opposite branching.

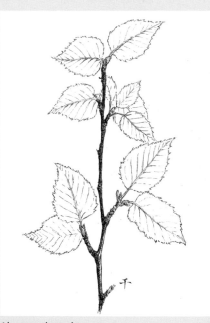

Alternate branching.

Whorled branching.

wood often appear brilliant red, due to the presence of a red pigment called *anthocyanin*, which is sensitive to light. The more intense the light, the redder this plant becomes. Thus, in early spring, before its leaf buds have opened, the red-osier dogwood branches are at their brightest.

Staghorn Sumac—*Providing a Food Resource*

This member of the Cashew family provides a great service to wildlife in winter and early spring,

Staghorn sumac fruit.

when food can be scarce and tiny red seeds still cling to its branches. Although not a first choice, sumac fruit is eaten by nearly 100 species of birds when other more desirable food is not available, particularly during the last half of winter. These include American robins, European starlings, wild turkeys, and ruffed grouse. Cottontail rabbits and white-tailed deer frequently feed on the bark, branches, and fruit of this plant, and many insects overwinter inside its clusters of hairy seeds.

Scarlet Cup Fungus—*Fruiting*

One of the very first bright colors seen in the spring is the scarlet cup fungus, often found growing on the ground in maple woods. The fruiting body of this particular fungus grows in the shape of a cup, which typically serves to catch raindrops that splash spores out and spread them. The curving sides enable wind to blow the spores out, as well.

Staghorn Sumac Lemonade

INGREDIENTS

2 quarts water

1 cup staghorn sumac berries

A cinnamon stick and/or cloves (optional)

A touch of maple syrup or honey (optional)

Cheesecloth or drip coffee filter

PROCEDURE

▶ Rinse seedheads and drain on a towel.

▶ Fill a container with cold water.

▶ Put sumac seeds and spices in water.

▶ Set aside at room temperature or in the sun for one to two hours.

▶ Remove berries and spices, and strain liquid through cheesecloth or coffee filter.

▶ Sweeten with maple syrup or honey.

(Note: Confirm the identity of staghorn sumac before consuming it, as it has close relatives that are inedible, including poison sumac.)

Scarlet cup fungus.

a closer look

Some signs of spring are so subtle you may not be aware of them, and others are so obvious they cannot be missed. Warm, wet spring nights usher in silent **spotted salamanders** (p. 20) under cover of darkness, returning migrant **wood ducks** (p. 22) seem to magically appear on ponds and lakes, and an examination of vernal pools may reveal the presence of **fairy shrimp** (p. 32). However, the vocal courtship of **spring peepers** (see below) loudly proclaims the arrival of spring, as do the passionate screams of **mammals mating** (p. 26), including **fishers** (p. 29), in the middle of a March night. Flowering **skunk cabbage** (p. 33) braves the cold days and nights, providing insects with shelter and some degree of warmth, and thanks to a variety of fruit, **American robins** (p. 25) survive until earthworms appear. The following pages present a closer look at each of these March phenomena—subtle and obvious, silent and shrill.

Spring Peepers—*Mighty Minstrels*

When the night air no longer dips below 40°F, and a gentle rain falls on the forest floor, certain hibernating amphibians begin to stir. Along with wood frogs, spring peepers are among the first woodland frogs to dig themselves out of their subterranean quarters. Heeding the urge to mate, they make their annual spring woodland migration to the nearest body of water. A single high-pitched piping whistle pierces the air. It is repeated roughly once every second. A second one joins it, then a third. Numbers continue to increase over the next few nights until a deafening chorus of shrill peeps emanates from the edge of the pond and spring is officially heralded in.

Curiosity may draw you to the pond, but as you approach the site, silence will ensue. There is literally not a "peep" from the

The spring peeper blends well with the leaf litter where it spends much of its time.

source of the overwhelming sound present moments ago. With patience, if you know where to look and what to look for, you will eventually see one or more of the tiny vocalists. In ground vegetation or perhaps a foot or two up in a shrub or tree near the edge of the pond sits a male spring peeper, only three-quarters of an inch from one end to the other. Along with his brethren he spends night after night serenading potential mates. When engaged in this endeavor, he takes air into his lungs, closes his mouth and nostrils, and pumps the air from his lungs back and forth over his vocal cords and into the loose skin under his chin. This loose skin fills with air every time he calls, creating a balloon-like pouch, or vocal sac, which acts as a resonating chamber,

Small, rounded discs on the end of each toe enable the spring peeper to adhere to vertical structures. Often a distinct "X" can be seen on a peeper's back.

amplifying his call. Locating this shiny quarter-size vocal sac inflating and deflating is one of the easiest ways to locate a singing peeper.

Different Calls, Different Messages

Female frogs are more or less silent. Male frogs do all the singing and different messages are conveyed with different calls. The call we associate with peepers—the high-pitched whistle that slurs upward at the end—is used by a male to attract a mate. According to biologists, each male repeats this call about 4,500 times a night during the breeding season. From a distance this chorus has been likened to the pleasant sound of sleigh bells, but up-close-and-personal it can be absolutely mind-numbing, it is so loud. Apparently, female peepers have no trouble hearing and distinguishing one peeper's peep from another, but—as unbelievable as it sounds—it is thought that male peepers *may not even hear* other males' calls.

In addition to the high-pitched whistle call that attracts a mate, the male peeper makes a distinctive lower-pitched trilled whistle when another male has moved too close to his territory. Other calls include those for defense, those given just prior to *amplexus* (or mating), and those telling one male frog that he's mistakenly grasping another male frog.

Annual Migration

Peepers spend most of the year inhabiting the forest floor. It's where they look for spiders, mites, ticks, and a variety of insects to eat throughout the summer and fall, and it's where they dig down below the frost line and hibernate, come winter. The one time they all leave the forest floor is in early spring when they make their annual migration back to their breeding ponds to mate and lay eggs. Peepers aren't fussy about the bodies of water that serve as their mating grounds—they frequent ditches, beaver ponds, marshes, vernal pools, bogs, wet meadows, swamps—any place that provides their eggs and tadpoles with at least three months' worth

of water. At the end of mating season, peepers leave the ponds and return to the woods.

Amplexus

While most salamanders have internal fertilization (the male deposits packets of sperm on the bottom of the pond, which the female then picks up into her body), most frogs and toads accomplish this externally. After attracting a female, the male peeper climbs on top of her and clasps her behind her front legs, around her belly. Herpetologists refer to this coupling as *amplexus*. While both frogs are locked together, they dive to the bottom of the pond where the female deposits 800 to 1,000 eggs one by one on vegetation as the male releases his sperm.

Spring peepers mating.

A few days later the eggs hatch and tiny tadpoles emerge. Within roughly three months these legless, plant-eating tadpoles transform into four-legged, insect-eating froglets that abandon the pond for the forest—until next spring.

"X" Marks the Spot

It is fairly easy to recognize a spring peeper when you see it. In addition to its small size (the female spring peeper measures up to an 1½ inches), it has a distinctive dark "X" mark on its back. No other New England frog is similarly marked. The peeper's mottled skin serves to camouflage it very well in leaf litter, and it can even change color from light tan to dark brown within just a few minutes to enhance this cryptic coloration. Each toe ends in a round, flattened disc or pad, which adds surface tension through mucous secretions, thus enhancing the frog's ability to climb vertical surfaces.

Spring isn't truly here until these mighty minstrels announce their arrival throughout our wetlands. If you should somehow miss this proclamation, don't despair, for although they aren't breeding, a few individuals resume their vocalizations in the fall, when climatic conditions are similar to spring. You will have a second, albeit brief, opportunity to hear them before cold weather ushers in their silence.

Spotted Salamanders—
A Midnight Mating March

There are many sights and sounds in the natural world that we humans anticipate, observe, and celebrate every spring. Year after year, the first red-winged blackbird's *"konk-la-ree,"* the first "quacking" courtship call of the wood frog, or the shrill peep of the spring peeper are welcome harbingers of spring. Even if our eyes don't spot the creatures making these pronouncements, our ears alert us to their presence. All these calls are precursors to procreation—love songs, as it were, that capture *our* attention as well as that of potential mates.

But not all spring courtship rituals involve such loud proclamations of love and, as a consequence, are much more secretive. One such ritual takes place under cover of darkness, in total silence, and, for the most part, on one given night. As a result, this event often escapes notice by most humans. It is the annual mass migration of a group of amphibians known as spotted salamanders to their ancestral breeding pools—a most magical event.

"Big Night"
"Big Night," as it's referred to by herpetologists, is actually fairly predictable, although it rarely occurs on the same date every year. On the first or second consecutive rainy night that reaches 45 to 50°F in late March or April, hundreds—in some locations *thousands*—of subterranean-dwelling, 6- to 9-inch shiny black salamanders with bright yellow spots awake from hibernation, crawl up out of the soil onto the forest floor, and begin their annual trek to the nearest pool, up to several hundred yards away, in order to breed. Although this process extends over a two-week period, the majority of spotted salamanders migrate on the first night. Every year each pool attracts the same individuals, plus the prior year's offspring. Generations of salamanders have repeated this ritual for thousands of years; a

Spotted salamanders are the largest members of the "mole" salamander family, so-called because of their subterranean existence in shrew, mole, or mouse tunnels. Usually the only time they come aboveground is in the spring, when they perform their annual spring migration and mating ritual. The spotted salamander in this photograph is a gravid female, heavy with eggs.

given salamander may make this same trip as many as 20 times in its lifetime.

Poolside Courtship

Spotted salamanders do not breed and lay their eggs in just any woodland pond or puddle; they are actually quite selective. The sites they choose are temporary bodies of water that usually dry up by mid-to-late summer. These *vernal pools* are essential to the continuation of several species of amphibians in addition to the spotted salamander, including the Jefferson salamander, the blue-spotted salamander, and the wood frog. These creatures rely on a fish-free environment in which to lay their eggs, as the lack of such aquatic predators gives their eggs, as well as their larvae, a fighting chance of survival. In fact, they are so dependent on vernal pools that their life cycles have evolved around the brief viability of such temporary watering holes, and breeding, egg-laying, and larval development must all occur within just a few months.

The male spotted salamander's arrival at the pool usually precedes the female's by at least a few hours. When they first arrive, males tend to form congregations of anywhere from 12 to 100 salamanders. These groups are called "congresses." Essentially they are writhing balls of slithering male salamanders weaving in and out and around each other. Every so often a single male will exit the congress for the express purpose of mating with a nearby female.

The newly-formed pair perform a courtship dance, circling each other on the pond bottom, placing their head under each other's tail as they do so. The male often climbs onto the female's back and repeatedly rubs his chin against her. Eventually he attempts to lure his chosen mate away by wiggling the tip of his tail enticingly as he swims in the direction of a sperm packet, or *spermatophore,* which he has previously deposited on the bottom of the pool. If he is successful, the female will straddle the spermatophore and pick it up with her *cloaca* (or vent), allowing her eggs to be fertilized internally. She then departs, possibly to collect other males' spermatophores, and he heads back to his congress in hopes of finding another "dance partner."

Metamorphosis

Even if you miss the night of migration and there are no signs of spotted salamanders or their spermatophores in a vernal pool, upon inspection, you may find one or more masses of up to 250 salamander eggs attached to grass stems or branches at the bottom of the pool. When the female lays her eggs, each mass is about 2 inches in diameter, but it often swells to more than twice this size once in the water. Each egg is enclosed in a sphere of jelly about the size of a marble; the entire cluster of eggs is also enclosed in one big gelatinous envelope. At times, algae can turn the salamanders' egg masses green and the presence of a certain type of protein can cause the eggs to turn white.

] FAST FACTS [
Spotted Salamander

▸ Spotted salamanders tend to arrive at a pool in the same order each year.

▸ They usually leave a pool near the same point where they enter.

▸ Each female lays up to 10 egg masses a year.

▸ An alga develops within the egg masses, which scientists feel benefits the developing larvae—they develop faster if it is present.

▸ The time it takes spotted salamander eggs to hatch decreases as their temperature rises.

▸ Spotted salamander larvae are voracious predators, eating everything from midges and mayfly nymphs, to fairy shrimp and caddisfly larvae.

▸ Predators of spotted salamander larvae include dragonfly and damselfly nymphs.

▸ When spotted salamanders breed in bodies of water that *do not* dry up in the late spring and summer, their larvae may overwinter instead of metamorphosing into adults in the summer or fall.

▸ Juvenile spotted salamanders leave the pool where they developed when it is raining.

▸ During non-breeding times of the year, spotted salamanders frequent subterranean rodent and shrew burrows.

▸ Individuals can be recognized by the pattern of their spots.

▸ The diet of adults consists mainly of earthworms, snails, slugs, insects (especially larval and adult beetles), and spiders.

▸ Spotted salamanders continue to grow throughout their adult lives.

▸ The adult life span can exceed 18 years.

The eggs hatch in approximately one month and gilled larvae emerge. One to four months later, the larvae metamorphose into juvenile spotted salamanders equipped with lungs that allow them to leave the pool and begin their largely subterranean life.

Wood Ducks—*Daredevil Ducklings*

As March progresses there is much to look forward to that has been either hidden under snow or absent from New England during the winter months. Male American woodcocks will soon spiral upward in the sky as they attempt to impress potential mates. Male woodchucks will wake up and leave their burrows in search of females still fast asleep in theirs. For most creatures, spring is a time to seek a mate, but some birds, including wood ducks, form couples in the fall or on their wintering grounds and return to our forested wetlands as mated pairs.

"Rainbow Iridescence"
Listen for the loud *"oo-eek, oo-eek,"* call of the female wood duck when she takes flight after being disturbed. You may not see her, as she is well camouflaged. It is typical in the bird world for the male to have more colorful plumage than the female, and wood ducks could well be the "poster birds" for this rule. If you've seen a male, or drake, wood duck, it is not a sight you are likely to soon forget. Feathers in metallic shades of red, orange, yellow, green, and blue cover his entire body—Roger Tory Peterson aptly refers to "rainbow iridescence" in his *Field Guide to Birds of North America* (Houghton Mifflin Harcourt, 2002). Even the drake's bill is multi-colored. The female? She is drab brown with a slight hint of blue on her wings. Of course, this makes perfect sense, for it is the female alone that incubates their eggs for the month that it takes them to hatch. She generally leaves the eggs twice a day to feed and is far less conspicuous going to and from her nest with this coloration.

Thanks to the Beaver

Wood ducks leave their more southern North American habitats and arrive back in New England in March. Look for them near streams, marshes, swamps, and beaver ponds. Wood ducks may, in fact, have beavers to thank for bringing them back from a sharply declining population in the late 1800s. They were overhunted and forested wetlands disappeared rapidly. But as the beaver population rebounded, more and more beaver ponds were created, providing wood ducks with ample habitat in which to nest and rear young.

Home is a Hollow Tree

The wood duck's common name reflects the location of its nest, for wood ducks are one of only seven North American waterfowl species that regularly nest in tree cavities. (They also nest readily in man-made wood duck houses, if available.) The female's slim body allows her to also take advantage of old pileated woodpecker holes, as well as the smaller holes of northern flickers. Wood ducks are known to reuse nesting cavities in successive years; in 1840, John J. Audubon found a wood duck nesting in the same abandoned ivory-billed woodpecker nest for a third consecutive year.

After investigating several potential nesting sites, the female wood duck chooses one (often over or close to water) and proceeds to pluck feathers from her breast to provide her eggs with a soft, insulating bed. She then lays 6 to 10 eggs and incubates them for the next 30 days or so. The hooded merganser, another cavity-nesting duck, has been known to share a nest with a female wood duck, with the two females taking turns incubating all the eggs.

An Early Leap of Faith

One thing that sets wood ducks apart from all other North American ducks is their ability to produce two broods (sets of offspring) in one breeding season in southern New England, where the breeding season is long enough to sustain this practice. There is something else that every wood duck does once in its life that few other birds do so dramatically, and it has to do with *fledging,* or leaving, its nest.

The cavities in which the young, *precocial* (born covered with down and fully active) ducklings are born are an average of 24 feet high in trees. Within 24 hours of birth, the young are ready to be on the water, but how do they manage to do this when they are this far off the ground? There are eyewitness reports of the mother wood duck ferrying her ducklings one by one from the cavity to water, with the young

March arrival of male (left) and female (right) wood ducks.

ducklings perched on her back. There are also those who have described a female carrying her young, one by one, with her bill and between her feet. However, most observers of this dramatic moment report that the mother does not assist her ducklings in any way, other than to encourage them vocally.

The adult female positions herself on the ground or in the water directly below the nesting tree. From this spot she softly calls to her young, "*kuk, kuk, kuk.*" The ducklings eventually emerge from the entrance of the cavity, having clawed their way up from the bottom of the nest cavity (a distance of up to 8 feet) with the help of their sharp nails. They then hurl themselves out of the tree, down into the water—that is, if there is water below. Wood ducks can nest over a mile from water, and when this is the case, the young are said to hit the ground and "bounce" like tennis balls. Ducklings have been known to leap from as high as 291 feet and still escape injury. The ducklings follow this daredevil act with a lengthy (average of a little over a mile) and dangerous hike over land to a suitable watery rearing spot.

Imagine starting out life by jumping—at the tender age of one day—off the roof of a two-story building, surviving the landing, and then hiking over a mile to reach the spot where your mother wants you to grow up. It sounds more than a little daunting, but this is a close approximation to what every duckling experiences. It's hard to believe that everyday life isn't a bit anticlimactic after an entrance like this.

] FAST FACTS [
Wood Duck

▶ The wood duck's genus and species names, *Aix sponsa*, mean "water bird" and "betrothed or bride," in reference to the male's exquisite plumage.

▶ Other common names for wood ducks include: acorn duck, bridal duck, squealer, swamp duck, tree duck, and woody.

▶ Because of loss of habitat and overhunting for their plumage, meat, and eggs, wood ducks were on the verge of extinction by the early 1900s. A closed hunting season from 1918 until 1943 in the US and Canada helped restore their population.

▶ About 90 percent of a wood duck's diet is plant life. It eats more fruits and nuts than any other North American duck. Its diet includes (among other things): duckweed; grass and sedge seeds; wild rice; water lily seeds; acorns; beechnuts; hickory nuts; grapes; and berries. The other 10 percent is largely comprised of aquatic insects, minnows, frogs, and salamanders.

▶ A total of 56 bur oak acorns were once found in an enlarged part of a male wood duck's throat in Minnesota.

▶ On land, the wood duck walks or runs with greater ease than most ducks and frequently perches in trees.

▶ The smallest opening a wood duck is capable of fitting through is 3½ by 4 inches wide.

▶ Clutches of 15 to 50 eggs can result from 2 to 10 females laying eggs in the same nest.

▶ If disturbed in the water, young wood ducks will either submerge or dive to reach cover.

American Robin—
A Diet for Winter Survival

How exactly do they do it? American robins—earthworm connoisseurs—routinely overwinter in New England where they face at least three cold months, and during which there is a stark absence of anything that resembles a worm. The secret to the robins' survival? The same as white-tailed deer and snowshoe hares (see p. 309)—they are opportunistic, making do with the food that is available. Their diet change, however, is much more drastic than that of the herbivores that move from herbaceous to woody plants. Robins switch from eating animal matter to eating plant material, and back again, every year.

The Seasonal Diet
For much of the spring, invertebrates, such as insects, earthworms, spiders, and millipedes, make up more than 90 percent of a robin's diet (the rest consists of fruit). Summer is a mixture of both plant and animal matter, but by fall, sometimes even before insects disappear, the robin shifts over to a diet that is more than 90 percent fruit to sustain it through the winter. (Robins that have consumed fermented fruit are a particularly amusing sight, as they react in much the same way as humans do, becoming obviously intoxicated—flapping, fluttering, and staggering around, and occasionally even passing out temporarily.) The actual shift in the kinds of food robins eat takes anywhere from one to two months—a relatively brief amount of time, considering how drastic a change it is.

Both seasonal diets include a wide range of food. N.T. Wheelwright, in an analysis of the US Biological Surveys published in the journal *The Auk* in 1986, showed that robins eat fruit in over 50 genera of plants and invertebrates from over 100 families. A diet this broad enhances their chances of surviving New England winters.

Not only does the spring-and-summer/invertebrate, fall-and-winter/fruit diet make seasonal sense

for a bird, it also makes nutritional sense. Robins require significant amounts of protein when females are producing eggs in the spring, and when both males and females are molting and growing new feathers prior to migrating. Thus, a protein-rich diet of earthworms, beetles, caterpillars, flies, sowbugs, spiders, snails, and millipedes suits the needs of robins during the spring and summer, when you often find them foraging on the ground for their meals. (They have also been observed supplementing their traditional invertebrate diet with small fish, snakes, mice, shrews, and damselfly nymphs.) A carbohydrate-loaded diet of 90 percent fruit, including that of sumac, dogwood, grapes, elderberry, red cedar, blackberry, Virginia creeper, and poison ivy, usually provides adequate fuel for the colder months.

American robin dining on staghorn sumac fruit in late winter.

Lean Times
Food-wise, late winter is the most stressful for robins, as well as other fruit-eating birds that occasionally overwinter here, such as eastern bluebirds. The branches of trees and shrubs bearing the most desirable fruits, such as that of red-osier dogwood (see p. 15), were stripped clean long ago, leaving the fruits of last resort, such as acidic high-bush cranberries and fuzzy staghorn sumac berries (see p. 17), for sustenance. Even though they aren't the food of choice for many birds, these bitter fruits tide the robins over until insects are once again available.

How can the relatively small amount of fruit that is available support the robin population? First of all, in New England, there is a much smaller

] FAST FACTS [
American Robin

▶ In a study cited in Cornell University's *Birds of North America* that took place from June through August, American robins spent 93 percent of their foraging time looking for invertebrates (78 percent in vegetation, 15 percent on the ground) and 7 percent looking for fruit.

▶ Earthworm-hunting techniques include "head-cocking" (focusing on the ground where the worm is, first with one eye, then the other) followed by "bill-pouncing," where the robin thrusts its bill into the soil in an attempt to seize the worm.

▶ Most ornithologists feel robins hunt visually. It is thought that the sounds of earthworms burrowing in the soil are of such a low intensity that they are masked by background noise at locations where robins normally forage.

▶ Robins are known to forage for earthworms most frequently in the early morning and late afternoon.

▶ They eat different types of food depending on the time of day—earthworms early in the day and fruit later.

▶ Robins prefer large fruits over small ones.

▶ Large, indigestible seeds are often regurgitated.

▶ Thanks to the large consumption of seeds, the robin is a very effective agent of seed dispersal.

winter population of robins than summer. Also, unlike during the spring and summer when they are nesting, robins are not territorial in winter. During colder months they tend to travel widely in large flocks, tracking sources of food, and do not usually remain in one location for very long.

It hasn't been determined whether the robins we see on our hawthorns, crabapples, and sumacs during winter are members of a New England summer population that choose to stay year-round, or if they are from even further north, and flew south to spend the coldest months in relatively balmy New England.

March Mating Rituals—
Screams, Bites, Leaps, and Punches

There is a reason why March is one of the noisiest months of the year, and it has everything to do with hormones. Many animals are now at the peak of their breeding season, and loud vocalizations are part of many courtship rituals. For anyone who has woken from a sound sleep wondering which neighbor was being killed outside their window, this should be reassuring. Much more than a few screams, however, are involved in attracting a four-footed mate. Fights, bites, leaps, and punches are also an integral part of March's courtship antics.

Fisher
Fisher courtship involves chasing, tail flagging by the female when she is receptive to advances, and incredible vocalizations by both sexes. An observer describes the noise made by one fisher in pursuit of another in a 1941 edition of *Fur Trade Journal of Canada*:

> *"...if there was anyone within a mile of us who did not think some large animal was being tortured to death, that person must have been deaf. Such noise! Such yowls! Such howling! No thousand cats caterwauling on a backyard fence at midnight ever could make such a noise."*

In addition to making a lot of noise, the male fisher is anything but gentle with his partner. When the time to mate arrives, he grips the female by the nape of her neck, sometimes dragging her considerable distances between multiple copulations.

American Mink
The mink, also a member of the weasel family but much smaller than a fisher, has a well deserved Romeo reputation. A rough-and-tumble courtship fight

often precedes frenzied and furious coupling, which can last as long as three hours, during which time both mink are said to make a "chuckling" noise.

Striped Skunk

A third member of the weasel family, the striped skunk, is a true diehard when it comes to finding a mate. A deep sleeper during most of the winter, the male awakens in early spring specifically to find a willing female. He roams far and wide on this quest, even on nights as cold as 10°F. One indication of this wandering is the number of road-killed skunks you often see during the third week of March, the peak of their breeding season.

Bobcat

Vocally, the bobcat is a close second to the fisher when it comes to breeding behavior. After considerable chasing, bumping, and "ambushing," copulation occurs, but not without considerable noise. Observers have likened bobcat breeding vocalizations to that of a woman screaming. It has been recorded as reaching as far as a mile, which is quite believable after reading Edmund C. Jaeger's 1961 account in *Wild Cats of the World*:

> "I was awakened near midnight by an interrupted series of ferocious hisses, shrill screams, harsh squalls, and deep-toned yowls. No alley strays could ever have half-equaled this cat concert...the loud and ludicrous serenade was kept up for almost half an hour, and it ended with a dual climax of discordant, frightening squalls as mating took place."

Red Fox

In the months preceding March, you may hear sharp, terrier-like barks from nearby fields or woods. If so (and if no terriers live near you) chances are great that you have a resident fox. Although they bark year-

Red foxes, normally somewhat solitary animals, pair up during the breeding season and rarely leave their mate's side. Historical records show that one trapper, upon returning and finding a fox captured in his trap, discovered its mate waiting patiently on a hummock nearby.

round, red foxes are most vocal during their long winter breeding season. In addition to their yapping, foxes have particularly pungent urine this time of year, which is noticeable to humans, as well as other foxes. A skunk-like odor can mean that a fox has been marking its territory, depositing its distinctive smell on bushes, stumps, or rocks. If there is snow, these scent posts are very obvious; without snow... just follow your nose.

Red foxes are normally solitary animals, but breeding pairs are known to be practically inseparable this time of year. More often than not you will notice two sets of tracks in the snow confirming this.

Raccoon

Like striped skunks, raccoons spend much of the winter in a deep sleep, venturing out of their log or tree cavity only during relatively mild weather, when night temperatures are 30°F or more. A male usually seeks out a female, and upon locating

Raccoons mate between January and March, right after emerging from their winter sleep. Copulation can last an hour or more.

her, moves into her sleeping quarters. However, it takes him from one to two weeks to win her over. Once breeding has taken place, the female usually goes back into her lethargic sleep for the rest of the winter, while males stay active for a period of time before settling down for a few weeks until spring arrives.

Meadow Vole
To say the reproductive activity of a meadow vole is impressive is an understatement. They are one of our most prolific mammals, producing up to 17 litters per year, should they be fortunate enough to live that long. Heavily preyed upon, the meadow vole must reproduce frequently and over a long period of time. In order to achieve

this, their breeding season is extraordinarily lengthy, beginning in March and continuing through to the following January, when a two-month hiatus generally occurs.

Eastern Cottontail Rabbit
Rabbits live up to their reproductive reputation, and then some, producing three to four litters a year. It is the

This young meadow vole, if it isn't consumed by one of its many predators, will produce anywhere from 13 to 17 litters in the next year.

manner in which the male attracts the female that is particularly unusual. When courting, the male approaches the female, who faces him. As the male moves closer to her, the female "boxes" or jabs him with her front feet. In response, the male dashes at the female, urinating in the process. A game of leapfrog ensues with her leaping over the onrushing male, after which they face off again. This sequence of moves is repeated several times before a chase ensues, ending with copulation.

Shared Courtship Traits
As different as their courtship behavior may be, many of these March breeders share certain reproductive traits. Most lead solitary lives except during breeding season. Many of the male carnivores grasp their mate by the neck and hang on for dear life during copulation. Many use vocalization in the pursuit of their mate, and most change partners every year (with a majority of males having multiple mates in any given year). Without exception, they each pass on their genes in a distinctive and memorable way.

] FAST FACTS [
Mating Rituals

► During their courtship ritual, male porcupines sometimes soak females with streams of urine while standing on their hind limbs. When the female is ready to mate, she and the male, both on their hind legs, perform a courtship "dance," embracing each other while whining and grunting loudly.

► Male and female coyotes may howl in a duet before mating.

► About 3 percent of mammals are monogamous.

► The courtship behavior of the eastern gray squirrel consists of chases, often involving several males in pursuit of a single female. A distinctive "buzzy" note accompanies these mating chases.

► Prior to mating, white-tailed deer does become very active at night, and bucks follow them continuously for five or six days. Does often stop to urinate, and the males smell their urine while curling their upper lip (referred to as a *flehmen response*) in order to analyze the scent (and pheromones) and thereby determine the does' readiness.

► Male little brown bats emit a special "copulatory call" that appears to calm the female and indicates reproductive rather than aggressive behavior.

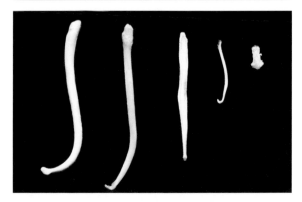

Many mammals, including raccoons, weasels, porcupines, foxes, and coyotes, possess penile bones, or *bacula*. The curvature of the bacula helps "get the job done." (From left to right: raccoon, fisher, coyote, mink, and porcupine.)

Fisher—*A Very Large Weasel*

Rotating its hind feet 180 degrees, the fisher descends head first from the spruce tree, having failed to catch the red squirrel it has been chasing. Shortly after reaching the ground, it crosses paths with a porcupine, and immediately the fisher begins circling the slow-moving rodent. The porcupine quickly turns its back, protecting its quill-less face. As the fisher circles repeatedly, the porcupine continues turning, always keeping its densely-quilled back to the fisher. Every now and again, the fisher rushes in and bites the porcupine in the face. Sometimes it fails to connect, but often it does not, and eventually, the severely wounded porcupine succumbs. The fisher moves in and flips the porcupine over, tearing into the only other part of its body that is not covered with quills—its belly. The next month's food supply has been procured.

The predator-prey relationship between fishers and porcupines is fairly well known. What may not be common knowledge is the fact that "fisher cat" is a complete misnomer. The fisher does not fish, and it is a member of the weasel—not cat—family.

The fisher is twice the size of an American marten (see p. 164).

Even though fishers are active both day and night throughout the year, one doesn't come across them all that often. They are similar to a fox in appearance, but with dark brown fur, very short legs, and less prominent ears and nose—in essence, a very large weasel. Fishers are solitary animals, relatively shy and secretive, and

The fisher's five toes each bear a strong, sharp, semi-retractable claw, which is useful in climbing.

Fisher scat containing porcupine quills, demonstrating the fisher's ability to ingest almost anything.

much of what is known about their life history has been gleaned from studying their scat and tracks.

Tracking the Fisher

Winter is the easiest time to find fisher sign. Fishers travel extensively, so there are plenty of tracks to be found in the right habitat. Often, especially in deep snow, they leave a series of diagonal, paired tracks, where the hind feet land directly in their front footprints as they bound. Fisher scat is usually very dark in color, and twisted with tapering ends.

In addition, fishers *scent mark* their territory in a very obvious way. They actually bite, rub, and roll on young trees, often conifers. Because the same trees are marked over and over, they often look very ragged (see photo on p. 421). Usually the fisher deposits urine and/or scat on or below the tree, and the snow surrounding the sapling is packed down in a fairly wide circle. Scent from the glands on a fisher's hind feet is also left at the site. Close examination almost always turns up a hair or two caught on a branch where the fisher rubbed its body. With luck you may also come upon a temporary den, such as a hollow tree, log, or brush pile, where a fisher found shelter for the night.

Population Control

Fishers have a long and tumultuous history in New England. Historically they ranged throughout the northern forests until, in the late 1800s and early 1900s, they were extirpated over most of the area due to overtrapping (their fur has always demanded a high price) and loss of habitat (via logging and agriculture). Numbers were so low that the trapping season for fishers was closed throughout the Northeast.

Around the same time, the logging boom came to an end and abandoned farmland began to return to forest. The remnant fisher population began to recover, but it was not stable during these years. It was noticed that during a decrease in the fisher population, the porcupine population climbed dramatically, and in the few locations where the fisher population was increasing, there was a decline in the number of porcupines. Thus, the idea of using fishers as a biological control for the high porcupine population was born in the late 1950s. With this purpose in mind, they were reintroduced in several states, including Vermont and Connecticut. By the 1970s, their population was healthy enough for trapping seasons to be reinstated, and today they are one of New England's more common land predators.

Fisher hair can often be found on branches used as scent posts.

Rabbits, Mice, and Squirrels—But Probably not the Cat

What are the chances that the woods near you have a fisher residing in them? Although fishers are

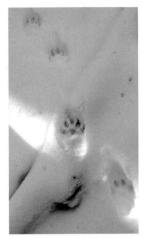

The fisher, like most weasels, often leaves diagonally-paired prints with five distinct toe marks when bounding through deep snow.

very adaptable and can be found in a variety of habitats, you frequently find them where there is a healthy population of snowshoe hares under a tall, closed, continuous canopy. Fishers have an aversion to open fields, as well as a preference for snowshoe hares in the northern part of their range. They are opportunists, however, and will eat any prey they can catch and overpower, including cottontail rabbits, squirrels, mice, meadow voles, shrews, ruffed grouse, blue jays and—of course—porcupines, for which there is little competition. It is estimated that a fisher requires about one snowshoe hare per week; a squirrel or two per week; from two to 22 mice per day; or one porcupine a month. Although not capable of killing an animal as large as an adult white-tailed deer, fisher tracks are often found near deer carcasses, for they do consume carrion.

It is true that a very hungry fisher will occasionally prey on a domestic animal. However, some biologists feel that fishers are scapegoats when it comes to the demise of cats, for other animals—including coyotes, foxes, and owls—also prey upon cats. In 1979 and 1980, the New Hampshire Fish and Game Department collected more than 1,000 fishers and checked their stomach contents to determine what they had been feeding on—cat hair was found in only one. (The one foolproof way to protect your cat from any predator is to keep it indoors.)

] FAST FACTS [
Fisher

► A fisher weighs over twice as much as its close relative, the marten.

► Fishers have both anal glands and glands on the pads of their hind feet, which they use for scent marking.

► The hind feet of a fisher can turn almost 180 degrees.

► Although at home in trees, fishers actually spend much less time there than they are reputed to.

► Fishers are active day and night.

► They are strong swimmers.

► Prey—other than porcupines—are usually killed with a bite to the back of the neck.

► Fisher copulation lasts approximately one hour.

► Fishers have been known to travel 56 miles in three days.

► Man is the fisher's primary enemy, due to the value of a fisher pelt.

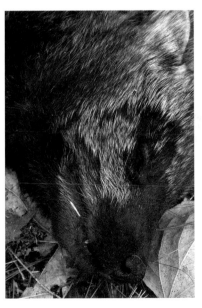

Although fishers are often found with quills imbedded in them—as seen on this deceased fisher's muzzle—infections rarely result due to the quills' antibacterial properties (see p.349).

Fairy Shrimp—
Tiny Residents of Vernal Pools

If you look very carefully into the water of shallow, temporary (vernal) woodland pools in March or April, you will discover a whole world of creatures you may never have seen before. With persistence and a certain amount of luck, you may come upon a small, delicate organism that looks something like a miniature shrimp swimming on its back. In fact, this crustacean is a shrimp—a "fairy" shrimp, so-called because of the way it seems to "magically" appear in these pools, sometimes after years of being absent.

Fairy shrimp are fascinating creatures. Our most common species is very small—about an inch—and translucent orange-red in color. Their back is so transparent, in fact, that it is often possible to see the beating of their long, tubular heart. Fairy shrimp have "stalked" eyes, and the males have modified antennae that form claspers with which they grasp the females during mating; females lack claspers and are often seen carrying egg sacs. They are remarkably graceful, and are most often observed swimming with their many long, leaf-like gill-feet (which are both breathing and swimming organs) beating in a series of wave-like motions, passing their diet of microscopic organisms toward their mouth.

Race against Summer

The entire life of a fairy shrimp (a few weeks) is spent in a vernal pool, usually formed in the spring by snow melt. With the approach of summer, the temporary pool starts to dry out, and the fairy shrimp must complete its life cycle before low oxygen levels and lack of moisture make the pool uninhabitable.

Fairy shrimp breed as soon as they mature and the females produce "resting eggs," which fall to the bottom of the pool and lie dormant in the mud. These eggs can endure drying and remain viable for

Fairy shrimp.

long periods—up to 14 years in one study, and possibly hundreds of years under certain circumstances. Usually, however, the eggs pass through one winter cycle of drying and freezing, and then hatch the following spring when the vernal pool again fills with meltwater. Biologists estimate that there is an average of roughly 960 fairy shrimp eggs per square foot in vernal pool sediment. Some years they all hatch, other years, a portion or none. They occur sporadically and unpredictably, appearing consistently in some locations year to year, but remaining absent from other pools except at irregular intervals.

Inherent Vulnerability

Because of the temporary nature of a vernal pool, only organisms adapted to long dry periods can inhabit it. Fish obviously cannot survive in this environment, making the pool relatively safe for fairy shrimp and other species subject to predation by fish.

Even so, fairy shrimp are quite vulnerable, for their very survival as a species depends on the existence of these ephemeral vernal pools. Human population growth and housing development threaten vernal pools' very existence, and many landowners do not recognize their uniqueness, or the need to protect them. In an attempt to record and monitor these bodies of water, vernal pool documentation, certification, and mapping projects have been undertaken in many New England states.

] FAST FACTS [
Fairy Shrimp

▸ Look for fairy shrimp early in the spring. While they can be present in vernal pools for weeks or months, when the water warms up to between 68°F and 72°F, they disappear.

▸ There are several species of fairy shrimp in the Northeast.

▸ Female fairy shrimp have two egg sacs where their thorax and abdomen meet.

▸ Species of fairy shrimp are identified by the shape of the second pair of antennae, used during mating, on the males.

▸ Fairy shrimp eggs, or *cysts*, lie on the bottom of vernal pools until hatching is stimulated by flooding.

▸ Fairy shrimp eggs in desert pools have been found to be viable after several decades.

Skunk Cabbage—
A Wetland Warming Hut

It defies logic but there exists a plant in New England capable of pushing up through the ice and snow-covered ground of March and sending forth a flower. How is it possible for our earliest "spring" wildflower, skunk cabbage, to survive and even flourish under these conditions?

Skunk cabbage is able to perform this feat because it produces heat as it's growing, which not only melts the ice and snow, but also prevents the plant's cells from freezing. The fact that the green parts of plants give off oxygen as a byproduct of photosynthesis is well known. What is not common knowledge is that in some plants the flower, through a process called *thermogenesis*, absorbs oxygen in order for the plant to produce heat. This is the case with skunk cabbage. For about two

weeks in early spring skunk cabbage increases its respiration and oxygen consumption and rapidly burns starch stored in its massive underground root system to produce the heat that enables it to survive the sometimes wintry conditions of March.

What stretches the imagination even more is that according to some botanists, skunk cabbage can actually vary its metabolic rate according to how cold the air is. On warmer days its respiration slows down, while on cooler days it may burn more starch to produce heat. A steady 72°F is maintained inside the cavity that the maroon-colored, pointed "monk's hood," or *spathe*, creates around the club-like flower head (*spadix*), regardless of how cold it is outside. A 60-degree difference has been recorded between the temperature inside and outside this cavity. If your timing is right, you are supposed to be able to put your finger on the flower head and notice that your finger is warming up.

One theory proposes that skunk cabbage was originally a tropical plant that has gradually moved northward, and its ability to produce heat may have evolved as a way for the plant to create a near tropical microclimate for its flower.

Skunk cabbage emerging from the ground in early spring.

Honeybee Haven
This ability to generate heat benefits far more than just the skunk cabbage. Its early flowering provides the first available food to emerging insects. Even though we associate honeybees with brightly colored, sweet-scented, nectar-filled flowers, the scarcity of food at this time of year means that a nontraditional looking (and smelling) flower that offers protein-rich pollen is able to lure honeybees from the warmth of their hive. Bees prefer to fly only after the temperature reaches 65°F or higher,

The "monk's hood" creates a warm cavity that provides early honeybees with food and shelter.

but they disregard this preference when it comes to skunk cabbage, not only because of the abundance of pollen it produces, but because each plant is a veritable "warming hut" where the honeybees can temporarily escape the cold. They fly from one skunk cabbage to another, savoring the warmth surrounding their food source.

It comes as no surprise that the heat produced by the skunk cabbage intensifies the smell given off by its flowers. The chemicals *cadaverine* and *skatole* give the plant its fetid odor. In addition to smelling like rotting meat, its maroon or liver-colored spathe, like the petals of red trillium and wild ginger, resembles the color of carrion in order to lure insects—such as carrion beetles, flesh flies, and blowflies—that are attracted to decomposing animal matter. This is no secret to the 11 species of spiders known to seek prey in and on skunk cabbage, sometimes even spinning a web across the opening of the spathe, through which pollinating insects must fly to reach the flowers.

Food and Shelter

Many animals in addition to insects and spiders are dependent on skunk cabbage as a source of sus-

tenance. In late spring the emerging rolled-up cabbage-like leaves of this plant are eaten by ring-necked pheasants. Perhaps because herbaceous plants are scarce this time of year, bears consume the leaves and roots, or *rhizomes*, with apparent relish. Slugs eat the leaves and pollen. Eventually the spadix turns black with age and releases heavy, marble-size seeds attractive to ruffed grouse, wood ducks, ring-necked pheasants, and northern bobwhites.

Skunk cabbage is known as an obligate plant of wetlands: if you find a skunk cabbage plant, you are 99 percent likely to find a wetland. A warbler of wetlands, the common yellowthroat, has been known to nest in the central hollows of the large leaves. Supposedly the foul odor of the plant masks the yellowthroat's scent and helps it avoid detection by predators.

Native American Uses

Although untreated skunk cabbage is toxic to humans due to the calcium oxalate crystals it contains, Native Americans found that drying it allowed them to use it in a myriad of ways—from treatments for epilepsy, toothache, and venereal disease, to birth control and headache relief. One of the more unusual ways in which it was used was as a tattooing agent. With the aid of a sharp fish tooth, Native Americans would insert a mixture of ground skunk cabbage root and pigment into their skin in order to ward off disease.

transformation

In New England, April experiences a greater degree of transformation than any other month of the year. An explosion of sights and sounds takes place from beneath the forest floor to the top of the forest canopy. In 30 days the hillsides can change from snowy white to a mosaic of greenery with the arrival of newly-emerged leaves. Birds and amphibians are suddenly everywhere, breaking the silence of the past winter months with their mating calls. Many trees take advantage of leafless canopies by flowering when the wind can easily disperse their pollen. Spring wildflowers, responding to the temporary sunny and warm forest floor, burst into bloom and carpet the ground. The earliest insects emerge and visit these flowers for sustenance, and there is a fury of hidden activity as the breeding and birthing of all forms of life take place.

nature notes

Here is a sampling of species that are emerging from hibernation, engaging in courtship, breeding, laying eggs, nesting, hatching, giving birth, and flowering in the month of April.

AMPHIBIANS

American Toad—*Breeding*

From April to July throughout New England the male American toad makes his presence known to females far and wide with his long, musical mating trill. Toads spend the winter hibernating up to 12 inches under the ground and emerge in late March or April. During spring nights they head for shallow water in fairly large numbers, often returning to the same breeding pool year after year. The peak of their breeding and egg laying is in late April, when they remain active in the day, even though they are nocturnal at most other times. The male mounts the female and clasps her around her chest, a posi-

American toads in *amplexus* (mating).

■ **Frogs Whose Calling Peaks in April or Early May**

Wood frog
Northern leopard frog
Spring peeper

■ **Amphibians Breeding in April**

Eastern newt
Jefferson salamander
Spotted salamander
Blue-spotted salamander
Northern dusky salamander
Eastern red-backed salamander
Slimy salamander
Northern two-lined salamander
Eastern spadefoot
American toad
Spring peeper
Green Frog
Wood frog
Pickerel frog
Northern leopard frog

tion referred to as *amplexus*. As she lays her eggs, he deposits his sperm on top of them. The eggs emerge in two jelly-like strings, one from each ovary. Just one of these long, curling strings contains between 4,000 and 12,000 eggs, which hatch after about four days. In just one-and-a-half to two months, when they have developed lungs and four legs, the tiny toadlets leave the pond. (See more about the American toad on pp. 55 and 159.)

Northern Leopard Frog—*Breeding*

The northern leopard frog usually emerges from hibernating in the mud at the bottom of a body of

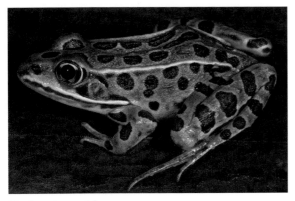
Northern leopard frog.

■ Frog and Toad Calls

Species	Call Description
Spring peeper	High-pitched peep, chorus like sleigh bells
Wood frog	Ducks quacking, two stones striking each other
Pickerel frog	Short snore
Northern leopard frog	Long snore, throaty croak
American toad	Musical, long trill
Green frog	Twang of a loose banjo string
American bullfrog	Deep "jug-o-rum"
Gray treefrog	Bird-like trill

water sometime in March. There have been occasional reports of sightings in the middle of winter during warm spells in southern New England. April is the peak of their mating season, when they gather in ponds, marshes, and slow, shallow streams to breed. The male's song resembles a drawn-out snore. After mating the female lays up to 6,000 eggs in oval masses, often in shallow water. Tadpoles wiggle their way out in two to three weeks and young adult leopard frogs leave the pond for wet meadows two or three months later.

Slimy Salamander—Breeding
The slimy salamander's name is derived from the slimy tail secretions it emits when it is mishandled. When disturbed, it produces a glandular skin secretion, which discourages predators due to its adhesive quality—when it dries, it sticks to your skin like glue. Silvery white spots and brassy flecks dot this otherwise black-skinned salamander.

The slimy salamander is found only along the western border of Connecticut and possibly southwestern Vermont. It is believed to have two breeding periods, one in the spring and one in the fall. Slimy salamander eggs, within which their entire larval stage is spent, are laid in protected areas such as rock crevices and rotting logs and hatch in two to three months.

Four-toed salamander.

Four-Toed Salamander—*Laying Eggs*
Although the four-toed salamander is present in every New England state, it is quite hard to find, being nocturnal and very secretive. It seeks out acidic habitats, where it often resides in sphagnum moss. During March, April, and May, while laying her eggs, the female four-toed salamander performs acrobatics: After creating a cavity in or near moss, the female turns upside down when depositing her individual eggs in the moss or on rootlets within the cavity.

REPTILES

North American Racer—*Breeding*

The North American racer is one of the earliest snakes to emerge from hibernation in the spring, appearing sometimes as early as late March in

North American racer.

southern New England. At this time winter retreats, including woodchuck burrows and rock crevices, are abandoned and sunny ledges are sought for serious basking. During their breeding season (April and May) racers are fairly aggressive. Typically they lay their 16 or 17 eggs in rotting stumps or under stones. Left to develop on their own, the young snakes use their "egg teeth" to cut through their rubbery eggshells in late summer or early fall.

Eastern box turtle.

Eastern Box Turtle—*Breeding*

Eastern box turtles, found primarily—but not exclusively—in low-lying coastal New England, emerge from hibernation in April. Box turtle sightings occur rarely, and generally happen during the breeding season when females often cross roads on their way to nest sites. Breeding takes place on land and extends over several months. During this time males are aggressive toward one another as well as toward females; they have been seen butting the female's shell and nipping at her limbs and head.

A fairly reliable way to determine a box turtle's sex is to look at the color of its eyes. Around 90 percent of males have red irises, while females have brown. Box turtles get their name from the hinge on their bottom shell, or *plastron*. This hinge allows both sections of the plastron to close tight against the upper shell, or *carapace*, providing excellent protection from most predators. During coupling, the male's concave plastron fits well over the female's domed carapace.

Box turtles have a life span similar to humans, with some individuals living more than 100 years. This compensates for the fact that it takes box turtles at least 10 years to become sexually mature and

Eastern musk turtle climbing out of the water.

Spiny Softshell—*Breeding*

Spiny softshell turtles are named for their soft, flat, rounded *carapaces* (upper shells), which lack *scutes*, or plates. The edge of the eastern subspecies' carapace is pliable and bears small spines toward the front. In New England the spiny softshell is found only along Vermont's western border, in the Champlain Valley. It moves north in September along a major tributary of Lake Champlain to hibernate, and migrates down to breed in the lake in April. An average of 12 to 18 eggs are laid near the edge of the lake, in sandy gravel. Hatchlings emerge either in late summer or fall, or overwinter in the nest and dig their way out in the spring.

Spiny softshell.

their clutches are relatively small, usually consisting of fewer than 10 eggs.

Eastern Musk Turtle—*Breeding*

The eastern musk turtle is also known as the "stinkpot" due to its musky smell. Within its range (the southern borders of all New England states except for Vermont, where it is found in the Champlain Valley) the eastern musk turtle can often be found in still water that has lots of vegetation. Look for this secretive, nocturnal, aquatic turtle basking in the sunshine on mats of vegetation, stumps, logs, and low tree limbs over the water.

The eastern musk turtle has an extensive breeding period, from April to October, with peaks in April/May and September/October. The only time it leaves the water is when the female lays her eggs, which she does in rotting logs, stumps, sandy soil, and mud on the edges of ponds.

APRIL

Chipping sparrow.

An American woodcock on its nest.

American Woodcock—*Courtship Displaying*

Soon after they return to New England in the spring, American woodcocks begin their courtship, with males performing acrobatics in the air to impress females. After mating, a shallow depression lined with dead leaves serves as a nest for the four eggs that are laid. Because of her cryptic coloration, the incubating female is extremely well hidden and rarely detected. (See p. 60 for more information on the American woodcock.)

engages in this behavior most ardently just prior to copulation, soon after the female has built her nest.

Sparrow—*Returning Migrant*

Many types of sparrows return to New England in April and in the following months nest and raise their young. Chipping, clay-colored, field, vesper, savannah, swamp, saltmarsh sharp-tailed, seaside, and white-throated sparrows all join the song sparrows that started arriving in March.

Male and female common grackles in courtship display.

Common Grackle—*Courtship Displaying*

Courtship displays vary among different species of birds. The female common grackle invites her mate to copulate by bending down and quivering her wings, behavior aptly referred to as a "wing-quivering display." The male participates by lowering his head in a "head-down display." The pair

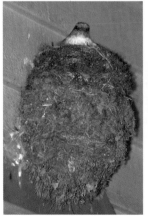

An eastern phoebe on top of multiple nests.

Eastern phoebe.

Eastern Phoebe—*Nesting*

The eastern phoebe, the earliest member of the flycatcher family to migrate back to New England, usually chooses to build its moss-covered mud nest on a protected, shelf-like projection under an eave, in a shed, or over a doorway. The female does most of the nest construction and occasionally builds a series of nests, one beside the other or on top of each other. Phoebe nests are heavily parasitized by the brown-headed cowbird, who avoids the labor of nest-building and the rearing of its young by laying its eggs in other birds' nests and letting the surrogate parents incubate its eggs and raise its young.

American Robin—*Nesting*

Mud is the main ingredient of an American robin's nest. If none is available, robins have been known to dip their feet in water and then stand in dry earth in order to make it. Easily recognizable, the nest is a deep cup, with a middle layer of mud, which

American robin nest and eggs.

the female molds by sitting in the nest and rotating her belly while the mud is wet and can be smoothed and shaped. Weed stalks, strips of cloth, and string may also be incorporated. It is always lined with fine grasses.

American robins usually have two or three broods in a summer. The first nest they build is usually located in a conifer, as deciduous trees often haven't leafed out at this early date, and needles afford some protection and camouflage. Subsequent nests are generally built in shrubs or deciduous trees. The robin is one of few species of birds that recognizes and removes a brown-headed cowbird egg when it appears in its nest (see further discussion above).

Killdeer—*Nesting*

In most of New England, killdeer begin breeding and laying eggs in April. They usually choose an open area for a nesting site, where they scrape a depression in the ground and lay their three to five eggs. Pigmentation on the eggs helps to camouflage them in this most vulnerable location. As

Killdeer nest and eggs.

incubation progresses, both adults add bits of material, often light-colored, to their nest. The young are *precocial*—covered with down and fully active at birth—and leave the nest soon after their down dries.

Nesting killdeer, as well as killdeer with young chicks, are known for their effective and dramatic distraction displays when they feel their nest or chicks are threatened. They have several types of displays, one of the most common being the "injury-feigning display." The killdeer leads the potential predator away from its nest or young, drooping its wings as it partially extends them on the ground, and fanning its tail, exposing its rufous-colored rump feathers. If in the vicinity, its mate often gives alarm calls throughout this performance. After the perceived threat leaves the

Killdeer giving distraction display.

Blue jay.

A hairy woodpecker with a moth.

A hairy woodpecker nesting hole.

area, the killdeer assumes an upright position and cautiously returns to the nest.

Blue Jay—*Nesting*
Both male and female blue jays participate in the building of their bulky nest of twigs, bark, mosses, and leaves, which they line with rootlets. Their nests are often located 10 to 25 feet high in conifers, well hidden from view, but you can also find them in deciduous trees. Although known for their noisiness, blue jays are uncharacteristically quiet while they are nesting. They actively defend their nest and young by dive-bombing marauders, such as red squirrels.

The blue jay is omnivorous, eating three times the amount of vegetable matter as it does animal. It has gained a bad reputation for supplementing its diet in the spring with the eggs and young of other bird species, but research has shown that the vast majority of blue jays do not engage in this activ-

ity and far prefer dining on acorns, beechnuts, and corn, when available.

Hairy Woodpecker—*Nesting*
Hairy woodpeckers pair up in late winter, performing "duet drumming" and courtship ritual flights. In early spring nest-building begins. Woodpeckers are among the best known excavators of nesting holes in trees. Both males and females do the excavating, which takes anywhere from one to three weeks, depending on the hardness of the wood. The smaller downy woodpecker creates a perfectly round nest hole, whereas the hairy woodpecker's tends to be slightly elongated, and a bit larger. No nest material is brought into the cavity; the eggs and nestlings have only a bed of wood chips.

Once the eggs are laid, the division of labor is quite equitable: The female hairy woodpecker incubates during the day; the male at night. The female does most of the brooding of the young, while the male forages and brings food back to the nest. Because the young of cavity nesters such as woodpeckers are relatively safe, they tend to leave their nest at a comparatively later stage of growth than young raised in "open" nests.

There are many hole-nesting species of birds that cannot excavate their own holes and depend on woodpecker excavations and other cavities for nesting sites. "Secondary" cavity nesters include the eastern bluebird, tree swallow, great-crested flycatcher, and saw-whet owl, among others.

Eastern Bluebird—*Inspecting Bird Houses*

In March and April eastern bluebirds begin appearing at nest boxes to evaluate them as future residences. In the late 1800s and early 1900s, displaced from tree cavity sites by the competing house sparrow and European starling, the eastern bluebird population dwindled. It decreased even

Male bluebird evaluating a birdhouse.

The female considers it, as well.

more as agricultural lands decreased and pesticide use increased through the twentieth century. However, through "bluebird recovery programs," thousands of new nest boxes were built and made available to these birds, allowing their numbers to grow. And, to a lesser degree, the rebounding of the American beaver population may have contributed indirectly to their recovery, as there were more ponds and thus more dead snags created by the flooding—which in turn provided cavities for birds (see p. 44 for more on beavers and p. 80 for a list of New England cavity nesting birds). Today, winter sightings of eastern bluebirds have become increasingly common throughout New England.

(see p. 44 for more on beavers and p. 80 for a list of New England cavity nesting birds)

] FAST FACTS [
Eastern Bluebird

- ▶ Typical eastern bluebird habitat is open land with a scattering of trees and low shrubs. The sparse vegetation allows for easier insect-hunting.

- ▶ By the late 1970s, bluebird-friendly farmland began reverting to forest, causing 90 percent of the eastern bluebird population to disappear from New England.

- ▶ Eastern bluebirds are secondary cavity nesters—they are not equipped to excavate their own nesting cavity, and thus are dependent upon woodpeckers (see p. 42) and rotting snags to provide them with suitable holes. When these sources become scarce, the bluebird population is governed largely by man-made birdhouses.

- ▶ A birdhouse with an entrance hole 1½ inches in diameter allows bluebirds to enter, but keeps out larger starlings, which are known to take over bluebird nest sites.

- ▶ If two bluebird boxes are erected on posts fairly close to each other (between 5 and 15 feet), tree swallows will usually nest in only one of them, leaving the other available to bluebirds.

- ▶ Eastern bluebird boxes should be cleaned and repaired by March.

- ▶ Grasshoppers, crickets, beetles, and caterpillars are among the eastern bluebird's favorite meals. A necessary switch to berries takes place if they overwinter in New England. Cold, freezing winter rains that cover fruit with a layer of ice can decimate their population.

- ▶ In the summer, the eastern bluebird's typical hunting style is to survey the ground from a perch, swoop down when an insect is spotted, and then return to the perch. This manner of feeding is called "drop feeding."

- ▶ Eastern bluebirds are unusual, in that both male and female sing.

- ▶ Year-old individuals often return to nest near where they were raised.

(see p. 42)

MAMMALS

APRIL

American Beaver—*Sign (Floating De-Barked Sticks and Scent Posts)*

When the April sun melts the ice on beaver ponds, an abundance of de-barked branches are usually floating on the surface. During the winter beavers swim out under the ice to the brush pile that serves as their food supply and chew off a piece of limb small enough to bring back to the lodge. There they eat it much like we eat an ear of corn: The beaver holds the stick in his front paws and twirls it around as he gnaws the bark down the length of it. Once the inner bark, or cambium layer, has been consumed, the piece of wood is dis-

Floating de-barked sticks on a beaver pond.

Beaver scent mounds.

carded—returned to—the water, where it surfaces and floats under the ice. Being of a very practical nature, beavers eventually recycle these chewed sticks, using them as construction material to repair their dam, as well as their lodge.

American beavers mark their territories by making piles of mud, leaves, and sticks near the boundaries of their territory. These piles range from just

a few inches high to over 3 feet. Once beavers have constructed the mounds, they add urine as well as the contents of their anal and castor glands to them. These secretions contain chemicals that allow beavers to communicate with each other conveying information scuh as the age and sex of the beaver that marked the mound. For example, the message relayed to transient beavers is "This pond is taken, please move on." A majority of scent mounds are constructed in the spring, when there are many two-year-olds dispersing and searching for ponds to claim for themselves. (To read more about beavers, see p. 321.)

River otter scat often consists of fish scales.

North American River Otter—*Sign (Scat and "Rolls")*

Of all the mammal scat found in New England, one of the easiest to identify is that of the river otter. Because of their largely fish diet, otters have scat that often consists of nothing but fish scales, which are obvious to the naked eye, in a small pile without much form. The scat smells very fishy, as well.

River otters tend to leave their scat, as well as urine, in one area known as a "roll," where they come on shore and roll around periodically. This spreads secretions through their fur and water-proofs their coat. Look for these rolls on narrow strips of land bordered by water on both sides, as well as on the banks of ponds and rivers. Sometimes the otter's urine kills some of the vegetation in the roll; this is referred to as a "brown out."

Being part of the weasel or mustelid family, otters possess well-developed scent glands. They often make mounds of vegetation or twist clumps of grass and then mark them with urine and scent gland secretions.

Common Muskrat—*Sign (Scent Post and Scat)*

The muskrat derives its name from glands that emit a smelly secretion into the urine with which the male marks his territory and advertises for a mate. Females have smaller, less active glands. In March and April this scent is liberally spread on mounds of vegetation, along runs, and throughout the area the muskrat inhabits. Muskrat scat varies

Muskrat scat varies in form, depending on the amount of moisture in the animal's diet.

quite a bit in appearance. It can be quite loose, shaped like a patty, clumped, or in individual pellets, depending on the moisture content of the muskrat's diet. Regardless of its consistency, muskrats create scent posts wherever they leave their scat—usually on a raised surface, such as a rock, stump, or clump of grass. (See more about the common muskrat on p. 143.)

White-Tailed Deer—*Sign (Browse Line) and Bucks Growing Antlers*

In the fall, when grazing on grasses and herbaceous plants is no longer possible, white-tailed deer begin browsing—feeding on the buds and bark of

Deer browse line on an eastern red cedar.

shrubs and trees, and the foliage of some conifers. They browse until spring, when they revert back to a more succulent diet. Often in April, when the snow is gone and deer are once again consuming greens, you can look in winter *deer yards* and detect a browse line on woody plants, which delineates the height the deer could comfortably reach while standing on the winter snow.

Antler growth usually begins in April for white-tailed bucks one year and older. The first year he grows antlers, a yearling usually produces a pair of single spikes, but in years to come, with good nutrition, his antlers may have up to five tines. Antlers are covered with a velvety skin, which is filled with nerves and blood vessels that carry nutrients to the fast-growing bone. Antlers, in fact, are the fastest growing mammal bones. They reach full size in four months or less, and if an injury occurs to them during this growth period, they are permanently scarred. When antler growth is complete, the bone hardens and the skin

A white-tailed buck in velvet.

or *velvet* dries up and falls or is rubbed off. Bucks in New England shed their antlers sometime between December and February. (Find out more about white-tailed deer antlers on p. 389.)

Mole and Vole—*Sign (Tunnels)*

By April much of the snow has melted in most of New England, and the busy work of small mammals on or just under the surface of the ground is highly visible, especially in fields and lawns. Raised ridges of soil are signs of mole activity that has occurred *since* winter, for the colder months are spent in a deeper tunnel system. During spring, summer, and fall, moles nest in the deeper tunnels, but create a second, shallow network of tunnels just under the surface of the ground, where they hunt for insects.

Black bear fecal plug.

Raised earthen mole tunnels.

Another small mammal, the meadow vole, leaves evidence of tunnels, but they differ from those of the mole in several ways. They are usually *above* the ground, not under it—tiny pathways chewed through the grass, right at ground level. Little piles of severed grass testify to this. Occasionally you even find little round balls of grass built on top of the ground (within the snow layer), which serve as aboveground nests, with nearby latrines interconnected to all their runs. An insulating layer of snow in the winter protects voles living in this *subnivian* layer. The runs are used year-round, but for the most part are obscured and hidden once grasses and vegetation begin to grow. (For more on these small mammals, see pp. 377, 379, and 392.)

American Black Bear— *Emerging from Hibernation*

Black bears usually emerge from their den in April, as the snow is starting to disappear. Adult males tend to be the first to wander, with females and cubs lingering at their dens a bit longer. At this time they eject a "fecal plug" of feces and hair, which has been in place all winter, during which time they neither defecate or urinate. Once the plug is gone, it takes several weeks for their metabolism and other body systems to resume normal function.

This is the most stressful time of the year for black bears because of the scarcity of food. They often are forced to continue living at least partially off the fat they accumulated in the fall and so lose a considerable amount of weight until grasses and other herbaceous plants begin to grow. (Read more about the black bear on p. 374.)

SCENT MARKING

The sense of smell is critical to communication among many species of wildlife. Using urine, feces, and secretions from scent glands, animals leave messages on prominently-placed "scent posts," where they are easily noticed by others. Deer, dog, cat, and weasel families, as well as black bears and beavers are some of our more active scent markers. Scent marking is used both for defining territory and keeping intruders out (foxes, coyotes, beavers), as well as for conveying social and sexual messages (bobcats, black bears, white-tailed deer). Many animals use it for both purposes.

Scent glands can be found in a variety of locations. For example, white-tailed deer have scent glands in at least seven different parts of their body. Those on their hind legs (tarsal), between their toes (interdigital), and forehead are the primary glands used for communication purposes. Information conveyed through the scent released by these glands includes the deer's individual identity, position in hierarchy, physical condition, and reproductive status. Several members of the weasel family, including North American river otters, fishers, and American martens, possess scent glands on some of the pads of their feet (*plantar*), which release scent along the trails that they travel. Beavers possess both castor glands as well as oil, or anal, glands, both of which produce secretions that they usually post near their lodge, dam, or trails.

Considerable time and effort is often made by animals in preparing a receptive scent-posting surface. Beavers build mounds out of leaves and debris (see p. 44). White-tailed deer rub the bark of saplings with their antlers, thereby creating a rough surface to which the scent from their forehead glands adheres. Moose scrape out a shallow depression, or pit, into which they urinate. They then splash the urine onto themselves or actually wallow in the urine, soaking themselves with its scent, which then wafts through the air, or is rubbed onto a tree. Porcupines drag their rear ends along the ground, leaving scent from their paired perineal glands. Black bears bite and scratch trees, and then rub themselves against the bark wounds. Bobcats often deposit scat and/or urine at one end of a scrape they've pawed in the ground, and spray urine on rotting and absorbent stumps.

While you may not often come upon an animal in the woods, these scent posts, due to the fact that they are intentionally located in prominent spots, are quite noticeable. Look for them on trees, in the ground, or on raised surfaces such as stumps and rocks, where they serve as "community bulletin boards" for resident animals.

Scent Gland Location

	White-tailed deer	North American river otter	Fisher	American marten	Common muskrat	American beaver	North American porcupine
Plantar (sole of foot)		X	X	X			
Interdigital (between toes)	X						
Tarsal ("ankle")	X						
Metatarsal (between ankle and toes)		X					
Forehead	X						
Abdominal			X				
Anogenital					X		X
Castor						X	
Anal			X			X	

INSECTS & ARACHNIDS

Isabella Tiger Moth—*Larvae Emerging and Pupating*

After spending the winter curled up under a log or in the leaf litter, woolly bear caterpillars emerge in April, definitely not looking their finest. They eat voraciously for a while and then pupate inside cocoons

A scraggily woolly bear in the spring.

made up of the caterpillars' hairs held together with silk. The adult Isabella tiger moths that emerge from these cocoons are tan and have a 1½ to 2-inch wingspread. These moths have two broods, or generations, each summer. They mate and lay eggs on a variety of plants. The larvae, or caterpillars, which hatch from these eggs then overwinter as woolly bears. (Read more about woolly bears on p. 293.)

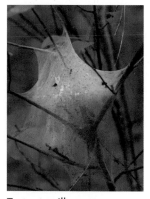

Tent caterpillar nest.

Tent Caterpillar—*Hatching*

Both eastern and forest tent caterpillar eggs hatch during the first warm days of spring, just as leaves are appearing on trees. This is no coincidence, as the caterpillars start to build their white web nest in the crotch of two or more branches about a week after hatching, and spend the next six weeks consuming the leaves (apple and black cherry are favorites).

The larvae leave the nest in order to feed on leaves, usually at night. As they travel among branches in search of food, they lay down a single strand of silk, accompanied by chemical signals, and follow these trails back to the tent after they finish feeding. The caterpillars molt their skins and defecate within the nest, and as they grow, they enlarge it around them. When ready to pupate, the larvae leave and the tent soon disintegrates.

The exact function of the nest is not known, although it's thought that it may offer protection against predators. Another unsolved mystery is why tent caterpillars often congregate on the outside of the tent—perhaps they are escaping from the heat and humidity inside, or are drawn to the warmth of the sun outside. (For more about tent caterpillars, see p. 175.)

Paper Wasp—*Nest Building*

Paper wasps are in the same family as yellowjackets and bald-faced hornets (*Vespidae*), but the nests of all three are easily distinguishable. Yellowjackets usually nest underground and hornets make a football-shaped nest in trees, surrounding the cells with several layers of paper. The cells in a paper wasp nest are exposed, forming a flat

A paper wasp collecting fiber from a wooden fence.

layer with the cell openings on the underside of the nest. Paper wasp nests are suspended, usually in a sheltered area, by a stalk.

Fertilized queens are the only members of the colony that overwinter and thus it is their job to start building a new nest in which to lay their eggs in the spring. Look for paper wasp queens collecting fiber from old fences, dead limbs, or weed stems in April. Each queen strips thin fibers from the wood as she walks backward, then she forms these fibers into a ball of pulp and carries it back to her nest in her

A bald-faced hornet nest (left) and paper wasp nest (right).

Water strider.

water. The bottoms of its feet, the only part of its body that touches the water, have water-repellent hairs that don't disrupt the surface tension of the water, and its claws are located not at the end of its legs, but a little way up them. These adaptations allow the water strider to swiftly "skate" on top of the water as it hunts for prey. Only the middle and hind legs of a water strider actually touch the water, with the middle legs doing the "rowing." Both the middle and hind sets of legs have vibration sensors that detect approaching ripples and can determine whether they are being made by a predator or prey. The front legs are held up above the water and assist when prey is captured.

Adult water striders that emerge in summer are often wingless; winged forms appear in the fall when they use their wings to reach the woods in which they hibernate.

mouth. A form of paper mâché is created with the addition of water collected at puddles.

Water Strider—*Preying on Other Insects*

April means open water and one of the first insects to appear is the water strider, which lives on, not in, the water. Having spent the winter hidden under leaf litter on shore or in nearby woods, the water strider returns to ponds and streams as soon as the ice melts. It is well adapted for life above the

■ Common Insect Defenses

Katydid.

Cryptic coloration (camouflage)	White-marked tussock moth; snowy tree cricket
Countershading (darker pigmentation on those surfaces exposed to the most lighting)	Hawk moth larvae
Disruptive coloration (stripes and spots that break up an insect's outline)	White admiral butterfly (white stripes
Eyespots	Polyphemus moth (on wings)
False head	Hairstreak butterfly; spicebush swallowtail larva
Warning coloration	Yellowjacket (black and yellow stripes);large milkweed bug (red and black)
Mimicry	Praying mantis (twig or leaf); walking stick (twig)
Disguise	Katydid (leaf); black swallowtail larva (bird dropping)
Toxins	Monarch butterfly (common milkweed cardiac glycosides)
Stinger	Bald-faced hornet
Mandibles	Dobsonfly

PLANTS & FUNGI

▨ Woodland Wildflowers Blooming in April

Coltsfoot
Hepatica
Spring beauty
Wood anemone
Bloodroot
Dutchman's breeches
Trout lily
Cut-leaved toothwort
Wild ginger
Red trillium
Blue cohosh
Trailing arbutus
Early saxifrage

▨ Trees and Shrubs Flowering in April and May

Red maple
Silver maple
Sugar maple
Boxelder
American elm
Slippery elm
American beech
Shadbush
Willows
Speckled alder
Beaked hazelnut
Quaking aspen
Bigtooth aspen
Eastern cottonwood
Balsam poplar
Black birch
Yellow birch
White birch
Gray birch
American hornbeam
Hophornbeam

Fiddlehead of an ostrich fern.

Fiddlehead of a sensitive fern.

Fiddlehead—*Emerging*

Ferns begin to push their way up out of the ground in April after lying dormant all winter. Because the young fern frond comes out of the ground curled up like the scroll on the end of a stringed instrument, such as a fiddle, it is referred to as a "fiddlehead." It is also called a "crozier," after the curved staff used by bishops and shepherds.

    The color, size, and appearance of fiddleheads of different species of ferns can vary tremendously. The Christmas fern starts out life as a stout fiddlehead covered in glistening white hairs. The edible ostrich fern fiddlehead is covered with shiny, bronze scales, and sensitive fern fiddleheads are a deep maroon color and very smooth.

Fiddlehead of a Christmas fern.

False Hellebore—*Leaves Emerging*

False hellebore, or Indian poke, may be the most commonly misidentified plant in New England. Often mistaken for skunk cabbage (Arum family),

False hellebore leaves.

False hellebore in flower.

Shadbush.

false hellebore is in a completely different family (Lily). Although these two plants do emerge from the ground at approximately the same time and in the same wet habitat, they are quite different. False hellebore produces leaves before flowering; skunk cabbage flowers first. When false hellebore eventually produces flowers they are green, star-shaped, and borne in large clusters on a stalk, whereas skunk cabbage's purple, hooded spathe contains a flowering *spadix*, or column, inside it (see more on skunk cabbage on p. 33). In addition, false hellebore's leaves clasp the plant's stem and are elongated and oval, while skunk cabbage's leaves do not clasp the stem and are rounded.

Shadbush—*Flowering*
Shadbush is in the Rose family. Known also as shadblow, its fishy names derive from the fact that it flowers when shad are swimming their way upstream to spawn. It also flowers around the time that colonists who died over the winter were buried, hence its other frequently-used name—serviceberry.

In the leafless days of early spring, a burst of white flowers on a shrub or small tree along a hedgerow, or in the woods often signals the presence of shadbush. At least 23 New England species of birds have been observed eating its purple fruit, including crows, Baltimore orioles, American robins, hermit thrushes, and cedar waxwings. Beavers, red squirrels, and black bears also dine on it.

Wild Ginger—*Flowering*
Growing close to the ground, wild ginger is easily overlooked. Under its heart-shaped leaves, a deep, three-pointed, maroon flower uses its "rotten meat" color and smell to lure potential pollinators, particularly early spring flies and gnats. Both shelter and copious amounts of pollen await these insects. The fruit of wild ginger has a small fatty deposit called an *elaisome* attached to it, which ants find irresistible. They haul the fruit into their underground tunnels where they eat the elaisomes and discard the seeds, thus giving the seeds a better chance of germinating than they have aboveground.

Wild ginger.

Trout lily.

Soldier beetles on a
trout lily flower.

Trout Lily—*Flowering*

New England's earliest flowering lily is a wildflower
of many common names: trout lily (the mottling
of its leaves is similar to markings on some trout);
adder's tongue (two emerging pointed leaves
resemble a snake's forked tongue); and dogtooth
violet (a misnomer—characteristics refer to
another species).

Trout lilies often carpet the forest floor in colonies that may have been there for a century or
more. Blossoming early, they take advantage of
the sun that reaches the forest floor before trees
leaf out. Only 1 percent of these plants produce a
flower in any given year. The bell-shaped blossom
attracts long-tongued insects such as queen bumblebees and soldier beetles.

Common Blue Violet—*Flowering*

The common blue violet—one of many species in
the genus *Viola* and Rhode Island's state flower—
shares many characteristics with other violets,

including the presence of "nectar guides." These
are lines on its petals that serve as a road map for
pollinating insects. All violets produce two kinds of
flowers. One is very obvious, grows on a stalk with
petals extended, and is visited by insects, which
usually pollinate it with pollen from another violet. The other, borne on the same
plant, grows close to the ground
and never opens. Instead of being
pollinated by an insect, it self-
pollinates. Violet seeds actually
explode out of their pods, travelling up to 4 feet away from the
plant. Like the seeds of wild ginger (see p. 51), violet seeds contain an oily substance highly
prized as a delicacy by ants.

Common blue violet.

Blue Cohosh—*Flowering*

Look for blue cohosh in rich, moist woodlands—
its leaves develop first, followed by tiny flowers that

mature into round, blue berries, which are much easier to spot. The dried root of this member of the Barberry family was used by Native Americans as a medicinal herb, specifically as a uterine tonic known to induce labor.

Trailing Arbutus—*Flowering*

Trailing arbutus, or mayflower, is the Massachusetts state flower. It inconspicuously creeps along the ground. Its woody stems and leathery, evergreen leaves belie the delicacy of its bell-shaped, pink flowers and the spicy scent of its blossoms. Queen bumblebees, seeking hard-to-find nectar and pollen during early spring, are its primary pollinator.

2- to 3-inch, pendulous, tassle-like structures bearing pollen. Above them, if you look closely, you can often find the much smaller female catkins. They are only about a quarter-inch in length and have fine reddish structures projecting from them. These are used to catch pollen grains blowing in the wind.

When pollinated, the female flowers form a woody fruit, which resembles a miniature pine cone. The prior year's fruit should still be evident on the shrub, although the seeds it once contained may well have been eaten by hungry black-capped chickadees or American goldfinches during the winter. This shrub is a popular nesting spot for many birds, including yellow warblers, red-winged blackbirds,

Blue cohosh flower and fruit.

Trailing arbutus.

Male (below) and female (above) speckled alder flowers/catkins.

Speckled Alder—*Flowering*

Speckled alder, a shrub that grows on the edges of wetlands, bears flowers that often escape notice. They are in the form of *catkins* (flowers that are drooping, lack petals, and are of one sex). The male catkins, reddish brown and roughly an inch long in winter, open and expand in the spring becoming

and American goldfinches. Speckled alders are also a substantial source of food for beavers, snowshoe hares, and grouse.

Speckled and common alder have the distinction of being the only common eastern shrubs that bear visible male and female catkins during the winter. The roots of speckled alder, together with nitro-

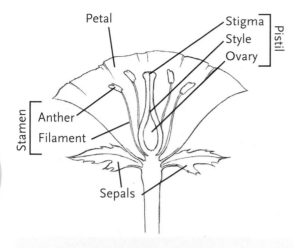

Petal

Stamen { Anther
Filament

Stigma
Style } Pistil
Ovary

Sepals

FLOWER STRUCTURE

Flowers can be male, female, or both. If a flower has both male and female reproductive structures, they are usually located in the center of the flower. The male pollen-producing part is called the *anther*. It is positioned on top of a stalk called a *filament*. The entire male structure is called a *stamen*. The female reproductive part of a plant, the *pistil*, consists of the *stigma*, which sits on top of a *style*, or stalk, and an *ovary* at the base. Fertilization and seed formation take place inside the ovary, which then develops into the fruit.

Each species of flowering plant produces a slightly different-shaped pollen grain. *Cross-pollination* occurs when pollen is transferred from the anthers of one flower to the stigma of another flower of the same species. *Self-pollination* occurs when the pollen from the anther of a flower is transferred to the stigma of the same flower. Because cross-pollinated flowers produce hardier and healthier seeds with greater genetic diversity (which is usually evolutionarily advantageous), different techniques are used by different plants to promote cross-pollination. Some plants bear male and female structures on separate flowers, some even on separate plants. When both male and female structures are on the same flower, they often mature at different times.

gen-fixing bacteria, enrich the soil surrounding them, much as plants in the legume family do.

Field Horsetail—*Dispersing Spores*

Horsetails are nonflowering plants that trace back to the coal-forming swamps of the Carboniferous period about 350 million years ago. They have hollow stems and distinct *nodes* (swollen areas along the stem where leaves are attached), giving them a bamboo-like appearance. When branches are present, they are whorled (three or more coming out of the same node—see p. 16).

Field horsetail has two kinds of stems: sterile and fertile. The sterile stem bears whorls of green branches, giving it a bushy appearance, even though it's only 6 to 24 inches high. The fertile stem is pale brown and bears a spore-filled cone at its tip. Both sterile and fertile stems have tiny leaves fused into small sheaths surrounding each node.

Field horsetail is the most common bushy horsetail, and can vary greatly in size and appearance (from upright to spreading along the ground). The fertile stems and cones of field horsetail appear in April and will wither and die by May. The vegetative stems persist through the summer.

Field horsetail showing both fertile (left) and sterile (right) stems.

a closer look

When one thinks of April, one conjures up images of the welcome colors of **spring wildflowers** (p. 66). **Coltsfoot** (p.62) is one of the first to greet us, lending splashes of gold to the drab, brown roadsides. This dandelion look-alike is just one of an explosion of woodland wildflowers that take advantage of the brief amount of time the forest floor is bathed in sunlight. Coltsfoot is joined by **hepatica** (p. 64)—its pink, blue, violet, and white blossoms can be seen braving some of the cold early days of April. If you look up, there are just as many flowers to find, although they are much smaller, less flashy, and produced by **trees** (p. 69). A spring ritual anticipated as eagerly as the first wildflowers is the return and courtship flight of the **American woodcock** (p. 60). **American toads** begin their courtship, too, (see below) while **painted turtles** bask and breed (p. 58).

Courtship and Mating of the American Toad—*Spring Serenaders*

Days are longer, temperatures higher, and wildflowers are blooming. Spring is announced in a myriad of ways, including the mating calls of some of our most familiar amphibians. First come the incessant "quacks" of male wood frogs from vernal pools deep within New England woods. Right on their heels, often simultaneously, the peeps of individual spring peepers, which build to a crescendo of sleigh-bell-like calls created by a multitude of males serenading their mates, can be heard. By April, musical, sustained, high-pitched trills lasting up to 30 seconds emanate from shallow pools and the edges of ponds. These are the mating calls of the American toad.

Mating Minstrels
Except for the two weeks each year that are devoted to courtship and breeding, American toads are solitary creatures. However, during their annual mating ritual, toads congregate—often in the hundreds—in permanent or temporary bodies of water. Males are the first to dig their way out of their underground hibernation chambers and migrate to nearby wetlands, where they return every year to breed.

The objective of the American toad's call is to attract females, far and wide. The calls increase in volume as more and more males join the chorus, and

The male American toad calls with his mouth closed, amplifying his trill by distending his throat into a bubble.

they travel great distances, thanks to the male's ability to distend his throat into a huge bubble, essentially creating his own sound amplifier. This is accomplished by closing the mouth and nostrils, and pumping air back and forth between the lungs and mouth, over the vocal cords. On the floor of the mouth is an internal opening. Air passes into this opening and enters the "pocket" or vocal sac formed by an extension of the mouth lining. The skin surrounding the vocal sac of an American toad (as well as the spring peeper and other frogs) is thin, and consequently a "throat bubble" is produced. The extra skin necessary for the formation

The eggs of the American toad resemble strings of black pearls. In just a few days, tiny, black tadpoles hatch from them.

It is not unusal to see two or more males attempting to breed with one female American toad (the reddish, larger toad on the bottom). She is often submerged for extended periods of time due to the males' ardor.

of this bubble darkens the color of the male toad's throat, so he is easily distinguishable from the light-throated female.

Soon females start appearing, lured by the males' trills. Apparently the larger the toad (and thus the deeper his trill), the more attractive he is to females.

One-Track Mind
Male toads are anything but shy when it comes to demonstrating their ardor, and they certainly are not particularly choosy when it comes to mate selection. Anything that even vaguely resembles another toad is likely to receive attention. Occasionally, a male toad is mistakenly grabbed from behind by another male. (When this occurs, the toad that has been grabbed objects vocally and is quickly released.)

Males grow dark, horny pads on the first and second toes of their forelegs during the breeding season, which allow them to get a better grip on their mate. Upon spying a nearby solitary female, the male leaps on top of her and wraps his front legs around her body, clasping her just behind her front legs. Sometimes more than one male clambers on the back of the poor female, who is often submerged due to their amorous attentions. The male toad retains a tight grip on his mate for days, securely attached to her until she releases her eggs into the water. He then fertilizes them and releases her.

Ribbons of Life

American toad eggs are noticeably different from frog eggs. They are not laid singly like spring peeper eggs (p. 18), nor in clumps like the wood frog (p. 2), but in two ribbon-like, clear, gelatinous strings, one from each ovary. If stretched out, each individual string would measure between 20 and 60 feet. They contain between 4,000 and 12,000 eggs that are countershaded in order to blend in with their background when viewed from above (dark) or below (light). The eggs hatch in 3 to 12 days into tiny, very dark tadpoles. Their development is relatively quick due to the warmth of the shallow water in which the eggs are laid. For protection, toad tadpoles have defensive chemicals in their skin, just as adult toads do in their warty glands.

After three to six weeks of eating vegetation and breathing through gills, the tadpoles begin to develop limbs and lungs, and metamorphose into carnivorous, terrestrial young adults, or toadlets, each of which will eventually be capable of eating up to 1,000 insects a day.

Warts and All

What some might call a rather homely, even unattractive creature (especially if it defends itself by urinating on a bothersome human's hand) is actually a vital part of our ecosystem. American toads have a rather pleasant call, consume thousands of mosquitoes and other insects, and alert us to potential environmental dangers. Just as a canary in a coal mine once alerted miners to the presence of carbon monoxide gas, the increasing number of malformed toads and frogs, as well as their decreasing population, give notice that something—be it depletion of ozone levels, pesticide residues, smoke, or smog—is adversely affecting the environment we all share.

] FAST FACTS [
American Toad

► There are three species of toads found in New England: the American toad (throughout the Northeast), the eastern spadefoot (localized spots of southern New England), and Fowler's toad (southern half of New England).

► Where their ranges overlap (southern New England), the American toad is easily mistaken for Fowler's toad. The American toad's spots contain one or two warts, while Fowler's toad has three or more.

► There is a large, bean-shaped parotid gland behind each of the American toad's eyes. These glands contain a substance that deters predators by acting as a neurotoxin.

► Because of its parotid glands, the American toad has few predators. Among the few are raccoons, striped skunks, northern watersnakes, and common gartersnakes. Toads are a staple food of eastern hognose snakes.

► American toads dig themselves backward into the soil in the fall, or find an abandoned burrow, and spend the winter hibernating up to 12 inches beneath the ground.

► Although American toads are primarily nocturnal, during the peak of their breeding season in late April they can be both heard and seen during the day.

► Male American toads have four different calls: the typical long trill, advertising for a mate; a shortened trill, more of a chirp, also used in courtship; a "release call," used when one male mistakenly clasps another male for breeding purposes; and an amplexus call, given very quietly while the male clasps a female and fertilizes her eggs.

Painted Turtles—*Part One: Days of Basking and Breeding*

One of the rewards of enduring a long, snowy winter is a long leisurely bake in the warm April sun. Warm-blooded or cold, hibernator or not, creatures of all shapes and sizes who remain in New England year-round celebrate spring by observing this ritual. In all likelihood the painted turtle, also known as the "sun turtle," devotes more time to this endeavor than any other animal, including human beings.

Buried Alive

Painted turtles remain active for more of the year than many other fresh water turtles and can even be seen swimming under the ice in late winter or early spring. However, in the northern part of their range, painted turtles spend at least four months buried in the mud at the bottom of ponds or streams. Unable to generate their own heat, all reptiles must find a fairly protected spot in which to spend the winter. The conditions under inches,

Painted turtle.

much less feet, of mud are less than ideal: little oxygen, cold temperatures, and darkness. Fortunately, painted turtles are very tolerant of low levels of dissolved oxygen and absorb what little

there is through their skin. Still, it's a delicate balance to keep from freezing and still survive several months with a significantly lowered metabolism.

After a winter of low light, no food, little oxygen, and even less heat it must be exhilarating to rise to the surface of open water, take a deep breath, and warm up in the sun. The appearance of painted turtles very early in the spring confirms that this may be the case. They are among the earliest reptiles to emerge from hibernation and can often be found lying in the sun on rocks or logs in a pond still partially covered with ice.

Professional Sunbathers

Basking is a priority in the life of a painted turtle. It spends a great deal of time—up to five or six hours a day in the spring—lying in the early morning and midday sun. The warmth of the sun not only raises its temperature, it also helps to metabolize vitamins in its diet.

Likely places to find these turtles are logs, rocks, and hummocks that are exposed to the sun's rays much of the day. While they make no attempt to hide themselves while they bask, that doesn't mean they aren't concerned about predators, such as raccoons, skunks, and foxes. They compensate for their show of bravado by being extremely wary, dropping off their perch into the water at the slightest movement. Unfortunately, this prevents most people from getting a close look at them.

When a pond lacks an adequate number of basking sites for its painted turtle population, the competition for those that exist is fierce. From a distance you may see several turtles piled up, one on top of the other. This occurs most frequently in ponds where sunning spots are few and far between. Occasionally these "turtle stacks" have been observed toppling; this is not by accident. The bottom turtle, when it has had enough of this weight-bearing exercise, often pushes with its hind legs to lift the rear part of its shell. It then rocks left

Painted turtles basking.

and right, as well as up and down, in an attempt to dislodge the turtles piled on top of it.

Synchronized Swimming
In addition to basking, painted turtles also have courtship on their mind soon after emerging from hibernation. While engaged in this activity, both male and female turtles exhibit movements and gestures reminiscent of water ballet. There is often a slow and lengthy chase, ending with both turtles facing each other in relatively shallow water. They extend their neck, arching toward each other until they are nose-to-nose, after which they sink to the bottom of the pond. They rise to the surface to repeat this series of movements until the female swims away. The male turtle leisurely chases and circles her, eventually stopping directly in front of the female and gently stroking her head and neck with the back of his claws. He then back-paddles away only to return shortly for more stroking and nose-touching. This continues until the female either rejects him or is receptive, indicating interest by stroking his outstretched front legs with the bottoms of the short claws on her front feet. She then sinks to the bottom, where the two turtles mate. (Read more about painted turtles on p. 96.)

(Read more about painted turtles on p. 96.)

Painted Turtle

► The painted turtle is New England's most familiar and conspicuous turtle.

► Larger turtles tend to bask for longer periods of time than smaller ones.

► The number of painted turtles in an ideal habitat (pond with many floating logs and rocks) can be extremely high. At a 151-acre lake in Connecticut a researcher caught and numbered 226 painted turtles one spring. Less than a month later the researcher returned to the same lake and in one day counted 246 basking turtles, of which only three were marked. Scientists surmise from these numbers that several thousand painted turtles reside in this lake.

► Painted turtles avoid swift flowing and rocky-bottomed streams.

► As spring moves into summer and ponds become warmer, painted turtles spend much less time basking and more time foraging.

► They are omnivorous, eating algae, aquatic plants, insects, fish, and tadpoles.

► Painted turtles are strictly diurnal (active in the daytime).

► Male painted turtles have long front toenails, and a long, thick tail with an anal opening beyond the rear margin of the shell; females have comparatively short front toenails, a thin, short tail, and their anal opening is under the rear margin of the shell.

► Juvenile painted turtles have a more circular and lighter-colored carapace (upper shell) than adults.

► Young painted turtles in New England emerge from their nest in both the fall and spring. There may be fall and spring-emerging turtles in the same nest.

► Unlike most New England turtles, painted turtles shed the *scutes* (plates or scales) on both their *carapace* (upper shell) and *plastron* (lower shell).

► Painted turtles can live for more than 30 years.

APRIL

The American Woodcock — *Secretive Sky Dancer*

A "mysterious hermit of the alders," a "recluse of boggy thickets," and a "wood nymph of crepuscular habits." These are the words that Arthur C. Bent, a renowned early twentieth-century ornithologist, used to describe the American woodcock nearly 100 years ago, and they still capture the essence of this forest-dwelling member of the Sandpiper family. These inhabitants of young, moist woodlands are very secretive and very well camouflaged. Often woodcock are not seen until they are flushed, when they burst into flight on twittering wings. As one of the earliest ground-nesting species of birds to return to New England, they appear along with eastern bluebirds and American robins, just as winter is beginning to lose its grip and the ground is starting

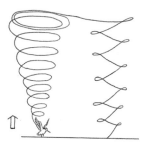

The stocky woodcock is surprisingly agile when it leaves the ground and performs its courtship display. Ever-widening, upward spirals are accompanied by a "twittering" sound produced by the wind passing through specialized wing feathers. The woodcock, having reached a desired height, then flutters downward in a series of zigzags, chirping melodiously as it descends to the ground.

to thaw. The American woodcock—or "timberdoodle," as some refer to it—loses no time in addressing the reason it has flown several hundred, if not thousands, of miles north. By April its courting has begun in earnest, and what a courtship it is.

Love in the Air

The aerial display that the American woodcock performs to attract a mate is somewhat incongruous, for one would hardly guess that this solid (some

The American woodcock's cryptic coloration resembling leaf litter permits this woodland shorebird to remain largely undetected.

might say "chunky") bird could transform into a remarkable "sky dancer." Its regular flight is certainly somewhat slow and clumsy, but something magical happens when love is in the air. Words cannot do justice to the performance—everyone should see and hear it at least once. But for those who may not have the opportunity, a brief description of the courtship display may help your imagination.

About half an hour after sunset, when it is almost—but not quite—too dark to discern anything in the sky, the male woodcock performs for his intended. (He will also do so at dawn, as well as on moonlit nights.) The female usually lurks in the brush at the edge of the clearing or field in which he is to put on his display. Silent except for occasions of courtship, the male woodcock arouses the female's interest with repetitive nasal "peent" calls from the ground. These usually occur regularly for several minutes. The calls suddenly stop, and the male takes off at an angle, circling higher and higher in increasingly large spirals until you can barely see him. During the upward flight a melodious "whistling-twittering" sound can be heard—it is produced by wind passing through three narrow flight feathers on each of his wings.

When he reaches the apex of his circular flight upward, somewhere between 200 and 300 feet, the male descends rapidly in a zigzag fashion, making a loud, musical chirping call that sounds like a high-pitched "chicharee-chicharee-chicharee." The song ceases shortly before he lands, within a short distance of where his flight began, and about a minute after he first took off. Moments after landing, he resumes his call from the ground, and usually within five minutes another flight begins. This pattern repeats itself for approximately half an hour, or until it is completely dark.

A few unobtrusive observers have actually witnessed female woodcocks walk out into the clearing in response to this display. If you are really stealthy, you can get close enough to hear the dove-like soft "coo" the male utters before his "peent" call. (One of my daughter Sadie's favorite past-times in her youth was creeping toward the spot where the woodcock took off while he was busy displaying in the air. Every aerial performance gave her a chance to get a little closer to the spot. The highlight of this activity occurred one evening when the male woodcock descended from the sky for the umpteenth time and all but landed on her back as she lay in the field, awaiting his return.)

Survival Skills
In addition to being an ardent suitor, the American woodcock is remarkably well adapted for survival. Many people walk right by nesting woodcocks, whose plumage blends in so well with the leaf litter on the forest floor that they are never even noticed. A devourer of earthworms, the woodcock has a specialized flexible tip on its upper mandible for grasping earthworms underground without having to open its bill. Because so much of its time is spent with its head down, probing the ground for food, the woodcock is especially vulnerable to predators. If you look at the placement of its eyes, you will see that not only do they "bulge," but they are located very high up on the sides of its head. This placement gives it "rear-view, binocular vision," allowing the bird to see over a large area and detect predators in any direction, even while bending over to search for earthworms.

American woodcock numbers have decreased to the point where the US Shorebird Conservation Plan lists it as a "Species of High Concern." Loss of habi-

] FAST FACTS [
American Woodcock

▶ The American woodcock eats more than its weight in earthworms daily.

▶ Woodcocks typically rock their body back and forth without moving their head as they step heavily with one front foot in an attempt to locate prey. It's considered likely that they locate earthworms on the surface of the ground visually, and those under the ground by feeling and hearing them. It is very possible that the rocking motion and heavy foot generate vibrations that cause shallow earthworms to move, a response then heard by a woodcock or detected by its bill as it contacts the soil.

▶ Across its northern range, woodcocks appear to be the earliest migratory species to breed.

▶ The three outer, narrow, primary feathers of each of the male's wings are modified to produce a "whistling flight song."

▶ Woodcocks usually nest within 300 feet of their courtship area.

▶ Unlike many precocial birds that leave their nest at hatching, newly hatched woodcocks cannot feed themselves. They are dependent on their mother for food for the first week. Male woodcocks do not care for their young.

▶ Other common names for the American woodcock include: timberdoodle, bog sucker, Labrador twister, and night partridge.

tat is thought to be the real culprit, as young forests age or are lost to development. Still, state wildlife agencies have made an effort to stabilize woodcock numbers by reducing the length of the hunting season and decreasing bag limits. With this in mind, I tend to agree with conservationist Aldo Leopold, who concluded that the American woodcock's emotive dawn and dusk displays are "a refutation of the theory that the utility of a game bird is to serve as a target, or to pose gracefully on a slice of toast."

Coltsfoot—*Dandelion Look-Alike*

Even though it has been written about, cooked with, and smoked, it is possible that you've never made the acquaintance of one of New England's earliest wildflowers, known by many as coltsfoot. This overlooked and underrated beacon of spring braves lingering winter patches of snow and endures rugged terrain found on the shoulders of roads, conditions under which few plants can survive.

Coltsfoot vs. the Common Dandelion

Because of its general appearance, coltsfoot flowers are often mistaken for dandelions. While both plants are in the Composite family (in which a single flower head is

Coltsfoot and dandelions are both in the Composite family and superficially look quite similar. However, coltsfoot (left) has tubular (disk) male flowers surrounded by flat (ray) female flowers, while dandelions (right) are composed of mainly flat (ray) flowers that possess both male and female structures.

actually hundreds of individual florets) and both bear brilliant gold flowers, their differences become apparent as soon as you take a closer look. Coltsfoot consists of flat yellow *ray flowers* (mostly female) surrounding tubular yellow-orange *disk flowers* (mostly male). Its hairy stem is stout and scaly, and leaves do not appear until the flowers have died back. A dandelion consists of mostly ray flowers (containing both male and female parts), has a slender smooth stalk, and both flowers and leaves appear at the same time.

When fully developed, the seeds of coltsfoot (left) are dispersed by the wind, traveling as far as 9 miles from their parent plant. Note the difference in appearance from the common dandelion seed head (right).

Rise and Shine

The techniques employed by coltsfoot to increase its chances of being pollinated are most noticeable in its manner of growth. As it is developing, the flower head bends down toward the ground. When it blooms, the head turns upward to greet visiting insects hungry for nectar and pollen, scarce in April. At night, as well as on cloudy or cool days when pollinators are in short supply, you will find coltsfoot flower heads tightly closed. After most of its flowers are pollinated, coltsfoot folds up its flower head and once again turns down toward the ground to protect the developing seeds.

Long-Distance Flyer

Once the seeds of coltsfoot are fully formed, its head is raised for the last time, displaying its seeds. The down, or *pappas*, that is attached to each seed acts as a dispersal mechanism and is similar to that of thistles, asters, and dandelions. Goldfinches line their nests with it (as well as with thistle down), and it has also been used as filler for pillows and mattresses in Scotland.

Leaves Come Later

Romans used to call coltsfoot *filius ante patrem*, or "son before father," in reference to the leaves appearing only after the flower has died back. In fact, most people don't even associate the flower with the leaf, as they never see them at the same time. The hoof-like shape of the leaves gives coltsfoot its prevalent common name, although it does have many others, including: ass's foot, horsehoof, foalfoot, sowfoot, and clayweed.

When young, the leaves are covered and somewhat insulated from the cold by a woolly fuzz that eventually falls off as the temperature rises. The white cottony hair that remains on the underside of the leaf is said to have been collected by English villagers and used as tinder.

► Look for coltsfoot by the sides of roads, shoulders of railroad tracks, and disturbed areas.

► In order to survive the harsh conditions of early spring, when it blooms, coltsfoot has a stem covered with hairy scales tinged with red. The hairs insulate the stem and one theory suggests that the red coloring helps the plant absorb heat from the sun.

APRIL

It's not hard to see how coltsfoot got its name, once you've seen the shape of its leaves. They do not emerge until the flowers have gone by.

Coughing Cure

Historically coltsfoot has served as a remedy for coughs. The leaves are said to contain a great deal of mucilage, which coats and soothes an irritated throat. This has been utilized in every form you can think of: A cough syrup is concocted from the leaves (along with a healthy dose of sugar); a fragrant tea is made from steeped leaves; coltsfoot extract boiled and sweetened with honey makes palatable cough drops; and dried leaves have even been smoked by asthmatics for relief.

Nothing announces spring's arrival like a bouquet of golden coltsfoot.

Hepatica—*Hardy Beauty*

When most of the snow patches have disappeared from the south-facing woodland slopes of New England, many spring wildflowers burst into bloom. One of the earliest flowers to do so is hepatica, whose delicate pastel blossoms belie this plant's hardiness. Its blue, white, pink, and lavender petals adorn many a barren woodland long before those of the more familiar spring wildflowers, such as bloodroot, dutchman's breeches, trillium, and wild ginger.

A Key to Medicinal Use
Hepatica comes from the Greek word *hepar*, for liver, having derived its name from the resemblance of its three-lobed leaves to a human liver. Some plant names, such as hepatica, are based on what is known as the Doctrine of Signatures, a theory proposed by a Swiss physician in 1657 suggesting that some plants have "signatures" that help you recognize their medicinal value. In other words, when a part of a plant physically resembled part of the human body, that was the key to its use and what it could cure. Thus, hepatica was used to treat ailments of the liver, first in Europe, and by the mid-1800s in the United States. In 1883 over 450,000 pounds of dried leaves were harvested for export or domestic use, although its effectiveness (or lack thereof) was often cause for debate among doctors. While no longer used to cure liver problems, hepatica leaves and flowers are still used as an astringent, as well as a diuretic.

"I find I have never admired this little firstling half enough. When at the maturity of its charms, it is certainly the gem of the woods. What an individuality it has! No two clusters alike; all shades and sizes...a solitary blue-purple one, fully expanded and rising over the brown leaves or the green moss, its cluster of minute anthers showing like a group of pale stars on its little firmament, is enough to arrest and hold the dullest eye." John Burroughs, *A Spring Relish*.

The Challenge of Pollination and Seed Dispersal
One of the first things one notices about this member of the Buttercup family is that its stems emerge from the ground covered with long, silky hairs that glisten in the sunshine. These hairs provide both warmth and protection, discouraging insects such as ants from crawling up to its blossoms and raiding the nectar supply intended for winged pollinators.

The two forms of hepatica seen in New England were once considered separate species, as one had pointed leaves (sharp-lobed hepatica) and the other rounded leaves (round-leaved hepatica). Today these two plants are considered subspecies of the same species. Their leaves live for an entire year, making and storing food in the plant's roots, thereby providing it with plenty of energy with which to blossom early the following spring. Year-old leaves turn liver-colored and die after the plant's flowers have withered, at which time new, green leaves replace the dead ones.

The flowers, some of which are very fragrant and some not, actually lack petals. Botanically the blos-

The resemblance of Hepatica's three-lobed leaf to a human liver led early botanists to conclude that this plant was to be used for the medicinal treatment of liver ailments. The pointed tips of the lobes of this leaf tell you that it is sharp-lobed hepatica.

soms consist of anywhere from six to twelve *sepals*, or leaf-like structures, which are usually green and form the outer layer of a flower bud, enclosing its petals and reproductive parts. In the case of hepatica, the sepals replace petals and can be white, pink, lavender, or deep blue. The fragrance and the colors attract potential pollinators that are out early in the spring, such as bees, flies, and an occasional early butterfly, such as the spring azure. However, this flower is perfectly capable of self-pollinating, an

Hepatica's *sepals*, substituting for petals, come in several colors, including pink, lavender, blue, and white.

ability that probably developed because of the lack of insects in April. At night and often on cloudy days, the flower closes in an effort to preserve and protect both its pollen and nectar.

Hepatica—along with several other spring wildflowers such as violets, anemones, wild ginger, and trillium—has evolved a very effective means of dispersing and planting its seeds. Through a process known as *myrmecochory* ("ant-farming"), hepatica has a symbiotic relationship with certain species of ants in which both plant and insect benefit. Each hepatica seed possesses a small protuberance called an *elaisome* that contain oils and possibly sugars, which ants (and chipmunks) find irresistible. The ants carry the seeds down into their underground nest where they consume the elaisomes, but discard the seeds, as the shells are too hard to open. Needless to say, the chances of seeds germinating are as good, if not better, underground than on the surface of the forest floor.

Look for this perennial, multi-colored wildflower in rich woods, often amongst American beech

] FAST FACTS [
Hepatica

▶ The two common New England species of hepaticas, sharp-lobed (*Hepatica acutiloba*) and round-lobed (*Hepatica americana*), are now considered two subspecies of the same species (*Hepatica nobilis*).

▶ Look for *sharp-lobed hepatica* in beech-maple woods and *round-lobed hepatica* in more acidic woods.

▶ Some hepaticas are scented, some not.

▶ Hepatica leaves are evergreen, which gives them the most time possible to make food for the plant and enables it to flower very early in the spring.

▶ Hepatica is a close relative of anemones, and was once classified as one.

The stems and buds of hepatica are covered with dense, silky hairs, which serve as a "fur coat" during cool days and cold nights in early spring. Carpeting the forest floor, hepatica ushers in spring.

and sugar maple trees. It is not nearly as delicate as its flowers would have you believe. Hepatica not only can endure the cold but thrives where there is a blanket of snow in the winter. The early appearance of its first blossoms illustrates hepatica's ability to tolerate cool temperatures. Not many other photosynthetic souls are strong enough to brave the potentially cold days and frigid nights of early to mid-April in New England—those that try include skunk cabbage, marsh marigold, and spring beauty.

A Rose by Any Other Name—
The Naming of Spring Wildflowers

The time between the thawing of the forest floor and leafing out of the canopy is of crucial importance to the early spring wildflowers of New England's woods and wetlands. It is during this time that most of the sun's rays reach the ground, and spring wildflowers cannot afford to miss a minute of this window of opportunity.

What's in a Name?
Flowering and photosynthesis on the forest floor start in March and are in full swing by mid-April. Skunk cabbage, marsh marigold, hepatica, spring beauty, bloodroot—the list of familiar friends that appear like clockwork every spring goes on and on. While we know exactly what plant we mean when we refer to these flowers by their *common names*, it is risky to assume that botanically-minded people in another part of the world, country—or even just another part of New England—would have the same plant in mind. This is because any given plant can, and usually does, have several common names by which it is well known. The same plant goes by the names cowslip and marsh marigold; trout lily is adder's tongue; and red trillium is also stinking Benjamin.

This naming business would be extremely confusing were it not for two fellows who came up with a foolproof way of eliminating the confusion. In the late 1500s a botanist by the name of Caspar Bauhin decided that every plant should have a specific set of two *botanical names* unique to it. Then along came a Swedish naturalist by the name of Linnaeus who set out to classify every living thing on earth using Bauhin's dual name system. With that, the practice of giving every plant both a *generic* and a *species* name became set in stone. This set of names, of Latin or Greek derivation, allows people wherever they are, whether on two different continents or just a few miles apart, to know for certain that they are referring to the same plant.

Bloodroot (*Sanguinaria canadensis*).

Have you ever wondered how bloodroot got its common name?

Of the two parts of the set of names given to each plant, the first is the *generic* or *group* name. Closely related plants usually share the same generic name (commonly referred to as the *genus*). The second part refers to the individual species. It is often descriptive of the plant's color or shape, but can also be derived from the name of a person or a geographical area. While two different plants can share the same genus or the same species name, they do not share both. Thus, every plant's botanical name is unique. Not only do the genus and species of a plant identify it, but, as previously mentioned, they also usually provide descriptive information about the plant, which can add insight into its natural history. Some of our more familiar spring wildflowers demonstrate this beautifully.

Spring beauty (*Claytonia virginica*).

Marsh marigold (*Caltha palustris*).

■ Common and Botanical Names of Seven Spring Wildflowers

Bloodroot (Red Puccoon, Indian Paint, Squaw Root)

Botanical name: *Sanguinaria canadensis* (*Sanguinaria* = blood-red juice; *canadensis* = Canadian)

Dutchman's Breeches (White Hearts, Soldier's Caps, Ear-Drops)

Botanical name: *Dicentra cucullaria* (*Dicentra* = two spurs; *cucullaria* = disguise, cap)

Marsh Marigold (Cowslip, Capers, Soldier's-Buttons, Meadow Boots, Kingcup)

Botanical name: *Caltha palustris* (*Caltha* = goblet—in reference to the shape of the flower; *palustris* = of marshes)

Sessile-Leaved Bellwort (Wild Oats, Merrybells, Straw Bell)

Botanical name: *Uvularia sessilifolia* (*Uvularia* = palate—the flower resembles the human uvula; *sessilifolia* = sessile—the leaves have no stalk or petiole)

Spring Beauty (Claytonia, Quaker Ladies, Patience)

Botanical name: *Claytonia virginica* (*Claytonia* = after John Clayton, an American plant collector; *virginica* = from Virginia)

Wild Red Columbine (Rock Bells, Red Columbine, Meeting House)

Botanical name: *Aquilegia canadensis* (*Aquilegia* = eagle—the flower spurs resemble eagle claws; *canadensis* = Canadian)

Wood Anemone (Windflower, Mayflower, Nimble Weed, Wood Flower)

Botanical name: *Anemone quinquefolia* (*Anemone* = windy habitation; *quinquefolia* = five-leaved)

Sessile-leaved bellwort
(*Uvularia sessilifolia*).

Wild red columbine (*Aquilegia canadensis*).

Dutchman's breeches
(*Dicentra cucullaria*).

Wood anemone (*Anemone quinquefolia*).

] FAST FACTS [
Spring Wildflowers

▶ Wood anemone was used by the Chinese in funeral rites, symbolizing death.

▶ Clintonia was named for DeWitt Clinton, a former governor of New York and a naturalist.

▶ Bunchberry is in the dogwood family.

▶ The smoke of burning false solomon's seal is said to have been inhaled for two purposes: to treat insanity and to quiet a crying child. (Could there be a connection?)

▶ Although marsh marigold flowers appear as plain yellow to humans, insects—which are sensitive to the ultraviolet (UV) wavelength—see nectar guidelines, leading them to a dark flower center.

▶ Red trillium is so-called because its flower is a maroon-purple color and the plant has three leaves; flowers with three petals; three sepals; three-celled ovaries; and berries with three ribs. It is also called wake robin (because it blooms about the time migrating American robins return) and stinking Benjamin (it has an odor similar to rotting meat in order to attract flies and other pollinating insects).

▶ Although both the bumblebee and the honeybee pollinate trout lily, only the bumblebee's tongue is long enough to gather nectar from the deep nectaries, where it is located.

▶ Bumblebees are also one of the few insects capable of reaching the nectar in the upper tip of wild columbine's spurs. The other major pollinators are hummingbirds. Short-tongued insects have been known to chew holes in the tips of the spurs in order to get to the nectar.

▶ Bloodroot, a member of the poppy family, is the only member of its genus in the world. Its red juice was used by Native Americans to dye clothing and baskets, as well as paint for their face.

▶ The young shoots of bellwort species are edible (minus the leaves) when boiled like asparagus.

▶ Many spring wildflowers, including bloodroot, hepatica, and spring beauty, close at night and on cloudy days—an adaptation for protecting and conserving pollen.

Flowering Trees—*Pollination by Wind and Wing*

While most of us are familiar with the blossoms on fruit trees and several other species, surprisingly few people are aware that almost all deciduous trees are flowering plants, and as such, have flowers. Some are just not as obvious as others because it's not necessary for them to be. It happens that many of these inconspicuously-flowered trees blossom in early spring, beginning in April. Trees and early woodland wildflowers both take advantage of early spring's leafless canopy, but for different reasons—trees benefit from the open space and wildflowers from the presence of sunlight.

Dependent Giants
Because trees are actually flowering plants, pollination must occur in order for them to produce viable seeds. A microscopic pollen grain from a given flower must reach the egg in the female structure of a flower on a different tree of the same species in order for a seed to form. Being stationary, trees are dependent upon other agents to transport their pollen. Some trees, such as black cherry, hawthorn, basswood, and black locust rely heavily on insects as their pollinating agents. In order to attract insects, many of these trees produce flowers with showy petals, sticky pollen that adheres well to an insect's body, aromatic blossoms, and nectar—attributes that increase human awareness of them, as well. These trees produce less pollen than wind-pollinated trees because their pollination process is less haphazard.

Blowing in the Wind
Many species of trees—including most conifers, as well as oaks, ashes, elms, birches, and black walnut—do not depend on insects to transport their pollen and so expend very little energy on adaptations designed to lure insects to their blossoms. In-

Speckled alder—male (bottom) and female (top) flowers.

stead, the flowers of these trees are dependent upon the dispersal of their pollen by the wind.

One of their crucial adaptations is the timing of their flowering, which occurs before leaves emerge, as the foliage would obstruct the wind (this is in contrast to insect-pollinated trees, which usually flower at the same time or after they leaf out). Likewise, flower petals would simply get in the way, so are greatly reduced or absent. Pollen is usually copious (more than five million grains are released from a single birch flower) and very light and fluffy—easily swept up and carried by even a slight breeze. In addition, the female stigma, where the pollen grain must land in order for fertilization to occur, is exceptionally sticky.

Often wind-pollinated trees, instead of having what are called *perfect flowers* (possessing both male and female structures), have *imperfect flowers* (separate males and females), either on the same tree or on separate trees. The male flowers of wind-pollinated trees are often in the form of pendulous catkins (named for their resemblance to cat tails) that hang suspended from the branches, free to blow in the wind. The female flowers are usually tiny and inconspic-uous. There are several wind-pol-linated trees and shrubs that flower in April, including poplars, willows, American elm, and speckled alder.

Poplar fruits.

Willows are unusual in that their flowers are structural-ly designed for wind pollination but are also pollinated by insects, such as the hover fly.

] FAST FACTS [
Flowering Trees

▶ Pollination by wind is very common in grasses, most conifers, and many deciduous trees. About 80 percent of all plant pollination is achieved with the help of liv-ing organisms. Of the 20 percent that aren't pollinated by living agents, 98 percent are pollinated by wind and 2 percent by water.

▶ Wind-pollination is more prevalent as the latitude and altitude increase.

▶ Apens, willows, oaks, birches, maples, and pines are all wind-pollinated.

▶ The pollen of wind-pollinated trees is usually copious, smooth, lightweight, and not sticky as opposed to the heavier and sometimes stickier insect-pollinated tree pollen.

▶ The male flowers of insect-pollinated trees, such as apple trees, have far fewer pollen grains than a typical wind-pollinated tree flower, such as that of oak, birch, or ash.

▶ In a research study in which people were skin-tested with pollen from 12 wind-pollinated tree species, boxelder, willow, and hickory elicited the highest allergic reactions.

▶ The abundant pollen from wind-pollinated trees (and grasses) irritates hay fever sufferers because of a protein it contains. While this protein causes an al-lergic reaction in some people, it serves an important function for the plant. Wind-pollinated plants are often "self-incompatible" and pollen grains will not germi-nate if they land on a stigma of the same plant. It is this allergen protein that inhibits self-fertilization.

▶ Ash trees are wind-pollinated and produce and shed copious amounts of pollen. Research shows that wind carries ash pollen as far as 110 miles from the point of dispersion.

▶ Many trees of colder climates, such as oak, poplar, birch, elm, walnut, alder, hazel, and conifers are wind-pollinated.

vitality

The stirrings of April intensify in May, with brighter colors, a greater variety of sounds and scents, and a rapidly increasing wildlife population contributing to the energy that spring brings to the earth. The forest floor slowly becomes shaded by the leaves of the trees above, and the earliest spring wildflowers develop seed-laden fruits. Birds stake out territories and attract mates; some, including cavity nesters, lay eggs. Trills, plunks, and snores announce the beginning of amphibian courtship rituals. Every shade of green imaginable can be found on New England hillsides. Nature announces her vitality in every way possible, overloading our senses wherever we turn.

nature notes

AMPHIBIANS

Eastern Spadefoot—*Breeding*

Eastern spadefoot toads are one of the region's rarest amphibians. They are not found in northern New England and are rare and very localized in southern New England. Those that do inhabit this area are seen infrequently due to their secretive and nocturnal habits. They spend much of their time underground, emerging once a week or so at dawn and dusk to feed on flies, spiders, crickets, worms, and snails. During very dry periods they have been known to remain underground for weeks or months in order to keep their skin moist. Usually in April or May on a single night during a heavy rain storm they gather at vernal pools to breed.

Pickerel Frog—*Calling and Breeding*

The pickerel frog is the most abundant and widespread frog in New England, with the exception of the green frog. It can be found in wet meadows and woodlands, as well as shallow ponds with thick vegetation at their edges. The pickerel frog is often confused with the northern leopard frog (see p. 37), as both have spots on their back and legs. While leopard frog spots are round or oval, those on the pickerel frog are square to rectangular in shape. In addition, the color of the inner thighs of the pickerel frog varies from yellow to deep orange.

Pickerel frogs seek shallow, clear bodies of water in which to breed in April and May. Their low snoring call, often followed by a series of grunts, is

Male pickerel frog.

very distinctive. Following breeding, the females lay masses of eggs, which they attach to underwater vegetation.

Pickerel frogs are very sensitive to water pollution; if you see them in a pond or stream it is indicative of clean water.

Northern Two-Lined Salamander—*Laying Eggs*

The northern two-lined salamander, named for the two black stripes running down its sides, is considered a brook-side salamander, for it usually is found under rocks and logs along stream banks. Unlike the northern dusky and spring salamanders, which are also found in the saturated soil beside streams, this salamander can occasionally be found wandering in the woods some distance from running water.

Northern two-lined salamander.

Eggs are usually laid singly in May and June on the bottoms of stones or logs in streams. Several two-lined salamanders have been known to deposit their eggs under the same stone, with one adult remaining with the eggs until they hatch—a period of 4 to 10 weeks, depending on the temperature of the water. Once hatched, the larvae remain in the water for the next two to three years before developing into adults.

■ Amphibians and Reptiles: Similarities and Differences

Amphibians (Frogs, Toads, Salamanders)

Ectotherm (cannot generate own body temperature)
Metamorphosis (different developmental stages)
Developmental stage with gills
External fertilization
Eggs often laid in water
Lay eggs
Gelatinous eggs
Soft skin with glands that secrete mucus
Usually live in or relatively near water

Reptiles (Snakes, Turtles, Lizards)

Ectotherm
No metamorphosis
No gills
Internal fertilization
Eggs laid on land
Lay eggs or live birth
Dry, leathery eggs
Dry skin with no glands; scales
Can live far from water

American toad.

Snapping turtle.

REPTILES

■ **Reptiles Breeding in May**

Snapping turtle
Eastern box turtle
Spiny softshell
Bog turtle
Painted turtle
Spotted turtle
Wood turtle
Common five-lined skink
Northern watersnake
Common gartersnake
Eastern ribbonsnake
Eastern hog-nosed snake
Ring-necked snake
Eastern wormsnake
North American racer
Smooth greensnake
Eastern ratsnake
Copperhead
Timber rattlesnake

■ **Reptiles with Teeth**

Snakes
Lizards

■ **Reptiles without Teeth**

Turtles

Spotted Turtle—*Breeding and Laying Eggs*

The spotted turtle is primarily a southern New England reptile. It lives in shallow water habitats as diverse as vernal pools, permanent ponds, slow-moving streams, and drainage ditches, and is well-known for its intolerance of polluted water. Found mainly in lowlands, it is distinctively marked with yellow-orange dots on its blue-black *carapace* (upper shell).

Spotted turtle.

The spotted turtle breeds from March through June, peaking in May. The females deposit an average of four or five eggs in sunny locations, such as fields and roadsides, as well as mossy hummocks (below which they often hibernate in the winter). One to eight eggs are often laid, and the hatchlings, like several other New England turtle species, often overwinter in the nest.

Common Five-Lined Skink—*Breeding*

The common five-lined skink is the only species of lizard that resides in and is native to New England. Contrary to its name, the "common" five-lined skink's population is very spotty in the Northeast, with records existing in Connecticut, Massachusetts, and Vermont. Due to its habit of spending

Common five-lined skink.

much of its time on ledges and rocky slopes, it is seldom seen.

Young skinks have a bright blue tail that turns dull gray as the lizard matures. During the time of courtship, the area around the males' jaw turns bright red. After breeding, the female skink lays her eggs under rocks and logs, or in rotting stumps, and remains with them until they hatch.

SNAKE SCALES

Milksnake.

Snakes are covered with plate-like scales connected by an elastic skin. The scales protect the snake from injury as it moves over rough ground, as well as from small predators and biting insects. Scales may aid locomotion by allowing the snake to grip the surface it is climbing or passing over, helping it pull itself forward horizontally or vertically. Scales also minimize water loss from evaporation.

There are different kinds of scales in different parts of a snake's body: dorsal (back and sides); ventral (underside); head; and subcaudal (beneath the tail).

BIRDS

American Bittern—
Calling, Breeding, and Laying Eggs
If you live in New England and you're a visitor of inland, freshwater marshes, you have a chance of seeing the elusive and well-camouflaged American bittern, but an even better chance of hearing one. American bitterns have a very distinct and audible courtship call referred to by birders as a deep pumping "oong-ka-choonk." The bird gets its nicknames "thunder-pumper" and "stake-driver" from the sound of this call.

When hunting for insects, small mammals, frogs, fish, or crayfish, the American bittern uses stealth—moving slowly and standing still for long periods of time. When alarmed, it often stands with its beak pointed to the sky, in an effort to blend in with the cattails and other vegetation.

American bittern.

Great Blue Heron—*Nesting*
Great blue herons, the largest and most widespread heron in North America, nest throughout New England in colonies ranging in size from a few to several dozen pairs. Their large, stick platform nests are usually located high up in trees and are repaired and reused every year. Most *heronries* (nesting sites) are located near water where ample fish can be found. The dramatic recovery of the beaver pop-

Great blue heron.

ulation in New England continues to provide additional nesting and foraging areas for great blue herons in the form of beaver ponds.

Ruby-Throated Hummingbird—*Returning to Breeding Grounds*

The ruby-throated hummingbird is the only hummingbird that nests east of the Mississippi River, and its return every spring is eagerly anticipated. The sexes migrate separately, with males arriving on their breeding territory several days before the females.

Males possess iridescent red

Ruby-throated hummingbird.

throats (in the right light) and females have tail feathers tipped in white. The roles of the two genders are even more different than their respective coloration. Males are polygamous and, after copulating with a female, assume no further responsibility for the building of a nest or the care of offspring. The female builds a lichen-covered nest, incubates and raises two, sometimes three, nestlings by herself.

Hummingbirds seek nectar primarily from tubular-shaped flowers (as well as feeders provided by humans), beating their wings 53 times a second as they hover and feed. Unlike most birds, their legs are so short that they can neither walk nor hop.

Males leave for their wintering grounds a full month before the females and the current year's young. They fly nonstop across the Gulf of Mexico to reach their wintering grounds in Central America.

American Kestrel—*Nesting*

The American kestrel, formerly known as the sparrow hawk, is the smallest, most numerous, and most widespread North American falcon. It breeds throughout the Northeast, and except for the northern New England states, is also found in the region in the winter.

Kestrels inhabit open fields with low ground vegetation— prime areas for the insects and invertebrates that they feed on. This falcon is well-known for its habit of hovering in the air while it surveys the ground below for grasshoppers, crickets, small rodents, and other prey, particularly when a perch is not available.

American kestrel.

Males and females have different plumage: the male has blue-gray wings and a lightly spotted chest, while the larger female has rufous wings and streaking on the chest. As a cavity nester, the kestrel uses old woodpecker holes and has adapted well to nest boxes when natural cavities are in limited supply. The kestrel appears comfortable with the presence of humans, often choosing to reside near them.

Ring-Necked Duck—*Nesting*

The ring-necked duck is named for a chestnut-colored collar on its black neck, visible only when

Canada goose gosling.

Canada Goose—*Hatching and Heading for Water*

Canada geese goslings hatch this month. Breaking out of an egg is a demanding task, which requires specific adaptations. Many birds have what is called a "hatching muscle" on the back of their head, as well as an "egg tooth" (a horny knob, or projection, near the tip of the upper half of their bill, which is only present for the first few days of a young chick's life). The hatching muscle provides the chick's head with the strong thrust that, with the egg tooth, breaks the shell, producing the "pip" in the egg that is the first sign of hatching. Gradually the chick enlarges the hole in the pipped egg, turning in the shell while puncturing all the way around it. It can take anywhere from a few hours to several days (depending on the species of bird) from when the egg is first pipped until the young bird actually hatches.

Ring-necked ducks.

you are very close to the bird. More obvious is the white ring around its bill. These birds breed in northern New England and overwinter along the coast of southern New England. They typically nest amongst dense low vegetation in the shallow, freshwater wetlands of Maine, northern New Hampshire, and the Northeast Kingdom of Vermont, usually in May.

After being incubated for roughly a month, the eggs hatch, and the down-covered ducklings are up and out of the nest within a day.

Red-Winged Blackbird—*Nesting*

Marshes and agricultural areas near wetlands are likely spots to find nesting red-winged blackbirds. Their well-camouflaged cup nests are made of grasses, cattail reeds, and rootlets, and are often woven into cattail stalks or low shrubs. Red-winged blackbird nests are commonly

Female red-winged blackbird with nesting material.

A red-winged blackbird nest and eggs.

found near or over water, anywhere from 3 inches to 14 feet above the water or ground. The female builds the nest in three to six days and then incubates the eggs, during which time she is fed by the male. Frequently you will find eastern kingbirds and red-winged blackbirds nesting in the same shrub or tree.

White-Breasted Nuthatch—*Nesting*

White-breasted nuthatches are often seen spiraling down the trunks of trees head first while probing for insects and storing seeds behind loose bark. They nest in dead limb holes or other natural cavities, as well as old woodpecker nesting holes. While white-breasted nuthatches remain paired throughout the year, courtship behavior

A white-breasted nuthatch "bill sweeping" at its nesting hole.

usually doesn't start until the end of winter. During the breeding season both males and females engage in behavior termed "bill sweeping"—they sweep their bills in a wide arc both in and outside their nest cavity, usually while holding an insect. This can go on for several minutes. There is speculation that this serves as a territorial defense mechanism; for example, one theory suggests that holding a crushed insect and sweeping it back and forth near a cavity could discourage squirrels from taking over the nest cavity.

Like many cavity nesters, white-breasted nuthatches have white eggs (there's no need for camouflage in a cavity); they hatch after 12 days of incubation by the female.

Baltimore Oriole—*Nesting*

When back on their New England breeding grounds, the female Baltimore oriole is treated to an extravagant courtship by the male. The male displays by singing, chattering, hopping from perch to perch

Male Baltimore oriole.

in front of the female, and bowing repeatedly with his wings lowered and tail fanned.

The nest of the Baltimore oriole is usually attached to the tip of a drooping branch, safe from most predators. It is a deep, water-resistant pouch, intricately woven from mostly plant fibers—it often includes milkweed, hair, yarn, string, and grapevine bark—with an opening at the top. It is usually lined with hair and/or

Female Baltimore oriole with nesting material.

white pine needles. The female builds the nest by herself, taking anywhere from four-and-a-half to eight days to do it. In New England, only orioles and vireos build nests that are suspended from their rims; other birds place them on top of branches.

Baltimore oriole nest.

A belted kingfisher nest in a bank.

Common Loon—*Nesting*

Since their return to the Northeast, many common loons have paired, mated, selected a nesting site, built a nest, laid two military-green speckled eggs, and now share the duty of incubating those eggs. Due to

Common loon on its nest.

the position of their legs (extremely far back on their body), loons have great prowess as divers, but very little when it comes to walking. Thus, their nest sites are usually at the very edge of an island or hummock, where they can easily slip on and off the nest into the water. Successful nest sites (from which loon chicks fledge) are often reused from year to year. Extreme caution should be taken to remain far from an active nest, as loons are easily disturbed.

Belted Kingfisher—*Nesting*

A pronounced rattling cry often announces the presence of a belted kingfisher at ponds and near streams where it feeds. The belted kingfisher is one of the few species of birds in which the female is more brightly colored than the male. She has two "belts," one of which is rust-colored, one blue, whereas the male only has one blue stripe across his breast. You can often see the belted kingfisher hovering above the water before it dives headfirst after fish, which it grabs with its beak. It then flies to a nearby branch and stuns the fish by pounding it against the perch. This allows the bird to align the fish in its beak and swallow it, head first.

Together, male and female kingfishers dig a 3- to 7-foot burrow and hollow out a chamber at the end, which serves as their nest site. While one bird digs, the other perches nearby and continuously gives its rattle call. Burrows usually slope upward from the entrance, probably as a flooding precaution, and have reached as far as 15 feet in length. They may make several burrows in one site, but they will only use one.

Although they are not lined, nesting cavities accumulate a layer of regurgitated *pellets* (undigestible parts of consumed fish and arthropods) between the eggs and the soil once incubation has started. You can tell if a nest is active by looking for two furrows at the entrance, made by the birds' feet as they enter and exit the tunnel. Just as they shared the digging of the burrow, belted kingfishers share incubation of the eggs, with the female incubating during the night and the male during the day. They also both rear their young. Nests are sometimes used for more than one breeding season.

Wild Turkey— *Laying Eggs*

Wild turkey nests are not elaborate; they are usually simple depressions in the soil, lined with dead leaves. Often they are located at the base of a tree or under

A wild turkey nest and eggs.

brush. As with most ground-nesting birds whose eggs are vulnerable to predation, wild turkeys have large clutches, laying anywhere from 8 to 15 eggs.

Pileated woodpecker scat in wood chips.

Pileated Woodpecker— *Sign (Scat)*

When you see a tree with fresh oblong pileated wood-pecker holes and a pile of wood chips at the base of the trunk, look for pileated woodpecker scat—usually consisting of the exoskeletons of carpenter ants. These insects are the reason why pileated woodpeckers make excavation holes in the trees—once reaching the dead heartwood in the center of the tree where the ants create their galleries, the pileated woodpecker scrapes them out with its barbed tongue. The larger the holes and piles of wood chips, the longer the woodpecker has been excavating in that location, and the greater the chances of finding its scat.

CAVITY-NESTING BIRDS

In some forests, 30 to 45 percent of bird species are cavity nesters. In North America alone, 55 avian species nest in cavities. Cavity-nesting birds are classified as *primary excavators* (can excavate hardwood—marked by a "P"); *weak excavators* (can excavate soft, dead wood—marked by a "W"); or *secondary cavity-users* (can utilize existing cavities—marked by an "S").

Red-bellied woodpecker.

Wood duck (S)
Common goldeneye (S)
Hooded merganser (S)
Common merganser (S)
American kestrel (S)
Eastern screech-owl (S)
Great horned owl (S)
Barn owl (S)
Barred owl (S)
Northern saw-whet owl (S)
Chimney swift (S)
Belted kingfisher (P)
Red-headed woodpecker (P)
Red-bellied woodpecker (P)
Yellow-bellied sapsucker (P)
Downy woodpecker (P)
Hairy woodpecker (P)
American three-toed woodpecker (P)
Black-backed woodpecker (P)
Northern flicker (P)
Pileated woodpecker (P)
Great crested flycatcher (S)
Purple martin (S)
Tree swallow (S)
Northern rough-winged swallow (S)
Black-capped chickadee (W)
Boreal chickadee (W)
Tufted titmouse (S)
Red-breasted nuthatch (W, S)
White-breasted nuthatch (S)
Brown creeper (S)
Carolina wren (S)
House wren (S)
Eastern bluebird (S)
European starling (S)
House sparrow (S)

Hairy woodpecker.

Pileated woodpecker.

Downy woodpecker.

Black-capped chickadee.

Eastern bluebird.

House wren.

Great crested flycatcher.

Tufted titmouse.

White-breasted nuthatch.

Hooded merganser.

European starling.

Red-breasted nuthatch.

THE RETURN OF THE SONGBIRDS

Chesnut-sided warbler.

Common yellowthroat.

One of the greatest pleasures of May is the welcome sight and sound of songbirds returning from their wintering grounds. (If you keep a record of when you first see each species every year, you may have noticed that many birds are arriving earlier each spring as temperatures warm along the East Coast of the United States.) Before the trees leaf out you have a prayer of seeing many of these returning migrants, but once tree buds have opened, viewing birds in the canopy is a great deal harder. A familiarity with some of the more common bird songs can greatly enrich the early riser's morning. What time of day a species of bird begins and stops singing is determined in large part by the amount of light—the songs of the American robin, wood thrush, and hermit thrush, for instance, are triggered by low light levels, and so they are often heard early as well as late in the day. You are more likely to hear insect-eating songbirds early in the day than seed-eaters, as insect-eaters can find food more easily in dim light. (Read more about songbirds in May on p. 101.)

Here is a sampling of some of the songs commonly heard in New England:

Eastern wood-peewee	"pee-a-wee"
Red-eyed vireo	"going up–coming down–going up–coming down"
Black-capped chickadee	"chick-a-dee-dee-dee-dee"
Tufted titmouse	"Peter–Peter–Peter–Peter"
Red-breasted nuthatch	"yank–yank"
Carolina wren	"tea-kettle–tea-kettle–tea-kettle"
Wood thrush	"ee-o-lay"
American robin	"cheer up, cheerily, cheerio, cheerily"
Yellow warbler	"sweet–sweet–sweet–I'm–so–sweet"
Chestnut-sided warbler	"pleased–pleased–pleased–to–meet–you"
Ovenbird	"teacher–teacher–TEAcher–TEACHER!"
Common yellowthroat	"witchity–witchity–witchity"
Canada warbler	"click! Turn-it-on-turn-it-off"
Eastern towhee	"drink–your–teeeeeeeeeeeeea"
White-throated sparrow	"poor Sam Peabody–Peabody–Peabody"
Red-winged blackbird	"konk–la–ree"
Eastern meadowlark	"sweet–spring–is–here"

Wood thrush.

MAMMALS

Woodchuck—*Giving Birth*

Woodchucks, being *diurnal* (active in the daytime) herbivores, begin to be seen with regularity once hibernation is over and herbaceous plants such as dandelions, clover, and grasses begin to grow in the spring. In April or May woodchucks give birth, usually to four, five, or six blind, naked young. Fur appears in about two weeks, young woodchucks are weaned in five or six weeks, and by early July they leave their parents to dig their own shallow burrows.

When not in fields or gardens devouring plants, woodchucks live in extensive (from 25 to 30 feet long) underground burrows, which they excavate 2 to 5 feet under the ground. During the process of digging a single tunnel, a woodchuck removes about 700 pounds of subsoil. In the summer woodchucks tend to live in burrows located in fields and

Woodchuck burrow and mound.

pastures, rarely straying more than 50 yards from them. Come fall, many move to woodland burrows where they hibernate through the winter months. Entrances to these winter burrows are often located under tree stumps and stonewalls. It is easy to tell when a woodchuck burrow is active by the mound of fresh dirt that accumulates outside its entrance.

This mound is the result of regular cleaning of the burrow by its resident. Other animals, including cottontail rabbits, Virginia opossums, raccoons, foxes, and skunks do use old woodchuck burrows as their home, but the dirt outside the entrance would be old, not fresh.

This largest member of the New England squirrel family shares its relatives' ability to climb and has been known to go up fairly high in a tree in order to survey the surrounding land. The woodchuck is also a proficient swimmer.

Woodchucks are most active in the early morning and late in the afternoon, often preferring to bask in the sunshine during the middle of the day.

Moose—*Giving Birth*

After being extirpated, or nearly so, in much of New England in the 1800s, the moose population has rebounded in the last century in northern New England, due in large part to a decline in agriculture

Moose.

and the resulting increase in moose habitat. In late May and early June cows give birth to one (on the rare occasion, two) young. The newborn calf weighs between 24 and 35 pounds, and can stand up within 12 hours of birth. During the first five months it gains over 2 pounds a day. The calf is weaned at six months but remains with its mother for a year, being driven off just before the mother gives birth to a new calf. Some yearlings return to their mother's side for a period of time after new young are born; some do not. (Read more about moose on p. 251.)

American Beaver—*Giving Birth and Leaving Lodge*

Young beavers are born fully furred, and their eyes open at or soon after birth. Each kit weighs roughly a pound. Some enter the water the day they are born, although most spend the major-

An adult and a young beaver.

A two-year-old beaver explores a shallow, leaf-littered pond in search of a new home.

ity of the first four or five weeks of their life inside the lodge. Initially the fur on the kits is not water-repellent. It takes about a month for their anal and castor glands to function and produce the oil and castoreum with which beavers "grease" and water-proof their fur. Even while still nursing from their mother, the kits usually begin gnawing wood—usually around 11 days of age. Other plants are eaten when they are a little over two weeks old. When they weigh about 7 or 8 pounds, the kits are big enough to regularly explore the world outside their lodge and feed with their parents and siblings.

Just before the birth of a new litter, two-year-old beavers are driven out, or they leave the beaver colony of their own volition to establish a new residence. Realizing that the food supply can feed only so many mouths, the parents encourage this departure.

Eastern Mole—*Giving Birth*

In southern New England, at the northern edge of their East Coast range, eastern moles give birth to litters of two to five young in their underground nests this month. Young moles are born blind and naked, but in a little over a week they are covered with a fine, velvet-like covering of light gray fur. They leave the nest and begin to excavate tunnels on their own in about four weeks. In crumbly soil eastern moles are capable of burrowing at a rate of up to 18 feet an hour. Thanks to their diet and activity, they make a significant dent in the Japanese and June beetle larvae population, as well as help control other insect pests and aerate the soil.

Bobcat—*Giving Birth*

Bobcats usually have their young between late April and mid-May, although births as late as September are not unheard of. Two to four young bobcats are born with spotted fur, weighing between one-half and three-quarters of a pound and

Bobcat.

measuring roughly 10 inches long. They are weaned when they are two months old, but remain with their mother until they are nearly a year.

Red Fox—*Playing Outside Den*

Although red foxes give birth in March and April, there is usually no sign of the pups outside the den until early May, when most are about five weeks old. For the first month their coats are dark gray but about the time they appear above ground they molt and have sandy-colored fur.

Red fox pup.

The mother begins to wean her pups now, and they start to eat solid food. Both parents, and occasionally "helper" foxes—usually daughters from a previous litter that remain in the area—bring food to them.

American Black Bear—*Foraging*

American black bear sign is not hard to come by if you live near forested wilderness. They leave very large tracks, trampled bushes, overturned logs and stumps, mud wallows, and tooth and claw marks on trees. Much of their activity and sign have to do with their omnivorous diet. Bears are opportunistic and will eat just about anything. They are partial to berries, grapes, apples, acorns, beechnuts, leaves of deciduous trees, jack-in-the-pulpit roots, jewelweed, and sunflower seeds. Although most of their diet is vegetative, they also eat frogs, fish, and mice, as well as colonial insects such as adult bees, wasps, and ants (and their eggs and larvae, too). In order to find these invertebrates, American black bears often tear apart rotting logs and stumps, leaving obvious evidence of their activity. It is common to find not one, but several, stumps or logs that have been visited by bears in a given location.

A log torn apart by a bear.

INSECTS & ARACHNIDS

American copper butterfly.

Spring azure butterfly.

■ **Butterflies Emerging from Chrysalises in May**

Black swallowtail
Eastern tiger swallowtail
Spicebush swallowtail
Cabbage white
Clouded sulphur
Brown elfin
Eastern pine elfin
Eastern tailed-blue
Spring azure
Meadow fritillary
American copper
Pearl crescent
Mourning cloak
American lady
Red admiral
Dreamy duskywing
Juvenal's duskywing
Cobweb skipper

■ **Insect Mouthparts**

Piercing and Sucking
Mosquitoes, leafhoppers, assassin bugs, squash bugs, and aphids

Sponging
Houseflies and most other flies

Siphoning
Moths and butterflies, and the leaf-footed bug

Chewing
Wasps, beetles, grasshoppers, dragonflies, lacewings, crickets, katydids, praying mantises, moth and butterfly larvae, and some bees

The grasshopper's mouthparts are specialized for chewing.

Lady beetles mating.

Lady Beetle—*Mating, Laying Eggs, and Eggs Hatching*

There are approximately 500 species of lady beetles in North America, many of which were introduced. Gardeners are particularly indebted to lady beetles, for they are responsible for consuming vast numbers of aphids, scale insects, mealybugs, and other soft-bodied insects that damage plants. The

Lady beetle pupa (left) and larval skin (right).

convergent lady beetle eats almost 60 aphids a day and consumes up to 500 aphids before laying hundreds of eggs. The majority of colorful lady beetles, both adults and larvae, are predators, but a handful of lady beetle species in New England are leaf-eating or fungus feeders. (Read more about lady beetles on p. 292.)

Deer Fly—*Laying Eggs*

Single-layered clusters of tiny, oblong, white eggs can be found this time of year on vegetation overhanging water or wet soil. Deer fly and horse fly egg clusters fit the description—they are similar, but not identical. Deer fly eggs are in a single

A close look at this egg-laying deer fly's eyes reveals their striking iridescence.

layer, whereas horse fly eggs are in clusters consisting of three or four layers.

Baltimore Checkerspot Butterfly—
Eggs Hatching and Larvae Feeding

The female Baltimore checkerspot butterfly lays her reddish eggs in clusters of up to 700 on a host plant—frequently, but not exclusively, turtlehead—during the summer months. When the eggs hatch the following May, the larvae form a silk nest on the plant, within which they feed and live until August. At that time the larvae stop eating and spin a new web on the ground within which they pass the winter. In the spring the larvae leave the nest independently and go off to feed on turtlehead, plantain, honeysuckle, lousewort, and viburnum. (It is hard

Baltimore checkerspot larva.

Baltimore checkerspot larvae on stalk.

to miss these boldly colored caterpillars marked with bands of orange and black and covered with black spines.) Eventually, the larvae pupate, emerge as striking black, orange, and white butterflies, mate, and begin the cycle all over again.

Female fishfly.

Fishfly—Emerging as Winged Adult

There are many insects that spend at least one stage of their life under water. Some, including fishflies, dobsonflies, dragonflies, damselfies, mayflies, caddisflies, and stoneflies, spend their larval stage in the water and emerge as winged adults. As a larva the fishfly is referred to—along with dobsonfly larvae—as a *hellgrammite*, and is an aggressive predator living in a narrow, clear stream or river. As an adult, a fishfly either does not feed at all or drinks small amounts of nectar and fruit juice. Most adult fishflies have pale wings, but the species pictured here (*Nigronia fasciatus*) is known for its blackish wings with white markings. Male fishflies have feathery antennae much like moths.

Dragonfly—Emerging as Winged Adult

After hatching from an egg, the dragonfly goes through two main stages in life—as an aquatic larva and a winged adult. These two forms couldn't be more different, with the exception that they are both voracious predators. Most of a dragonfly's life (several months to several years, depending on the species) is spent in the larval stage, underwater. Different

Dragonfly emerging.

species have different body shapes and the larvae are classified accordingly, as "claspers," "sprawlers," "hiders," or "burrowers." It is possible to identify the species of dragonfly in its larval form as well as by the final skin that is molted.

At the end of the larval stage, metamorphosis takes place. The larva emerges from the water and clings onto nearby rocks or vegetation while its skin splits down the center of its head and back and the adult dragonfly pulls itself out. As soon as it emerges it pumps its body full of air and sends fluid into its wing veins, causing them to expand. Initially, the adult dragonfly is pale, soft, and its wings have a definite sheen. It flies weakly for cover shortly after the wings are fully expanded. Over the course of the first day, it gradually hardens, develops richer colors, and improves its flying ability as the wings lose their sheen and become more rigid. (For more about dragonflies, see p. 146.)

(For more about dragonflies, see p. 146.)

Crane Fly—*Emerging*
Crane flies are often mistaken for giant mosquitoes, but fortunately, crane flies do not bite. Some species have mosquito-like beaks, but these mouthparts are used to obtain nectar, not drink blood. (To determine whether you are looking at a crane fly or a mosquito, examine the middle section—the thorax—of its body closely, just above where the wings attach. Crane flies have a "V"-shaped demarcation, while mosquitoes are covered with scales.) You often find these insects in cool, shady areas. Of the 15,000 species of crane flies in the world, 1,500 are found in North America. Some of them

Crane fly.

Eastern tiger swallowtail butterfly.

have aquatic larval stages, but not all. Many species metamorphose into winged adults in May.

Eastern Tiger Swallowtail Butterfly—*Emerging*
Eastern tiger swallowtail butterflies spend the winter as *chrysalises*—inch-long structures that rest their bottom tip against a supporting plant. They are anchored to the plant by a button of silk spun during the larval stage. The upper portion of the chrysalis is then suspended at about a 30-degree angle from the plant's stem, supported by a silk strap woven by the larva prior to pupating.

In May or June, when there are enough flowers blossoming to provide necessary nectar, eastern tiger swallowtail butterflies emerge. Although common, the young larvae of this species are rarely seen, as they feed at night and hide in curled up leaves during the day.

There are two species of tiger swallowtails whose ranges overlap in New England: the Canadian tiger swallowtail, which is abundant across Canada, and the eastern tiger swallowtail, common in the Northeast. These two butterflies are extremely similar in appearance and have been known to hybridize.

PLANTS & FUNGI

False morel.

True morel.

Red maple.

American beech.

False and True Morel—*Fruiting*

True morels are considered a delicacy by some— these mushrooms, with distinctive honeycomb-like caps, are indeed edible, but not all morels are. Another group of fungi, referred to as *false* morels, somewhat resemble the edible species, and also appear in the spring, but they are considered potentially toxic. One difference between the two is that true, edible morels have a hollow stem, whereas false morel stems are usually filled with cotton-like fibers or are fairly solid (although there are exceptions). The caps of true morels are honeycombed whereas the caps of false morels are convoluted, bearing some resemblance to a human brain. It's wise to check with a mycologist (a biologist who studies fungi) before eating any wild mushroom, including morels.

Deciduous Tree—*Leaves Emerging*

If you are very observant you know that buds on trees don't magically appear in the spring; they are present on tree limbs all winter, having developed over the previous summer. Miniature branches and leaves are tightly wrapped in protective "bud

scales" until the lengthening days of spring break their dormancy and they open. This response to the changing *photoperiod* (the duration of an organism's daily exposure to light) by trees (as well as other plants) is a great evolutionary adaptation that helps to prevent tree buds from opening prematurely in the fall or during a January thaw, which would be catastrophic.

Yellow, pink, and showy lady's slippers.

Lady's Slipper—*Flowering*

Three species of lady's slippers (yellow, pink and showy) can be found in New England. They all belong to *Cypripedium*, a genus of hardy orchids. Other members of the Orchid family grow here, but these are the only common *pouched* orchids in the Northeast. (Read more about the lady's slipper on pp. 92 and 150.)

Painted trillium.

Painted Trillium—*Flowering*
Painted trillium grows in acid woods and bogs, where it brightens the forest floor with its white and red blossoms in May. It is often found in the shade of acid-loving trees such as eastern white pine, red maple, red spruce, and balsam fir. The petals are white with a blaze of crimson at the center, and they are slightly wavy along the edges. The blossoms have a slightly fetid odor, but nothing compared to their relative, red trillium. Over the summer painted trillium develops a single, bright red, berry-like fruit (see photo p. 208).

Miterwort—*Flowering*
This slender-stalked, 4- to 8-inch-tall member of the Saxifrage family, also known as bishop's cap, is one of the most delicate-looking spring wildflowers in New England. Its lacy flowers are reminiscent of tiny snowflakes. The fruit of this plant resembles a mitre,

Miterwort.

or bishop's cap, hence, its common names. Look for it in moist, calcium-rich woodlands.

Orange Cedar Rust Gall—*Producing Telia*
The strange orange growths on the eastern redcedar tree pictured here are a form of fungus called cedar-apple rust. The fungus spends part of its life cycle on one host, usually a member of the *Juniperus* genus (in this case eastern redcedar), and part on another host in the Rose family. It requires both hosts to complete its life cycle. Rusts spend the winter on their juniper hosts as stem galls. In the spring, bright orange, gelatinous, horn-like growths one-half to three-quarters-of-an-inch long emerge from the galls. These orange structures are called *telia* and they produce bright orange spores, called *teliospores*, which spread by wind to infect the Rose family host. Apple, crabapple, hawthorn, quince, serviceberry, and pear all serve as host plants. The teliospores infect their leaves, fruit, and stem tissue, and produce bright yellow- or orange-colored lesions. From these lesions more spore-producing structures form, which then infect cedars, continuing the cycle year-round.

Orange cedar rust galls.

Clintonia—*Flowering*
Clintonia's three-parted flower helps to identify it as a member of the Lily family. It grows in acid soil in moist woods, and its yellow flowers, if pollinated, develop into round, bright blue berries (see photo p. 173). Because of Clintonia's fruit, it is also referred to as blue bead lily. Clintonia occurs commonly with Indian cucumber root, red trillium, hobblebush, and striped maple. The genus this flower

Clintonia.

Cut-leaved toothwort.

Superficially this plant resembles a wild strawberry; it only grows to a height of 3 to 6 inches and has dark, shiny leaves and a single, star-shaped, white flower. The plant is appropriately named after the long, slender, creeping, much-branched bright golden-yellow roots that run just beneath the surface of the forest floor. Native Americans chewed on the roots to treat mouth sores. Ruffed grouse feed on goldthread's leaves.

Goldthread root.

belongs to was named after DeWitt Clinton, an eighteenth-century botanist and politician.

Cut-Leaved Toothwort—*Flowering*
Chances are good that if a plant has flowers with four petals in the shape of a cross, it is in the Mustard family. Cut-leaved toothwort, named for its deeply divided leaflets as well as tooth-like projections on its underground stem, or *rhizome*, is just such a plant. You will find most members of the Mustard family growing in fields and sunny habitats, but toothworts actually prefer the forest floor.

Goldthread—*Flowering*
Goldthread, a member of the Buttercup family, is found in damp, mossy swamps and woods.

Goldthread flower.

Blue-Eyed Grass—*Flowering*

Blue-eyed grass.

There are eight species of blue-eyed grasses in the Northeast, all of which have stiff, grass-like leaves and wiry stems—but none of them is actually a grass. These beautiful members of the Iris family have six blue-violet petals, each tipped with a bristle-like point. Dark lines, possibly *nectar guides*, on these petals, lead pollinating insects, mostly bees, to the golden center of the flower. Individual flowers stay open only for a day or less, and never open at night. Look for them in meadows and pastures.

Bigtooth aspen catkin with seeds.

Poplar/Aspen—*Dispersing Seeds*

You may have noticed little bits of white fluff floating through the air when May breezes are blowing. These are the tiny, wind-dispersed seeds of various *Populus* (poplar) tree species—quaking aspen, bigtooth aspen, eastern cottonwood—which are blown from pendulous catkins hanging from their branches. These catkins are covered with female flowers early in the spring, and those that are pollinated develop into seeds. Their cotton-like threads catch the wind, ensuring their dispersal far and wide. Every four or five years, abundant seed crops are produced; however, most poplars reproduce vegetatively from suckers, rather than from seeds. (See more about flowering trees on p. 69.)

THE ORCHID POLLINATION PROCESS

Pink, yellow, and showy lady's-slippers (see p. 89) all possess an inflated sac, or labellum, which is actually a modified petal. This "pouch" is crucial to the lady's slipper's survival, for it is what attracts the insects responsible for pollination. Without pollination, there are no seeds. If you look closely you can see faint lines on the pouch that guide insects to the opening at its top. The leaf-like twisted lateral petals that twirl out from the top are also thought to be insect guides. If neither the lines nor the petals are successful, the lady's slipper's heavy nectar scent may lure the insects in (although disappointment awaits them, for they will find no nectar).

A showy lady's slipper and an insect pollinator.

Once inside insects are met with a bit of an obstacle course. Hairs grow toward the exit hole (much smaller than the entrance hole) at the back of the labellum, encouraging trapped insects to head in that direction. Prior to escaping out of this chamber, however, the insect must enter a constricted passage where it rubs against a comb-like structure (*stigma*) that removes pollen from its body, thereby pollinating the flower. It then passes by *anthers*, which deposit pollen back onto the insect. (See p. 54 for a diagram of flower parts.) This enables cross-pollination to occur when it visits another lady's-slipper.

Occasionally you see a pouch with a hole in it, which is usually evidence of a frustrated (often large) insect chewing its way out. Some insects not fortunate enough to ever reach the exit, nor equipped to chew an escape hole, perish inside.

Wild ginger (position—on ground for easy beetle access).

Red trillium (smell and color).

Wild red columbine (design).

Jack-in-the-pulpit (smell).

New England aster (color).

■ Examples of Wildflower Pollination Techniques

Color
New England aster, marsh marigold

Smell
Jack-in-the-pulpit, skunk cabbage, trailing arbutus

Smell and Color
Red trillium

Design
Wild red columbine, dutchman's breeches

Position
Wild ginger (on ground for easy beetle access)

CROSS-POLLINATION

Cross-pollination occurs when pollen is transferred from the anthers of one flower to the stigma of another flower of the same species. *Self-pollination* occurs when the pollen from the anther of a flower is transferred to the stigma of the same flower. Because cross-pollinated flowers produce hardier and healthier seeds, different techniques are used by different plants to promote cross-pollination. Some plants bear male and female structures on separate flowers, some even on separate plants. When both male and female structures are on the same flower, they often mature at different times.

a closer look

There are signs of life everywhere you look in May. The air is full of hatching **mayflies** (p. 109), pesky **black flies** (p. 108), and an immense variety of **bird songs** (p. 101). The tree canopies are alive with **wood warblers** (p. 98) darting here and there, gleaning insects from the leaves and branches. **Common gartersnakes** (see below) emerge from hibernation and immediately seek mates. **Painted turtles** (p. 96) leave their ponds to lay eggs, while **white-tailed deer** give birth to **fawns** (p. 105). Wildflowers continue to blossom on the increasingly shady forest floor, none with a more intriguing life history than **Jack-in-the-pulpit** (p. 112).

Common Gartersnake Courtship and Mating—*Love over Food*

About a week or two after wood frogs and spring peepers begin their very vocal courtship, the first reptiles start awakening from their winter hibernation. Being slightly less hardy than frogs and salamanders, they linger a bit longer in their burrows and crevices until the temperature of the ground's surface is warmer than that of the subsurface. Like their amphibious relatives, New England's reptiles—snakes, lizards, and turtles—have mating foremost on their minds at this time of year, so much so that it takes priority over food (even after a winter's fast). Because the gestation of young, whether inside an egg or the female, takes roughly three to four months, timing is everything—the threat of autumn's cool weather makes mating a relatively urgent assignment.

Having recently emerged from hibernation, common gartersnakes are often found this time of year basking in the sun to warm up their body.

Slow-Moving Slitherers

The first reptile we're likely to see in the spring is the common gartersnake, and it's usually a male, as males emerge before females. Males tend to exit en masse, as opposed to the females, which appear individually over a longer period of time. In order to activate their mating behavior, male gartersnakes have to experience a rapid rise in body temperature. This is achieved by basking in the sun, most often fairly near their den and usually in open areas such as fields, roadsides, and on rocks and logs. Perhaps because their need to absorb heat is so vital, gartersnakes tend to slither away more slowly, and not as far, as they might when approached later in the summer.

"Mating Ball"

Having reached the required rise in body temperature, male gartersnakes proceed to diligently pursue females. Because of their emergence pattern, there are usually far more males than females in any one area. As many as 100 or more male gartersnakes actively seek out a female, and upon finding her become intertwined in a writhing mass surrounding her, each one vying for access. Herpetologists (zoologists who study reptiles and amphibians) refer to this cluster of frenzied suitors as a "mating ball" for obvious reasons.

The male that succeeds in getting closest to the female rubs his chin on her head, back, and sides to stimulate her as he simultaneously attempts to align his body with hers in order to mate. (Meanwhile, the other males continue their struggle around them.) When she is ready to mate, the female gartersnake stops forward motion and raises the rear part of her body ever so slightly, exposing her *cloaca* (the chamber into which the digestive and reproductive systems empty). Once one male couples with the female, the mass of frenetic snakes dissipates, with the males heading off in search of another possible mate. According to some herpetologists, female gartersnakes only mate once (not so for the males). In some populations, males are known to insert a substance into the female's cloaca that repels other males for several days.

Clearly there is a lot of competition for the female gartersnakes, as there are never a lot of them in one place at one time (due to the manner in which they emerge from hibernation). Scientists have discovered one strategy used by certain males in order to have an edge over others—they mimic a female in the hopes of attracting and confusing their competition. Apparently some male gartersnakes are even capable of emitting pheromones similar to the ones that females produce. Research has shown that the males that produce these pheromones succeed in mating a greater number of females than those that do not.

] FAST FACTS [
Common Gartersnake

▶ Common gartersnakes are *viviparous*, giving birth to live young.

▶ Mating takes place at or near their hibernation site.

▶ Females reach sexual maturity when they are two years old.

▶ Mating takes place not only during the first few warm days after they emerge from hibernation, but also just prior to entering hibernation in the fall.

▶ In New England, the gestation period of common gartersnakes is three to four months, or longer.

▶ Anywhere from 3 to 85 young are born between July and September. Older gartersnakes usually give birth to more young.

▶ Newborn common gartersnakes tend to gather together in small groups for several weeks.

▶ 80 percent of the common gartersnake's diet is composed of earthworms.

▶ Common gartersnakes are very cold-tolerant and are active from February through October in southern New England.

▶ When picked up or threatened, common gartersnakes emit a foul-smelling liquid as a defense mechanism.

▶ The life span of the common gartersnake is at least eight years.

Portable Incubator

All of this intense activity results in the production of 3 to 85 young gartersnakes come August or September. Female snakes like the common gartersnake that produce live young, not eggs, have the luxury of providing a portable incubator for their developing offspring, as they can transport them to sunny warm spots throughout the summer. Look for the wide girth of a pregnant female toward the end of summer, but in May, keep your eyes peeled for those optimistic, diehard males.

Painted Turtles—*Part Two:*
A Mother's Work Begun and Done

Painted turtles are considered an aquatic species, but they occasionally venture onto land. Males only rarely wander from ponds during the spring and early summer, but females make an annual pilgrimage to dig a nest in which to bury their eggs.

In Search of a Nesting Site

Sometime in May or June, after breeding in water takes place (see p. 58), females head onto dry land. Their destination is a patch of ground that receives a lot of sunlight and has sandy soil that is easily excavated. These site requirements are often met in gravel pits, railroad beds, roadsides, sand banks, and lawns.

It is not unusual to come across a turtle (painted and snapping turtles are the most common species in the Northeast) crossing a road this time of year in search of such a nesting site. Although they usually choose a spot within a few yards of their pond, female painted turtles have been found depositing eggs as far as half a mile away from any sizeable body of water. What guides a female turtle to a suitable nesting area remains unknown, but the journey usually takes place in the afternoon, often when it's raining.

Once she locates a suitable site, the real work begins. Slowly and methodically the female painted turtle excavates a depression in the ground, using her hind feet to loosen the soil and fling it backward out of the deepening hole. Painted turtles, as well as other species of turtles, often urinate on the soil as they dig so as to soften it and make excavation easier. Eventually a hole close to 4 inches deep and 2 inches wide is dug, and she proceeds to lay anywhere from 2 to 20 (typically 4 to 8) round, roughly one-inch-in-diameter eggs. The eggs are then covered with the soil she's removed, and the turtle tamps it down firmly with her hind feet and

Unfortunately, raccoons, skunk, foxes, and other predators make short work of turtle eggs, as well as hatchlings. It is estimated that 90 percent of all turtle nests are destroyed by such predators.

the edge of her shell every now and then. Next she scrapes vegetation such as grasses and leaves over the spot, leaving it looking so undisturbed that human observers have difficulty locating it even moments after the deed is done.

The female turtle never so much as glances over her shoulder the entire time she is laying and burying her eggs. Maternal responsibilities end once the nest is covered to her satisfaction and, her job done, she then heads back to the pond, leaving her progeny to survive and find a suitable body of water on their own.

Although turtle nests are difficult for the human eye to detect, other creatures with a greater sense of smell can locate them with ease. Raccoons, skunks, foxes, and other predators dig up and eat turtle eggs (and hatchlings) regularly. It is estimated that 90 percent of turtle nests are lost to predation.

Most painted turtle hatchlings in New England overwinter several inches under the ground in the nest in which they hatched. They dig themselves out of the soil in the spring and find their way to the nearest pond, where they spend the rest of their life.

] FAST FACTS [
Painted Turtles

▶ The *plastron*, or lower shell, of hatchlings is often reddish-orange. It turns yellow during the turtle's first summer.

▶ In the summer, larger turtles tend to bask for longer periods of time than smaller ones.

▶ Painted turtles are relatively inactive at night and sleep on the bottom of the pond.

▶ At least five different species of algae have been found growing on the shells of painted turtles.

MAY

Bright Lights in the Night Sky

Turtle embryos stop developing shortly after fertilization, while still inside their mother. Their growth doesn't resume until the eggs have been deposited in the ground. For the next two-and-a-half to three months the eggs are incubated by the sun and kept moist by the rain. The temperature of the nest influences both the development of the eggs (warmer equals faster) as well as, in many species—including painted turtles—the sex of the hatchlings. Typically, very high and very low nest temperatures produce female turtles, and moderate temperatures produce males. In species that lay a lot of eggs, such as snapping turtles, one nest can produce hatchlings of both sexes, with the upper and lowermost eggs containing females and the eggs in the middle containing males.

With the exception of very few species, turtles in the Northeast hatch and emerge from their nest between mid-August and mid-October, "pipping"

their eggs open with the help of a horny growth called an "egg tooth" that appears on their upper beak for the first week of their life (turtles have no real teeth). While painted turtle hatchlings break out of their egg in late summer or early fall, only some of them crawl up out of the soil right after hatching. The vast majority remain in their nest throughout the winter and emerge in the spring, usually at night after the ground thaws. Once a hatchling reaches the surface it immediately heads for the nearest pond. Hatchlings appear to be strongly drawn to the brightest part of the night sky. The surface of a body of water reflects light back into the sky and turtles have learned to recognize this. Unfortunately, lights from houses and roads in more developed areas can confuse hatchlings and draw them in the wrong direction.

If you know of a sandy location near a pond, keep your eyes peeled this month and next. A turtle on land at this time of year usually indicates that a nest is either about to be dug or has just been completed in the immediate vicinity. However, unless the turtle is in the process of laying her eggs, don't expect to find the nest—you need the nose of a raccoon to do that.

Wood Warblers—
Butterflies of the Bird World

If you've never scanned the branches of trees for movement and you haven't made a habit of listening carefully to sounds emanating from above your head, you could conceivably live your entire life without being aware of the wave of wood warblers that arrive in New England every year around the middle of May. It's likely that most people fall into this category. If you are among them you have much to look forward to, for as a group, wood warblers are among the most colorful and active birds in the world. A distinguishing behavior is their tendency to migrate north in the spring in large numbers over a relatively short period of time. This concentrated annual spring warbler arrival from wintering grounds in Central and South America is a highlight for every New England birder. It is during migration that we have the opportunity to see not only the warblers that stay and nest here, but also those species that are just passing through on their way to their breeding grounds further north.

Tiny Songbirds

The term "wood warbler" refers to a family of diminutive birds that are found only in North and South America. It is next to the largest family of North American songbirds (more than 100 species), second only to finches. Over 50 species occur regularly in North America, and close to 30 of them nest in New England. The term "wood warbler" is actually somewhat misleading; many are found in wooded habitats, but some reside in wetlands, and few actually "warble." In fact, many have very high, thin, squeaky or "buzzy" voices.

Most wood warblers are insectivorous and, due to the sharp, pointed shape of their beaks, are very efficient at gleaning insects (mostly moth and butterfly larvae) from the branches and leaves of trees. This is most fortunate, for they consume between

A prairie warbler sings with gusto.

30 and 80 percent of their body weight in food every day, making a significant dent in the arboreal insect population. Perhaps because of their diet, wood warblers are almost constantly moving, which makes them quite challenging to locate, even with binoculars—and especially once the trees are fully leafed out.

Warblers reduce competition against one another by foraging for their food in different ways and in different locations. Some, such as the blackburnian warbler, feed high in the trees, while others, such as the ovenbird, look for ground insects. Some, including the pine warbler, forage for insects at the tips of twigs, and others, such as the black-and-white warbler, stay close to the trunk. The American redstart often flies out to catch insects in midair, but the Louisiana waterthrush (despite its name, a warbler, not a thrush) teeters along stream beds looking for

The male yellow, black-throated blue, and blackburnian warblers (top to bottom) illustrate why wood warblers are referred to as "butterflies of the bird world."

insects. Interestingly, warblers that inhabit treetops are often brightly colored and those living near or on the ground tend to be quite drab.

The Warbler Playlist

Each species of bird has its own specific song and warblers are no exception. During the breeding season males are very vocal in order to attract a mate as well as defend their territory. High-pitched sounds have shorter wavelengths than low-pitched and are more easily blocked by solid objects, so a sound that travels through an area of many obstacles, such as trees, will travel farther if low in pitch. Warbler songs illustrate this principle well. Species that sing from the tops of trees (blackburnian warblers, blackpoll warblers) where their songs encounter few obstacles, tend to have very high-pitched voices. Species singing from the ground or

very close to it (ovenbirds, waterthrushes) have the lowest-pitched songs. The songs of species singing from shrubbery or low trees (yellow warblers, common yellowthroats) are, as you would expect, pitched somewhere in the middle.

Identifying warblers by ear rather than eye is the method of choice for many birders in the spring. Audio files and CDs exist that allow anyone to gain the expertise necessary to identify birds by sound (see p. 441 for some recommendations). Putting familiar words to bird songs can also be helpful when first learning them. Some of the well-known interpretations of warbler songs include:

Yellow warbler: *"sweet–sweet–sweet–I'm–so–sweet."*

Chestnut-sided warbler: *"pleased–pleased–pleased–to–meet–you."*

Common yellowthroat: *"witchity–witchity–witchity."*

Black-throated green warbler: *"trees–trees–mur-muring–trees."*

Black-and-white warbler: *"weesee, weesee, weesee"*

Canada warbler: *"click! Turn–it–on–turn–it–off."*

Ovenbird: *"teacher–teacher–TEAcher–TEACHER!"*

What wood warblers lack in size they more than compensate for with the diversity of their plumage, feeding techniques, and song patterns and pitches. To many birders, spring—when both the songs and bright plumage of male warblers are very much in evidence—is synonymous with the arrival of these "butterflies of the bird world." (Read more about bird songs on p. 101.)

] FAST FACTS [
Wood Warblers

▶ Like most insectivorous birds, wood warblers have short, thin bills.

▶ New England wood warblers are migratory, flying mostly at night.

▶ The warblers that migrate from Central America up to New England for the summer tend to lay more eggs than those that remain in Central America year-round, due to the fact that they have only one clutch in the Northeast's shorter breeding season.

▶ Many male warblers have distinct and colorful plumage that aids in territorial defense and mate attraction.

▶ The plumage of wood warblers and vireos can be quite similar, making identification tricky. Birders take careful note of bill shape.

▶ The greatest variety of wood warbler species is usually found in coniferous/deciduous mixed forests.

▶ Most North American wood warblers are closely related, and there are a number of hybrids where certain species' ranges meet. One such example in New England is Brewster's warbler and Lawrence's warbler, hybrids of the blue-winged and golden-winged warblers.

▶ Identifying warblers in the fall is most challenging since adults molt out of their colorful breeding plumage, and immature warblers tend to sport drab colors. Roger Tory Peterson accurately referred to fall migrating wood warblers as "confusing fall warblers" in his *Field Guide to the Birds* (Houghton Mifflin Harcourt, 2002).

▶ It is often possible to tell whether a warbler is immature or an adult from the shape and color of its tail feathers. The tail feathers of first-year birds are narrower and more pointed than adults, as well as more brown, according to David Sibley in his book, *The Sibley Guide to Bird Life & Behavior* (Knopf, 2009).

▶ Several of our breeding wood warblers—including black-throated blue warblers, magnolia warblers, American redstarts, and northern parulas—separate by sex into different habitats on their wintering grounds.

▶ There are 14 subspecies of the common yellowthroat warbler.

▶ The black-and-white warbler creeps along the bark of tree trunks much like nuthatches do, in search of insects in bark crevices.

▶ American redstarts have well-developed stiff feathers called *rictal bristles* either side of their bill, which aid them in capturing insects in flight.

▶ Waterthrushes found near streams have been known to occasionally consume small fish.

▶ In the fall, fruit is an important source of food for many wood warblers. Yellow-rumped warblers fill up on nutritious bayberries when insects are scarce.

▶ Wood warblers are generally monogamous.

▶ Although usually only the male of a species sings, there are at least 10 species of wood warblers, including the yellow warbler, in which the female is vocal.

▶ Many wood warblers are threatened by the loss and fragmentation of habitat, both for breeding and over-wintering, including blue-winged, cerulean, and Canada warblers.

MAY

Bird Songs—
A Choir Singing on the Wing

And where the shadows deepest fell,
The wood thrush sang his silver bell.
—HENRY WADSWORTH LONGFELLOW

One of the most ethereal performances on earth takes place right outside our homes every spring morning when most of us are fast asleep. In the hour before dawn a lone melodic voice breaks the silence, quite possibly that of an American robin. *"Cheer up, cheerily, cheerio, cheerily,"* he seems to sing. Gradually more voices join in, each one different in pattern, pitch, and tone, for they are sung by different species of birds. By sunrise a magnificent chorus greets the day and lucky are those who are privileged to hear this concert.

Who?

Are all birds songsters? No, not all. Some are mute. They have no voice boxes, or *syrinxes*, and their utterances are rudimentary (such as the hiss of the turkey vulture). Other birds, such as raptors and crows, are vocal but don't actually "sing," as we define it.

It is the *passerines*, or perching birds, also referred to as songbirds, which consistently have one or more songs in their repertoire. These include familiar species such as the American robin, cardinal, and black-capped chickadee.

The vast majority of singing birds are male. There are some species in which females also sing (Baltimore oriole, northern cardinal, white-throated sparrow, song sparrow, and rose-breasted grosbeak), but for the most part, if you hear a bird singing, it is a male.

Thrushes are considered the master singers of the Northeast, as anyone who is familiar with the wood or hermit thrush's flutelike song can testify. Male thrushes are quite dull in color and closely resemble the females.

Why?

Most songbirds use song to communicate with other birds of their own species. A song usually conveys more than one message. For the majority of songbirds the male's song establishes and defends his nesting territory against other males of his species as well as attracts a mate and maintains a pair bond.

Song sparrow (abrupt, well-spaced notes ending with a buzz or trlll).

What?

Many birds sing more than one song, but most species have a primary song that differs from every other species' primary song. Some are simple (eastern phoebe); some are more complex (winter wren). Some are bell-like (dark-eyed junco); some are a series of clear whistles (Baltimore oriole). Some songs are mechanical (chipping sparrow); some are hard to describe (purple finch). Some are soft and sweet (eastern bluebird); some are harsh (common grackle). Each species of bird has a song as distinctive as its appearance, and in some cases, such as with the willow and alder flycatchers, it is more so.

In addition to one or more songs, each bird species also has up to a dozen "calls." As a rule calls are unmusical, one-syllable notes given by both males and females throughout the year, and each call has a different meaning. Among other things they can signal alarm, aggression, food location, and begging.

When?

As spring progresses in New England, increased daylight triggers the hormones that prompt birds to sing. Different species vary as to the amount of light needed for them to start and stop singing. The

American robin sings in very low light levels and as a result is often one of the first and last birds you hear singing each day. There is a rough sequence in which the songs of different species are heard in the morning. Those familiar with this sequence can almost tell the time simply by noting which birds are singing.

Birds usually sing most vigorously and frequently early in the morning. Sound is transmitted better at this time because the air is usually still. Following the early morning burst of vocal activity, the majority of birds quiet down during the middle of the day, especially when it's very hot, and resume singing in the late afternoon. Northern mockingbirds and white-throated sparrows occasionally sing in the middle of the night as well as during the day.

The red-eyed vireo, a *diurnal*, or daytime, singer, typically doesn't take any kind of a vocal break during the day. It is also known as the "preacherbird"—at risk of offending readers who may be pastors or priests, the root of this nickname is the red-eyed vireo's habit of singing non-stop. Rain or shine, early in the day or late, hot or cool, it matters not. The red-eyed vireo will sing without fail and often without stopping. Biologist Louise de Kiriline Lawrence counted the number of times a red-eyed vireo sang its song in a 10-hour period. The number was an incredible 22,197. For comparison, a typical song sparrow sings a little

Chestnut-sided warbler (*"pleased–pleased–pleased–to–meet–you"*).

American goldfinch (*"Potato chip–potato chip–potato chip"* while in flight).

over 2,000 songs over an entire day.

In addition to attracting a mate and establishing territory, song also maintains the bond between a male and female while they raise their young. More often than not, when the fledglings leave the nest, songs gradually taper off. Some species only sing during certain parts of the breeding season, perhaps only during courtship, or through nest building, but almost all songbirds wind down their singing by mid-summer. Come fall, there is a brief resurgence of song for some species, especially gray catbirds, American robins, and white-throated sparrows.

Where?

Anyone who has spent some time listening to birds singing in the woods is aware that the higher-pitched songs are often sung by birds that spend a lot of time high up in the canopy of trees, such as blackburnian and blackpoll warblers. Birds that inhabit the understory or stay even closer to the ground, such as ovenbirds and northern waterthrushes, often sing lower-pitched songs. As explained on p. 99, high-pitched sounds have shorter wavelengths than low-pitched sounds and are more easily blocked by solid objects. Thus, high notes are

Ovenbird (*"teacher–teacher–TEAcher–TEACHER!"*).

sung by birds that spend most of their time in the tops of trees where tree trunks won't interfere with the broadcasting of their songs. A sound that must travel through an area of many obstacles travels farther if it is low in pitch.

Most songs are sung while the bird is perched, but there are a few species, such as the bobolink, that have flight songs. Most birds do not sing near their nests, for the same reason that most females—who do the majority of incubating and caring for their young—are often duller in color than their mates: The less attention the nest gets from potential predators the better.

How?

Birds communicate through a variety of sounds, not always songs. Woodpeckers hammer on hollow trees; ruffed grouse beat their wings creating a drumming sound; and snipe, woodcock, and night-hawks produce noise when air passes through their wing or tail feathers during courtship flights. Vocal songs are produced by the muscles of the syrinx —a structure unique to birds—which allows some birds to produce more than one song at a time. Mimics (gray catbirds, brown thrashers, northern mockingbirds) and other birds that produce a wide variety of sounds, such as the common crow and starling, have the highest number of syringeal muscles.

Development

How exactly does a bird learn its species' song? Does it hatch knowing it or must it hear the song first in order to learn it? The answer is not simple, and no one rule applies to all species. Some birds begin calling even before they hatch, when they pierce the membrane inside the eggshell, giving them access to the air space within the egg. For these species, such as the northern cardinal, their songs and calls are entirely inherited. Young of other species learn their songs by listening to other birds. If these young birds routinely hear a song different from their parent species, some—such as the song sparrow—will still sing their own species' song, while others—such as the white-crowned sparrow—will sing whatever song they've heard. Regardless of how they developed their song, most birds learn their own species' song during their first year. Few birds, other than mimics, develop new songs or calls later in life.

As mentioned before, most species of songbirds have their own unique song. It is possible to learn the individual songs of the common species of birds in New England, and being able to identify a bird

White-throated sparrow (*"poor Sam Peabody–Peabody–Peabody"* unless you're in Canada, where it is *"oh sweet Canada–Canada–Canada"*).

Indigo bunting (a series of paired, warbling notes).

Rose-breasted grosbeak (exuberant whistled phrases, thought by some to resemble the song of a robin who took voice lessons).

Hermit thrush (single note followed by flutelike trill).

Eastern towhee (*"drink–your–teeeeeeea"*).

terson Field Guide's *Birding by Ear* and *More Birding by Ear* audio files or CDs are very helpful (see my recommendations on p. 441).

Don't rest on your laurels, though. While the phrases of an American robin may be similar within the species, they are sung in a different order by different robins. You will know that you've graduated to a higher level of attention and birding expertise when you can tell one singing robin from another simply by the pattern of the phrases that are sung.

The birds pour forth their souls in notes
Of rapture from a thousand throats.

— WILLIAM WORDSWORTH

without setting eyes on it is particularly helpful once the trees have leafed out. As a learning device, birders have put words to many songs. You can find some of the most common renditions in the sidebar on p. 82. There are, of course, songs which don't lend themselves to this practice and are a bit more of a challenge to learn. Aids such as the *Pe-*

- Bird song is at its height an hour or two before sunrise.

- Birds such as owls, shorebirds, and woodpeckers make sounds that serve the same purposes as the songs of songbirds.

- Many warblers, sparrows, and finches have special songs they sing during flight; it is often an extended or excited version of their normal song.

- In addition to their primary song, male ovenbirds also sing a flight song, but in their case, the name "flight song" is inappropriate because the vocalization is often given when the bird is *not* in flight. It is most commonly sung at twilight, but sometimes also at dawn.

- Males and females of some species, including Baltimore orioles and northern cardinals, are known to sing "duets."

- European starlings are very accomplished imitators of other birds' songs.

- The eastern towhee has about five different song types that he sings in succession, over and over.

- In addition to its typical *"yank–yank"* call, the white-breasted nuthatch has a melodic song.

- Many warblers and certain sparrows sing special songs at dawn that they don't sing at other times of the day.

- Northern mockingbirds, gray catbirds, marsh wrens, ovenbirds, and white-throated sparrows, among others, have been known to sing in the middle of the night, particularly during a full moon.

White-Tailed Deer Fawns— *A Fragile Early Existence*

With May coming to a close and June around the corner, the white-tailed doe's time arrives. She seeks a spot within the woods to give birth to the (most likely) two fawns she's carried for seven months. At two years of age the doe may have had a single fawn, but with an adequate food supply, twins are the norm in ensuing years. Reproductively, twins are most common, but triplets and quadruplets occur, and there are actually several recorded instances of quintuplets.

The unborn fawns' father disappeared long ago, and the prior year's fawns are temporarily driven off so that the birthing process can take place in solitude. A month after the doe gives birth, yearling daughters will rejoin their mother and stay with her until the following spring, but the males who were driven from the family unit must seek out new territory of their own.

Birth
The restless doe, standing and then laying down on the ground, eventually gives birth to her young.

Does give birth either standing up or lying down.

MAY

White-tailed deer fawn.

No more than 30 minutes elapses from start to finish for the first birth, and the second fawn follows within the hour. Both emerge front feet first, followed quickly by the head—much like foals or calves. The fawns have spotted hair, four lower incisors in the front of their bottom jaw, open eyes, and hooves that have yet to dry and harden. A female fawn weighs about 5 pounds, the male closer to 7 pounds.

As soon as the fawns are born, the mother removes and eats the fetal membranes and afterbirth for its nutritional value, at the same time removing material that might otherwise attract predators to the birth site. She then proceeds to lick each fawn inch by inch, from one end to the other, concentrating on their anal and genital areas. Again, she is taking precautions and consuming rather than leaving their waste for predators to detect. In roughly half an hour they begin nursing, and within an hour of birth the fawns stand on their own, wobbly though they may be.

Fragile First Days

The doe intentionally stays away from her young as much as possible in the days just after their birth, so that her body scent (the fawns have little scent

for the first hours of their life) won't give away their location. She returns 8 to 10 times in a 24-hour period to nurse, often lying down to make it easier for them (they remain unsteady when they stand). While nursing, fawns often quiver all over and wag their short tails vigorously, again, much like foals or calves. Nursing usually continues for about a month, but weaning can take place as late as September or October. The young are very vulnerable during the time they are nursing, for if a fatal accident should befall their mother, chances are great that they will die, too. Only rarely will a doe adopt and nurse fawns other than her own.

When a doe leaves her young, she discourages them from following her either with her voice, or with a nudge from her head or front foot. People often mistakenly assume that a lone fawn has been abandoned. Rarely is this the case. The parent may be out of sight, but she is definitely still tending her young, much like a parent bird continues to feed and keep an eye on her fledglings for several weeks after they leave the nest.

For the first three or four days of their life, the fawns are relatively inactive. Instinctively they seem to know that stillness increases the ability of their dappled coat to camouflage them. During these motionless hours, while their mother is off eating in order to keep up her supply of milk, the fawns lie still with their head on the ground and their ears flattened against their neck to reduce the apparent bulk of their body.

Adolescence and Adulthood

At two weeks of age, the fawns start playing with each other, and at three weeks they feed on grass and join their mother and older sisters, who by now have rejoined the family unit. By about two months they are as active as the older does and are usually weaned and capable of eating and digesting plant material. Their growth has been rapid, due in large part to the milk they've been raised on, which has

] FAST FACTS [
White-Tailed Deer

▶ White-tailed deer have a gestation period between six and seven months.

▶ Food availability on wintering grounds affects the number of offspring a doe will have.

▶ The average length of a doe's labor is half an hour.

▶ Twin fawns tend to lie apart from one another in thickets as well as fields when the doe leaves them to feed. The fawns, not their mother, choose the bedding sites, and they often change from day to day.

▶ The doe feeds her young one to three times a day.

▶ Fawns remain with their mother well into the fall, and frequently through winter or longer. Female fawns often stay with their mother up to two years.

White-tailed does leave their fawns hidden in thickets or fields during the day, while they go off to feed and drink, returning several times so that their young can nurse.

about three times as much protein and butterfat as the milk of most cows.

In the autumn the fawns shed their russet dappled coats. Protective camouflage is no longer necessary, as they can easily outrun most predators. Although the new coats of most six-month-old deer resemble the adult coat, occasionally a row of spots on either side of the backbone remains.

The following spring, approximately half the fawns born the previous year will have survived. At this point, male yearlings are coerced into leaving their family, while female fawns may remain. Females can expect to live about 10 years while males only around five—due in large part to the stresses that accompany the lack of adult protection that young males experience at an earlier age, as well as the energy expended to defend their territory and secure a mate. It has been documented that after fawns, mature dominant males have the highest winter mortality rate.

Males become sexually mature during their second autumn. Females are likely to breed and give birth to their first fawn at age two. Males, because of their rigid breeding hierarchy, will not be permitted to breed until they can out-compete other male deer for breeding privileges.

If you should come upon a fawn in the next month or so, the kindest, and perhaps hardest, thing you can do is to walk the other way. It is illegal to transport or possess wildlife, and besides, its mother is fully capable of caring for it. She just needs you to disappear in order to do so.

Black Flies—
A Cause for an "Itchy Spring"

Most of what spring brings delights us, but there are a few negative aspects to this season—and black flies are one of them. Male black flies are not a problem; most feed exclusively on nectar. In order to lay viable eggs, however, the females of some of the three-dozen or more resident black fly species must dine on warm-blooded animals prior to mating...and human blood is apparently the blood of choice for some.

The Anatomy of a Bite
The female black fly alights onto a host, often a bird, but occasionally a domestic animal or (as we well know) a human. If the body temperature of the host is between 82.4 and 98.6°F, she will begin to probe. First she anchors her mouthparts into the skin with a pair of small hooks. With sharp, saw-toothed mandibles she slices rapidly in a scissor-like motion into the skin, proceeding to cut until she reaches a capillary, which she then sucks blood from until she is satiated (or squashed by a human hand). Most of us are familiar with the itching, swelling, and considerable discomfort that this feeding process can cause. It is due primarily to the strong anticoagulants in the saliva of the black fly, which also explains why black fly bites bleed so much.

Emerging Swarms
Adult black flies have a life span of only about three weeks once they hatch in the spring (having spent perhaps two weeks developing from an egg to an adult underwater), so there is no time to waste. Often upon emerging from the water, adult black flies form swarms. Instead of directly seeking the females, swarms of 5 to 15 males often head for spots where the females are most likely to be—the flapping of the ears of a cow, for instance, caused by the biting of female flies.

Black fly.

After mating takes place the female lays 100 to 600 eggs, which are placed on the surface of a fast-running stream, or attached to objects under water such as rocks (this differs from the laying habits of mosquitoes, which seek out stagnant pools of water). It is thought by some that the shimmering that occurs off the surface of running water acts as an egg-laying stimulus to females.

The eggs hatch in four to five days if the water is 70°F. The cooler the water, the longer it takes for the eggs to hatch. (Eggs laid in autumn hatch the following spring when the water warms up.) The slender, bulbous-bottomed larvae attach themselves to submerged stones, branches, and leaves by means of a series of "hooklets" that grab onto a silk pad spun by the larvae's salivary glands. Larval numbers can be so great that they resemble moss growing on these surfaces. Most species possess delicate structures called *cephalic fans* on either side of their head, which serve as filters for food (organic matter, bacteria, algae) that is swept past them by the moving water.

After a few days each larva spins a cocoon, fastens it to a rock, and transforms into an adult black fly. When this transformation is complete, the cocoon fills with gas, and the adult black fly emerges and bobs to the surface of the water in this "bubble." The life cycle thus begins all over again,

MAY

resulting in up to four generations of black flies in any given season.

Tips for Going Bite-Free

At the very least we can be thankful that, unlike black fly species in Mexico, Central America, and Africa, New England species don't transmit a disease that causes blindness. At the other end of the spectrum, you could join the residents of the Vermont town of Adamant, which holds an annual festival in May celebrating the arrival of black flies. Because of the adaptations of this fly, there is no magic formula for avoiding its bites. Hopefully, though, some of the following suggestions will make your spring a bit less itchy.

1 Wear white or light-colored clothing. Black flies are strongly influenced by color, and dark hues are more attractive to them than pale ones.

2 Don't wear perfume or aftershave. Black flies are attracted to it like bees to honey.

3 Avoid the shade. Black flies are far more common in shady areas than out in the open.

4 Better yet, stay indoors. Black flies, unlike mosquitoes, do not like the sensation of being trapped that a house or vehicle gives them. Once they sense that they're trapped, all their attention is directed toward escaping.

5 Grow up. Children are particularly susceptible to black flies.

6 Pollute your stream (not really). Black flies are very sensitive to water pollution. Generally the better the water quality the more likely there will be black flies, although they supposedly can also be an indication of too many nutrients, such as nitrogen and phosphorus, in the water.

► Male black flies don't bite.

► Black flies are daytime insects and rarely bite indoors.

► Bird blood is preferable to human blood for most black flies.

► Most New England species of black flies have only one generation per year.

7 Become nocturnal. Limit your activity to the hours just before and after midnight. Black flies are most prevalent two hours after sunrise and two hours after sunset. Rarely do they feed at night. Midday is an improvement over dawn and dusk, but to truly escape them, become a night person.

8 Don't exhale. Black flies are attracted to the carbon dioxide and moisture in exhaled breath. This is why they tend to concentrate around your head.

Mayflies—*A Life in a Day*

With the seasonal warming of streams, rivers, lakes, and ponds in New England, millions of winged insects that have spent their immature stages clinging to underwater rocks are now emerging as adult mayflies. While familiar to fly-fishermen who tie flies that mimick these inch-long insects, mayflies are unfamiliar to many of us, perhaps be-

Mayfly nymph.

Mayfly subimago.

cause 99 percent of their one-year life is spent underwater.

Underwater Existence

The mayfly's common name comes from the fact that the majority of the species emerge from their watery environment as adults this month. They are also referred to as shadflies and willowflies, as they emerge around the time shad are migrating upstream into fresh waters to spawn, and when willows are flowering. The scientific name for the order of mayflies is *Ephemeroptera,* which comes from a combination of two Greek words: *ephemeros,* meaning "lasts for a day," and *ptera,* meaning "wings." This name refers to the brevity of the adult stage of a mayfly's life.

All members of this order are aquatic as nymphs and terrestrial as adults. Adult female mayflies, regardless of species (there are 500 in North America) lay their eggs in water. In anywhere from a week to several months (the average is two to three weeks) their eggs hatch and the young nymphs spend the next three to six months (and in some species, up to a year or more) living under the water. During their nymphal stage, many mayflies feed on algae and rotting vegetation on the stream bottom. Some species, however, are predaceous. Feeding voraciously, they grow rapidly and must molt their skin often—up to 45 times—more than any other aquatic insect.

Mass Emergence

During the last days before emerging from the water, many changes occur in the mayfly's body: the digestive system degenerates; mouth parts atrophy; and eyes, wings, tails, and legs mature. Just prior to emergence, the nymphs tend to congregate behind rocks or logs, where the water is calm. It is common for members of the same species in the same area to all emerge on the same day or within a few days of each other. Such mass emergences overwhelm their predators and increase an individual's odds of survival.

Mayfly adult.

Emergence occurs in one of two ways. A mayfly can float to the surface of the water and extract itself from the last nymphal skin by using it as a raft. When this occurs, it usually takes place very rapidly, in just a few seconds, as the mayfly is extremely vulnerable to being eaten by a fish in this situation. Alternatively, the mayfly crawls to the edge of the stream and out of the water onto a rock or vegetation. It then proceeds to shed its skin, taking a few minutes to do so, as the risk from fish is not as great.

Although the winged insect that emerges looks like an adult, it is not. Mayflies are unique among insects in that they have a stage, the *subimago,* between the nymph and adult stages, in which they possess functional wings. The subimago looks like the adult, except for its wings, which are dull and opaque, thanks to a coating of fine hairs. In short order the subimago molts one more time and its wings become shiny and transparent, the mark of an adult mayfly. It's difficult to imagine, but included in this molt are the outer coverings of the subimago's delicate wings.

Mayfly adults have nonfunctional mouthparts, so do not feed—their sole reason for being is to breed.

One Reason for Being
The adult stage, or *imago*, is a very short one. It can last anywhere from 90 minutes to a few days. Generally speaking, most mayflies live for about 24 hours, a much shorter period of time than the adult stage of any other insect, aquatic or terrestrial. Adult mayflies have nonfunctional mouthparts and so do not feed. Their sole reason for being is to reproduce. Some species of mayflies are *parthenogenic*—there are no males, and the females alone can lay viable eggs—but the majority of species have both males and females, and reproduce through fertilization. Males of these species employ an unusual means of visual communication, called "swarming," to perpetuate their species.

Male mayfly courtship takes place in the air and competes with the aerial displays of avian performers such as the American woodcock (see p. 60) and Wilson's snipe. Often thousands, and sometimes millions, of males of the same species of mayfly congregate over the water in which they spent their youthful nymphal days, and together perform a synchronized dance. They move horizontally and vertically as one shimmering body, attracting the at-

(see p. 60)

] FAST FACTS [
Mayfly

▶ As aquatic nymphs, mayflies have wing "buds," which remain undeveloped until they emerge from their nymphal skins as winged subimagos.

▶ Adult mayflies have large, almost triangular forewings that they hold together above their body, and two or three long, thin tails. They have either no hind wings at all, or very small ones.

▶ Like many insects that form male swarms, male mayflies have proportionately large eyes.

▶ The male mayfly's stomach is basically an air sac that serves as an aid in maneuvering as he performs his swarming dance.

▶ Most of the mayflies found pressed against the underside of rocks in streams are in the "flat-headed" mayfly family.

▶ The tails of mayfly nymphs serve to keep them oriented into the current of fast-moving streams.

▶ The leaf-like gills along the sides of mayfly abdomens sometimes act as suction cups, helping the insect stick to rock surfaces.

▶ Mayflies are very sensitive to changes in concentrations of dissolved oxygen in water, and because of this are used as an indicator species. The disappearance of mayflies in a body of water indicates that the quality of the water is changing.

▶ Male mayflies are attracted to lights.

tention of female mayflies that recognize their own species by the time of day this dance takes place, the altitude of the swarm, the number of males present, and the motion of the swarm. Females enter the group and the males quickly grasp them and mate. Very soon thereafter the females lay 50 to 1,000 eggs on the surface of the water, and—having accomplished their mission—both they and their mates die.

Jack-(or Jill)-in-the-Pulpit?
A Story of Sex Determined by Diet

Imagine for a moment that each year your gender is determined by the previous year's diet. If you consume ample nutritious food one year, you are a female the next; if your diet is found lacking, you are a male. If you are practically starving, you are neither male nor female, but asexual. Your sex, or lack thereof, is entirely dependent upon the amount of energy you are able to store in any given year. Over a lifetime, you would spend approximately half your time on earth as a male, the other half as a female. Sound plausible? Most of us know a spring wildflower that has this exact life history—the familiar Jack-in-the-pulpit.

Flowers in Hiding
Most Jack-in-the-pulpits bear either male or female flowers. Each plant begins life as a male (bearing male flowers) for the first year or two, and then the diet factor starts to influence the sex of the plant. It's actually quite an ingenious and flexible way to deal with varying environmental conditions. Enough sun, moisture, and particularly nutrition, and the

Dissected female flower ("Jill").

plant can make and store the necessary energy to produce female flowers and the resulting seeds the following year. With a shortage of any of these, less energy is stored and male flowers result. It makes sense if you think about it—in mammals, it takes a lot more energy to produce a baby than it does to produce sperm.

Dissected male flower ("Jack").

It is easy to go through life without ever setting eyes on the actual flowers of Jack-in-the-pulpit, for unless you actively (but gently) look for them, they are not visible. The "pulpit," or *spathe*, provides a protective umbrella for "Jack" (the *spadix*), which bears the flowers that encircle its base. The spathe wraps around the spadix and has an overlapping flap in the front. By carefully opening the flap, you can inspect the flowers. If they resemble little green berries, you are looking at a female Jack-in-the-pulpit ("Jill"). If they are more threadlike and not green, you have found a male plant. Although it doesn't always hold true, in general a female produces two leaves, a male only one. A single leaf with no Jack or "pulpit" is a flowerless, and therefore sexless, plant.

A Jack-in-the-pulpit that has stored very little food will produce no flower at all and only a single leaf ("asexual").

Botanically speaking, the "pulpit" is the spathe, and "Jack" the spadix. The spathe provides protection from the elements for the flowers found at the base of the spadix.

Poor Plant Design

It is thought that the purple coloring and perhaps the odor of the Jack-in-the-pulpit help attract pollinators—particularly fungus gnats. Often, if you're looking at the flowers, you will notice one or more insect bodies at the bottom of the spathe. While it is easy for insects to get down to the flowers, it is apparently more difficult to get out—slippery walls and a projection above the flowers in the stalk of the spadix make a winged exit very tricky. An insect must locate the flap of the spathe and squeeze its way out to freedom if it is to pollinate another Jack-in-the-pulpit. Some botanists feel that the poor design of this plant may result in the eventual evolution of an insectivorous lifestyle.

Caustic Crystals

Jack-in-the-pulpit, although fascinating to examine, is not considered edible (although black bears love the underground *corm*, or stem), for all parts contain large quantities of needlelike crystals of calcium oxalate. To a much lesser extent this is found in some of the vegetables we eat, including spinach, beets, broccoli, parsley, and brussel sprouts, as well as peanuts and even chocolate. The amount in Jack-in-the-pulpit, however, is sufficient to cause a severe burning sensation in the mouth and throat, causing blisters to form, and possibly death from suffocation due to a swollen tongue.

Often, but not always, the female Jack-in-the pulpit develops two leaves due to the ample amount of food stored by the plant the previous year.

▶ Native Americans called Jack-in-the-pulpit "Indian turnip," due to their custom of boiling the underground corm, or stem, and eating it.

▶ Jack-in-the-pulpit is in the Arum family and is closely related to skunk cabbage, calla lily, and philodendron. The word *Arum* comes from the Arabic word for "fire," in reference to the peppery hot root of plants in this family.

▶ Because of the chemicals it contains, Jack-in-the-pulpit has few insects that feed on its leaves.

▶ Ring-necked pheasants, wild turkeys, and wood thrushes are among the birds that consume Jack-in-the-pulpit berries.

Native Americans learned that drying the pulverized root would destroy the crystals. After months of drying it, they used it as a source of flour for their bread. Medicinal uses included the Chippewa's balm for sore eyes, the Mohegan's throat gargle, the Shawnee's cough medicine, and the Pawnee's headache cure.

Jack-in-the-pulpit has quite a number of common names that reflect its various characteristics: Indian turnip (the underground corm, or food storage tuber, is the shape of a turnip); dragonroot; marsh pepper; memory root (all referring to its unforgettable burning properties); and starchwort (high in starch, it was used as such in Elizabethan times until gentlemen complained about getting rashes from their starched ruffs).

The male Jack-in-the-pulpit usually bears only one leaf because the previous year's food supply was insufficient for the formation of two.

engagement

June is a month full of possibilities. A walk in any habitat has the potential to reveal many forms of life. The sounds and sights of courting animals are everywhere: frogs calling, turtles performing water ballet, birds singing, mammals leaving signs, insects "dancing." Food is beginning to be plentiful for the first time in months, with the fruit of early-flowering shrubs and trees such as dogwoods and black cherries ripening, herbaceous wetland plants providing nutrient-filled leaves and tubers, and fields full of flowers offering nectar and pollen to lure pollinators. Hatches and births are constant, from beavers and moose to stoneflies and silk moths; the air and land are filled with new life.

Here's a sampling of species that are breeding, laying eggs, nesting, hatching, fledging, giving birth, emerging, and flowering in June.

AMPHIBIANS

Green Frog—*Breeding and Laying Eggs*

There are several ways to quickly tell what gender a green frog is. Their circular eardrums, or *tympana*, which are located just behind their eyes, are different sizes: in males, they are larger than the eyes; in females, they are the same size or smaller than the eyes. In addition, males have bright yellow throats, which females lack. During the breeding season, male thumbs enlarge and sometimes develop dark growths to help them clasp their mate.

Male green frog.

Female green frog.

Male green frog singing with throat extended.

After emerging from hibernation in March or April, green frogs breed through August, with peak mating and egg-laying occurring in most locations in late May through July. Only males sing, at which time their throat swells into a resonating chamber, expanding when they make their loose-banjo-string-like "plunk" call to attract a mate and defend their territory.

Somewhere between 3,500 and 5,000 eggs are laid by each female in floating masses of jelly attached to underwater sticks and vegetation in ponds. Green frog eggs hatch in three to six days, and most tadpoles mature into frogs in one or two years. Herbivorous tadpoles consume algae, while adult green frogs are primarily insectivores, devouring large numbers of beetles, flies, caterpillars, and grasshoppers.

Throughout the summer, look for green frogs in or along the edges of ponds—they rarely stray far from water.

Mink frog.

Mink Frog—*Breeding and Laying Eggs*
The mink frog is only found in northern New England and only in permanent bodies of water home to water lilies. The water lilies are a prerequisite, apparently because mink frogs use them as platforms from which they prey on insects. A mink frog can easily be mistaken for the more common green frog (see p.116). However, if handled roughly, mink frogs produce a musky scent.

Gray Treefrog—*Breeding and Laying Eggs*
Nighttime temperatures must reach around 50°F or so for the male gray treefrog to begin calling in earnest in an effort to attract a mate. Although

Singing male gray treefrog.

the gray treefrog's singing isn't limited to its breeding season, it is most pronounced now. Its trilling is very distinctive—loud and prolonged—and often mistaken for that of a bird. Treefrogs often call during the evening hours from shrubs or small trees near shallow water. Their enlarged, specialized toes act as suction cups, allowing them to cling to vertical branches. During the summer, it is common to hear a single gray treefrog calling during warm, humid weather (see photo p. 327).

Gray treefrogs have the ability to change color, depending on temperature, humidity, and light intensity. They can range from bright green, to pale white, to dark brown, although most of the time they remain gray. Juveniles are generally green in color and develop their gray adult coloration as they mature.

Mudpuppy—*Laying Eggs*
Mudpuppies are rather bizarre-looking nocturnal salamanders that are strictly aquatic. Although they have been found in ditches and canals, they usually prefer the running water of rivers and large streams. The average mudpuppy is about a foot long and has obvious and permanent external gills behind its head. The resemblance of the gills to ears perhaps influenced the individual who gave this salamander its common name.

Mudpuppies, found in all six New England states, are native to Vermont's Lake Champlain and its tributaries but are generally assumed to have been introduced into the rest of New England. They mate in the fall and lay their eggs under rocks and logs in May and June. Females attend their eggs until they hatch in mid-to-late summer.

Aquatic insects make up about a third of the mudpuppy diet, crustaceans another third, and fish eggs, leeches, plant material, and other species of salamanders—including red-spotted newts, northern two-lined and northern dusky salamanders—make up the rest. Most active in the winter, mudpuppies have been known to be caught by ice fishermen. (Read more about the mudpuppy on p. 314.)

Mudpuppy.

JUNE

■ Amphibian Eggs—Form and Number

Single
Spring peeper (up to 800)
Eastern newt (up to 375)
Marbled salamander (up to 200)

Clumps
Wood frog (up to 2,000)
Northern leopard frog (up to 6,000)
Gray treefrog (up to 2,000)
Green frog (3,000–5,000)
American bullfrog (up to 80,000)
Mudpuppy (up to 190)
Spotted salamander (up to 250)
Eastern red-backed salamander (up to 15)

Wood frog eggs.

Strings
American toad (4,000–8,000)
Eastern spadefoot (up to 2,500)

*Estimates from Tom Tyning, Stokes Nature Guides—*A Guide to Amphibians and Reptiles* (Little, Brown, 1990).

REPTILES

Northern Red-Bellied Cooter—*Laying Eggs*
The only population of northern red-bellied cooters (formerly known as Plymouth redbelly turtles) known to exist today is in Plymouth County, Massachusetts. This turtle's population is estimated to be between 200 and 300, putting it on the Federal Threatened and Endangered Species list. From mid-June to early July it deposits its 12 to 17 eggs, often in disturbed areas. Look for it basking on mats of floating vegetation in ponds during the early morning.

Milksnake—*Breeding and Laying Eggs*
The milksnake is found throughout New England, except for northern parts of Vermont, New Hampshire, and Maine. It is rarely encountered due to its nocturnal habits. When it is discovered, it is often

Milksnake.

mistaken for a poisonous snake, specifically a copperhead, due to similar coloration. It is nonpoisonous and actually beneficial, as it consumes quantities of small rodents. The milksnake breeds and lays its eggs in June, depositing them in soil, under rotting vegetation, and in other similar sheltered spots that will keep them relatively warm. Several milksnakes often lay their eggs in the same location, where they will hatch in August or September. (Read more about milksnakes on p. 213.)

Eastern Hog-Nosed Snake—*Laying Eggs*
The eastern hog-nosed snake, named for its upturned snout, is found primarily in southern New England, often near sandy soil. Having bred in April or May, the hog-nosed snake lays its eggs in June and July, either in soil or in rotting logs, where the eggs remain until August, when they hatch.

This harmless species is best known for its display of aggression when threatened, which is 100 percent bluff; it rears its head and makes striking movements, but if you look closely you will notice that its mouth is not even open. If faux

■ **Snapping Turtle Egg-Laying—Step-By-Step**

A snapping turtle laying her eggs.   The egg, close-up.   The turtle uses her claw to bury the egg.

1. Leave pond to locate sandy soil suitable for digging.

2. Urinate on soil to make it easier to dig.

3. Dig several holes approximately 12 inches deep with hind legs (multiple holes confuse predators).

4. Choose one to use as a nest.

(Read more about snapping turtles on p. 139.)

5. Lay 11 to 83 eggs (the average is 20 to 30).

6. Cover each egg with soil immediately after it is laid, using hind claws as shovels.

7. Pat down soil surface with feet and shell.

8. Return to pond.

aggression fails, the snake feigns death by flipping over on its back, opening its mouth, and hanging its tongue out. This defensive behavior is instinctive, and is displayed even by young snakes that have just hatched.

BIRDS

Cliff swallow.

Cliff Swallow—*Nesting*

Cliff swallows are primarily colony nesters, building up to 3,700 nests in one location (colonies in New England tend to be smaller than those in the West). Look for their gourd-shaped nests on the sides of buildings, under eaves of barns, and occasionally on the sides of cliffs.

The nests consist of lumps of mud and clay that the swallows gather at puddles, often in pairs, and carry in their beak to the nesting site. A typical nest consists of 900 to 1,200 mud pellets and is lined with grass, hair, and feathers. It takes longer to build than most perching bird nests (one to two weeks). Fortunately, the male assists the female in both building the nest and incubating the young.

Within a colony, some swallows lay eggs in other swallows' nests. They have even been known to lay eggs in their own nest and then carry one of the eggs (with their beak) and place it in another female's nest.

Barn Swallow—*Nesting*

Barn swallows, like cliff swallows, use mud as their primary nest-building material. Originally barn swallows nested in caves, but they converted to artificial sites after the European settlement of North America. Like the cliff swallow, this species attaches its nest to a verticle wall under a sheltering overhang, but it can also place its nest on a ledge

Barn swallows.

or beam of a barn, shed, or bridge. If the nest is built on a verticle wall, it is usually semicircular and more or less half-cup shape; if it is built where the bottom is supported (as on a beam), it can be circular in shape. Both male and female participate in nest construction and commonly reuse an old nest from the previous year, adding new mud to the rim and removing old feathers.

Bank Swallow—*Nesting*

Bank swallow nests.

A number of birds that breed in New England excavate their nests in sandy banks, most notably belted kingfishers (see p. 79) and bank swallows. Using their beak and feet bank swallows hollow out cavities that measure anywhere from 1 to 4 feet deep. As they dig tunnels near the top of the vertical side of a bank, they kick the earth out with their feet. Straw and grass stalks line the nest, and feathers are added to it after the birds begin incubating their eggs. Most bank swallows return to nest in the same bank year after year. Old nests may be spruced up and reused.

Scarlet Tanager—*Nesting*

With the return of deciduous woodlands in New England, the scarlet tanager population has increased, particularly in mature woods. The hoarse robin-like song of the male can be heard throughout the nesting period. Its call note, "chick-burr" continues to be given throughout the summer. As in most bird species, the male is more brightly colored than the female; he is scarlet red while she

Scarlet tanager.

is yellowish-green, blending in well with the foliage. Their nest is usually located well out on a branch, commonly in an oak tree. It is somewhat flimsy and occasionally you can see the eggs from the ground through its shallow bottom. These colorful birds can often be found foraging for insects in the outer tips of branches, particularly of beeches and oaks.

Bobolink—*Nesting*

Visually, vocally, and behaviorally, the bobolink is a fairly obvious resident of New England fields in June. The male's plumage is very conspicuous— so much so that this bird is referred to as

Male bobolink.

the "skunk blackbird" due to the light-colored feather on the back of its head and its black and white body. The song sung by the male bobolink is long and bubbly and is often emitted as he flies in a helicopter-like fashion over his territory.

Predation of eggs and young, as well as bad weather, are the primary cause of bobolink mortality, but these birds—as well as all other grassland birds, such as eastern meadowlarks and savannah and vesper sparrows—are also at the mercy of farmers. Not only are the number of hay fields declining in New England, but farmers cut them two to three weeks earlier now than they did in the 1940s and 1950s, a practice which coincides with the peak nesting period. Within their North American breeding range, more intensive agriculture; the shift from hay crops to corn, wheat, and soybeans; and declines in dairy farming have resulted in decreasing population sizes of field-nesting birds.

Wood Duck—*Nesting and Fledging*

Female wood duck.

Female wood duck on a snag.

Without the help of American beavers, wood ducks would have a much harder time finding an adequate number of nesting sites. When streams are dammed and flooding occurs, trees that were formerly growing on dry ground suddenly stand in the middle of a pond. Many of these flooded trees die, and it is these snags that provide cavities (where limbs have fallen off) in which wood ducks nest. Even with the comeback of the beaver population and the resulting increase in the number of ponds and snags,

Female wood duck and ducklings.

nesting cavities are scarce. To help remedy this situation, humans build and set out wood duck houses in wetlands, which the birds readily use. The wood duck is the only North American duck that, in the southern part of its range, regularly produces two broods in one year. (See more on wood ducks on p. 22.)

Red-Winged Blackbird —*Fledging*

Red-winged blackbird nestlings.

Typically, red-winged blackbird eggs hatch after 12 days of incubation, usually just minutes after sunrise. Born naked, blind, and poorly coordinated, it takes 10 or 11 days for the chicks to grow feathers and leave the nest. The parents continue to feed their fledglings for the following two weeks while they remain in their territory, as well an additional three weeks after they've left the nesting area.

Red-winged blackbird fledgling.

The fledgling in the photograph here had fallen into water as it left the nest— a common occurrence with red-winged blackbird fledglings—which might explain the flustered look on its face. Although adult red-winged blackbirds cannot swim, fledglings can, for a short duration.

American Woodcock—*Fledging*

American woodcocks build their leafy nest in a shallow depression in the ground. Little is known about the construction process, as it's rarely been observed. The eggs are brooded for three weeks before hatching. When the young woodcocks start to pip their eggs open with their egg tooth,

SEXUAL DIMORPHISM IN BIRDS

In some species of birds—such as the house wren, eastern kingbird, and ruffed grouse—differences in male and female plumage is nonexistent or very slight. In many New England bird species, however, there is a distinctive difference between the plumages of the male and female of a given species. Usually (belted kingfishers are one exception) the male is more brightly-colored than the female (for instance, during the breeding season, male scarlet tanagers are brilliant red and females are a drab olive green). These bright colors play a part in male breeding displays, warnings, and other social interactions. The female usually broods the eggs and raises the young, either alone or with her mate; the less noticeable she is when entering and leaving the nest, the less likely predators are to discover it.

In some species, such as ruby-throated hummingbirds and cardinals, color differences are permanent. In others, such as black-throated green warblers, an early spring molt allows the male to replace his usually unremarkable coloration with a bright, breeding plumage. After mating and the raising of young is over, another molt returns the male to his "quiet" winter plumage, which is similar to the female's.

A male black-throated green warbler in breeding plumage (left) and his female counterpart (right).

A male (left) and a female rose-breasted grosbeak.

"HOUSE-CLEANING"

While they are in the nest, the young of many species of *passerines*, or perching birds, produce droppings in the form of whitish sacs with black tips, called *fecal sacs*. The parents of the nestlings either eat them or carry them off and drop them while in flight, some distance from the nest.

A house wren (left) and a white-breasted nuthatch (right) rid their nest of fecal sacs.

American woodcock nest and eggshells.

Red-shouldered hawk nestling.

the mother begins to softly cluck. The chicks remain in the nest until all their thick down is dry (usually no more than 24 hours), at which point they leave the nest.

Red-Shouldered Hawk—*Fledging*

Red-shouldered hawk nests are usually located in mixed deciduous-coniferous woods, below the canopy but more than halfway up a tree, in a crotch of the main trunk. In addition to sticks, leaves, and bark, the nest usually contains living sprigs of conifers. The easiest way to detect a red-shouldered hawk nest is to look at the forest floor: As early as five days of age, the young birds begin ejecting their droppings over the edge of the nest, and the ground surrounding the nesting tree appears "white-washed." At around six weeks of age, young red-shouldered hawks leave their nest, but continue to be fed by their parents for another 8 to 10 weeks.

Brown-Headed Cowbird—*Laying Eggs*

Brown-headed cowbirds are what are known as *brood parasites*—they lay their eggs in the nests of many different species, and then depart, leaving the raising of their young to the host bird, sometimes to the detriment of the host bird's own young. Cowbirds frequently remove one or more host eggs from the nest in order to increase the chances of

their offspring successfully fledging.

Originally cowbirds followed herds of roaming buffalo and fed on the insects kicked up by the buffalo as they scuffed the dirt and grass. As land opened up, cowbirds expanded their range, but this did not result in them building their own nest, incubating their own eggs, or raising their own young.

The female cowbird lays up to 40 eggs in one summer, which explains why there are 214 species of birds known to have been parasitized. The impact on local breeding bird populations can be considerable. The yellow warbler and song sparrow are two of the species that are most heavily victimized. Most birds do not recognize that a cowbird egg is not their own, or if they do, they disregard this fact. However, some species—such as the gray catbird and American robin—*do* recognize that the cowbird egg is not theirs and discard it. Yellow warblers have been known to build up to six nests, one on top of the other, in order to cover over cowbird eggs deposited in their absence.

Female brown-headed cowbird.

Male brown-headed cowbird.

Ruffed Grouse—*Hatching*

This is the month when you are most likely to see ruffed grouse mothers with their broods of chicks hunting for insects along the forest floor. The young, like the offspring of most ground-nesting birds, are *precocial*—born with a covering of down, open eyes, and the ability to walk and feed themselves

An alarmed female ruffed grouse protecting her chicks.

soon after birth. The mother still broods and guards them as they travel together searching for food, issuing a vocal command for all to hide in tall vegetation whenever a potential threat appears. She then confronts the source of danger with a show of bravado.

Common Loon—*Hatching*

In late June and early July, common loon eggs are hatching. Within hours, one or two black, downy chicks make their way to the water from their nest and are immediately able to swim. By day two they are diving and chasing after minnows. Both parents care for the chicks, and at this stage one of the adults

A loon chick tries a minnow as its mother looks on.

Female loon with chicks on her back.

always stays near them. The parents catch fish, crayfish, and other aquatic food for themselves as well as their young, whom they continue to feed for the next

three months. The chicks tire easily, and are not efficient at regulating their body temperature for the first two weeks of their life, so often are brooded on top of a parent's back, under their wings. In good weather they come out from under their parents' wings.

Female mallard and ducklings.

Mallard—*Hatching and Heading for Water*

Mallards lay up to 13 eggs in a shallow depression, which the hen makes on the ground, pulling surrounding vegetation in for bedding, and adding down plucked from her breast. The chicks can be heard vocalizing from within the egg 24 hours before they start to hatch and their

Mallard duckling.

mother responds with her own soft calls as they "pip" their way out. The ducklings hatch fully covered with down, which usually dries in about 12 hours. Within 24 hours after birth the hen makes repeated vocalizations (200 times per minute) as she leads her brood to water. Ducklings feed on animal food for the first few weeks and eventually include seeds and other vegetation in their diet. Their mother continues to brood her young for two weeks, as they are not able to maintain their body temperature for long periods of time.

Canada Goose—*Families Remaining Together*

Geese are among the very few birds in which the family does not break up at the end of the breeding season. Not only do the parents mate for life, but usually the entire family stays together for almost a year. In the fall, migrating flocks of Canada geese consist of several families. They winter together, and the following spring migrate northward again. When they reach the parents' nesting territory, the prior year's young (which don't breed until they are two or three years old) form flocks with other yearling geese and usually relocate several hundred miles from their parents.

Canada goose and goslings.

■ Types of Bird Nests

(Note: Material and location are species-specific.)

No Structure
Description: Egg laid with no supporting or sheltering structure
Location: Leaf-covered ground, rooftops, gravel areas
Material used: No nesting material
Examples: Common nighthawk, eastern whip-poor-will

Scrape
Description: A slight depression in ground—natural or scraped by bird
Location: On ground, in vegetation or soil
Material used: Lining includes leaves, grasses, pine needles, twigs, pebbles, feathers
Examples: American woodcock, wild turkey, ruffed grouse, killdeer

Cavity
Description: Chamber inside a tree
Location: Inside dead or living wood
Material used: Lining includes wood chips, feathers, dried grasses, leaves
Examples: Woodpecker, tree swallow, wood duck, eastern screech-owl, eastern bluebird

Burrow
Description: Excavated tunnel, several inches to several feet in length, with a chamber hollowed out at the end
Location: Dirt banks
Material used: Lining includes grasses, feathers, leaves, stones
Examples: Belted kingfisher, bank swallow, Atlantic puffin.

Platform
Description: Loose (largely stick) platform, often used and enlarged in consecutive years
Location: Trees, cliffs, man-made structures such as telephone poles and buildings, on ground
Material used: Sticks, bark, grasses, vines, leaves, mosses, mud, feathers
Examples: Osprey, bald eagle, great blue heron, black-billed cuckoo

Cup
Description: Cup-like structure
Location: In trees and shrubs (inside trunk, sitting on or suspended from branches), dirt banks, buildings, bird houses, on ground
Material used: Grasses, rootlets, mud, leaves, mosses, twigs, plant fibers, bark, vines, lichen, pine needles, feathers, animal fur, snake skins, spider webs
Examples: Baltimore oriole, red-eyed vireo, black-capped chickadee, American robin, chipping sparrow

■ Unusual Man-Made Materials Found in Bird Nests

Kleenex®
Yarn
String
Cellophane
Aluminum foil
Cigarette butts
$5.00 bill

Barbed wire
Paper clips
Straight pins
Rubber bands
Thumb tacks
Shoelaces
Match sticks

Darning needle
Light bulb
Pocket knife
Pipe
Comb

■ Natural Materials Found in Bird Nests

Snake skins
Spider webs
Mammal hair
Saliva
Fresh herbs
Carnivore scat
Shells
Cow patties
Lichen
Mud

A nest with snake skin.

■ Common Number of Eggs per Clutch and Broods per Season

Bird Species	Size of Clutch	Number of Broods per Season
Ruby-throated hummingbird	2	1–2
Common loon	2	1
Red-tailed hawk	2	1
Turkey vulture	2	1
Great horned owl	2–4	1
Osprey	3	1
American robin	3–4	2–3
Song sparrow	3–5	2–3
Downy woodpecker	4–5	1–2
Great blue heron	4–5	1
Eastern phoebe	5	2
Eastern bluebird	4–6	2–3
Tufted titmouse	5–6	1
Ruffed grouse*	9–12	1
Ring-necked pheasant*	10–12	1
Wild turkey*	8–15	1

(* Ground nesters)

Turkey eggs.

MAMMALS

American black bear bite marks on a beech tree.

American Black Bear— *Breeding*

The black bear breeding season extends from June through mid-July, and begins with males advertising their presence to females by biting the bark of trees within the females' range. The females, who have just separated from their year-and-a-half-old cubs, come into heat and leave a scent trail of urine as they travel. Males track down the females in estrous and mating takes place. The resulting cubs, however, are not born until January or so because of a process called "delayed implantation"—the fertilized eggs are more or less in an arrested state of development until late fall, when they implant in the uterus and the embryos start growing. If there is not an ample summer and fall supply of food prior to hibernation (that would allow the mother and cubs to survive the winter), the embryos simply don't implant. (To find out more about an American black bear birth, see p. 374.)

Southern Flying Squirrel—*Breeding*

Most of New England has both northern and southern flying squirrels. We don't often see them due to their nocturnal habits and their arboreal life. Pointing a flashlight at your bird feeder on a winter night may reward you with a glimpse of one, however, for they forage on the ground after dark. The south-ern flying squirrel is smaller and more gray in color than the browner northern variety. Southern flying squirrels have two breeding periods, one in early spring and one in June.

These soft-furred rodents do not actually "fly"; rather, they "glide." They have two flaps of skin, one on either side of their body, extending from their front feet back to their hind feet. After climbing a tree they stretch all four limbs out and glide to another tree, where they repeat this process all over again. With the right air currents, they have been known to glide 150 feet from a height of 60 feet.

Eastern Mountain Lion—*Breeding*

You may know this animal as a puma, cougar, cat-amount, panther, or mountain lion, depending on where you live. Up until the late 1800s, mountain lions occurred throughout the eastern United States, but by 1891 they were extirpated in New England. There have been no ironclad confirmations of a wild mountain lion breeding population in the Northeast in over 100 years. Mountain lions are shy, solitary animals that seek remote habitats that are hard to find in New England any more.

Southern and Northern Bog Lemming— *Mating and Giving Birth*

It may come as a surprise to learn that there are bog lemmings in New England. In fact, there are two species: The southern bog lemming is found throughout New England and the northern bog lemming in only northern New Hampshire and Maine (its population is quite small). It would be hard to distinguish the two without examining their teeth, which have slight differences. Bog lemmings dig shallow burrows several inches underground and have "runways" on the surface of the ground as well. They are found in a variety of habitats, including sphagnum bogs and other places where grasses and sedges grow.

Bobcat scrape.

Bobcat—*Sign (Scrape and Scat)*

At times, bobcats will cover their scat, but more often they don't. In areas of relatively high bobcat density, they often make "scrapes" where they paw the ground, creating a pile of leaves and debris at the end of a bare patch upon which they deposit their scat and urine. These scented leaf piles are often placed near ledges. In addition, bobcats frequently back up to an object, such as a stump or rock, and urinate on it, anywhere from 9 to 17 inches from the ground.

Eastern Chipmunk—*Collecting Young Seeds*

Eastern chipmunks have specially adapted internal cheek pouches that allow them to carry large amounts of food at one time. As soon as they are

Eastern chipmunk.

beginning to ripen, nuts and seeds are being collected and stored by chipmunks in underground chambers. Eastern chipmunks have been seen emptying their cheeks pouches by squeezing them with their front feet. (Read more about eastern chipmunks on p. 288.)

Red Fox—*Kits Becoming Independent*

In June, red fox pups spend a great deal of time playing and mock-fighting with each other near the den entrance. Litter hierarchy has been established, with food going to those that are dominant. By mid-June the young foxes accompany their parents on hunting trips. In late June they acquire the red coat we associate with adult foxes and at this point are referred to as "kits." By fall they will strike off on their own.

Red fox pups play outside their den.

INSECTS & ARACHNIDS

Sphinx Moth—*Emerging*

Most sphinx moths, or hawk moths, are night-flying and pollinate pale, tubular flowers, often hovering in front of the flower as they feed. Because of their nocturnal habits, we usually only see them early in the day when they linger near outside lights that have been on during the night. (An exception to this rule is the diurnal hummingbird clearwing sphinx moth, whose appearance and ability to hover at flowers while sipping nectar gave it its name.) Sphinx moths are stout-bodied and have

Hummingbird clearwing sphinx moth.

Big poplar sphinx moth.

long, narrow forewings with wingspans ranging from 2 to 8 inches. The big poplar sphinx moth has a 4¾-inch wingspread, feeds on poplars and willow leaves in its larval stage, and does not feed at all as an adult. In most species, the larva is called a "hornworm" because the caterpillar's posterior end has a harmless hook, or hornlike appendage, protruding upward. When disturbed, this moth rears up its head in sphinx-like fashion, hence, its name. (Read more about hornworms on p. 184.)

Rosy Maple Moth—*Emerging*

The larvae of rosy maple moths are sometimes referred to as green-striped mapleworms, due to the pale blue-green stripes that run the length of

Rosy maple moth.

their light green bodies. These caterpillars eat oak leaves as well as maple and are capable of considerable defoliation, particularly of red, silver, and sugar maples.

After pupating all winter underground, the pink and yellow adult moths emerge in May and June, producing caterpillars that are present from May to November. If handled, they often pull the old opossum trick of feigning death—lying on their side and curling their abdomen up under the thorax.

White Admiral Butterfly—*Emerging*

Most species of admiral butterflies possess broad white bands across the wings, and white admirals are no exception. Their distinctive flight, alternating quick wing beats and flat-winged glides, can help identify them at a distance. White admiral butterflies are often found on dirt roads, near mud, along streams, on rotting fruit, and on mammal scat. White admirals and red-spotted purple butterflies

White admiral butterfly wings—the view from above and the underside.

are both considered subspecies of the same brush-footed butterfly. The ranges of both forms of butterflies meet in New England, where you find many

THE MATING WHEEL

When mating, damsel-flies and dragonflies, form a "mating wheel": The male grasps the female at the back of her head with the tip of his abdomen, and the female then curls her

Mating damselflies.

abdomen forward so the opening at the end comes in contact with the male's reproductive organs (which are at the base of his abdomen, in the middle of his body). Prior to forming this "wheel," the male transfers a packet of sperm from the end of his abdomen to his sexual organs. It is not unheard of for him to remove sperm present in the female from previous matings with his copulatory organ (it has two spoon-shaped projections at its end) before transferring his sperm to her. In addition, he may

Mating dragonflies. (The little red balls on the female's abdomen are harmless mites.)

continue to grasp her neck while she lays her eggs in the water or on nearby vegetation, guarding her in order to prevent other males removing his sperm.

THE POWER OF UV LIGHT

Insect pollinators see color differently than we do because they are sensitive to ultraviolet (UV) light. UV light makes the reproductive areas of some flowers stand out. To human eyes a buttercup appears as a uniform yellow, but to a bee's eyes the flower's center (where the reproductive structures are) is darker because it reflects UV light.

A buttercup appears differently to humans than it does to insect pollinators.

intermediate forms. The larvae are the only horned bird-dropping mimics in New England. Look for them on willows, poplar, and birches.

June Beetle—*Emerging*

The June beetle—or June bug or May beetle—as it is commonly called, belongs to a group of beetles called scarabs, along with rose chafers and Japanese beetles, all of which have root-feeding larvae and leaf-eating adults. They also share club-like antennae tips, consisting of three sensory lobes that can be opened and closed, a characteristic unique to scarab beetles. We rarely see these beetles in the daytime, for they are active at night, and bury themselves in the soil during the day.

There is not even a slight resemblance between the fat, white, "C"-shaped, larval grubs, which are found underground feeding on the roots of grasses and other plants, and the adult June beetles they become. You can tell it's a June beetle larva from the double row of tiny spines on the underside of its last body segment, which other beetle larvae lack. Striped skunks find these larvae delectable, which is fortunate for the oak, hickory, ash, birch, maple, and willow tree whose leaves might be eaten by the adults that the larvae would eventually become.

June beetle.

Firefly—*Pupating and Emerging*

There are 2,000 members of the family *Lampyridae*—beetles known as fireflies or lightening bugs. As a group, fireflies are fairly easy to identify in the daytime as well as at night, due to the "plate," or *pronotum*, that usually conceals the head. If you look at a firefly from the side, you can see its head and its large eyes, which are typical of nocturnal creatures.

Firefly.

Larval fireflies, commonly called glowworms, overwinter under the ground. They emerge in the spring and glow like the adults as they search at night for snails and other prey. About this time of year they pupate and adults emerge. Each species of firefly has its own pattern of flashes that it uses during courtship. In June, the males, flying in the night sky, flash this pattern to females perched on the ground.

In addition to having their own pattern of flashes, each species has a particular time of night when they emit these flashes, and a particular habitat where they do so. The length of time spent flashing also varies between species. Although there are other species that can produce light, no insect other than the firefly flashes on and off using distinct signals. (Read more about fireflies on p. 185.)

Polyphemus Moth—*Emerging*
The Polyphemus moth is a member of the giant silk moth family, *Saturniidae*, and can be found throughout New England. It has an "eyespot" on

Polyphemus moth.

each of its two hind wings, and when disturbed or threatened, these eyespots are displayed with a quick flash in an attempt to startle an approaching predator. Its name comes from the mythological one-eyed Cyclops Polyphemus.

The wingspan of a polyphemus moth is enormous—6 inches from wing tip to wing tip. As a larva it is equally impressive, consuming up to 86,000 times its weight at emergence in a little less than two months. It is unusual to see this moth during the day.

Damselfly—*Emerging as Adult*
Damselflies spend their youth underwater, preying on aquatic organisms. Constantly growing, they shed their skins an average of 11 or 12 times before reaching maturity. At this time, after roughly 10 months as aquatic larvae, they climb up out of the water and cling to emergent vegetation, rocks,

Adult damselfly emerging.

or tree roots while they experience their final molt. Over a period of about three hours their skin cracks open down the middle of their back, and they slowly withdraw their abdomen and then their head. Pale, soft, and vulnerable for a day or so after emerging, damselflies eventually harden and acquire coloration.

Different species of damselflies emerge throughout the spring, summer, and early fall. On average they live about a month, longer than many aquatic insects. (See p. 148 for more about damselflies.)

Spittlebug—*Sucking and Growing*
Inside those little white bubbles of froth that you see on the stems of herbaceous plants in the summer dwells an immature insect called a spittlebug, a relative of the cicada that belongs to the order *Hemiptera*. There are many species of spittlebugs, often with common names that reflect the plant they feed on (for example, pine spittlebug and dogwood spittlebug). The most common species in New England is the meadow spittlebug, which was introduced

Spittlebug nymph.

Recently emerged adult spittlebug and skin of nymph.

These bubbles dry up to form a protective dome in which the nymph molts to a winged adult, leaving its nymphal skin behind.

Some species of adult spittlebugs are referred to as froghoppers, due to their superficial resemblance to frogs. The adults also suck sap from plants, but are able to eject droplets of excess water away from their bodies, rather than have it dribble over them, as is the case with the nymphs.

Jumping Spider—*Hunting Prey*

Not all spiders stay in one place and wait for prey to be trapped in the silken webs they've spun.

Jumping spider with prey.

accidentally from Europe. It is found on a variety of plants, and has no known enemies.

In the fall, female spittlebugs lay their eggs (masses consisting of up to 30 eggs) on plant stems, where they overwinter. In June, spittlebugs are suddenly everywhere you look. If you gently push aside some of the bubbles in one of the frothy masses, you will find a spittlebug nymph, often head down, with its syringe-like mouthparts inserted into the stem of the plant. It taps into the xylem, which has .005 percent sugar compared to the 10 to 25 percent of phloem sap. Because of this, the spittlebug nymph has to pump an enormous amount of fluid in order to obtain enough nutrients to survive. Essentially what it is doing is sucking up the plant's sap and pumping out excess water from its abdomen. It pumps 150 to 300 times its own weight every 24 hours. The nymph contracts its muscles and forces air and glandular secretions into the excess watery sap, producing a bubbly mass that covers its body. The abdominal gland secretions make the bubbles tough and sticky enough to form a spittlebug "shelter," which protects and keeps the spittlebug from drying out. When the flightless nymph has matured it makes a new shelter of somewhat more gelatinous bubbles.

Some, like jumping spiders, hunt their prey. Unlike some web-spinning spiders, jumping spiders generally have excellent eyesight. Their eyes are usually arranged in two or three rows, with the front eyes somewhat enlarged and facing forward. This heightened vision, along with their ability to spring quickly into action when necessary, makes them formidable predators. When the jumping spider spies prey, it quickly pounces upon it while attached to a silken safety line it uses to retreat if it misses. They have been recorded jumping as much as 80 times the length of their body.

■ Complete vs. Incomplete Metamorphosis

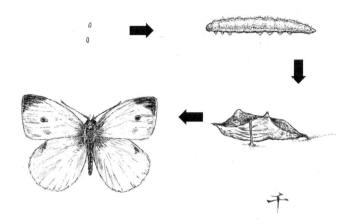

Complete metamorphosis (holometabolism): egg, larva, pupa, adult.

Complete Metamorphosis

Beetles
Flies
Ants
Bees
Sawflies
Wasps
Butterflies
Moths
Dobsonflies
Lacewings
Antlions
Fleas

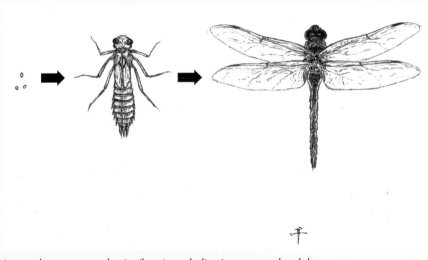

Incomplete metamorphosis. (hemimetabolism): egg, nymph, adult.

Incomplete Metamorphosis

Scale insects
Aphids
Whiteflies
Cicadas
Leafhoppers
True bugs
Grasshoppers
Crickets
Praying mantises
Cockroaches
Dragonflies
Damselflies
Caddisflies

PLANTS & FUNGI

Eastern White Pine—*Maturing, Shedding Male Cones, and Candles Emerging*

White pine tree buds open and send forth new shoots (bearing new needles) at this time of year. Because of their initial compact appearance these shoots are referred to as "candles." At the same time that candles appear, their tiny, pollen-bearing male cones emerge. Look for them at the base of the new shoots. Cone pollen is very light and fluffy, and it is dispersed by the wind onto nearby female cones, usually located at the tips of the branches. If fertilized, they develop into the larger seed-bearing cones we are most familiar with. After their pollen is dispersed, male cones fall to the ground, often leaving conspicuous gold patches beneath the tree. (Read more about pine cones on p. 360.)

Shed male white pine pollen cones.

Eastern white pine candles.

Indian Cucumber Root—*Flowering*

Indian cucumber root is a member of the Lily family that grows to be 1 to 2 feet tall and has one or more whorls (several leaves coming off stem at same point—see p. 16) of leaves. Plants that are going to flower usually put out two tiers of leaves, with their distinctive flowers arising from the second tier. The flowers nod down below the leaves, while the dark purple fruit that forms later in the summer rises above them. As its name implies, the small root

Indian cucumber root plant (left) and flower (right).

tuber of this wildflower is edible, and resembles a cucumber in both texture and taste, but should be harvested sparingly.

Spatterdock and Sweet-Scented Water Lily—*Flowering*

Despite their common names, these two aquatic plants do not belong to the Lily family. Spatterdock (also known as bull-head lily, yellow pond lily, and beaver root) is in the genus *Nuphar* (in which there are 50 species), and sweet-scented water lily is in the genus *Nymphaea*. Both of these aquatic mem-

Spatterdock (left) and sweet-scented water lily (right).

bers of the *Nymphaeaceae* family possess leaves that float on the water and are connected by a long stalk to a horizontal, underground *rhizome*, or stem that grows from the bottom of the pond. Although their leaves resemble each other and they are both commonly referred to as water lilies, the flowers

JUNE

of these two plants are very different. Spatterdock has a rounded, yellow flower, and sweet-scented water lily has a white or pink multi-petal flower. The fruit of spatterdock is held above the water until it matures, while that of sweet-scented water lily sinks below the water after the flower has gone by.

Spatterdock leaves are grazed by deer and the rhizomes are consumed by moose, beavers, and muskrats. Seeds are consumed by ducks and other waterfowl.

Purple-Flowering Raspberry— *Flowering*

Purple-flowering raspberry is a member of the Rose family, but unlike many members of this family, it lacks thorns. Purple-flowering raspberry can be found blossoming along woodland edges and in moist thickets. The strik-

Purple-flowering raspberry.

ing purple blossoms are up to 2 inches wide and are very fragrant. Flowering raspberry continues to flower through the summer, producing flat, edible, but relatively tasteless raspberries in the fall.

Black Raspberry— *Flowering*

Black raspberries quickly move into open, disturbed areas such as roadsides and recently-cut woodlands. This perennial

Black raspberry.

plant bears biennial stems or canes. In its first year a stem arches away from the plant and bears no flowers. The second year the stem doesn't grow any longer, but its buds open and produce flowering lateral stems. Both first- and second-year stems have short, curved, very sharp thorns.

Blackberry plants can be mistaken for black raspberries. One easy way to distinguish the two plants is to notice the shape of their stems. Black raspberry stems are round; blackberry stems have ridges.

Male (top) and female (bottom) cattail flowers.

Cattail— *Flowering*

While cattails reproduce *vegetatively*—forming clones by sending shoots off their creeping *rhizomes*, or horizontal stems—they also reproduce *sexually*, developing seeds. Separate male and female cattail flowers form in cylindrical spikes located at the tip of a stalk, with the female flowers located directly below the male. Timing is such that the male flowers tend to mature and produce pollen (which rains down on the female flowers below) sooner than the female flowers are fully developed and receptive to it, thus discouraging self-pollination. However, the timing of their maturity often overlaps, so that most cattail flowers are self-pollinated (resulting in only a 50 percent seed success rate). Approximately 220,000 seeds per spike are produced. The male flower spike dies soon after producing clouds of pollen, leaving the seed-laden, sausage-like female spike below. Each seed has tiny hair-like appendages that aid in its dispersal. These hairs form on the outside of the spike, giving it a felt-like surface.

Bunchberry—*Flowering*

Bunchberry is the smallest member of the Dogwood family and is referred to as dwarf dogwood by some. It is a plant of the cool, acidic soils of northern New England. If you look closely at a flowering bunchberry, you see that it is not a single white flower with four petals, but many tiny flowers surrounded by four white *bracts*, or modified leaves. Bumblebees, solitary bees, and syrphid flies are the main pollinators of bunchberry. Each flower has one petal with a bristle-like extension that, when triggered by an insect, releases an explosion of pollen. When pollinated, the flowers develop red fruit that is eaten by moose as well as several birds, including spruce grouse, veeries, and vireos.

Bunchberry.

COMMON FIELD FLOWERS IN BLOOM

Red clover.

Buttercup.

Red hawkweed.

Yellow hawkweed.

White campion.

Yellow goatsbeard.

Cow vetch.

Oxeye daisy.

Bird's foot trefoil.

JUNE
a closer look

For the most part, food is plentiful in June. Temperatures are mild and plants and creatures of all kinds are engaged in the continuation of their species. Female **snapping turtles** (p. 139) leave their ponds in search of sandy, sunny spots where the digging isn't too laborious and where their eggs will receive some warmth. The bird songs you began to hear in May are peaking. But this month songbirds are busy not only singing, but nest-building, mating, laying eggs, incubating them, and raising **baby birds,** (p. 141). People lucky enough to live where the soil is somewhat acidic and contains certain fungi may be treated to the flowering of one of three species of **lady's slippers** (p. 150) this month. It is this time of year when pitcher plants, one of several New England **carnivorous plants** (p. 151), flower in bogs. Along the edges of ponds, where there is emergent vegetation, **dragonfly** larvae (p. 146) crawl up plant stems and shed their skins for the final time, emerging as winged adults. A glimpse into a pond might well reveal mating **eastern newts** (see below), and following a rain, a walk in the woods is often rewarded with a sighting of a red eft. And, the ever-elusive **muskrat**, primarily nocturnal, is more active during the day this month, (p. 143)

Eastern Newt—*One and the Same*

Who would ever guess that the orange, terrestrial red eft is related to the olive-green, aquatic eastern newt—much less that it is the same species of salamander? Both appearance- and behavior-wise, the eastern newt has three distinct stages in its development, none of which closely resembles the others. (The third and earliest stage is the rarely-seen aquatic green larva that emerges from the egg.)

Changing Form, Changing Setting
Many aquatic creatures go through the process of *metamorphosis* (a change in form as a result

of development) including the damselfly—which progresses from egg to nymph to adult—and the frog—which hatches into a tadpole before developing into an adult. Pond occupants undergoing metamorphosis either remain in the water throughout their lives (whirligig beetles, giant water bugs, predaceous diving beetles) or become terrestrial once they have metamorphosed into adults (wood frogs, mosquitoes, American toads), returning to water only to breed. An exception to this rule is the eastern newt, which, after emerging from an aquatic larval stage onto land for a period of two to three years, returns to the water for the rest of its life.

The red eft is the juvenile land stage of the eastern newt.

The eastern newt in its adult aquatic stage.

Toxic Juvenile

After developing inside an egg attached to submerged pond vegetation for three to five weeks, the olive-green, larval newt emerges. Barely half-an-inch long, it is fully aquatic and breathes with the help of feathery gills that extend from either side of its head. Most of its time is spent resting on the bottom of the pond, partially covered with mud so as to avoid detection by hungry predators.

The eastern newt's two subsequent stages are more familiar, but many people are not aware that they are actually one and the same species. After two to five months, usually in late summer, the gilled larva metamorphoses, absorbing its gills and developing a third heart chamber that can support the lungs, which then develop. At the same time, it turns from a greenish color to the brilliant orange-red of the juvenile terrestrial stage—at this point is referred to as a red eft. Efts are active both day and night, especially during or after a rain. They have relatively few predators, for this is the most toxic stage in their development; their bright coloring is a warning to all that their skin has toxic secretions that should be avoided.

Return to Water

After two to three years on land, the red eft transforms, often in the fall, into the mature, breeding stage of the eastern newt, retaining its lungs but

becoming olive-green and returning to the water where it will live for the rest of its life. Its skin retains enough toxic chemicals to discourage most predators, including fish (which often eat other species of salamander). During most of the year, and especially during the breeding season, males can be identified by enlarged hind legs that bear raised black structures on the inner surfaces of the thighs and toe tips (used for gripping the female during mating), swollen vents, and broad tails (used to wave and disperse pheromones to attract females).

Rare Exceptions

It should be said that there are exceptions to this life cycle. Some coastal populations of eastern newts do not experience a terrestrial red eft stage—the larvae immediately transform into breeding adults, feathery gills and all. There are also red efts that never undergo a second metamorphosis, and continue to live on land for the rest of their life, returning to water only to breed. But these are not common occurrences.

It is typical for some species, including many frogs, toads, salamanders, and insects that start life in the water and then leave it, to return to the water to breed. Rarely, however, does a species that has metamorphosed from an aquatic stage to a terrestrial one revert back permanently to an aquatic life, to say nothing of changing its appearance so dramati-

- Only 2 percent of eastern newt larvae survive to become red efts.

- It is common to see red efts traveling through the woods after a rainstorm. The moisture allows them to expose themselves.

- The eastern newt used to be known as the red-spotted newt.

- A terrestrial red eft can have as many as 21 red spots encircled with black. Different subspecies have different patterns of spots.

- After returning to the water, the eastern newt remains aquatic for the rest of its 5- to 15-year life span.

- The skin of eastern newts secretes a poisonous substance when the newt is threatened.

- The female newt lays her eggs singly and wraps each one in vegetation.

- The eastern newt is the state amphibian of New Hampshire.

cally when it does so. Some scientists feel this life history can be traced back to serving as an adaptation to temporary and ever-changing habitats, such as beaver ponds. Whatever its origin, the series of metamorphic stages experienced by the eastern newt makes human development seem relatively simple and straightforward by comparison.

Snapping Turtle— *An Overland Journey*

At this time of year, sightings of snapping turtles crossing the road are not unusual. "Snappers" emerge in May and June from their resident ponds to lay their eggs on land, preferably in sandy soil. Because they are more susceptible to predation out of the water, snapping turtles tend to pursue their nesting activity in the very early morning or late afternoon, often on a rainy day, making their presence less noticeable. They are on land only long enough to excavate one or more holes and lay their eggs in one of them, returning to water without ever setting eyes on the hatchlings that climb up through the dirt and emerge several months later.

Female snapping turtles complete an overland journey to lay their eggs. They usually seek well-drained, sunny areas as nesting sites.

An Unappealing Individual

Snapping turtles can grow to an impressive size. Their shell reaches 18 inches in length, and males can weigh up to 75 pounds. They have a prehistoric appearance, with jagged points at the hind end of their upper shell (*carapace*) and spikes along the ridge of their tail, which is appropriate, given the fact that they were around 200 million years ago, before dinosaurs even existed.

The disposition of a snapping turtle is not much more appealing than its appearance, so keep your dis-

JUNE

The snapping turtle doesn't have teeth, but its sharp beak is strong enough to sever a finger. The good news is the "snapper" generally only bites in self-defense or if provoked.

tance. Because their bottom shell, or *plastron*, is small, snappers are unable to retreat into their shells for protection; this accounts for their somewhat defensive nature (usually only evident if provoked). While turtles don't have any teeth, their jaws are bony and quite sharp, and can easily cut through a finger.

Eggs Against the Odds
Once on land the female snapping turtle often investigates several sites before deciding where to lay her eggs. She may excavate several so-called "false nests," perhaps as decoys for potential egg predators. Eventually, with the help of her hind legs, she digs a "true nest," roughly 4 to 7 inches deep. (If the soil is very hard, snappers have been known to urinate on it in order to make it easier to excavate.) She then deposits an average of 20 to 50 eggs (sometimes as many as 80) in the nest. Each egg is 1 inch in diameter, and could easily be mistaken for a ping-pong ball. Interestingly, turtle species such as the snapper that lay more than 10 eggs to a clutch generally lay round eggs, due to the space efficiency of the spherical shape (it takes up less). Those that lay fewer than 10 tend to produce oval, somewhat elongated eggs.

After each egg drops into the nest, the female snapping turtle slowly scrapes soil over it before laying the next one. When she is finished laying, she scoops more sand into the nest hole, again with her hind legs, and often drags her plastron over the area to cover up any signs of her presence (see photos on p. 119). She then returns to the pond, swamp, marsh, or river from whence she came.

A fascinating aspect of turtle reproduction is the influence of temperature on the incubating eggs; in some species, it actually determines what sex the turtles will be. Researchers have discovered that if the eggs are kept at 58°F, all the turtles will be females. At 73°F they all become males. If the temperature is raised a mere four more degrees to 77°F, once again all the young become females. There's only a short developmental period during which this phenomenon occurs. Because the temperature of the eggs near the surface of the ground is different from those deeper in the nest, different nests will have different combinations of males and females.

It has been estimated that 75 to 90 percent of all snapping turtle nests are destroyed by predators, primarily skunks, raccoons, foxes, and mink. Raccoons have actually been seen sitting behind female snapping turtles, grabbing their eggs as they appear and immediately eating them. Scattered white, wrinkled, egg shells will litter the ground around the nest if it has been preyed upon. (See photo of raided painted turtle nest on p. 96.)

Tiny Hatchlings
Sometime in late August or September you might be fortunate enough to see the tiny $1\frac{1}{8}$-inch hatchlings emerge from the ground. Occasionally the young remain in the nest all winter, emerging in the spring. After crawling their way up through the dirt, the young snapping turtles migrate without any guidance from an adult to a pond or wet area that can be as near as a few feet or as far as a quarter-mile away. After maturing for the next six years these hatchlings will mate, and the females will repeat this seasonal overland journey.

- ▶ The snapping turtle is found throughout New England, with the exception of the Northeast Kingdom of Vermont and northern New Hampshire and Maine.

- ▶ Snapping turtles can live in fresh, brackish, or even salt water.

- ▶ Muddy-bottomed ponds are particularly attractive to "snappers."

- ▶ They are actually quite timid in the water and will swim away from humans.

- ▶ Muskrat houses have been used by snapping turtles as nest sites.

- ▶ One snapping turtle was recorded walking over 4 miles from her pond to her nest site.

- ▶ Turtles sometimes shed tears as they lay their eggs.

- ▶ This omnivorous reptile forages mainly at night.

- ▶ Snapping turtles have been seen walking on and under ice.

- ▶ They will tolerate high levels of water pollution.

- ▶ Snappers are harvested for soups and stews.

"Abandoned" Baby Bird— *Is It an Orphan?*

Much happens in the natural world during the month of June—turtles migrate to sandy patches to lay their eggs, young fawns begin exploring their surroundings, treefrogs start trilling, and as the month progresses, young birds are frequently discovered on the ground, looking helpless and abandoned. Our first reaction when we see such a bird is to "rescue" it, for if it were supposed to be out of its nest, it would be capable of flying away, would it not? In fact, this is not necessarily so. Many misconceptions exist about young birds, and there's no better time of year to separate fact from fiction.

Stages of Development

Birds are categorized by their state of physical development at hatching. The young are referred to as *altricial* (born naked, with eyes closed, and dependent upon parents for warmth and food for a number of weeks) or *precocial* (born with downy feathers, open eyes, and capable of obtaining their own food within hours of birth). The young songbirds most commonly found "lost" on lawns are altricial. For a period of time after they are born they are in need of parental care. Sometimes it is not blatantly obvious to us humans whether or not a bird is receiving this attention—in fact, we're quick to assume that it is not.

The very first thing that you should do upon finding a young bird on the ground is to determine whether or not it belongs there. Human intervention might be appropriate if the bird in question is a *nestling* (a young bird that belongs in a nest). However, a *fledgling* (a bird that has intentionally left the nest) often spends several days hopping around on the ground before it acquires full flight capability, and during this time it is cared for by its parents. If the bird in question is a fledgling, the crucial issue becomes whether or not it is truly an orphan.

JUNE

The first week to 10 days that a young bird spends out of its nest are filled with parental lessons that are crucial for its survival. Unbeknownst to most human passersby, at least one of this fledgling robin's parents is probably hiding in some nearby shrubs, responding to the fledgling's calls, feeding it, and teaching it valuable survival techniques. Even the most skilled humans cannot equal this specialized care.

There is a very simple way of finding out which stage a young bird is in. It involves handling the bird. Although you often hear that adult birds will not have anything to do with their young if they have been handled by humans, it is not true. Birds have a very poor sense of smell and actually appear to not recognize (nor become concerned) when their young have had contact with humans.

Helping a Nestling

If you find a very young bird on the ground that has closed eyes, lacks many feathers, and is unable to hop around, you can assume it belongs in a nest. If feathers have developed and its eyes are open, but you're unsure if it's a nestling or fledgling, pick it up in your hand and attempt to have it perch on one of your fingers. A general rule is when the bird is incapable of firmly gripping your finger, it is a nestling prematurely out of its nest.

Nestlings fall out for a variety of reasons—wind, predators, jostling from other birds in the nest, and human interference. If the nestling is chilled, warm it in your hands and then, if it appears healthy, try to locate its nest. Usually it is close by and well hidden. (Nestlings don't often take a second tumble right away, so if you find the bird on the ground again soon after returning it, you can assume it's time for it to fledge.) If you can't find the nest, construct a makeshift one out of a berry basket or a butter tub—add drainage holes and line it with tissue (not fresh grass, as it contains moisture that can chill the bird) and tie it to a nearby branch. Then leave the area. Once you are out of sight, the parent bird should return to feed the nestling. It may take an hour or two. If you watch the nest from a distance for several hours and there is no sign of a parent, or if the young bird is injured, then other measures—such as calling a local wildlife rehabilitation center—are appropriate.

Helping a Fledgling

If you find that the young bird is capable of perching on your finger, it is a fledgling and should quickly be returned to the spot where you found it, where its parent will hear its calls. It should not be put back into a nest nor adopted by humans. As mentioned previously, most fledglings leave the nest before they are capable of sustained flight and before their parents are finished caring for them. They can hop and perhaps fly short distances, but for the next week to 10 days their parents feed them and teach them skills they need to survive. If the likelihood of predators (such as house cats) is high, try to find a bush or thick cover in which to place the bird. If you're looking for a mission, educate your outside-cat-owning neighbors about the high predation rate (National Audubon Society estimates that cats kill 100 million birds each year in the United States) and encourage them to keep their cats inside.

Although fledglings out of the nest but not yet skilled at flying are extremely vulnerable, it's not as though they were a great deal safer in their nest. While nests serve to contain the heat of the parent bird as well as offer the young some protection from the elements, they are a magnet for predators. Think about it from a raccoon or sharp-shinned hawk's point of view—a nest is a goldmine of relatively helpless, concentrated packages of protein. Consequently, the goal of parent birds is to have their young fledge, or leave the nest, as soon as possible in order to disperse and increase their chances of survival.

The reasons for not trying to play Nurse Nightingale to a fledgling are many. To begin with, more often than not there is no need for human intervention—as already mentioned, the parents are usually caring for it, even if it is not evident to you. Secondly, even with the best of intentions the most skilled humans do not have a high success rate in raising young birds. Birds start out life with only a 50 percent chance of surviving long enough to leave their own nest. Being raised by humans rather than their own parents further decreases their chances.

The Legalese

There are other reasons to let nature take its course

► The time between hatching and acquiring flight feathers is only two or three weeks for most birds.

► Only a small fraction of nestling birds that humans try to raise become fully functional adult birds.

► Most birds have developed a fear response that causes them to prematurely leave their nest if disturbed, even though they may be several days from fledging.

► Only 30 percent of young songbirds survive their first year of life.

► All birds, except non-native species (house sparrow and European starling, for example) are protected by federal laws under the Migratory Bird Act of 1918.

rather than bringing home an "orphaned" bird, including the legality of adopting a young bird as well as the time commitment involved. To have possession of a young bird, you must have federal and state permits. Wildlife rehabilitators have such permits. In addition, the amount of time that is required to care for a young bird is staggering. Parent birds feed their young every 15 to 20 minutes from sunrise to sunset for several weeks. An adult robin makes about 400 trips every day to feed its young. Finally, for a week or two after leaving the nest, fledglings are not only fed by their parents but are also taught such valuable skills as how to procure food, avoid predators, and communicate with other birds—experience humans obviously can't teach.

The vast majority of young birds that are found looking helpless and abandoned on our front lawns and in our backyards are young fledglings. Before giving in to your nurturing instinct, stop and observe the bird from a distance for a period of time. It will most likely call to its parents who will respond by appearing with food. By not taking any action at all, you may very well save its life.

Muskrat—*An Elusive Mammal*

Many rodents are encountered frequently—striped chipmunks, red and gray squirrels, woodchucks, meadow voles—but there are some that are more elusive, due primarily to their nocturnal habits. Among these is the semi-aquatic muskrat. Marshes with equal amounts of emergent vegetation and water, as well as a water level that doesn't fluctuate significantly, are likely spots to find muskrats. Your chances of glimpsing one are greatest in the spring and early summer, when they tend to be more active during the day.

What's in a Name?
Their name says it all: "musk-rat." Like all rodents, muskrats have a pair of incisors in the front of both upper and lower jaws, followed by a space, or *diastema*, between these teeth and their distinctively-grooved molars. At this time of year, during their breeding season, the "musk" comes into play, for these rodents have paired glands that secrete a musky-smelling liquid that mixes with their urine and is then deposited throughout their territories on scent posts—raised objects such as stumps or tufts of grass—and along travel routes, advertising the availability of the muskrat that left its scent. Although both sexes possess these glands, the odor of the males' secretion is much stronger.

Striking Similarities
Although more closely related to voles and lemmings, muskrats share many characteristics with another semi-aquatic rodent: the American beaver. The muskrat, while lacking the fully-webbed hind feet of a beaver, has partially-webbed hind feet that are fringed with short, stiff hairs. Both of these rodents swim by propelling themselves with their hind feet while holding their front feet under their chin. The beaver's tail is flattened, whereas the muskrat's is laterally compressed. Both are known to use their tails as

JUNE

Muskrats are very clean animals, and spend a great deal of time grooming themselves as well as each other.

rudders when turning in the water, and believe it or not, the muskrat, like the beaver, uses its skinny tail as a warning device by slapping it against the water.

Beavers and muskrats are able to close their upper lips behind their incisors; this allows them to chew underwater without swallowing any water. They both have dense, soft, waterproof "underfur" that traps air and thus helps insulate them, as well as make them more buoyant, and long, glossy guard hairs. These characteristics are what put a price on the pelts of both animals and make them attractive to trappers.

Even the dwellings of beavers and muskrats have many similarities. Both animals construct houses of vegetation in the middle of ponds. Both hollow out a cavity above the water level inside their respective houses, and have one or more plunge holes that lead to the water. There are differences, though, too. Muskrats seldom build where the water is more than 2 feet, whereas beavers prefer much deeper water. Beavers use sizable limbs and mud as building material; muskrats are more apt to use cattails and other aquatic vegetation. Muskrat

houses are anywhere from 1 to 4 feet high, and often 8 to 10 feet in diameter at water level. They can have several cavities so that multiple families can dwell within the same structure.

Beavers and muskrats also build shelters in the banks of rivers, streams, and ponds. These bank burrows end with a lined cavity. Some sources say that, all things being equal, muskrats will choose to dig a bank burrow over building a house, but others have found the opposite to be true.

Both beavers and muskrats build canals, although their purposes differ. Beavers use these channels to transport limbs and branches to their lodge; muskrats use them during periods of low water levels to swim from their house to deeper water.

Although both these rodents are, for the most part, *herbivores* (eating primarily vegetation), their diet preferences differ. Whereas beavers dine on the leaves, buds, and branches of trees, and the cambium layer just under the bark (as well as other vegetation), muskrats prefer aquatic vegetation, such as the roots and stalks of cattails and other plants growing in the water.

"Feeders" and "Push-Ups"

In addition to their primary house, muskrats erect two other kinds of structures, also conical in shape and built out of vegetation. One is called a "feeder"—a hut where they bring food to eat. Feeders are smaller than houses, and basically consist of a roofed-over platform that provides an area where muskrats, protected from the elements and predators, can consume food, warm themselves, and replenish their oxygen supply after swimming submerged for up to 20 minutes. "Push-ups" or "breather houses" are the third kind of shelter you find in muskrat habitat in the Northeast. The muskrat cuts a 4- to 5-inch hole in thin ice and pushes fine roots and vegetation from the bottom of the pond up through this hole onto the ice surface, forming a pile anywhere from 12 to 18 inches high.

Muskrat

- Muskrats are in the subfamily *Arvicolinae*, which also includes voles and lemmings.

- The skull of a muskrat closely resembles that of a meadow vole, but is much larger.

- Muskrat predators include man, mink, raccoons, red and gray foxes, coyotes, bobcats, striped skunks, snapping turtles, great horned owls, northern harriers, pickerel, large-mouth bass, and northern pike.

- In addition to vegetation, muskrats eat freshwater clams, fish, and crustaceans.

- They eat roughly a third of their weight a day.

- Most foraging is done within 50 feet of a muskrat's house. Rarely does it travel more than 500 feet from home unless dispersing to a new location.

- Muskrats are very territorial.

- Muskrats need a minimum of 6 inches of water in order to build a house and be able to enter and exit underwater.

- In the southern part of their range, muskrats usually do not put a roof on top of their feeding platforms.

- In the male muskrat, musk secretion is emitted through openings in the foreskin of the penis into the urine.

- The muskrat is still considered the most important of our native furbearers.

- Most researchers find that muskrat populations follow a 10-year cycle, although 4- to 5- and 6- to 10-year cycles have also been documented.

- Muskrats can swim backward and up to 3 miles per hour.

- Most young muskrats stay with their family until they are a year old.

- A muskrat house can lodge up to 10 muskrats.

- The temperature inside a house in the winter is about 36°F *above* the outside temperature.

- The inside chamber of a muskrat house is roughly 12 inches in diameter.

- The size of a muskrat's litter correlates with latitude—the further north, the larger the litter.

The muskrat then excavates a cavity in this pile at ice level. Push-ups serve as shelters and breathing space, as well as feeding stations during bad weather. When the ice melts in the spring, these structures collapse (while feeders and houses remain useable year-round).

If you know of a heavily vegetated marsh, there's a very good chance you may find it has resident muskrats. While you may not see the animals themselves, one or more of their shelters may well be visible. You may also catch a glimpse of a mink or raccoon, busily trying to locate their next musky meal.

Roughly the size of a housecat, the muskrat inhabits marshes where it occasionally appears during the day in the spring and early summer.

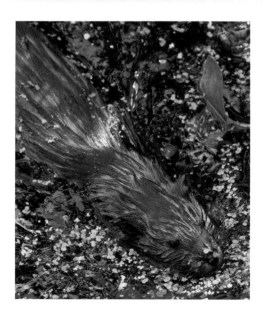

Dragonfly—*A Modern Day Dragon*

Perched on a cattail at the edge of a pond, a dragonfly moves its head left, then right, as it follows the flight path of a blood-seeking mosquito. Suddenly, the dragonfly darts out into the air, snatches the unsuspecting mosquito in its bristly legs, and consumes its prey on the wing. Below the surface of the pond, a sudden flash of movement occurs as a tiny minnow is seized and disappears into the jaws of a young dragonfly nymph.

Two Life Stages—One Aquatic, One Terrestrial
Immature dragonflies (nymphs or *naiads*) inhabit ponds, swamps, large rivers, brooks, and other wetlands, whereas winged adults are airborne much of the time. A majority of the dragonfly's life is spent underwater: Most dragonflies lay their eggs in water or nearby vegetation, and the nymphs that hatch from these eggs spend anywhere from several months to five years in an aquatic environment. When they do eventually develop wings, they become terrestrial for only the last few days or months of their life.

Masters of both sky and water, dragonflies come by their reputation as fierce predators honestly. The adaptations that allow nymphs and adults to obtain their prey and survive are as different as the habitats in which the two stages reside.

Nymphs
Extensible Toothed Lower Lip
The aquatic nymph bears little resemblance to the adult dragonfly it will become. Squat with a broad, brownish abdomen, the nymph possesses a lower lip or *labium* that is hinged and greatly elongated. The forward end of this lip bears a pair of grasping organs that have "teeth" or spines. (Dragonflies, as well as the more slender damselflies—see p. 131 —belong to the order *Odonata*. "Odon" means "tooth" in Greek.) Due to the hinge, this lip can be

The immature dragonfly (nymph), resides underwater and possesses an extensible toothed lower lip that enables it to prey successfully on other aquatic insects, small minnows, and tadpoles.

extended outward almost half the length of the dragonfly in order to capture prey, which it then draws into its powerful mandibles (or jaws). When at rest, the lip folds beneath the dragonfly's head, sometimes with one portion covering its face like a mask. Small fish, tadpoles, crayfish, and a variety of aquatic insects are quickly seized with this remarkable device.

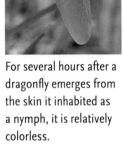

For several hours after a dragonfly emerges from the skin it inhabited as a nymph, it is relatively colorless.

Sensory Organs and Perception
Dragonfly nymphs possess sensory organs on their legs that allow them to perceive currents in the water caused by other aquatic animals. As a result, enemies such as frogs and fish have a difficult time approaching them without being detected.

Jet Propulsion
One of the challenges of underwater life is obtaining the oxygen necessary for survival. Some insects, such as predaceous diving beetles, travel up to the surface of the water, trap a bubble of air, and then dive back down with it, returning to the water's surface every few minutes to retrieve another bubble. Mosquito larvae have an appendage

Two abandoned dragonfly skins cling to the same blade of vegetation.

or siphon on the tip of their abdomen that they stick above the surface of the water to obtain oxygen as they float, head down. Dragonfly nymphs have devised a way to extract oxygen directly from the water. Unlike adults, nymphs possess gills that line the inside of their rectum. Water is sucked into the tip of the abdomen, the gills extract the oxygen, and the dragonfly expels the water, sometimes quite violently, causing the dragonfly to move suddenly. If necessary, this process can be utilized by the nymph to quickly propel itself away from predators.

Although males and females of the same species usually resemble each other, they can look quite different, in which case the male is usually the more colorful. Here you see a male (left) and female (right) common whitetail.

Adults
Multi-Faceted Eyesight
After growing and shedding their skin several times, dragonfly nymphs climb up on shoreline vegetation and emerge as winged adults through a slit that appears on the back of the larval skin. After pumping their body full of air and sending fluid into their wing veins, the dragonflies expand into their familiar adult form.

Eyesight is of crucial importance to any predator, especially one that is moving at great speed. The size of an adult dragonfly's compound eyes indicates the large role that they play. Through a hand lens you can see that each eye consists of up to 30,000 individual hexagonal facets, each of which focuses on one portion of the visual field (most insects have only hundreds). Just as more pixels produce a sharper photographic image, more facets in a compound eye result in better resolution. Scientists have discovered that 80 percent of a dragonfly's brain is reserved for analyzing what it sees. It is believed that in addition to being able to rotate their head almost 360 degrees, some dragonfly species can see objects up to 30 feet away and detect movement as far away as 60 feet.

Speed, Agility, and Maneuverability
Dragonflies depend on their flight ability as much as their vision when capturing prey, as well as when escaping enemies. Adaptations include extra strong venation on the front of all four wings, causing the wings to twist as they beat up and down and imparting forward thrust. In addition, eight pairs of muscles are attached to each wing to allow incredible maneuverability. Of all winged insects, only dragonflies do not beat their two pairs of wings up and down at the same time. While the hind wings are rising the front wings are moving downward. Consequently, each pair of wings encounters undisturbed air and as a result dragonflies can hover and fly backward, as well as dart quickly away in pursuit of prey or to dodge enemies. Their agility and speed is unexcelled in the insect world.

Capturing Prey

The legs of dragonflies are equipped with spines, and during flight they dangle their legs in such a way as to form a "basket" with these spines. They use this basket to scoop up prey.

Passing on Genes

Mating is somewhat convoluted with dragonflies (and damselflies), due to the fact that the male's genital opening and his copulatory organ/storage sacs are not located in the same place. Sperm is produced near the tip of his tail, and the male transfers it to the storage sacs located behind his last pair of legs by bending his abdomen up and around. He uses his tail to grab the female right behind her head. She then has to bend her body up under the male's and place her genital opening (on the tip of her abdomen) up against his storage sacs. They can stay coupled in this position for several days. (See photo on p. 130.)

It's hard to think of an organism that has adapted in more ways than male dragonflies in order to assure that their genes are passed on. Because female dragonflies usually mate with more than one male, the challenge for males is to make sure that it is *their* sperm, and not another's, that is used to fertilize their mates' eggs. Male strategies of different species include: 1) using a blunt penis to squash down any sperm already inside of the female, thereby allowing the squasher's sperm to be positioned front-and-center for fertilizing eggs; 2) using a spiked, bristly penis to scrape out competing sperm before replacing it with the scraper's; 3) keeping a grasp on the back of the female's head after copulation, guiding her to an egg-laying spot and holding her there until she has completed the task (therefore preventing other males from mating with her); 4) hovering over a spot where the female is likely to lay her eggs and driving away other males.

Damselfly.

Dragonfly.

■ Damselfly vs. Dragonfly

Damselflies and dragonflies are both in the order *Odonata*, but have several distinct differences:

Damselfly	Dragonfly
Delicate and small-bodied with narrow abdomen	Stout and large-bodied
Head wider than long	Head rounded
Eyes separated by more than their own width	Eyes cover much of top and sides of head
Forewings and hind wings similar shape	Forewings and hind wings different in shape
Wings pressed above body or only partially open at rest	Wings held straight out to the sides at rest
Weak fliers	Strong fliers

*Facts from *A Field Guide to the Dragonflies and Damselflies of Massachusetts* (Little, Brown, 2003).

Because dragonflies, like all insects, cannot internally control their body temperature, they are dependent upon external conditions for regulation. In order to avoid over-heating, adults often lift their abdomen toward the sun, a position that exposes the minimum amount of body surface to the warmth of the sun's rays.

Dragonflies Close-Up

For an up-close look at a dragonfly, visit a pond early on a cool summer morning. Look for dragon-flies perched on vegetation along the shore. (Most of those you see will be males, as females gener-ally only visit ponds during the brief period of time when they are ready to mate.) When you approach a dragonfly at this time of day, chances are great that it won't move, for in order to be able to fly, a dragonfly's body temperature must be warmed to 85 to 95°F. Sometimes vibrating their wings for a while and exercising their flight muscles raises their temperature high enough for the wings to develop their full power, but more often than not the sun's help is necessary. Enjoy this opportunity to investi-gate one of nature's most impressive predators.

► The size and relative position of the eyes helps deter-mine a dragonfly's family.

► The eye color, wing coloration, and markings, and the shape, color, and markings of the abdomen, are important in species identification.

► Dragonflies at rest hold their wings straight out to the sides because they lack the hinge at the base of the wing that allows most other insects to fold them back against the body.

► The males of some species of dragonflies are territo-rial.

► Most female dragonflies are found in wetlands only when they are breeding and laying eggs.

► When a dragonfly emerges from its skin it is pale and soft and the wings have a "sheen" to them. Within a day or two the wings lose this sheen, the body becomes hardened, and colors appear.

► Dragonflies are usually most active from mid-morn-ing to mid-afternoon on sunny days, but some prefer late day and a few come out only at dawn and dusk.

► Dragonflies in New England are flying from about mid-April to mid-November.

► Dragonfly nymphs can be classified by their body shape as *claspers* (long and cylindrical), *sprawlers* (elongated legs and flattened body), *hiders* (flat-tened), or *burrowers* (stout).

► Insects in the order *Odonata* are the only aquatic insects that have a lower jaw (*labium*) that can be extended outward for capturing prey.

JUNE

Lady's Slipper—
A Fragile Flower Blooms

Lady's slippers, moccasin flowers, whip-poor-will's shoes—these are some of the common names given to certain members of the Orchid family whose lowest petal is enlarged and inflated into a "pouch," or *labellum*. There are about 10 species of lady's slippers in North America, with the yellow, pink, and showy the most common in New England. (See photos p. 89.) These three orchids flower during May and June, usually yellow first, then pink, followed by showy. Theirs is a display of colors, textures, scents, and shapes unlike any other.

Fungi-Dependent
Yellow and pink lady's slippers are found in both wet and dry sites, whereas showy lady's slippers are most likely to grow strictly in wet areas, such as swamp openings and fens—wetlands similar to bogs, but not as acidic. Even if you know the kind of habitat in which to look for different species of lady's slippers, there is no guarantee that you

A showy lady's slipper emerges.

will find them, as they have very specialized needs. The soil in which these flowers grow must be somewhat acidic, and it must also contain a certain type of fungus (*Rhizoctonia*), which is vital to the survival of all lady's slippers.

Rhizoctonia fungi and lady's slippers have a symbiotic relationship. Lady's slippers produce minute seeds that lack the food supply most seeds contain. *Rhizoctonia* digests the seeds' outer coats so that they can access soil nutrients. The fungi must penetrate far enough to digest the outer coat, but not the inner cells, in order for the seeds to germinate. The fungi also integrate themselves with the orchids' underground *corms*, or stems, allowing

the corms to obtain minerals and other nutrients from the soil. Lady's slippers return the favor by sharing the food they photosynthesize with the *Rhizoctonia* fungi.

Laws of Attraction
In five to seven years, when a lady's slipper seed matures into a flowering plant, it uses color, design, and scent to attract potential pollinators. Attraction is simple and straightforward compared to the challenges the insects must tackle once they arrive at the flower. The easier it is for an insect to obtain pollen and nectar from a flower, the more likely it is to return to the flower. Flowers with landing platforms and easy access to nectaries and pollen-bearing anthers, such as dandelions and asters, are likely to be revisited frequently. Flowers that present pollinators with time-consuming hurdles to overcome are not as likely to receive multiple visits from the same insect.

Although lady's slippers involve some difficult maneuvering and provide no nectar reward after an insect does so, they succeed in attracting a sufficient number of pollinators, after which the lady's slipper's blossom fades and seeds develop within the swollen ovary. This capsule splits and releases hundreds of thousands of some of the tiniest seeds of any flowering plant. Not even half these seeds

► The hairs along a lady's slipper's stem contain a fatty acid that is toxic to many animals, and in large amounts, to people. For this reason, handling lady's slippers may cause a rash.

► There are two varieties of yellow lady's slipper: greater yellow lady's slipper and lesser yellow lady's slipper.

► Lady's slipper tea is recommended by some herbalists for nervous headaches.

► Native Americans used this plant to ease toothaches.

After pollination, the lady's slipper's blossom fades, and seeds develop within the swollen ovary, a capsule containing hundreds of thousands of seeds.

will germinate, and of those that do, only 2 percent of the flowers they produce will be successfully pollinated. Fortunately, however, a lady's slipper lives an average of 20 years (occasionally up to 150 years) and one pod contains up to 60,000 seeds, so with adequate protection they will continue to grace our woodlands for years to come.

Because of their popularity, lady's slippers have received a lot of attention from horticulturalists, but efforts to grow them from seed have been successful only within a laboratory environment. Transplanting often fails, as fungi have to be in the new location in order for the lady's slipper to survive. These factors have led to the protection of lady's slippers growing in the wild.

Carnivorous Plants—*Fatal Attraction*

Throughout the glaciated Northeast there are wetlands, referred to as bogs, in which acidic *peat*—dead plant material (often mosses)—has accumulated. Many of these bogs were originally glacial "kettle holes" caused by huge chunks of ice breaking off a glacier and then being buried by sediment. When the ice melted, it left depressions containing water, with no inlets or outlets. If decomposing plant material renders this water acidic, the resulting wetland is called a bog.

The stagnancy of a bog has a significant impact on the plants that live there. It contributes to oxygen deficiency and a relative lack of nutrients (that would be carried in by a stream) as well as an accumulation of acids (since there are no means of flushing them out of the system). This type of bog is a "closed ecosystem." Most plants in these bogs are totally dependent upon precipitation—rain, fog, and snow—for their limited supply of nutrients. Those that survive under these acidic, and nutrient- and oxygen-poor conditions have adapted to them. One such group—that of carnivorous plants—has evolved unique ways to actually supplement the nutrients available to them.

There are more than 20 species of plants in New England that trap insects, mites, and spiders to supplement their nutrient intake. Some of these carnivorous plants have evolved a passive means of entrapment; others more actively catch their prey. The three groups, or *genera*, of plants that illustrate the range of these different trapping techniques are also the most common carnivorous plants in northeastern bogs: pitcher plants (passive), sundews (semi-active), and bladderworts (active).

Pitcher Plants—Passive Persuasion
Many plants have flowers that use fragrance, nectar, and coloration to attract pollinators, and the purple pitcher plant is no different. However,

the modified leaves of pitcher plants found in the Northeast that use these techniques to attract insects. Pitcher plants aren't luring visitors solely for the purpose of pollination; they are attracting potential meals, which, if caught and ingested by the plant, allow it to flourish.

The pitcher plant's common name derives from its modified, pitcher-shaped leaves, which are not only photosynthesis factories, but also serve as very efficient traps. Prior to the nineteenth century botanists had no idea that the leaves had this function. Carl Linnaeus (Swedish botanist and the "father of taxonomy") believed the leaves might be designed to hold water that sustained the plant during droughts. But closer examination revealed that the liquid-holding vessels served as traps. Because the majority of sweet-smelling, sugar-exuding nectaries are located near the mouth of the pitcher, insects and other visitors are attracted to it and occasionally fall in.

The chances of escaping from the pitcher are minimal, thanks to a number of clever adaptations on the part of the plant. Tiny downward-pointing hairs prevent all but the most determined insects from getting out. Below the hairs, the vertical walls of the leaf are smooth and quite slippery, causing insects to slide down into the rain water that collects at the bottom of the pitcher, where they usually drown. (Insects that attempt to fly out of the narrow confines of the pitcher rarely succeed.) Glands along the lower walls secrete digestive

The deep maroon petals of the pitcher plant blossom wave like tiny flags throughout many New England bogs.

The bright colors and sweet nectar of the pitcher plant's modified leaf lure unsuspecting insects to its rim.

Downward-pointing hairs on the interior surface of the pitcher plant's leaf prevent insects from escaping this watery trap once they have fallen in.

enzymes that break down and digest the dead insects. When rain dilutes the water, or if there is an abundance of prey to be broken down, the plant injects extra amounts of acidic digestive fluids into the water. Bacteria living in the water also help to decompose the prey organisms.

The pitcher plant's leaf is not a death trap to all who enter it. The larva of one mosquito actually thrives in the water and even hibernates through the winter in the leaf-trapped ice. The larva of a species of fly takes advantage of leftovers and lives off of the insect remains left inside. And, it is not unusual, especially in the fall, to find the mouth of the leaf covered with the silk web of a spider that is capitalizing on the ability of the pitcher plant to attract insects.

Sundews—Semi-Active Seizure

Sundews, a second group of carnivorous plants in the Northeast, are more active than pitcher plants in catching their prey. The leaves of this "fly paper" plant have hairs, often referred to as "tentacles," that are tipped with a lethal, sticky fluid that is very effective in capturing small insects that come in contact with it. The aroma, color, and visually attractive glistening of the droplets of fluid on the tips of the longest hairs lure creatures to the sundew's leaves. The struggle that ensues when the insect gets mired in the adhesive fluid stimulates the leaf to produce more fluid, thereby sealing the organism's fate. Nearby hairs grow toward the prey and hold it firmly in place. Glands on the tips of the shorter hairs then secrete an anesthetic to debilitate the prey and within just a few hours enzymes will have done their work and the plant will ingest its meal.

There are 100 species of sundew, five of which are found in New England. The three species we're most likely to encounter in bogs and other acidic environments are named for the shape of their leaves: round-leaved sundew, spatulate–leaved sundew, and thread-leaved sundew.

Bladderworts—Sudden Suction

Of the 14 species of bladderworts in New England, the two most common bog species are horned bladderwort and common bladderwort. This unique group of plants is rootless; their flowers are supported by a stem and finely-divided leaves that are located under or floating on the water. If you look closely at their leaves, you will notice tiny sacs (or "bladders") interspersed throughout them, which were once thought to be flotation devices. We now know that they are, in fact, highly specialized traps.

The bladders—1/5 to 1/100 of an inch in diameter—capture, hold, and digest food for the plant (picture miniature oval balloons with a double-sealed, airtight door on one end). When this door is closed, the

Many insects and other small organisms find the glistening drops of adhesive liquid on sundew hairs irresistible...and inescapable.

bladder expels water through its wall, creating a partial vacuum inside. A leafy, feather-like structure hangs down adjacent to the door and the instant an organism bumps against this feathery trigger, it twists and breaks the seal of the door. The vacuum inside causes water to rush in, pulling the victim along with it. As the bladder fills with water, the pressure is equalized inside and out and the door automatically closes, caging the plant's prey. This entire process takes a fraction of a second. As enzymes digest the victim, special cells in the bladder's wall pump out the water and reestablish a partial vacuum inside, preparing the trap to spring again.

The beauty of the horned bladderwort flower belies the lethal nature of the traps that lie beneath it.

The survival of carnivorous plants isn't dependent upon their ability to trap and ingest animal matter. They will live and, if pollinated, produce seeds, but their vigor as well as their flower and fruit development, are greatly enhanced when their diet is supplemented with nutritious little bodies. As impressive as our New England carnivorous plants are, they are tame in comparison to one tropical pitcher plant that is capable of holding several quarts of water in its leaf and has been known to capture and digest giant rats.

] FAST FACTS [
Carnivorous Plants

- ▶ More than 600 species and subspecies of carnivorous plants have been identified.
- ▶ Pitcher plants capture foraging insects—especially flies, moths, wasps, butterflies, beetles, and ants.
- ▶ Bladderworts capture very small prey like rotifers and daphnia, as well as larger aquatic prey, such as mosquito larvae and even fish fry.
- ▶ Sundews tend to catch flying insects like gnats, flies, and moths.
- ▶ Most carnivorous plants, such as sundews, make their own digestive enzymes. Some carnivorous plants rely on bacteria to produce the enzymes to digest captured prey. The species of pitcher plant found in New England, *Sarracenia purpurea,* uses enzymes that it has manufactured as well as bacteria-generated enzymes.
- ▶ Pitcher plants grow smaller leaves where humans have increased the concentration of nitrates in rainwater.
- ▶ Charles Darwin wrote the first well-known treatise on carnivorous plants in 1875.

■ Types of Carnivorous Plant Traps

Pitfall traps of pitcher plant leaves form deep, slippery pools filled with digestive enzymes.

Flypaper traps (or sticky, adhesive traps), like those of sundews and butterworts, are leaves covered in glandular hairs that exude sticky mucilage.

Snap traps (or steel traps) of the Venus flytrap plant are hinged leaves that snap shut when trigger hairs are touched.

Suction traps, unique to bladderworts, are highly modified leaves in the shape of a sac or bladder with a hinged door lined with trigger hairs.

Lobster-pot traps of corkscrew plants are twisted tubular channels lined with hairs and glands.

Galls—*Edible Houses*

Imagine being able to reproduce without the pressure of providing a home for your offspring, much less feeding them three meals a day, because that part of the process is all taken care of for you. There are many insects, bacteria, mites, fungi, and nematodes (round worms) that are in this enviable position. The plants on which they lay their eggs, or where their spores germinate, produce abnormal growths called galls, which serve as "edible houses" for the next generation.

An Unusual Plant Reaction

Most of the agents responsible for this type of plant reaction are insects. Of 2,000 gall-producing insects in the United States, 1,500 of them are wasps or gnats. Certain plant families are more attractive to gall insects than others—the Oak family (over 800 species of insects), Daisy family (nearly 200 species of insects), Rose family (over 100 species of insects), and Willow family (over 100 species of insects) top the list.

A given species of gall-making insect always chooses the same species of plant as host, and the resulting gall has a certain shape, size, and color. Thus, all galls associated with a given species of insect look the same. A naturalist can note the species of plant as well as the appearance of the gall and often immediately know what insect resides within the gall. Different insects lay their eggs in different parts of their host plant—on buds, leaves, stems, or roots.

As a rule, galls are formed by a plant in reaction to an insect laying its eggs on or in it. This usually occurs in the spring, during the plant's growing season, as mature plants do not appear to react to gall-making insects. Scientists are still trying to understand what stimulates a plant to form an insect gall. Mechanical irritation (of the larva boring into the plant) and chemical substances secreted by

Pine cone willow gall (caused by a midge).

Spruce pineapple gall (caused by an aphid).

Wool sower gall (caused by a wasp).

JUNE

Oak apple gall (caused by a wasp) and a view of its interior.

Poplar leaf stem gall (caused by an aphid).

the egg-laying insect both appear to be involved. In defensive reaction to the presence of the egg-laying insect and/or her eggs and larvae, the plant grows specialized cells to contain them. These cells form a mass of tissue, and this we refer to as a gall.

Having hatched and bored their way into the host plant, most larval insects spend this stage of their life inside the gall that has formed around them. Most, if not all, of the eating they will do in their life-

Grape aphid or grape *phylloxera*: While most galls do not significantly harm their host plant, the grape aphid, which appeared in France around 1860, destroyed more than 2.5 million acres of grapevines in 25 years.

time occurs while they are a larva and have chewing mouth parts. The host plants are very accommodating, as the tissues that form the gall are very nutritious and provide the larva with food, sometimes for as long as an entire winter. Some galls house a single larva, while others are colonial in nature. After pupating, often in the spring, the adult insect emerges from the gall, leaving a tiny exit hole.

Predators, such as downy woodpeckers and black-capped chickadees, have learned that they can obtain a high-protein morsel in the middle of winter inside these growths. Often you can detect when they've dined on the resident larva by a fairly large hole "drilled" into the gall. (See photo on p. 422.)

A Win-Win

Galls are actually a win-win proposition. The larval insect derives both food and shelter (from wind, storms, and temperature extremes) from the gall. While the host plant appears not to benefit from the presence of galls on its leaves, buds, or branches, it usually doesn't suffer severe damage from them either, and humans have found a number of ways to utilize galls, including the making of medicines, insecticides, and permanent inks, due to the large amount of tannic acid they contain.

maturation

July is a time of growth and development in the natural world. The young of most species are born, raised, and taught how to survive on their own within a few short months. Birds fledge. Insects hatch and mate. Tadpoles mature. Young turtles and snakes, most without parental guidance or protection, learn how to secure food and avoid predators. On the other hand, most young mammals receive intense instruction from their parents on everything from avoiding detection to hunting techniques. Flowering plants that were successful in attracting pollinators produce fruit. The spore-bearing structures of non-flowering fungi pop up and disperse their spores. Plants and animals alike make the most of the warm summer days.

nature notes

Here's a sampling of species that are breeding, laying eggs, hatching, caring for young, fledging, giving birth, emerging, molting, shedding, flowering, and fruiting in July.

AMPHIBIANS

American bullfrog.

American Bullfrog— *Breeding*

The bullfrog is the largest *anuran* (frog or toad) in the United States and has the longest developmental period (up to two years from egg to adult). It is one of the last frogs to emerge from hibernation and breed, and it is the most aggressively carnivorous frog in New England. The highly aquatic bullfrog is found throughout most of New England with the exception of northern Maine, but its once abundant population has diminished in many areas.

Bullfrogs are silent for up to a month after emerging from hibernation. Their "jug-o-rum" calls signal the onset of courtship. The bullfrogs' breeding area is referred to as the "booming ground" for obvious reasons; within it males defend an area 20 feet in diameter. Peak breeding occurs during the month of July when mated females lay up to 80,000 individual eggs in a large, gelatinous mass that floats on the surface of the water. The tadpole stage of the bullfrog usually lasts through two winters, which is why it is possible to see very large tadpoles in a pond in the early spring. Transformation from tadpole to frog takes 10 to 20 days—this usually happens in July. The bullfrog tadpole is largely vegetarian, while the adult preys on a wide range of animals, including salamanders, young turtles, small birds, mice, and other frogs—even its own young. The bullfrog is the only amphibian to have acquired "game species" status in North America.

Fowler's Toad— *Breeding*

Fowler's toad is found primarily in southern New England and the southern half of New Hampshire. It resembles the American toad (see photo, p. 159),

Fowler's toad.

but there is a way to quickly tell them apart. Look at the black spots on its back. Fowler's toads usually have three or more warts in each dark spot on their back, as opposed to the one or two that American toads have. Fowler's toad has a long hibernation—up to seven months—and emerges later than the American toad. And as you would expect, Fowler's toad breeds later, as well. The existence of hybrids between the two species indicates there is some overlap in their breeding seasons. When it comes to the two species' breeding calls, the American toad's melodious trill is easier on the ear than the Fowler's toad's short nasal "waaaaah," said to resemble the "caw" of a crow.

American Toad—*Transforming*
American toad eggs hatch within a week of being laid, and small, dark tadpoles cluster together in groups, or "schools," for the next three to six weeks in the shallow water near the edge of a pond. There often are several schools in a pond; scientists have discovered that most of the tadpoles in a given school hatch from the same egg mass. When the tadpoles transform into tiny toadlets, they come out on land and can be found by the hundreds in the vegetation around the pond, where they may linger for days or weeks before moving away. Look very closely and you'll see remnants of a tadpole tail and the beginning of mottled adult coloration.

American toad toadlet.

Green frog.

American toad.

■ Frogs vs. Toads

Frogs	Toads
Moist skin	Dry skin
Smooth skin	Warts on skin
Long hind legs (for jumping) and webbed hind feet	Short hind legs, feet are not webbed
Live in or near water	Live on land, breed in water
Eggs laid in gelatinous mass or singly	Eggs laid in two strings
A group of frogs is called an army	A group of toads is called a knot

REPTILES

Eastern ratsnake.

■ New England States with Poisonous Snakes

Copperhead Massachusetts (localized and rare), southern and central Connecticut

Timber Rattlesnake Vermont, New Hampshire, Massachusetts, Connecticut (rare and localized in all of these states)

Bog Turtle—*Laying Eggs*

In the southwestern corner of Massachusetts and along Connecticut's western border, in unpolluted sphagnum fens or wet meadows, lives the smallest turtle in New England—the bog turtle. Its upper shell, or *carapace*, rarely measures more than 4 inches in length and is brown in color and lightly sculptured. In addition to its small size, a bright orange spot on each side of its head is an identifying feature. The bog turtle is restricted to valleys having calcium or lime bedrock. Because of a number of factors, including the filling of wetlands and collection by humans, this once abundant turtle is now classified as threatened and protected.

After breeding in late May or June the bog turtle lays two to five eggs in June or July, often in shrubby tussocks or on sphagnum moss out in the open. Some bog turtles have been known to pass the summer in a dormant state (*aestivation*); as a rule they aren't out and about during the hottest part of the day. They often hibernate in tunnels located in the tussocks where they bask in the summer. Bog turtle eggs hatch in August or early September.

Eastern Ratsnake—*Laying Eggs*

The eastern ratsnake, formerly known as the pilot snake or pilot black snake, is well known for its large size (5 to 6 feet in length) and its ability to climb trees. With the exception of New Hampshire and Maine, it is found in every New England state. Its diet is 60 percent warm-blooded vertebrates, including rodents (hence, its name), small birds and their eggs, amphibians, and insects. It has also been known to consume young opossums, weasels, owls, and American kestrels. It kills its prey by constriction. In July or August it lays 5 to 44 eggs in loose soil, decaying wood, manure, or sawdust piles.

As a cold-blooded (*ectothermal*) reptile, the ratsnake must avoid the freezing temperatures of New England winters, and does so by hibernating in ledges and other rocky areas. It is not unusual for eastern ratsnakes to hibernate with copperheads and timber rattlesnakes when they inhabit the same area.

SHEDDING AND "SPECTACLES"

Snakes never stop growing. Throughout their life, all snakes regularly shed their outer layer of skin to allow for this growth, baring a new, larger skin underneath. The frequency of shedding is determined by the rate of growth. Young snakes grow more quickly than adults, so shed more often.

When you look closely at the head of a shed snake skin, you can see the transparent "spectacles" that cover the snake's eyes.

A snake sheds its skin much as we peel a banana. It usually rubs its snout on a rough surface to loosen the skin, and as it crawls forward the skin is turned inside-out. Often the snake intentionally catches it on a log or branched stick, which then holds it in place as the snake crawls out of it.

Snakes have no eyelids, but they do have protection for their eyes in the form of "spectacles," or "eye caps"—transparent scales that cover their eyes. Like eyelids, spectacles keep dirt and debris off the surface of the eye and prevent the cornea from drying out by holding a layer of tears in place. The spectacles are replaced every time the snake sheds.

A shed snake skin.

BIRDS

Hairy Woodpecker —*Feeding Young*

After about a month of life inside a tree cavity, hairy woodpecker nestlings fledge. After leaving the nest, a fledgling is often seen with one parent—the fledgling is dependent upon it for several weeks for food. Right after fledging the young woodpecker often remains on a tree branch for several hours, waiting

An adult male hairy woodpecker feeding a fledgling.

for its parents to come feed it. In time it explores its surroundings, and it is not unusual to have the two birds visit feeders, with the adult feeding its young.

An adult loon catches a fish and places it in a chick's beak.

Common Loon— *Feeding Young*

At about three weeks of age, the sooty black down on newborn loon chicks is replaced with gray/brown down. The parents continue to feed their young for several weeks. Initially the adults place the food in the chick's beak,

A tree swallow feeds its young.

but as time goes on, in an effort to wean the chicks from being fed, they drop it in the water for the chicks to retrieve. By summer's end the chicks are totally independent.

Tree Swallow— *Feeding Young*

As they age, tree swallow nestlings come to the entrance hole of their nest cavity—be it a tree or bird house—to be fed, often sticking their head out of the hole. Both parents feed their young. They carry food in their bill and throat and place it directly into the open mouth of the begging nestling. A variety of insects are fed to the nestlings, but flies make up a major part of their diet. Young tree swallows can fly when they leave the nest for first time, and do not return.

Wild Turkey—*Sign (Dust Bath)*

In dry weather, especially during nesting and molting, adult wild turkeys (as well as ruffed grouse, ring-necked pheasants, wrens, and others) spend considerable time "dusting" in ant hills, leaves, or decayed logs. The turkey rakes in dirt all around its body with its beak, and then works the dust into its feathers by flapping, kicking, and rolling. It then stands and shakes itself thoroughly (often leaving traces of its actions in the form of loose feathers). Although the function of this behavior is not known, it appears to improve the alignment of the barbs of

the feathers. It also makes the outer contour feathers dry and fluffy so the interior down feathers fill the space between the contour feathers and the birds' skin, improving the insulating quality of the plumage. It is also possible that dusting rids birds of fleas, mites, lice, and other parasites.

Turkey dust bath.

Eastern bluebirds feed their nestling.

Eastern Bluebird— *Feeding Young*

As is often the case with birds, the female eastern bluebird does most of the nest-building and incubating of eggs, although the male helps feed the young once they've hatched. Clutch size varies with latitude and longitude, with bluebirds farther north and farther west having larger clutches, and eastern bluebirds typically have more than one brood each year. Young produced in early nests usually leave their parents in the summer, but young from later nests frequently stay with their parents over the winter.

Here you see a female song sparrow on her nest; the song sparrow eggs; nestlings at two stages of life (just-hatched and older); and an adult bringing food back to the nest.

Song Sparrow—*Feeding Young*

Quietly and secretly, early in the morning, the female song sparrow builds her nest in a secure, concealed spot. In roughly four days she finishes construction of the nest, which is composed mostly of grass and weed stems, leaves, and strips of plant bark. Rootlets, grasses, and hair are used to line the nest. After laying three to five eggs, the female incubates them without help from the male. Both parents feed the hatchlings high-protein meals consisting of insects; eventually the young birds' diet expands to include seeds and fruits.

Common Raven—*Sign (Inside-Out Carcass)*

Even though their bills are impressive, common ravens are unable to tear open the carcasses of deer, or even smaller animals such as raccoons, rabbits, and foxes. Usually they wait for carnivores or other scavengers to rip open these tough-skinned carcasses, and then they eat them. Occasionally, though, you will come across the carcass of a gray squirrel that has been turned inside-out. Instead of tearing them open, ravens often get at the flesh by turning the squirrel inside-out through the squirrel's mouth.

Common ravens sometimes turn squirrel carcasses inside-out in order to get at the flesh.

THE QUIETING OF BIRD SONGS

Indigo bunting.

By July, the woods and fields of New England have quieted down. Although some birds are still singing, the number of individuals and frequency of their songs has declined since June. Male birds sing in order to stake out their territories and announce their availability to females (some females, such as Baltimore orioles, cardinals, and rose-breasted grosbeaks, sing too, but they are in the minority).

By July most birds have mated and their young have fledged. Because their songs have performed their intended function, they cease to be sung. Among the birds whose voices you can still hear are the indigo bunting, eastern wood peewee, red-eyed vireo, scarlet tanager, and common yellow-throat. (For more on songbirds, see p. 101.)

MAMMALS

American Marten—*Breeding*
The American marten, or pine marten, is an arboreal weasel smaller than a housecat and slightly larger than a mink, with a long, bushy tail. During colonial times it could be found throughout New England's coniferous forests, but due to over-trapping and habitat reduction, the current New England population is limited to the boreal forests of northern Maine, New Hampshire, and Vermont. You are most likely to find the marten in woods with forest floors littered with branches and leaves that provide good habitat for rodents such as the red-backed vole and the red squirrel, the American marten's chief prey. Martens have few predators, due to their agility in trees.

Breeding takes place in late July and early August, but due to delayed implantation, young martens aren't born until the following March or April.

Virginia Opossum—*Giving Birth and Raising Young*
Until recent decades the Virginia opossum was unknown in New England. However, its range has expanded northward and westward in the past 100 years. Opossums are abundant in Connecticut, Rhode Island, and Massachusetts, and can be found even further north. However, in Vermont, New Hampshire, and Maine it is not unusual for opossums to suffer from frostbite on their naked ears and tail—North America's only marsupial is ill-equipped for northern New England's low winter temperatures. Even so, the opossum is usually out and about even when it is as cold as 32°F.

Opossums give birth from February to July, bearing an average of six to nine very underdeveloped young after a gestation of just 12 to 13 days. They crawl up their mother's belly to her *marsupium*, or pouch, where they remain for two months,

Virginia opossum.

The hind foot of a Virginia opossum.

each attached to one of her 13 teats. These "living embryos" weigh only one-or-two tenths of a gram, are less than half an inch long, and lack fully developed hind limbs. They are smaller in size than a honeybee. In New England, most opossums only have one litter as opposed to the two litters they have in the south. Northern litters tend to be larger than southern ones.

The opossum is shy and secretive, as well as nocturnal. The innermost toes, or "thumbs," on its hind feet are clawless and opposable and it has a prehensile tail capable of grasping onto limbs or carrying leaves and other nesting material.

Opossums are well known for their ability to feign death when threatened by a predator. This is actually caused by a temporary paralysis brought on by shock, a condition that is similar to fainting.

New England and Eastern Cottontail Rabbit—*Breeding*
New England has two species of cottontail rabbits and they greatly resemble one another. The eastern cottontail is the familiar rabbit of New England, with the exception of the state of Maine. The New England cottontail's range overlaps the eastern cottontail's but is much smaller. Although it's hard to distinguish the two, the eastern cottontail is lighter in color and often has a white spot on its forehead, whereas the New England cottontail rarely has this white spot and instead tends to have a black spot between its ears. Eastern cottontails have relatively

long, large ears while New England cottontails have shorter, black-rimmed ears.

The eastern and New England cottontails not only look, but behave, similarly. Both spend most days sitting still in a "form" at the base of a tree, or in a clump of grass or berry thicket, and become active at dusk. Both eat grasses and herbaceous plants in the summer, browse on woody plants in the winter, and re-ingest their feces so as to extract all possible nutrients. Both engage in elaborate courtship antics and dig shallow depressions in the ground to serve as a nest, lining it with fur and grass.

There has been a relatively rapid decline in the New England cottontail population, while eastern cottontail numbers have increased dramatically.

American Black Bear— *Teaching Cubs*

An American black bear cub.

Black bear cubs are born between late December and February, weighing less than a pound and measuring about 7½ inches. Mother and cubs emerge from their den usually from late March through early May, at which time the cubs weigh about 10 pounds. The cubs stay with their mother throughout the summer and fall, learning how to survive and gaining weight rapidly.

Striped Skunk—*Young Dispersing*

A young striped skunk.

Striped skunks give birth sometime between late April and early June in most of New England. At birth, young skunks' eyes are closed, they have little hair, and they don't hear until they are two weeks old. Now, two months later, they are bright-eyed and bushy-tailed. Weaned from their mother, this year's young are starting to disperse, heading off on their own to find insects, small mammals, and fruit to dine on.

Moose—*Summering Near Wetlands*

During the summer moose browse on aquatic vegetation and other plants, such as fungi, mosses, and lichens, in addition to tree leaves and twigs. Look for moose on the shores of ponds with aquatic plants, as well as in clear-cuts and clearings. In the summer you often find females near wetlands, in lowland coniferous woods, and in clear-cuts, while males are more likely to be in deciduous or mixed woods near a pond or lake. Wetlands are sought after not only because of the

A moose cooling off in the water.

aquatic vegetation, but because moose can cool off in the water, as well as escape from biting mosquitoes and deer flies. (Read more about moose on p. 251.)

Woodchuck—*Gaining Weight*

Instead of storing up food for the winter in its extensive underground system of burrows, the woodchuck eats voraciously all summer long in order to acquire a thick layer of fat that will sustain it through the four or five months that it hibernates. Everyone who has a vegetable garden, and many who don't, are well acquainted with New England's largest member of the squirrel family. Too well acquainted, some would say, for in addition to dandelions, plantain, clover,

A woodchuck considers its choices in a summer garden.

and grass, the woodchuck relishes fresh vegetables.

Just about the only time humans see a woodchuck is when it is eating, for other than when it is looking for food, it remains underground. Its tunnel system usually has four or five entrances. Many of these holes have conspicuous mounds right outside them, where dirt was removed from underground and deposited. Some woodchucks make separate burrows for their winter quarters, often on wooded slopes near the fields where they live in the summer. (See photo on p. 12.)

By July, red fox kits look more "grown up."

Red Fox—*Becoming Independent*

By July red fox kits no longer remain close to their den during the day. More often, they go out to catch their own meals and return to their den to sleep. They have lost their "baby" look and now closely resemble adults in both color and head shape, although they are still noticeably smaller in size. (Read more about red foxes on p. 415.)

■ Mammal Activity Chart

Diurnal (Active During the Day)	Nocturnal (Active at Night)	Crepuscular (Most Active at Dawn and Dusk)	Active Day and Night
Red fox (winter)	Red fox (summer)	White-tailed deer	Meadow vole
Woodchuck	Coyote	Coyote (early morning)	Common muskrat
Eastern chipmunk	Fisher	Fisher	Southern bog lemming
Red squirrel	American beaver	American beaver	American marten
Eastern gray squirrel	American black bear	Moose	North American river otter
American black bear	Virginia Opossum	American black bear	
Bobcat (winter)	Gray fox		
	Bobcat (summer)		
	Canadian lynx		
	Raccoon		
	North American porcupine		
	American mink		
	Ermine		
	Striped skunk		
	Woodland and meadow jumping mice		
	North American deermouse		
	White-footed deermouse		
	Masked shrew		
	Northern and southern flying squirrels		

The eastern gray squirrel is *diurnal*—most active during the day.

INSECTS & ARACHNIDS

Dobsonfly—*Emerging and Breeding*

Dobsonflies are not actually flies. They are closely related to antlions, fishflies, and lacewings, and belong to the order *Megaloptera*, meaning "large wing" in Greek. The 3-inch long dobsonfly larva, called a *hellgrammite*, lives in a stream or lake. It possesses conspicuous mandibles, or mouthparts, that can deliver a nasty bite if the insect is handled or stepped on.

Male dobsonfly.

Hellgrammites live under rocks in streams for several years, swimming forward and backward as they prey on other aquatic insects. Eventually they crawl onto land and burrow into rotting logs or the ground where they overwinter and emerge, often in July, as 5-inch-long (from the tips of mandibles to the tip of the abdomen) winged adults. The adult dobsonfly only lives for seven days, just long enough to mate, and it doesn't appear to feed during this time. Females retain the same mandibles they had as larvae, which are imposing-looking and deliver a mean bite, but they are nowhere near as large as the "tusks" that males use to grasp the females during mating (because of the size and shape of these tusks, males are not able to bite humans). Thousands of eggs are laid on rocks and plants situated next to or over water.

Both sexes defend themselves with an irritating and foul-smelling anal spray.

Pelecinid Wasp—*Laying Eggs*

If you see a shiny, black, slow-flying wasp with a disproportionately long abdomen crawling on your lawn in late July, August, or September, shout for joy. It is North America's one species of pelecinid

Female pelecinid wasp.

wasp, and it is a *parasitoid*—an insect, with larvae that complete their development at the expense of a single host organism that is killed in the process. Using her long, flexible abdomen, the female pelecinid wasp lays her eggs in June beetle larvae (which are busy consuming plant roots beneath your lawn—see p. 130). These eggs hatch into wasp larvae that devour their host, thereby decreasing next year's June beetle infestation.

Leafcutter Bee—*Lining Cells and Laying Eggs*

Leafcutter bees are about the size of honeybees, but are darker and have stripes on their abdomen, so they resemble small bumblebees. Unlike honeybees and bumblebees, leafcutter bees are solitary, not colonial. Once the temperature rises above 70°F, female leafcutter bees become very active building "cells," in which they lay their eggs. Females find a suitable cranny where they construct a "nest

A leafcutter bee hole in a sugar maple leaf.

tunnel" consisting of 12 to 15 cells. Before laying the egg and sealing the cell, the bee cuts circular pieces roughly half an inch in diameter out of leaves with her mandibles. Usually only one or two pieces are cut from each leaf. Each time a round segment of leaf is cut, the bee folds it under her abdomen and grasps it with her legs while flying back to the cell. Approximately 15 pieces of leaf are used to line each cell. The female leafcutter bee lays one egg and deposits a little pollen and nectar in the cell for the developing larva to eat once it hatches; she then seals the cell, never to return.

The perfectly round holes in leaves that result from this activity are quite obvious, and are often found in rose, lilac, and Virginia creeper foliage. Different species of leafcutter bees collect different material, including woolly plant hairs and resin, with which they line their cells.

Nursery Web Spider and Wolf Spider— *Carrying Egg Sacs*

Unlike most spiders, which leave their eggs to hatch unattended, wolf spiders and nursery web spiders carry their egg sacs around with them. Wolf spiders attach their egg sacs to their *spinnerets*, the structures at the tip of their abdomen through

A nursery web spider with its egg sac.

which silk is spun, and newly-hatched spiderlings can be found riding around on their mother's abdomen. Nursery web spiders carry their egg sacs in their jaws and *pedipalps* (the short, leg-like structures in front of their other appendages). When the eggs are about to hatch, the mother spider builds a nursery tent of silk in which she puts her egg sac. She remains nearby protecting it until the eggs hatch. Many species are able to walk on the surface of ponds, and may even dive beneath the surface to escape enemies.

The female nursery web spider sometimes attempts to eat the male after mating with him. To minimize this threat, the male often presents the female with an insect when approaching in the hope that it satisfies her hunger.

Potter Wasp—*Building Pots and Laying Eggs*

A potter wasp building pots to hold its eggs.

Potter wasps are named after the mud pots they build to hold their eggs. These wasps capture and paralyze caterpillars, place them inside a pot, lay an egg, and then seal up the structure. When the wasp egg hatches, the larva has several caterpillars to eat before pupating into a wasp and gnawing its way out.

Stonefly—*Emerging as Adult*

Species of stoneflies that emerge during the summer months in New England appear now. They crawl out of the water onto rocks and vegetation, where they split their skins and begin life as winged adults. American robins and eastern phoebes congregate near wide sunny rivers to feed on them.

Stonefly larva.

CAMOUFLAGE— CRYPTIC COLORATION

Camouflage is an effective survival mechanism for all kinds of organisms, including insects. Because they have so many predators, insects employ many devices to avoid detection. Blending in with their surroundings—whether by color, pattern, movement, or structure—is crucial to their survival.

Note how this sphinx moth blends in with the bark of the tree.

Cicada—*Emerging as Adult*

Cicadas are called "locusts" in some parts of the country, although they are unrelated to true locusts, which are a kind of grasshopper. Males are heard more than seen in the Northeast, for they are usually calling their mate from a treetop where they can't be spotted. The cicada call is among the loudest of any insect call. Instead of rubbing one part of their body against another, as many insects do (including crickets and grasshoppers) cicadas have

Cicada skin.

BUTTERFLY "PUDDLING"

White admiral and crescent butterflies on coyote scat.

Canadian tiger swallowtails on wet ground.

"Puddling" is a term used for the behavior of butterflies when they gather on wet soil (including dirt roads), scat, and carrion to obtain nutrients such as salts and amino acids. These nutrients are often transferred to the female during mating as a "nuptial gift," resulting in an increased survival rate of her eggs. As a rule, butterflies that gather on animal droppings, such as white admiral and crescent butterflies, are interested in obtaining ammonia, while those that puddle on wet soil like the Canadian tiger swallowtail seek salt ions.

loud, drum-like noisemakers called *tymbals* on the sides of their middle section, or *thorax*. Muscles attached to the tymbals cause them to vibrate, and the male's relatively empty abdominal cavity acts as a resonating chamber. (Read more about insect songs on p. 226.)

After mating, female cicadas cut a slit in the bark of a twig and deposit their eggs. When they hatch, cicada nymphs drop to the ground and burrow anywhere from 1 to 8 feet down in the soil, where most stay for two to five years, sucking sap from tree roots. Some cicadas, in an attempt to avoid predators such as cicada killers and praying mantises, stay underground for 13 to 17 years—the large, prime number is thought to make it difficult for a predator to time its life cycle to match the cicada's. Eventually, nymphs crawl up through the soil onto a plant where they molt, or shed their skin, for the last time. We see these shed skins far more often than we do the winged adults that emerge from them.

Primrose Moth—*Feeding*

Summer nights are filled with moths that visit flowers, which open in the dark to receive them. Usually light-colored, these flowers are easily visible to moths, and their *nectaries* are positioned so that moth tongues can reach them. One such flower is the

Primrose moth.

evening primrose, a common "weed" of disturbed roadsides and fields. If you rise early enough, you have a good chance of seeing the brilliant pink-scaled primrose moth head-down in a primrose flower, obtaining nectar and pollinating it at the same time.

Great Golden Digger Wasp—
Preparing Meals
The great golden digger wasp builds several nests, often underground, each with several compartments, in which she lays her eggs. She then finds and paralyzes other insects and carries them back to the nests. This ensures her wasp larvae have an instant meal of live but immobilized insect prey upon hatching.

■ Butterflies vs. Moths

Butterflies	Moths
Diurnal (active during day)	Nocturnal (active at night)
Slender body (tight scales)	Plump body (longer, looser scales)
Slender antennae with recurved knobs at tips	Slender or feathery antennae without knobs at tips
Wings upright when resting	Wings open when resting
Eggs upright	Eggs flat or oblong in most (upright in cutworms, tiger moths, and gypsy moths)

Common ringlet butterfly.

Crocus geometer moth.

A great golden digger wasp with its prey.

Leaf Miner—
Tunneling
At this time of year you can easily find leaves with white "squiggle marks" on them. These trails are the diagnostic sign of leaf miner insects—larvae of flies, moths, or beetles that feed or "mine" between the upper and lower surfaces of a leaf. The

A mined poplar leaf.

larvae tunnel through the leaf eating the juicy, green layers, creating a narrow, whitish-colored winding mine. The tunnel is clear, except for the trail of shed larval skins and black fecal material left behind as the larvae feed.

SPIDER WEBS IN THE GRASS

About this time of year small silk webs are noticeable in the grass, especially in the early morning, when dew covers the ground. These are the work of young spiders (born this spring). As spiders grow, their webs increase in size, making them more obvious. (See more about spider webs on p. 228.)

Spider web.

PLANTS & FUNGI

Partridgeberry— *Flowering*

In July it's possible to find partridgeberry bearing both this year's flowers and last year's fruit. This evergreen, woody vine produces twin, hairy, white

Partridgeberry flower and fruit.

flowers. In one flower the pistil is short and the anthers long, and in the other the opposite—a long pistil with short anthers. This arrangement discourages self-pollination. The ovaries of the two flowers fuse, so there are two flowers for every berry. If you look closely at the fruit, two red spots are evident at one end, one from each ovary. Ruffed grouse, northern bobwhites, red foxes, raccoons, and white-tailed deer feed on these berries.

Common yarrow.

Common Yarrow— *Flowering*

This familiar member of the Aster family can be found growing in most New England fields. Its flat-topped cluster of flowers makes a suitable landing platform for the many insects that come to drink its copious nectar and inadvertently pollinate it.

Over the years yarrow has been a popular medicinal and spiritual herb. It has been used to treat more than 25 ailments, including colds, fever, indigestion, toothache, infections, and wounds.

At one point it was used to repel witches and demons, as well as fleas and lice. Even today a yarrow compound is used in the treatment of viral hepatitis and *Staphylococcus* bacterial infections. Yarrow's finely cut, fern-like leaves give off a pungent odor when crushed. (Read more about common yarrow on p. 397.)

Queen Anne's Lace— *Flowering*

Queen Anne's lace is the delicate, lacy white flower that adorns most fields in the summer. It belongs to the carrot or parsnip family, *Apiaceae*, and is sometimes referred to as wild carrot. Botanists do not know whether the cultivated carrot was derived from Queen Anne's lace, or vice versa. Along with parsnips and fennel, Queen Anne's lace is related to the highly poisonous water hemlock and poison hemlock.

Queen Anne's lace.

Several small deep purple flowers that often appear in the center of the flower help identify Queen Anne's lace. It was once hypothesized that these flowers served as a "bull's eye," helping guide pollinating insects. However, research shows that this is not the case and that insects do not have a preference for these marked flowers. At this point, the purpose of the darker flowers is unknown.

After fertilization occurs and seeds start developing, the remaining structure (the *umbel*) curls inward, becoming concave, and resembles a bird nest. Spiny seeds are held within this "nest." As they mature, the umbel opens up again, flattens, and empties the seeds (1,000 to 40,000 per plant). It is worth examining one of these seeds under a hand lens or microscope, for their intricate design is beautiful.

Chicory—*Flowering*

The cornflower blue of the roadside chicory flower is unmistakable. Like its close relative, the dandelion, it belongs in the Aster family, and what we refer to as one blossom is actually

Chicory.

composed of many flowers—all flat ray florets. It is found primarily in poor soils, where it doesn't have much competition from other plants.

Just about every part of this plant is edible. Young leaves have been cultivated as greens. The root of chicory is roasted, ground, and flavored with burnt sugar to make a drink resembling coffee. Young roots are also boiled and eaten like carrots, as well as used for medicinal purposes.

Wintergreen.

Wintergreen—*Flowering*

Wintergreen—along with blueberries, trailing arbutus, and mountain laurel—is a member of the Heath family. Its shiny, evergreen leaves creeping along the forest floor indicate that the soil is fairly acidic. In July you're likely to spot its dangling, waxy, bell-like, white flowers that sometimes have a hint of pink to them. If pollinated, wintergreen flowers produce red fruit that often remain on the plant through the winter. Both the leaves and the fruit of this plant taste like wintergreen and are a favorite of ruffed grouse. White-tailed deer and American black bears feed on the foliage.

Chanterelle—*Fruiting*

Chanterelles are orange, funnel-shaped fungi that are collected by foragers and considered a delicacy. Their gill-like folds extend down their *stipes* (see illustration on p. 209), which is a good characteristic for indentifying this mushroom, as is their distinct apricot-like odor. There are many varieties of chanterelles, the first of which usually appear in July. (Have a mycologist or someone very familiar with edible mushrooms identify any mushroom before you eat it.) See more about fungi on p. 295.

Chanterelle.

Clintonia—*Fruiting*

In July, the beautiful, yellow, lily-like blossoms of clintonia have set seed and the round, blue fruits that give this plant its nickname blue bead lily are much in evidence. (See photo of a clintonia flower on p. 91.)

Clintonia fruit.

JULY

GRASS FLOWERS

Because they are tiny and inconspicuous, the two rows of flowers on grass plants are rarely noticed. Grasses are wind-pollinated, and have no need for the colorful petals and fragrance used to attract insects to plants that are insect-pollinated.

Each grass flower, or floret, has both male and female reproductive parts. The male stamens bear many smooth, light, pollen grains on their tips, or anthers. Often you can see the ripe pollen-laden anthers hanging outside the bracts, or scales (lemma and palea) that protect the reproductive parts of the flowers. The feathery stigmas, or tips

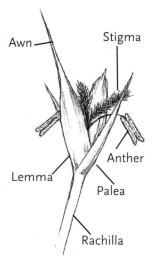

A grass spikelet.   A close-up of grass flowers.

of the female pistils, also protrude outside the bracts, so that pollen carried by the wind has a better chance of landing on them.

There are often several flowers, or florets, on a single stem, or rachilla. At the base of this inflorescence (flower head) are structures called glumes, which enclose the florets before they are mature. Together the florets and glumes are referred to as a spikelet.

Bunchberry—*Fruiting*

The four-petalled white bunchberry flowers of June (see p. 136), if pollinated, develop into bright red fruit in July and August. Veeries, members of the thrush family of birds, as well as warbling vireos, consume the fruit. The fruit is edible, both raw and cooked, but doesn't have much flavor. Native Americans used it in puddings and sauces.

Bunchberry fruit.

Rye.

■ Grains that Belong in the Grass Family

Wheat
Rye
Corn
Rice
Oats
Barley
Sorghum
Millet

JULY
a closer look

July is a month filled with insects as well as insect-eaters. As dusk arrives and mosquitoes and moths begin to fill the air, **bats** (p. 177) emerge and take advantage of the meal that is presented them. Many of these insects, such as **caddisflies** (p. 180), spent their youth underwater. Others, like the **tiger beetle** (p. 188). Between the aerobatics of bats and the flickering courtship of **fireflies** (p. 185), every New England evening presents displays that one never tires of. During the day, fields are full of flowers such as **common milkweed** (p. 190), which lure all kinds of **insect visitors** (p. 193). The leaves of plants are consumed by herbivorous **caterpillars** that have a multitude of defenses (p. 183). Predators such as **crab spiders** (p. 189) recognize the gold mine of prey that can be found wherever flowers advertise their presence with sweet fragrances. The "*cu-cu-cu*" of the **black-billed cuckoo** (see below) is often heard on hot, humid days, prior to rain.

Cuckoos and Tent Caterpillars—
Integrated Life Cycles

Every decade or so New England is subject to an influx of tent caterpillars, both eastern and forest. Distinguishing one from the other is fairly simple if you know what to look for and have a specimen close at hand. Both species are very hairy, but forest tent caterpillars are bluish with cream-colored, keyhole-shaped spots down their back, and eastern tent caterpillars are black with a cream-colored stripe down their back (see illustration, p. 176). Forest tent caterpillars seek out sugar maple, trembling aspen, and oak, and they tend to spin silk "mattresses" that lie directly on the branches. Eastern tent caterpillars prefer black cherry and apple trees, and they build silk "tents," within which they seek shelter from predators and inclement weather.

When their numbers build, there is no doubt to the density of larvae, as the defoliation of the trees in which the tents are built can be significant.

Close scrutiny of the host tree species in the fall or winter will tell you if an irruption is likely to take place the following summer. The shiny, brown egg masses of tent caterpillars encircle the branches through the winter, and larvae emerge as early

An abundance of hairs makes the forest tent caterpillar unappetizing to many birds.

as May. (See more about eastern tent caterpillar egg masses on p. 310.) You can almost hear the caterpillars' mandibles crunching on leaves overhead during one of these peak

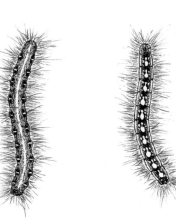

Eastern (left) and forest (right) tent caterpillars.

Black-billed cuckoo.

years—newly formed openings in the canopy and their copious droppings confirm their presence.

We Are Not Alone

Fortunately, humans aren't the only ones aware of the onslaught of moth larvae. The soft, monotone "cu-cu-cu," "cu-cu-cu," "cu-cu-cu," of the insect-eating black-billed cuckoo, as well as the "ka-ka-ka-ka-kow-kow-kow-kow-kowlp-kowlp-kowlp-kowlp" of the yellow-billed cuckoo from the edges of woods and overgrown fields confirm that they, too, are tuned-in to the life cycle of the tent caterpillar.

Far more frequently heard than seen, black-billed cuckoos—and to some degree, the less common yellow-billed cuckoo—experience years of peak population density. It appears that it is not pure coincidence that the influx of tent caterpillars coincides with higher-than-usual numbers of cuckoos, especially black-billed. However, the erratic fluctuation in the numbers of cuckoos is not considered wholly proportional to the incidence of tent caterpillars. For one thing, eastern and forest tent caterpillars pupate by late June, before young cuckoos ordinarily fledge. While parents may have an easier time of providing their nestlings with meals, the caterpillars are gone by the time the fledglings can

feed themselves. It is felt, however, that an increase in the breeding rate of cuckoos is somehow related to the simultaneous outbreak of tent caterpillars.

Caterpillar Bingeing

The fact that cuckoos eat tent caterpillars has been known for many years. Over 100 years ago an observer watched a black-billed cuckoo eat 36 forest tent caterpillars in five minutes. He then watched another cuckoo eat 29 caterpillars, rest a short while, and proceed to eat 14 more. While not limited to tent caterpillars, the diet of a cuckoo definitely reflects a preference for them—the remains of over 100 tent caterpillars have been taken from a single cuckoo's stomach.

You might well ask why cuckoos find these hairy caterpillars so delectable when most other birds avoid them like the plague that they are. How is it that cuckoos are able to digest all those hairs? In fact, they can't. The hairs become embedded in the lining of the cuckoo's stomach, creating a felt-like mass. The cuckoo sheds this hairy lining periodically after growing a new one to replace it. This adaptation allows both black-billed and yellow-billed cuckoos to fill a niche in which there is (understandably) little competition.

- Black-billed and yellow-billed cuckoos lay eggs in each others' nests. Black-billed cuckoos have also been known to lay eggs in nests of the yellow warbler, chipping sparrow, eastern wood-pewee, cardinal, cedar waxwing, gray catbird, and wood thrush.

- Cuckoos are relatively quiet, shy birds that usually remain concealed in the foliage of trees and shrubs.

- During their breeding season they often call through the night.

- In many parts of the United States cuckoos are called "rain crows" because their calls are thought to predict wet weather.

- Only 17 days pass between when a black-billed cuckoo egg is laid and when the young bird fledges—a remarkably short time compared to most other birds.

- The black-billed cuckoo was formerly much more common in the United States. Their population decreased dramatically in the 1980s and 1990s, perhaps due to the growing use of pesticides.

Bats—*Hard Work on the Night Shift*

Myths about these nocturnal fliers abound: Bats will head for your hair and get tangled in it; bats are blind; bats are rampant with rabies and will aggressively attack humans and infect them. Not one of these claims has an ounce of truth to it. The only reason for a bat to ever swoop near the head of a person is to catch dinner in the form of an insect that is hovering close by.

Bats make up a significant portion of life on earth. There are nearly 1,000 species in the world, and they are the only mammals capable of flying. Bats belong to the order *Chiroptera* (Greek for "hand-wing," reflecting the wing's bone structure—see

p. 178) and have been divided into two suborders: *Megachiroptera* (the large, fruit-eating bats of Old World tropics that seek food by sight), and *Microchiroptera* (mostly insect-eating bats that hunt by echolocation—see below). New England has nine species of bats, all in the suborder *Microchiroptera*, including bats that live in houses (little brown bat and big brown bat); forest dwellers (eastern pipistrelle, northern long-eared bat, Indiana bat, and eastern small-footed bat); and those that migrate south for the winter (silver-haired bat, red bat, and hoary bat).

Insect Eaters
Around 70 percent of all bats in the world eat insects, consuming half to three-quarters of their weight each night. They seize insects with their mouth while flying or use their wings and/or the membrane around their tail to scoop them up. With the exception of three species of nectar-feeding bats that live along the Mexican border of Arizona and Texas, all bats in the United States and Canada are insectivorous. According to the US Fish and Wildlife Service, some species of bats consume up to 3,000 flying insects a night during the summer months. It's estimated that the 20 million free-tailed bats living in Bracken Cave in Texas eat 250,000 pounds or more of insects in a single night.

Contrary to common belief, only a small percentage of these insects are mosquitoes. For the most part, large numbers of mosquitoes are not found at the level of air where bats feed. Bats do, however, consume large numbers of crop-harming and disease-carrying insects. Spotted cucumber beetles, scarab beetles, stink bugs, cutworm moths, and leafhoppers are heavily preyed upon by the bat population.

Navigating by Sound
Due to their use of *echolocation*, bats are extremely accurate navigators. They emit high-frequency pulses of sound through their mouth or nose that are

beyond the range of human hearing. These sounds strike objects and come back as echoes. By interpreting the echoes, a bat can tell what an object is, where it is located, and how fast it's moving. Amazingly, the bat is doing this not for one or two objects a minute, but for hundreds, while flying as fast as 15 miles per hour or more. Bats not only locate prey this way, but deftly maneuver around objects in the dark. In pitch blackness they can detect obstacles as fine as a human hair.

Although bats locate insects primarily by echolocation, they are not blind, and many have excellent vision. Because they are nocturnal, most do not depend upon locating prey and navigating by sight.

Female bats gather together in maternal colonies, each giving birth to one pup during June or July. The young bats are not capable of flight until they are a month old. Mothers recognize their young by the high-frequency sounds their pup emits. Once the young can fly, they and their mothers still return to roost during the day.

Big brown bat.

Specialized Wings

A bat's maneuverability is a result not only of echolocation, but also the design of its wings. Each wing consists of two layers of skin, which form a membrane that is supported by the bones of the bat's arm and four elongated fingers. The thumb is in the form of a small hook at the junction of the finger bones on the leading edge of the wing. The second and third fingers, along with the membrane in between, give the wing a stiff leading edge. The third finger also forms the wing tip. The membrane is attached to the bat's hind legs as well as its tail in some species.

Speed and maneuverability are often at odds with one another—some bats are swift (long, thin wings), and others are slower but have greater maneuverability (short, wide wings).

Rabies

Bats, like many other animals, can and do contract rabies. They can also transmit it to humans. However, the extent to which this happens is tremendously exaggerated. Bat rabies accounts for approximately one human death in the United States per year. Compare this to the average 95 people a year who die from bee stings. Even when bats do contract rabies, they do not become aggressive like other animals that have the disease. Bats rarely bite except in self-defense when handled.

White Nose Syndrome

Something is killing whole populations of bats in the eastern United States as they hibernate in caves and mines. Scientists have determined that bats are losing their fat reserves (which are crucial to winter survival) long before winter is over, causing them to die of starvation. It is estimated that over a million bats have died in this manner since 2006—little brown bats, our most common species, have a mortality of 90 percent, more than any other species. Afflicted bats are infected with a fungus,

QUICK-N-EASY BAT SHELTER

A quick and easy option for providing bats with shelter is to staple an 18-inch-wide piece of tar paper (or similar material) completely around a tree trunk so that it's tight at the top and flares out about 2 inches at the bottom. Bats like to crawl up inside tight quarters and the tar paper allows them to choose the shady or sunny side of the tree, depending on their temperature needs at a particular time of day.

Geomyces destructans, which is white in color and grows on the bats' noses (and occasionally on wings, ears, and tail); hence, the name "white nose syndrome."

Much is still being learned about white nose syndrome. Scientists don't know if the fungus is the actual cause of death, or if it's present because of a weakened immune system. They have learned that the syndrome is probably transmitted from bat to bat. Hopefully more research will reveal the cause and cure of this condition in the very near future.

Coming to the Rescue

More than 50 percent of the bat species in the United States are declining or already endangered. The causes of this decline may be the result of one or more factors, including disease, pesticides, loss of winter fat stores, pneumonia, and the interruption of hibernation and feeding schedules due to warm and variable winter weather.

The decreasing number of large dead or dying trees in which bats roost in the daytime and form maternal colonies only adds to these pressures. Land owners can help by leaving snags standing as well as providing suitable man-made housing for bats. You can buy or easily find directions on building a bat house and erecting it on your property. In order to make sure the design and placement of the

] FAST FACTS [
Bats

▶ Bats are not the only mammals that navigate by echolocation; dolphins and whales use it as well.

▶ The sound pulse a bat emits returns to its ear in 0.006 of a second.

▶ Tiger moths produce ultrasonic signals to warn bats that their body is chemically-protected.

▶ While other mammals have one-way valves in their veins to prevent their blood from flowing backward, bats also have this mechanism in their arteries.

▶ Bat teeth are very tiny and very sharp, adapted for crunching through insect exoskeletons.

▶ The cartilage in a bat's "finger bones" lack calcium and minerals, especially near the tips, making them easier to bend without splintering.

▶ The bat's "thumb" is a claw on the front edge of its wing that it uses when crawling over surfaces.

▶ A baby bat is referred to as a pup.

▶ Many bats have small eyes, but bats are not blind and some have excellent vision.

▶ Most New England bats mate in the fall, but delayed fertilization takes place in the spring.

bat house meet the criteria to successfully attract and support bats, you can go to Bat Conservation International's Web site, www.batcon.org, and check their list of certified models. (Your state's Fish and Wildlife Department is also a good source for information on how to attract bats.) Bats, the primary predators of night-flying insects, can use all the help we can give them.

"Sleep all day. Stay out all night. No wonder kids like bats."
—BAT CONSERVATION INTERNATIONAL

Caddisflies—*Master Architects*

Many insects are master architects, designing and building complex structures within which they live. The nests of social insects such as honeybees, paper wasps, and bald-faced hornets come to mind. Equally impressive, if not more so, are the creations of caddisfly larvae, insects that can be found throughout New England. (Note: they are not true flies.) Not only do the larvae use a variety of material—including bits of plants, twigs, leaves, grains of sand, and pebbles—to build their individual "cases," but construction and habitation take place underwater.

Although caddisflies are found almost anywhere there is open water, they are most common in clean, cool, northern streams and ponds. In general most caddisfly larvae living in flowing streams make their case out of sand and pebbles, which are heavy enough to help anchor the case in strong currents. Those living in the still water of ponds tend to build lighter cases out of plant material.

p. 133). They are all aquatic as eggs, larvae, and pupae, and terrestrial as adults. Caddisflies are best known for their larval stage, which lasts anywhere from two to three months, to two years. Have you ever looked down through the water of a pond or stream and thought you saw a tiny clump of plant material or stones inching its way along the bottom? Or turned over stones in a fast running stream and found little clumps of pebbles attached to them? If so, you have seen the portable and well-camouflaged home of a caddisfly larva.

Not all caddisflies build these cases. Some are "free-living," others build shelters and spin silken webs from rocks in fast running streams to catch tiny particles of food. The majority, however, construct tubular cases around themselves made of the materials mentioned earlier. Most case-making caddisfly larvae attach themselves to their case with two hooks at the end of their abdomen, then haul their case around as they feed on both plant and animal matter. A fewer number of caddisflies attach their case permanently to an object, such as a large rock (often on the bottom of it), and remain there through their pupal stage.

Each species of larva always constructs the same type of case, using the same materials, just as each species of bird builds the same type of nest out of identical material. Each species' case is unique, enabling you to identify the species of caddisfly purely from the case's size, shape, and base mate-

Caddisfly larvae construct portable homes using their own silk, as well as available plant and mineral material. These two species are in the northern caddisfly family, the members of which use leaves, stems, sticks, pebbles, and sand as building material for their cases. One looks like a log cabin (left) and the other is a tube of pebbles (right).

Larvae

Caddisflies go through all four stages of complete metamorphosis—egg, larva, pupa, and adult (see

One species of caddisfly cuts bits of vegetation and assembles them in a square case.

rial. Many are about the width of a pencil and from a quarter of an inch to an inch long. Some resemble a log cabin, with criss-crossed sticks stuck together and a hollow cavity chewed through the middle where the larva lives. Others consist of tiny pebbles linked together in the shape of a hollow tube. There are fine-grained cases made of sand that resemble trumpets and snail shells. One species builds around a long stick that hangs out the back and is thought to spin the case naturally so that it faces into the current. Another uses pieces of vegetation cut very precisely and arranged so as to form a perfect square in cross-section. Silk is the common denominator in all, as it is used to spin the tube shape in which all these different materials are embedded.

If you want to be entertained, watch a caddisfly larva build its case. Begin by carefully removing a larva from its current case. (Gently squeeze the case and the larva's head and thorax will appear; a tiny tug extracts the insect.) Put the larva in a tank or container filled with water, along with tiny particles such as bits of leaves, sticks, and stones—anything tiny that isn't completely smooth (one British woman provided her larva with gold dust). Watch what happens next. With luck, construction will take place under your very eyes.

Pupa

When it has matured, a case-making caddisfly larva creates an underwater silken cocoon, which is basically a modification of its case. It spins a sieve-like silk screen for the back opening of the case and uses stones or plant material for the front. The larva then attaches its cocoon with silk to a large rock or other immovable object in the water. Eventually it sheds its larval skin for the last time, revealing the pupa. All of this takes place inside the cocoon, underwater. This pupa has as much need of dissolved oxygen as it

Certain species of caddisfly larvae gather in one spot before sealing themselves inside their case and pupating. When the larvae have almost finished transforming into adults, the pupae float to the surface of the water and adult caddisflies emerge.

did as a larva, so in order to create a current of water (containing dissolved oxygen) that will pass through the cocoon, the pupa wiggles, drawing water in the front and out through the back of the case. The silk strainer covering the rear opening not only allows water to run through the case, but also prevents predators, such as dragonfly larvae, from getting into it. After two or three weeks the adult caddisfly, still inside its pupal case, cuts its way out of the cocoon with its sharp mouthparts and swims or floats to the surface of the water. (There are some who believe it is aided by a bubble of air surrounding it.) It emerges as an adult either by splitting its pupal skin and using it as a raft from which to fly away, or by wiggling its way to a rock and then molting.

A recently emerged adult caddisfly drying its wings.

Adults

The winged adults bear a close resemblance to moths—in fact, the two are closely related. Both are predominantly nocturnal and usually quite dull in color. Caddisflies and moths do have their differences, however, the most visible being the covering of their wings. Caddisfly wings are covered with hairs, whereas moth wings are covered with scales. In addition, caddisflies don't have a long, straw-like *proboscis* through which they drink nectar, as moths do. Instead, they suck it up with hairy, finger-shaped mouthparts that serve as sponges during the month or so that they are alive.

Adult caddisflies fly mostly at night as well as at dusk and dawn, and usually spend the day hiding in vegetation; consequently, many people are not familiar with them. The adults live only a few weeks, and are most frequently sighted near outdoor lights at night between late spring and early fall. Their most distinctive characteristic is the way in which they fold their wings like a tent over their back when resting.

Males often congregate and form mating swarms, easily noticed by females. After mating takes place, females lay anywhere from just a few to 800 eggs (depending on the species), often in a gelatinous mass or in strings underwater. Because adult females are covered with hair, they can maneuver underwater as they lay their eggs without becoming water-logged.

Caddisflies fill a significant niche in their aquatic environment. Both adults and larvae are a

Adult caddisflies are distinguishable from other flying insects by the way they fold their wings in a tent-like fashion over their body when at rest.

popular food for fish. (As a consequence, fishermen often tie flies mimicking both of these stages.) Some birds, such as swallows, take advantage of courting swarms of male caddisflies, consuming many at one time in the early morning hours or late afternoon. Scientists consider caddisflies biomonitors of pollution. The number of species and their relative abundance compared to the number of other aquatic insects indicates the environmental condition of a body of water. Clean streams and ponds support a diverse caddisfly population.

JULY

Caterpillar Defense Strategies— *When Everyone's Out to Get You*

It sounds like the perfect stage of life. Your only two jobs are to eat and grow, eat and grow. What is there not to envy about being a caterpillar? Actually, predators are just as busy trying to eat caterpillars as caterpillars are trying to eat vegetation.

While all four stages that butterflies and moths go through (egg, larva, pupa, and adult) are vulnerable to predation, it is the larval, or caterpillar, stage that demonstrates perhaps the most innovative physical, chemical, and behavioral strategies for avoiding detection or, if discovered, warding off predators.

Masters of Disguise

The most common tactic caterpillars use to avoid detection is camouflage. How many heads of broc-

coli have made it to your table without at least one green cabbage butterfly larva being discovered? And who knows how many you missed! Color is one way to avoid detection. Mimicry is another. There are caterpillars that are next to impossible to distinguish from twigs. Their color, shape, and position (they can extend their bodies without support at one end for many minutes) can fool most predators, most of the time. Other caterpillars are known to mimic bark and leaves (going so far as to "paste" bits of vegetation on themselves so as to resemble lichen and leaves), as well as buds, flowers, fruits, and tendrils. One of the most convincing examples of mimicry is the resemblance of several swallowtail larvae to bird droppings. What better way to avoid being eaten by birds?

The master of disguise in New England could arguably be the monkey slug or hag moth caterpillar. In its larval stage it resembles the cast skin of a tarantula. No, there are no tarantulas in New England, but we do have birds that winter in the Neotropics where there *are* tarantulas (plus this genus of moth is primarily tropical). In addition, the adult female monkey slug mimics a bee, complete with pollen baskets made of scales, and the adult male, a wasp.

Bristly "Armor"

Different strategies meet different needs. An effective way to avoid predators as well as parasitizing insects is to arm one's exterior with hard-to-

The milkweed tussock moth caterpillar (left) and Baltimore checkerspot butterfly caterpillar (right) use bristles to deter predators.

penetrate bristles or "hairs." They are a successful deterrent to most predators (cuckoos are one of the few New England consumers of tent caterpillars, a feat made possible by an ability to shed their bristle-embedded stomach linings—see more about this on p. 175). Older larvae are prime targets for insects looking for a host in which to lay their eggs (when the eggs hatch the larvae feed on the insides of the caterpillar). Because some parasitic insects locate their hosts by smell, camouflage is not as effective a defense as bristly "armor."

Standing Out from the Crowd

Some larvae display *disruptive coloration*—prominent markings that break up the caterpillar's recognizable shape and appearance—while others

Monarch (left) and black swallowtail butterfly (right) caterpillars use warning coloration to ward off enemies.

use *warning coloration* to announce their toxicity to would-be predators. Often a combination of red, orange, or yellow with black and white markings indicates the inedibility of a caterpillar. Monarch butterfly caterpillars, which contain cardiac glycosides from the milkweed plants they consume, illustrate this strategy. In addition to warning coloration, there are also designs that are intended to scare potential predators, such as the false "eyes" of the spicebush swallowtail.

Combining Defenses

Rarely does a caterpillar utilize just one defense mechanism. A perfect example of this is the Abbott's sphinx moth larva. It employs a multitude of mechanisms to avoid detection as well as to discourage any predator that is clever enough to notice and disturb it. Initial efforts are made to disguise and break up its outline with patches of color on its back. Should this not succeed, and it is noticed by a potential predator, the magnificent false "eye" on its hind end will hopefully scare off the enemy. Unbelievably, this "eye" depicts not only a pupil and an iris, but also a white spot on the pupil, which makes it appear moist and shiny.

If the predator is bold enough to peck at the

"eye," the caterpillar then produces a mouse-like squeak by forcing air out of its *spiracles*, or breathing holes, which surely must surprise if not alarm a hungry bird. Last but not least, if the squeaking doesn't discourage the predator, the caterpillar proceeds to actually bite the source of its disturbance.

The spicebush swallowtail caterpillar is another employer of multiple defense mechanisms. Prior to its fourth molt, the young caterpillar mimics a bird dropping. As it matures, it becomes a snake mimic and lives within a leaf shelter. As a last defense, it extends a tentacle-like structure loaded with butyric acid, a very effective weapon against predators.

The Carolina sphinx moth (left) and Abbot's sphinx moth (right) caterpillars combine defenses—note the Carolina sphinx moth larva's horn and multiple false "eyes," and the Abbot's sphinx moth's disturbingly realistic "eye" and patches of color along its back.

Certainly the larval stage of moths and butterflies cannot be faulted for lack of originality when it comes to outwitting predators, but in fairness to the predators, it's their skill that drives the creative juices of natural selection. John Himmelman put it best in his book, *Discovering Moths* (Down East Books, 2002):

> *It's tough being a caterpillar, and evolution has provided an ever-changing contest of adapt, fool, hide, catch on, re-adapt. The defenses we see are the result of this, and none*

is one hundred percent effective...The invisible will be found and the undesirable will be consumed by those with strong constitutions and an indiscriminate palate. Even the pain-givers will meet their match. This keeps the balance and makes sure that everyone, predator and prey, can at some point grab a meal.

■ Summary of Caterpillar Defenses

Physical

Camouflage Mimicry, countershading, disruptive coloration

Warning coloration Bright colors, false "eyes"

Toxicity Chemicals from plants eaten

Acidic fluid Secreted from tips of spines

Defense gland Emit bad smell

Spines and hairs Prevent ingestion from predators, prevent parasites from laying eggs

Warning sounds Emit squeaks via forced air

Behavioral

Hiding Leaf nests, bore into food source

Shelter Spin/live in silk tents

Camouflage Attach bits of plant material to body, extend body out from branch unsupported, "blow" back and forth like a dead leaf in the breeze

Get "backup" Enlist ants for protection

Surprise/frighten Twitch, regurgitate, drop from plant or tree, attempt to bite

Nocturnal feeding Safety in the dark

Communal feeding Safety in numbers

Fireflies—*Lighting Up for Love*

Nocturnal insects have adapted in many ways to the challenges of communication that darkness poses. Their courtship, for instance, takes place during the night. How does one recognize a member of one's own species, much less a member of the opposite sex, in the pitch dark? Crickets "sing" by scraping their wings together. Moths use pheromones, detectable with the help of antennae. Fireflies, or lightning bugs, opt for visual communication. They have evolved a signal system visible in the dark—a series of light flashes by which males and females of the same species identify each other prior to mating. Because of fireflies' ability to produce light and their very obvious display of it during their nocturnal courtship ritual, humans have the privilege of witnessing this mating game.

Alight with Life
Although these glowing insects are referred to as "fireflies" and "lightning bugs," they are neither flies nor bugs, but beetles. Fireflies (family *Lampyridae*) and related insects in the family *Phengodidae* are the only *bioluminescent* (living organisms capable of producing light) beetles in the Northeast. There are other bioluminescent organisms, particularly in warm, humid climates, as well as in the ocean. These include a tropical species of click beetle that has two "headlights" and the railroad worm, a wingless female beetle that has a row of lights along each side of her body and a glowing red "headlamp."

All fireflies share certain characteristics. These include soft, flexible forewings, a somewhat flattened body, and a shield, called a *pronotum*, which covers and protects their head. There are 20 to 30 species of fireflies in New England, most of which produce light (about two-thirds of the 2,000 known species of fireflies are bioluminescent). Many, but not all, of the fireflies that are active during the day lack this ability to create light. The larval stage

The large size of a firefly's eyes indicates that it is a nocturnal creature.

Many male fireflies produce light in the last two segments of the abdomen.

(glow-worm) and sometimes even the eggs of nocturnal fireflies produce light (continuously, not at intervals), in order to warn predators of the bitter chemical that makes them an unappetizing meal.

years ahead of humans.

Luciferin and luciferase are used in medical research related to cancer, multiple sclerosis, muscular dystrophy, cystic fibrosis, heart disease, and antibiotic testing. Detectors made with these chemicals warn that milk, food, or water may be contaminated with bacteria. Fireflies used to be the only source of these chemicals, and massive numbers of insects were collected for this reason, but (fortunately for fireflies), they now can be made synthetically.

Energy Efficiency

The firefly creates light through a chemical reaction in its abdomen. *Luciferin* (a chemical compound that reacts with oxygen to produce light) is stored in the cells of the firefly's light organ. These organs are richly supplied with air tubes. When oxygen comes in contact with luciferin in the presence of an enzyme called *luciferase*, it reacts chemically to release energy in the form of light. Fireflies are able to control light production by regulating the oxygen supply to the light organs. A layer of reflector cells in the light organs intensifies the effect. Perhaps the most amazing thing about this reaction is its efficiency, for it creates very little heat (given off as wasted energy). At least 90 percent, and some scientists say up to 96 percent, of the energy a firefly uses to create light is actually converted into visible light. In comparison, an incandescent electric bulb converts only 10 percent of total energy used into visible light and the rest is emitted as heat. In terms of energy conservation, fireflies appear to be light

Patterns that Mean Something

The flashes of light that fireflies emit are not produced randomly. Each species has a unique pattern of flashes—a bioluminescent Morse code of sorts. The flash patterns of different species have distinct differences, including color, length, number of flashes, interval of time between flashes, and the time of night they are flashed. The flight pattern flown by the firefly while flashing also differs.

As a general rule in the Northeast, females become active around dusk, when they settle on vegetation, often in open fields. Male fireflies then begin flying above the field, intermittently flashing while patrolling for females, signaling their identity as well as availability. (Males of some species in the

The firefly's shield, or *pronotum*, protects its head.

tropics synchronize their flashes, creating quite the light show.) These signals can take many forms—a continuous glow, brief single flashes, or a series of multi-pulsed flashes known as "flash-trains." Once a female—usually perched on a blade of grass—detects her own species' flash code within 10 or 12 feet of her, and if she is receptive, she flashes back the same signal after a brief interval (the length of which depends upon the species of firefly). Females are known to respond to several males, eventually choosing to mate with the male whose flash, due to its rapidity or length, she finds most attractive. Upon mating, the male firefly injects a nutritional package of protein along with his sperm.

While for the most part males signal in flight and females from perches near the ground, the sex of a firefly cannot always be determined by where you see it flashing. Males sometimes begin the evening by flashing from a perch and some females flash while in flight. A more dependable way to sex a firefly is to examine the tip of the abdomen. Males of many species have light organs on the last two sections of the abdomen, while many females have them on the second-to-last segment of the abdomen.

"Girl" Power

In contemplating life as a firefly, one might choose to be female, for they seem to have most of the advantages. To begin with, most females can sit and relax without having to expend as much energy

as the male on flight. If they're not romantically inclined on any particular night, females simply don't flash their tail ends in response to the males patient signals. Finally, they are intelligent enough to lure unsuspecting suitors to their death in order to dine on them.

Some female fireflies utilize their bioluminescence in a very unromantic way. The females of some species in the genus *Photuris* have been known to mimic the female responses (flash patterns) of other fireflies in the area in order to attract males of the mimicked species. Once a duped male descends into the grass to meet his supposed mate, the mimicking female pounces upon him and eats him. In addition to a tasty snack, the female firefly gains access to the male's supply of defensive chemicals, which she uses to protect herself as well as her eggs. Each *Photuris* can consume several unsuspecting fireflies in one night. (There is also at least one species of firefly in which the male does the mimicking to lure others as prey.)

Female fireflies are outnumbered by males, 50 to 1, so whether they're looking for a mate or a meal, the odds are in their favor.

JULY

Tiger Beetles—
The Fast and the Furious

Picture a predatory creature with huge, bulging eyes and large three-toothed mandibles that can reach a speed of at least 200 to 300 miles per hour (relatively speaking). Fortunately for us, this creature is a tiger beetle, an insect measuring only half to three-quarters of an inch in length, and it is far more interested in preying on ants and flies than on humans.

Twelve-spotted tiger beetles are ferocious predators—fast-moving and quick to crush their prey upon capturing it.

There are many different species of tiger beetles. The most familiar in New England, due to its brilliant green iridescent coloring, may be the six-spotted tiger beetle, which, true to its name, usually bears six white spots on its outer wing covers. Often this species is seen in the early spring in open woodlands. Another common species is the twelve-spotted tiger beetle, which usually has 12 spots on dark wing covers and resides in dry, sandy areas with little or no vegetation.

Built for Speed, Built to Kill

Tiger beetles are voracious predators, as larvae and as adults, capturing prey both on the ground as well as in the air. If you look closely at a tiger beetle (they are wary, and it is hard to get closer than within about 3 feet) it is easy to see that they are built for speed. Long, slender legs lift their body off the ground, allowing them to be swift. When a potential meal is spotted with their large eyes, tiger beetles rush after the insect, seize it in their powerful, sickle-like mandibles, and bang it against the ground several times until it is dead. They then

JULY

] FAST FACTS [
Tiger Beetle

▶ Both larvae and adults (after they pupate) overwinter in the tunnels they dig, which can be as deep as 4 feet underground in order to avoid freezing temperatures.

▶ Although two New England species of tiger beetles are nocturnal, most are active during the day. Look for them on sunny days running around ambushing unsuspecting insects on sandy patches of earth. They tend to run for cover whenever clouds move in.

mash the insect with their mandibles and suck up its liquids, filtering out chunks of exoskelton with hairs located on their upper "lip."

The immature tiger beetle is just as formidable a predator as the adult, both in looks as well as behavior. Eggs are laid just under the surface of the ground in summer and hatch after about two weeks. The larvae immediately begin digging, turning their egg chamber into a shallow vertical tunnel. They scoop out the soil with their mandibles and fling it away from the tunnel, leaving level ground surrounding the entrance. The larvae go through several molts, digging deeper (usually an inch or two) into the earth as their size increases. They back into the tunnel until their entire body except their head and the enlarged area right behind their head (the *prothorax*) is under the ground. From this position they keep a lookout for prey, with their mandibles wide open. If they see an insect go by close to the tunnel, their head whips out, often backward, and in a couple of hundredths of a second they grasp their prey. They then anchor themselves inside their tunnel with a pair of hooks on their back, located just behind the middle of their abdomen, and pull their prey down into their burrow where they crush it, liquify it with regurgitated digestive fluid, and proceed to drink their meal.

Crab Spiders—
Delivering a Sweet Surprise

Imagine, if you will, a life of leisure that allows you to be surrounded by natural beauty and sweet perfumes. The only interruptions in your days of repose are the timely delivery of sumptuous meals. Sound too good to be true? Not for members of the *Thomisidae* family of arachnids, otherwise known as crab spiders. Like crabs, these spiders are more adroit at moving sideways and backward than they are at moving forward; hence, their name. And, they have a life of ease compared to most of their relatives who actively stalk their meals, or at the very least construct a silk trap in which to catch them. Crab spiders are capable of stalking and, like all spiders, can spin silk. However, their *modus operandi* for catching prey relies not on these more energy-expending methods, but on the element of surprise.

Because of the toxicity of their poison and the speed with which it paralyzes prey, crab spiders can successfully capture insects such as honeybees, moths, and flies, some much larger than themselves.

Tools of the Trade

Certain species of crab spiders are referred to as "flower spiders" due to their habit of spending time in or on flowers. This tendency is not accidental, for the spiders' very survival depends on being in a location frequented by insects—their primary source of food. Once a flower site has been chosen, the crab spider sits in waiting, remaining relatively motionless until a pollinating insect happens by. Immediately the spider (which often has its first two pairs of legs stretched out at right angles to its body in attack position while it waits) grabs the unsuspecting insect and with its hollow fangs injects paralyzing poison and digestive enzymes into its prey. After the spider's enzymes have turned the insides of the insect into liquid, the spider sucks the prey dry until only the exoskeleton of the insect remains.

The tools that allow crab spiders to be successful predators are numerous. They include the two long and enlarged pairs of front legs that possess the strength necessary to firmly grab and hold onto prey. Eight eyes produce sharp images only at very short distances, but they perceive motion as far as 8 inches away. Although crab spiders possess relatively small jaws, or *chelicerae*, their paralyzing poison is very toxic and quick-acting (but not harmful to humans). Because of this crab spiders can prey upon insects much larger than themselves, such as butterflies, moths, and honeybees. Perhaps the best-known adaptation of certain species is the ability to change color to match their surroundings, thus camouflaging themselves very effectively, both from their prey and any predators interested in an eight-legged meal.

The Art of Blending In

One of the most common species of crab spider in New England is the goldenrod spider, a fairly small spider that frequently bears a red band on either side of its abdomen. It turns out that this species of spider contains a pigment that is sensitive to white

The goldenrod crab spider often turns white when waiting and watching for prey on white flowers and yellow when on yellow flowers.

Common Milkweed—
Overlooked and Underappreciated

Think of the word "milkweed" and immediately images of floating silk parachutes come to mind. For generations children have been entertained by providing wind power to aid in the dispersal of milkweed seeds. The pod itself has sailed who knows how many seas, or cradled how many tiny dolls. Adults have been equally creative in their use of the fruit of this plant, particularly the silken "wings" of milkweed seeds. Over the years it has provided: mattress stuffing (8 to 9 pounds of fluff per bed); a substitute for life preserver filling during the Second World War (26 ounces of the waxy, hollow threads packed inside a life jacket will keep a 150-pound person afloat for 48 hours); and cloth (the silky hairs, mixed with flax or wool, were woven to create a softer thread than either fiber alone). As impressive as the ingenuity of humans has been in finding uses for milkweed, the way in which the plant accomplishes the production of its fruit is even more so.

Attracting Winged Pollinators

Although common milkweed propagates not only by seed, but by budding on lateral roots under the ground, seed formation is crucial to its survival. Not being wind-pollinated, milkweed requires agents to carry the pollen grains of one plant to the eggs or ovules of another in order for pollination to take place and seeds to be formed. The objective then is luring potential pollinators to its flowers. If you've ever smelled a milkweed flower, you know it does this very effectively. The scent of milkweed is something everyone should experience—its sweetness is beyond description. In addition to its appealing scent, the milkweed flower produces copious amounts of nectar, far more than most North American flowers, which numerous insects feed upon (see sidebar, p. 193). Between its scent and prodigious amounts

or yellow reflected light, and as a result, the spider changes color according to the color of its background. As far back as 1870 the female goldenrod spider was observed changing color from white to yellow when moved from a white flower to a yellow flower. Recent research shows that, if placed on a yellow flower, a white goldenrod spider will turn yellow within 20 days. It can reverse this color change, as well. While they may be found on a variety of colored flowers, a very high percentage of goldenrod spiders occur on white or yellow flowers, and a significant number of these match the color of the flower upon which they sit. Researchers found that 84 percent of all white crab spiders found were on white flowers and 85 percent of yellow crab spiders were on yellow flowers. Only 6 to 10 percent of the spiders were found on flowers of other colors.

The next time you're walking by a field of oxeye daisies, Queen Anne's lace, mullein, or goldenrod, stop and take a closer look at the flower heads. Chances are great that somewhere in the sea of sweet-smelling white or yellow flowers, a crab spider patiently waits for the perfect moment to surprise a pollen or nectar-seeking insect. With luck you may even witness the ambush.

Each milkweed blossom has five cups, or hoods, each of which holds nectar for visiting insects.

of nectar, milkweed is virtually assured of many insect visitors.

Common milkweed is selective, however, when it comes to which insects are allowed easy access to its flowers. Because milkweed flowers need to receive pollen from a stand of milkweed other than their own in order to produce viable seeds (*cross-pollination*), the plant encourages flying insects, especially the honeybee, with nectar and sweet smells. In addition to attracting insects that are beneficial in distributing its pollen far and wide, milkweed actually discourages nonflying insects—such as ants—as they are less likely to travel the necessary distance to another milkweed patch. The sticky milky latex within the plant (for which it is named), is not only toxic to many creatures, but it also clots once it comes in contact with the air. The tiny spikes on the bottom of an ant's feet puncture the outer layer of tissue on the milkweed stalk as the ant climbs toward the flower. When the milky sap is released through these tiny pinholes, it usually gets the ant's feet tangled up, thus preventing the ant from reaching the flower.

Crown of Horns

With a hand lens in one hand, and a needle in the other, you will readily discover the cleverness and efficiency of the milkweed flower's design. Each individual flower possesses five "horned" or hooded sections, which contain nectar. The actual petals hang down beneath this crown of horns. If you look closely with your hand lens you see a tiny slit between each of these five hoods, within which is the stigmatic chamber where pollen must be

delivered in order to reach the ovaries and fertilize the ovules. Insert your needle into the slit and up past it, and with luck you will snag two tiny yellow pollen sacs called *pollinia* that are connected by a thread (rotator arms), and which resemble miniature saddle bags. A pair of pollen sacs hangs over each of the five slits, with one sac located on either side of it. Each pollinium contains enough pollen grains to pollinate an entire milkweed pod (80 to 200 seeds).

Pollination Process

One of the most remarkable aspects of the common milkweed plant is the number of ways in which its flower promotes cross-pollination. In addition to other adaptations, the milkweed flowers are quite slippery, so that an insect landing on one to get a drink of nectar often finds its six legs slipping and sliding down between two of the nectar-filled hoods into the previously mentioned slit. When this happens, the insect attempts to pull its leg free, and if it is successful, the pollinia usually become attached to the leg as it is extracted from the slit. If you look closely at the legs of insects, particularly honeybees, as they hover near or land on milkweed flowers, you are almost sure to see up to a dozen pollinia dangling from their legs.

Bumblebees are one of the many insects that visit a milkweed patch, attracted by the sweet scent and copious nectar.

While the insect makes its way to another milkweed plant (honeybees and other insects are known to concentrate on a plant species during its peak flowering time so they don't need to learn the structure of another type of flower) the pollinia

Between each hood on the milkweed blossom is a slit into which the pollen sacs must fit in order for pollination to take place. A visiting insect's foot slips easily into this slit, and the pollen sacs often slip off once the foot is inside the flower. Sometimes an insect such as this moth cannot extract its foot, and is trapped. Eventually it dies from starvation or predation.

begin to dry, contracting and rotating 90 degrees to the proper position to fit in the slit and into the stigmatic chamber of another milkweed flower, where ovules await the pollen grains' arrival. The drying and rotation process takes a bit of time, and thus pollination of flowers in the same patch, that are likely to be visited immediately after securing the pollinia, is hampered. By the time the insect has

MONARCHS THREATENED?

The pollen from corn that has been modified with *Bacillus thuringiensis (Bt)* as an internal organic pesticide has been found to be moderately toxic to monarch butterflies, affecting their growth and survival rates. Monarch butterfly larvae feed solely on milkweed plants, and the adult butterflies drink nectar from milkweed flowers. A large percent of milkweed grows along roadsides and, to allow for easy access, many corn fields are also adjacent to roads. Given the frequent proximity of these two plants, corn pollen, distributed by the wind, is very likely to settle on milkweed leaves, thus adversely affecting the monarch population if the pollen has been altered to serve as a pesticide. Future decisions regarding this issue will hopefully be made with an awareness of the inter-connectedness and value of all forms of life.

] FAST FACTS [
Common Milkweed

▶ The scientific name for members of the milkweed family is *Asclepiadaceae*, after Asklepios, the Greek god of healing.

▶ Most of the 2,000 to 3,000 species of milkweed occur in the tropics.

▶ There are 110 species of milkweed in North America.

▶ Grazing animals, such as cows and horses, avoid eating milkweed growing in pastures because its sap contains a toxic alkaloid called cardiac glycoside.

▶ The insects that have adapted to tolerate this toxic alkaloid benefit by being protected from most predators by its presence in their systems.

▶ Milkweed becomes quite fragrant at night, attracting several species of moths, which pollinate between 5 and 25 percent of milkweed plants.

moved on to another milkweed patch, where cross-pollination can potentially take place, the pollinia will be ready for insertion.

The Unlucky Few
Unfortunately, not all the nectar-seeking insects that visit milkweed flowers succeed in extracting their leg from the slit once it is caught. They simply don't have the strength, and after struggling for a considerable amount of time, perish, either from exhaustion, starvation, or predation. It is not unusual to see dead honeybees hanging by one leg from the occasional milkweed flower—studies show that approximately 5 percent of milkweed flowers visited by honeybees trap them permanently in this manner.

Gossamer Wings
Even with sweet lures, intricate flower mechanisms and the beneficial timing of the drying and rotating of the pollinia, only 2 to 4 percent of milkweed flow-

Close to 300 seeds are arranged in a spiral pattern inside each milkweed pod. All of these seeds came from the pollination of one milkweed flower.

ers produce mature pods, each of which contains roughly 80 to 200 seeds. Milkweed patches are large, and less energy is needed to visit the flower next door (which won't result in the production of viable seeds) than the one down the road (which will). Even so, with an average of four to six pods maturing on any given milkweed stalk, each plant produces an average of 700 seeds—more than enough to keep children busy blowing "gossamer wings" for the foreseeable future.

MILKWEED VISITORS

The reasons insects visit milkweed patches vary considerably, depending on species. Some come to drink or collect nectar; some to eat or collect pollen; some to eat flowers, leaves, pods, or roots of milkweed; and others to prey upon the former. This photographic sampling of some of the insects that visit a milkweed patch illustrates the diversity of their size, shape, and color. Note the prominence of red, or orange and black coloration—a warning to predators that although these insects have adapted to the toxic alkaloids of the milkweed plant, those contemplating eating them would be adversely affected.

Large milkweed bug (nectar, leaf, pod, and seed eater): These red and black insects are herbivorous and equipped with piercing-sucking mouthparts, which are used to eat the ripe seeds of common milkweed available in late summer. They also feed on the pods, nectar, and leaves. The large milkweed bug overwinters in leaf litter. The adults seen in New England most likely migrated south the prior summer and returned in the spring.

Red Milkweed Beetle (leaf eater): Several species of longhorn beetles use milkweed as a host plant. The arrangement and number of black spots on their body distinguish one species from the other. One of these species, the red milkweed bee-

tle, is herbivorous and leaves characteristic chew holes on the tips of common milkweed leaves. It lays its eggs on milkweed stems near the ground, and upon hatching, the larvae burrow into and eat the stems and roots. If disturbed, the beetle makes squeaking noises by rubbing together rough spots on its *thorax*, or middle body section. The larvae overwinter on milkweed roots, pupate underground in the spring, and emerge as adults. Early summer is when they are most active and noticeable.

Robber fly (predator): Robber flies prey on other insects. Keen vision, a head that swivels left and right, fast flying capability, and alertness allow them to prey on the flies, bees, grasshoppers, butterflies, and beetles that visit a milkweed patch, many of which are larger in size than they are. Prey is paralyzed with chemicals inserted with the robber fly's beak, and their insides consumed.

Crab spider (predator): Named for the similarity of its stance and movements to those of a crab, the crab spider does not spin a web to catch its prey. It hides in amongst the flowers of the milkweed (as well as many other flowers) and awaits the visit of unsuspecting nectar or pollen-gathering insects. When opportunity knocks, it pounces, grabbing its prey with its fangs and secreting a digestive enzyme, which dissolves the prey's inner tissues, which the spider then proceeds to drink. (Read more about crab spiders on p. 189.)

Lady beetle (predator): There are 5,000 species of lady beetles worldwide, over 350 of which reside in North America. Their eggs are bright yellow, and are often laid on milkweed leaves. When they hatch, the spiny, spotted larvae immediately begin to consume any available insects. Lady beetles can be the most abundant predator in a milkweed patch, with both larvae and adults preying on aphids, mealy bugs, scale insects, and small caterpillars.

Black-and-yellow argiope (predator): Orb weaver spiders, such as the black-and-yellow argiope, are quite common in milkweed patches, due to the abundance of prey. Unlike crab and jumping spiders, orb weaver spiders have poor vision and depend upon the vibrations of their webs to alert them to the presence of prey. These spiders usually incorporate a zigzag pattern called a *stabilimenta* into their web. While the function of this thicker strip of silk is not known, one theory is that it might be a means of protecting the web by alerting low flying birds to its presence.

Yellowjacket (predator, nectar eater): Some species of yellowjackets drink nectar as well as catch and chew up insects to feed to their developing larvae. A milkweed patch provides plenty of both.

European honeybee (nectar and pollen eater): Honeybees are one of, if not the most, important pollinators of common milkweed. Their abundance in a milkweed patch is apparent from the humming buzz that emanates from the patch when the flowers are in full blossom. Worker honeybees are either pollen or nectar collectors. It is easy to tell one from the other in a milkweed patch, as the pollinia caught on their legs are usually very apparent.

Great spangled fritillary (nectar eater): The great spangled fritillary, like the monarch, is a member of the brush-footed butterfly family, whose forelegs are greatly reduced in size, quite hairy, and useless for walking. The larva of the great spangled fritillary hibernates soon after hatching, and the following spring feeds at night on violets. After pupating and emerging as an adult butterfly, its long *proboscis*, or tongue, allows it to reach deep within flowers and drink the sweet nectar.

Monarch butterfly larva (leaf eater) and adult (nectar eater): The monarch butterfly caterpillar has one, and only one, source of food—milkweed. The female monarch butterfly lays each of her eggs on the underside of a milkweed leaf, usually one per plant. Upon hatching the larva consumes first its shell and then eats the leaf on which it was born, simultaneously ingesting the cardiac glycosides that milkweed leaves contain. Insect foliage feeders of milkweed, such as monarch larvae, have evolved special physiological adaptations that enable them to tolerate these toxic glycosides in the milkweed plant's latex. This has proven an effective means for warding off predatory insects that lack this tolerance. The adult monarch butterfly retains the toxicity it acquired in its larval stage.

Slug (leaf and flower eater): Insects are the most common, but not the only, visitors to a milkweed patch. Other creatures, including slugs, find sustenance among the leaves and flowers of this remarkable plant.

dispersal

The nature of the activity that surrounds us changes as summer progresses. Fledglings are, for the most part, now independent of parents and feeding on their own. Some birds are beginning to disperse from their breeding grounds and others, especially shorebirds, are migrating south. While the decrease in bird songs is very noticeable, this avian silence is filled by the songs of male grasshoppers, katydids, crickets, and cicadas, which persist through the day and well into the night. There is no time to lose, as these insects must attract mates in order to breed and lay their eggs before temperatures begin to drop significantly. Nearly every step taken along the shore of a pond or lake is greeted with the startled jump of a young frog, now fully equipped with four legs and breathing with lungs. Eggs of turtles and snakes buried several months ago are hatching. Trees, shrubs, vines, and wildflowers are producing fruit, often packaged to entice would-be seed dispersers. The miniscule spores of moss, ferns, and fungi ripen and drop to the ground, or are blown about by the wind. Summer has done its work; the next generation of plants and animals is well on its way.

nature notes

Here's a sampling of species that are breeding, nesting, laying eggs, hatching, caring for young, fledging, giving birth, migrating, pupating, emerging, shedding, flowering, and fruiting in August.

AMPHIBIANS

Duration of Tadpole Stage for Frogs and Toads*

American toad: 3 to 6 weeks

Fowler's toad: 6 to 9 weeks

Eastern spadefoot: 2 weeks to 2 months

Spring peeper: 6 to 8 weeks

Gray treefrog: 4 to 8 weeks

Green frog: 3 months to 2 years

American bullfrog: 4 months to 2 years

Mink frog: 1 to 2 years

Northern leopard frog: 3 to 4 months (occasionally overwinter)

Pickerel frog: 2½ to 3 months

Wood frog: 60 to 70 days

*Estimates from *Stokes Nature Guides—Guide to Amphibians and Reptiles* by Thomas Tyning (Little, Brown, 1990)

A young green frog that still has its tail.

American toad tadpoles congregate near the shore.

Marbled Salamander—*Breeding*

The range of marbled salamanders doesn't extend as far as northern New England, and even in southern parts of the region, these salamanders are fairly uncommon. The marbled salamander is unusual in that it breeds in the late summer or fall in dried-up temporary ponds. Females often remain with their eggs, guarding them until the fall rains fill the vernal pools in October and November, at which point they head back into the woods and their eggs hatch. (If there is no rain, the eggs will not hatch until spring, when flooding occurs.) The larval salamanders overwinter at the bottom of the pools, metamorphosing into adults the following summer and dispersing in the woods up to half a mile away. Both the aquatic larvae as well as the terrestrial adults are nocturnal.

Slimy Salamander—*Eggs Hatching*

The northern tip of the slimy salamander's range reaches just into New England, and even within this range, it is quite rare. It can be found in the southwest corner of Connecticut and up along the state's western border, possibly into Massachusetts. When disturbed, slimy salamanders produce a slimy glandular skin secretion that discourages predators due to its adhesive quality (when it dries, it sticks to your skin like glue). Silvery white spots and brassy flecks dot this otherwise black-skinned salamander.

Slimy salamanders mate and deposit their eggs in the late spring, with the first eggs hatching in August. During hot, dry spells adults congregate underground, coming out at night to hunt, particularly for ants and beetles.

A wood frog on the forest floor—can you find him?

Wood Frog—*Blending In*
Many animals utilize camouflage as a means of protecting themselves from predators. While there are many forms of camouflage, cryptic coloration—being similar in color and/or pattern to one's surroundings—is the most common form. Wood frogs, with their earthy colors, are well hidden on the forest floor, where they reside most of the year.

REPTILES

Northern Map Turtle—*Eggs Hatching*
The map turtle is primarily a midwestern species, but its range extends eastward as far as Lake Champlain, along Vermont's western border. Its name comes from the fact that the markings on its *carapace*, or upper shell, resemble a system of waterways laid out on a chart. The eggs of this aquatic species hatch in late August and

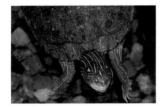

Northern map turtle.

Snakes: Live Young or Eggs?

Viviparous (give birth to live young)	Oviparous (lay eggs)
Northern watersnake	Eastern hog-nosed snake
DeKay's brownsnake	Ring-necked snake
Red-bellied snake	Eastern wormsnake
Common gartersnake	North American racer
Eastern ribbonsnake	Smooth greensnake
Copperhead	Eastern ratsnake
Timber rattlesnake	Milksnake

early September, with the young usually emerging at this time (occasionally they overwinter in their nest and appear in the spring). Their primary diet consists of snails, clams, and crayfish. Look for groups of these shy turtles basking in relatively remote areas with aquatic vegetation.

Blanding's Turtle—*Eggs Hatching*
Blanding's turtles are found in eastern New England, including sections of southern Maine, southeastern New Hampshire, and eastern Massachusetts. This mostly aquatic turtle is named after William Blanding, a Philadelphia naturalist, and is considered threatened or endangered over much of its range. It is often referred to as the "semi-box turtle" due to its hinged *plastron*, or lower shell. Unlike the true box turtle, it cannot close its upper and lower shells tightly together.

In the spring Blanding's turtles leave their shallow ponds or wetlands to lay their eggs, often in nearby plowed fields. Their eggs hatch in the fall, emerging either at this time or the following spring.

Eastern Wormsnake—*Eggs Hatching*
The eastern wormsnake is rarely encountered, due to its nocturnal habits and secretive manner. It spends a majority of its time underground as well as under logs, stones, and leaves, and is almost never seen in the open. Named for its resemblance

to an earthworm, the eastern wormsnake is plain brown and measures 7½ to 11 inches in length. It feeds primarily on its namesake, as well as larval insects and slugs. In June or July, eastern wormsnakes lay two to six eggs under leaf litter and other vegetation. The eggs hatch in August or September.

Timber Rattlesnake—*Giving Birth*

The timber rattlesnake, one of two poisonous snakes in New England (the other being the copperhead), can be found in every state but Rhode Island and Maine, but only in small numbers in a very few, localized spots. It is the only species of rattlesnake in New England, and although it used to be quite common, its numbers are far fewer today than in the past, due to extirpation. In late August and September female timber rattlesnakes return to their hibernation den and give birth to 5 to 17 live young. They enter hibernation soon afterward. At this time they often congregate with other timber rattlesnakes—as well as copperheads and other snakes—in rocky ledge dens. More often than not the rocks where the dens are located have a southern exposure, where the snakes bask prior to and immediately after going into and coming out of hibernation.

Timber rattlesnakes in their den.

BIRDS

■ Shorebirds Migrating in August

Semipalmated plover
Greater yellowlegs
Lesser yellowlegs
Solitary sandpiper
Upland sandpiper
Ruddy turnstone
Semipalmated sandpiper
Least sandpiper
White-rumped sandpiper
Pectoral sandpiper
Short-billed dowitcher
Wilson's phalarope
Red-necked phalarope
Red phalarope

Upland sandpiper.

■ Major Shorebird Migration Staging Areas (support 20,000 birds or more)

Ripley Neck (near Harrington, Maine)
Parker River National Wildlife Refuge
   (Newburyport, Massachusetts)
Monomoy National Wildlife Refuge
   (Chatham, Massachusetts)

Cedar Waxwing—*Nesting*

The name "waxwing" comes from the waxy red appendages found on the tips of the secondary wing feathers (those behind the leading, or primary, wing feathers) of these birds. The exact function of these red tips is not known. Cedar waxwings are one of the latest nesters in New England—they take advantage of the ripening fruits in August by nesting and

Cedar waxwing.

raising their young now. Occasionally the fruit cedar waxwings ingest is fermented, in which case they can actually become intoxicated, and even die.

While the tip of the waxwing's tail is usually bright yellow, occasionally in New England it is orange. This coloration is the result of a red pigment picked up from the berries of an introduced species of honeysuckle. If a waxwing eats the berries while it is growing a tail feather, the tip of the feather will be orange.

A male American goldfinch feeds a fledgling.

American Goldfinch—
Nesting and
Rearing Young

The American goldfinch is another one of the later nesting birds in New England. It usually does not start nesting until late June or early July (the peak is during the second half of July), when most other songbirds are finished breeding. The late timing may be related to the availability of suitable nesting materials (often the down of thistle or other composite plant material) and seeds for feeding their young. After young American goldfinches fledge, they remain dependent upon their parents for food for two or three weeks.

Great Blue Heron—
Fledging and Wandering

If you happen to be anywhere near a great blue heron nest during late July or early August and there are still young in the nest, you will hear a loud ruckus whenever a parent returns with food. By late August most

Great blue heron.

SHOREBIRD MIGRATION

Fall migration begins in July and August for many shorebirds, including plovers, killdeer, yellowlegs, and certain species of sandpipers, dowitchers, and phalaropes.

Lesser yellowlegs.

Many shorebirds travel thousands of miles in their biannual migrations at speeds of approximately 30 to 50 miles per hour.

Shorebird migration extends over a long period of time. Research shows that failed breeders depart a week or more before successful breeders, adult females up to a week before adult males, and adult males a week or more before juveniles. Most shorebird migration takes place at night and at altitudes of up to 20,000 feet or more, so it is not common to observe them while they are flying. You will have more luck finding them at food-rich spots—referred to as "staging areas"—along their migratory route, where they rest and refuel (see p. 198).

young great blue herons have fledged or will soon do so, but unlike most birds, great blue heron fledglings return to their nest to be fed for approximately three weeks, and there is still much vying for the food brought to them—as their guttural cries attest. Both adults and young wander beyond their breeding grounds well into the fall, with those in northern New England eventually migrating to coastal areas off Massachusetts, Connecticut, and Rhode Island.

Great blue heron tracks.

A common loon chick losing its down.

Common Loon—*Chicks Losing Down*

By August most of the common loon chick's brown down has been pushed out by new feathers growing in, giving the young molting bird a very unusual look. By the end of the month the chick has a sleek new coat of brown feathers and is referred to as a juvenile bird.

Eastern Towhee—*Feeding and Calling*

Eastern towhees are more often heard than seen, for they spend most of their time on or near the ground in densely shrubby areas where they search for insects by scratching the ground with both feet simultaneously. This large member of the sparrow family is probably best known for its call, which is the source of its name. (Many people feel that this song resembles "drink–your–t-e-e-e-e-e-e-e-a" as much or more than "towhee.")

Eastern towhee.

Northern Flicker—*Feeding and Calling*

The northern flicker is a medium-sized, ant-eating woodpecker. Its name is derived from its "wik-wik-wik" call. The northern flicker has two color forms, which used to be considered different species: In eastern North America, the shafts of the flicker's feathers are yellow (formerly known as the yellow-shafted flicker) and in the western part of its range, they are red (formerly called the red-shafted flicker). They have now been combined into one species. This bird is most often seen on the ground. It is capable of climbing and drilling into trees, but its preference is for ground-dwelling ants, which it spears with its barbed tongue. The flicker is one of the few North American woodpeckers that is strongly migratory in parts of its range. Most of those found in northern New England migrate south for the winter, whereas others can be found in southern New England year-round.

Northern flicker.

Green Heron—*Hunting*

The green heron is a small, stocky heron found in wetland thickets throughout New England. It is a very patient hunter, standing motionless for long periods of time, both in the water and on nearby perches, waiting for unsuspecting fish to swim by. The green heron's hunting techniques include the use of tools—a trait very few birds possess. It commonly drops bait, in the form of feathers, insects, earthworms, twigs, or bread crust, onto the surface of the water and grabs the fish it attracts.

Green heron.

INSECT-EATING BIRDS

Insects are a bountiful source of protein for birds in the summer. Once a butterfly or large moth is caught in its beak, a bird often "flicks" the insect to remove the wings before consuming the body. In addition to being a challenge to swallow, insect wings are not particularly nutritious.

Cecropia moth wings leftover from a bird's insect meal.

MAMMALS

Brown Rat and Black Rat—*Breeding*

The brown rat, formerly known as the Norway rat, and the black rat were introduced to the United States around the time of colonization, and they have become well established throughout the country. In New England they are primarily found near humans and along rivers. Unlike the brown rat, which inhabits all of New England, the black rat is found only in southern parts of the region. These two species are very similar in looks; however, it is possible to tell them apart by the relative size of the tail, for the black rat's tail is longer than the length of its head plus its body.

Because of their enormous consumption of grain, as well as their ability to transmit diseases as deadly as the bubonic plague, rats are not high on most humans' list of favorite mammals. Their abundance is not necessarily obvious, for rats are largely nocturnal and not encountered all that often. Although rats are hunted by hawks, owls, and weasels, they are so prolific that their population remains strong. In fact, they are known to breed throughout the year. Rats seldom overpopulate, though, for when their numbers start increasing they give birth to fewer young. And, if the competition for food becomes strong enough, they will attack and even kill each other.

One of many impressive things about rats is their appetite. They will eat a third of their weight in 24 hours and are not at all choosy about what they ingest—soap, meat, eggs, grains, aquatic plants... they are true omnivores.

House Mouse—*Breeding*

The house mouse was introduced to the United States—along with rats—when Europeans first arrived in the New World. It is often mistaken for a deermouse, but an easy way to tell the difference is that house mice are grayish brown all over, whereas our native deermice are dark on top and light on the bottom, with a fairly distinct line of demarcation.

These small rodents breed from early spring until late fall. Houses, barns, and city dwellings are likely spots to find them. House mice can sense salts, sugars, and other chemicals at low concentrations, which is why their droppings are often found in kitchen cupboards. Due to their nocturnal habits, house mice are rarely seen, but those with sensitive noses can recognize the distinctive and rather unpleasant odor indicative of a small rodent resident, and occasionally they are heard singing a surprisingly melodious, canary-like song.

Coyote—*Howling*

It starts with high-pitched yips that develop into chattering howls said to resemble maniacal laughter by some. You are more likely to hear coyotes howling in

Coyote howling.

late August or September than any other time of year, due to the fact that families haven't dispersed yet, and the young are very excitable. It is now that they are also most likely to yip and howl in response to high-pitched human sounds. Group choruses are thought to have more than a single function: One is to call the pack—the family group—back together again after a period of individual hunting; a second is to advertise their presence to other packs and warn against trespassing across territorial boundaries.

American Black Bear—*Sign (Scat)*

American black bears are too slow and large to consume enough meat to gain the weight they need to hibernate (generally speaking, only a small portion of a black bear's diet is animal matter, and most of that is carrion)—thus they rely on sugars and carbohydrates in fruits and mast crops to add bulk. Their late summer and fall diet consists of a variety of nuts, including acorns, beechnuts, and hickory nuts. Fruits such as apples, raspberries, blackberries, blueberries, wild grapes, and chokecherries are also eaten in great quantities. During years when their usual "crops" are scarce, black bears are famous for raiding bird feeders in order to consume sunflower seeds. Fish and Wildlife Departments recommend not filling birdfeeders until late November, when most black bears have retired for the winter.

A close look at a black bear's scat reveals exactly what it has been dining on—it varies throughout the spring, summer, and fall, depending on what's ripe at the time.

Bear scat exposes a bear's diet, which changes with the season. From top left: 1) hair (likely from carrion), 2) apples, 3) sunflower seeds, 4) chokecherries, 5) black raspberries, and 6) wild grapes.

American Mink—*Sign (Scat)*

This wetland member of the weasel family feeds heavily on fish, frogs, and crayfish during the summer months. Close inspection of its scat often reveals the pink exoskeleton and body parts of consumed crayfish. The overall appearance of mink scat is usually twisted, folded, and tapered on both ends.

Mink scat often contains crayfish shells.

It is fairly unusual to come across a mink latrine, where scat is deposited on a regular basis, as they are usually quite well hidden. They tend to be near the mink's den site, and occasionally near a muskrat scat depository, as mink sometimes prey on muskrats.

◼ Dietary Division of Mammals

Herbivores (plant eaters)	Carnivores (meat eaters)	Omnivores (plant and meat eaters)	Insectivores (insect eaters—a type of carnivore)
Rabbits and hares	Bobcat	Raccoon	Moles
White-tailed deer	Coyote	American black bear	Shrews
American beaver	Fisher	Virginia opossum	Bats
North American porcupine	North American river otter	Red and gray fox	
Woodchuck	Ermine	Striped skunk	

An American beaver consuming an aspen leaf.

INSECTS & ARACHNIDS

Organ Pipe Mud Dauber Wasp—*Laying Eggs*

Mud daubers belong to a large family of solitary hunting wasps, many of which prey on spiders. Most mud daubers specialize in a single type of prey, and many build highly characteristic nests. Organ pipe mud dauber wasps make tubular nests of mud, carrying individual balls of mud back to the nest, which they often build on the outside of buildings or sheds. Look for nest-guarding males hovering near these tubes. Inside each tube is a series of individual cells, in which the female wasp lays a single egg, and then stuffs it full of spiders it has paralyzed. These spiders provide the wasp larvae with ample food until they chew their way out and

Open cells in a mud dauber's tubular nest, exposing the spiders stored to nourish the wasp larvae (left) and a wasp egg (right).

emerge as adults. There are other species of mud daubers that close the opening of their nest with a moveable stone, and return periodically with fresh caterpillars.

Burying Beetle—*Burying Carcasses, Laying Eggs, and Hatching*

When an organism dies, both beetles and flies are quick to move in and get the decomposition process under way. The most colorful and smelliest beetle you are likely to find crawling on or under a dead body is the burying beetle, a bright-reddish-orange and black insect. Burying beetles and other carrion beetles are called "nature's

An organ pipe mud dauber wasp adding on to its nest.

undertakers," and the name is well deserved. Usually in pairs, burying beetles dig the soil out from under small cadavers, sinking the bodies in the resulting holes where they are quickly covered and sealed into a chamber, well hidden by the beetles from competing flies. With the aid of small red mites that cling to adult burying beetles, any eggs or maggots that were on the carcass before it was buried are killed off. The female burying beetle then lays her own eggs on the body and chews the remains, preparing it for consumption by her young. When the eggs hatch into larvae, they move into a pocket the female makes on the outside of the masticated body, and thus they have an instant meal at their disposal. Few insects receive this much care after they are born.

Burying beetle.

Dogbane Beetle—*Emerging, Feeding, and Mating*
The dogbane beetle is usually found on dogbane and milkweed, for these are its only food sources. Dogbane beetle larvae eat the roots of these two plants and the adult beetles feed on the leaves. Metallic reds, greens, blues, and yellows reflect off the dogbane beetle's outer wings and body parts, giving this insect a jewel-like appearance. The colors actually change as the beetle or the person viewing it changes position. This iridescence is due to both the beetle's body structure as well as the light. The surface of this beetle is made up of stacks of tiny, slanting plates, under which there is pigment. Some light rays reflect

Dogbane beetle.

from the surface of the plates and other light rays reflect from the pigment beneath the plates. At different angles the light reflects at different speeds, which ultimately causes us to see different metallic colors.

Black Swallowtail Butterfly Larva—*Feeding*
Black swallowtail butterflies, one of the largest butterflies in North America, are most abundant around farmlands and along the coast. The stages of their metamorphosis are very distinct. If you grow dill, parsley, parsnips, carrots, or fennel in your vegetable garden, you may be familiar with their tiny yellow eggs or the larvae that hatch out of them.

One distinguishing characteristic of black swallowtail larvae is that the stages,

Black swallowtail larva.

or *instars*, between each shedding of their skin, do not all look alike. The caterpillar that hatches out of the egg is dark brownish-black, has a white band around its middle, and is covered with spikes, resembling a bird dropping (effectively discouraging hungry birds from eating it). It repeatedly outgrows its skin, sheds, and grows a new one, and after three molts it becomes green with black stripes and yellow markings. After its fifth molt the caterpillar pupates inside a green (during the summer) or brown (during the fall) chrysalis, in an attempt to match the color of the surrounding vegetation. The butterfly—depending on when the egg it developed from was laid—emerges in the summer or the following spring.

The black swallowtail caterpillar has an orange "forked gland," called the *osmeterium*, located behind its head. When it is alarmed, its osmeterium sticks up and releases volatile chemicals to repel predators.

AUGUST

Mating insects, from left to right : red milkweed beetles, lady beetles, skippers, and Japanese beetles.

MATING INSECTS

Throughout the summer, but especially late summer, you can find any number of insect species mating, from butterflies to beetles. Some are together only for a few seconds, others for minutes, hours, or even days. Often the male positions himself on top of the female and grasps her with his legs, but others join while facing opposite directions. The eggs that are then laid are frequently so well camouflaged that they remain undetected until they hatch. Some insect eggs overwinter, others hatch and the newly born insects spend the winter in a larval, pupal, or even adult stage.

Ant—"Farming"

Ants and aphids have a very interesting relationship that is easily observed on milkweed plants during late summer. Aphids are tiny insects that often congregate on a plant, pierce its stem, and suck its sugary sap, usually causing reduced plant growth. Often ants are attracted to these clusters of aphids; it turns out that both

Aphids and ants on milkweed.

species of insect benefit from the other's presence. The ants protect the aphids from predators, such as lady beetles, by patrolling the plant; aphids, when stroked by ant antennae, exude droplets of a sweet liquid, or "honeydew," from the tip of their abdomen, which the ants readily consume. This practice of ants herding a mass of aphids is referred to by naturalists as "farming."

Snowy Tree Cricket—*Telling Temperature*

The chirping of snowy tree crickets, a vital part of their courtship, is accomplished by males rubbing their wings together. An entomologist by the name of Amos Dolbear came up with "Dolbear's Law" in 1897, which stated that the snowy tree cricket's call can be used to determine the temperature when it is between 45 and 90°F—just count the number of chirps in 15 seconds and add 40. The warmer the temperature, the more rapid the chirps. (Read more about insect songs on p. 226.)

Once the female snowy tree cricket has selected a singing male, she approaches him and nudges him until he stops singing. He then lifts his wings and presents her with an aphrodisiac glandular secretion. While she is busy eating, he initiates copulation. After mating, the female snowy tree cricket cuts pin-like holes in the thin bark of trees or shrubs, deposits a little excrement as well as an insulating secretion inside the hole, and embeds her banana-shaped eggs in it. They hatch in the spring.

A spined soldier bug preying on a monarch caterpillar.

Spined Soldier Bug—*Feeding*

Spined soldier bugs are a kind of stink bug—bugs that exude a very bad smell. (If you pick one up, you will smell the unpleasant odor.) On the bug's thorax, near its hind legs, is a wick-like surface over which scent glands discharge bad-smelling chemicals. Immature bugs have these glands on their abdomen. Research shows that this smell not only repels would-be predators, but alerts other stink bugs to the presence of these predators. It is not hard to find these shield-shaped insects; they are all over plants and make little attempt to hide due to this effective defense mechanism.

About a third of stink bugs are predators and the remaining two-thirds are plant feeders. The spined soldier bug is predacious, easily identified by its sharp, pointed shoulders. Although some stink bugs are significant pests, the spined soldier bug is beneficial in that it preys mainly on webworms and tent caterpillars, which they spear right through the caterpillars' silken tents. Occasionally other prey, such as monarch caterpillars, are taken.

Carolina Sphinx Moth Larva—*Eating, Pupating, and (Occasionally) Being Parasitized*

If you grow tomatoes (or tobacco) you are probably aware of the larva of the sphinx moth, referred to as a tobacco hornworm. It is green and quite large (up to 4 inches in length) with a pointed, reddish "horn" on its hind end and seven diagonal white stripes on its sides. It feeds voraciously on the leaves of tomato and tobacco plants. It closely resembles its relative, the tomato hornworm, but is easily distinguished from it—the tomato hornworm, also green, has eight "V"- or "L"-shaped white marks on its sides. Both larvae feed on plants in the *Solanaceae* family, including eggplant, potatoes, and peppers (in addition to tomatoes and tobacco) and after pupating 3 to 4 feet underground all winter, emerge as winged adults in the hawk moth family.

Carolina sphinx moth larva, known as the tobacco hornworm.

Specifically, the tobacco hornworm overwinters underground as a shiny, brown pupa with a "handle." This handle is actually the developing *proboscis*, or mouthpart, of the Carolina sphinx moth, which emerges in the spring. If you grow tomatoes, you can often find these pupae buried in the ground beneath where the plants grew in the summer.

Tobacco hornworm pupa.

Both the tobacco and tomato hornworms are parasitized by braconid wasps. The wasp lays its eggs inside the hornworm. After they hatch, just before the caterpillar dies, the wasp larvae emerge and pupate on the outside of the caterpillar. (Timing is everything; if the wasp larvae inside the caterpillar kill their host before they are ready to transform into adults, they are trapped in

A tobacco hornworm covered with braconid wasp pupal cases.

AUGUST

■ **Deciphering Stinging Insects**

Wasp Family (*Vespidae*)

Subfamily	Type of Nest
Hornet and yellowjacket (*Vespinae*)	Enclosed paper nests (hornets in trees; yellowjackets underground)
Paper wasp (*Polistinae*)	Open paper nests suspended by stalk
Potter wasp and mason wasp (*Eumeninae*)	Mud

the host's dead body without any food.) You occasionally see the tobacco hornworm covered with the white pupal cases of wasp larvae, from which adult wasps will emerge.

NORTH AMERICAN MILLIPEDES
Detritus Feeders

You don't see millipedes all that often, for they are usually hidden beneath the decaying leaves on the forest floor, which they are busy consuming. Most species (there are 10,000 worldwide) eat dead plant material by moistening it with secretions and then scraping it into their mouth. Millipedes have two pairs of legs on most body segments and

North American millipede.

move relatively slowly, unlike centipedes, which have one pair of legs on most body segments and move quite quickly. Like spiders, insects, and crustaceans, millipedes are arthropods, a group that comprises 80 percent of all described living species of animals.

PLANTS & FUNGI

Cardinal Flower—
Flowering
There may not be a flower that is redder than the cardinal flower. A member of the Lobelia family, the cardinal flower is pollinated primarily by ruby-throated hummingbirds, which brush their forehead against the tube that projects above the petals as they drink the nectar below. The repro-

The female stage of the cardinal flower.

ductive parts of the flower are located in this tube. The male pollen-bearing stamens emerge from the tube first. As they wither, a Y-shaped female pistil appears. This staggered development of the male and female flower structures is an adaptation called *protandry*, which discourages self-pollination.

Broad-Leaved Helleborine—
Flowering
It's hard to believe, but there is an orchid that grows in New England that is classified as an invasive plant. Broad-leaved helleborine, or epipactis, as it is now referred to, was introduced from Europe and

Broad-leaved helleborine.

AUGUST

can be found growing in a number of habitats, from roadsides to woodlands and meadows. It is so common that it is sometimes called the "weed orchid." Like all orchids, broad-leaved helleborine is dependent on underground fungi for much of its nutrients. Because of this, some species in the genus *Epipactis* have reduced leaves and need little chlorophyll.

Round-Leaved Sundew—*Flowering*

Round-leaved sundew, a carnivorous plant found in bogs and acidic wetlands, is usually closely identi-

Round-leaved sundew flower.

fied with its glistening, glandular hair-covered leaves that capture insects. It is, however, a flowering plant, that bears delicate pink or white flowers in August, when the thinnest of stalks appear all curled up—much like fern fiddleheads (see p. 50). As these flower-bearing stems unfurl, their blossoms open from bottom to top so that the open blossom is always at the top of the curled stem. (Read more about the round-leaved sundew on p. 151)

Painted Trillium—*Fruiting*

Approximately 70 plant families worldwide have species that have ant-dispersed seeds. Trilliums belong to a genus of one of these families. Each seed within the fruit of a trillium has a fatty appendage called an *elaiosome*, which ants consider a choice treat. Ants collect trillium seeds and

Painted trillium fruit.

carry them into their underground tunnels where they eat the elaiosome and discard the remaining part of the seed. Thanks to the ant, the seed is then in a prime germination location. Yellowjackets and white-tailed deer also disperse trillium seeds.

Basswood—*Fruiting*

The fragrant yellow-white flowers of basswood, or American linden, are borne on modified leaves, called *bracts*. At least 66 species of insects are known pollinators, many of which are bees, flies, and moths. Fruits ripen in the late summer and early fall, and are soon dispersed by such mechanisms

Basswood fruit.

as wind, gravity, and animals. Although one would assume the flower bracts, which persist through the fruiting stage, aid in wind dispersal, basswood fruits are rarely carried more than one or two tree-lengths from the parent. In addition to their limited role in seed dispersal, bracts may act as "flags" to attract pollinators (especially nocturnal ones).

Common Blackberry–*Fruiting*

Blackberries.

Common blackberry plants are easily distinguished from their relatives, red and black raspberries, by their ridged (not rounded) stems. They have a perennial rootstock that sends up canes that live for two years, producing leaves the first year and flowers and fruit the second. Ripening blackberries in August are at the very top of most animals' list of favorite summer foods—they are a significant portion of the diet of at least 100 species. Even the dried or drying berries are eaten into the late fall or winter. Consumers

THE AMANITA GENUS

When a mushroom (the fruiting body of a fungus) of the *Amanita* genus first emerges from the ground, it is often enclosed in a capsulated sheath called a *universal veil*. As the mushroom matures and expands, the veil splits, often leaving bits on its cap and a sac-like cup called a *volva* at the base. Most species also have a *partial veil*—a membranous structure that protects the developing gills of the young mushroom. When the mushroom cap expands, the partial veil breaks and is left as a ring (*annulus*) on the stipe.

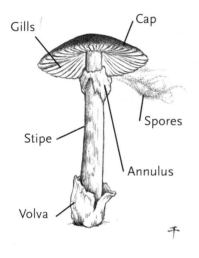

Gills
Cap
Spores
Stipe
Annulus
Volva

Amanita species.

Parts of the Amanita.

include ruffed grouse, ring-necked pheasants, bob-white quail, gray catbirds, cardinals, pine grosbeaks, American robins, brown thrashers, thrushes, eastern towhees, raccoons, chipmunks, squirrels, and black bears. (An examination of the scat of various animals in August confirms the blackberry's popularity.) Its stems are browsed by rabbits, hares, and white-tailed deer in the winter. In addition to being a valuable food source, blackberry bushes are a very effective cover for wildlife, providing an impenetrable thicket for birds and many other prey animals.

Caesar's Mushroom—*Fruiting*

As you might guess from the name, Caesar's mushroom was a favorite of the emperors of the Roman Empire, the Caesars. A member of the *Amanita* genus (see above), many consider it to be the most

Caesar's mushroom—three stages.

beautiful fungus found in New England. Its bright scarlet cap stands out in the dry oak and pine woods where it grows. You can find a single Caesar's mushroom growing by itself, or several in a "fairy ring." The remains of the *universal veil*, within which it was enclosed when it first emerged, can be seen as a sac-like cup, or *volva*, at its base. Books often identify this mushroom as edible, but caution should be taken, as there are many very similar Amanitas that are not.

Eyelash Cup—*Fruiting*
The fungus known as eyelash cup is very brightly colored, and grows in clusters on rotting logs or damp ground. A form of cup fungus, eyelash cup possesses long, stiff, dark, hair-like structures, resembling eyelashes, around its edges. (Read more about fungi on p. 295.)

Eyelash cup.

Velvety Earth Tongue—*Fruiting*
Velvety earth tongue is an easily overlooked fungus, as it is only half an inch or so tall and often mistaken for dead organic matter (it grows on rotting wood or in the soil). The fruiting body looks like a black club with a velvety stalk and a lance-shaped, flattened head.

Velvety earth tongue.

Smooth-stalked helvella.

Smooth-Stalked Helvella—*Fruiting*
The most distinctive characteristic of smooth-stalked helvella is its saddle-shaped cap. Look for this mushroom growing on the ground in both deciduous and coniferous woods.

Wild Cucumber—*Fruiting*
Once you've seen the fruit of wild cucumber, you know how its name was derived. However, its green prickly fruit is not edible. Eventually it matures into a brown pod containing four large seeds. A vine with distinctive star-shaped leaves, wild cucumber can be found growing along stream banks and roadsides.

Wild cucumber fruit—green (unripe) and brown (ripe).

Native Americans used wild cucumber seeds as beads, and pulverized the root for treatments for rheumatism, chills, kidney ailments, and headaches.

FERNS GROWING IN AUGUST

(For illustrations depicting parts of the fern, see p. 212.)

Sensitive fern (grows in moist areas and has a winged *rachis*—main midrib of the fern blade).

Interrupted fern (the fertile frond is interrupted by two to five pairs of fertile *pinnae*—leaflets—in its middle).

Cinnamon fern (small tuft of cinnamon-colored hairs at the base of the pinnae).

Ostrich fern (the shape and form of the sterile fronds resemble feathers).

Christmas fern (individual pinnae resemble tiny Christmas stockings).

Narrow beech fern (the bottom two pinnae angle downward).

Marginal wood fern (clusters of *sporangia*—spore-bearing structures on underside of frond—are on the edge of the pinnae).

Intermediate or evergreen wood fern (*sori*—groups of sporangia—are in middle of pinnae).

Bracken fern (tall, three-parted, triangular fern).

Maidenhair fern (a circular pattern of delicate, finely-divided fronds with a black, wiry stipe and rachis).

AUGUST

PARTS OF THE FERN

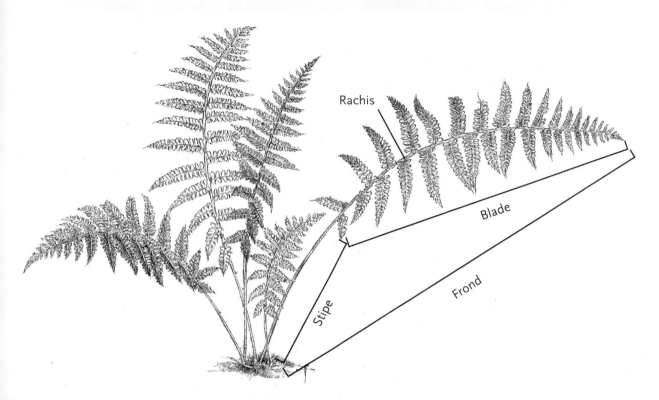

Rachis

Blade

Stipe

Frond

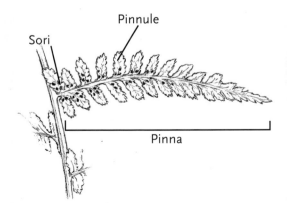

Sori

Pinnule

Pinna

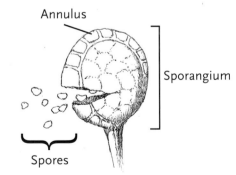

Annulus

Sporangium

Spores

a closer look

The highlight of late summer for many is the sight of **monarch butterflies** in the air (p. 222). The eggs they lay at this time of year hatch into a new generation of monarchs that live six to nine months and migrate to Mexico in the next few weeks. Ears as well as eyes are aware of increased insect activity, as a flurry of late summer courtship **singing** takes place (p. 226). Predators take advantage of the abundance of insects, none more so than spiders that create silk **webs** (p. 228) to trap the insects. **Yellow-bellied sapsuckers** (p. 215) also prey upon the insects that are attracted to the sap-filled holes that they drill. **European honeybees** (p. 219) are busy storing food for the winter, before nectar-bearing flowers disappear. Although many flowering plants are producing fruit in August, it is the peak flowering season for several non-photosynthesizing plants, including **Indian pipe** and **pinesap** (p. 231). Only if you are lucky will you catch a glimpse of one of New England's most beautiful reptiles, the **milksnake**, which tends to stay hidden under cover until the dark of night (see below), or the **star-nosed mole**—also out-of-sight, beneath our feet (p. 218).

Milksnake—*A Secretive Serpent*

There is movement in the grass. You catch a glimpse of a snake—just enough to determine that it has a dark pattern on a lighter background. This distinctive coloration helps narrow down the list of possible species. Which New England snake has brown "saddles" on its gray back? The pattern is similar to the copperhead's, but unless you live in one of the few spots in Massachusetts or Connecticut where copperheads exist, you've most likely had a chance encounter with our native, nonpoisonous milksnake, often referred to locally as a checkered adder. (Juveniles of a few other species—including the eastern ratsnake, North American racer, and northern watersnakes—do superficially resemble the milksnake, but they are also harmless.)

A Milky Myth

Milksnakes have a history, not only of being misidentified, but also of being misunderstood. Because they were (and continue to be) frequently seen in and around cow barns, people reasoned that a fondness for milk was what brought them there. Tales of milksnakes attaching themselves to cow teats and sucking them dry were commonplace, to the point where these snakes were actually named for this misconception. There's no disputing their presence in dairy barns, but milksnakes are anything but the scourge of dairy farmers—just the opposite. It is rodents,

The common but secretive milksnake is harmless to humans. The poisonous copperhead, for which it is often mistaken, is found in localized spots in Massachusetts and Connecticut.

The underside of a milksnake has a checker-board appearance.

attracted by the grain kept in barns, that encourages the milksnake to take up residence.

The Mimic Serpent

While the milksnake physically resembles the copperhead, it imitates the timber rattlesnake behaviorally by coiling up and vibrating its tail, and making a buzzing sound when threatened, or occasionally when trying to attract prey. These similarities with the copperhead and timber rattlesnake are examples of what biologists call *Batesian mimicry*, where a harmless species resembles another species that is armed with spines, stingers, or toxic chemistry. The harmless species is afforded protection from certain predators by its resemblance to the potentially dangerous species. While these forms of mimicry serve the milksnake well as far as most predators are concerned, they often lead to its demise when it is confronted by a fearful human.

Squeeze of Death

Although milksnakes are quite common in the Northeast, it is fairly unusual to see one, for they tend to be quite secretive, hiding under the bark of rotting logs, flat stones, or boards. Snakes, like all reptiles, cannot regulate their body temperature and warm themselves by basking in the sun. Milksnakes, however, tend to obtain their body heat by having contact with the underside of sun-warmed objects, such as stones, logs, and lumber. In addition to not lingering out in the open where we might see them more frequently, milksnakes are not active when we are, for they tend to hunt mainly at night when mice, their favorite prey, are active.

The milksnake feeds primarily on small rodents, birds, and small snakes (including poisonous species, where they both inhabit the same area). Being a constrictor, it kills with a physical squeeze: The snake grasps its prey by the head and rapidly wraps itself around it; each time the prey exhales, the milksnake coils a little tighter. Suffocation is the result, after which the snake swallows its prey whole. Occasionally, if the prey is small enough and doesn't pose a threat to the snake, it is swallowed alive.

Proper Incubation

After emerging from hibernation and mating in late April or May, the female milksnake lays 6 to 18 leathery, oval, white eggs. Once laid, the eggs are left to develop and hatch on their own, so the site in which they are deposited must provide a degree

► A milksnake grows to be roughly 3 feet in length.

► There are two color phases of the eastern milksnake: one has brown "saddles," and one has red.

► Unlike most nonvenomous snakes, which have black tongues, the milksnake's tongue is red. Molecular particles are collected in the air by the snake's tongue and then analyzed in a cavity called *Jacobson's organ* in the roof of the snake's mouth. This alerts the snake to its surroundings, and as to whether it should give chase or slither away.

of heat and protection. In addition, the nesting site must also have enough humidity to prevent the eggs from dehydrating. A decomposing log that sits in warm afternoon sun fulfills all these requirements. Occasionally these nesting sites are communal, with several female milksnakes gathering together to lay their eggs. The young snakes hatch this month or next and are at their most colorful; all 8½ inches are covered with bright rusty red blotches. Within an hour of birth the young snake sheds its skin and adds about three-quarters of an inch to its length.

There is no shortage of small rodents in New England, and it's not just dairy farmers who are plagued by their presence. Wherever there is grain, there are mice. Milksnakes, as well as other species of snakes and predators—such as coyotes, foxes, hawks, and owls—deserve credit for keeping our rodent population under control. Rather than reacting to this harmless snake with fear, we should acknowledge its contribution to the food chain and the balance of nature.

Yellow-Bellied Sapsucker—
Winged Well-Driller

Most woodpeckers make holes in trees, but only the yellow-bellied sapsucker creates horizontal rows of holes, or "wells," on a tree's trunk and limbs. The where and why of this well-drilling is not at all haphazard; sapsuckers have it down to a science. The timing of drilling, as well as the depth of the wells drilled, are coordinated with the nature of the sap.

Seasonal Sap Collecting

The sap in a tree is drawn up from the roots to the leaves through *xylem cells*; the products of photosynthesis travel down from the leaves through *phloem cells*. Both types of cells are located in the *cambium layer*, which lies under the bark of a tree. Within the cambium, the phloem cells lie closer to the outside of the tree and xylem cells closer to the center. In the spring, sapsuckers tap deep into trees to get at the xylem cells. The sap they tap is thin, watery, and fast-flowing. It bubbles out of the wells without further intervention from the sapsucker, which laps up the sap with its fringed tongue, much as a paint brush collects paint when dipped in a can. (Humans, perhaps from observing sapsucker activity, have learned to take advantage of a tree's pattern of sap flow, extracting xylem sap for maple syrup in the spring.)

During the summer, sapsuckers go after the slower moving sap that takes nutrients through phloem cells down to the roots. These wells must be continually maintained in order for the thicker sap to continue to flow. They begin as rectangular lateral slits and—because phloem cells are closer to the surface of the tree—they are not as deep as the xylem holes. They are continuously enlarged while the sapsucker is feeding from them. After three or four days, the sap flow stops and new wells must be drilled, usually just above the previously used row of wells. This pattern continues, often until the group of

AUGUST

Look for yellow-bellied sapsucker holes just beneath the lowest branches of deciduous trees, particularly maples, birches, and apples. It is common for these birds to visit their wells several times a day. Multiple horizontal rows of wells indicate repeated visits from a sapsucker.

cells form a rectangle on the trunk or branch.

Yellow-bellied sapsucker holes have been found in nearly 1,000 species of perennial woody plants, including trees, shrubs, and vines. Sapsuckers have tree preferences, which are most likely related to the varying amounts of sugar in different trees' sap. A sapsucker's species preference changes as the summer progresses. In the spring, red maple is a favorite, as are birches in summer, and red oaks, apples, and maples in the fall.

It has been estimated that sap makes up roughly 20 percent of a sapsucker's diet, though the exact amount is very difficult to determine given that there is no evidence of sap in their droppings. Despite their name, they also consume phloem and cambium tissue, as well as wasps, ants, flies, hornets, butterflies, and other insects vying for access to their sap-filled wells. In addition, when the sap supply dwindles in the fall, sapsuckers eat fruit, including that of black cherry, redcedar, and dogwood trees, as well as Virginia creeper.

Share and Share Alike

Yellow-bellied sapsuckers provide a source of sustenance not only for themselves and a wide range of insects, but for many other animals, as well. The summer phloem sap of deciduous trees can be 20 to 25 percent sugar, making it very attractive to por-

Juvenile yellow-bellied sapsuckers quickly learn that drilled wells provide them with sap, insects, and both phloem and cambium tissue.

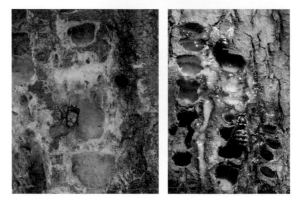

Sapsucker wells attract a variety of insects, including flies and yellowjackets.

cupines, bats, and squirrels, and at least 35 species of birds—including phoebes, warblers, kinglets, nuthatches, and other woodpeckers.

By far the most frequent visitor to sapsucker wells, other than sapsuckers, is the ruby-throated hummingbird. Like the sapsucker, it is in search of sap as well as insects that are attracted to the sap, and has been seen following sapsuckers as they visit their wells. Tree sap is similar to flower nectar in the amount of sugar and nutrients it contains. When hummingbirds first return to New England in early May, flowers are few and far between, so tree sap, available to hummingbirds thanks to yellow-bellied sapsuckers, is a lifesaving substitute. It seems more than coincidental that the spring arrival of ruby-throated hummingbirds and the height of yellow-bellied sapsucker drilling occur at the same time.

Bad for the Tree
Sapsucker wells do allow fungi and bacteria to enter a tree and potentially do some damage. Loggers, particularly, are not great fans of this woodpecker, for their drilling causes distortions in the grain of the wood, lessening the value of the timber. Occasionally, if sapsuckers attack the same area of a tree, large patches of bark may be removed. If this occurs all the way around the trunk, and the tree is girdled, the tree will die above this point. Both limbs and trunks can be affected in this way. Most often, however, damage is minimal.

Because trees tend to heal wounds by growing scar tissue over them, sapsuckers rarely kill trees, although they may weaken them. If you discover a favorite yellow birch or apple tree riddled with fresh holes, you can discourage the sapsuckers by wrapping the tree with burlap or hardware cloth.

If you find that sapsuckers are inhabitants of nearby woods (listen for a "Morse code" of irregular tapping in the spring), keep an eye out for drilling activity. Often trees that are selected by sapsuckers in the spring continue to be visited several times a day throughout the season, and sometimes are used as a food source for several years.

] FAST FACTS [
Yellow-Bellied Sapsucker

▶ Because yellow-bellied sapsuckers are taught to drill wells and drink sap upon fledging, they are only dependent upon their parents for one to two weeks after leaving the nest.

▶ Yellow-bellied sapsuckers maintain their drilled wells daily so as to ensure sap production.

▶ Sometimes prey items, such as ants, are dipped into the sap-filled wells by sapsuckers before they are consumed.

▶ Xylem sap is usually 2 to 3 percent sucrose; phloem sap is usually more than 10 percent sucrose.

▶ Yellow-bellied sapsuckers prefer trees that yield higher sucrose concentrations over trees that have higher sap flow rates.

▶ Yellow-bellied sapsuckers usually choose weakened or wounded trees in which to drill their wells.

▶ Yellow-bellied sapsuckers feed their young a mixture of sap and insects.

▶ Frank Bolles, a naturalist who lived in the late 1800s, raised three young sapsuckers and recorded that each consumed eight teaspoonfuls of diluted syrup every 24 hours.

▶ During migration very little drilling is done by sapsuckers.

▶ Yellow-bellied sapsuckers have been observed acting "drunk" after drinking the sap of mountain ash.

Star-Nosed Mole—*Tentacles that Touch*

A streamlined body; strong, wide front feet; lack of external ears; short appendages; velvety fur that can lie flat in two directions—everything about a mole is built for its subterranean existence. All seven North American species of moles share these characteristics, but there is one—the star-nosed mole—that has an additional, unique adaptive feature, for which it is named.

A Nose with Feeling

Moles possess numerous tactile hairs on their nose, as well as highly sensitive tactile organs called

The star-nosed mole bears many characteristics best suited for its primarily subterranean existence.

Eimer's organs, which are very sensitive to touch. Due to poor eyesight, (not an important sense when one's life is spent mostly in pitch-black tunnels), moles are dependent upon these structures to navigate and locate prey. Whereas most moles have a few thousand Eimer's organs surrounding their nostrils, star-nosed moles have as many as 25,000 to 30,000. In addition, their nose has 22 fleshy, pink rays of varying lengths. All of these rays contain nerves and blood vessels and are very sensitive to touch. They are constantly in motion when the mole is active.

The actions of these rays are quite complex. In general, the more excited the mole, the faster the rays move. The rays can all point forward, or can fan out. Star-nosed moles have been observed moving their head and nose side-to-side, and sweeping their star's rays forward and backward, while they feed in shallow water or soil. The centermost, short

rays repeatedly touch prey before and as it is being eaten. One study suggests that these rays may allow the mole to sense electrical stimuli, such as that given off by earthworms, a favorite food, but this has not been

This species of mole's remarkable nose enables it to thoroughly examine its environment, despite its poor eyesite.

confirmed conclusively. What is known is that while the rays seem to assist in locating prey, they are not used to capture prey, manipulate objects, or position food that is being eaten. In addition to being an aid in securing food, the entire nose, including all of the rays, can be elevated in order to form a "snorkel," which the star-nose mole uses when swimming underwater.

Fine Swimmers

The star-nosed mole is rarely responsible for the tunnels and molehills found in lawns, for the soil there is usually too dry for it. The star-nosed mole is *semiaquatic,* as much at home in the water as it is on land. Thus, it is found in wetter environments than other species. Look for these moles in swamps, wet fields, and other wetlands that could be described as "mucky." The star-nosed mole is a skillful swimmer, using its broad front feet as oars and its tail as a scull. An average dive lasts about nine seconds, but these moles have been known to remain submerged for up to 47 seconds. Star-nosed moles have even been observed swimming under the ice in winter.

Tunnel Specifics

Earthworms are a primary source of food for star-nosed moles, but they also consume a variety of

Star-Nosed Mole

- ▶ It is thought that star-nosed moles are quite social and reside in colonies.

- ▶ Star-nosed moles are functionally blind.

- ▶ The star-nosed mole's long thick tail appears to function as a fat storage reserve for the spring breeding season.

- ▶ Star-nosed moles possess the ability to smell underwater. They do so by exhaling air bubbles onto objects or scent trails, and then inhaling the bubbles to carry scents back through the nose.

- ▶ Star-nosed moles are active year-round, both day and night.

- ▶ Some scientists consider the star-nosed mole the fastest-eating mammal, taking as little as 120 milliseconds to identify and consume individual food items.

- ▶ When a star-nosed mole consumes prey, it clumps its nose tentacles together, so as to facilitate eating.

- ▶ The star-nosed mole propels itself in water, even under ice, by moving its feet and tail in unison.

aquatic prey, including leeches, caddisfly and midge larvae, crustaceans, and even small fish. Much of the food they eat is gathered by rooting in the mud of a stream bottom.

Like other species of moles, star-nosed moles dig two types of tunnels—deep, permanent tunnels and more shallow tunnels. The soil that is removed during the construction of the deeper tunnels appears as small, conical piles of earth, much like those that a crayfish produces (the star-nosed mole's piles lack the obvious opening that the crayfish's has). It is not unusual for the tunnels to lead directly into a stream or pool.

The chances of your coming across a star-nosed mole are not great, for they tend to forage aboveground only at night, but occasionally they emerge during the day. If you should be lucky enough to spot one, watch the constant motion of the ring of rays on its nose. Thanks to these appendages and their sensitivity, star-nosed moles can zero-in on prey quickly and accurately.

European Honeybees—
The Essential Lives of Worker Bees

You are a social being living with 50,000 of your siblings, all but roughly 300 of which are sisters. You work nonstop from the minute you become an adult until the day you die, a span of anywhere from 32 to 140 days, depending on what time of the year you are born. Your life is

In its lifetime a single honeybee collects enough nectar to make about half a teaspoon of honey.

devoted to caring and providing for your family, and in so doing you inadvertently provide an invaluable service to humans. Who are you? A female European honeybee.

Family Dynamics

For those not familiar with this nonnative insect and its social family structure, there are three main categories of honeybees within a hive: queen, male *drones*, and female *workers*. There is one, and only one, queen. She never sees the light of day after she takes her nuptial flight, during which she often mates with several males. She spends the next three to five years laying eggs within the hive (up to 2,000 eggs per day at the peak of her summer laying).

AUGUST

After swallowing nectar, the worker bee carries it back to the hive in her "honey stomach." She then regurgitates it into a wax cell where other workers fan it so it evaporates until it's the consistency of honey.

There are usually about 300 male bees, otherwise known as drones, in a hive. A select few get to mate with the queen, but they perish as a result (their reproductive part is ripped out of their body during mating, killing them). The rest of the drones lead a life of luxury, and are fed and cared for by the third category of bee: the sterile females, or worker bees. The drones' sweet life is short, however, (90 days) and comes to a sudden end in the fall when, in order to make the honey supply last the winter, the workers force them out of the hive. (One wonders if this behavior might also result from the workers tiring of inequity in the division of labor.)

Call Them "Cinderella"

Worker bees come by their name honestly, for they literally do all the work in the hive: repairing and building the wax cells that contain pollen, nectar, eggs, and developing young bees or larvae; feeding the queen and the young larvae; cleaning the hive; keeping the hive around 94˚F (collecting water and fanning their wings to cause cooling evaporation in the summer, and clustering and fanning warmth in the winter); guarding and defending the hive from robber bees interested in stealing honey, as well as other predators; and, finally, collecting the nectar and pollen so crucial to the development of the larvae, as well as the hive's ability to survive the winter.

The Most Important Job of All

Each worker bee performs the same series of jobs in her lifetime in the same sequence, culminating with the most dangerous (to bees) yet most beneficial (to humans) job of all—that of leaving the safety of the hive and collecting nectar and pollen (as well as *propolis*, a wax-like resinous substance found on some tree buds that bees use to seal cracks in their hive). In the process of gathering pollen and drinking nectar to bring back to the hive, workers rub against the *anthers* (male pollen-producing structures) of a flower.

Pollen that has collected on the front legs, head, and body of the worker bee is brushed to the *pollen comb* on the hind legs. There it is combed, pressed, and compacted, and transferred to the outside surface of the hind legs where a concave cavity (the *pollen basket*) is surrounded by a fringe of hairs that holds the pollen in place. Often the color of the pollen can identify the flower from which it came.

Because the pollen of the flowers visited by honeybees is somewhat heavy and sticky (and thus is not able to be dispersed by the wind as is the light, fluffy pollen of many tree and grass flowers), a considerable amount gets stuck on the bee's body. When the bee visits another flower, some of the pollen inevitably falls off, a portion of which often lands on the flower's *stigma* (the top of the *pistil*, or female flower structure) and travels down the pistil to unite with an *ovule*, or egg. This transfer of pollen, called *cross-pollination*, enables plants to produce seeds and fruit. (For an illustration depicting the parts of a flower, see p. 54.)

Once they've learned the structure of a flower, and where the nectaries and pollen-bearing anthers are, honeybees tend to return to the same kind of flower repeatedly, in an effort to save the time and energy needed to learn their way around a new plant. This enhances the chances of cross-fertilization occurring within the same species of plant.

In a single day a honeybee can fly up to 12 miles and pollinate as many as 10,000 flowers. To make a pound of honey (derived from evaporated nectar), bees must visit two million flowers. It should come as no surprise to find that honeybees perform 80 percent of insect pollination. The average hive needs at least 60 pounds of stored honey to sustain it through the winter months.

Humans reap the benefit of the honeybee's diligence in the form of honey, as well as many other products. Fully a third of the food we consume exists because of honeybee pollination. A number of agricultural crops are all but totally dependent on honeybee pollination, including almonds, apples, avocados, blueberries, cranberries, cherries, kiwi fruit, macadamia nuts, asparagus, broccoli, carrots, cauliflower, celery, cucumbers, onions, beans, peas, pumpkins, and squash.

Colony Collapse Disorder

The mysterious disappearance of entire bee colonies has been observed in many countries for several years. Since the last few months of 2006, this phenomenon—called Colony Collapse Disorder (CCD)—has occurred in the United States, as well. For unknown reasons, foraging worker bees never return to the hive, which results in the death of the brood (larvae) and queen. Entomologists

are doing their best to determine whether a virus, fungus, mites, poor bee nutrition, pesticides, or a combination thereof are responsible for the demise of up to 30 to 60 percent of honeybees on the West Coast and up to 70 percent on some parts of the East Coast and in Texas. In a survey taken during the winter of 2009/2010, 28 percent of beekeeping operations nationwide reported losing hives due to CCD; they lost an average of 44 percent of their hives. According to the Agricultural Resource Service, losses of this magnitude are economically unsustainable for commercial beekeeping.

Human research into this disorder is far from altruistic. Honeybees are the most economically valuable pollinators of agricultural crops worldwide. The monetary value of honeybees as commercial pollinators in the United States is estimated at about $15 billion annually (*Congressional Research Service Report for Congress*, March, 2007). About a third of this value is in alfalfa production, primarily alfalfa hay. Nearly 10 percent of the value of honeybee pollination is in apples and almonds. Citrus, cotton, and soybeans each comprise 6 to 7 percent.

Between their production of honey and their pollination prowess, honeybees' contribution to our palate is significant. Thanks to their work ethic and the help of beekeepers, our sweet tooth is satisfied and fruits and vegetables abound. That a small, seemingly insignificant insect has such a large impact on creatures thousands-of-times its size speaks to the interconnectedness of every living thing on this planet. Hopefully, we can repay the favor that honeybees have bestowed upon humans for the past several thousand years by solving the mystery of their recent disappearance and providing a solution—for their sake and our own.

- Honeybees are members of the *Apidae* family along with other bees, wasps, and ants, which all belong to the order *Hymenoptera*.

- There are seven species of recognized honeybees. Our honeybee, *Apis mellifera*, is the most common domesticated species.

- The honeybee is not native to North America; it was brought to the United States by European settlers. (No honeybees are native to North or South America.)

- Native Americans called the honeybee "white man's fly."

- Drones hatch from unfertilized eggs, females (queens and worker bees) hatch from fertilized eggs.

- Honeybee eggs are laid only by the queen. Workers emerge from their cell in 21 days, drones in 24.

- All larvae are fed "royal jelly" (a secretion from the glands of young worker bees) in addition to pollen and honey. A larva chosen to become a queen is fed only royal jelly for the first four days of its life.

- Worker bees of a certain age secrete beeswax from a series of glands on their abdomen.

- Worker bees communicate the location of nectar and pollen sources by doing a dance inside the hive.

- Nectar is 80 percent water; after evaporating in cell hives, it is 16 percent water and referred to as honey.

- Swarms of bees consist of a mated queen and workers seeking to start a new hive, often due to overcrowding of the old hive. Swarming hives tend to be docile.

- Alarmed bees release a pheromone that stimulates an attack response in other bees.

Monarch Magic—*Great-Great Grandchildren in a Single Year*

The monarch butterflies that visit New England fields this month are among the select few monarchs whose life span exceeds six weeks. They are part of this year's only generation of monarchs that can live up to nine months—long enough to migrate to mountainous fir forests in central Mexico, spend the winter, mate, and in March, begin a return flight to the Northeast. Unfortunately, they don't live long enough after mating to reach their destination. Along the way, in northern Mexico or the southern United States, the females lay eggs and both the males and females die. In a little over a month, the second generation of adult butterflies (hatched from these eggs) continue flying toward New England. It is the third and fourth generations that eventually reach their destination and lay their eggs in our fields in July or August. So, the monarch butterflies we see in late August are the great-great grandchildren of the monarchs that left us last fall and overwintered in Mexico.

The fact that an insect weighing half a gram can actually survive a flight of 2,500 miles, to say nothing of finding its way to one of approximately a dozen groves of fir trees in the mountains of central Mexico when it's never been outside New England, stretches the imagination. Equally impressive is the series of transformations a monarch butterfly experiences during its life cycle.

Egg
Female monarch butterflies lay an average of 700 eggs over a two- to five-week period after mating numerous times. Because the hatching monarch larvae's diet is restricted to milkweed plants, this is where the eggs are laid (see p. 190 for more on milkweed). There is a preference for younger, more palatable plants, and it is unusual to find more than one egg on any given plant. Look for a very small,

Monarch metamorphosis (from left to right): egg; larva exiting and eating the egg; larva hanging from leaf in "J" position; the larval skin splits, revealing the green chrysalis; the chrysalis; and the adult monarch butterfly.

oval-shaped, light yellow, and longitudinally-ridged egg—easily mistaken for a small drop of the plant's milky juice—glued to the bottom of a leaf near the top of a young milkweed plant.

Larva

About four days after it is laid the egg hatches and a tiny translucent, black-headed larva (caterpillar) proceeds to eat the egg shell from which it hatched. It then dines on fine hairs on the surface of the milkweed leaf before consuming the leaf itself. As it eats and grows, the caterpillar goes through a series of five stages or *instars*, shedding its skin at the end of each one. Because the length of each instar is known (most are one to three days), and the appearance of the caterpillar is distinctively different in each instar, it is possible to age a monarch caterpillar with some degree of accuracy. Eating only milkweed leaves, the monarch larva ingests toxic chemicals called *cardiac glycosides*, which

■ Length of Monarch Butterfly Stages*

Stage	Length
Egg	4 days
Larva (caterpillar)	9 to 14 days
Pupa (chrysalis)	10 to 14 days
Adult	Summer generations: 2 to 5 weeks; late summer/early fall generation: 6 to 9 months

* Estimates from the Monarch Lab (University of Minnesota), "Monarchs in the Classroom"

protect it both as a larva and an adult butterfly from predators. (After consuming one monarch butterfly, a blue jay threw up nine times in 30 minutes.)

Pupa

By the time the fifth and final shedding of the caterpillar's skin takes place the larva has increased its body mass about 2,000 times since hatching. At this point it usually crawls away from the milkweed plant on which it's been feeding and travels several feet to find a stable, sheltered spot—such as the underside of a branch—to attach itself and hang, head down. As its skin splits, a green, wiggling chrysalis (or pupa) is revealed. Changes that started to occur while it was still a larva continue inside the chrysalis for the next 9 to 15 days.

Adult

Toward the very end of the pupal stage scales that cover the butterfly's wings develop and become pigmented; they are now visible through the chrysalis shell or *cuticle*. Usually within 24 hours of when the wing colors are clearly detectable, the adult monarch emerges (often early in the day). The first indication that *eclosure*, or the escape of the adult butterfly from the chrysalis, is beginning is the splitting of the cuticle. It splits along a line of weakness from air being pumped into the space between the adult and pupal cuticle. Once the cuticle is split, the adult pulls itself out, with the head

appearing first from the bottom of the chrysalis. Its small, crumpled wings slowly emerge, and eventually the swollen abdomen, which has occupied the topmost portion of the chrysalis, drops down below the head. With the help of gravity, the wings unfold while the butterfly hangs from the chrysalis. As the butterfly pumps blood from its body into its wings, the abdomen dramatically decreases in size and the wings increase. Eclosure can take up to 20 minutes, from the initial splitting of the chrysalis cuticle to the expansion of the butterfly's wings. Several hours must pass before the wings are dry enough for flight to be possible.

Determining the gender of a monarch butterfly is fairly simple. Males have a dark spot on a vein on each hind wing, made of specialized scales; females lack these spots. (In some of the monarch's relatives, these scales produce *pheromones*—chemicals used in courtship—but they don't appear to perform this function with monarchs.) Males are also usually brighter orange than females and have thinner black wing veins.

If you peer under the topmost leaves of young milkweed plants in a field that hasn't been mowed since early summer, you may have the good fortune of finding a monarch egg—and thus the opportunity to observe all four stages of its life cycle. Second best is finding a caterpillar and witnessing three of the four stages. Observing monarch metamorphosis is relatively easy, as all that's involved is providing larvae with fresh milkweed leaves to eat; they take care of the rest. However, unless you want your house adorned with little green chrysalises, you might want to keep them in a screened container.

■ **Male vs. Female Monarch Butterflies**

A male (left) and female (right) monarch butterfly.

Male	Female
Black spot on hind wing vein	No black spot on hind wings
Thin wing veins	Thick wing veins
Pair of "claspers" at end of abdomen	No "claspers"

Eclosure—the adult monarch emerges (from left to right): clear chrysalis; the first crack; the butterfly halfway out; the butterfly out with wings folded; wings open but crumpled; wings dry and ready for flight.

▶ Monarch butterflies usually arrive in New England in June or July.

▶ Monarch eggs and larvae have a mortality rate of over 90 percent. Predators, diseases, parasites, bad weather, and pesticides all contribute to this.

▶ The primary source of human-caused mortality for monarchs is habitat loss.

▶ The monarch butterfly is the only butterfly that makes a long (up to 3,000 miles in the fall), two-way migration.

▶ Monarchs migrate at a rate of 40 to 100 miles per day.

▶ Most monarchs east of the Rocky Mountains migrate to the Transvolcanic Mountains of central Mexico to overwinter; those west of the Rockies overwinter in more than 200 sites along the California coast.

▶ Eastern monarch butterflies, which breed over an area of approximately 247 million acres in size, migrate to and spend the winter in an area that is less than 50 acres.

▶ No one knows exactly how monarchs navigate from breeding grounds to wintering grounds and back. It is thought that an internal sun compass, the magnetic field, and topographic cues such as rivers and mountain ranges, contribute to the monarch's navigational ability.

The novelty of metamorphosis may have worn off a bit for some of us, and with it perhaps an appreciation for the miracle that it allows us to witness. If that's the case, introduce a child to the process for the first time. Seeing it through his or her eyes is a guaranteed way to recapture a sense of wonder.

AUGUST

Singing Insects—
Serenading Songsters of the Night

As evening approaches during late August afternoons, the bushes and trees seem to come alive with the songs of various insects. It's almost hard to believe, but many of us live our entire lives bearing witness to this late summer orchestration, but never set eyes on the musicians, much less learn who plays which instrument. In fact, we become so accustomed to this nightly serenade that we almost don't hear it. If late summer nights in New England were suddenly silent, however, we most certainly would take notice.

The Instruments

The chirps and trills that dominate the nights of August and September are made primarily by members of the insect order *Orthoptera*, particularly crickets and grasshoppers. The songs of these insects come not from their mouth, but are instead produced chiefly by what entomologists refer to as *stridulation*—the rubbing of one body part against another. Crickets and long-horned grasshoppers (including katydids), which are responsible for the majority of our night sounds, produce their songs by rubbing a sharp edge (the "scraper") at the base of one front wing along a ridge (the "file") on the underside of the other front wing (much the way we run a finger down a comb). When the song is produced, the front wings are elevated and move back and forth, with the closing stroke of the wings producing the sound.

As with birds (see p. 101), male insects do most of the singing. Although insects may have more than one song, the loudest and most commonly heard serves primarily to attract females. The female is able to hear and recognize the song of her species with the aid of her "ears," which are located on her front legs. She responds to the song by moving toward the male, and mating soon follows.

Katydid.

True or ground cricket.

Species-Specific Songs

Each species tends to live in a particular environment and gives its calls at specific times of the day or night. For instance, some insects sing only at night (katydids), many sing both day and night (most crickets), and a few sing only in the daytime. Again, as with birds, each species of insect has its own distinctive call or song by which it may be identified. Three songs that you might encounter on any given late summer night in the Northeast—and that are fairly easy to distinguish—are those of the rattler round-winged katydid, the ground cricket, and the snowy tree cricket.

It's not too difficult to identify these three common species, as their songs are distinctive. If you've determined that the call you're listening to is pitchless, sounds somewhat mechanical, and is sung in evenly paced intervals, it probably is the long-horned (referring to long antennae) grasshopper we know as the katydid. Even if the common true katydid (possessing a loud rasping "katy-did" call, from which this group of insects derived its name) were to sing in broad daylight (which it rarely does), you would have a hard time finding its green, leaf-like body, so well does it camouflage itself in the grasses where it lives. In several species of katydids, the female actually answers the male with a call of her own.

▩ Insect Song Production Method

Stridulation
(rubbing one body part against another)

Crickets: wing against wing
Katydids: wing against wing
Grasshoppers: wing against wing and wing against hind legs

Muscle Contraction

Cicadas: contract abdominal tymbal muscles, causing tymbal membrane to buckle and "click"

If you find you can hum a matching note to an insect song, chances are it's one of three types of crickets: true crickets, mole crickets, or tree crickets. The most common sound of the night is the steady call of a true cricket, known as a ground cricket. Unlike the katydid, which produces evenly spaced rattles or bursts of song, the ground cricket creates a continuous high-pitched trill, familiar to almost everyone who has spent any time outdoors after dark.

The melodic regularly repeated chirps of the snowy tree cricket are, in contrast, given intermittently. They are quite high in pitch and their evenly spaced timing is a dead giveaway as to their identity. Entomologists say the snowy tree cricket can help tell the temperature (see p. 205 to find out how).

Tuning Your Ear
The songs of other night-singing insects have

(see p. 205 to find out how)

] FAST FACTS [
Insect Songsters

▶ Crickets, katydids, and grasshoppers have oval eardrums, or *tympana*, on their front legs.

▶ Cicadas have exposed ear drums on their abdomen.

▶ Each insect species has its own distinct song, which is recognized by all individuals of the same species.

▶ Insects are cold-blooded; therefore, the pulse rate of their songs varies with the temperature—speeding up as the temperature rises and slowing down as the temperature falls.

▶ After attracting a mate, the male insect stops singing or switches to a special "courtship song."

▶ Singing insects sometimes form choruses and are known to synchronize their songs.

▶ Most insect sounds occur in the upper two octaves of human hearing. As we age we lose our high-frequency sensitivity and therefore lose our ability to hear the highest insect singers.

subtle differences that you can learn, ideally with the help of audio recordings. The book and CD *The Songs of Insects* by Lang Elliott and Will Hershberger (Houghton Mifflin Harcourt, 2007) is an excellent aid to the identification of insect songs. The next evening you are out airing the dog, stop and listen—a symphony awaits you.

▩ Time of Insect Singing

Day and Night	Day	Night
Field crickets	Grasshoppers	Tree crickets
Ground crickets	Cicadas	Most katydids

Spider Webs—*Spin Control*

Every spider is capable of producing silk. Glands inside the abdomen of the spider produce it in the form of a liquid, but once it is exposed to the air, it hardens into silk. Seven different gland types have been identified (although no spider possesses all seven), and each gland produces a different kind of silk, for a special purpose, and is connected to an appendage called a *spinneret*—a flexible spigot-like device located at the end of the spider's abdomen. Most spiders have three pairs of spinnerets.

A barn spider on its web.

Under a hand lens they look like hose nozzles covered with tiny holes, and it's these holes through which silk is spun.

We associate spider silk with the webs they spin, but spiders have many other critical uses for this super-strong material. Every spider continuously spins a "dragline" as it walks along—a double strand of silk that is occasionally glued down. This line allows the spider to find its way back to where it was, and it serves as a means by which the spider can suddenly jump from a high spot to avoid a predator.

Female spiders spin silken egg sacs that protect their enclosed eggs from predators and adverse weather conditions. (See photo on p. 372.) Newly born spiderlings, in order to disperse, often climb to a high spot and spin one or more threads of silk that are then caught by the wind. This act of gently being lifted up and carried away by the breezes is referred to as "ballooning." Silk is also often used when prey is caught, to wrap and im-

Common Spiders in New England

Web-Spinning Spiders

Orb web spiders
Cobweb or tangled web spiders
Sheet web spiders
Funnel web spiders

Hunting Spiders

Crab spiders
Jumping spiders
Wolf spiders
Nursery web spiders

mobilize the insect until the spider's paralyzing venom takes effect.

Non-Web Spiders

Most, but not all, spiders spin webs in which they capture prey. There are some species, however, that don't. They hunt their prey by sitting, waiting, and pouncing, or by actively stalking or even fishing for it.

Web Weavers

However, 85 percent of spiders use silk to spin webbed traps. Often they hide off to the side of the web, clasping a signal thread that enables them to feel the web's vibrations. Accurate analysis of these vibrations is crucial—breezes are ignored, violent shaking is run from, and somewhere in the middle of the two are the beckoning movements of an ensnared insect. When suitable prey is detected, the spider usually rushes out and crushes the insect with its *chelicerae* (jaw-like structures), wraps it in silk, and injects paralytic and digestive juices, which essentially turn the insect's insides into liquid. Spiders cannot eat solid food, having no way of chewing it, and thus must drink their meals.

There are many different web designs, depending on the species of spider that creates them. Sheet webs, funnel webs, cobwebs, and of course, the "wagon wheel" orb web are some of these designs.

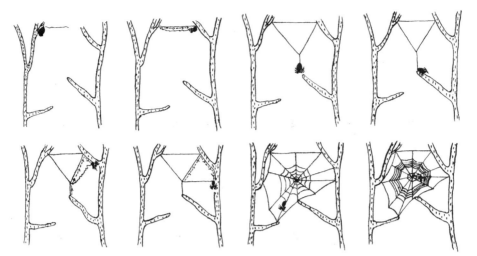

Weaving an orb web, step-by-step (left to right, beginning with the top left).

Orb Web Construction

The weaving of an orb web is very methodical. Although many different species of spiders build orb webs, all orb weavers use basically the same strategy in constructing them. *Amazing Spiders* by Claudia Schnieper (Lerner Publishing Group, 1989) describes the process as follows: The spider starts by making a bridge thread and uses the wind to carry it. With some luck the silk is released from the spider's spinnerets and lands on a suitable adherent surface. The spider strengthens it with a second thread, and the process is repeated until the primary thread is strong enough to support the rest of the web.

Orb web.

The next step is making the first "spokes" of the circular web. The spider crawls across the bridge thread trailing a loose thread behind it, attaches it to the opposite support, then moves to its center and starts a new thread. Dropping down on this thread to yet another support point, the spider pulls the thread tight and attaches it. The web now has a "Y"-shaped frame that can be used in making the other spokes and support lines. The number of radials in a web directly depends on the size of the

spider, plus the size of the web—each one must be close enough to the next for the spider to cross.

Once the spokes are completed, the spider starts at the center and moves outward in a circle, attaching a thread of dry silk (temporary) to the spokes, then spirals back toward the center of the web, eating the temporary thread while laying down a thread of sticky silk that serves as the permanent spiral. The spider carefully attaches the thread to each spoke. It is this sticky, tightly woven spiral that serves as a trap, catching insects that fly into

Sheet web.

Funnel web.

Bowl web.

it. (Spiders have to be careful to only climb on the non-sticky strands of their webs.)

Web Maintenance

Webs allow a spider to catch prey without having to expend energy chasing after it. Thus, it is an efficient method of gathering food. However, constructing the web is energy-demanding due to the large amount of protein required for silk production. In addition, after a time the silk loses its stickiness and becomes inefficient. It is not uncommon for spiders to eat their own web daily, thereby gaining back some of the energy used in spinning silk.

Damage to the web is not unusual, due to the struggles of captured prey. Many orb weavers make new webs every night, often using the old bridge threads, a process which takes approximately an hour. Occasionally spiders repair damage by replacing threads and patching up holes.

If you live near an overgrown field or have an old shed or barn, you may be lucky enough to observe a spider in the process of weaving its web. The sight of the silk emerging and being attached in a very meticulous fashion by the spider's legs to existing threads is one that is not easily forgotten—nor is the speed with which the web materializes. A means of survival for the spider, the silken web is an architectural work of art to those of us unable to duplicate these efforts. Who among us would even try, using just our feet and rear ends?

Parasitic Plants—
Indian Pipe and Pine Sap

Everybody gets by with a little help from their friends—some more than others. The same is true in the plant kingdom.

Ghosts of the Forest Floor

Typically a flowering plant has green leaves that make food through a process called *photosynthesis,* and this food gives the plant the necessary nutrients and energy to produce flowers and seeds. There are, however, some flowering plants that do not make their own food, but instead rely on the energy of other plants in order to produce flowers and fruits (*epiparasites*). These plants lack the chlorophyll necessary, not only for them to be green, but for the process of photosynthesis to take place.

Two such plants are flowering this month, thanks to the food they obtain from nearby green plants. They are almost translucent, and have a ghostly look about them, especially in the dark, shaded woods where they are found. We know them as Indian pipe and pine sap. Indian pipe's resemblance to a clay pipe and pine sap's association with pine trees are reflected in their common names. It's hard to believe, but blueberries and trailing arbutus are some of their closest relatives. Indian pipe is the better known species, as it is more abundant and thus more frequently seen.

Making Up for What They Lack

Like the parasitic brown-headed cowbird—which lays its eggs in another bird's nest, leaving the incubating and raising of its young to another (see p. 123)—Indian pipe and pine sap have evolved ways to avoid some of the basic work of survival. Unlike the cowbird, however, they do not depend directly on their host for sustenance; there is a middleman (or "middle plant") involved. Both plants associate with underground fungi that derive their food from

Because it does not make its own food, Indian pipe has no need for chlorophyll or leaves. It does have a single, five-petaled flower at the end of its stalk that produces both nectar and pollen. When young, it faces downward (left). As soon as it is pollinated, the flower becomes erect and points to the sky (right).

decaying plant material or nearby green plants, and then pass some of this food on.

This is how it works: Indian pipe and pine sap grow on the forest floor. Many of the nearby trees have *mycorrhizal fungi* (fungi in a mutually beneficial relationship with other plants) attached to their roots. The fungi facilitate the decay of organic matter and provide nutrients for the trees' roots to absorb, and the trees help nourish the fungi. Thus, a symbiotic, or mutually beneficial, relationship exists between the fungi and the trees. At the same time, the root systems of Indian pipe and pine sap are coated with the fungi that are attached to the trees. All the nutrition that the flowering plants need is obtained from the trees via the fungi. Whether or not the fungi gain anything from the plants is unknown.

Indian pipe flowers produce both nectar and pollen. Botanists don't know which species of insects pollinate it, but they do know that the position of its terminal waxy flower conveys its pollination status. An unpollinated Indian pipe flower nods downward.

AUGUST

As soon as it is pollinated, the flower becomes erect, eventually forming a dry fruit capsule. As fall approaches the entire plant turns black or dark brown and often persists through the winter.

Look for both Indian pipe and pine sap in shaded woods. They are rarely found in open habitats, as they don't need sunlight for pho-

After producing seeds, Indian pipe turns brownish-black, and its texture goes from fleshy to woody. It often persists through the winter.

tosynthesizing food. As a result, they also have little use for leaves, the plant's food-making structures. (Along their stalks you can see vestiges of leaves in the form of scales.) Indian pipe favors beech woods, although it can be found elsewhere. Pine sap usually grows beneath pines or oak trees. A particularly fruitful time to go "ghost hunting" is after a heavy rain.

] FAST FACTS [
Parasitic Plants

► Non-photosynthetic flowering plants are referred to as *heterotrophic*; they obtain their food from organic material only.

► There are about 3,000 species worldwide of non-photosynthetic flowering plants.

► Many of these plants, including Indian pipe and pine sap, are members of the family *Ericaceae*, which also includes blueberries, cranberries, heath, arbutus, rhododendron, and azaleas.

► Pine saps that bloom in summer tend to be yellow, while those that bloom in fall are reddish.

► Indian pipe can be an indication of rich woods.

► Experiments using radioactive isotopes of carbon and phosphorus injected into trees have shown that the marked carbon and phosphorus are taken up by the Indian pipe, with the help of fungi.

► Some non-photosynthetic flowering plants, like mistletoe and dwarf mistletoe, are directly parasitic on other plants and don't use an intermediary fungus, like Indian pipe and pine sap do.

Pine sap can be white, reddish pink, lavender, or yellow. The flowers at the tip of the stalk are nodding and vase-shaped.

preparation

All our senses can detect a change in the air. There are fewer and fewer hours of daylight, more crickets chirping, fewer birds singing, and berries ripening. Creatures that are tuned in to the seasons to a greater degree than humans are preparing for the months ahead by migrating, laying eggs, breeding, gorging, caching food, and finding shelter.

nature notes

AMPHIBIANS

Northern Two-Lined Salamander—*Breeding*

The mating of northern two-lined salamanders takes place in streams from September through May and is quite involved. The male initially pokes a potential mate with his head, and then encircles her head with his body. Next he scratches her skin with his teeth, an action thought to perhaps create a way for his glandular secretions to enter her bloodstream. Sufficiently aroused, the female places her head at the base of the male's tail and together, entwined, they walk a short distance. The male then releases a packet of sperm, referred to as a *spermatophore*. Internal fertilization takes place after the female picks the spermatophore up into her *cloaca*.

Northern two-lined salamander.

Spring Peeper—*Calling*

Often on warm September days you will hear a lone spring peeper calling, sometimes far from any body of water. This loud, high-pitched call can be heard for up to half a mile. Typically males use their voice to attract females during the spring breeding season, but it is occasionally heard in autumn. These late-in-the-year vocalizations are called the "fall echo." Scientists speculate that peeper calling is spurred by light and temperature, and occur when fall climate conditions are very similar to those in the spring.

Spring peeper.

Northern Dusky Salamander—*Entering Hibernation*

Northern dusky salamanders can be found in woodlands near streams or *seeps* (where water oozes from the ground to form a pool) during the summer months. Their preference is saturated soil, and they usually only stray from streams in wet weather. In September they seek deeper water and hibernate under logs and rocks.

Northern dusky salamander.

REPTILES

Snapping Turtle—*Hatching*
Newly-hatched snapping turtles climb up through several inches of soil, leaving discarded eggshells as evidence of their subterranean summer. A close look reveals the temporary "egg tooth" with which the hatchling breaks out of its shell. Young snapping turtles, like other species of aquatic turtle hatchlings, instinctively find their way to the nearest body of water. Occasionally hatchlings in areas further south overwinter in their nest and emerge in the spring. Although this does occur in New England, it is less likely to happen at higher latitudes. (Read more about snapping turtles on p. 139.)

A snapping turtle or "snapper" hatchling.

Ring-Necked Snake—*Hatching*
Although common throughout New England, with the exception of northern Maine, ring-necked snakes are seldom seen due to their nocturnal habits. Eggs laid in June or July hatch in late August and September, just prior to the start of hibernation. In late September or October ring-necked snakes seek out woodchuck, vole, and chipmunk burrows, as well as foundations of old stone dwellings, and go into hibernation. Winter temperatures in these specially chosen sites range anywhere from 32 to 50°F.

Ring-necked snake.

Copperhead—*Giving Birth*
There are only two poisonous snakes that inhabit parts of New England—the copperhead and the timber rattlesnake. Copperheads occur only in southern New England. Their range reaches as far north as Massachusetts, where they are considered extremely localized and rare; they are also found in Connecticut. Usually in September copperheads give birth to five or six live young. Then in late September or October, most seek dens where they hibernate until April. These sites are often used year after year and are sometimes shared with other snakes.

BIRDS

Common Loon—*Pre-Migratory Rafting*
Prior to migrating in late fall, common loons tend to gather in groups. This behavior is referred to as *rafting* and is thought to enhance their feeding. One theory is that if the loons feed in groups, they do not spend time chasing each other out of their respective feeding territories. By sharing the same feeding area, a group can feed more efficiently. Most of the Northeast's common loon population shifts from freshwater inland breeding locations to coastal marine wintering locations, although some

Common loons rafting.

remain at inland freshwater sites throughout winter. Adults usually migrate before juveniles. Young loons remain on the ponds where they were born, or on adjacent lakes, until late in the fall, just prior to when these bodies of water freeze.

MOLTING

After several months feathers become worn, frayed, and in need of replacement. The process of shedding old feathers and growing new ones is called *molting*. Most birds molt at least once a year, sometimes twice, and three times is not unheard of. During a molt, feathers are dropped in a regular sequence. This can take a few weeks or several months. Not all feathers are shed at once; enough must remain to protect the bird from rain and cold weather. Growing new feathers takes a great deal of energy, and thus rarely occurs during nesting or migration.

A molted feather.

Most birds molt after the breeding season, in late summer or early fall, in order to have their feathers in good condition for migration. For this reason, you will find more feathers on the ground at this time of year than any other.

A molting male eastern bluebird.

Tree Swallow— *Migrating*
Through the month of September, tree swallows can be found by the thousands in bayberry patches along the southern New England coast. Some spots to look for these concentrations include Block Island

Tree swallow.

and Little Compton, Rhode Island, and Cuttyhunk Island, Massachusetts. More than 300,000 tree swallows were seen in the Elizabeth Islands, Massachusetts, on September 26, 1994.

Black-Crowned Night-Heron—*Migrating*
The black-crowned night heron, which breeds on every continent except Australia and Antarctica, is the most widespread heron in the world. It is most active at dusk and at night, when it feeds on a wide variety of food, including crustaceans, earthworms, fish, insects, eggs, birds, lizards, snakes, and rodents. Because of its nocturnal habits, this heron is seen far less often than the more common *diurnal* (active during the day) species of herons. Immature black-crowned night-herons look very different from adults; the young lack the black crown and back of the adult, and instead are brown with streaks.

Black-crowned night-herons breed along the coast of New England, as well as in the Lake Champlain Valley in Vermont. After nesting season, they

SONGBIRD MIGRATION

Migrants account for 75 percent of the more than 650 bird species that nest in North America. In New England, a large number of birds usually migrate the day following the passage of a cold front—the accompanying brisk north winds, dropping temperatures,

A chestnut-sided warbler in fall plumage.

rising barometer, and clearing skies often herald waves of birds passing through on their way south. Shorebirds start migrating in August (see p. 199) and passerines, song, or perching birds begin to migrate in earnest in September. (Most raptors and waterfowl soon follow—see p. 249.) Eastern wood-pewees, eastern kingbirds, most swallow species, veeries, many species of warblers, bobolinks, and Baltimore orioles are among the earliest song birds to head south. Most of these birds winter in South America and need a lot of time to make the long and dangerous journey. (See more on bird migration on p. 285.)

disperse widely and are seen far from their summer breeding grounds. Black-crowned night-herons that breed in Massachusetts and further south have been known to overwinter there.

A juvenile black-crowned night-heron.

However, those whose breeding range is further north usually begin migration in late September or October. Most of these herons follow either coastal or Mississippi River pathways when migrating.

Broad-Winged Hawk—*Migrating*

The passage of a cold front and wind from the north or northwest can trigger mass movements of raptors (birds of

Broad-winged hawk.

prey) in New England, beginning in September. The southward migration of different species of raptors peaks at different times. Most broad-winged hawks migrate during mid-September when thousands of birds may pass overhead on any given day. They are often seen in "kettles"—groups of birds ranging from a couple of individuals to thousands. These birds take advantage of rising thermals of warm air by riding them up and then peeling off in order to glide toward their destination. According to the Cornell Laboratory of Ornithology, information from radio-transmitters placed on four broad-winged hawks revealed that they migrated an average of 4,350 miles to northern South America, and travelled an average of 69 miles each day. Other raptors migrating in September include the osprey, northern harrier, sharp-shinned hawk, Cooper's hawk, red-tailed hawk, American kestrel, and merlin. (Read more about hawk migration on p. 249.)

Blue Jay—*Staying Year-Round*

Blue jay.

Most New England blue jays are year-round residents. Although not a great deal is known about blue jay migration, it is likely that no more than 20 percent of the breeding population migrates. Seeds and fruits from trees and shrubs, particularly acorns, provide enough sustenance for them to survive winters in the Northeast.

■ New England Hawks

Buteos
(broad wings, broad rounded tail; soar in wide circles)

Red-tailed hawk
Red-shouldered hawk
Broad-winged hawk
Rough-legged hawk

Falcons
(long pointed wings, long tapered tail; rowing wing beats)

Peregrine falcon
Merlin
American kestrel

Accipiters
(short wide rounded wings, long tail; "flap-flap-flap-glide" flight)

Goshawk
Cooper's hawk
Sharp-shinned hawk

■ Fall Hawk Watch Sites in the Northeast

Maine
Cadillac Mountain, Acadia National Park, Bar Harbor
Mount Agamenticus, York

Massachusetts
Mount Tom State Reservation, Easthampton
Mount Watatic, Ashburnham
Wachusett Mountain State Park, Princeton

Vermont
Putney Mountain, Putney

New Hampshire
Little Round Top, Bristol
South Pack Monadnock, Miller State Park, Temple

Connecticut
Lighthouse Point Park, New Haven
Quaker Ridge, Greenwich

Rhode Island
Napatree Point, Westerly
Lewis-Dickens Preserve, Block Island

New Jersey
Cape May State Park, Cape May

Pennsylvania
Hawk Mountain Sanctuary, Kempton

Cooper's hawk.

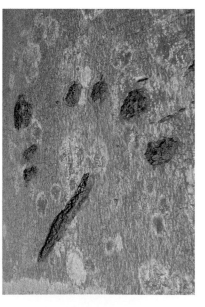

Black bear claw marks on a beech.

MAMMALS

American Black Bear—*Foraging and Making "Bear Nests"*

In addition to feasting on berries in the fall, black bears feed heavily on *mast*, the nuts and seeds of oaks and American beech trees (among others), in order to accumulate a thick layer of fat. (See more about mast on p. 256.) Black bears have been known to increase their weight 100 percent in preparation for winter.

In bear habitat, the smooth bark of American beech trees often clearly shows claw marks made by generations of bears climbing to reach the nuts.

They often remain in the crown of a tree for a period of time, eating every nut or acorn in sight. Because the slender tips of branches cannot support their weight, bears frequently break or chew off these ends. After eating the acorns or beechnuts the bear discards each

Black bear "nest."

branch, sometimes stacking them in a pile (resembling a "nest"), often in an upper crotch of the tree. Occasionally bears have been observed sitting or standing on this pile of branches, but it's not known whether the nest is made for this purpose.

Raccoon—*Sign (Scat)*

Raccoon sign in the form of tracks and scat are evident in New England throughout spring, summer, and fall. Raccoon scat usually has blunt ends,

A raccoon latrine.

a uniform width, and in the summer consists mainly of insect and crustacean parts, fruits, and seeds. Raccoons often establish communal latrines—areas where several raccoons deposit their scat. They are often located at the base of a large conifer tree, near well-travelled paths and denning areas. You should not handle or smell raccoon scat, as it could contain a parasite dangerous to humans.

Striped Skunk—*Sign (Raided Yellowjacket Nest)*

Yellowjackets often construct their tiered paper nests in abandoned rodent burrows. From above, the nest appears to be a simple hole in the ground, frequently hidden within groundcover. But below the surface of the ground the nest houses up to several thousand yellowjackets. Inside each nest cell the queen lays an egg. The hatching yellowjacket larvae are fed by adult female workers before pupating and emerging as adults.

Striped skunk.

Striped skunks (as well as black bears and raccoons) have a taste for yellowjackets and are known to dig into the burrows, and excavate and tear apart the nest as they consume the larvae and adult insects. These raids usually take place in the late summer and early fall.

An excavated underground yellowjacket nest.

American Beaver—*Increasing Activity Level*

Beavers in New England leave unmistakable signs wherever they find a source of food. These can be in the form of well-travelled paths, wood chips, cut trees, and debarked limbs. In the fall you are more likely to notice these signs, as beaver activity ramps up now, due to impending confinement ("life under the ice").

Starting the winter with a good layer of fat, as well as building up a supply of winter food, is of vital importance. The

Beaver-cutting sign—note incisor marks on tree.

SEPT

BAT MIGRATION AND HIBERNATION

Three of New England's nine species of bats are long-distance migrators, traveling to the Gulf or Mexico for the winter. The remaining six species travel less than 300 miles to find a suitable cave or mine (referred to as *hibernacula*), where they remain up to six months or more, surviving solely on stored fat reserves. More often than not these bats mate before entering hibernation. (Ovulation and fertilization occur in the spring as females emerge.)

Come fall, some New England species of bat migrate, but most hibernate.

Some hibernating species are extremely hardy and capable of surviving subfreezing body temperatures. The big brown bat is the only North American species that commonly overwinters in walls or attics as far north as Canada.

All six species of bats that hibernate in New England are found in its largest hibernaculum, the Dorset Bat Cave on Mt. Aeolus in Dorset, Vermont. This cave attracts bats from as far away as Rhode Island and Cape Cod, Massachusetts. Over 20,000 bats hibernate in its inner recesses where the temperature remains around 43°F. Most bats hibernate until May, when they emerge and give birth. Because North America's bat population is decreasing, extra care must be taken not to disturb these animals. Of the 45 species of bats found in the continental United States, six are federally-listed as endangered under the Endangered Species Act. (Read more about bats and the problems they are facing on p. 177.)

Beaver in front of its dam.

inner bark of willows, alders, and poplars is particularly appetizing to beavers. Like all rodents, they possess four incisors—two in the front of the upper jaw and two in front of the lower jaw. An adult beaver's incisors are large—roughly a quarter-inch in diameter—and they never stop growing. Debarking is accomplished with these teeth. The beaver usually turns his head sideways when working on a standing tree. Each bite leaves four grooves, one for each incisor, that meet in the middle. The grooves are just deep enough to reach the *cambium* layer of the tree (the green growth just under the bark), which is what the beavers are after. (See more on beavers on p. 321.)

Moose—*Rutting*

By mid-September moose have entered the rutting, or mating, season, which will last for several weeks. This is the time of year when bull moose are seen with regularity, as they are busy charging through the woods and across back roads in search of females.

Early in the breeding season, small groups of bulls have sparring matches to determine social rank, with age to their advantage. Much of this confrontation consists of shoving matches. Later in the season, when two bulls are

Muddy bark on a rubbed tree is a common sign of moose in rut.

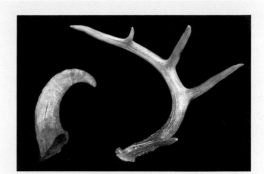

A horn (left) and an antler (right).

vying for the same cow they often have quick, vicious fights, using their antlers as weapons. Eventually one moose acquiesces and departs, leaving the "spoils" to the victor.

This time of year bull moose also paw out depressions, or "wallows," in the ground, in which they urinate and then roll, soaking themselves. Females seek out and roll in these wallows as well. Information about the sexual state of the moose is conveyed through the pheromones in its urine. Moose have been known to rub their head and neck against a tree after rolling in a wallow, leaving telltale sign in the form of muddy bark, which serves as an effective scent post. (Read more about moose on p. 251.)

Common Muskrat—*Building Lodges*

As fall approaches, muskrats begin working on new lodges for the coming winter. Using reeds, cattails, and mud, muskrats form mounds in fairly shallow water that is deep enough to allow an underwater entrance and exit hole. A burrow runs from this hole up to the center of the mound, where a chamber is hollowed out above water level, much like a beaver lodge. Muskrat lodges are usually 2 to 4 feet above the water, depending on the number of muskrats overwintering in them. The number of lodges in an area is a good indication of the density of the muskrat population. (See more on common muskrats on p. 143.)

A common muskrat lodge.

INSECTS & ARACHNIDS

Harvestman—*Mating and Laying Eggs*

A harvestman, or daddy longlegs, is an arachnid, but it is not a spider. Harvestmen have two body parts that are nearly joined, so much so that they appear to be one; spiders have two distinct body parts. Harvestmen have no venom, fangs, or silk glands, all of which spiders possess. Unlike

A harvestman, or daddy longlegs.

spiders, which must drink their meals, harvestmen are capable of eating solid food.

Harvestmen are omnivorous, eating mostly insects, plants, and fungi. Some species are scavengers and feed on dead organisms. Most are nocturnal. If threatened by a predator, some species play dead. They are also capable of detaching their legs, which continue to quiver long after separation, distracting the predator and allowing the harvestman to escape.

This is the time of year that harvestmen mate, lay eggs, and then die.

Monarch Butterfly—*Migrating*

Monarch butterflies that emerge in New England (as well as most of the country east of the Rocky Mountains) in August and September migrate to the Transvolcanic Mountains in central Mexico. This flight is up to 3,000 miles in length, a trip that takes approximately two months. (Monarch butterflies west of the Rocky Mountains migrate to several locations along the California coast.) Monarchs spend the winter clustering on oyamel fir trees in one of about a dozen sites. (Read more about monarch butterflies on pp. 192 and 222.)

INSECT OVERWINTERING STRATEGIES

Insects have evolved different strategies for dealing with New England's cold winters (see examples on p. 277). Some migrate, but most remain here in an inactive state referred to as *diapause*. In this state, their growth, development, and activity are suspended temporarily, and they maintain a metabolic rate that is just high enough to keep them alive. Some insects overwinter as adults or larvae. Some pupate in the ground, in logs, or under bark, and many breed,

A red-legged grasshopper with an abdomen swollen with eggs.

lay eggs, and perish with the arrival of a hard frost.

Common Green Darner—*Migrating*

Darners are a type of large dragonfly that have big eyes that meet in a long seam at the top. The common green darner dragonfly is one of only two darners in the Northeast with an entirely green *thorax*, or middle section of its body, and the only darner that frequently remains joined with

Common green darner.

its mate during the egg laying process. Thousands of common green darners gather in swarms when migrating south in early fall. (Read more about dragonflies on p. 146.)

Fall Webworm—*Making Nests*

The fall webworm is an insect in the same family as the woolly bear (see p. 293). Both are moths known primarily for their larval stages. This time of year, the larval silk webs that encompass the tips of tree branches (the foliage of over 100 species of trees is eaten) are very noticeable. These webs are often mistakenly attributed to eastern tent caterpillars (see p. 48). Although similar in appearance, the nests of the tent caterpillar and the fall webworm

Webworm nest.

can be distinguished from one another quite easily by both where and when they are built. Eastern tent caterpillar nests are built in the forks of branches in the spring; fall webworm nests enclose leaves at the tips of branches during late summer and fall. The difference in where they are placed reflects the different uses of the nests. Tent caterpillars leave their nests to feed on leaves, returning to safety to digest their food, whereas fall webworms build their nests around the leaves they feed on. As their supply of food is consumed, the larvae simply enlarge the nest, extending it down the branch toward the trunk to envelop more leaves.

Aerial Yellowjacket—*Remaining Active*

While many species of yellowjackets build their nest underground in the burrows of animals, there are species that build paper nests aboveground that resemble those of the bald-faced hornet. Unlike hornets, which usually build their nests high up in shrubs and trees, yellowjacket nests are usually just a few inches aboveground, in bushes.

With the queen no longer laying eggs, yellowjacket workers do not need to provide larvae with protein-rich insects, and instead often seek out sugary substances—such as the juice of decaying apples—for themselves. Workers can be found flying in and out of their nests until there are several hard frosts, at which point they die. The queen

YOUNG SPIDERS "BALLOONING"

Baby spiders.

As you read on pp. 228–230, spiders use silk for a variety of purposes, including making egg sacs, capturing prey, extending a safety dragline, and transferring sperm during mating. Recently-hatched spiders (as well as some mites and caterpillars) also use it to disperse from the area they are born. They spin several threads of silk and float away as breezes catch them. This is called "ballooning."

Spider silk can withstand the same amount of stress before breaking as steel but is much less dense, making it about five times as strong as the same weight of steel. A strand of spider silk long enough to circle the earth would weigh less than 16 ounces.

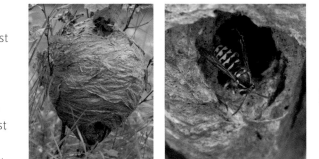

An aerial yellowjacket nest and a yellowjacket worker.

hibernates through the winter in a protected spot, such as a rotting log, and begins laying eggs in the spring.

■ Insects vs. Spiders

Bumblebee.

Insects	Spiders
Three body parts: head, thorax, abdomen	Two body parts: cephalothorax, abdomen
Six legs	Eight legs
Compound eyes	Simple eyes
Antennae	No antennae
Mouthparts: mandibles	Mouthparts: chelicerae (fangs)
Undergo metamorphosis	Do not undergo metamorphosis
Most have wings	No wings

Barn spider.

Black-and-Yellow Argiope—*Catching Prey*

All spiders are capable of spinning silk, but not all spiders use it for spinning webs. Those that do are often categorized by the type of web they spin (orb,

A black-and-yellow argiope wrapping its prey.

funnel, or sheet, for example). A large orb-spinning spider, the black-and-yellow argiope, can often be found in overgrown fields in the fall, where it finds an ample supply of insects to trap in its silken, spiral web. After the web catches an insect, the spider grasps it with its third pair of legs while its fourth pair draws silk from its spinnerets. After the prey is wrapped in silk, the spider bites it, injecting a paralytic venom. After a few more wraps, the spider often snips its catch out of the web and carries it to a more convenient location for future consumption.

Spiders don't get stuck in their own webs partly because of the nature of the different threads used in construction. Spiral threads are sticky; radial threads are dry. Spiders travel on the dry radial threads. In addition, spider legs are coated with an oily substance that makes it hard for the silk to adhere. (Read more about spider webs on p. 228.)

PLANTS & FUNGI

Canada Goldenrod—*Flowering*

In September, 50 different species of goldenrod color New England yellow—more than any other part of the country. A close examination of one of this plant's plumes or "rods" reveals as many as 1,000 tiny, star-like flowers, belonging to the Aster family. Each of these flowers is actually a composite of many *ray* (strap-like) and *disk*

Canada goldenrod.

(tubular) florets, and one plume is said to produce more than 10,000 seeds.

Goldenrod is a favorite host for several gall-making insects (see p. 261), as well as the goldenrod spider, a crab spider capable of changing color in order to camouflage itself among flowers of different colors (see p. 189). A few species of birds consume goldenrod seeds, including swamp sparrows, tree sparrows, and pine siskins.

SEPT

New England Aster—*Flowering*

New England aster.

The New England aster is one of fall's most colorful wildflowers and a vital source of nectar and pollen for many insects late in the season, particularly butterflies, moths, and honeybees. As is typical of the Composite family, what looks like a single flower is actually a cluster of strap-like *ray* flowers, surrounding *disk* or tubular flowers.

Turtlehead—*Flowering*

Turtlehead.

The white and pink-tinged flowers of turtlehead are pollinated primarily by large bees that are strong enough to push between the "lips" of the flower and reach the nectar and pollen within. The derivation of this plant's name becomes even more obvious when you see the movement of its "lips" as a bee moves around inside the flower. The Baltimore checkerspot butterfly frequently lays its eggs on the leaves of turtlehead, providing its larvae with a meal as they emerge.

Beechdrop—*Flowering*

Beechdrops are flowering plants that lack green chlorophyll and consequently are unable to make their own food. They are called *epiparasites*—plants that feed indirectly from the roots of green plants. Epiparasites derive nutrients from fungi below the

A beechdrop plant next to an American beech tree, and an up-close look at the beechdrop flower.

ground, which in turn connect with and derive nourishment from green plants. Beechdrops are often found near (and obtain nutrients indirectly from) American beech trees, as well as oak and chestnut trees. (Read more about epiparasites on p. 231.)

Canada Thistle—*Flowering and Going to Seed*

Canada thistle, a member of the Aster family, is North America's most abundant thistle and the only species that has male and female flowers on separate plants. It begins flowering only when days have reached 15 hours in length. Although

Canada thistle down.

Canada thistle produces quantities of seeds (a single plant produces an average of 1,500), it also reproduces vegetatively, through underground stems. Over 100 creatures feed on Canada thistle. The American goldfinch not only eats the seeds, but uses thistledown as the primary building material for its nest.

SEPT

White (left) and red (right) baneberry fruit.

Bunchberry fruit.

White and Red Baneberry—*Fruiting*

White and red baneberry are members of the Buttercup family and are both found in New England. Their white flowers appear during the months of May and June. White baneberry has oblong flower heads and red has more rounded ones. By this month it is much easier to distinguish between these two species, as they are named for the color of their poisonous fruits—white and red, respectively. Ruffed grouse, American robins, yellow-bellied sapsuckers, white-footed deermice, and red-backed voles are some of the animals known to eat these berries. White baneberry fruits are referred to as "doll's eyes," for the berries have a black spot on one end and bear some resemblance to the ceramic eyes of old-fashioned china dolls.

False Solomon's Seal—*Fruiting*

Unlike Solomon's seal, which bears paired flowers and fruits beneath its leaves, false Solomon's seal's white flowers and red fruits occur in terminal clusters.

False Solomon's seal fruit.

Bunchberry—*Fruiting*

This low-growing member of the Dogwood family produces a milk-white flower very similar to that of flowering dogwood, on a much smaller scale (see photo p. 136). When pollinated (usually by bees and small flies), these flowers produce a vibrant cluster of scarlet fruits in the middle of a whorl of six leaves. Look for bunchberry in coniferous woods, along with partridgeberry, clintonia, and goldthread. Veeries and warbling vireos eat the fruit, as did Native Americans, who used them in puddings, sauces, and tea.

American Beech—*Fruiting*

The American beech tree, along with the sugar maple and yellow birch, form one of the primary

Beechnut.

climax forest types (the succession of one species replacing another ends with these species) in New England.

Mast is a broad term that refers to the various nuts and fruits produced by woody plants. Peak fruiting or mast years can be cyclical in some species, but American beech trees are very sporadic producers, and tend to produce bumper crops some years and then fail almost completely for the next several years. Beechnuts have high protein content (22 percent) and are eaten by

■ Seed Dispersal Agents

Wind	Animal	Mechanical (propulsion)
Common dandelion	Violet	Witch hazel
Common milkweed	Black cherry	Jewelweed
New England aster	Mustard	
Sugar maple	Common burdock	
American basswood	Wild grape	
Trembling aspen	Blackberry	
Virgin's bower	Painted trillium	

Highbush cranberry fruit.

a variety of mammals and birds. Lean fruiting years often result in a decrease in chipmunk and squirrel populations the following spring. (Read more about mast on p. 256.)

Red Oak—*Fruiting*

Red oak is the fastest growing of all oaks and one of the largest and longest lived. In general, oak, hickory, and black walnut trees produce mast fairly regularly, although they can vary year to year with little predictability. Insect species foraging on red oak number over 1,000 and include gypsy moth larvae, many gall-making

Red oak acorns.

insects (see p. 155), and 50 species of leaf miners that chew tunnels between the upper and lower surfaces of oak leaves. Mammals, including white-tailed deer and black bears, as well as many birds—from ruffed grouse and wild turkey to blue jays and common grackles—consume acorns.

American Highbush Cranberry—*Fruiting*

The fruit of American highbush cranberry, while not a preferred fruit, persists through the winter, providing birds such as the ruffed grouse, wild turkey, and cardinal with an emergency food resource.

Virginia Creeper—*Fruiting*

The grape-like clusters of Virginia creeper fruits are important fall and winter food for wildlife, including songbirds such as northern mockingbirds, American robins, eastern bluebirds, and brown thrashers. The leaf of this vine has five leaflets, distinguishing it from the three leaflets of poison ivy. Virginia creeper sends out tendrils,

Virginia creeper fruit.

the tips of which develop adhesive discs when they touch the nearest surface. Five of these tendrils can support a weight of 10 pounds.

Gray birch fleur-de-lis fruit.

Gray Birch—*Fruiting*

Gray birch's seeds hang from a pendulous structure called a *catkin*. They mature in the fall, and are, like those of every species of birch, distinctively shaped. Look for tiny *fleur-de-lis* on the forest floor beneath or close to gray birches. These seeds are consumed by ruffed grouse, redpolls, pine siskins, black-capped chickadees, fox sparrows, purple finches, and squirrels, among others.

Gray birch can be distinguished from white birch by its tight, non-peeling bark. Other key characteristics include tapered, sharp leaf tips and black triangular bark patches at the base of branches. Typically several trees occur in a cluster.

Virgin's Bower—*Fruiting*

Virgin's bower is a woody vine in the Buttercup family. Often climbing 10 to 20 feet high, it bears four-petaled white flowers in August that eventually form beautiful seed heads in the fall. It is best known for these silky fruits, which can completely cover the bushes that this vine grows on.

Earthstar—*Dispersing Spores*

An earthstar fungus is so named because the outer wall of the spore-bearing body splits open into a star-shape as the fungus matures. Spores are dispersed through a tiny hole on top of the central round structure. (Read more about fungi on p. 295.)

An earthstar. (The points of the "star" are curled underneath the fungus in this photograph.)

Virgin's bower fruit.

a closer look

Moose (p. 251) are very much in evidence this time of year, due to their rutting season, as are **soaring raptors** (see below), as they head south for winter. Instead of leaving New England to escape the cold, many insects, such as the **walking stick** (p. 258), mate, lay eggs that will overwinter, and then die. There are other insects, including the tiny fly that inhabits the **goldenrod ball gall** (p. 261), that spend the winter as larvae, protected by their spherical shelter as well as their production of *glycerol*—an antifreeze-like substance. Some insects, such as the **western conifer seed bug** (p. 260), take advantage of the shelter our human homes offer and overwinter as adults inside them. A good **mast** year (p. 256) leaves many signs that indicate who benefits from the nut explosion. Flowering plants are fruiting, some more dramatically than others. **Bottle gentian's** blue blossoms are a welcome extension of summer (p. 267). **Jewelweed**, with its explosive pods, efficiently disperses its own seeds (p. 264).

Soaring Raptors—*Southward Bound*

The fall migration of raptors is an event much anticipated by birders in the Northeast. Relatively large concentrations of hawks, eagles, harriers, falcons, ospreys, and vultures migrate through New England in September and October every year. A sunny day following the passage of a cold front with winds coming out of the northwest is more than likely to produce waves of migrating raptors. Three of the most abundant species are broad-winged, sharp-shinned, and red-tailed hawks. Broad-winged hawk numbers peak in mid-September, sharp-shinned hawks the latter part of September and first part of October, and red-tailed hawks in mid- to late October.

Groups and Divisions

Migrating birds can be divided into two groups: those that migrate at night and those that migrate during the day. Birds of prey are typically diurnal migrants, which may explain why so many other species of birds migrate at night. Diurnal migrants can be divided into *non-soarers* (species propelled by the flapping of their wings) and *soarers,* many of which are hawks. Many of the migrant soaring hawks are classified as *buteos*—robust-bodied hawks with broad tails and round-ended wings (the broad-winged, red-tailed, red-shouldered, and rough-legged hawks are examples). Although these birds are capable of sustained flight, during long migrations they try to conserve energy and muscle reserve by utilizing two types of rising air currents: *thermal* and *deflective*.

Although there are red-tailed hawks that remain in New England year-round, red-tails will usually outnumber all other migrating raptors during the last three weeks of October. They frequently soar on updrafts along mountain ridges, although occasionally you see them spiraling upward in thermals.

Going Thermal

It is not just coincidence that most soaring migrants are seen passing overhead during the middle of the day, for it is usually late morning by the time "columns" or "bubbles" of rising air warmed by the sun, referred to as "thermals," are created. These thermals are crucial to certain soaring migrants. With outstretched wings hawks effortlessly gain height by circling ever higher within these bubbles of rising air before peeling off and gliding, with little or no wing movement, until they encounter the next thermal. They repeat this process over and over, soaring from one thermal to another as they work their way toward their wintering grounds. It is pri-

marily broad-winged hawks that make extensive use of thermals during migration. Their dependence on them sometimes results in hundreds of circling birds—commonly referred to as a "kettle."

In addition to thermals, on windy days many soaring hawks take advantage of updrafts created by strong horizontal winds striking the side of a mountain and being forced upward. Hawks are propelled along by these updrafts, sometimes reaching speeds of 60 miles per hour as they soar along mountain ridges running north-south. When riding a thermal, a hawk's wings are usually widespread in order to maximize lift, but in an updraft it tucks its wings in somewhat in order to control the lifting power of the air current. This gives the bird a more streamlined appearance.

James Brett, in his book *Feathers in the Wind* (Hawk Mountain Sanctuary Association, 1973), compares hawks riding thermals and updrafts to "a swimmer riding a wave toward shore where the water acts as a buoyant. The birds are riding on the vast sea of air with its varying currents and are buoyed upward by convection and updraft." With the help of these air currents, on an ideal day with plenty of sunshine and winds out of the northwest, ornithologists have found that migrant soarers are able travel 240 miles, flying for six hours at an average speed of 40 miles per hour.

Soaring Views

There are prominent points where birders gather every fall to participate in a "hawk watch," when birds of prey are counted as they soar overhead (see sidebar on p. 238). First-time hawk watchers be warned, however. As Bryan Pfeiffer and Ted Murin warn in their book *Birdwatching in Vermont* (UPNE, 2002), "most migrating hawks are observed only at a considerable distance, at first appearing more like gnats than raptors."

Moose—*Thinking "Big"*

When you think of a moose, think "big." It is the biggest member of the deer family, the biggest antlered animal in the world, the biggest animal in the Northeast, and second in size only to the bison in North America as a whole. Roughly 6 feet tall at the shoulder, a moose dwarfs most other mammals, with a bull moose weighing in at around 1,000 pounds. Historically in the Northeast, moose were found as far south as Pennsylvania. However, the moose population has experienced a bit of a rollercoaster ride in the past 400 years.

Habitat and Moose Population
When European settlers arrived in the Northeast in the 1600s, forested land stretched uninterrupted from the East Coast to the Mississippi River, and moose were plentiful. By the mid-nineteenth century, only 30 percent of that forest remained, due to the growth of an agrarian society that cleared the land for pastures and farming. Hunted and deprived of habitat, many animals, including bears, wolves, and moose, all but disappeared.

Today New England is 80 percent forested—more than at any other time in the past 200 years. As farming decreased, forests reclaimed the land and moose made a comeback. In northern New England, forest cutting practices and a halt to the harvest of moose fostered high reproduction and survival rates. From an estimated 200 animals in 1980, Vermont's moose herd increased approximately twenty-fold over the next 25 years to over 5,000 in 2005. New Hampshire's current population is estimated at 6,000. Maine has gone from an estimated 2,000 moose in the early 1900s to 29,000 moose in 2007. Gradually, as their population has increased, moose have moved southward into their historic range; as of the 1980s they were starting to breed as far south as Massachusetts and were first seen in Connecticut in 2000.

SEPT

If you only get a quick glimpse of a moose, and it's during the winter or early spring when bull moose don't have antlers, there are ways of determining its sex. A bull moose (left) typically has a dark muzzle—the color of his coat—whereas a female's muzzle (right) is lighter in color than the rest of her body. If you only get a view of the hind end, look for a white patch under the tail. If there is one, it's a cow.

Diet

The word "moose" in Algonquin means "eater of twigs" or "one who strips the bark off trees," and this is precisely what moose do. Like other members of the deer family, moose are herbivorous and lack upper incisors at the front of their jaw. They grab their food (leaves, twigs, buds, bark, aquatic vegetation, and other herbaceous plants in the summer; bark, buds, and twigs in the winter) with their lower incisors and the hard pad in the front of their upper jaw, and strip off browse and bark, rather than cutting it neatly as rodents do. Willows, balsam firs, aspens, and birches are favored trees.

Sign

While seeing a moose is still an unusual event in southern New England, you can find moose sign with regularity in northern New England. Being a large animal with a large appetite (consuming roughly 44 pounds of food a day), moose often leave not-so-subtle traces of their presence. They

are creatures of coniferous forests, swamps, and aspen thickets that border lakes and rivers. Although active throughout the day and night, moose often seek vegetation to eat as well as refuge from flies in the shallow water of ponds early and late in the day.

Tracks

When you look at the track of a moose, or any member of the deer family for that matter, the impression you see is made by the ends of their toes, or hooves, which are analogous to our toenails. Two smaller dew claws are found on either side of these toes, higher up on the backside of each leg. In soft mud or snow, they sometimes leave an imprint as well.

The moose's track is very similar to the white-tailed deer's track, heart-shaped with the sharper end of the heart pointing in the direction of travel. However, there are distinct differences, the greatest being size: A moose track is roughly 5 to 7 inches long, compared to the deer's 1½ to 3½-inch track. More subtle are the rounded tips on the hooves of older bull moose, due to age and use. According to Paul Rezendes, noted Massachusetts tracker, it is safe to assume that any track over 4¾ inches wide is a mature bull moose.

Browsing

Sometimes it is very evident that a moose has been browsing on trees and shrubs, as moose often pull branches down in order to reach the foliage and buds, and in so doing break the branch. They also frequently straddle a sapling and feed on it as they walk forward over it. This often results in the sapling's thin trunk being snapped. Another telltale sign is bare branch tips; moose often take a branch and strip leaves from the last foot or so by running it through their mouth. The height of the browsing can be a clue as to whether a white-tailed deer or moose was dining on the branches and buds. Moose often browse up to 7 feet above the ground; white-tailed deer usually feed on woody plants 4 feet or fewer from the ground.

Incisor Scraping

Moose consume large amounts of bark, particularly that of red and striped maple, willow, quaking aspen, balsam fir, and mountain ash. Because they lack upper front incisors, moose must grip the bark with their lower incisors and scrape upward. This leaves grooves in the tree trunk where the bark has been removed. The

The height and width of the incisor grooves left after bark has been scraped from a tree can often tell you whether a moose or white-tailed deer made them. Scars remain years after the bark is eaten.

Moose scat consists of individual pellets slightly larger than a grape. In the winter they contain wood fiber (top). In the spring, due to the herbaceous plants moose consume, the pellets tend to adhere to one another, and they are less fibrous (bottom).

width of the incisor grooves (in white-tailed deer, 1/8 to 3/16 inch; in moose , 3/16 to 3/8 inch) as well as the height of the scraping helps differentiate deer from moose sign (take into account the additional height a snowpack affords in winter).

Scat

Scat is one of the more common signs of wildlife and one of the most informative. Like that of all animals, moose scat reflects the nature of the food that the moose has been eating and digesting. The size and shape of moose scat is altered by the change in diet that moose undergo seasonally. In the summer, due to the high moisture of the largely herbaceous diet of moose, scat is more or less in the form of a "plop" or cow patty 7½ to 11 inches in diameter. In the winter, when their diet is drier and

From left to right: a cow, young bull in velvet, and a bull shedding his velvet in late summer.

more fibrous, moose scat consists of individual pellets, each 1 to 1¾ inches long. In spring and fall the pellets are often soft and clumped together.

Antler Rubs

As mentioned, fall is a particularly productive time for looking for moose sign, as it is their mating season, or "rut." Bull moose carry around antlers that are roughly 5 feet wide and that weigh as much as 40 pounds. Their value as a weapon for fighting other bulls during breeding season apparently justifies the energy expended lugging them.

In the fall, the velvet skin covering that supplies nutrients to the growing antler bone dries up and falls off. At this time moose (and deer) rub their antlers against trees, removing bark while they do so. Biologists used to think that the drying up of the velvet caused an itching sensation that the moose satisfied by rubbing. It is now known that moose (and deer) rub their forehead against trees as much as they rub their antlers, leaving scent on the tree from the glands located there. By rubbing their antlers against the tree, some of the scent from their forehead gets on the antlers and is distributed into the air as the moose travels through the woods. These rubs, therefore, provide not only visual sign to potential mates, but also a scent that conveys vital information, such as the bull's health and dominance status.

Marks left by antlers rubbing against a tree can be confused with incisor scraping. If there is shredded bark at both ends (top and bottom) of the markings, they are the result of antlers being rubbed up and down. Incisor scraping leaves frayed bark only at the top, due to the upward direction of the scraping motion.

Wallows

Toward the end of September or beginning of October, when their mating season is well underway, bull moose scrape out hollow depressions in the ground with their hooves. These *wallows* or *rut pits* are roughly 3 to 6 inches deep, 2 to 4 feet long, and 1 to 3 feet wide. The bull then proceeds to urinate in them. The cow moose is so attracted to these pits that frequently she not only approaches them, but lies down and wallows in them, often repeatedly. Occasionally the male wallows in it as well, after which mating takes place.

Disease

White-tailed deer carry a parasite known as a "brain worm," a nematode that is harmless to them, but potentially lethal to moose. The parasite passes from deer scat to land snails, which moose ingest while feeding on browse. If the snail is contaminated, the moose can contract a neurological disease that causes a lack of coordination, stiffness, circling associated with blindness, paralysis, and eventually death. The greater the number of white-tailed deer (the primary hosts), the greater the likelihood of moose contracting this disease. Continued global warming could result in an increase in these snails, leading to more moose fatalities.

Moose and Man

An herbivore as large as a moose living in close proximity to humans inevitably poses potential problems. Prized possessions such as gardens and hardwood trees are attractive to moose. While there has been heavy over-browsing in northern New England due to the high density of moose, management of the population is bringing numbers down to a sustainable figure. Losing a portion of hardwoods is unavoidable and part of the package if we are to coexist with this animal.

Of more concern is the rising population increasing the risk of running into a moose on the highway, especially in the fall when they roam far and wide in search of mates. Each year approximately 700 moose-car collisions occur on Maine highways, approximately 225 in Vermont, and 250 in New Hampshire. The dark color of the moose's coat blends well with dark pavement, and often their eyes do not reflect off car headlights. Fish and Wildlife Departments urge drivers to slow down this time of year, especially at dusk and at night, when our vision is compromised.

If you are fortunate enough to have the opportunity to observe a moose, it's best to do so with binoculars. Approaching a moose, even an apparently docile individual, is not wise. The moose may well perceive you as a threat, and moose are known to attack without warning, especially cows defending calves.

] FAST FACTS [
Moose

- Young aspen stands and mature stands of balsam fir and white birch are the preferred habitat of moose.
- Moose tend to spend summers near water and winters in mixed conifer-hardwood forests, often at higher elevations.
- Submerged aquatic plants are a source of sodium for moose.
- Moose are partial to spatterdock, eating their *rhizomes*, or underwater stems, petioles, and leaves.
- Moose are *crepuscular*—most active at dawn and dusk.
- Moose are known as "elk" in Europe.
- The bull moose's "bell," or dewlap, which hangs from its throat, is soaked with urine when the moose lies down in its wallow. The moose's scent is then distributed through the air wherever the moose goes.
- Moose antlers are used for thrashing through brush, fighting for mates, and rooting plants from the bottom of ponds.
- Moose are powerful swimmers.
- Bull moose "croak" and "bark" during rut.
- The peak of moose mating season is the last week of September and the first week of October.
- Young moose gain an average of 2.2 pounds per day during their first five months.
- Moose lead a solitary life except during the breeding season.
- The home range of a moose is 1½ to 10½ square miles.

SEPT

"Masticators"—Harvesting Nature's Hard and Soft Crops

Mast refers to the edible fruit of woody plants. There are two categories: hard (acorns, beechnuts, hickory nuts) and soft (berries). Hard mast ripens in September and October, and the ramifications of a bumper acorn crop are enormous. Acorns are considered the most important form of mast in the eastern deciduous forest. Percentages vary from species to species, but all acorns contain large amounts of protein, carbohydrates, and fats, as well as the minerals calcium, phosphorus, and potassium, and the vitamin niacin. These high-powered packages comprise 25 to 50 percent of the fall diet of black bears, white-tailed deer, raccoons, eastern grey squirrels, mice, wild turkeys, wood ducks, and blue jays.

Mast Production Variables
In general, mast production—especially hard mast—is unreliable. It varies greatly from year to year with little predictability. The black oak group (oaks with sharp-pointed leaf lobes), hickories, and black walnut are generally more reliable producers than the white oak group (oaks with rounded leaf lobes) and American beech.

White oak, American beech, and northern red oak are very sporadic producers, tending to produce bumper crops some years and then failing almost completely for the next several. When there is mass mast production, wildlife survival and birth rates reflect it. In order to take a look at some of the animals that rely on and benefit from a good oak mast year, we need to take a close look at the signs they leave behind.

A Visit to the Woods
A recent visit to nearby oak woods was rewarded with the sound of acorns "thudding" on the ground every few seconds. A quick look up into the canopy determined that a flock of blue jays had discovered a productive stand of northern red oaks and was harvesting the acorns fast and furiously. Whether or not they intended to eat them up amongst the branches and accidentally dropped them, or intentionally let them fall to the ground so they could collect them later, is unknown. What was noticeable was the silence with which these normally raucous birds went about harvesting their meal. Blue jays flew every which way and acorns rained down all around, but other than the sound of the acorns hitting the ground and one "chucking" chipmunk, it was perfectly quiet. (Perhaps the blue jays didn't want to tip their competitors off by announcing their presence.)

In addition to the acorns that littered the forest floor, oak branch tips were scattered about the ground. A quick look at the cut end of some of them indicated that a rodent, most likely an eastern gray squirrel, had severed them. Perhaps their fruits were too far out to reach safely and nipping the end of the branch allowed the squirrel to eat and collect the acorns on the ground.

Signs of Gathering
Signs of who takes advantage of this kind of "windfall" can be very obvious, or extremely subtle, depending on the consumer. White-tailed deer leave one of the most easily interpreted signs, in the form of crushed acorns. Deer forsake all other types of food, even apples, to stuff themselves with acorns. Often, when they are eating mouthfuls, they crunch

◼ Mast Producers

Hard Mast
Oaks
Hickories
American beech
Black walnut
Hazel

Soft Mast
Flowering dogwood
Viburnums
Hawthorns
Black cherry
Sumac
Wild grape
Virginia creeper
Greenbriar
Spicebush
Blackgum
Poison ivy
Sassafras

down with their molars and some of the acorns are forced out and fall to the ground. The pieces of acorn that spill out are crushed, and bear indentations from the deer's molars on the outside of the shell. They have a very distinctive "mangled" look.

In addition, deer often scrape and dig through the leafy forest floor to find acorns that have fallen down between the leaves. In doing so they leave patches of earth exposed. Occasionally you even find the imprint of a hoof in the patch of dirt.

The Bird List
Wild turkeys also shuffle up leaves when digging for acorns, but they do not leave crushed nuts scattered nearby, for they swallow acorns whole, and their gizzard grinds them up at a later

Acorns that have been chewed by deer have a very ragged appearance.

time. It's hard to imagine muscles that could make short work of acorns, but believe it or not, it took one turkey a mere four hours to internally pulverize several walnuts.

Other birds that relish acorns include black-capped chickadees, white-breasted nuthatches, and common grackles—10 to 25 percent of a grackle's diet consists of acorns. Inside a grackle's mouth there is a hard ridge that runs the length of the upper mandible. The grackle secures the acorn and then rotates it in its bill, biting down and cutting the shell with each turn. A groove is cut around the middle of the acorn, allowing the grackle to split it in half and eat the exposed meat.

Rodent Connoisseurs
Distinguishing smaller rodents that consume acorns can be tricky. Eastern chipmunks (see p. 288) and eastern gray squirrels tend to peel shells into strips in order to get at the nut inside (particularly the thin-shelled white oak acorn). Gray squirrel peelings are larger than those of red squirrels, and chipmunk peelings are smaller than either squirrel's. The way a chipmunk opens an acorn actually depends to a large extent on the thickness

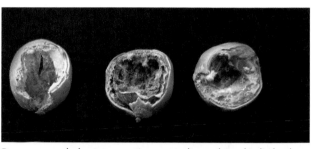
Deep, narrow holes into a nut's meat indicate that a bird's beak has been at work.

of the shell, which varies according to the species of oak it is from. White oak acorns have much thinner shells than red oak, so stripping them is far easier. Chipmunks sometimes chew holes in the side of thick-shelled acorns, such as those of the northern red oak. Both squirrels and chipmunks are known to leave *middens*, or piles of acorn shells, on exposed rocks or logs where they have eaten.

Mice tend to open acorns at the top and continue off to one side, usually only removing as much shell as necessary to get at the meat inside, leaving more than half the acorn intact. A hand lens can help you confirm that a mouse has been at work on an acorn. Tiny white dots usually line the outside edge of the chewed hole—these are where the mouse grasped the shell in its lower incisors while it scraped the meat out with the upper ones. Unlike chipmunks and squirrels, mice usually seek shelter while eating and their acorn

SEPT

] FAST FACTS [
Mast

► Mast was historically a critical source of carbohydrates and fat calories in the Native American diet. The fruits and nuts of at least 30 hard mast tree species were used, the most important being oak, hickory, and chestnut, which dominated much of the eastern forest. The fleshy fruits, or *soft mast*, of over 20 species of trees were also commonly utilized.

► The greater the variety of *soft mast* (fruits) and *hard mast* (nuts) in an area, the greater the diversity of wildlife is likely to be.

► Insects generally damage or destroy more than 50 percent of the hard mast crop; in some years it is 90 percent or more.

► With many species, mast production begins when a tree is between 20 and 40 years of age. Production is greatest at mid-age and size, and tapers off between 100 and 200 years.

► Warm early spring temperatures followed by cooler summer temperatures tend to produce the best mast crops.

remains—quite small—are often found under a rock or log.

A mast year, when many trees are producing heavily, not only affects the primary consumers. Excess food availability and resultant nutrition allows squirrels, chipmunks, and mice to have larger and more frequent broods. This enlarged rodent population, in turn, benefits predators, such as hawks, owls, foxes, and coyotes—and their populations grow accordingly.

Acorns provide wildlife with a valuable food source that can drastically influence populations. They also provide us with the means to identify exactly who inhabits our woods and frequents the oaks within them.

Walking Sticks—*Clever Camouflage*

Have you ever seen a walking stick? If so, count yourself among the lucky few. Even though this insect is common in New England, both its ability to camouflage itself and its nocturnal habits allow it to escape detection.

Hard to Spot
While the world's largest known insect is a species of walking stick that measures over a foot in length, our species is a mere 3 inches. Still, one would think that a 3-inch insect might be easy to spot. However, the full grown adults are rarely seen due to the fact that they inhabit the forest canopy where they dine on the leaves of deciduous trees, such as black cherry, black locust, and oaks.

Although immature walking sticks (*nymphs*) reside in shrubs and low vegetation, we don't often notice them, primarily because of their extraordinary adaptations. A long, thin *thorax*, or middle section, bears three sets of legs set far apart from each other, which create the illusion of several slender sticks. The name of the walking stick order, *Phasmatodea*, is derived from the Greek word *phasma* (meaning apparition or phantom), and refers to the insect's ability to disappear in the foliage. Young nymphs are miniature versions of the adults, but they are light green in color (as opposed to a shade of brown like most adults). In the fall when green leaves have turned color and fallen off the deciduous trees, they turn brown. Some species are capable of changing coloration on a daily basis, appearing light green during the day and turning several shades darker at night.

More than Appearance Alone
Not only does the walking stick look like a twig of its host tree in both color and structure, it acts like one, too, staying motionless for long periods of time, or gently swaying back and forth as it clings to

After mating, walking sticks often stay coupled for a considerable amount of time. This is the male's way of insuring that his own genes are responsible for egg fertilization. Although most adults are brown in color, one of these walking sticks remains a well-camouflaged green.

a branch, as if wafting in the breeze. Even so, there are birds and other predators that are not fooled, and there's enough to the walking stick's skinny body to make a decent meal. So, another ploy walking sticks use is to drop to the ground and extend their legs and antennae together in front of their head so that they resemble a single twig. If all else fails, some species of walking sticks (although no New England species) spray a substance that can cause an intense burning irritation of the eyes and mouths of predators. Should a predator persevere and manage to remove a limb from a young walking stick, all is not lost—nymphs are able to regenerate a leg after several molts of their skin. Because adults are fully grown and no longer shed their skin, they do not possess this ability.

Eggs Falling from the Sky

Most walking sticks reach maturity in August and mate and lay eggs before a hard frost hits. Most females lack wings, unlike the males, and therefore populations tend to be somewhat localized. Some

species of stick insects (there are over 3,000 worldwide) are capable of *parthenogenesis*: When males are not available to fertilize eggs, the females can lay eggs that develop into other females that also lay unfertilized eggs.

Whereas many insects are quite particular about where they lay their eggs, walking sticks are surprisingly casual. Females simply drop them onto the forest floor while feeding and moving about in the treetops. Each female lays up to 150 small (less than 3 millimeters), shiny, brown eggs at a rate of three per day. Individuals in Illinois who witnessed a walking stick population explosion in the late 1800s reported that the sound of their eggs dropping in the forest was like the constant patter of rain (and trees were defoliated twice in one season due to this herbivore's appetite).

Walking stick eggs are just as adapted for survival as the walking stick is at every other stage of its life. Although they would appear to be very vulnerable to predation lying exposed on the forest floor, the eggs are well protected. Each has an extra edible segment attached to it, called the *capitulum*, similar to the *elaiosome* that some plant seeds have, and which ants find delectable (see p. 208). Again, ants haul the eggs to their underground nest, eat the capitulum, and then discard the eggs—leaving them intact and safe underground until they hatch.

Before cold weather sets in, take a walk in the woods and listen for the patter of tiny eggs dropping. You are bound to discover something you might not have seen otherwise—perhaps even a walking stick.

SEPT

Western Conifer Seed Bugs—
Harmless Household Visitors

They appear when you least expect them—lurking behind the curtains on a windowsill or perhaps balancing on the top of a banister. What are these odd-looking brown insects that appear in our home sometime after the weather turns cold in the fall? They are western conifer seed bugs, insects with an outdated common name, for they are no longer restricted to the West. Around 30 years ago they began moving east and didn't stop until they reached the Atlantic Ocean (some have even invaded Europe). Due to their size and habits, western conifer seed bugs are a common winter sight in many New England houses.

In the last 15 years the western conifer seed bug has become a common sight indoors during winter in New England. Listen for a loud, buzzing noise when it is airborne.

Give Me Shelter
The first thing you should know about these bugs is that they do no harm. They simply seek shelter from the winter elements and have discovered that houses are the perfect habitat in which to spend the winter in a semi-dormant condition. During this winter hiatus they do not bite or sting humans, breed, or feed (they live off fat reserves). Unless disturbed by being picked up, they do not smell. (If threatened they do emit a noxious odor for defense purposes.) Come spring they leave to feed, mate, and lay eggs in conifers, and you and your house will be none the worse for wear.

A "True Bug"
All bugs are insects, but not all insects are bugs. The words "insect" and "bug" are often used interchangeably, but entomologically speaking, they are distinct and different terms. "Insect" refers to the class of creatures (*Insecta*) with six jointed legs, three body parts, antennae, (usually) two pairs of wings, and an exoskeleton. Within this class there are different orders, one of which is "true bugs," or *Hemiptera*. The western conifer seed bug is a true bug.

This bug's name derives from the fact that the adult emerges in the spring to feed on the sap of one-year-old cones and flowers from a variety of conifers, including eastern white pine, red pine, Scotch pine, white spruce, and eastern hemlock. During summer months the immature nymphs (hatched from eggs adult females laid on conifer needles in the spring) feed on the seeds of conifers with their piercing-sucking mouthparts (which all true bugs possess). These insects find the seed-containing cones that they feed on by detecting the infrared radiation that the cones emit; this causes the cones to be much warmer than the needles, and they stand out like candles on a Christmas tree.

Western conifer seed bugs belong to the family *Coreidae*, which consists of leaf-footed bugs and squash bugs. They are well suited to their alternative name, "leaf-footed bug," as they possess a specialized, flattened tibia section on their hind legs, which some species display during courtship and others are thought to use for defense purposes. Bugs from this family are numerous in the tropics, where their flattened tibias can reach an enormous size.

- The flight pattern and loud buzz produced by this strong flying bug resemble those of a bumblebee.
- Western conifer seed bug eggs are laid in chains on conifer needles.
- The western conifer seed bug produces a single generation each season.
- Eggs laid on host conifers hatch in 10 days, and young caterpillars feed on the needles and tender tissue of cone scales. Later, nymphs use their piercing-sucking mouthparts to feed on developing seeds.
- The western conifer seed bug does not bite or sting.

Coming Home

In the fall, after cold weather has arrived, the adult bugs stop eating and seek shelter. If a warm house is in the vicinity, it often wins out over loose bark, leaf litter, or the nest of a hawk or rodent. Western conifer seed bugs have been known to congregate in large numbers on the outside walls of houses prior to entering. Pest controllers will tell you the only way to keep them out is to seal off all possible cracks and crevices where they might enter, such as around loose-fitting windows, chimneys, and attic vents. This seems a bit unrealistic, to say the least. Consider their harmlessness and maybe even allow free room (and no board) to these peculiar-looking bugs. Or, you could always help them fulfill one of their other common names, "flick bug," and send them flying out the door.

Goldenrod Ball Gall—*A Study in Plant and Insect Relationships*

Ingenious doesn't begin to describe the nature of the relationship between certain plants and insects. Imagine for a minute that you had the means to create an edible house for yourself that provided you with not only a source of food, but shelter and protection from most of those who would do you harm. Fanciful, you say? Not so. This very situation exists right outside your front door.

Galls

Step into the nearest overgrown field and look for goldenrod stalks that have a spherical swelling midway up their stem. These hard, round "balls," found on at least two goldenrod species, Canada goldenrod and giant goldenrod, are referred to as goldenrod ball galls. They are the year-round and year-long homes of the goldenrod ball gall fly.

A goldenrod ball gall on flowering goldenrod.

Double goldenrod ball galls on goldenrod (the bottom gall precedes the top gall in formation, and is usually larger).

SEPT

A gall is an abnormal growth on a plant that starts forming in reaction to the egg-laying or feeding (scientists aren't sure which, but it's been suggested that perhaps larval saliva mimics plant growth hormones) of the gall-making insect (read more about different kinds of galls on p. 155). Of the 2,000 gall-producing insects in the United States, 1,500 are either wasps or gnats. The Oak, Rose, Composite, and Willow families are hosts for most of these insects. Usually a particular insect forms a distinctly-shaped gall on a single species of plant, although in the case of the goldenrod ball gall, several species of goldenrod serve as hosts. Galls can resemble seeds, cones, flowers, balls, fur, witches' hats, and fingers, among other things. Any part of the plant can form a gall during the growing season, depending on where the gall-making species lays its egg—on the stem, bud, leaf, twig, flower head, fruit, or roots.

Goldenrod ball galls are very evident this time of year.

Goldenrod ball gall fly larva inside a gall.

There are actually three different goldenrod galls that we commonly see: goldenrod ball gall—stem (fly); elliptical goldenrod gall—stem (moth); and goldenrod bunch gall—apical leaf bud (gnat). The goldenrod ball gall and its inhabitant have been so thoroughly investigated, examined, photographed, dissected, frozen, and thawed that the fly's adaptations, predators, and life cycle are well known to the scientific community.

A goldenrod ball gall fly pupa. Note the tunnel excavated during its larval stage when it had chewing mouthparts.

Late Spring
Adult goldenrod ball gall flies emerge from galls in late spring. During the next 14 days, the only two weeks of their life that they spend outside the gall, the male and female do not eat, but mate and the female lays her eggs. Thanks to special chemical sensors on her feet and antennae, the female locates the correct species of goldenrod and deposits one egg in the leaf bud at the tip of the stem just before the goldenrod leaves open.

Summer
Ten days after being laid the egg hatches, and the larva bores into the tissue at the base of the goldenrod bud, and it begins to feed. In response to the larva's chewing or secretions, the stem begins to thicken and grow. Approximately three weeks elapse from egg deposition to the beginning of gall formation. As the gall grows and swells, the larva inside consumes the nutritious interior walls, forming a small cavity in the middle of the sphere. During this time the larva increases greatly in size. The formation of the gall itself takes three to four weeks.

Fall
Triggered by the cooling temperatures of late fall, the larva produces glycerol, a type of antifreeze, which prevents the liquid interior of its cells from freezing. The glycerol also protects the larva's delicate cell membranes from being destroyed by ice crystals.

Winter
The resting larva remains dormant for the duration of the winter, able to withstand New England's freezing temperatures. This state of suspended animation is often referred to as *diapause*.

A downy woodpecker hole in the side of a gall.

Spring
Prior to pupating, the larva (the only stage in which the fly has chewing mouthparts) chews a tunnel to, but not quite through, the gall's outermost layer of tissue and then crawls back into the central cavity of the gall. When warm weather arrives it pupates. Two weeks later the adult emerges, crawls out through the excavated tunnel, and pumps body fluids into a portion of its head, causing it to inflate. The fly uses this "balloon" to burst through the thin layer of outer tissue remaining on the gall and emerges for the first time since it bored its way into the stem a year prior.

Predators
Although most predators are thwarted by the thick, hard walls of the galls, downy woodpeckers and black-capped chickadees manage to penetrate them in order to extract the nutritional larval nugget that lies within. Many researchers have suggested that downy woodpeckers tap on galls to locate the fly's emergence tunnel, in order to reduce the amount of drilling necessary to reach the larva. While the downy woodpecker leaves a tidy little hole as evidence of its predation, the black-capped chickadee, lacking the powerful chisel-like bill of the wood-

] FAST FACTS [
Goldenrod Ball Galls

► Goldenrod is host to more than 50 species of gall-making insects.

► Gall-making insects lay their eggs near the growing points of goldenrod stems. You can tell how tall the goldenrod was when the egg was laid by looking at the height of the gall.

► Goldenrod gall flies do not fly very well, so they do most of their travelling by walking up and down goldenrod stems.

► The adult goldenrod gall fly is tawny in color with speckled wings and is about 5 millimeters long.

► The male goldenrod gall fly attracts the female by dancing or making a special display that consists of flicking his wings.

► The seed production of plants with galls drops up to 40 percent.

pecker, usually makes a larger, messier hole on the side of the gall.

Several species of wasp are known to lay their eggs in the gall chamber or even on the gall larva, with the help of the long ovipositor that extends from the abdomen of the females. Hatching wasp larvae feed on gall fly larvae, as well as the inner gall tissue.

The Good Life?
All in all, the goldenrod ball gall fly has a relatively carefree life. Food is plentiful and close by. Although the shelter that the gall provides does not insulate the larva from freezing temperatures, it does provide some relief from snow, wind, and rain. Lastly, protection from most predators is provided. There are certainly worse fates than living the life of a goldenrod ball gall fly—although two weeks of freedom with nary a meal might not be considered paradise by some.

SEPT

Jewelweed—*Precious Plants*

Jewelweed, also known as spotted touch-me-not, can be found along many wet roadsides in New England.

A second species of jewelweed, yellow in color, is called pale touch-me-not.

Imagine a single plant that could provide all of the following: nonstop entertainment (whether you are two or 102), relief from the itching and spreading of poison ivy, copious amounts of food for hummingbirds, and untold beauty for the eye to behold. Jewelweed, a common plant of New England's shady, wet areas, has all of these attributes and more.

Seed Dispersal

Jewelweed is known by many as touch-me-not. This name, as well as its generic name *Impatiens*, alludes to the manner in which jewelweed's mature pods burst open and scatter tightly coiled seeds several feet away with little more encouragement than a good breeze. Several of this plant's common names can be attributed to this mechanism: Jack-jump-up-and-kiss-me, snapweed, kicking horse, and quick-in-the-hand, are just a few. If you haven't had the fun of witnessing this process, head for the nearest patch of jewelweed and look for the biggest, fattest pod that you can find. Gently place your thumb and forefinger on either side of it, and you will feel the sudden unwinding of its tightly coiled

spring and see the next generation of jewelweed promptly dispersed.

"Jewel" Weed

Jewelweed's magical properties do not end with its explosive pods. If you take a leaf and submerge it underwater, not only will the underside of the leaf have a shimmering silvery sheen, but once removed from the water, the leaf will be absolutely dry. How can this be? Microscopic hairs on the leaf's surface trap a thin layer of air, causing these effects.

Nature's Calamine Lotion

One of the results of our warming climate and increased carbon dioxide is the abundance of poison ivy. Fortunately, relief for this ailment is as close as the nearest jewelweed patch, for the juice of jewelweed has been scientifically proven to reduce the itching of poison ivy. Simply by crushing the

Mature jewelweed pods waiting for a passing breeze to help release their seeds (left). Tension is released as the pods' sections spring open (right).

Although ruby-throated hummingbirds pollinate a majority of jewelweed flowers, small insects, such as flies and bees, also help transport pollen.

succulent plant and spreading the resulting juicy pulp over a poison ivy or poison sumac rash, you can often feel better in seconds. If applied to the skin soon after contact with poison ivy, jewelweed purportedly can neutralize poison ivy's oil and prevent a rash from forming.

Two Types of Flowers

Unlike most wildflowers, jewelweed is an annual and thus its survival as a species is totally dependent on the production of seeds. It compensates for not being able to vegetatively reproduce by having two different types of flowers. One type receives pollen from another jewelweed plant through the process of *cross-pollination*, which joins the genes of two plants in the formation of highly adaptable seeds. The other type of flower, which is relatively small and green in color, is *cleistogamous*—it never opens, is *self-pollinated*, and contains only the parent plant's genes. Both flowers produce viable seeds, but because a seed resulting from cross-pollination is better at adapting to a variety of situations, cross-pollination is encouraged by having

the male structures in the open flowers mature and decline before the female parts mature.

Haven for Hummingbirds

One of the more prominent features of jewelweed is its long "spur." The flower's nectar, which it uses to lure pollinators, is located deep within this spur and is fairly difficult for most insect visitors to reach. Insects that can't reach the nectar by entering the plant from the front have been known to cut holes in the tip of the spur and "steal" nectar without taking away pollen.

Although bumblebees, honeybees, yellowjackets, and hover flies are attracted to jewelweed, its primary pollinator, at least until fall migration, is the ruby-throated hummingbird. Able to reach and drink the nectar, the hummingbird is a frequent visitor.

Food for Wildlife

The seeds of jewelweed are popular with ruffed grouse, white-footed deermice, short-tailed shrews, and immature stink bugs, and the entire plant is consumed by white-tailed deer, snowshoe hares, and—particularly during dry spells—black bears.

Because jewelweed quickly wilts when the temperature drops consistently below 40°F, seize the opportunity and investigate the wetter areas near you this month.

Abnormal plant growths called galls form on jewelweed and house immature gnat larvae (see p. 155). After hatching from an egg inside the jewelweed gall, the gnat larva, *Cecidomyia impatientis*, eventually chews a tunnel and emerges from the gall.

Fine hairs on the underside of the jewelweed leaf collect a film of air, creating a silvery sheen when the leaf is submerged in water.

- ▶ The nectar of the jewelweed flower is about 40 percent sugar.
- ▶ Rub crushed leaves and stems on a mosquito bite for quick relief.
- ▶ Look for holes cut in the back of the flower by insects that aren't able to reach the nectar from the front.
- ▶ The inside of jewelweed seeds is colored turquoise.
- ▶ Colonial Americans used the juice of the jewelweed plant to dye wool yellow.
- ▶ Most jewelweed plants cannot survive temperatures of 40°F or less.
- ▶ Jewelweed is usually found in moist soil near springs, streams, and swamps.

SEPT

Bottle Gentian—
Autumn's Burst of Blue

Nature's last burst of colorful blossoms before flowering plants close down for the winter includes one of its most beautiful flowers—bottle, or closed, gentian. Think of the bluest sky you've ever seen, and apply its hue to a cluster of flowers shaped like Christmas tree bulbs and you have a good image of these blossoms. The petals only open very slightly to allow insects to enter and drink their nectar, thereby pollinating them.

The scarcity of this flower, the time of year it blossoms (August through October), its structure, and the intense blue pigment of its petals combine to make it unique. Up to six or seven flowers cluster at the tip of the plant, with additional flowers in the axils of the lower leaves. Although it can grow to a height of 2 or more feet, the stem of this perennial plant often collapses on the ground, with only the flowering tip stretching up toward the sky.

Peculiar Flower
The most unusual characteristic of bottle gentian, other than the lateness of its blooming, is the closed nature of its petals. One advantage of not opening is that it prevents its nectar from being diluted by the rain. Due to this structure, naturalists wondered for years how the plant could possibly become pollinated. Closed flowers makes entry a major challenge for any small insects searching for nectar or pollen. Most of them don't even attempt to force themselves through the petals. Even large, strong bumblebees, which make up the majority of bottle gentian's pollinators, have a difficult time pushing themselves in.

There can only be one reason why they would exert this kind of effort—what they find once they get in there. This theory has been confirmed by scientists who have determined that bottle gentians are one of the richest of all flowers in nectar

Bottle gentians are unusual because of their closed flower petals, which provide an obstacle for pollinators to overcome.

quantity (up to 45 milliliters) and sweetness (40 percent sugar). As the bees back out of the flower, they comb the pollen that has gathered on their head and abdomen into baskets made of hairs on their hind legs, some of which falls out when the next gentian is visited, potentially pollinating it. Flowers such as bottle gentian and lady's slippers, which present pollinators with significant obstacles to overcome, often have holes in the flower base chewed from the outside by frustrated bees. (Read more about lady's slippers on p. 150.)

Visual Coding
Bottle gentian has a trick up its sleeve to make life

Bumblebees are strong enough to push their way into bottle gentian blossoms in order to reach the sweet nectar inside.

easier and collection quicker for visiting bees. The flowers tips are coded to let bees know which ones have nectar left, and which ones don't. A blossom that hasn't been visited is marked with white at the tip of its petals, which acts as a signal and nectar guide for the bees. Older flowers, from which nectar has been extracted, lack this white marking, and are bluish-purple at their tips. This visual coding saves bumblebees a great deal of time as they fly from flower to flower.

Look for bottle gentian near wetlands. You don't often find it, but when you do, there may be several plants in the area. Bottle gentians, as well as their cousins, fringed gentians, are classified as threatened throughout New England and are legally protected in most places. The loss and shrinkage of wetlands appears to be the primary factor causing this diminishing population.

SEPT

adaptation

The summer has come to an end and hints of the coming winter remind us of changes brewing. For many plants and animals, these changes are life-threatening. They include the disappearance of the food that many relied on over the past six months; the cooling of the air that determines the body temperature of cold-blooded animals; and strong, cold winds that can quickly desiccate plants. This time of year provides many examples of ways in which both plants and animals have adapted to New England's changing seasons.

Here's a sampling of species that are breeding, laying eggs, hatching, flocking, migrating, preparing for winter, molting, entering hibernation, dropping leaves, and dispersing seeds in October.

AMPHIBIANS

Eastern red-backed salamander.

Eastern Red-Backed Salamander—*Breeding*

The eastern red-backed salamander is the most abundant and most widely distributed terrestrial salamander in New England. In the fall, when they breed, females have been observed brooding (caring for) the clutch of eggs they lay under logs or in cavities under rocks.

Spring Salamander—*Breeding, Laying Eggs, and Hatching*

The spring salamander is much more common in most of northern New England than in southern parts, where it's quite rare. It's not seen that often, due to its tendency to hide under stones near clear, cold streams and its nocturnal habits. Spring salamanders breed in the late fall and the eggs that result are attached to the undersides of rocks. After hatching, the young salamanders have been observed lingering in the nest area for several months. These aquatic larvae spend the next four years or so in the water before metamorphosing into terrestrial salamanders. Adult salamanders remain active through the winter.

Spring salamanders.

REPTILES

Wood Turtle—*Hatching*

Wood turtles are known to breed in March, May, and October, with a majority of their eggs hatching during late summer and fall. While some of the hatchlings, particularly in northern New England, may remain in their nest until the following spring, a number of the young turtles make their way up through the soil to the shallows of slow-moving streams and brooks, where wood turtles spend a majority of their time.

Frequently, often in the middle of the day, adult wood turtles wander away from the water, foraging for fruits, berries, mushrooms, snails, slugs, earthworms, and insects. Wood turtles have been observed stamping the ground, first with one front foot and then the other, which causes earthworms to surface. After quickly snatching a worm and eating it, a wood turtle is apt to move a few feet away and repeat the process.

Smooth Greensnake—*Hibernating*
Look for this beautiful, delicate, emerald green, foot-long snake in the fields and meadows of all but northern-most New England. The smooth green-

snake enters hibernation earlier than many species of snakes and has usually already disappeared by this time of year. It is experiencing a population decline in southern New England, which may be partially attributed to diminishing grassland habitat and pesticides.

Smooth greensnake.

BIRDS

Blue jay.

Blue Jay—*Caching Food*
Several species of birds store seeds and nuts in the fall for consumption later in the winter and early spring. Blue jays have been known to collect more than half the acorns produced in an oak stand and bury them up to a mile away. (In contrast, squirrels only carry acorns up to 100 feet from their source.) It is no wonder that oaks have a dispersal rate of 1 to 2 miles per year. It is estimated that one blue jay can bury (individually) as many as 4,500 acorns a year and only retrieves a quarter of them for food. (See more about blue jays harvesting food on p. 256.)

European starlings.

Blackbird—*Flocking*
European starlings, red-winged blackbirds, rusty blackbirds, and common grackles are communal roosters, particularly outside of the breeding season. They often spend the night in mixed-species flocks and depart for their respective feeding grounds at dawn. These roosting flocks increase in size during the summer and often join other flocks, resulting in fewer but larger roosts of birds that overwinter in New England. In some parts of North America, roosting aggregations of more than a million birds are not uncommon. This flocking is thought to provide group protection against predators ("safety in numbers") and to increase chances of finding food.

Eastern Bluebird—*Flocking*
Late in the summer pairs of eastern bluebirds often gather with the young from the current year's broods while they feed. In the fall this "extended family" may join other bluebird families and form

Female eastern bluebird.

OCT

an even larger flock (usually 5 to 20 birds), which then migrates south together. A small number of eastern bluebirds remain in New England throughout the winter, feeding on berries and roosting together in cavities during periods of extremely cold weather.

Swamp sparrow.

Sparrow—*Migrating*

Many species of sparrows are on the move during October, including white-throated, white-crowned, swamp, Lincoln's, chipping, field, song, and savannah. The number of birds migrating on any given day—sparrows as well as other species—increases dramatically after a cold front has passed through and high pressure is accompanied by northwest tailwinds.

Migrating waterfowl.

WATERFOWL MIGRATION

In transit from the major breeding grounds in the Midwest, Canadian prairies, and the Arctic, to their wintering grounds along the Atlantic Coast, many species of waterfowl migrate in substantial numbers down the Hudson and Connecticut rivers and/or along the Atlantic Coast during October. (Read more about migratory patterns on p. 285.)

Common loons begin molting prior to migrating.

■ Migratory Birds—Miles Traveled*

Species	Weight	Miles Traveled
Ruby-throated hummingbird	1/10–1/8 oz	0–3,500
Blackpoll warbler	1/3 oz	2,500–5,000
Tree swallow	2/3 oz	600–3,400
Eastern bluebird	1–1¼ oz	0–2,500
Bobolink	1¼–1 2/3 oz	5,000–6,800
American robin	2¾ oz	0–4,000
Killdeer	3–3½ oz	0–6,000
Belted kingfisher	4–7 oz	0–4,700
Broad-winged hawk	7 oz–1 lb 3 oz	1,000–8,700
Common loon	6 lb 3 oz–9 lb 15 oz	60–4,000

*Estimates from the *Atlas of Bird Migration*, ed. John Elphick (Firefly Books, 2007).

OCT

Sandhill Crane—
Migrating

Sandhill crane.

Sandhill cranes—long-necked, long-legged birds of grasslands and freshwater marshes—are thought by some to have been New England residents when the Europeans arrived, but within 100 years they were gone in the East. The western population of cranes remained strong and proceeded to grow and expand eastward. New England sightings became more common by the 1990s, and their nesting was confirmed in Maine in 2000, in Vermont in 2005, and Massachusetts in 2007.

The majority breed in northern central and western states, Alaska, and Canada, and winter in Georgia, Florida, New Mexico, Arizona, Texas, or Mexico. Other than the few individuals breeding here, most New England sightings are of migrating birds. Sandhill cranes are well-known for their distinctive bugling call (often heard before they are seen), as well as their elaborate courtship dance.

Owl—*Sign (Pellet)*

Most birds excrete both solid waste and uric acid from the same opening. However, some birds, such as raptors, gulls, crows, shorebirds, kingfishers, and others do not defecate to get rid of their solid waste. Instead, they regurgitate the indigestible parts of their diet in the form of little packages called *pellets* that can easily be mistaken for scat. The barred owl, as well as other birds of prey, coughs up oblong pellets consisting of fur, bones, teeth, and nails. Usually these hard, sharp fragments are wrapped inside the hair of the prey. Close examination of a pellet's contents can often reveal the identity of the owl's prey.

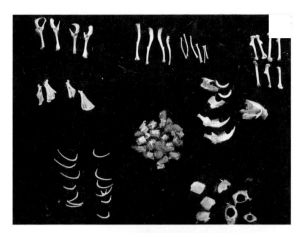

Barred owl pellets (right) and the bones found during dissection of several pellets (above).

MAMMALS

White-Tailed Deer—*Rubbing Antlers*

In the fall, shortening day length triggers a rise in the level of hormones in male white-tailed deer, or bucks. This signals the beginning of the breeding season, or *rut*, which peaks between mid- to late November. In the weeks leading up to rut, antlers harden and the blood and nutrient-supplying velvet skin covering them dries up. Bucks proceed to rub it off by scraping their antlers against saplings and shrubs (usually the bigger the buck, the larger the diameter of the tree), removing portions of bark as well as velvet. While not necessarily using the same tree every year, bucks usually return to the same vicinity for this ritual. Young, strong bucks usually make the most rubs.

OCT

White-tailed buck antler rub.

White-footed deermouse.

Bucks are rubbing not only their antlers on trees, but also their foreheads and the area beneath their eyes, where scent glands are located. When the buck rubs his antlers where he has previously rubbed his scent glands, the scent is transferred to the antlers and information contained in the scent (such as the buck's health and breeding status) is then broadcast far and wide to competing males, as well as potential mates. Similar information is also communicated when bucks scrape the ground and then urinate in it.

Ermine—*Molting*
During October the ermine, formerly called the short-tailed weasel, sheds its brown summer coat and replaces it with a white one, effectively camouflaging itself for the snowy New England winter. By April, it will have shed its white coat and grown a new brown one. During all seasons of the year, the ermine's belly remains white and the tip of its tail, black. (See more on molting on p. 290.)

White-Footed and North American Deermouse—*Preparing for Winter*
Some mice become torpid in winter, but the majority of both white-footed and North American deermice stay active, caching food in the fall to sustain themselves through the colder months. This supply of food includes the seeds of black cherry, jewelweed, clover, shadberry, and viburnum, as well as hickory nuts, acorns, beechnuts, and many others.

Communal nesting for both species begins around mid-October, often in trees. When the temperature drops, nests frequently are relocated underground. The combination of communal nesting, nesting below ground, and torpor contributes to an energy savings of nearly 75 percent for these small rodents. (Read more about small mammals on p. 377.)

Red Squirrel—*Caching Food*
Red squirrels remain active throughout the winter and eat a variety of foods, depending on what is available: acorns, hickory nuts, beechnuts, hemlock cones, conifer buds, and bark, as well as many berries and fungi. In early fall they cut the green cones of pines and bury them in damp earth so that the seeds won't dry and blow away before the squirrel is ready

Red squirrel.

to eat them. During fall and winter the rusty-red band that extends down the back of the red squirrel is very apparent. During the summer its fur is a duller color.

OCT

Woodchuck—*Entering Hibernation*

The woodchuck is one of New England's true hibernators. It prepares for this state in late summer by putting on a half-inch layer of fat equaling about a third of its weight, which sustains it through the winter. When the temperature dips below 50°F, woodchucks retreat into their winter burrows, often located in woodlands as opposed to the fields where they live in the summer.

Significant metabolic changes take place in the hibernating woodchuck's body. Its heart rate plummets from 100 beats per minute to just 15, and its body temperature drops from 96°F to 47°F. A woodchuck's weight drops by 20 to 37 percent by the time it emerges in the spring. (Read more about winter survival on p. 355.)

Meadow and Woodland Jumping Mouse—*Entering Hibernation*

Because they are true hibernators like the woodchuck, jumping mice do not store food. Rather, they must accumulate a substantial layer of fat to sustain themselves. Due to the difficulty in acquiring enough fat to achieve this, only about a third of meadow jumping mice survive to emerge in

Woodland jumping mouse.

the spring. The woodland jumping mouse is considered the most profound of eastern hibernators, spending roughly six months in dormancy. It curls into a little ball and sleeps for two or three weeks at a stretch, briefly awakens, then resumes its torpor. Its temperature hovers only a few degrees above freezing, its respiration slows, and its heart rate is reduced to a few beats each minute. (Find out more about small mammals on p. 377.)

■ Mammals and Their Most Developed Senses

	Sight	Smell	Hearing	Touch
Bat			X	
Virginia opossum		X	X	
White-tailed deer	X	X	X	
Red fox		X	X	X
American beaver		X	X	
North American porcupine		X		X
Coyote	X	X	X	
Raccoon		X		X
Bobcat	X		X	
American black bear		X	X	
North American river otter	X			X

A North American porcupine in its winter tree den.

INSECTS & ARACHNIDS

Field Cricket—*Mating*

What we commonly call field crickets are actually six or seven species of crickets in the genus *Gryllus* that are almost indistinguishable until they start to sing. As with birds, frogs, and other animals that engage in choral courtship, each species of cricket has its own unique call. (See p. 226 for more about cricket "singing.") At this time of year, it's imperative that mating occur so that egg-laying can take place before winter sets in.

As pleasant as it is to have a cricket singing on the hearth, bear in mind that there is almost nothing a cricket won't eat: seeds, dead insects, paper, fur, wool clothing, books—anything and everything is fair game.

March Fly—*Swarming and Mating*

On warm October days, slender male March flies (so-called because of their early appearance in the spring as well as the fall) of the genus *Bibio* form conspicuous swarms in the air. If a female is attracted to this constantly moving cloud of insects, a male, with his larger eyes, spots her, attaches to her, and together they leave the swarm and mate. You often see joined pairs on the ground near a swarm; the male remains with the female for quite some time in order to discourage her from mating with other males. This habit caused one species in this genus to be called the "lovebug."

March flies mating. Notice how much larger the male's eyes are than the female's.

Earth-Boring Scarab Beetle—*Hiding under Scat*

Rarely do we see earth-boring scarab beetles, for they usually are located underneath scat or carrion. In order to escape detection, this beetle digs a deep burrow into the earth, with the opening located directly under its food of choice. Sometimes known as "dung beetles," these insects provide a valuable service by rapidly decomposing organic waste.

Earth-boring scarab beetle.

The burrow of an earth-boring scarab beetle, exposed when the scat in this photo was moved.

OCT

■ Examples of Insect Overwintering Strategies

Some species overwinter in more than one stage of development; hence, you will see their name more than once on the charts below.

Leave New England

Migrate

Monarch butterfly

Painted lady butterfly

Red admiral butterfly

Question mark butterfly

American lady butterfly

Common buckeye butterfly

Clouded sulphur

Queen butterfly

Bee-fly or twelve-spotted skimmer dragonfly

Black swallowtail butterfly chrysalis.

Overwinter in New England

Egg	Larva	Pupa	Adult
Walking stick	Isabella tiger moth (woolly bear)	Cecropia moth	Mourning cloak butterfly
Praying mantis	Great spangled fritillary butterfly	Silver-spotted skipper butterfly	Question mark butterfly
Red-legged grasshopper	Common wood nymph butterfly	Black swallowtail butterfly	Water boatman
Field cricket	Viceroy butterfly	Cabbage butterfly	Water strider
Snowy tree cricket	Caddisfly	Hover flies	Whirligig beetle
Bush katydid	Japanese beetle	Polyphemus moth	Lady beetle
Eastern tent caterpillar	June beetle	Luna moth	Paper wasp queen
Gypsy moth	Giant predaceous diving beetle	Sphinx moths	Bald-faced hornet queen
Bagworm moth	Goldenrod gall fly	Caddisfly	Honeybee queen and late summer workers
Some aphids	Burying beetles		Bumblebee queen

THE MATING OF SOCIAL INSECTS

Bumblebees, hornets, yellowjackets, and wasps seen this late in the year are usually queens and attending drones (males). Mating takes place in the fall, but eggs won't be laid until spring. Workers (unfertilized females) in the colony die soon after the first hard frost, as do the drones; only the fertilized queen lives through the winter, hibernating in cracks or crevices, or in the ground. In the spring she will start an entirely new colony.

Mating bumblebees.

PLANTS & FUNGI

Poison Ivy—
Chlorophyll Disappearing

Beautiful foliage can be found on the ground as well as in the canopy, come fall. Poison ivy leaves turn a brilliant red before falling off. The oil on the surface of this plant's leaves is responsible for their metallic shine in the fall.

Red poison ivy leaves.

Deciduous Trees—*Losing Chlorophyll and Forming Abscission Layer*

The coloring of fall leaves is no mystery—photosynthesis ceases and the production of chlorophyll stops, allowing previously hidden pigments such as *xanthophylls* (yellows) and *carotenoids* (red, orange, yellow) to be revealed. In addition, *anthocyanins* (red and purple) are produced in the fall if conditions are right (bright, sunny days and cool nights). New England experiences the turning of its deciduous trees, such as maples, birches, and aspens, every fall. But why does a deciduous tree close down its production in October? Because water will be in short

Bigtooth aspen leaf.

supply through the winter, and a tree cannot afford to lose (through its leaves) what little it has.

Deciduous trees form a corky abscission layer where leaf stems join the branches. This layer effectively cuts off water and nutrients to and from the tree's leaves, causing them to change color and fall off the tree, bringing photosynthesis to a halt in most cases. In order to survive the winter, it is essential that this process take place, for it is a means of protection against winter water loss. Unlike most conifers, or evergreens, there is less waxy coating on the leaves of deciduous trees to prevent the escape of water vapor. (See more about foilage on p. 282.)

Eastern White Pine—*Losing Leaves*

White pine trees are continuously shedding old needles and growing new ones. Their needles, or leaves, have a life span of approximately one-and-a-half years. After this period they turn yellow, then brown, and then fall off the tree. If you look at a white pine in the fall, you will see that about a third of its needles, usually those furthest from the tips of its branches, have turned yellow/brown. In the spring leaf buds will open at the end of the branches and new needles will emerge.

Eastern white pine needles.

Eastern Larch—*Losing leaves*

Eastern larch, also known as tamarack and hackmatack (from the Algonquin word "akemantak," meaning "wood used for snowshoes"), is the only softwood species in New England that drops all of its

A small eastern larch tree and an up-close look at its leaves.

Hay-Scented and Sensitive Fern—*Dying*

Both hay-scented and sensitive fern are affected by the cold and will start turning yellow, and then brown, after the first frost of the season. (See more about ferns on p. 211–212.)

Hay-scented fern.

needles each year. Prior to falling off, the green leaves (needles) turn a beautiful golden bronze. The inner bark of eastern larch has been used as a poultice to treat cuts, infected wounds, frostbite, boils, and hemorrhoids.

Common Milkweed—*Dispersing Seeds*

Only 2 to 4 percent of milkweed flowers produce pods and all of the seeds in a given milkweed pod are produced by one flower. (Read more about common milkweed on p. 190, and about seed dispersal on p. 300.)

Grape Fern— *Dispersing Spores*

Grape ferns, members of the genus *Botrychium*, are small, non-flowering evergreen fern relatives that usually produce only one leaf per year. Their common name comes from the Greek word for "cluster" and refers to the grape-like bunches of spore cases (*sporangia*) that are on the fertile spikes they produce in the summer or fall.

Cut-leaved grape fern.

Common milkweed pod.

FUNGAL GROUPS

Mushrooms, or toadstools, are the fruiting body or reproductive structure of a fungus. They are usually the only part of a fungus that is visible. What you don't see is the vegetative body of the fungus, or *mycelium*, which consists of a mat of fine filaments called *hyphae* and is often located underground (see also p. 295). Fungi break down organic matter in the soil and extract the digestion product for their own use. Mycologists have divided fungi into different groups, primarily according to their reproductive structures and the appearance of their fruiting bodies.

Jelly fungus. When the weather is dry these fungi are quite hard; in rainy weather they become gelatinous and rubbery to the touch.

Puffball. These can be anywhere from the size of a grape to larger than a soccer ball, depending on the species. The "smoke" that comes from the holes in mature puffballs is actually the reproductive spores of this fungus. Long ago, these spores were used to stop nosebleeds and treat wounds.

Polypore. All polypores produce their spores on the inside walls of tubes located under their caps (they do not have gills). Usually they are found growing on wood and lack a distinct stem.

Coral fungus. Its name is derived from its resemblance to underwater coral. Coral fungi come in many colors, including white, yellow, pink, orange, red, and purple. Look for them on the ground and on logs and stumps in coniferous woods.

Tooth fungus. Tooth fungi produce their spores on "teeth" instead of gills or tubes. Comb tooth fungus is the most widespread and common species of tooth fungus in North America (pictured here). It is often found on decaying deciduous wood.

Bolete. Instead of gills, boletes have a thick, sponge-like layer consisting of fleshy tubes where their spores are produced. Boletes are mainly found growing on the ground near trees.

Stinkhorn fungus. You may smell stinkhorn fungus before you see it. The spores are embedded in a green slime that smells increasingly putrid as the fungus matures. Unlike those of most fungi, stinkhorn spores are not dispersed by the wind; rather, they adhere to the bodies of insects that are attracted to the smell.

OCT

Chanterelle. These include some of the best known edible mushrooms in New England. Most are orange or yellow, and they are often vase-shaped. Chanterelles lack gills; they bear their spores on ridges, folds, or on a smooth surface.

True morel. Some species of morels are edible and highly sought after by mushroom foragers. This group of fungi have honeycomb caps. They are often found in old apple orchards and in association with dead elms and ash, oak, and beech-maple woods.

False morel. Whereas true morels have honeycombed caps that are hollow, false morels have convoluted, brain-like caps. Most false morels are poisonous.

Cup fungus. Fungi in this group produce their spores on the inner or upper surface of a cup- or saucer-shaped fruiting body. When the spores are ripe, the fungus forcibly discharges them into the air, which sometimes causes the spores to form a visible cloud. There are reports of people actually hearing these discharges, as well as seeing them.

Gilled agaric. Agarics are gilled mushrooms of many colors and include the common cultivated mushroom that is sold in stores. While in the wild many gilled fungi are edible, there are also deadly poisonous members of this group. The genus *Amanita* includes many of

these inedible (by humans) fungi. All develop from an egg-like enclosure called a "universal veil"—a tissue that is quickly outgrown but often leaves patches on the cap and a cup at the stalk's base. A "partial veil," which initially encloses the gills, leaves a ring or "skirt" on the upper stalk. (See more on this on p. 209.) Toxic amanitas have caused 90 percent of fatal mushroom poisonings.

Earth tongues and allies. The spore sacs of these fungi are often club-shaped and expel their spores through a hole in the tip of the club, or "tongue."

OCT

FALL FOLIAGE COLORS—A MATTER OF PIGMENT

The quintessential New England scene—fall foliage reflected along the shore of a lake.

Three types of pigments are responsible for the summer greens as well as the brilliant reds, yellows, oranges, and purples of fall leaves in New England:

Chlorophyll: This gives leaves their basic green color and is necessary for photosynthesis—the chemical reaction that enables plants to use sunlight to manufacture sugars.

Carotenoids: These produce yellow, orange, and brown colors in such things as corn, carrots, buttercups, bananas, as well as fall foliage.

Anthocyanins: These produce the red, blue, and purple colors of cranberries, red apples, concord grapes, blueberries, cherries, strawberries, plums, and fall foliage.

Woody Plants and Leaf Color

Purple: White ash, hobblebush

Yellow: Aspens, larch, elm, striped maples, birches, hickories

Red and orange: Sugar maple, red maple, sumacs, blueberry, poison ivy, Virginia creeper

Red maple leaves.

Sequential Order of Fall Foliage

Black gum
Red maple
Sumac
Virginia creeper
Poison ivy
Birches
Sugar maple
Aspens
Huckleberry
Oaks
Eastern larch

OCT

a closer look

There is a flurry of activity this time of year, most of which can be detected through one or more of our senses. Looking up is often rewarded by the sight of **vultures migrating south** (see below), while looking down reveals **woolly bears** (p. 293) on a mission and **eastern chipmunks** (p. 288) busily collecting nuts and seeds to store for winter snacks. Woodlands are alive with the bright yellow blossoms of **witch hazel** (p. 297) and the **dispersal** of many **seeds** (p. 300). Many houses increase their population dramatically at this time of year, when **multi-colored Asian lady beetles** (p. 292) move in for the winter. The fruiting bodies of **fungi** (p. 295) are popping up everywhere. What we don't detect as easily are the **molting mammals** (p. 290) that are starting to replace their brown summer coats with white winter ones, hopefully in time for the first snow of the cold season.

Turkey Vulture —
Nature's Winged Recycler

Awkward on land and not much to look at, the turkey vulture probably isn't on anyone's list of Top 10 birds. However, if you can get beyond the featherless head and a taste for carrion, there is a great deal to admire about this gentle scavenger.

A Sense for Death
Most people associate the turkey vulture with rotting carcasses, and rightly so. It has an uncanny ability to find both wild carrion and dead farm animals. For years scientists wondered which played a bigger part in the turkey vulture's detection of decaying bodies—sight or smell. Most birds have a very poor sense of smell—if they have any at all. However, research has proven that both senses are highly developed and are of great importance

to turkey vultures. While road kill is highly visible, bodies decomposing under the canopy of a forest require other means of discovery. This is where the turkey vulture's impressive ability to detect odors comes into play. They are sensitive to the gas *ethyl mercaptan*, which is emitted by carrion. This was confirmed when some enterprising engineers put ethyl mercaptan in a gas line to detect leaks and then found them when they saw turkey vultures begin to circle over part of the gas line.

Although turkey vultures prefer relatively fresh carrion, they do occasionally eat aging carcasses. Their beaks aren't equipped to open thick skin, so in the case of a larger body, they must either wait until it decomposes further, or until a predator comes along and opens it up, providing access to the inside. In most ways, however, turkey vultures are extremely well equipped for their dining practices. The scarcity of head feathers is not coinci-

OCT

dental; feathers would only collect rotting flesh and bacteria every time a vulture thrusted its head deep within a decomposing cavity. With the turkey-like adaptation of a comparatively featherless head, the turkey vulture simply finds a sunny spot after dining where it bakes off the relatively minor debris that has accumulated. The nature of its diet appears not to be lost on the turkey vulture. In times of danger, such as when a predator approaches its nest, the turkey vulture's primary defense is to regurgitate the half-digested, putrid remains of its most recent meal, which serves as a very effective deterrent.

Not Guilty

The turkey vulture has been much maligned as a carrier of livestock diseases, when the opposite is actually true. Most of the bacteria found in decomposing matter that are responsible for diseases such as anthrax and hog cholera are destroyed in the turkey vulture's digestive tract before reaching its intestines. Because of this, the turkey vulture actually prevents the spread of these bacteria, for the same bacteria remain alive as they pass through the systems of other animals.

A relative of storks, the turkey vulture is a familiar sight in New England's October skies. Look for a large, black soaring bird with its wings in the shape of a "V."

Avian Glider

In addition to being a very effective recycler, the turkey vulture is considered one of the most skillful North American avian gliders. You can easily recognize the "V"-shape dihedral that a turkey vulture's 3-foot wings form as it soars overhead looking for and attempting to smell its next meal. Chances of your spotting one this month are great, for many of these birds are passing through New England on their way south during October.

You rarely see turkey vultures flapping their wings, as they conserve energy in the same manner as many raptors—by riding *thermals* (masses of rising hot air) up to their tops and then peeling off and gliding in the direction of flight until they come upon another thermal. According to the Turkey Vulture Society (yes, there is one, and its mission is to rid us all of the "unmerited images of death, filth, and cruelty" that turkey vultures conjure up), the turkey vulture can glide for over six hours at a time without a single flap of its wings. They don't appear to sacrifice speed as a result of soaring, for turkey vultures have been recorded flying over 600 miles in six days. Look for their characteristic "teetering," which gives the bird lift as well as stability as it flies low enough to detect the scent of carrion.

Turkey Vulture

- The turkey vulture's common name comes from the red skin of its head and its dark body feathers, which resemble those of wild turkeys.

- Immature turkey vultures have a black rather than a red head.

- The turkey vulture soars up to 5,000 feet in altitude when it migrates.

- When searching for food, turkey vultures usually soar about 200 feet above the ground, where they are close enough to use both sight and smell to detect carcasses.

- Turkey vultures do not build a nest; they lay their eggs on the floor of caves, rock ledges, and hollow trees.

- Two species of vultures are seen in New England: the turkey vulture and the black vulture. Both are relatively new transplants. The turkey vulture's range didn't extend north of New Jersey until the 1920s and the black vulture, an even more recent arrival, is rarely seen north of Massachusetts.

- Both species of vulture have two-toned underwings. The turkey vulture has silvery flight feathers on the trailing edge of its wings; the black vulture has silvery wing tips.

The turkey vulture has another interesting trick up its sleeve. When overheated, it excretes its waste onto its own legs and the evaporation of the moisture in its droppings serves to lower its body temperature. The acidity also kills bacteria that may be present. Certain turkey vulture habits may be unappetizing, even disgusting, to some, but one has to admire this bird's resourcefulness.

Bird Migration—*A Simple Overview of a Complex Phenomenon*

From 500 to 2,000 feet above our heads, 24 hours a day, one of Mother Nature's greatest magic tricks takes place this time of year. Every fall over half of the species of birds that breed in New England disappear, only to return in the spring.

Humans have been aware of this phenomenon for centuries, and entertaining explanations have been proposed. Aristotle surmised that some of our birds, such as swallows, hibernated at the bottom of ponds through the winter months. It was thought by some that one species of bird turned into a different species in the fall, and then turned back into its original species in the spring. Another commonly held belief was that birds migrated to the moon, a trip estimated to take approximately two months. By the early 1800s many clues (including German storks that appeared in the spring with African arrows imbedded in their body) led scientists to an understanding of the true nature of migration: annual seasonal flights made by many birds—not to the moon or the bottom of ponds—but to much closer and more hospitable environs.

Origin
Many factors are thought to have contributed to the origin of migration, the primary one being the succession of six ice ages over the past two million years. The southward advances and northward receding of ice sheets affected the location of suitable habitat for birds, causing similar movement within their populations.

Who?
Approximately five billion land birds, consisting of 500 species, leave their North American breeding grounds for more southern wintering grounds every year. This group includes 62 percent of the species that breed in the deciduous forests of New

OCT

England. Species of songbirds, birds of prey, inland and coastal water birds, and shorebirds are among these migrants.

Where?
Most New England birds fly to Central America or the Caribbean for the winter, but a few go as far as southern South America. (This is one reason why environmental conditions in southern locals are of great concern to ornithologists.)

Why?
The primary reason birds in the northern hemisphere migrate south in the fall is a dwindling supply of food. They return in the spring to lengthening days and a food supply that allows them to provide for their young as well as themselves—so much so that the clutches of migratory birds in New England are larger than related non-migratory species that remain in the tropics year-round.

When?
Shortening days and a bird's internal clock trigger the onset of migration preparation. This includes accumulating an extra amount of fat (hummingbirds more than double their weight before crossing the Gulf of Mexico); molting and growing new wing and tail feathers; and building up the size of flight muscles. While the approximate time a bird migrates is determined by these hormonally-induced physiological changes, weather conditions influence the exact day an individual migrant chooses to begin its journey. Favorable winds, an extended high-pressure system, a lack of star-obscuring clouds—these are some of the cues birds appear to be aware of and take into consideration when beginning their flight.

There are birds that migrate only during the day, some of which, including hawks, use the rising air of thermals to support them in their travels. (This eliminates the need for flapping their wings,

Yellow-rumped warbler in fall plumage.

thereby conserving precious energy—see p. 249.) Others travel by night, when the temperature is cooler. Most species do both.

How?
Most birds can navigate to within 6 to 12 miles of their destination, after which they use landmarks to find the exact spot where they will spend the winter. Scientists have been asking how they do this for hundreds of years and researchers still don't have a definitive answer.

Even if the whole puzzle hasn't been solved, however, bits and pieces of the mystery of migration have been put in place. A simplistic and partial explanation of how migratory birds navigate would have to include night fliers using the stars as a compass and day fliers the sun, both in combination with an internal clock and the earth's magnetic field. Sight (landmarks such as coastlines, rivers, mountain ridges); sound (waves crashing on the shore, wind created by mountain ranges); and even smell (yes, most birds have a poor sense of smell, but apparently petrels and

OCT

vultures are exceptions to the rule) have been implicated as navigational tools.

Look and Listen

Many times migratory flocks come in waves that are visible during the daytime, but it's the night fliers that capture the magic and mystery of this annual event. How do you observe birds flying in the pitch dark? Listen—they call back and forth to one another, maintaining social contact, and these sounds can be heard by the human ear, even without magnification. Especially on cloudy nights after a cold front has passed through, it is possible to hear hundreds of birds calling to each other as the pass overhead.

Each species has a distinctive call note (usually calls have only a single note), just as they have species-specific songs. The call note of a rose-breasted grosbeak resembles a mellow whistle, while a wood thrush sounds more like a bedspring squeaking. The ability to discern one species' call note from another allows ornithologists to track not only relative numbers, but the timing of a species' migration, as well as its migratory route.

Best of all, look up at the next autumnal full moon, and hold a steady gaze on it with either binoculars or a spotting scope. You are likely to be rewarded with the sight of more than one migrating bird silhouetted against the orb, heading for a warmer clime.

] FAST FACTS [
Bird Migration

► Migration is the regular movement of individuals between their breeding and wintering grounds.

► Bird migration is seasonal, predictable, and repeated each year.

► When migrating birds are forced to stop and wait for bad weather to pass, it is referred to as a *fallout*.

► Nocturnal migrants (warblers, vireos, and thrushes, among others) begin migrating about half an hour after the sun sets, when the first stars are visible and the location of the sun can still be detected. Perhaps they use both of these aids in navigation.

► At least 75 percent of the slightly more than 650 species of nesting North American birds engage in some form of migratory behavior.

► Research techniques on migrating birds include bird banding, radar, seasonal censuses, radio transmitters, geolocators, satellites, and observation.

► Major migration routes, or *flyways*, are defined by geographic features, but birds also use a great many other routes to get to their wintering grounds.

► American golden-plovers make a cross-Atlantic flight of roughly 2,500 miles from the northeastern United States to northeastern South America.

► The total weight of non-migrating birds is 5 percent or less fat. The weight of short-distance migrants is roughly 15 to 25 percent fat and that of long-distance migrants is 50 percent or more, at the onset of migration.

► There are aerodynamic advantages for birds flying in a flock.

► Spots where migrating birds stop to rest and refuel are called *staging posts*.

OCT

Eastern Chipmunk—
Caching and Chattering

A chorus of soft chucking reverberates throughout New England woodlands these late summer and early autumn days, making it next to impossible not to be aware of the activity of eastern chipmunks. Their increased vocalizations and frenzied gathering and storing of nuts and seeds as winter approaches dominate the forest scene.

The chipmunk's activity this time of year is an integral part of its winter survival strategy. Unlike its relative, the woodchuck, which gorges in the fall, accumulating a life-sustaining layer of fat that allows it to hibernate continuously through the winter months, the chipmunk takes a series of "naps," waking every couple of weeks to eat from its stored cache. These differing strategies achieve the same end: Food stored inside (woodchuck) and outside (eastern chipmunk) the body is used as fuel to survive a long, cold winter.

Supreme Gatherers

Chipmunks are adequately equipped for collecting and transporting their winter food supply, for their two large cheek pockets or pouches serve as "backpacks." The amount and variety of food the pouches can hold is truly impressive. Biologists have documented each of the following contents in the pouches of four chipmunks: 31 kernels of corn, 13 prune pits, 70 sunflower seeds, and 32 beechnuts.

The efficiency and speed with which this scavenging and storing is done is impressive. In 1982, researchers watched one chipmunk carry six white oak acorns at a time to its burrow 200 feet away in two minutes. It carried three acorns in one pouch, two in the other and one in its mouth. A total of 116 acorns were moved in an hour (the return trip from the burrow to the food supply used up some time). In a large storage chamber off its 2½-foot-deep tunnel system, as much as half a bushel of food may be

The enlarged cheeks of eastern chipmunks enable them to carry large amounts of food to storage chambers in their underground burrows.

cached, all of which is consumed by the one chipmunk inhabitant of the burrow. Smaller chambers hold far less—during a study in 1974, 308 acorns and one hickory nut were found in one small chamber and 82 acorns and one hickory nut in another.

Surviving by Communication

During this period of intense food collection in the fall, chipmunks are more exposed and therefore more vulnerable to predation. They employ a communication system that may make us more aware of their presence, but at the same time warns other chipmunks of potential danger. There are basically three types of calls that we hear them giving regularly: chips, chucks, and trills. The general consensus is that all three are predator alarm calls, but that they indicate different sources as well as degrees of danger.

Biologists have not yet determined the meaning of the chipmunk's many calls. The high "chip" can be repeated as many as 130 chips a minute over as long as a 10-minute period. The soft "chuck"

OCT

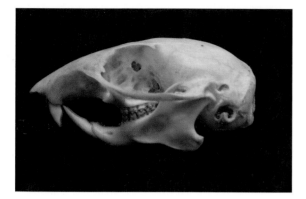

Like all rodents, the eastern chipmunk has a pair of continuously growing upper and lower incisors in the front of its jaws (see left side of photo), separated from the molars by a wide gap or *diastema*. These incisors have a layer of dentine that is covered by enamel on the front of the tooth. When gnawing hard nuts and seeds, the incisors grind against each other, wearing away the softer dentine in the back of the tooth, but leaving the enamel edge, which acts as the blade of a chisel—a very effective self-sharpening system.

can go on for many minutes as well, with a chorus of other chucking chipmunks often joining in. It is thought these might be warning signs to other chipmunks. The "trill," consisting of a loud chip followed by a startled, upturned whistle, is sounded when imminent danger exists and is heard as the chipmunk disappears down one of the entrances to its burrow.

A fun pastime during September and October is eavesdropping on these chipmunk conversations. You haven't much time, for as the mercury starts dropping, so does the frequency of chipmunk chattering.

From left to right the contents of three sets of eastern chipmunk pouches examined by the author contained: 287 young maple seeds with wings nipped off (collected in June); a mixture of 149 maple seeds and 34 elm seeds (collected in June); and 37 (older and larger) maple seeds (collected in November).

OCT

Mammal Molts—
Keeping Hidden, Keeping Warm

Winter in New England can be brutal. Temperatures can and often do dip below zero, and food can be difficult to come by. Animals that remain active year-round undergo many changes in order to survive a winter with such challenges. Diets are switched, habitats changed, and behavior altered. Adaptations are numerous and varied, but one of the most apparent is the change in color of three of our resident mammals.

Camouflage and Insulation
The ermine (formerly called the short-tailed weasel), the long-tailed weasel, and the snowshoe hare all go through two complete molts every year. In the fall, when snow is starting to cover the ground, their brown hairs are replaced by white ones, and in the spring, as the snow melts, white hairs are shed and brown hairs grow in.

The obvious explanation for these molts is that they help camouflage the animals that undergo

animals retain their body heat. Even though dark colors absorb heat and white reflects it, there is an insulating advantage to white fur. As anyone who has worn a down jacket knows, dead air space is a good insulator. Because white is actually the absence of pigment, the cells in white hairs (as opposed to brown) are filled with air, not pigment, and thus provide additional thermal insulation.

The Molt Process
As a general rule, it takes a weasel approximately a month to shed and replace all its hair, while a snowshoe hare completes its molt over a period of roughly three months. In New England, most fall molts begin and end between October and December and then occur again in the spring between March and May.

There is a set progression to this process. As winter approaches and daylight decreases, a molt begins on the abdomen and white hair then progresses up the sides and onto the back of the animal. In the spring, the molt takes place in reverse order, beginning on the back and progressing

An ermine in its summer (left) and winter (right) coat.

them. By blending in with their surroundings, these animals often avoid being noticed by both predators and prey. But there is more to this adaptation than camouflage—this change in color helps these

downward over the sides to the belly. Except for the weasel's black-tipped tail, and the black-bordered ears of the snowshoe hare, the coats of these three animals are completely white. (Note: Only the very tips of the winter hairs of a snowshoe hare are actually white; the lower two-thirds are a tawny-gray—see photo on p. 291.)

Although the snowshoe hare appears to have a white coat in the winter, only the outer half of each hair is white. The half nearest the hare's skin is brown and gray.

] FAST FACTS [
Mammals Molting

▸ The process of molting does not involve a given hair changing color; rather, a hair of one color is shed and replaced with a hair of another color.

▸ Seasonal molt, when the coat of an animal is shed and a different colored coat grows in, is believed to be a photoperiodic phenomenon governed by lengthening or shortening periods of daylight.

▸ The snowshoe hare's white winter coat is 27 percent more insulating than its brown summer coat.

▸ The mink, a slightly larger member of the weasel family than either the ermine or long-tailed weasel, has a brown coat year-round.

The timing of these mammals' molts is governed by hormones, which, in turn, are triggered by the length of daylight. Thus, the timing of a molt is predictable every year. Our weather, however, can vary greatly from year to year. Consequently there are times when molting is not a very effective survival mechanism. If snow arrives very late in the fall, or lasts unusually long in the spring, both weasels and hares (which have molted on schedule) may be particularly conspicuous. Research shows that snowshoe hares that have turned white before snow flies, or remain white after the snow has melted, spend more time in dense underbrush than they would if snow was on the ground, indicating that habitat selection may be determined by predator avoidance.

Ermine undergo these molts regardless of where they live (in the East they range throughout New England, New York, and Pennsylvania). On the other hand, the molts of long-tailed weasels (which range from Maine to Florida in the East) vary according to their geographic location. Those individuals living north of Pennsylvania turn white in the fall. There is a 600-mile-wide belt across their continental range, however, in which some long-tailed weasels undergo a molt, and others don't. In Pennsylvania less than half turn white, and south of the Maryland/Pennsylvania border all long-tailed weasels remain brown year-round. Apparently this process is genetically determined. Scientists captured long-tailed weasels in northern New England, transported them south, and found that they continued to molt every winter, while southern long-tailed weasels that were transported north did not undergo a molt.

If the frequency with which we set eyes on an ermine, long-tailed weasel, or snowshoe hare in New England is any indication, the energy they spend on these biannual molts is well worth it. A multitude of both weasel and hare tracks in winter tells us these animals are plentiful, even if they usually escape our detection. (Read more about mammal winer adaptations on p. 355.)

OCT

Multicolored Asian Lady Beetles— *Creatures of the Good God*

Is your home inundated with tiny, colorful, six-legged (uninvited) guests? Fear not, for as far as company goes, the beetles that are the likely culprits are fairly unobjectionable. They don't take up much room, they don't eat, nor do they reproduce while under your roof. What more could you ask of any guest?

These visitors come in a variety of colors and bear the appropriate common name of multicolored Asian lady beetles. (Many of us know them as ladybugs, but because they are technically beetles, entomologists refer to them as lady beetles.) This particular species is also sometimes called the Halloween ladybug because some adults are a pumpkin yellow-orange and large populations often occur in late October or early November.

Friendly Infestation

For the most part, lady beetles are beneficial predators that consume aphids, scale insects, and many other pests that injure plants. While humans have historically had a fondness for these diminutive insects, current infestations are testing even the most ardent lady beetle admirer.

Why, in the past decade, have our houses become infested with lady beetles in the fall and again in the spring? Have they suddenly discovered the protection a house can provide during the cold winter months? The answer lies in the exact type of lady beetle we're seeing; it is an entirely different species from the one most of us grew up with. While there are over 350 kinds of lady beetles in North America, only the multicolored Asian lady beetle has chosen to cohabit so conspicuously with humans. And as is often the case, it is humans who are responsible for this phenomenon.

Through both accidental and planned releases, the multicolored Asian lady beetle has firmly estab-lished itself throughout North America. Originating in China, Russia, Korea, and Japan, this insect was very effective in controlling aphids and soft-bodied insects that inhabited Asian trees. As a result, the US Department of Agriculture imported tens of thousands of them during the late 1960s through the 1990s in an effort to control insect pests that injure North American trees, particularly apple and pecan. Only recently have the beetles become established in the Northeast, so much so that they are commonly referred to as a "seasonal nuisance pest."

Our native species of lady beetle hibernate under logs, leaf litter, and other outdoor sites, whereas the multicolored Asian lady beetles, in their native habitat, congregate in cracks and crevices within cliff faces. Apparently the south and southwest-facing sides of light-colored houses are the next best thing, as that is where they most often appear in the Northeast. After a beetle has found a suitable site it emits a "come hither" pheromone—a chemical that attracts other beetles. Once the signal is sent, hundreds of beetles may gather in this spot. Cracks around windows, doors, and siding allow them access to the inside and even more protection.

"Creatures of the Good God"

As far as humans are concerned, there really is very little objectionable about these little insects, which the French call *les betes du bon Dieu* or "creatures of the good God." They are beautiful to look at. Once hibernating they don't move unless disturbed. They do not eat wood, building materials, or human food. In fact, as mentioned previously, they neither eat nor mate during the winter months. Come spring, they voluntarily move back outside where they consume quantities of injurious insects. Consider that the convergent lady beetle, one of our common native species, consumes up to 350 aphids per day during its month-long larval or immature stage. The adult female consumes up to 75 aphids per day while the smaller male may con-

OCT

Multicolored Asian lady beetles come in all shades of yellow, tan, and orange, with many or no spots. Females tend to be heavily spotted; males often with fewer, if any, spots.

sume 40. With a life span of up to three years, any species of ladybug takes quite a toll on the aphid population and makes a highly desirable neighbor. There is such a demand by gardeners that you can even mail order certain species of this voracious aphid-eater.

The only word of warning one might heed is that to disturb a multicolored Asian lady beetle is to ask for trouble. It is not by chance that they have few natural enemies, for as a defense mechanism they exude a liquid (actually blood) from their joints. This behavior is referred to as *reflex bleeding*. Unfortunately, this blood has a distinctly unpleasant odor. In addition to its smell, their blood also permanently stains whatever surface it is on. All in all, it pays to be hospitable to these pint-size boarders. They are harmless if left alone and will vacate the premises come spring.

Woolly Bears—*Winter's Fortune-Tellers*

Woolly bears. Just their name connotes something you'd want to pick up and cuddle. However, they prefer to have the exact opposite effect on potential predators. As members of the *Arctiidae* family, woolly bears possess coats of dense bristles or *setae* (insects don't technically have "hair"). If you've ever disturbed a woolly bear, you know that their immediate reaction is to curl up in a ball, effectively protecting their soft, bare underparts. This has led to the nickname hedgehog caterpillar—because hedgehogs curl into a tight ball and "play dead" when picked up or disturbed. Woolly bear bristles are unappetizing to most predators, which

OCT

avoid them fastidiously, with one known exception. Striped skunks are clever and patient enough to carefully pick off the bristles with their paws before downing the naked caterpillars, which they apparently relish.

Meteorological Legend

As many of us know, the woolly bear is renowned for its ability to forecast the length and severity of the coming winter. According to Yankee legend, the longer the black bands at either end of the caterpillar, the longer, colder, snowier, and more severe the coming winter. On the other hand, the longer the middle brown band, the milder the winter will be.

Although it didn't strictly follow scientific method, a bit of informal research was done on this theory back in the 1940s when Dr. C. H. Curran, the Curator of Insects at the American Museum of Natural History in New York City, decided to collect as many woolly bears as he could find in one day every year for eight years. Once he had them in hand, he would count the number of segments per caterpillar that were colored brown (each caterpillar has 13 segments). Depending on the average ratio of brown to black segments, he would issue a forecast for the coming winter. Much to the delight of meteorological legend believers, his predictions bore out 70 percent of the time. Whether or not you accept this theory, one cannot question Dr. Curran's observation that the proportion of brown versus black coloring on woolly bears does differ. The question is, "Why?"

Stages of Development

Many insects go through four stages in their lifetime: egg, larva (moth larvae are called "caterpillars"), pupa (moths pupate inside "cocoons"), and adult. The larval or caterpillar stage is the only stage that has chewing mouthparts, and thus, it eats constantly from the day it hatches until shortly before winter arrives. At this time it seeks shelter often

Woolly bear caterpillar (larva).

under a rock, a log, or leaf litter and hibernates until spring, when it pupates inside of a cocoon fashioned from the bristles of its last larval coat held together with silk. It emerges in one to two weeks as a rather non-descript pale, dull orange-brown moth with a 2-inch wingspread—the Isabella tiger moth.

As the caterpillar eats, it grows, and as it grows, its skin (which is actually its exoskeleton, and can't increase in size) becomes very tight. The caterpillar forms a new, larger skin under the old one and then sheds the outgrown older skin, a process referred to as *molting*. Woolly bears go through six molts before their growth is completed and each successive molt not only produces a new exoskeleton, but also an additional brown segment. If spring comes early, allowing the wooly bear a longer span of time in which to consume available food and thus grow larger and complete more molts, the fall caterpillar will have a greater percentage of brown segments than it would have had it been a late spring. Thus, the amount of brown on any given caterpillar is more an indication of the length of last year's winter than a forecast of what's around the corner. While it would be nice to think that winter's going to be balmy if we see a mostly or totally brown woolly bear, it would be unwise to assume anything other than perhaps the previous winter was fairly short.

Even though woolly bears are able to tolerate subfreezing temperatures, protection from the elements is crucial. Late September and October

► Often there are two generations of Isabella tiger moths a summer that produce mature caterpillars, or larvae.

► The woolly bear eats a variety of low-growing plants, including dandelion, grass, meadowsweet, and nettle.

► The woolly bear caterpillar travels at a rate of .05 miles per hour (4 feet per minute).

► The woolly bear caterpillar overwinters as a nearly mature larva under leaf litter, loose bark, and boards.

► In the spring the woolly bear caterpillar resumes eating, spins a cocoon made out of its setae and silk, and pupates inside it.

► There are at least 120 species of woolly bears in North America.

► Woolly bears feed on over 30 species in 21 families of plants.

Isabella tiger moth.

is when they are apt to be observed out and about seeking their winter shelters or *hibernacula*. Although we know the real reason for their broad and narrow black and brown bands, it's still fun to believe that a tiny fuzzy creature has the power to predict something that humans, so far, haven't been able to—at least, without a great degree of inaccuracy.

Fungi—*A Tree's Best Friend*

Toadstools, mushrooms, fungi—call them what you will, they're everywhere this time of year, popping up from under leaves and out of rotting logs in myriad shapes, colors, and sizes. However, other than brightening the forest floor and providing an occasional meal for the brave of heart, mushrooms don't attract a great deal of attention. Why would anyone wish to celebrate a family whose relatives are responsible for the demise of our elm and chestnut trees, peach rot, powdery mildew, athlete's foot, and an untold number of other infections?

The Tip of the Iceberg

Why? Just imagine a life without penicillin, insulin, bread, beer, wine, or Brie cheese. Or picture all the organic matter that falls to earth every day piling up miles high in the sky rather than decomposing and being recycled. This is what life would be like for humans in a world without fungi. It's possible that trees, shrubs, and other green plants would actually be even *more* at a loss without these organisms than humans, for their productivity relies heavily on them.

The structure we refer to as a mushroom is but the tip of the fungal iceberg (see photos of different kinds of mushrooms on p. 280). Producing reproductive seed-like spores, a mushroom is merely the fruiting body of a massive organism called a fungus that resides within the leaves, logs, and soil of the forest floor. In other words, mushrooms are to a fungus what apples are to an apple tree. The entire fungus consists of a vast network of filaments (called *hyphae*), which grow in a cobweb-like net throughout the organic matter and soil beneath our feet (the *mycelium*), in an attempt to obtain food from it.

The relatively diminutive size of a typical mushroom belies the voluminous nature of both spores and mycelia. An average field mushroom produces about 16 billion spores, which are released at the rate of about 100 million per hour, while a large

OCT

BIRD'S NEST FUNGUS

This fungus was named for its obvious resemblance to a nest and eggs. The "eggs" are actually cases containing spores, which are splashed out of the "nest" and dispersed when it rains.

Bird's nest fungus.

When a tree is in poor health, it is common to find fungi growing in it and fruiting on it.

puffball the diameter of a foot can produce up to 700 billion spores. Mycelium size can be as extensive as spore production. A honey fungus discovered in Michigan extended over 38 acres, weighed over 100 tons, and had an estimated age of approximately 1,500 years. The mycelium of another fungus in the state of Washington is thought to extend well over 2 square miles.

The Feeling's Mutual

Although fungi were originally classified as plants, they no longer are, in part because fungal cells have cell walls that contain *chitin* (also in exoskeletons of crustaceans and insects), unlike the cell walls of plants, which contain cellulose. Today they are considered to be more closely related to animals than plants.

Because of an inability to manufacture their own sugars and starches, fungi had to arrive at a way to obtain them in order to survive. The solution for many was to establish mutually beneficial, or symbiotic, associations with plants, called *mycorrhiza*. The individual hyphae of the mycelium colonize the roots of a host plant, which allows the fungus to have access to a renewable source of food. In return, the plant gains the use of the mycelium's tremendous surface area to absorb mineral nutrients and water from the soil. Believe it or not, 95 percent of all plants that have been examined have access to nutrients and water they obtain through a relationship with fungi. Research has shown that

plants with a mycorrhizal relationship not only have additional nutritional benefits, but are also more resistant to disease and the effects of drought.

The symbiotic path was not taken by all fungi. There exist *saprophytic* fungi that break down dead or dying organic matter, without which recycling of essential nutrients would occur at a much slower rate. There are also *parasitic* fungi that grow on living organisms and can cause severe damage.

Even though most plants are dependent upon a mutually beneficial relationship with fungi, we are generally unaware of this activity, for much of it takes place out of sight. If you dissect a rotting log, or poke through the leaf litter, you can sometimes find the white or black thread-like hyphae, but many are microscopic and not visible to the naked eye. The limited interactions we have with fungi are primarily with the fruiting bodies that form when the necessary nutrition,

Around 95 percent of all plants have access to nutrients and water they can obtain only through a relationship with fungi.

humidity, temperature, and light conditions are met. Although beautiful and occasionally edible, they tell only a fraction of the toadstool tale. The next time you notice a mushroom in the woods, picture the network of potentially acres of filaments that may be helping to create the robust canopy above your head.

Witch Hazel—
An "Explosive" Autumn Flower

While it's true that trees no less noble than the sugar maple—whose dissipating supply of chlorophyll allows the red, orange, and yellow pigments in its leaves to boldly announce its presence—are a sight to behold, there is a more subtle and infinitely more rewarding finale to the annual foliage festival. It lingers long after the splashes of color on the hills and valleys of New England fade away. Those familiar with the woodland understory look forward to this annual event with great anticipation, for just when the colorful leaves of maples, birches, and ashes start raining down on the ground after the first hard frost, making the woods relatively stark and bare, a twinkling of gold catches the eye. It is the flowers of witch hazel, which bring life and light to the dreary late-autumn woods.

Strap-Like Flowers
This multi-stemmed, 20-foot-high shrub is not the most commanding woody plant in the forest. It is often overlooked, in fact, except for this time of year, when, unlike most other trees or shrubs, it is not only dispersing its seeds, but also opening and displaying its flowers. This unprepossessing shrub now takes center stage, for it is the last native plant in the Northeast to flower. Hundreds of bright yellow "whiskery" flowers adorn its branches, often appearing in clumps of three. The sunnier the spot in which it grows, the more apt it is to bear many flowers. Four yellow strap-like petals, each about half an inch in length and resembling tiny bits of twisted ribbons, announce the end of the growing season. So late is it that these flowers have their work cut out for them attracting pollinators, for insects are scarce after the first hard frost. The flowers linger long enough, often past Halloween, so that any insects still active, such as gnats and hover flies, have ample opportunity to visit them.

OCT

The undulating, wavy edges of witch hazel leaves are distinctive and help to identify it in the summer, before its flowers open.

Coiled tightly inside each tiny, round flower bud are four petals that spring into bloom this time of year. It is not unusual to find the "spidery" flowers of witch hazel (appropriately) still in bloom on Halloween.

Potential witch hazel pollinators, such as the hover fly, are few and far between this late in the season. To compensate for the scarcity of insects, witch hazel has a lengthy flowering period, which often extends well into November.

branches reveals various lumps and bumps. There are two species of insects, both aphids, that specifically seek out witch hazel as a host for their young. The activity of both of these insects causes a reaction in the shrub that results in the formation of a gall—an abnormal plant growth that houses the developing aphid offspring (see more about galls on p. 155). The cone gall aphid causes a cone-shaped gall to be formed on the upper side of witch hazel leaves. Equally distinct is the spiny gall found on witch hazel branches. It is shaped like a miniature pineapple and results from the actions of the spiny witch-hazel gall aphid.

There are also several moth larvae that take up residence in and on the leaves of witch hazel, rolling the leaves into cylinders or cones and developing within these shelters.

Flower Buds and Fruits

When you come upon a flowering witch hazel in the woods, enjoy the flowers, but look closely at the surrounding leaves and branches, as well. The tiny cylindrical spheres you see on the witch hazel branches are the flower buds. The petals inside are rolled inward in a closed spiral, much like a watch spring, and are coiled so tightly that each bud is a solid little ball no larger than a BB.

The larger nut-like growths are seed pods that have persisted on the branches for an entire year, ever since the flowers were pollinated. They shrink in the warmth and dryness of fall and eventually explode with an audible "pop," scattering two shiny, black seeds up to 45 feet away. After lying on the ground for two years, if conditions are right—and if the seeds haven't been eaten by scavenging ruffed grouse or turkeys—they germinate.

Aphid Nurseries

A close examination of witch hazel's leaves and

Legends and Lore

Whether witch hazel derived its name from the Anglo-Saxon word "wych," meaning "bending" (the branches are very flexible), or from the fact that its forked branches were used as "divining" or "witching" rods to find water or precious metal beneath the ground, is not known. What has been ascertained is that regardless of its name, it is not a member of the hazelnut family. It does have a cousin, springtime witch hazel, which (true to its name) flowers in the early spring.

The velvety nut-like fruit of witch hazel ripens and expels its two shiny black seeds a full year after first appearing on the shrub. Look and listen for this event as you walk through the autumn woods. The empty husks remain on the shrub for another year.

The cone gall aphid causes the formation of cone-shaped galls on the upper surface of witch hazel leaves. The winged adult aphids escape through openings in the lower surfaces of the leaves in the autumn and spend the next stage of their life cycle on birch trees.

Witch hazel may ring a bell with readers over the age of 50 or so, as many of us grew up with bottles of an extraction from this plant (combined with more than a little alcohol) in our medicine cabinets. The Onondaga Indians of New York are credited with teaching settlers how to extract sap from witch hazel by boiling the leaves, twigs, and bark. When added to alcohol it was once a very popular hair tonic, liniment for aching muscles, and lotion for soothing skin irritations. The extract was also used as a cure for all sorts of ailments, from hemorrhoids to varicose veins, and to this day,

When the spiny witch-hazel gall aphid lays its eggs inside a witch hazel bud, the plant reacts by forming a spiny, pineapple-like gall that houses the developing insect.

even though chemical analysis confirms that it is inert, the extract is still available in many drugstores.

Whether celebrating its late-blooming, delicately aromatic flowers, the powerful explosion of its seeds, or its skin-healing powers, we are indebted to this humble shrub for putting life into a season not known for its vitality.

OCT

Seed Dispersal—*A Flower's Real Job*

What is the point of a flower? Its *raison d'etre*? Although flowers enrich our landscapes, they do not have humans in mind when they flash their brilliant colors and exude fragrant odors. These appealing qualities are a means to a much more important end—if flowers can attract insects, the insects pollinate them, and fertilization takes place, than the flowers have successfully performed their main job, which is to produce seeds.

Flowers don't produce just any size or shape of seed. Each species of flowering plant adapts their seeds in a way that maximizes the seeds' chances of getting away from the plant on which they grow. To disperse is to avoid the severe competition for sunlight, water, nutrients, and space that exists directly underneath the parent plant. The adaptations that seeds have evolved ensure that they can take advantage of a number of dispersal agents, including wind, water, animals—and yes, force—in the form of an "explosion."

Wind

Wind disperses more seeds than any other agent. One of the reasons for this is that many plants whose seeds are wind-dispersed produce large numbers of seeds that are very small and weigh very little.

Some of these small seeds have tufts of silky hairs, called *pappus*, attached to them. The pappus acts as a parachute, allowing the wind to carry the seed a considerable distance. Often the silky hairs of the pappus close up on rainy days and open back up as the air dries, for only then can they function as a dispersal mechanism. Cattails, dandelions, asters, goldenrod, thistles, poplar trees, and willows all produce seeds that are dispersed by the wind via these parachutes. One of the most familiar plants with wind-dispersed parachute seeds is common milkweed. Each seed has about

A single cattail spike contains about a million seeds, each of which possesses a silky parachute. Breezes over a one-acre cattail marsh disperse up to a trillion seeds.

900 silky hairs attached to it. These hairs are well designed for floating through the air—they are hollow and weigh very little. (Read more about common milkweed on p. 190.)

Wind-dispersed seeds that are relatively large tend to use "wings," not parachutes, to catch the breeze. These wing-like outgrowths have a slight pitch that causes the seeds to spin as they fall from the parent plant. The spinning lengthens the time the seed is in the air, just as the pappus does for a smaller seed, thereby allowing the wind to carry it further away. Both ash and maple tree seeds have these wings. Although they develop from woody cones, not flowers, the seeds of many pines, firs, spruces, and hemlocks also have wings.

Water

Many aquatic plants and plants that live near water have seeds that can float. One of the largest seeds in the world, the coconut, is dispersed in this way. Water lilies produce seeds that float away in little cases of jelly. After a while the jelly dissolves and the seeds fall to the bottom of the pond, where they then sprout and grow.

Animals

Animals are the agents of dispersal for a number of seeds, in a number of ways. Hitchhiking seeds such as stick-tights, or beggar's ticks, and burdock are familiar to humans. Often the fruit surrounding the seeds or the seeds themselves have hooked tips that get tangled in clothing, animal fur, or feathers. In this manner the seeds get dispersed, sometimes miles from where they first hitched a ride.

Some plants surround their seeds with brightly-colored and sweet-tasting pulp, which helps attract hungry animals. After being eaten and passed through the gut of the animal, the seeds are expelled in its droppings. Some seeds actually cannot germinate unless they have had their outer seed coat scraped as they travel through the digestive system of an animal. Many seeds are gathered and carried underground by ants, due to an appetizing fatty structure (the *elaiosome*) attached to the seed. After eating this morsel, the ants discard the seeds, leaving them in an ideal environment for germination.

Animals such as blue jays and squirrels collect huge numbers of seeds and nuts and bury them for future consumption. A study at Virginia Polytechnic Institute found that in 28 days, about 50 blue jays transported 150,000 acorns. Inevitably, some buried seeds are forgotten, and a portion of them germinate.

Explosion (Force)

Some plants don't depend on outside agents such as wind, water, or animals to disperse their seeds, and instead manage to perform this feat by themselves. There are several methods that plants use to fling their seeds out of their seed pods. All of them rely on the effect of evaporation of water in the seed pod. This time of year, for example,

The seeds of the maples and ashes (boxelder is pictured) are wind-dispersed, but are too large for a parachute. Instead, there is a "wing" attached to each seed, which the wind catches and twirls away from the parent plant.

witch hazel is shooting out two large, shiny black seeds from each of last year's capsules. The drying out of the capsule shrinks it, causing it to press on the seeds, which in turn, causes the seeds to be discharged with considerable force. (See more about witch hazel on p. 297.)

Jewelweed, also known as spotted touch-me-not, is famous for its seed pods, which burst open at the slightest touch when the seeds are ripe. The pods are made up of strap-shaped pieces, each of which is like a stretched spring. As the seeds become bigger and mature, the straps are stretched more and more. If an animal brushes against the pod at this point, it explodes; the straps swiftly recoil, sending the seeds flying away from the parent plant. (Read more about jewelweed on p. 264.)

A flowering plant's objective is to produce and disperse its seeds to a location that maximizes their chances of germinating, maturing, flowering, and

OCT

Brightly-colored, succulent fruit, such as pokeweed, is ir-resistible to many birds and animals. The indigestible seeds within these fruits pass through the digestive system of the consumer and are deposited in its droppings.

producing another generation of seeds. Because they are stationary, most plants are dependent upon wind, water, or animals for transporting their seeds, and the ways in which seeds have adapted to these dispersal agents are as creative, or more so, than any man-made invention.

OCT

quiescence

New England temperatures can fluctuate greatly in November. Within a given state, climatic conditions can be wildly erratic. First snows may fall in northern New England, yet balmy days are not unheard of. Throughout the Northeast most deciduous trees have lost their leaves and many animals have disappeared from sight. Reptiles and amphibians that didn't enter hibernation last month do so in November. Insect sightings become more and more scarce. The last of the migrant birds are leaving. Mammals that don't remain active through the winter have entered hibernation or dormancy. The natural world is bracing for winter.

nature notes

Here's a sampling of species that are breeding, migrating, preparing for winter, entering hibernation, or remaining active in November.

AMPHIBIANS

Northern Leopard Frog— *Hibernating*

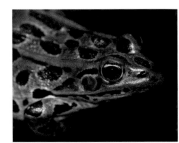

Northern leopard frog.

Northern leopard frogs, so-called because of the roundish, dark, leopard-like spots on their back, sides, and legs, spend the summer in fields and meadows. When winter approaches, they retreat to the mud at the bottom of ponds and streams. Here they hibernate, occasionally digging a small pit in which to spend the colder months. They have been observed making slight movements throughout the winter, although they don't appear to feed. Unlike the spring peeper, wood frog, and gray treefrog, the northern leopard frog cannot withstand being frozen.

Eastern newt.

Eastern Newt— *Remaining Active*

Most adult eastern newts spend the colder months underwater in streams or on the bottom of ponds, where they have been seen swimming throughout the winter. While not as active as during the summer months, they continue to feed and move about, and often gather in groups. (Read more about eastern newts on p. 137.)

REPTILES

Northern Watersnake —*Hibernating*

Northern watersnake.

Northern watersnakes are active from April to October. At this time of year many hibernate in crevices of rocky ledges, riverbanks, abandoned wells, and inside the lodges of muskrats and beavers.

North American Racer—*Hibernating*

As days shorten in late October, North American racers tend to migrate up forested slopes to communal den sites, where they overwinter. They often return to the same den year after year. Typically they can be found hibernating in deep rock crevices on southeast facing slopes, abandoned woodchuck burrows, and red fox dens. For weeks prior to entering hibernation, they bask outside the entrance to the den. They often hibernate with other species of snakes, including (within their range) timber rattlesnakes, copperheads, and eastern ratsnakes. North American racers are often the earliest spe-

North American racer.

cies of snake to emerge from their *hibernacula* in the spring. They tend to linger near the den until the danger of frost disappears and then proceed to mate in April or May.

BIRDS

White-Crowned Sparrow—*Migrating*
We see white-crowned sparrows as they migrate through our area on their way to and from their more northern breeding grounds on the Canadian tundra and their wintering grounds to the south and west of New England. (Their wintering range actually extends as far north as southern Connecticut). While stopping over to refuel, these sparrows can be observed hopping along

White-crowned sparrow.

NORTHERN BIRD IRRUPTION

Although pine siskins are found year-round in the northern coniferous forests of Vermont, New Hampshire, and Maine, they are an unpredictable winter visitor to the rest of New England.

Pine siskin.

There are a number of other seed-eating bird species (pine grosbeak, red crossbill, white-winged crossbill, and common redpoll) that don't normally overwinter in central and southern New England, but every so often their numbers explode at this time of year. This irregular influx of birds unusual to the area is referred to as an "irruption." It is thought that irruptions are related to the available supply (or lack thereof) of cones and other types of seeds in these birds' more northern wintering grounds. A failing seed crop in Canada can mean many unusual winter visitors to New England bird feeders. (See more on irruptions on p. 347)

the ground with both feet moving forward and backward simultaneously as they forage for insects and seeds.

Ruffed Grouse— *Growing Toe Fringes*
Some birds' arsenal of winter survival techniques include caching food in the fall, seeking tree cavities for protection from the cold, and flocking together. Others adapt physically to winter by fluffing their feathers, creating air pockets that will help insulate them, or by

■ Birds that Irrupt in New England

Pine grosbeak
Red crossbill
White-winged crossbill
Common redpoll
Pine siskin

NOV

going into a torpid state—a relatively brief period where their metabolism slows down in order to conserve energy.

Ruffed grouse—in addition to plunging into snow banks, which serve as snow caves on very cold nights (see p. 345)—grow fringe-like projections a mere sixteenth of an inch in length along both sides of each toe. The fringes resemble miniature combs. These projections increase the surface of the foot that is supported by the snow, thus serving as "snowshoes" for the grouse and keeping it on top of even the fluffiest snow. In addition, grouse spend a portion of every day "budding" in trees—perching on branches, often quite high up, gorging themselves on buds and bits of twigs. The toe fringes help the grouse grip icy or snowy branches more securely.

Biologists have found that grouse in the northern part of their range grow longer fringes than those in the southern part, confirming the fact that they are most likely an adaptation. When spring comes, these fringes are shed. (Read more about how snow affects wildlife on p. 392.)

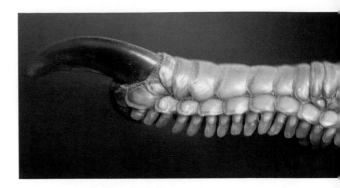

Ruffed grouse toe fringes.

Bird Predators—*Leaving Clues (Sheared Feathers)*

You can narrow down the identity of a predator when a large bird is killed and feathers are left at a kill site. After killing their avian prey, raptors often pluck the feathers out before consumption. This usually leaves creases at the quill end of the plucked feathers, where the raptor grasped them in order to pull them out, but leaves the tips of the feather shafts intact. (Frequently the feathers are arranged in circular fashion on the ground.)

On the other hand mammalian predators shear feathers off their prey, so examination shows the tips of the feather shafts missing. You often find clumps of feathers at canine kill sites, each clump having been sheared off en masse; these clumped feathers frequently remain

VISIBLE BIRD NESTS

VISIBLE BIRD NESTS

Red-eyed vireo nest.

After leaves have fallen is the ideal time to look for bird nests. If you take note of the building materials used, the habitat and specific location in which a nest is found, as well as its interior and exterior dimensions, it is often possible to determine the identity of the nest builder using field guides and nest keys. (Find out more about bird nests on p. 318.)

The carnivore-sheared feathers of a crow.

A turkey feather, plucked by a bird of prey.

BIRD DROPPINGS

Unlike mammals, which have two separate openings that evacuate solid waste and urine, birds have only one—a *cloaca*. Their droppings consist of both solid, undigested material as well as *uric acid*, resulting in the familiar whitewash often associated with gulls and birds of prey.

A great blue heron dropping.

Many larger birds, like the great blue heron, regurgitate most of their solid waste in the form of pellets, so that their droppings are almost entirely uric acid.

North American porcupine.

stuck together due to the predator's saliva. Each feather in the clump is cut at the same angle, distinguishing the canine predator from a member of the weasel family, whose shorter cuts leave different angles on the feathers' quills. Just to confuse the issue, canines also occasionally leave both sheared and plucked feathers. Other predators, such as bobcats and weasels, do not leave as clean a cut on the quill as canines, due to their tooth structure.

MAMMALS

North American Porcupine—*Breeding*

An elaborate courtship takes place between porcupines prior to mating in the fall. With considerable vocalization the male squirts urine all over his mate, thoroughly soaking her. When she is ready, mating takes place. There are only 8 to 10 hours during which time the female's body is physically receptive to the male. If fertilization takes place, one offspring is born the following spring.

Porcupine, White-Tailed Deer, Moose, Snowshoe Hare, and Cottontail Rabbit—*Shifting Diet*

Many of the herbivorous animals that remain active throughout the winter are forced to adapt to the changing climate by shifting their diets to food that is available. Porcupines spend the summer eating leaves, grasses, fruits, and flowers; in winter they consume woody vegetation, favoring the bark, buds, and needles of hemlock, as well as the bark of sugar maple and birch. White-tailed deer and moose switch from grasses, sedges, and other herbaceous plants to acorns, beechnuts, twigs, buds, and

A white-tailed deer eating acorns.

the bark of woody plants. Snowshoe hares and cottontail rabbits also go from succulent summer greens to the twigs, bark, and buds of woody shrubs and trees in winter.

NOV

American Beaver—*Storing Food and Renovating Lodge*

Late summer and fall is when beavers must prepare for the coming winter months, as their movement will soon be restricted to the water below the ice that forms on the pond's surface. While the pond is frozen, the only food available will be that which they have stored. Beavers eat two pounds of bark a day and there can be up to 10 beavers occupying a lodge over the winter, so an ample supply of food is essential to their survival. In November beavers cut and store a large pile of branches on the bottom of the pond, near their lodge. After felling a tree beavers remove the branches that are within reach.

A beaver's winter food supply pile, stacked with heavy logs on top to weight it down.

A beaver lodge with an adjacent winter food supply pile.

The interior chamber of a beaver lodge

A cross-section of a beaver lodge.

Usually they select branches that are 5 inches or less in diameter and then cut them into shorter lengths for easier transport. Their storage pile is usually visible, as it rises above the water level, and it is often weighted down with larger limbs. The presence or absence of this pile is a good indication of whether or not the lodge is active.

In addition to gathering a winter food supply and transporting it to their pond, beavers must also make any necessary repairs to their lodge and dam (and build both if establishing a new lodge). Although beaver lodges can be built on river banks or on the edges of ponds, or even tunneled into a bank, most are constructed in the middle of a pond, providing the beavers with maximum protection. A pile of branches is made and then the interior hollowed out with the aid of the beavers' incisors, providing a sleeping area and a platform on which to feed. Usually there are two or three underwater entrances. The pond's depth and the impenetrability of the lodge are both essential to the beaver's survival. There is so much to do that this normally nocturnal mammal is frequently active both day and night at this time of year. (Read more about American beavers on p. 321.)

White-Footed Deermouse and North American Deermouse—*Storing Food*

Because they do not hibernate, mice must store enough food to sustain themselves through the winter months. Berries, nuts, and seeds, particularly black cherry seeds, are a favorite of these omnivorous rodents and are stored under logs, behind bark, and in abandoned bird nests. While both of these species of mice cache food, the white-footed

A white-footed deermouse larder—black cherry seeds in a catbird nest.

deermouse usually has the larger larder. Impressive collections by a single white-footed deermouse include several quarts of clover seed and, in another instance, a peck of beechnuts.

American Black Bear—*Denning*

Black bears feed heavily in the fall, increasing their weight as much as 100 percent. As long as food is plentiful—abundant beechnuts and acorns, for instance—and temperatures are mild, bears remain active. When food becomes scarce they retire to their winter dens and enter a period of dormancy. In New England this can occur any time between October and December, but most often it begins in November. Females usually den first, as finding a protected spot is even more crucial to them than to the males (they give birth in these dens). Cavities under stumps, logs, and brush piles, and holes dug in banks are typical den sites. For bedding, bears drag leaves, twigs, wood chips, and bark into the sleeping area.

Hibernation for black bears is not the same as it is for rodents, such as jumping mice and woodchucks. Their body temperature drops only a few degrees below normal while their metabolic rate is cut in half. They do not defecate or urinate while in the den.

American black bear.

They can also awaken very quickly if danger threatens and occasionally will emerge from their dens during warm spells for a look around. Active bears in winter have been documented, even in northern New England. (See more about American black bears on p. 374.)

(See more about American black bears on p. 374.)

■ Mammal Winter Adaptations

Color of new coat changes dramatically with molt (brown to white)	Diet changes (herbaceous to woody) or herbivores store food	Hair structure changes with molt (solid to hollow)	Foot hair amount changes (increases)	Density of new coat changes with molt (denser in winter)
Long-tailed weasel	New England cottontail rabbit, eastern cottontail rabbit	White-tailed deer	Canadian lynx	American beaver
Ermine	North American porcupine	Moose	Eastern gray squirrel	Weasel family: long-tailed weasel, ermine, American mink, fisher, North American river otter, American marten
Snowshoe hare	Snowshoe hare		Red squirrel	Red fox, gray fox
	White-tailed deer		Eastern chipmunk	Coyote
	Moose		Fisher	
	American beaver			

NOV

Striped skunk.

Striped Skunk—*Entering Dormancy*

Striped skunks spend the fall eating and storing body fat to be used for fuel during cold periods in winter, when they may sleep for weeks at a time. The female and young of the year are the deepest sleepers, but even they are not true hibernators, for their body temperature drops just a few degrees. During warm spells striped skunk tracks can be found in the snow, and in the southern part of New England they remain active year-round.

Raccoon—*Dormant*

Raccoons generally become dormant at this time of year, and remain so through the winter in most

of New England, often holing up in tree cavities. During colder weather several raccoons may den together. Like the striped skunk, during periods of milder weather they become active; by March their tracks can be found with regularity.

Raccoon.

INSECTS & ARACHNIDS

Eastern Tent Caterpillar—*Laying Eggs*

Eastern tent caterpillar moths lay up to 2,500 eggs in the fall, often on the slender branches of black cherry or apple trees (the leaves of which the larvae will consume in the spring), as well as plants in the Rose family. The foam in which the eggs are laid forms a ring around the branch, firmly attaching the eggs to the tree. Once the foam hardens, it gives the

Eastern tent caterpillar egg mass.

egg mass a shiny, brown, varnished appearance. The mass is rain- and snow-proof—protection that is particularly advantageous, as the eastern tent caterpillar spends as long as nine months as an egg.

Cecropia Moth—*Spinning Cocoons and Pupating*

The silken protective covering of the pupal stage of a moth is referred to as a *cocoon* (a butterfly's pupal stage is referred to as a *chrysalis*). Cecropia moths are giant silk moths and spin the largest cocoons—about 3 inches long—in North America. As a cater-

Cecropia moth cocoon.

pillar it spins its cocoon lengthwise to the branch of a shrub or tree with modified salivary glands, using copious amounts of silk (this is where the term "silk moth" originated). It then pupates inside the cocoon, through the winter. Because of the strength of the silk from which it was woven and an insulating layer between its inner and outer walls, the cocoon is very tough and nearly impenetrable. While it protects the pupa very well, it makes escaping from the cocoon in the spring problematic for the moth, so before transforming from a caterpillar into a pupa, the caterpillar spins a one-way exit in the top of the cocoon. This allows the adult moth—which no longer possesses the chewing mouthparts it had as a larva—to squeeze its way out of the cocoon in the spring.

Mourning Cloak Butterfly—*Hibernating*

There are several species of butterflies in New England that overwinter as adults, hibernating under loose bark and similar protected spots. Among

them are the mourning cloak, eastern comma, question mark, and compton tortoiseshell. Because they do not go through a larval or pupal stage prior to emerging in the spring, they are one of the earliest butterflies you see when warm weather returns.

Mourning cloak butterfly.

Monarch Butterfly—*Arriving in Mexico*

Monarch butterflies born in the fall live six to nine months, as opposed to the four-to-six-week life span of those born in the spring and summer. The monarchs that begin their migration east of the Rocky Mountains in the fall migrate as far as 3,000 miles over a two-month period, arriving in one of about a dozen sites in the Transvolcanic Mountains of central Mexico in November. There they overwinter, clinging to the evergreen branches of oyamel fir

trees. Unbelievably, these butterflies arrive weighing more than when they began their migration. The nectar they drink along the migration route sustains them through the winter. Beginning in mid-March the monarchs will leave Mexico and head back to the northeastern United States, mating and dying along the way. Although these butterflies will never see New England again, some of their great-great grandchildren will. (Read more about monarch butterflies and their journey on p. 222.)

Monarch butterfly.

PLANTS & FUNGI

American Beech and Oaks—*Retaining Leaves*

Unlike most deciduous trees, which shed all their leaves in the fall, young oaks and beeches—both members of the Beech family—tend to retain their tan leaves well into the winter months.

American beech.

British soldiers.

British Soldiers

The lichen referred to as British soldiers, which bears a bright "redcoat" fruiting body of spores, consists of a symbiotic union of an alga (*Trebouxia erici*) and a fungus (*Cladonia cristatella*). Both contribute to their mutual survival, with the fungus retaining water and providing structure, and the green algae photosynthesizing necessary nutrients. Look for British soldiers on stumps and in poor soil. Spores are produced by their red tops—fruiting bodies called *apothecium*. (Find out more about lichens on p. 325.)

Snags serve an important function in an ecosystem, providing many species of wildlife food, shelter, nesting space, and a means of communication.

NOV

SNAGS IN SERVICE

A snag is any dead or dying standing tree. Tree snags serve as critical habitat for many species of wildlife in North America. They have a number of uses, including nesting cavities (woodpeckers, which excavate holes, and secondary cavity nesters, which use old woodpecker holes and natural cavities); hunting perches (raptors and insect-eating birds); resting and singing perches (songbirds); tool for communication (woodpeckers drumming); location for food storage (small mammals); protection from weather (many animals); food source (insect-eating birds); and roosting sites (birds of prey and many cavity-nesting birds). Over 85 species of birds, 35 of which occur in New England, use cavities in dead or dying trees.

Species	Snag Use
Double-crested cormorant	Nest (cavity)
Wood duck	Nest (cavity)
Hooded merganser	Nest (cavity)
Osprey	Nest, perch
American kestrel	Nest (cavity), roost, perch
Wild turkey	Perch
Eastern screech-owl	Nest (cavity), roost
Great horned owl	Nest (cavity)
Barred owl	Nest (cavity)
Belted kingfisher	Perch
Hairy and downy woodpeckers*	Food, nest (cavity), roost, communication
Pileated woodpecker*	Food, nest (cavity), roost, communication
Northern flicker*	Nest (cavity)
Great crested flycatcher	Nest (cavity), roost
Eastern kingbird	Perch, nest
Tree swallow	Nest (cavity), perch, roost
Black-capped chickadee*	Nest (cavity), roost
Tufted titmouse	Nest (cavity), roost
Red- and white-breasted nuthatches	Food, nest (cavity), roost
Brown creeper	Nest, food
House wren	Nest (cavity), food
Eastern bluebird	Nest (cavity)
Cedar waxwing	Perch
Raccoon	Den
Fisher	Den
North American porcupine	Den
Northern/southern flying squirrels	Nest
Bats	Roost
Snakes	Safe spot to shed
Opossum	Den
American black bear	Den
Mourning cloak butterfly	Hibernation site
Engraver beetle	Nursery

*Excavates holes

NOV

a closer look

With most deciduous trees lacking leaves and shrubs having lost their leaves, plants and animals are much easier to observe this time of year. **Sensitive** and **ostrich fertile fronds** (p. 324) stand out amongst their dying sterile fronds. Evergreen **club mosses** (p. 328) carpet the forest floor and **lichens** (p. 325) adorn rocks and trees. **Bird nests** (p. 318) are much more obvious without their leafy cover. **American beavers** (p. 321) are active even in daylight trying to repair dams and lodges for winter before ice forms, and **mudpuppies** (see below) are breeding on the bottoms of select bodies of water. Recently arrived **northern shrikes** (p. 316) are very obvious, perched on top of a prominent tree or post, searching for prey.

Mudpuppies—*They Don't Bark*

Even if you saw one, you might have trouble believing it was real: a creature scooped from the depths of the Connecticut River, Lake Champlain, or one of very few other bodies of water in New England, roughly a foot long, with four short legs, slimy skin, and gills like ostrich plumes coming out of both sides of its neck. This strange amphibian is none other than the aquatic salamander best known as a "mudpuppy." The main reason we rarely happen upon these bizarre-looking salamanders is that they are largely nocturnal. During the day, when we tend to be in the water, mudpuppies take refuge under rocks and logs on the bottom of ponds, lakes, rivers, and streams.

Debunking the Myths
As is the case with many animals that are rarely encountered, mudpuppies remain somewhat mysterious, and myths about them abound. Mudpup-pies were named perhaps because their external gills look something like "ears," and there exists an erroneous belief that they bark. Although rumor has it they occasionally squeak, salamanders are, for the most part, silent. Some fishermen claim mudpuppies are competitors that consume large numbers of fish. While they do eat small fish, a much larger portion of the mudpuppy's diet consists of aquatic insects, insect larvae, earthworms, crayfish, and snails. Lastly, contrary to the belief of some, mudpuppies are not venomous.

Most mudpuppies live to the west and south of New England, with the majority located in tributaries of the Mississippi River and the Great Lakes. While their historic range does extend to Lake Champlain, it is thought that mudpuppies were introduced to the Connecticut River—and the few other scattered locations where they are currently found in New England—through migration via canals or after being released from laboratories.

NOV

A Different Kind of Salamander

There are several characteristics (in addition to being much larger) that make the mudpuppy strikingly different from most other New England salamanders, one of which is that the mudpuppy remains in its larval form throughout its life. The metamorphosis that most frogs, toads, and salamanders experience never takes place in the mudpuppy. The large, maroon-colored, bushy gills remain intact, and although the mudpuppy does possess lungs, their primary function is thought to be related to positioning the salamander in the water by inflating and deflating, rather than obtaining oxygen.

Unlike most salamanders, mudpuppies never develop eyelids or molt their skin. The only noticeable change in their appearance takes place around two years of age, when they lose the two yellow stripes running from snout to tail that they have at birth. After this, the mudpuppy's back is rusty brown with scattered blue-black spots, and it is considered a juvenile. Mudpuppies are also unusual, though not unique among salamanders, in that they are active year-round. Ask your ice-fishing friends and you're bound to find someone who has hooked one at one time or another.

Breeding and Growing

Mudpuppies breed in the fall, between September and November. This month males are courting females on the bottom of rivers and streams. The males swim and walk all around, over and under the females, before depositing a packet of sperm on the bottom of the stream, which the female picks up into her *vent* (cloaca). She waits to lay her fertilized eggs until next spring, when she attaches 30 to 200 of them individually to the bottoms of rocks and logs. An area roughly 6 to 12 inches in diameter is peppered with her eggs. The female mudpuppy's maternal duties extend beyond egg laying; she remains with her eggs through their five-week to two-month incubation. Occasionally

---

] FAST FACTS [
Mudpuppy

▶ The mudpuppy is New England's only strictly aquatic salamander.

▶ Mudpuppies are also referred to as water dogs.

▶ During the day mudpuppies are usually found in deep water (up to 60 feet) that has rocks or other cover.

▶ Although they can swim quite well, mudpuppies tend to live on the bottom of their aquatic habitat, burrowing under submerged objects.

▶ In warm or oxygen-poor water, the mudpuppy's gills are more extensive and more brightly colored, whereas they are smaller and paler in oxygen-rich water.

▶ Mudpuppies are thought to migrate to shallow streams or the shallow parts of lakes and rivers to breed in groups.

▶ Mudpuppies are particularly sensitive to pollutants.

Mudpuppies are large, aquatic salamanders that are found in the Connecticut River, Lake Champlain, and a few other scattered bodies of water in New England. They grow to an average of 12 inches in length, but have been reported to reach 19 inches. (For a photo of a mudpuppy, see p. 117.)

she even stays with the larvae for a period of time after the eggs hatch.

The 1-inch larvae grow about 1½ inches a year. They are sexually mature at five years of age, when they are about 8 inches long, but it will be approximately three more years before they are full grown. The life span of a mudpuppy is a matter of uncertainty, but they are known to live at least six years. That is, of course, if they do not fall prey to large fish, raccoons or snapping turtles.

If your curiosity is piqued and you'd like to see a mudpuppy in the flesh, head for the Connecticut River or Lake Champlain and try looking in shallow water after sunset, when they are most likely to be foraging for food on the sandy bottom.

Northern Shrike—*The "Butcher Bird"*

Matching the bravest of the brave among birds of prey in deeds of daring, and no less relentless than reckless, the shrike compels that sort of deference, not unmixed with indignation, we are accustomed to accord to creatures of seeming insignificance whose exploits demand much strength, great spirit, and insatiate love for carnage. We cannot be indifferent to the marauder who takes his own wherever he finds it—a feudal baron who holds his own with undisputed sway— and an ogre whose victims are so many more than he can eat, that he actually keeps a private graveyard for the balance.

—ELLIOTT COUES, ORNITHOLOGIST AND AUTHOR

From its nickname "butcher bird" to its reputation as a wanton killer, the northern shrike is not one of the more stellar members of the avian community in the eyes of many. If you consider its behavior as an adaptation for survival, rather than a blood-thirsty personality trait, you may see this bird in a totally different light.

A Patient Hunter

During the winter months New Englanders often coexist with this Arctic visitor. If and when their food supply of small rodents and birds becomes scarce, northern shrikes venture as far south as necessary to find prey. Historic records show that the prey population of northern shrikes suffered low numbers on more or less a four-year cycle during the nineteenth and early twentieth centuries, resulting in heavy visitation by shrikes at those times, but in recent decades their visits have been relatively sporadic. Small numbers can occur in northern New England during the colder months, but many years shrike sightings are rare and occasionally entirely absent or localized.

Even in good years (for shrike-spotters, not shrikes), spotting a northern shrike is an exciting event. Often their perch of preference is the top of a tree from which they survey surrounding fields for the songbirds, voles, and mice that comprise their winter diet. If you see a bird that resembles a chunky mockingbird with a thick beak and a black band through the eye, sitting upright at the top of a tree adjacent to a field, chances are great that you've discovered a northern shrike. Northern shrikes have been known to perch for several days from the same tree, scanning the ground from on high, intent upon finding a rodent running through the fields or a hapless songbird feeding on grass seeds. Occasionally they have been seen hovering in the air in one spot for extended periods of time while they look for prey.

Storing Victims for Leaner Times

Although northern shrikes are predators and are said to have eyesight comparable to that of diurnal

The northern shrike is a predatory bird but is not considered a bird of prey because it lacks talons. It uses its curved beak as a means of delivering quick death blows to its victims.

raptors, they are not classified as birds of prey, primarily because they don't possess talons—the powerful claws raptors have that are so well adapted for killing. Instead, shrikes use their notched beak as a weapon. They have been known to eat birds larger than themselves, such as blue jays, mourning doves, and hairy woodpeckers, but also smaller species such as black-capped chickadees and American goldfinches. After spotting prey from a perch, a shrike makes a rapid dive from above, which usually ends with a stunning blow to the prey bird with the shrike's beak, often proving fatal. If this isn't the case, the shrike then kills the victim by severing several neck vertebrae with its beak.

Much of the shrike's reputation is built upon one of its more unusual habits, that of killing more prey than it can eat at one time. Rather than look with disdain upon this practice, consider the practicality of storing extra food for a time when food is a lot harder to come by, such as when snow covers the fields and hides the mice from view. North-

ern shrikes often hang their prey up to "cure" by impaling it on the spikes or thorns of trees such as hawthorn. If thorns are not available, shrikes have been known to use barbed wire or to wedge their prey in the crook of small branches. At one time this practice reminded people of their local meat market, where meat was hung from hooks to age, and led to the nickname butcher bird.

Arthur C. Bent was an ornithologist who collected various firsthand accounts of bird observations in the field from the late 1800s through the mid-1900s. He relates the tale of a farmer who, while shucking corn for days on end in his cornfield, was witness to a shrike who perched in a nearby tree, then would suddenly swoop down, pin a mouse, and quickly end its misery with a bite to its neck. The shrike would then fly off with the prey in its beak, across a nearby river into the adjacent woods. This occurred several times a day, for days on end. Later in the season the farmer happened to meet a logger who had been working in these same woods, and who told of a honey locust tree he had come upon that had mice hanging from thorns on nearly every branch.

The Hunter becoming the Hunted
The shrike has only recently gained a modicum of respect from humans. There was actually a time when house sparrows were protected, shortly after they were first introduced to North America in the mid-1800s, and northern shrikes in Boston apparently developed a taste for them. The shrikes became so abundant on Boston Common that men were employed to shoot them so as to preserve the house sparrows. One man killed over 50 northern shrikes in one winter. Today the shrike might well be considered heroic for preying on this bird, which competes for limited nesting sites with less common, native birds.

Bird Nests—
Building Home Sweet Home

Imagine attempting to build a house very much like the one you grew up in—roughly the same size and shape, and made of similar materials. Even if a builder drew up plans and walked you through the process step-by-step, and even if you possessed state-of–the-art tools, would you be up to the challenge? Most of us would not. And yet this is precisely what most birds do—minus the instructions, and the tools, to say nothing of hands.

Evolution of Warmth and Shelter
Birds have not always performed this remarkable feat. There was a time when they were cold-blooded, like their reptilian ancestors, and adapted easily to the surrounding temperature. Eventually, however, birds became warm-blooded, and it was then necessary for them to keep their eggs and hatchlings warm, all the while protecting them from predators and inclement weather. It was only a matter of time before nests evolved as an answer to most of these needs. Nests serve as a structure to hold the eggs as well as the nestlings, while the sparsely-feathered belly of the incubating bird serves as both a furnace and a roof, sealing in the heat that emanates from it. Nests also provide eggs and young with shelter from the elements and a degree of protection from predators, depending on where they are located and how well they are camouflaged.

Scrapes
The complexity of most creations increases over time, and bird nests are no exception to this evolutionary rule. The earliest nests are referred to as *scrapes*—mere depressions in the ground to which little, if any, nesting material is added. There still exist birds that use this form of nest—the eastern whip-poor-will and killdeer are two of them.

Platform Nests
Platform nests are a bit more advanced, in that nesting material, largely sticks, is gathered and assembled to form a plate-like collection located in a shrub or tree, which provides added protection from predators. Many herons and hawks build platform nests.

Cup Nests
Cup nests, with raised sides, are considered the most evolutionarily advanced form of nest. They are by far the most common type and are built by most *passerines*, or perching (song) birds. Cup nests are built in a variety of locations—sitting on top of forked branches or in the crotch of a tree (American robin); in amongst grasses and shrubs (song

NOV

Nests are thought to have evolved as a means of keeping eggs and nestlings warm; they entrap the parent bird's body heat. This is a photo of American robin nestlings.

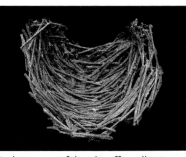

A chimney swift breaks off small twigs while on the wing and then glues them together with sticky saliva. In Asia, swifts build their nests entirely of hardened saliva, and a soup made from these nests is considered a delicacy.

Sometimes it is quite easy to determine the habitat in which a nest was built. Here you see how an urban northern mockingbird took advantage of discarded cigarette filters.

One bald eagle's nest measured 20 feet deep and 9½ feet in diameter.

A ruby-throated hummingbird's nest is roughly 1 inch deep by 1 inch wide, as the penny illustrates.

A gray catbird's nest usually contains shredded grape vine and is lined with rootlets.

sparrow); high in treetops (Blackburnian warbler); on the ground (ovenbird); and tucked behind loose bark (brown creeper); to name just a few examples.

Burrows and Tree Cavities
There are even species of birds that excavate burrows in sand banks (bank swallow, belted kingfisher)

as well as tree cavities (woodpeckers) in which they lay their eggs.

Following the Crowd
Wherever bird nests are located and whatever form they take, they are species-specific. In other words, birds of the same species build nests very similar to

each other and quite different from other species' nests. In general, the nests of a given species of bird tend to have roughly the same dimensions, consist of the same kind of material, and are usually located in similar habitats.

For instance, most red-winged blackbirds nest in marshes, preferably near or over water, weaving their 4-inch-diameter nests out of sedge leaves, rushes, grasses, and rootlets, and binding them to surrounding vegetation with milkweed fibers. There are always exceptions, but if someone brings you a nest and you know where it was built (habitat as well as specific location), what material was used in its construction as well as its dimensions, identification of the builder is often possible, especially with Richard Headstream's *A Complete Field Guide to Nests in the United States* (a dichotomous key) in one hand and Hal Harrison's *Peterson Field Guide: Eastern Birds' Nests* (contains photographs) in the other.

Building Materials

The typical songbird nest takes approximately six days to complete—three days spent on the exterior and three days on the interior. Nesting material consists of whatever is available in the habitat of choice, including grasses, twigs, and plant fibers. A quick glance at any nest tells you that the materials used for the lining are much finer and softer than those used for the base and exterior. While twigs often form the base, hair, pine needles, fine grasses, and thistledown are often the surface on which eggs and nestlings rest. There are certain species that seem to have a predilection for certain building materials, including: great crested flycatcher—shed snake skins; wood thrush—rootlets; chipping sparrow—horsehair; ovenbird—dried spore stems of mosses; ruby-throated hummingbird—lichens attached with spider silk; yellow warbler and American goldfinch—plant down from willows, poplars, and thistles; and chimney swifts—sticky saliva (their own) with which sticks are glued together.

Sometimes an inspector of a bird nest is rewarded with the unexpected. For example, the following materials have been found incorporated into osprey nests: shirts, bath towels, arrows, a rake, a broom, barrel staves, a fish net, a toy boat, light bulbs, old shoes, a straw hat, a rag doll, bottles, and tin cans. Off the coast of Labrador, near a sunken trading vessel, a nest of double-crested cormorants (fish-eating birds known for their diving prowess) was found to contain pocketknives, men's pipes, hair pins, and ladies' combs, all of which had been retrieved by the birds from the sunken ship. Equally impressive was the white-throated raven nest in Texas that consisted of nothing but interwoven barbed wire.

Moving House

Most birds build a new nest not just every year, but for every brood, and some birds manage to fit in two or three broods a summer. This can mean a lot of work for the parents; one patient researcher counted more than 1,200 trips a barn swallow made carrying mud to its nest. Sometimes a species that nests multiple times in a given summer, such as an American robin, will reuse its nest, but this is the exception for most songbirds.

Eagles, ospreys, and some hawks, on the other hand, usually return to the same nest year after year, repairing and adding on to it until, in some instances, it collapses from its own weight. Some birds of prey, however, take over nests built by other birds of prey. One such nest constructed by Cooper's hawks was occupied the next year by a pair of great horned owls, the following year by red-tailed hawks, and the next year by barred owls.

A bird nest is worthy of close examination in the fall or winter after all breeding birds have finished nesting. (A federal permit must be obtained in order to legally possess a bird's nest.) By this month, you can safely assume that the feathered occupants have left, but watch out—you wouldn't

▶ The average songbird nest is constructed in less than a week.

▶ For protection, nests are often located in inaccessible locations such as rock cliffs (raven) or at the tips of slender branches (Baltimore oriole).

▶ Smaller birds sometimes nest in the lower parts of the nests of larger predatory birds. Common grackles have been found nesting in active osprey nests, house sparrows in an occupied great horned owl nest, and mourning doves in a heron nest.

▶ A pair of great horned owls and a pair of bald eagles were observed sharing a bald eagle nest and incubating their respective eggs within feet of each other.

▶ The largest nests on record in North America were built by bald eagles. One such nest in Ohio was occupied by bald eagles for 35 years and was estimated to weigh about 2 tons when it fell to the ground.

▶ A pair of canyon wrens in California built a nest inside an office building, constructing it totally out of office supplies (paper clips, straight pins, safety pins, rubber bands, thumbtacks, and paper fasteners).

be the first person to be surprised by the sudden appearance of a resident white-footed deermouse who has made a cozy winter shelter by roofing over an abandoned bird nest.

American Beaver Adaptations—
Clever and Comfortable on Land and Underwater

Picture a beaver silently gliding across a pond, head tilted ever so slightly upward as it cuts a smooth path through the water. Something on shore startles it, and immediately the beaver brings its tail up, slaps it down on the water, and dives below the surface. As soon as its nose hits the water its body automatically adapts and adjusts to the new environment below the surface.

The beaver, North America's largest rodent, is extremely well adapted to its semi-aquatic life.

So, What Happens?
Valves in the beaver's ears and nose instantly close, sealing out all water. A transparent third eyelid, a *nictitating membrane*, slides across both eyes, providing protection from debris. Loose upper lips close behind the beaver's four front incisors permitting underwater gnawing without water or splinters entering its mouth. The beaver's large, webbed hind feet propel it forward at speeds up to 5 miles per hour. Its smaller and more dexterous forefeet, which aren't webbed, are balled up against its chest while swimming (above the surface they are used to carry mud and sticks, dig

NOV

The beaver's sense of smell is acute and essential to its nocturnal habits. Research shows that beavers can identify palatable trees by smell alone. In addition, their primary means of communication with each other is through chemicals left on *scent mounds*—piles of mud and vegetation marked with oil and pungent *castoreum* from their castor glands.

Beavers' incisors are constantly growing. It is necessary for them to chew wood as well as grind their incisors against each other in order to keep them filed down.

Special Out-of-Water Features
Specialization of body parts is not limited to adaptations for an aquatic existence. All rodents possess two pairs of incisors at the front of their jaws, which are constantly growing throughout the life of the animals. A beaver's incisors are particularly large, orange, and prominent. After looking at these teeth, the discovery that a beaver is an herbivore, consuming only vegetation, often comes as a surprise. The outer orange material is hard enamel, behind which there is a softer layer of dentin. As the beaver chews on hard bark, the inside layer wears down faster than the outside, resulting in very sharp, chisel-edged incisors, well suited for chewing through wood. The upper and lower incisors also keep each other paired down. If one of these teeth is injured or lost, the opposite incisor (above or below the missing tooth) continues to grow, sometimes in a circular fashion, which ultimately causes the beaver's death through starvation or piercing of the brain cavity.

The webbing between the toes of a beaver's hind feet enhances its ability to swim but the

burrows, handle food, and comb fur). The broad, flat, scaly tail regulates the beaver's temperature, stores fat, and performs as a rudder, helping the beaver swim in the desired direction. It also is used to deliver a warning signal when it is slapped against the water.

The beaver's skin remains dry, thanks to the dense wooly underfur and the water-repellent oil that the beaver has applied to its fur. If it chooses, the beaver can remain submerged for up to 15 minutes (although one or two minutes is more typical) and swim as far as half a mile underwater. This is due in part to its ability to use as much as 75 percent of the oxygen it breathes in as opposed to the 15 percent humans use. Beavers also seem to be able to increase the oxygen flow to their brain, tolerate high levels of carbon dioxide, and reduce their heart rate when diving.

Just one of these adaptations would be impressive. Together they have enabled the beaver to adapt to a mostly aquatic existence.

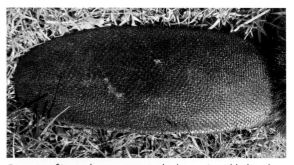

Because of its scaly appearance, the beaver's tail led to the beaver's misclassification as a fish many, many years ago.

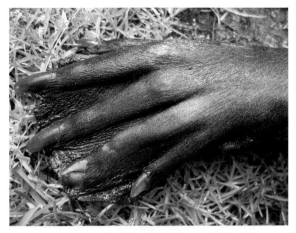

Here you see the webbed hind foot of an American beaver. A specialized split nail (see close-up below) on each hind foot allows the beaver to comb debris and parasites out of its fur, as well as apply water-repelling oil to its coat.

] FAST FACTS [
Beaver Adaptations

▶ The beaver's tail is used as a prop for balance when cutting down trees.

▶ The beaver's tail acts as a heat exchanger. In the summer a beaver loses up to 25 percent of its body heat via its tail; in the winter it only loses 2 percent.

▶ All beavers possess *two castor glands*, often called musk glands or castors. They use the secretion, or *castoreum*, from these glands to mark scent mounds in their territory.

▶ The beaver produces dilute urine, which is concentrated in the castor glands, and becomes castoreum.

▶ A beaver's intestine is very long—about six times its body length—reflecting its herbivorous diet.

▶ A beaver's sense organs are aligned in a row so that it swims with only its nostrils, eyes, and ears above the waterline, allowing it to escape detection by predators.

▶ The body of a beaver is tear-drop-shaped for maximum streamlined maneuverability in the water.

▶ The beaver's *cloaca* is the only opening to serve the reproductive tract, excretion, and scent glands. This is thought to be an adaptation for minimizing risk of infection from the water.

hind feet have other uses. A great deal of debris accumulates in a beaver's fur and a large amount of time is spent removing it. In addition, beavers are known to be hosts of a number of parasites that reside in their coats. The beaver rids itself of the debris as well as the parasites primarily with the inner toe on each of its hind feet. The nails on these toes are split in such a way that they make very effective combs. The beaver uses these nails to preen itself, as well as to apply waterproofing oil from its oil glands to its fur.

If you were to design a creature that was supremely adapted to its environment in every conceivable way, you would be hard-pressed to surpass the beaver. Eyes, ears, nose, teeth, feet, tail, and fur are all specialized to enable the beaver to thrive, both in and out of water.

Fertile Fronds—
Reproductive Strategies Exposed

If you've been near a stream or wetland recently, chances are that you've encountered the reproductive remnants of ferns, perhaps without recognizing them as such, for their resemblance to the leafy, green fern fronds of summer is negligible. As non-flowering plants, ferns do not develop seeds; instead, they bear spores. In a majority of ferns, these spores are located on the underside of the leafy fronds. (See p. 212 for the parts of the fern.) Many of these fern fronds die back in the fall after dispersing their spores. In the spring new fern fronds, tightly coiled into fiddleheads (see p. 50), emerge and unfurl.

Holding on through the Winter

There are a few species of ferns, however, which do not bear spores on the underside of their sterile, green fronds, but instead develop separate structures called *fertile fronds* on which their spores are borne. They do not look anything like the green fronds we're familiar with; fertile fronds are usually some shade of brown and often have a woody appearance. Two common New England species that possess these highly specialized fertile fronds are ostrich fern and sensitive fern. During the summer these ferns form both *sterile* (leafy) fronds and *fertile* (spore-bearing) fronds. While their sterile fronds die back in the fall, the fertile fronds persist through the winter, releasing spores in the early spring before new fronds appear and make wind dispersal more difficult. It is these fertile fronds that you may notice this time of year, as they're no longer hidden by the green fronds of summer.

Ostrich fern favors the flood plain of rivers, where its tall, gracefully arching sterile fronds do, indeed, resemble ostrich plumes (see p. 211). Although all ferns appear as curled-up fiddleheads in the spring, it is those of this particular species

The ostrich fern's fertile frond contains thousands of spores that are dispersed in the spring.

The spore-bearing fertile fron[d] of sensitive or bead fern pers[ists] through the winter.

that are foraged and eaten. The fertile fronds of ostrich fern also look something like feathers, and their spores are contained inside modified structures that vaguely resemble segmented worms. The fertile fronds are initially green but turn brown by summer's end.

Sensitive fern is so-called because of its sensitivity to frost. Green, sterile fronds immediately turn brown and die back with the first frost, leaving only the erect, brown, fertile fronds. It is the size and shape of the spore-bearing structures on these fronds that give sensitive fern its other common name: bead fern. When these "beads" mature and dry in the spring, they burst, scattering thousands of chlorophyll-containing green spores.

If you have access to a microscope or strong hand lens, you might enjoy getting a closer look at the individual spores. Inside each "bead" you will find many spore cases, or *sporangia*. They are round, with a distinctive ring of cells, or *annulus*, encircling three-quarters of their perimeter. If you gently break open these sporangia, you find individual spores. With an electron microscope, the different shapes and structures of different species' spores are visible—some are roundish, some elliptical, and some kidney-shaped. Many have intricate lattice work, spines, or crests on their surface and are quite beautiful. The appearance of each species' spores is unique to that species.

From Thousands to Few
A single fern can produce thousands of spores, only a small percentage of which develop into spore-producing ferns. Spores are viable from a few days to a few months, but they have the challenge of finding just the right conditions that allow them to successfully develop two very different stages or "alternating generations." In the best of circumstances, the spore develops into a minute, heart-shaped plant called a *gametophyte* or *prothallus*—the sexual

stage of a fern's life cycle. Fertilization must then take place between two gametophytes in order for the second stage, or *sporophyte* (spore-producing stage), which we recognize and refer to as a fern, to form. These processes need a very specific set of conditions, including a certain humidity, ground moisture, temperature, and proximity of gametophytes, in order to be successful. Just as ground-nesting birds lay large clutches of eggs due to the vulnerability of their young to predation, ferns produce a plethora of spores in order to assure that a fraction of them will survive to reproduce.

Lichens—*Hardy, Ancient, Beyond Classification*

Tiny though they are, lichens cover 8 percent of the Earth's surface—more than tropical rainforests. They are found on some of the most inhospitable surfaces, or *substrates*, known to man; lichens are the dominant form of vegetation in the Arctic, as well as the Antarctic. Although their growth is slow (a lichen in northern Alaska was documented as growing an eighth of an inch a century), they can live thousands of years.

What Are They?
The more one learns about lichens, the more complicated they become. Even classifying them is a tricky business. Lichens lack flowers, leaves, and roots, so technically, they are not a plant; neither are they considered part of the animal kingdom. Lichens are a separate category of organism, which taxonomically falls under the umbrella of fungi (which are also neither plants nor animals).

Most lichens are composed of fungi and algae. Usually the algae are sandwiched between two layers of fungi. There is a *symbiotic* (mutually beneficial) relationship between these two organ-

NOV

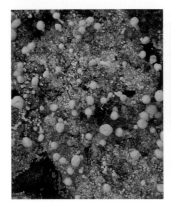

Fruticose lichen.

Crustose lichen.

rock, tree, or ground, and resembles spray paint); *foliose* (leaf-like appearance, often with lobes); and *fruticose* (bushy growth). Both the lichen's form, as well as the sub-

Foliose lichen.

isms, with the fungi getting the lion's share of the benefits. Lacking *chloroplasts* and the pigment necessary for photosynthesis, fungi cannot make their own food and therefore need to locate and attach themselves to a food source. Often this source is organic material, such as rotting logs or living trees; in the case of lichens, fungi rely on photosynthetic algae for their food.

Fungi provide structure as well as water retention for lichens. They also protect the algae, which can be quite sensitive, from harmful ultraviolet (UV) rays. When the weather is dry (and thus, possibly sunny), the fungi (which surround the algae in a majority of lichens) is usually opaque, and thus protects the algae within from UV light. When it rains, the *thallus*, or lichen body, becomes translucent, allowing any available light to penetrate through to its photosynthetic partner, which utilizes the light in manufacturing food. This characteristic explains why lichens change color. The translucence of wet fungi allows the colorful algae within to be seen, and thus, most lichens appear more vibrantly colored when it rains.

Three Basic Forms
For simplification, lichenologists have grouped lichens into three basic categories based on their form: *crustose* (attaches very closely to surface of

strate on which it grows (ground, tree bark, or rocks), are helpful identification characteristics.

Reproduction
Lichens reproduce both sexually and asexually (vegetatively). In order for a lichen to reproduce sexually, a fungal spore must land on an alga cell. The chances of this happening are thought to be quite limited. (This process has actually never been observed, in or out of the laboratory.)

Vegetative reproduction can happen in one of two ways. One is for a fragment of the lichen, containing both fungal and algal cells, to separate and fall from the lichen. A second way is for special reproductive structures (*soredia* and *isidia*), containing both fungal and algal cells, to detach from the lichen and land on the right substrate.

Human Applications
Lichens can live where other forms of life cannot, in part, because of the acids and pigments they produce to compete in a hostile environment. Their talents include far more than breaking down rocks with acids, and humans have adapted many of them for their own use. The chemicals lichens produce to repel insects have been found to be effective bacteria-fighting antibiotics for humans. (When you're next in the grocery store, check

Bristly beard lichen.

the list of ingredients in natural deodorants; you will find lichens listed in many of them.) Chemicals produced by lichens to inhibit the growth of neighboring lichens have been utilized in natural herbicides. Thousands of tons of lichens are harvested annually for use as fixatives for perfumes. In India, foods such as curries and masalas are flavored with lichens. Up until fairly recently, lichens were the source for the dye in Harris tweed; their chemicals not only colored the wool, but mothproofed it as well.

In addition, lichens are used by many kinds of animals in New England for food and shelter. White tailed deer and moose feed on lichens that grow mainly on trees, while slugs, snails, mites, and snow fleas feed mainly on terrestrial lichens. Northern flying squirrels feed on and line their cavity nests with lichen, and over 50 species of birds use lichen as nest-building material.

Lichens absorb all their nutrients directly from air and rainwater. Unfortunately, they have no filtering device, and therefore absorb any and all pollutants the air and water contain. Lichens have no way of getting rid of these pollutants, a fact which humans use to their advantage. By monitoring the presence or absence, size, and health of lichens, scientists can monitor pollution very

► Neither the alga nor fungus species that are found in lichens could grow on their own.

► Lichens are named (scientifically) for the fungus component, for it determines the form the lichen takes.

► Many lichens reproduce asexually, through fragmentation or by dispersing *soredia*, diaspores containing both algal and fungal cells. Lichen fungi also reproduce sexually, dispersing spores that must then unite with algal partners in order to form another lichen.

► Lichens do not have roots, and therefore do not need a constant supply of water. Consequently, they can tolerate longer dry periods than most green plants. Because of this they are able to grow on surfaces where other plants could not, such as bare rock.

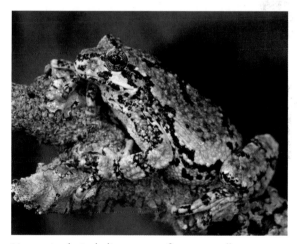

Many animals, including gray treefrogs, are well camouflaged on lichen-covered trees.

accurately. David Richards, of St. Mary's University in Halifax, Nova Scotia, refers to *Parmelia caperata* as the "30-mile-per-hour lichen," in reference to the fact that along roads with higher speed limits and more traffic, these lichens disappear, as they cannot survive the car fumes.

NOV

Clubmosses—*Relics of Ancient Forests*

The primary characteristic that distinguishes ferns from many plants is that they produce spores, not seeds (or flowers). They are not the only group of spore-producing plants, however. The "fern allies" or clubmosses, are another; they consist of plants which, while not ferns, were believed to be close relatives. Relatively recent DNA research has resulted in a regrouping of these fern relatives, due to the fact that many of them have been found to be only distantly related to ferns. They are now commonly referred to as clubmosses.

Currently botanists divide all plants with vascular tissue (a system that transports water and nutrients) into three different groups. The first group (*Spermatophyta*) has not changed—it consists of all seed-producing plants. The other two groups consist of spore-producing plants: the *Monilophyta*—true ferns and horsetails; and the *Lycophyta*—clubmosses, spikemosses, and quillworts. A closer look at clubmosses examines some of the evergreen plant life of the forest floor.

Ankle-High "Conifers"

Most of us are familiar with clubmosses, even though we may not know them by this name. Perhaps you are acquainted with "princess pines." If so, you have met a clubmoss. When you walk through the woods, particularly where the soil is acidic and conifers such as eastern hemlock are growing, there are often large expanses of the forest floor that are green year-round. This miniature forest of ankle-high evergreen plants usually consists of clubmosses. At first glance they may remind you of miniature conifers such as pines and spruces. Apparently the botanist who first discovered and named this group of plants felt they resembled mosses. (While mosses do produce spores, they do not have a vascular system, and thus are in an entirely different group.)

Bristly clubmoss is a common plant in acidic, coniferous woods, forming large colonies of erect branches that rise from a running stem. When young, the upright stems or branches are unforked, but as the plant ages it may divide. If you look closely, you can see where leaf constrictions indicate annual growth. The cone of bristly clubmoss is terminal and does not have a stalk; rather, it forms where the leafy tip of the branch ends.

Clubmosses were not always so diminutive. Long before dinosaurs roamed the earth there were forests of tree-size clubmosses. Today there are roughly 12 species (and many hybrids) of much smaller clubmosses in the northeastern United States. Most have horizontal stems, either above or

Running clubmoss, also known as wolf's claw or staghorn clubmoss, is one of the world's most widely distributed plants. Its forked branches have dense leaves that each have long, whitish to colorless, hair-like tips. Like bristly clubmoss, the leaves produced later in the season are more closely placed than those formed earlier in the season, producing annual growth markers in the form of these compressed leaves. The cones of running clubmoss are borne on long, slender stalks.

The branches of southern ground cedar or fan clubmoss are two-parted, flattened and fan-shaped, giving the plant a very distinctive look. This species can be found in deciduous as well as coniferous woods. Three or four cones are found at the tip of long stalks.

below ground, which grow longer each year, sending up erect branches as they do so.

An Infinite Number of Uses
The name clubmoss is derived from the club-like shape of the plant's fertile stalk. Referred to as the *strobilis*, this spore-bearing club often develops at

the tip of vegetative, leafy branches. The process of developing from a spore to a mature clubmoss with strobili takes approximately 20 years. Within recent memory many species of clubmoss were collected for Christmas decorations, but partially because of the time it takes a plant to establish itself, they are now protected in many states.

When the spores mature in the fall, enormous amounts of them are released—a light tap on a clubmoss strobilis produces a visible yellow cloud of spores. Over the years clubmoss spores have

NOV

Princess pine or tree clubmoss looks just like one of its more familiar common names—a miniature pine tree with spreading branches bearing needle-like leaves. Its cones develop at the tips of the branches, but lack stalks. Three varieties of tree clubmoss exist.

been used in a variety of ways. Because they are of such uniform size, they were once used as an aid to microscopic measurement. As soon as it was discovered that the spores repelled water, they were used to coat pills and stop the bleeding of wounds. Another property of clubmoss spores is their high flammability. They were used in the early days of photography as a source of flash, as well as for fireworks and theatrical displays.

▶ Clubmosses are protected from herbivores by chemicals called *alkaloids* (nicotine and caffeine are examples of alkaloids) that cause them to taste bad.

▶ The remains of ancient giant clubmosses in their petrified form constitute much of the coal we use today.

▶ Clubmoss has a stem that runs along the ground and can reach a length of up to 4 feet when fully grown.

▶ A powder known as *lycopodium*, consisting of dried clubmoss spores, was used in Victorian theaters to produce stage lightning, since the high aluminum content of the plant causes a bright, fast-burning fire when ignited. It was also used as a baby powder and even as an absorbent dusting powder in the early days of surgery.

▶ The classification of clubmosses is still being debated by botanists.

Reminder of Generations Past
These small evergreen plants are well adapted for winter. Their leaves are covered with a waxy material, minimizing water loss, essential for winter months when water is in short supply. In addition, clubmosses contain an antifreeze-like substance that prevents their cells from freezing and bursting.

When it's cold outside and you come upon a "forest" of these hardy plants, let them be a reminder of warmer days gone by. Hundreds of millions of years ago when the earth was steamy and plants thrived, clubmosses were among the dominant plants on earth, with some species measuring over 100 feet tall.

NOV

signage

Many creatures have disappeared from sight. Those that remain include "feeder birds," whose interactions present an opportunity to assess hierarchy within a flock as well as between species. While there are fewer mammals around, the signs of those that remain active are more evident, and change daily. As soon as the first snow falls, animal signs—be they tracks, scat, scent posting, feeding holes, or markings of any kind—offer the observer an intimate look at animal activity. Plants, for the most part, are dormant, with next year's growth safely sealed within protective buds, awaiting lengthening days.

DECEMBER
nature notes

Here's a sampling of species that are preparing for winter, entering hibernation, waking periodically, remaining active, and retaining leaves in December.

AMPHIBIANS

Wood frog.

Wood Frog—*Hibernating*

Wood frogs are now hibernating under the leaf litter, rocks, and logs on the forest floor. New England is in the southern part of their range, which extends further north than any other cold-blooded amphibian or reptile—beyond the treeline in Alaska and Canada to within the Arctic Circle. Because of this cold tolerance, they are one of the first frogs to emerge from hibernation and migrate to vernal pools to breed in the spring. The wood frog has been seen migrating as early as February in Connecticut, even crossing over ice to get to open water where it calls for a mate. (Read more about wood frogs on p. 343.)

Four-Toed Salamander—*Hibernating*

The four-toed salamander, having bred in the fall, often spends the winter hibernating in the decaying roots of trees. Even during the warmer months, this salamander is hard to find, due to its secret and nocturnal habits. Look for it in sphagnum moss of swampy areas.

Four-toed salamander.

The four-toed salamander is known for its habit of shedding its tail when a predator attacks it. The accepted theory is that the wiggling, detached tail distracts the predator while the salamander escapes. The tail grows back.

REPTILES

DeKay's brownsnake.

DeKay's Brown-snake—*Hibernating*

Often many DeKay's brownsnakes hibernate together during the winter in mammal burrows, decaying logs, rock crevices, or beneath buildings below the frost line. Common gartersnakes frequently share these communal dens with DeKay's brownsnakes. The advantage in forming these clusters is that it reduces water loss from the snakes' bodies.

Painted turtle.

Painted Turtle—
Hibernating

These aquatic turtles remain active longer into the winter than most other freshwater species of turtles, even in northern New England. The length of their hibernation in the mud at the bottom of ponds ranges from one to more than four months, depending on how far south or north they are (their range extends from southern Canada to Louisiana). Painted turtles have been seen basking during warm spells in winter when the water temperature is above 50°F, as well as swimming under the ice during cold spells. (Read more about painted turtles on pp. 58 and 96.)

BIRDS

Hairy and Downy Woodpecker—
Staying Year-Round

Many people have trouble distinguishing between our two most common woodpeckers— the hairy and the downy. The hairy woodpecker is very similar in plumage to the downy woodpecker, but is larger, has a proportionately larger bill, a longer and more dis-

Male downy woodpecker (left) and male hairy woodpecker (right) on the same tree.

tinct black mark on the shoulder, and, in most populations, has completely white outer tail feathers (downy woodpecker outer tail feathers are barred in black, which gives them a spotted appearance). If you can see both species together these differences stand out. Hairy and downy woodpeckers occur together throughout most of their respective ranges. Look for downy woodpeckers on smaller branches; hairy woodpeckers tend to spend more time on tree trunks.

Wild Turkey—*Sign (Scratching)*

The wild turkey is non-migratory, although it does make seasonal shifts, changing its range according to the availability of food and snow depth. Turkeys forage year-round on the ground looking for mast (acorns and nuts), and scratching through the snow in winter into the leaf litter below.

Turkey scratching.

Periods of deep snow are particularly difficult for wild turkeys, as they are not equipped to forage well in these conditions. When several feet of snow lie on the ground, it is not unusual to see them perched in shrubs or trees, particularly apple, looking for food. Fortunately, turkeys can go without food for about a week, even in the middle of winter, without damaging effects. They seek out wind-swept fields and other areas where the snow is not as deep. Often you can find signs of wild turkeys near spring-fed brooks, which because of warmer spring water, don't freeze as readily as surface-water brooks. Both water and grit, which turkeys need in their gizzards to help grind up the hard nuts and food that they eat, are available in these areas. The significant size of their tracks (4 to 5 inches in width and length) alerts you to their presence.

Pileated Woodpecker—
Sign (Feeding Holes)

A favorite meal for the pileated woodpecker, New England's largest woodpecker, is carpenter ants, which often live and form galleries in the center of living trees. This center, or heartwood, is dead; its only function is to support the tree. When pileated woodpeckers feed they excavate large holes

Pileated woodpecker holes.

that extend into the tree's *heartwood*, where they find and scrape out carpenter ants with their long, reverse-barbed tongues. You often see these rectangular holes in a vertical line up a trunk, one above the other. When the ants are consumed and the woodpecker is long gone, white-footed deermice may take up residence in these holes.

Cooper's Hawk—*Seeking Feathered Prey*

Along with sharp-shinned hawks and goshawks, Cooper's hawks are classified as *accipiters*—birds of

Cooper's hawk with winter victim. This pileated woodpecker is quite a bit larger than most of the birds this accipiter preys upon.

prey with short, broad, rounded wings and a long tail that helps them maneuver in the forests where they often reside. Long legs and sharp talons, along with powerful flight capabilities, enable them to ambush their prey—often birds, small and mid-size, as well as small rodents. Most female raptors are larger than their male counterparts; this size difference is particularly pronounced with Cooper's hawks. (See more about birds of prey on p. 249.)

Tufted Titmouse—*Remaining Year-Round*

It is not surprising to find that the spritely tufted titmouse is in the same family as the black-capped chickadee. Both are lively, industrious, little birds that frequent bird feeders year-round. The chickadees have a dark cap and bib, while the titmice have a crest. Both species start to move about in family groups in the fall. Prior to the 1940s the farthest north tufted

Tufted titmouse.

titmice ranged in the eastern United States was southern Pennsylvania and New Jersey. An expansion further north into New England has been attributed to an increased number of winter bird feeders, global warming, and farmland reverting to forest.

Unlike chickadees, tufted titmouse pairs do not join other titmice and form larger flocks outside of the breeding season. Instead, most remain on their territory as a pair. Frequently one of their young from the current year remains with them and occasionally other juveniles join them. Tufted titmice do, however, form mixed-species flocks with chickadees, nuthatches, and small woodpeckers during the winter months.

BIRD BILLS

Most birds catch and hold their food with their bill. Because their diets are varied, birds have evolved different-shaped bills. Raptors, or birds of prey (hawks, falcons, eagles, owls, ospreys), have sharply hooked bills equipped to tear flesh. Foliage gleaners (brown creeper, nuthatches, many warblers, vireos, orioles) have relatively long, thin bills with which they can reach to pick an insect off a leaf, or probe under loose bark. Seed eaters (finches, grosbeaks, cardinals, sparrows) have short, thick bills that can crush hard seeds. Birds that catch and eat flying insects (swallows, flycatchers, swifts, whip-poor-wills) have flat bills with a broad base.

Left to right: The red-tailed hawk (raptor), brown creeper (foliage gleaner), purple finch (seed eater), and tree swallow (insect eater) have developed different-shaped bills to best suit their diet.

Red fox tracks in the snow and along a log, and the bottom of a red fox's foot, showing the hair that interferes with a clear track.

MAMMALS

Red Fox—*Sign (Tracks)*

Due to the amount of hair on the bottom of a red fox's foot, it is often difficult to see details of a fox's track in the snow. Instead, identification can often be made from the pattern of the tracks. Trotting foxes often leave a clean, straight-line pattern, due to the fact that their hind feet register directly in the tracks made by their front feet. What looks like a single mark is actually two tracks—the imprint of a front foot as well as the impression of a hind foot placed directly on top of it. A domestic dog does not usually direct register and its track pattern is quite messy. In addition, unlike a fox, a dog can afford to wander here and there, because it knows its dinner will be provided; its energy doesn't need to be conserved and the stealth of a predator is not necessary. (See more about tracks on p. 385.)

Fisher—*Sign (Scat)*

Unlike many predators, the fisher does not usually defecate along a trail, but rather seeks higher ground, such as a rock or tree stump, on which it leaves its calling card. Because scat passes by scent glands inside most animals before being deposited, it is a very efficient means of com-

This fisher scat was deposited inside a tree stump on top of wood chips that woodpeckers had made searching for insects.

munication. Fishers are very faithful to their scent posts and regularly loop back to check on old scats and deposit new ones if they need refreshing. They are able to deposit very small amounts of feces for use as scent markers. (Read more about fishers on p. 29.)

Moose—Sign *(Scraping Bark)*

Bark is a staple food of both moose and white-tailed deer in the winter. Because they have no teeth in

their upper jaw at the front of their mouth, moose are forced to scrape bark upward with their bottom incisors. Often areas where moose have been feeding on bark resemble antler rubs. You can tell one from the other by noticing where the bark is torn and fragmented. If it is messier at the top than at the bottom, chances are it is incisor scraping. (Moose and

Moose "barking."

deer grip the tree with their bottom incisors, scraping the bark upward and leaving frayed ends at the top, where it is ripped off the tree.) If both upper and lower ends of the debarked area are shredded the mark was probably caused by the up and down movement of antlers.

Often the species of tree can help determine which of these two ungulates has been eating. Moose prefer red and striped maple, quaking aspen, and balsam fir, while white-tailed deer like young hemlock, birches, sumac, witch hazel, and viburnum. Don't be fooled by the height of the sign—moose have been known to kneel in order to feed just a foot off the ground. (Read more about moose on p. 251.)

Coyote—*Sign (Bed)*

Like most carnivores, coyotes don't have a permanent home, other than the maternal dens where their young are raised (which they tend to reuse year after year unless disturbed). During especially bad storms they will seek cover in

Coyote bed.

these dens, but for most of the winter they bed down in the snow, just like foxes.

White-Tailed Deer—*Sign (Scat)*

White-tailed deer scat can vary tremendously due to different seasonal diets and their moisture content. Herbaceous plants eaten during the spring and summer produce relatively loose scat, often in the form of patties. In the fall deer are eating dry as well as succulent vegetation, and their scat often consists of pellets clumped together. The twig and bark

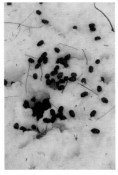

White-tailed deer winter scat.

diet of white-tailed deer in winter results in hard, individual, fibrous pellets.

A bird nest with a down roof addition, courtesy of a resident mouse.

White-Footed and North American Deermouse—*Sign (Winter Home)*

Although the nests of most songbirds are used by their builders only once, they do not go to waste. Before they are recycled as prime nest-building material in the spring, many serve double duty as winter shelters for industrious white-footed and North American deermice that roof them over with milkweed or thistledown. This addition converts the nests into snug homes well insulated and protected from winter elements.

WINTER AWAKENINGS

Big brown bat.

Most hibernating bats and jumping mice wake periodically, on an average of every two weeks throughout the winter. When they do so, precious stored energy is used up. It is not known why they wake up— neither feeding nor evacuation takes place. Scientists hypothesize that the large amount of energy is expended in order to keep their muscles from atrophying.

North American Porcupine—Sign *(Trail and Feeding Trees)*

Porcupines leave distinctive trails as they travel through deep snow. In shallow snow, their pigeon-toed tracks are more obvious. Usually these trails lead from a den to feeding trees, where patches of missing bark are evident; the bright yellow color of freshly-chewed bark stands out. Incisor marks can often be seen upon close inspection. (Read more about porcupines on p. 349.)

A porcupine trail in deep snow.

A porcupine feeding tree and a close-up of the incisor marks in the freshly chewed bark.

Common Muskrat—*Preparing for Life below the Ice*

At this time of year, muskrats, like beavers, have a limited number of days in the open air, for once the pond or marsh they inhabit freezes, they are locked under the ice. By December a family of up to 10 or more muskrats has built a lodge and several nearby roofed feeding platforms. These structures are made of cattails, sedges, and other available aquatic plants, and have underwater entrances. Through the winter the muskrats leave their lodge and collect food such as cattails, bulrushes, and water lilies to eat in the relative safety of their feeding platforms. (See more about the common muskrat on p. 143.)

A muskrat enjoying the last few days above the ice.

A muskrat lodge (left) and feeding platform (in background on right).

■ Winter Activity Chart for New England Animals

There is a continuum between the deep sleep of raccoons and Virginia opossums and the true hibernation of woodchucks, whose bodily functions markedly slow down. The term "hibernation" is therefore reserved in this chart for those animals whose metabolism is greatly reduced.

	Migrate	Hibernate	Dormant	Active	Semi-Active (den up in extreme cold)
BIRDS	X			X	
AMPHIBIANS					
Frogs		X			
Toads		X			
Salamanders		X			
REPTILES		X			
Snakes		X			
Turtles		X			
Lizards		X			
MAMMALS					
Jumping mice		X			
Mice				X	
Lemmings				X	
Voles				X	
Shrews				X	
Moles				X	
Bats	X	X			
Virginia opossum					X
Eastern cottontail rabbit				X	
New England cottontail rabbit				X	
Snowshoe hare				X	
Eastern chipmunk			X		
Woodchuck		X			
Eastern gray squirrel				X	
Red squirrel				X	
Southern flying squirrel				X	
Northern flying squirrel				X	
American beaver				X	
Common muskrat				X	
North American porcupine				X	
Coyote				X	
Raccoon					X
Fisher				X	
American mink				X	
Ermine				X	
Long-tailed weasel				X	
American marten				X	

MAMMALS CONTINUED	Migrate	Hibernate	Dormant	Active	Semi-Active (den up in extreme cold)
North American river otter				X	
Striped skunk			X		
Red fox				X	
Gray fox				X	
American black bear			X		
Moose				X	
White-tailed deer				X	
Bobcat				X	
Canadian lynx				X	

INSECTS & ARACHNIDS

Bagworm pupa case.

Bagworm Moth—*Overwintering as Eggs*

Bagworm moths are rarely seen, but their egg-laying site and larval home, or "bag," is evident on trees and shrubs, especially in the winter. These bags are made by the larvae and consist of plant material that they eat, bound together with silk that they spin. At this time of year bagworm moth eggs reside inside the bags. In the spring the larvae leave the bag they hatch in and create their own, which they live inside, feeding on plant material, with only their head and feet protruding. As they eat and molt and increase in size, the bag is enlarged. Eventually the larvae attach the bags to a branch and pupate. Adult male bagworm moths must seek out adult females, which, unlike the males, are wingless and remain in their bag emitting pheromones to which males are attracted. The males fertilize the females through the tip of the bag and the females lay their eggs there. Soon after, the females exit the bag and die.

Eastern Spruce Budworm—*Sign (Dead Branch Tips)*

Spruce budworm sign.

One notices the harmful effect of spruce budworms in New England coniferous forests far more often than the insect itself. Contrary to what its name implies, the spruce budworm does the most damage to balsam firs, although it does feed heavily on red, black, and white spruce. Because it bores into and feeds on expanding buds and developing shoots, it is considered one of the most destructive native insect pests in the Northeast. Waves of outbreaks of spruce budworms have occurred every three decades or so since at least the sixteenth century; quite possibly this has been the case for thousands of years.

Eggs are laid on needles in the fall and hatch shortly thereafter. The larvae spend the winter months inside tiny silk shelters that they spin. In the early spring they emerge from hibernation and feed on spruce needles, eventually moving on to the developing shoots, where they do the most damage. If you shake a spruce limb in May, chances are you will dislodge numerous brown larvae with yellow stripes down their back. These larvae are a preferred food of Cape May, bay-breasted, and Tennessee warblers.

By the end of June spruce budworms are usually pupating and emerge as adults in mid-summer. A shake of spruce or fir limbs in the fall often produces masses of small, bell-shaped adult spruce budworm moths. Massive amounts of insecticides have been used on spruce fir forests, in part because of the loss of timber resulting from these insects.

Carpenter bee nesting holes.

Carpenter Bee—Sign (Nest Holes in Wood)

Carpenter bees are large bumblebee-like insects. Their name is derived from the fact that in the spring mated females chew perfectly round, quarter-inch diameter tunnels into the solid wood of both trees and unpainted siding. Carpenter bees don't eat the wood—they use bits of it to construct six to eight cells at the end of the tunnels, each of which is filled with pollen and a single egg. Non-stinging males can often be seen hovering near the nest site. These insects have extended their range northward to the Canadian border in recent years, and signs of their work can be seen throughout New England.

PLANTS & FUNGI

Intermediate Wood Fern—Leaves Persisting

There are nine species of wood ferns in New England, the most common species being intermediate wood fern, also known as evergreen wood fern. As its common name implies, its fronds remain green throughout the year. It also bears glands on the leaf stems or rachis as well as the flaps (indusia) covering its reproductive spores (see p. 212 for a diagram of the parts of a fern). Because it hybridizes with all eight other wood ferns, identification to species is sometimes challenging. Look for its large, delicately cut fronds in moderately moist woods, bogs, and along swamp margins.

Intermediate wood fern.

Common Polypody—Leaves Persisting

Common polypody is an evergreen fern that is seen frequently throughout New England and can be found growing in colonies on rocks, cliffs, and ledges, in both sun and shade. Its deeply lobed leathery blades are quite distinctive. In the summer it can look withered during dry spells, but rain quickly refreshes it.

Common polypody.

Rose hip.

Rose Hips—Fruit Persisting

Because they are available when other fruits are covered with snow, rose hips, the fruit of plants in the Rose family, are a staple winter food for many species of birds in New England, including wild turkeys, ruffed grouse, mockingbirds, American robins, cedar waxwings, cardinals, evening grosbeaks, American goldfinches, dark-eyed juncos, tree sparrows, and fox sparrows. In addition, American black bears, cottontail rabbits, white-footed deermice, red squirrels, striped skunks, and white-tailed deer eat the fruit, stems, and/or foliage of wild roses.

Boxelder—*Seeds Persisting*

Boxelder, also called ash-leaved maple, is one of the hardiest species of trees in the Maple family. It is the only species of maple that has compound leaves like an ash (one leaf consists of several small leaflets). Like all maples, it has winged fruit called *samaras*, which are typically "V"-shaped. Boxelders are known for their prolific production of seeds every year. Because they hang in clusters on branches through the winter, boxelder seeds are an important winter resource for wildlife. They are the preferred food of evening grosbeaks and are also consumed by pine grosbeaks, purple finches, mice, and squirrels. (See photo on p. 301.)

Common Burdock—*Dispersing Seeds*

Common burdock, a biennial, sends up a rosette of leaves its first year. It grows erect stalks the sec-

Common burdock fruit.

ond year that bear flowers and then fruit, which are covered with modified leaves, or *bracts*, that are barbed. These barbs serve as an effective aid in dispersing the seeds, as anyone who has come in contact with burdock well knows. In fact, in the mid-1950s, after observing how burdock burs caught on his clothing, George de Mestral, a Swiss engineer, developed Velcro™, a fastening device consisting of hooks and loops.

Burdock flowers are visited by insects searching for nectar in summer, and the seeds that the fruits contain are eaten by birds in winter. Wild turkeys are particularly fond of burdock seeds, and it is not unusual to come upon a cluster of empty burs stuck together, each of which have been turned inside out by turkeys extracting the seeds.

■ Conifers In-a-Glance

▶ Retain leaves year-round
▶ 20 percent of leaves new each year
▶ Individual needle's life span is two to five years
▶ Leaves have thick, waxy, watertight protective layer (*cuticle*)
▶ Leaves structurally stronger than broad leaves
▶ *Stomata* (openings for gas exchange and water vapor from transpiration) located in depressions in leaf, far from surface; stomatas close tightly
▶ Relatively low rate of photosynthesis
▶ Smaller surface area than deciduous trees
▶ Many species have high tolerance for low temperatures

■ Broad-Leaf Trees In-a-Glance

▶ Drop leaves annually
▶ 100 percent of leaves new each year
▶ Individual leaf's life span is one year
▶ Cuticle is thinner and not as watertight
▶ Leaves structurally weaker than conifer leaves
▶ Stomatas on surface of leaf; stomatas don't close as tightly as on conifers
▶ High rate of photosynthesis
▶ Larger surface area than conifers
▶ Many species have low tolerance for low temperatures

A sugar maple (broad leaves) turning color next to a conifer in the fall.

CONIFER VS. BROAD-LEAF TREE LEAVES

Eastern hemlock (conifer) leaves.

American beech (broad-leaf) leaves.

The best possible arrangement for a tree is to have broad leaves that remain in place year-round. This type of tree is common in the tropics, but not in the Northeast. New England winters pose a challenge to trees, as water is in short supply, and a tree transpires a large percentage of the water it takes up. Different types of trees have adapted to this need to conserve water in the winter in different ways.

In order to prevent a loss of water at a time of year when they can least afford it, broad-leaf or deciduous trees drop their leaves. This prevents water from being transpired through them. The tree forms a corky abscission layer where the leaf stem attaches to a branch, so that when the leaf falls, the opening in the bark that it leaves is sealed off, limiting water loss. Because photosynthesis stops (for the most part—the bark of some tree species photosynthesizes, but minimally), the need for water uptake, as well as the resulting transpiration, is greatly decreased.

There are a number of adaptations that enable conifers to survive freezing temperatures. Many of them have to do with the retention of water and because, as mentioned, water loss is largely through a tree's leaves, the adaptations are found primarily in a conifer's needles. The most crucial of these is the thick, waxy *cuticle* (outer layer) on the surface of needles, which greatly reduces water loss through transpiration. (Conifers do not photosynthesize year-round, though they sometimes do on warm, winter days; they can get an earlier start than broad-leafed trees in the spring and can extend the season in the fall.) Structurally, needles have greater strength than broad leaves, and can withstand the weight of snow and ice. The biggest evergreen advantage is thought to be the conservation of nutrients. These trees don't need to make a whole new set of leaves each year and thus don't need as many nutrients as deciduous trees. This puts them at an advantage in nutrient poor environments such as the upper slopes of mountains, mountain tops, and bogs.

Trees also undergo cellular changes that allow them to survive the cold, dry conditions of winter. There is a given temperature at which ice crystals form within cell structures, resulting in cell death. This temperature varies among different species, between populations of the same species, and even among different tissues. In some cases, killing temperatures are limiting factors for species' ranges. In general, conifers can tolerate lower temperatures than broad-leaf trees.

DECEMBER
a closer look

Winter offers opportunities found no other time of year. Animal signs such as **bald-faced hornet nests** (p. 358) that are easily overlooked when there is foliage are suddenly very apparent. A lack of **cone** production (p. 360) in Canada occasionally results in an **irruption** of northern birds in New England (p. 347), seeking food south of their range, which adds to our winter wildlife viewing. Animals such as **North American porcupines** (p. 349) and **ruffed grouse** (p. 345) remain active, as their food is adequate year-round, but they have to make accommodations in order to survive the climate change from summer to winter. Many mammals **have to adapt to survive the cold** months ahead (p. 355), while **wood frogs** (see below), are frozen solid beneath our feet. Time indoors can be spent examining mammal **skulls** (p. 352) and trying to deduce the nature of a mammal's diet from its dentition.

Wood Frog in Winter—
Amphibian Cryogenics

Right beneath our feet, under the snow and just a few inches deep in the leaf litter, hardy amphibians known as wood frogs spend the winter. Their ability to withstand cold temperatures is responsible for their being the only species of frog found north of the Arctic Circle. This hardiness is apparent in every season and in most stages of the wood frog's development. The adults emerge very early in the spring to breed, sometimes gathering at ponds before the ice has completely disappeared. Even their eggs have exceptional temperature tolerance. Those that are laid in water that freezes are able to begin developing once the temperature rises again.

The "Frogsicle"
This adaptation to cold temperatures has allowed

Extremely cold-tolerant, wood frogs can survive completely freezing in the winter and then thawing when warm weather returns.

wood frogs to achieve something humans have yet to master. In order to deal with the protracted deep cold of January and February, which drives frost through the leaf litter as well as under logs where adults overwinter, wood frogs have perfected the "cryogenic freezing process." They can literally survive being frozen. In the winter as much as 45 to 60 percent of a wood frog's body may freeze and turn to ice. As the temperature drops below 32°F, ice crystals start to form just beneath the frog's skin. What up until now has been a pliant and slightly slimy body turns into slush. As the temperature drops, ice forms in the frog's arteries and veins. Its heart and brain stop working. Eventually the entire frog is solid to the touch and is said to make a small thud when dropped. It can spend two to three months in this frozen state, with its body temperature ranging between 21 and 30° F. Unbelievably, this does not kill the frog. When a thaw comes and temperatures rise, it can "melt back into" its normal state over a period of several hours, restart its heart, and hop away, none the worse for wear.

How?

This miraculous ability to withstand freezing is the result of both behavioral and chemical changes. Prior to winter, wood frogs gorge themselves and store the resulting starch in their livers. A freeze triggers their body to convert the starch into glucose or blood sugar. The glucose—which is about 100 times the normal concentration—acts as antifreeze, preventing dehydration and lowering the freezing temperature of water inside the frogs' cells. Because of this the cells stay liquid, even as ice fills the space around them. If the water inside the cells froze, it would be curtains for the frog, as the jagged ice crystals would destroy everything.

As of the time of writing, that which a wood frog is capable of doing with *all* its organs—freezing them, and then returning them to a normal state—humans can't do with *a single* organ. The fact that this amphibian is able to adapt to and survive freezing temperatures has thus caught the attention of scientists—not just herpetologists (those who study reptiles and amphibians) but

] FAST FACTS [
Wood Frog

▶ Wood frogs do not hibernate below the frost line; they hibernate just a few inches under the leaves on the forest floor.

▶ There are three species of frogs in New England that tolerate being frozen: the wood frog, spring peeper, and gray treefrog.

▶ Up to 65 percent of total body water in a wood frog can be frozen and the frog can still survive.

▶ At about 18° F, ice forms outside of and between of the frog's cells (as opposed to forming in the cells, which is lethal).

▶ Unlike insects, which prepare for winter by producing the chemicals necessary to prevent freezing prior to winter, frogs wait until the freezing process begins to trigger the production of glucose, which acts as antifreeze within the cells.

medical researchers, seeking for a way to preserve donated organs for longer periods of time. Today a harvested organ is packed in a special solution and kept on ice, but it can't be frozen due to the damage that ice crystals would do to the cells. Without freezing, a kidney can last a mere 48 hours, and a heart only four. Adding hours or even days between the time an organ is removed and when it must be implanted would be of great value.

Winter Adaptations of the Ruffed Grouse—*Ingenious Survival Tactics*

Winter in northern New England is challenging even for the most cold-hardy birds. Most species (62 percent) avoid the lack of food and the cold by migrating to a warmer climate where food is plentiful and the demand for energy not as extreme, according to Jonathan Elphick in his book *Atlas of Bird Migration* (Firefly Books, 2007). Birds that remain here in the winter have several basic requirements: an adequate source of food, protection from the elements, and refuge from predators.

Overwintering species of birds use a number of techniques to meet these needs, such as excavating roosting cavities in trees (downy woodpecker), lowering body temperature at night (black-capped chickadee), and shivering. When it comes to winter adaptations, however, one of the most ingenious birds is the ruffed grouse, which employs several survival tactics.

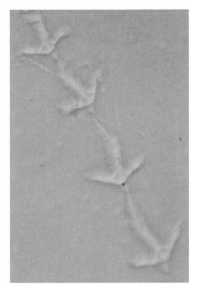

The single-file, three-toed tracks of the ruffed grouse are quite distinctive.

other. Grouse are also heavy winter consumers of bigtooth aspen buds and catkins, as well as those of birch, alder, willow, hazel, and hophornbeam. In order to digest this woody diet, a grouse has a *gizzard*—a hard, horny gland that grinds, with the help of grit swallowed by the grouse, tough cellulose fibers.

Ruffed grouse store very little fat, and thus must eat frequently—usually twice a day, at dawn and dusk. It is in the grouse's best interest not to linger while eating, as it is fully exposed while feeding on the buds of leafless deciduous trees. Predators such as red-tailed hawks, goshawks, and great horned owls are quick to spot such vulnerable prey. The ruffed grouse has devised an efficient way of minimizing risk while obtaining the necessary amount of food. Within 20 minutes the grouse rapidly picks and swallows enough buds to make it through the night. These buds go directly to the grouse's *crop*, a widening of the esophagus that acts as a storage chamber. The grouse then flies to a more protected area to leisurely digest the food.

Behavioral

In the spring, summer, and fall, ruffed grouse eat the leafy vegetation of over 100 kinds of plants, most of which are groundcover. Because these sources of food are not accessible in winter, the ruffed grouse is forced to change its winter diet to buds as well as twigs. By far the most nutritious and sought-after winter food sources are the sugar- and protein-rich flower buds of male trembling aspen. It is not a coincidence that the range of ruffed grouse is almost identical to that of trembling aspen; where you find one, you will usually find the

Physical

Every September a fringe of fleshy projections, called *pectinations*, begin to grow on either side of a grouse's toes (see p. 306 for a photo). These comb-like nubs act as snowshoes, increasing the surface area of the foot, allowing the grouse to walk on top of the snow and thereby expend far less energy than it would without them. It is likely that these pectinations also give the grouse a better grip on the icy branches where it perches while feeding. By April or May, these growths fall off.

In the background you can see where a grouse flew into the snow. After creating a cavity at the end of a tunnel and spending at least one night in it, the grouse burst out, leaving wing prints when it took off, which you can see in the foreground.

Two additional physical attributes benefit the grouse in winter. Feathers extend down its beak far enough to cover its nostrils. These feathers warm up the cold air before the grouse inhales it. Ruffed grouse also have feathers partially covering and insulating their legs.

Snow Divers

The ruffed grouse is notorious for its winter roosting routine. If there is no snow, or just a few inches of it, grouse often roost in conifer stands, which offer some protection from the wind and cold. However, when the snow is at least 10 inches and lacks a thick crust, the grouse's preference is to spend the night insulated by this air-filled white blanket. Whenever conditions permit, the grouse flies directly into the snow, leaving no tracks or scent behind for predators to detect. After landing in the snow, the grouse often extends the tunnel made by its trajectory by 3 to 10 feet and then hollows out a small cavity where it spends the night. The temperature under the snow is significantly warmer than on its surface. According to Michael Furtman, in his book *Ruffed Grouse: Woodland Drummer* (Stack-

pole Books, 2004), the temperature in a grouse's hideaway may warm to 32°F and rarely falls beneath 20°F, no matter how cold the outside air is. This represents an energy savings of 30 percent or more compared to spending the night in the open. Less expenditure of energy means less food is required, which in turn means less time spent in the open, exposed to predators. There is also the advantage of being hidden from view while under the snow.

When exiting this burrow, the grouse often bursts out of the snow, startling many a snowshoer or skier. Look for the impression of the grouse's feathers left by its wings as it takes off.

Bird Irruptions—*Hello, Strangers*

Occasionally in New England we have an influx of birds that normally do not stray this far south. When species of birds that regularly winter in the boreal forests of Canada appear in large numbers south of their normal wintering grounds, it is called an *irruption*. While a migration consists of a seasonal, predictable movement that is repeated each year, an irruption is defined as an unpredictable and erratic appearance of large numbers of birds in the non-breeding season into regions beyond their usual winter range. Ornithologists feel that these movements are, at least in part, a response to food shortages, such as poor cone crops on coniferous trees in the wintering grounds of seed-eating birds or rodents. As a result of a seed crop failure, rodent populations crash and seed-eating birds are forced to look elsewhere for food, as are the birds that prey on seed-eating rodents. A good mast year followed by a very prolific spring with lots of young birds, can also contribute to the occurrence of irruptions.

Triggers

There is sometimes a synchronization of seed crop failures in some high-latitude tree species to the north of New England. When this occurs, states bordering Canada, and often further south, can expect to have unusual birds at their feeders and fruit trees. For example, if there happens to be an unusually high number of boreal finches in southern Canada due to a successful breeding season, as well as a shortage of essential winter seeds, it can trigger a major irruption of these birds in New England. Pine grosbeaks, red crossbills, white-winged

The pine grosbeak is a large, unwary finch from the north and a less frequent visitor to New England than other members of the finch family. It has a short, conical bill well adapted for crushing seeds and nipping buds and tips of conifer branches. It is a voracious eater and a flock can strip the fruit off of a crab apple tree within hours. When pine grosbeaks are not stuffing themselves with crab apples, they can often be found feeding on the buds and the seeds of mountain ash, boxelder, and ash. The male's reddish plumage (left) readily distinguishes it from the female's yellow-bronze head and rump (right). At night these birds often roost very close to one another in dense conifers and may be seen sunbathing during the day.

crossbills, common redpolls, pine siskins, and evening grosbeaks are the primary seed-eating birds affected by these crop failures. When you consider the appetite of these birds (a white-winged crossbill eats 3,000 seeds a day) it is not surprising that they are forced to look farther afield when the Canadian crops fail. Cedar and bohemian waxwings are not members of the finch family, but they also sporadically shift from their typical wintering grounds into other areas to search for fruits.

According to the National Audubon Society, it is a rare winter without an irruption of at least one bird species in North America. Sometimes it is very

White-Winged Crossbill
Main food source: Smaller-coned spruce and larch seeds in boreal forest; eastern hemlock and cedar seeds during Northeast irruptions (also feed these seeds to their young, which allows them to breed and raise young in winter).

Red Crossbill
Main food source: Conifer seeds, primarily those of eastern hemlock and white pine during Northeast irruptions.

Pine Grosbeak
Main food source: Crabapples, European mountain-ash berries, conifer and maple seeds.

Evening Grosbeak
Main food source: Conifer seeds, boxelder seeds.

Common Redpoll
Main food source: Seeds of birches and alders.

Pine Siskin
Main food source: Seeds of birches and alders.

Bohemian Waxwing
Main food source: European mountain-ash berries, crabapples, buckthorn berries.

Crossbills and redpolls (a common redpoll is pictured) possess a two-lobed pocket in their neck in which they store seeds that they have gathered. The use of this pocket late in the day and during severe winter weather saves energy by shortening the birds' foraging time and allowing them to feed in sheltered areas.

localized; at other times there are simultaneous irruptions of several species into more than one area. A major winter finch irruption, or *superflight*, occurred during the winter of 1997–98, when the Northeast was inundated with northern birds.

Food Source Magnets
Certain species of trees and bushes seem to attract certain species of birds. If you have a crabapple tree on your property, your chances of seeing a pine grosbeak during an irruption winter are very high. Once they discover a tree laden with fruit, they are apt to eat every apple on it, and then move on to the next tree. If you have a white or yellow birch tree that has produced seeds, you may very well be

treated to the sight of a flock of common redpolls, and, if you're fortunate, maybe even the more rare hoary redpoll in the midst of them.

Northern owls also experience irruptions. A crash in the small rodent population (due to a lack of seed production) can cause great gray owls, northern hawk owls, and snowy owls to move southward. Red-backed vole numbers often decline when the deermouse population declines, and because saw-whet owls and barred owls eat significant numbers of red-backed voles, there can be a large influx of these species, too.

There are many opportunities to learn about and contribute sightings of irruptive bird species. The National Audubon Society and Cornell Laboratory of Ornithology sponsor Birdsource (www.birdsource.org), a database for bird information that records bird sightings throughout North America. It coordinates and publishes results from Project FeederWatch, Christmas Bird Counts, and the Great Backyard Bird Count—programs that utilize volunteer sightings. Another excellent program that collects and provides information on dates and numbers of irruptive as well as other bird species is eBird, a program begun in 2002 by the Cornell Lab of Ornithology and National Audubon Society. It provides rich data sources for basic information on bird abundance and distribution. (More information on how to participate in and use this program this can be found at http://ebird.org.)

The North American porcupine cannot move very fast, nor see very well, yet it has been very successful as a species. What is the secret to its survival? Modified hairs, primarily, which serve a variety of purposes, including sensing, insulating, navigating, and self-defense.

North American Porcupine—*Slow Moving, but Thoroughly Armed*

Porcupines are not highly favored by humans, not only because domestic dogs seem to be repeatedly outwitted by their quills, but also because of the porcupine's love of salt. It is this craving that spells disaster for any tool that has been handled by a person's sweaty palm, or for any piece of building material cured with sodium nitrate. The porcupine's constant conflict with humans hasn't always been the case. Before the colonists arrived many woodland tribes of Native Americans in the Northeast revered the porcupine. Not only were its quills used for decoration and jewelry, but it was an easily-caught source of food, which helped Native Americans stave off starvation.

Superhero Hair Coat

There are many things a porcupine is not, such as fast-moving and keen-sighted, but when it comes to adaptations, it rules. What other mammal has hair modified in five different ways to serve five differ-ent purposes? Dark, woolly underfur insulates the porcupine in winter. Long guard hairs are sensitive to touch and help the nearsighted porcupine maneuver on branches high in the canopy. Stout whiskers, called *vibrissae*, located near the porcupine's nostrils, are also thought to be very sensitive to touch. The short, stiff bristles on the undersurface of a porcupine's tail assist stability by gripping the bark as the mammal ascends trees, preventing it from slipping downward. Last, and most unusual, are the roughly 30,000 quills that cover most of the porcupine's body. With the exception of its face, ears, and a portion of its belly, the porcupine is protected with approximately 100 quills per square inch of body surface. These modified hairs—mini-spears with microscopic barbs at their free end—allow the porcupine to survive despite its slow movement and myopic eyesight. Most animals—with the exception of the fisher and, to a lesser degree, red foxes, bobcats, coyotes, and great horned owls (and, of course, dogs)—have learned to keep their distance.

There are many misconceptions about porcupines, one being that they shoot their quills.

Porcupines usually feed within several hundred feet of their den. Well-worn runways between the den and feeding areas are conspicuous any time of year.

Female and juvenile porcupines usually retreat to a den (rock crevice, hollow tree, or log) during the colder six months of the year. Although solitary animals, porcupines may gather in groups of 12 or more in these dens. For reasons that have yet to be determined, they usually move to a new den site every three weeks or so. It's easy to recognize a porcupine den by the ever-growing mound of scat outside its entrance. Shed quills, white with black tips, can often be found lying amongst the curved, fibrous scat.

The quills are extracted quite easily as soon as something comes in contact with them, but they are not "shot" from a distance. In all fairness to porcupines, they, like striped skunks, do not employ their most severe defense mechanism without fair warning. In fact, these two mammals both announce their potential to do harm with their black and white warning coloration. Most porcupines have a dark line up the middle of their tail, which is bordered by white, in addition to their whitish head. Should a potential predator fail to take notice of this and approach a porcupine, it is met with furious teeth-chattering. If the predator persists, the porcupine may then produce a pungent odor thought to emanate from fatty acids produced near the base of its tail. By this time the porcupine is facing away from the predator and special muscles in its skin have caused its quills to become erect; in this position they readily penetrate the mouth and face of an attacking animal when it attempts to bite.

The porcupine also thrashes its tail back and forth, causing loose quills to fall out.

Porcupine quills can be deadly weapons. The barbs on the end of a quill serve to lodge it in the skin of a predator and cause it to be propelled through tissue, where it can keep moving until it reaches a vital organ. The short quills under a porcupine's tail are considered the most dangerous, as they tend to be driven deeper than longer quills and travel faster once imbedded. The quills on a porcupine's back and tail have a greasy coating that allows them to continue to move forward once the quill has penetrated an animal's skin. This grease contains antibiotics, which prevent porcupines from becoming infected by their own or by another porcupine's quills.

Capable Climbers
Porcupines are well equipped for their largely arboreal existence. Their long claws grip crevices in the bark when ascending and descending a tree and enable them to pull the slender bud- or nut-bearing tips of branches within reach. In addition, the pads of porcupines' feet are very wrinkled; this increases friction when their feet grip a surface. Even with these adaptations, however, porcupines are not accident-free. A survey of museum porcupine skeletons revealed that 35 percent had evidence of healed fractures.

While we don't see porcupines regularly, there is no shortage of them in New England. Being nocturnal, they are out and about mostly at night but occasionally can be found during the day hidden in the tops of trees where they obtain their preferred food—buds and leaves in the spring; acorns and beechnuts in the fall; and the inner bark, or *cambium*, of sugar maples, aspens, red oaks, beeches, spruces, and especially eastern hemlocks in the winter. The bright yellow patches of trees whose bark has recently been chewed by porcupines are easy to spot. It is not unusual for a porcupine, particularly a male, to spend several days feeding in the same tree, high up in the crown, where the outer bark on branches is thinner and the cambium easier to get to.

Of Questionable Pleasure

Porcupines have quite an elaborate courtship, and one of questionable enjoyment, at least for females. With much vocalization the male approaches the female on his hind legs and tail. In order to determine whether or not the female is receptive (there is only an 8 to 10-hour window of receptivity) the male squirts her with his urine, ejecting it in a high-pressured stream that thoroughly soaks her from nose to tail. If the timing isn't right, she merely shakes herself off and ambles away. If she remains, mating ensues, often after a second soaking. One young porcupine is born roughly seven months later, emerging in a sac that protects the mother from its spines. Actually, the quills are quite soft at birth, but harden within an hour.

When there is an established fisher population, it is felt that they keep porcupine numbers under control, for this large member of the weasel family is very effective at overpowering porcupines by repeatedly attacking their quill-less faces. However, it is thought by some biologists that bobcats kill as many porcupines as fishers.

] FAST FACTS [
North American Porcupine

▶ Porcupine quills are not hollow—they are filled with a spongy material. Cutting the tips of quills that are embedded in you or your dog does not make them easier to extract.

▶ In winter porcupines feed on bark; during the rest of the year they feed on leaves and buds at the tips of branches as well as fungi and herbaceous plants.

▶ The porcupine is one of very few strictly vegetarian rodents.

▶ None of the trees that the porcupine consumes contain much sodium, which is why porcupines so actively seek it. Road salt satisfies much of their craving, along with aquatic plants and the handles of garden tools.

▶ Sometimes the accumulation of scat at the entrance to a porcupine den is so great the porcupines have to dig their way through it in order to get into or out of the den.

▶ In late spring porcupines dig for false truffles in the forest floor, creating conical holes that are 6 to 8 inches in diameter.

▶ In the spring porcupines molt all their underfur (not quills or guard hairs) at one time, leaving masses of woolly hair behind.

▶ Up to 100 porcupines were found denning in ledges within a single 4- to 5-acre area in Massachusetts.

▶ Porcupines are quite vocal, whining, grunting, moaning, and even screaming like a human at times.

It is relatively easy to find signs of porcupine activity, for they remain active in the winter, seeking shelter only during the most severe weather. Look for their pigeon-toed tracks when there are a few inches of snow; in deep snow they leave a 5- to 9-inch-wide trough (see photo on p. 337). Occasionally you can see where their tail dragged, and in especially good conditions the individual quills make fine lines in the snow.

Skulls and Dentition—
The Tales Teeth Tell

"Reading the landscape" includes interpreting all that your eyes and other senses detect, including tracks, scat, and skeletons. While all of these animal signs offer the observer insight into the environmental life style of an animal, none exceeds that of a skull. It is capable of telling you much more than just the identity of an animal. A skilled skull-reader—especially one with Mark Elbroch's book, *Animal Skulls* (Stackpole Books, 2006), in one hand—can often determine the animal's relative age, size, and diet, along with details related to its reliance on smell, visual acuity, ability to hear, whether it was active at night, whether it was a predator or prey animal, and possibly even its relative intelligence. The teeth alone—their shapes, sizes, and position—can provide you with considerable knowledge about the animal's diet and life style.

Dentition
The eating habits of New England mammals can be categorized into four groups: *carnivorous* (meat eater), *herbivorous* (plant eater), *omnivorous* (meat and plant eater), and *insectivorous* (insect eater). Because of the nature of their respective diets, these groups have different dentition. Each kind of tooth performs a different function, including grasping, killing, chewing, nipping, grinding, and crushing. Most carnivores and omnivores have four kinds of teeth: incisors, canines, premolars, and molars (the latter two are often referred to as "cheek teeth"). Herbivores such as rodents and some hoofed animals (*ungulates*) lack canines, and the teeth of insectivores are distinctly different from those of the other three groups.

Incisors are the small chisel-shaped teeth (except for in rodents and *lagomorphs*—cottontail rabbits and hares, where they are larger) located at the front of the jaws, which are used for cutting, scraping, and tearing. Canines are the conical, pointed teeth associated with carnivores, although omnivores also possess them. They are used to capture and kill prey. Premolars and molars are located at the back of the jaws and are primarily used for grinding and shearing.

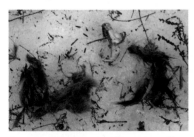

Sometimes even a small portion of a skull can help identify a species. If the reddish-brown glossy fur didn't tell you that a muskrat had been killed here, the segment of upper jaw containing incisors and distinctively-shaped molars would have.

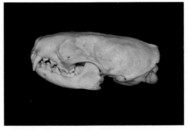

American mink (carnivore): A mink's skull is like that of other members of the weasel family, relatively long and slender. Most mustelids have long and slender canines, well-developed carnassial teeth (specialized for shearing flesh into small pieces), and short, rounded mandibles.

Masked shrew (insectivore): The masked shrew has to capture the insects it eats, and it does so with the aid of two front incisors that project outward (seen here in this upper portion of a shrew's skull). Note the reddish-brown coloring on the tips of its teeth, especially the incisors. This is diagnostic for all shrews in North America.

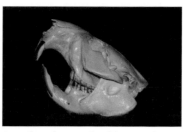

North American river otter (carnivore): Otter skulls are flattened and rounded. Their teeth are specialized for their diet: incisors tear off small pieces of flesh, canines hold slippery fish, premolars shear through flesh, and molars are capable of grinding crayfish and crushing fish bones.

American beaver (herbivore): The incisors of all rodents, including those of North America's largest rodent, the beaver, grow throughout the life of the animal. The outer orange layer of enamel is harder than the dentin in the rest of the tooth, allowing the beaver to create a sharp, beveled edge on its front teeth when it moves its upper incisors against the lower ones.

Woodchuck (herbivore): A woodchuck's skull is large, flattened, and heavy. Like all other rodents, a woodchuck has no canine teeth. Unlike other rodents, its incisors are white, not orange.

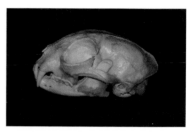

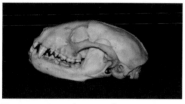

Raccoon (omnivore): The raccoon's skull is rectangular in shape. An omnivore, the raccoon possesses four types of teeth—incisors, canines, premolars, and molars—none of which are very specialized. An opportunist, the raccoon is well equipped to eat everything from clams and insects to acorns and grapes.

Virginia opossum (omnivore): The Virginia opossum has 50 teeth, more than any other North American land mammal. Its teeth most closely resemble those of a carnivore, with 18 incisors for cutting off bites, canines for tearing, and molars for grinding. Although classified as an omnivore, the opossum eats primarily animal matter.

Bobcat (carnivore): The bobcat's prominent sharp canine teeth are typical of most carnivores. Although they seldom do so, bobcats are capable of killing full-grown deer.

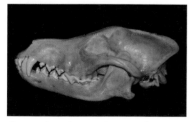

Coyote (carnivore): Coyotes, along with other fellow canids (foxes, wolves, and domestic dogs) have large canine teeth that are slightly blunted for grabbing and holding prey. Their *carnassial* teeth (specialized molars), shear off pieces of flesh small enough to swallow.

Fisher (carnivore): Nearly all carnivores and omnivores have *sagittal crests*—ridges running the length of the cranium—but male fishers have particularly massive ones. The powerful temporal muscles, responsible for closing the jaw at the front of the mouth, are attached to this crest.

Red fox (omnivore): Although equipped with impressive canine teeth, the red fox is very much an omnivore, consuming large amounts of fruit such as grapes, apples, and berries when they are available. Close inspection of a red fox's upper incisors reveals that they are lobed, with tiny, rounded points. The gray fox's incisors do not have these lobes.

Carnivores

As mentioned, carnivores, who survive as meat eaters by predation and scavenging, have four types of teeth, with specializations that allow them to be successful predators. One very noticeable distinction is the size of many carnivores' canines. They are usually very large and considerably longer than their other teeth—well adapted for seizing prey, as well as fighting. Many carnivores' cheek teeth have sharp points and serrated edges, ideal for tearing and cutting flesh. Some of these are very specialized premolars and molars, which act as sharp, shearing blades. These jagged, serrated teeth (last upper premolar and first lower molar on both sides of both jaws) are called *carnassials* and are especially well developed in the cat family.

Herbivores

Herbivores may lack canine teeth, but they have evolved the perfect tools for snipping off and grinding up tough vegetation. Their incisors have very sharp edges, excellent for cutting. The grass that many of them eat contains hard, abrasive silica in its fibers. As a result, the cheek teeth (molars and premolars) of many rodents, rabbits, and hoofed animals are large, have high crowns (so that they last a long time even with intense use), and flat surfaces that are good for grinding. These molars are reinforced with hard enamel ridges that become apparent as an animal ages. The shape and size of molars can reveal much about an animal's diet—one look at the very sharp cheek teeth of a white-tailed deer explains how it can live on a winter diet of woody browse, buds, and nuts.

Rodents (mice, voles, lemmings, squirrels, chipmunks, woodchucks, porcupines, and beavers) are a specialized group of herbivores that possess a single pair of long, curved, chisel-edged, continuously-growing incisors in both lower and upper jaws. These enable them to gnaw, nip, and bite plant material. There is a wide gap between these incisors and the cheek teeth. Being herbivores, they lack canines. If you find a skull and it has prominent incisors as well as a gap before the cheek teeth, take a close look behind the upper two incisors. Hares and rabbits have a second, smaller set of incisors directly behind the ones, and for this reason (among others) are classified as *lagomorphs*, not rodents.

Omnivores

As you would expect, the dentition of omnivores is a combination of herbivorous and carnivorous features. Usually there is a full compliment of incisors, canines, premolars, and molars. The canines may not be as pronounced as those of carnivores, but they are present. The cheek teeth of omnivores may not be as flat as those of herbivores, nor as sharp as those of carnivores. The teeth of animals such as raccoons, American black bears, and Virginia opossums equip them to survive in situations that strict carnivores and herbivores might find challenging.

Insectivores

Moles and shrews often have squarish cheek teeth with sharp cusps and edges designed to crunch the hard *chitin* (a carbohydrate similar to the protein *keratin*) in the exoskeletons of insects. Shrews have long front teeth that are projected forward so that they may be used as forceps in grasping small insects or as weapons for attacking larger animals. Their teeth are very distinctive with reddish-brown tips.

If you can overcome your reluctance to pick up a skull that you come upon in the woods, or that your cat drops on your doorstep, and take the time to scrutinize the shape, size, and position of its teeth, you can discover, at the very least, its identity as well as its diet. Even easier (and possibly less distasteful), look in the mirror and open your mouth—see what you think *your* teeth were designed to chew. Looks like meat and potatoes to me.

Skulls and Dentition

- More than any other skeletal feature, the skull is the greatest source of information about an animal's lifestyle.

- Mammals have two lower jaws—one on the right and one on the left. These jaws are also called *mandibles* and they are moveable. What is commonly referred to as the upper "jaw" is actually the *maxilla*; it is fused to the main portion of the skull.

- Eye socket position in a mammal's skull can face forward or can face outward from the side of the head. Forward-facing eyes permit the field of vision in each eye to overlap, producing binocular, three-dimensional vision. Side-of-the-head eye sockets restrict an animal to flat, two-dimensional vision, but allow for greater peripheral vision and increased sensitivity to motion. Often the eyes of predators face forward, and those of prey face to the sides.

- The location of major muscle group attachments to the skull can tell you which teeth are of primary importance to the animal, as different muscles provide power to different portions of the mandibles.

- The reason more skulls (and bones and antlers) are not found is that they are consumed by rodents for their calcium content.

- Owl pellets under owl roosts can contain whole skulls of small prey in pristine condition.

Surviving Winter— *Adaptations of Active Mammals*

Humans living in northern climates adapt as best they can to the rigors of the cold season—wood stoves and fireplaces, an extra layer of fat and/or clothing, snow tires—but these measures pale in comparison to those of our four-footed relatives. Mammals utilize different strategies in order to survive winter in northern New England. Some

overcome the cold temperatures and lack of food by avoiding them altogether. They enter differing levels of dormancy—from true hibernation like that of jumping mice (their metabolism practically comes to a halt for six months of the year), to the torpor of raccoons (they arouse themselves periodically to wander about hunting for food when the weather is suitable). Many bats, our only flying mammals, choose to migrate to a protected spot, or *hibernaculum*, for the winter. There they enter a state in which their body temperature hovers just above freezing until insects are once again available.

Considering that it takes approximately 10 times the energy to run a given distance than to fly, most mammals do not choose migration as a winter survival strategy; they not only stay in New England through the winter, but most remain active. This means that they face numerous challenges. Temperatures are low and food is scarce. How do non-dormant, non-migrating mammals produce the necessary amount of heat during the coldest months of the year, while still conserving it efficiently so gathering enough food or fuel is manageable? The answer is that over time they have adapted in extraordinary ways to their environment.

Year-round, red and gray foxes hunt primarily at night and sleep out in the open during the day, curled up, using their tails as protection in the winter against the cold, wind, and snow.

White-tailed deer change their herbaceous diet to a woody one, browsing on available shrubs and trees during the winter.

Insulation

An insulating covering of fur that traps dead air next to their body is crucial for mammals that remain active in winter. The thicker the layer of fur, the greater its insulating value. The thick coats of the hollow-shafted winter hair of white-tailed deer keep them warm at –30°F. However, as body size decreases, the ratio of surface area to volume increases, as does the amount of heat loss. Small mammals, unable to physically carry around thick, heavy coats, have evolved other tactics to stay warm. One is to live where temperature fluctuation is minimal—not up on the surface of the snow, but down at ground level, in what is known as the *subnivian layer*, where the temperature remains very stable under an insulating blanket of

The snow on top of an active beaver lodge in winter is melted because beavers intentionally leave a vent where warm air from inside the lodge escapes and fresh air enters.

snow. (See more on this on p. 392.) If there are 6 or more inches of snow on the ground, temperatures at ground level rarely fall below 32°F, regardless of air temperature.

Large or small, mammals in northern New England must set priorities in order to survive. The metabolic cost is too great for a mammal to keep its entire body warm. Therefore, most animals keep their core warm, as that is where their vital organs are located, while they allow the temperature of their outer layers as well as their extremities to drop.

Huddling or clustering together in small groups also helps small mammals retain as much of their body heat as possible, for less of each individual's body surface is exposed to the air. In addition, more bodies equal more heat production. Many small mammals that are solitary during summer months, such as flying squirrels and meadow voles, become social in winter for this very reason. (Read more on this subject on p. 377.)

Food and Fat

Some animals, such as eastern chipmunks and American beavers, store food for winter consumption in underground tunnels, hidden caches, or in the beavers' case, in a pile at the bottom of their pond. Increased fat levels are essential for animals that don't demonstrate this kind of instinctive behavior, as well as those that do. Taking this one step further, scientists have discovered that moose actually have high concentrations of unsaturated fat in their feet. The advantage of this is that unsaturated fat remains liquid at cooler temperatures than saturated fat, and for animals that spend hours standing on cold ground, this is a very useful adaptation.

Some animals—notably eastern and New England cottontail rabbits, snowshoe hares, white-tailed deer, and moose—actually change their diet to accommodate whatever food is most available in a given season. Herbaceous and aquatic plants in summer give way to buds and twigs in winter.

Staying Out of Sight

Camouflage certainly enhances survival rates. In New England, this adaptation benefits ermine and long-tailed weasels, as well as snowshoe hares. Two annual molts, one in the fall and one in the spring, turn their coats from brown to white and back again. Not only does the color change to white in winter decrease their chances of being detected, but it also has been shown to increase the insulating quality of the animal's coat (by 27 percent in snowshoe hares). The color white indicates an absence of any color or pigment; cells that hold pigment in brown hairs are filled with air in white hairs, creating an additional layer of insulation. (Read more about molting on p. 290.)

Surviving winter in the Northeast is a daunting task for any mammal, but particularly those that remain active. The diversity and ingenuity of their adaptations are equal to the challenges they face during the coldest months of the year.

] FAST FACTS [
Mammals in Winter

▶ Mammals spend New England winters *hibernating* (those that cannot obtain necessary food and whose metabolism drops significantly); *dormant or semi-dormant* (those whose body temperatures do not fall significantly and who are active during mild spells); or *active* (those who can find suitable food, or have stored enough food prior to winter to sustain them until spring). See the chart on p. 388.

▶ Bobcats were historically the only wild predator in New England that regularly killed white-tailed deer in the winter, when deep snow impairs the deer's ability to flee. However, coyotes have replaced them as the primary winter hunters of deer, and bobcats more often hunt smaller prey.

▶ Rabbits and hares pack down regularly traveled trails in order not to expend more energy than necessary traveling through snow.

▶ In deep snow deer remain in a "yard," an area where they create a network of trails that they use to reach food. South-facing slopes and cedar swamps are frequently used for this purpose.

▶ American mink feed through holes in the ice of lakes and streams where they can find fish, crayfish, and hibernating frogs in the mud during winter months.

▶ North American river otters keep one or two holes open in the winter for fishing purposes. They often reside in old beaver or muskrat dens in stream banks.

▶ The striped skunk is active in early and late winter, but is usually dormant during midwinter.

▶ Red squirrels make leafy winter nests in treetops and often line them with redcedar bark. In New England many if not most remain in underground nests during the winter months.

▶ Eastern gray squirrels bury nuts individually in the fall, retrieving them during the winter when food is scarce.

Bald-Faced Hornets—
Cooperative Construction Workers

Most trees are no longer bearing leaves and the formerly hidden secrets within their crowns are revealed this time of year. In addition to the smaller bird nests that become apparent, an occasional large, gray, papery structure—the

Bald-faced hornets are black with white markings on the front of their head and at the end of their abdomen.

Bald-faced hornet nests can measure up to 3 feet in length.

Each color seen in this close-up represents a different source of wood fiber used to make the nest.

summer home of bald-faced hornets—is noticed. This structure is built strictly as a nursery for the queen hornet, her eggs, and developing larvae. This relatively small insect (which is not a true hornet, but rather belongs to the genus of wasps called yellowjackets) not only works in cooperation with hundreds of its kin to construct a nest, but it also creates the material of which the nest is built.

Paper to Live In
Most of us have seen these structures at least once. They are usually gray, somewhat oval, 2 to 3 feet in length, and attached to the branches of shrubs or trees, often out of reach. Made out of paper, they are formed by many hundreds of hornets' mandibles masticating on wood fibers that were stripped from logs and weathered fence posts. The combination of chewed wood and hornet saliva containing

starch forms a pulpy material resembling papier-mâché, which the hornet shapes into a ball and then carries back to its nest where it dries as soon as it is exposed to the air. Slowly over the summer months the size of the nest is increased from that of a golf ball to an overly large football. Careful examination of the outside of the nest reveals white fibers along with many shades of grays, browns, and even reds and greens. Each of these colors represents a different source of wood from which the building material was made.

Reared by a Queen
The visible part of the nest is one of several "envelopes" surrounding the cells in which eggs are laid and young hornet larvae develop. Multiple layers enveloping the cells create protection from the elements and provide excellent insulation. Several horizontal tiers are constructed within the nest, each consisting of a layer of identical hexagonal cells.

Although impressive in size by the time most of us notice them, hornet nests have very humble beginnings. In the spring the overwintering young

DEC

A paper shell consisting of multiple layers envelops the three or four tiers of cells within a bald-faced hornet nest. A single opening at the bottom allows the hornets to fly in and out. The queen lays one egg in each cell, and workers feed the developing larvae once the eggs hatch. When the larvae are ready to pupate and develop into adults, the cells are covered with white silk "domes," through which the adult hornets will emerge.

queen emerges from a rotting log or leaf litter and performs the only work other than laying eggs that she will ever perform in her lifetime: She builds several cells and an enveloping shell roughly 1 to 2 inches in diameter. She then lays one egg in each of the cells. When the eggs hatch, she rears the young hornets, or larvae, preying on insects (mainly crane and other species of flies) and then chewing them into fine bits to feed to her young. The sole purpose of the egg-laying is to create *workers* (infertile females) whose lives will be devoted to building more cells and enlarging the nest, feeding the young, and guarding the nest. The size of the nest increases as the workers eat away the inner layers of the shell and add this material, as well as newly-chewed fibers, to the exterior. As soon as the initial eggs hatch, pupate, and emerge as adults, the queen reverts to just laying eggs, which she will continue doing until the end of the summer. Up to 400 workers can occupy a nest, which explains how its size can increase so dramatically in just a few months.

Come fall the workers raise several new queens, which when mature, leave the nest to mate with the few males, or *drones*, in the colony that exist for this purpose. The drones' single contribution is to fertilize these young queens in the fall before the queens seek shelter and hibernate until spring. After mating occurs and very cold weather arrives, the drones—along with all the workers and the old queen—die.

Recycled Architecture
Even though the nest is not occupied by hornets during the winter, its usefulness is not over. The many layers surrounding the interior cells provide excellent insulation for creatures wise enough to seek shelter within (such as the deermouse I once encountered—it is hard to say which of us was more surprised). Come spring, the durable paper

walls are a prized source of building material for many songbirds.

Although bald-faced hornets aren't as aggressive as most other wasps, they will definitely defend their nest. The workers' *ovipositors*, or egg-laying devices, have been modified into stingers, as workers do not lay eggs. Unlike a honeybee, a hornet can sting repeatedly without losing its stinger or its life. Those anxious to inspect the inside of a nest would be wise to wait until late November or December, when active inhabitants (at least those possessing stingers) are no longer in residence .

Cones—*Conifer Cradles*

At this time of year, cones are everywhere—in wreaths, around candles, and in many holiday displays. Their function is far more than decorative, however—at least for the cone-bearing tree, or conifer, on which they grow. Essentially cones are the "cradles" in which conifer seeds develop and mature, protected by hard, woody scales.

Naked Seeds
There are two kinds of seed-producing plants: non-flowering, or *gymnosperms* (in the United States these include cycads, ginkos, and conifers) and flowering, or *angiosperms*. Angiosperms—be they trees, wildflowers, or vegetables—have seeds that are encased in a protective covering, or *ovary*. They are more numerous than gymnosperms, with approximately 300,000 species identified at the present time. As gymnosperms, conifers have what are called *naked seeds*—seeds that have no protective covering and are not as evolved as flowering plants. Although they were the dominant plant form from about 300 million years ago to 50 million years ago, only about 630 species of conifers exist today. (Even so, they make up as much as a third of the world's forested area.)

The seed cones of many conifers, like these young black spruce cones, are positioned at the tips of the uppermost branches, where they are most likely to receive wind-borne pollen.

Eastern hemlock cone.   White spruce cone.

Cones are the reproductive structures of conifers, and as such, they are either male or female. The cones we are most familiar with are the *seed*, or female, cones. *Pollen*, or male, cones produce pollen and are typically very small and inconspicuous. We've all seen the piles of tan, quarter-inch-long, papery structures beneath eastern white pines (see photo on p. 134). These male cones fall off the tree within a few days of having their pollen dispersed. Female cones, containing the developing seeds, are much larger than the male cones (size and shape depend on species of conifer, with one of the largest, the sugar pine cone, being nearly 2 feet in length). They usually consist of woody scales and persist on the tree for varying amounts of time, from months to years—again, depending on the species. (There are some conifers, including junipers and yews, whose seed cones are greatly modified, so much so that they resemble berries far more than cones.)

Old-Fashioned Pollination

One of the ways in which conifers are more primitive than flowering plants is the way in which pollination takes place. Conifers depend on the wind to disperse their copious amounts of pollen grains. In the spring, when the pollen is mature, the tiny male cones open, allowing the wind to blow their pollen grains far and wide. You may have noticed a yellow dust-like coating on your car, or clouds of yellow "powder" blowing from conifer stands in the spring—this is pollen, and it is responsible for many of the allergic reactions people have at that time of year. Pollination is a game of chance for any plant, but especially for conifers, as the wind is not as reliable a pollinator as a hungry insect. In order to assure that at least one pollen grain lands on an *ovule*, or egg cell, inside the female cone of the same species, conifers must produce volumes of pollen, and it must be very light so that it will disperse in the slightest of breezes. Therefore, one pine or spruce cone releases up to 2 million grains of pollen into the air.

The techniques conifers have evolved for increasing the likelihood of healthy seed produc-

Eastern white pine cones (left) and pollen cones (right).

Yew trees do not bear typical cones. They produce single seeds, fully or partly enclosed by a fleshy covering, or *aril*. The seeds are poisonous to humans and are dispersed by birds attracted to the fleshy, sweet, red pulp of the berry-like cone.

tion are varied. Seed cones, which are most often located on the same tree as pollen cones, usually form at the tips of the tree's uppermost branches, above the conifer's own pollen cones. This position decreases the chances of the tree pollinating itself, as the pollen grains can't just drop down on its own tree's seed cones. In addition, the seed cones are in the most likely spot to receive airborne pollen from other trees.

When a seed cone is developing, it opens and closes according to reproductive needs. Initially the scales of the cone are closed, but during the few days that its species' pollen is being dispersed, the scales open up, allowing pollen grains to enter the cone and with luck, land on one or more ovules that rest on top of each scale. After

Northern white cedar cone.

Red pine cone.

] FAST FACTS [

Cones

- All cones are either male or female.

- The cones of pines fall off the tree in one piece after the seeds have been shed, whereas cedar and fir cones usually disintegrate on the tree.

- The cones of firs stand erect on the branches.

- After falling apart on the tree, all that is left of a balsam fir cone is a spike-like axis.

- When the larch's golden leaves fall off in autumn, greenish young cones are visible near the tips of the branches; older brown cones are further back on the branch.

- Spruce cones are smooth and slightly flexible, unlike hard pine cones.

- An eastern white pine cone has between 50 and 80 scales.

- It takes up to three years for a female pine cone to fully develop.

- Pine seeds develop in pairs, with two seeds attached to each scale in the cones; attached to each seed is a thin, delicate "wing," which aids in its dispersal.

pollen dispersal for this species is over, the cone closes up again, re-opening only to release mature seeds, which are also dispersed by the wind.

The maturation of a cone's seeds can take anywhere from several months to several years, depending on the species of conifer. After the seeds are mature, the cones of some species go so far as to open and close according to the likelihood of their seeds successfully dispersing; they close on damp, rainy days and open in dry weather. For this reason cones have historically been used as weather forecasters. There are some conifers that even need the heat of a fire to open up, thus giving the seeds a chance to germinate in a burned-over area where competition is less severe.

In addition to contributing to the survival of their species, these mature seeds are a vital part of the food chain. Many birds and small mammals depend upon them. A case in point is the red crossbill—70 percent of its diet consists of pine seeds. If there is a poor seed crop in a given year in eastern Canada, we often see the consequences the following winter in the form of seed-eating species of birds, such as pine grosbeaks, white-winged crossbills, and common redpolls, irrupting in New England in search of an adequate food supply (see more on this subject on p. 347).

JANUARY

endurance

Although January occasionally provides us with a thaw, most years New England is locked into winter during this month. Food is scarce for wildlife and any snow on the ground usually compounds the difficulty of finding it. Mammals that remain active rely on stored caches or must secure enough food to fuel their energy needs. The hibernation of reptiles and amphibians allows them to escape the rigors of winter, which they could never tolerate. Insects, too, are deep into their dormancy, whether adults, larvae, pupae, or eggs. Birds are active soon after dawn, foraging for food, and activity heightens a few hours before sunset as they eat in preparation for the long, cold night ahead. For the most part, plants are still in their dormant stage. In most of New England, most years, they are provided protection from wind and desiccation by a blanket of snow.

nature notes

Here's a sampling of species that are courting, breeding, giving birth, migrating, arriving from the north, hibernating, and remaining active in January.

AMPHIBIANS

Gray Treefrog—*Hibernating*

Although there are two species of gray treefrogs in eastern North America, the common species in New England is *Hyla versicolor*. This beautifully mottled frog spends the winter hibernating beneath

Gray treefrog.

leaf litter, rocks, and rotting logs. Along with the spring peeper and wood frog, the gray treefrog can withstand temperatures as low as -20°F for several days, thanks to the glycerol that accumulates in its blood. It is able to freeze up to 40 percent of its body, thaw, repeat the cycle several times, and still survive.

Red Eft—*Hibernating*

The red eft, the land stage of the eastern newt, spends the winter hibernating under logs and leaf litter. It remains on land for two to seven years, after which it returns to the water and transforms into a green, aquatic adult. The skin secretions of red efts are about 10 times more toxic than those of adult newts. (Read more about red efts on p. 137.)

REPTILES

Eastern Ribbonsnake—*Hibernating*

When the eastern ribbonsnake's diet of frogs, toads, and salamanders disappears in the fall, it soon follows, vanishing from October to March. It often hibernates near ponds and streams, where it leads a semiaquatic existence in the summer. Muskrat bank burrows and lodges, ant mounds, crayfish burrows, and vole tunnels serve as hibernation sites. The body temperature of a hibernating ribbonsnake averages 43°F.

Eastern ribbonsnake

Eastern Musk Turtle—*Hibernating*

The aquatic eastern musk turtle, or stinkpot, as it is also known, is more common in southern

Eastern musk turtle.

New England than further north. When hibernating, musk turtles tend to gather in groups in the muddy bottoms of ponds, beneath large rocks in rivers and in riverbank burrows. They retire to these locations when the temperature goes below 50°F and remain there until spring.

BIRDS

Dark-Eyed Junco—*Remaining Year-Round*

Dark-eyed juncos are year-round residents throughout most of New England. Their white outer tail feathers are distinctive and their counter-shading

Dark-eyed junco.

(dark above, light below) makes them harder for predators to detect. Five different forms of juncos that were once considered separate species are now lumped into one. The form that resides in New England is known as the slate-colored junco. It is one of the most common species of birds found at feeders during winter in the Northeast, but its numbers may vary from one winter to the next.

American Goldfinch—*Remaining Year-Round*

It is much harder to tell a male from a female American goldfinch in the winter than in the summer, for the male loses his bright yellow breeding feathers in the fall and both sexes have rather drab tan winter plumages. If you look very closely during the winter months, you can distinguish some yellow-tinged feathers at the base of the male's slightly blacker wings, next to his body, and a barely perceptible yellow wash on his throat; the female has buff-colored wing bars with not much hint of yellow anywhere. Unlike any other members of the finch family, the American goldfinch

Male (left) and female (right) American goldfinches in their winter plumages.

has a second molt in the spring, when the male turns bright yellow and black again.

Evening Grosbeak—*Irruptive Winter Visitor*

The evening grosbeak is a large, colorful member of the finch family. This stocky, heavy-billed bird of northern coniferous forests has gradually extended its range eastward. It currently breeds in northern New England and winters throughout the Northeast. There is often a biannual *irruption* (an unusual appearance in the non-breeding season outside their usual range) of evening grosbeaks in New England during the winter, when a lean northern food supply drives them southward.

Male evening grosbeak.

Frequently they take command of bird feeders, emptying them in very little time with their seed-cracking bills. (Find out more about bird irruptions on p. 347 and bills adapted for different diets on p. 335.)

Ruffed grouse scat.

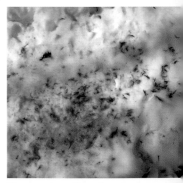

The remains of a red squirrel. Note the ejected droppings of a hawk in the upper right hand corner, approximately 6 feet from the kill site.

Snowy owl.

The dry segments are between ¾ and 1½ inches long, and each one usually has an end that looks as though it has been white-washed, due to uric acid. Usually a pile of scat is deposited, as opposed to a single segment.

The second form of ruffed grouse scat is soft and semiliquid. It is produced by the *ceca*, two pocket-like appendages in the upper gut, which among other things, aid in the digestion of cellulose. The consistency of grouse scat reflects the degree to which food has been digested. The softer scat is usually evacuated after the harder segments, but the two forms of scat can also be found in separate locations. Burrowing holes, which grouse create when they fly into a snow bank for shelter during extremely cold nights, often contain this second form of scat. (Read more about ruffed grouse on p. 345.)

Snowy Owl—
Irruptive Winter Visitor

Lemmings are the primary prey of snowy owls. Many boreal rodents, including lemmings, have a four-year cycle during which their populations explode and then crash. When the lemming population crashes in Canada it forces avian predators, including snowy owls, to move further south into New England in search of alternate prey. (Read more about bird irruptions on p. 347.)

Ruffed Grouse—*Sign (Scat)*

Grouse scat comes in two forms. The more common form is fibrous droppings that reflect the bird's dietary preference for buds and small twigs.

Hawk—*Sign (Kill Site)*

As a rule, birds of prey rid themselves of solid waste by regurgitating pellets consisting of the indigestible parts of the prey they've eaten. Their droppings consist mostly of uric acid, which looks like whitewash. Often the location and pattern of an avian predator's uric acid waste at a kill site can help you determine whether the predator

BIRDS OF PREY

Many birds are predators, including hawks, owls, shrikes, some gulls, jays, crows, and ravens. Predators are carnivorous, feeding on small mammals, especially rodents, birds, snakes, fish, and frogs. "Birds of prey" is a subcategory of carnivores, and includes meat-

Bald eagle.

eating birds that possess large and powerful curved beaks adapted for tearing flesh, and strong, sharp *talons*, or claws, such as hawks, eagles, falcons, owls, and osprey. Birds of prey—or raptors, as they are sometimes called—have been admired by humans over the years. Vikings adorned their helmets with the wings of hawks; Cherokee, Sioux, and Apache used hawk and eagle feathers for their headdresses, and the bald eagle is the emblem of the United States. Birds of prey have also been vilified and persecuted in the past, as predators of farm animals and game birds. Today's laws protect them, as well they should. One pair of meadow voles could be responsible for a million offspring within a year. This extended family might well consume 23 million pounds of vegetation in 12 months, were it not for the birds of prey that consider them a staple food and help keep rodent numbers in check.

was an owl or a hawk. Owl droppings tend to land directly beneath the owl, whereas hawks and falcons raise their tails and squirt uric acid quite a distance away.

■ **New England Owls**

Barn owl
Eastern screech-owl
Great horned owl
Snowy owl (irregular
    winter visitor)
Northern hawk owl
    (regular winter visitor
    in northernmost
    Maine)
Barred owl
Great gray owl (very rare
    and irregular winter
    visitor)
Long-eared owl
Short-eared owl
Boreal owl (very rare and
    irregular winter visitor in northern New England)
Northern saw-whet owl

Eastern screech-owl.

MAMMALS

Coyote—*Breeding*
Coyotes often remain in pairs throughout the year. During January and February both markings and tracks of coyotes are prevalent throughout much of New England. As breeding time approaches, the male and female "tandem mark," both mark-

Marking of a female coyote in estrus (urine and blood present).

ing (primarily with urine) in the same spot, with increasing frequency. This is done most often at the edges of their territory, and serves to ward off trespassing coyotes. It is thought that this habit may also strengthen pair bonding and synchronize breeding. Coyotes have been known to keep the same mate for several years, sometimes for life.

The coyote population has grown tremendously due to its ability to adapt to new habitats and to man, as well as the absence of wolves in New England. Their wariness and their preference for small rodents enable them to survive in an environment increasingly populated with humans. In addition, the coyote's reproductive strategy enhances its success; when its numbers decrease, the remaining coyotes produce larger litters that have a higher rate of survival.

Black bear den.

American Black Bear—*Giving Birth*

The process that leads to the birth of black bear cubs this month is an extended one. Mating takes place in June or July, but implantation doesn't occur until late fall and is followed by a 70-day gestation period. The female bear gives birth to up to five cubs (most often two) in late January or early February. The cub of a 200-pound black bear sow weighs less than half a pound and measures about 7½ inches in length. This year's young remain with their mother through the coming summer, fall, and into next winter. Because female black bears are not sexually receptive while nursing, they ordinarily have young only every two or three years. (Read more about American black bear birth on p. 374.)

Northern and Southern Flying Squirrel—*Huddling*

During cold periods in the winter, both species of flying squirrels in New England are known to form groups and huddle to keep themselves warm. As many as 50 flying squirrels have been found in a cavity clustered together in a snug ball. On rare oc-

casions both species have been found sharing the same space. (See more on active mammal winter adaptations on p. 355.)

White-Tailed Deer— *Sign (Eaten Fungus)*

As opposed to the summer when white-tailed deer consume herbaceous foods such as grasses and leaves, in winter they become browsers, feeding on the buds and twigs of maples, birches, viburnums, and many other woody

A shelf fungus eaten by white-tailed deer. Note the incisor marks.

plants. In addition, acorns, ferns, wild grapes, and fungi are eaten. White-tailed deer spend more time eating than on any other activity—each deer consumes from 5 to 9 pounds of food per day.

American Beaver—*Sign (Tracks)*

Most winters, beaver ponds freeze over, limiting beaver activity to beneath the ice. Occasionally during a January thaw, a portion of the pond will open up, allowing its resident beavers to access land and obtain fresh food. Signs of this activity, such as tracks, cut trees, and wood chips, can be seen near open water. (Find out more about beavers on p. 321.)

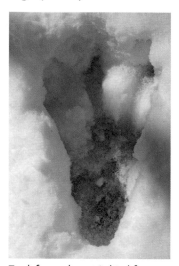

Track from a beaver's hind foot.

Raccoon tracks.

Raccoon—*Sign (Tracks)*

When cold weather arrives in New England, raccoons often seek out a protected spot such as a hollow tree or den and remain there for several weeks. They don't hibernate (their metabolism isn't greatly lowered), but instead enter a dormant state in order to conserve energy. If the temperature rises above 32°F raccoons rouse themselves and wander about in the snow. Little or no food is consumed by raccoons in the winter in New England; they survive on the fat that they accumulated in the fall, which can be as much as 30 percent of their body weight. By spring many raccoons will have lost up to half of their fall weight. (See more about tracks on p. 385.)

Ermine—*Sign (Tracks)*

Members of the weasel family stay active in winter, and the ermine (short-tailed weasel) is no exception. Although its population is healthy and it actively hunts for mice, shrews, and other small mammals both day and night, the ermine

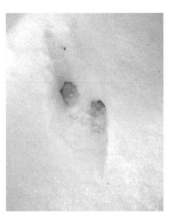
Ermine tracks.

is seldom seen. This is largely due to its white winter coat, which provides effective camouflage in the northern part of its range. Its paired tracks frequently lead to the burrow of another animal, where the ermine often builds a winter nest out of the feathers and fur of its prey. (Read more about winter camouflage on p. 290.)

A red fox marking.

Red Fox—*Sign (Marking)*

Beginning in January a skunklike smell is often detectable as you walk through woods and fields. Chances are, however, that a skunk is not the culprit. Look for saplings, rocks, or stumps that poke out of the snow in the middle of trails, especially at the junction of two or more trails. Chances are your nose will guide you to the yellow urine markings of a red fox on one or more of these objects. Mating season has begun for red foxes and their frequent territorial marking is done with particularly strong-smelling urine at this time of year. (See more on red foxes on p. 415.)

Red Squirrel—*Sign (Midden)*

Red squirrels often have a favorite spot where they bring food and eat it. Frequently a red squirrel brings cones to such a spot, strips off the scales of the cone, and eats the inner seeds, discarding both the cone as well as the empty scales on the ground. These uneaten portions

A red squirrel midden. Note the tunnel in the background.

THE BEAR AND I—A MORNING ENCOUNTER

Early one morning as I passed the window looking out onto the porch of my log cabin, out of the corner of my eye I saw a large, dark moving object and quickly realized it was a bear. What I did next was without conscious thought, as if I were on automatic pilot: I headed out the door, grabbing my camera on the way, and took off after the bear. It had lumbered off the porch and then on into the woods beyond it. Although I had seen black bears before (at a distance) I had never seen one in Vermont, much less managed to get one in my camera's viewfinder, so I was in hot pursuit. By this time I had noticed that there did not appear to be any cubs around. Because I knew that for the most part the only time black bears were known to be aggressive was when they were protecting their cubs, I felt fairly comfortable giving chase. Had I stopped to consider my actions, I probably would not have had the courage to continue, but by then it was too late for rational thinking.

I didn't really believe I would set eyes on the bear again, so when I stumbled upon it a short distance into the woods, my heart pounded against my chest, my hands shook, and I'm sure I was more frightened than it was. We were about 50 feet apart when it looked up and saw me; our eyes met and it proceeded to rise up, grunt, whine, and chatter its teeth at me. Hoping that what I'd read and been told was accurate, I assured myself that this was all "for show" and that I had little to fear. Still, I made sure, at this point, that there was a solid tree (for what good that would do) between me and the bear.

After a few short moments of bravado, the bear calmly turned and walked away on all fours, heading further into the woods. There was never a question in my mind as to what I was going to do next—I followed at a healthy distance, keeping an eye on the bear at all times so as to gauge whether I should retreat or continue in pursuit.

The bear was fully aware that it was being followed. After several minutes it stopped at an old white pine tree and climbed to a height of about 20 feet. It was amazing to see how it could balance itself, much less get comfortable enough to settle down on the spoke-like dead limbs of the pine, but settle it did, resting its very large body on what looked like very thin branches. There were several yawns and much shifting of position. When the bear finally was satisfied with its purchase, it closed its eyes and appeared to go to sleep. Every now and then the bear would open its eyes, and shift the position of its head, so I was aware that this "sleep" was not a deep one. But I crept closer and closer to the tree. The bear whined a lot of the time its eyes were closed and remained somewhat restless throughout its stay in the pine. Even so, the fact that it trusted me enough to close its eyes in my presence was humbling. I worked my way up to a distance of 10 or 15 feet, and as I stood there I found myself curious to see what effect the sound of my voice would have, so I began to speak. Its eyes remained closed; however, when I picked up the smallest of sticks and broke it, the bear's eyes immediately flew open and it became totally alert.

After an hour-and-a-half of rest, the bear yawned several times, stood up on the branches and stretched, placing its front feet against the trunk of the tree while sticking its rump way out in the air. I knew it was only minutes before the bear would be on the ground again and it had been so tolerant of my presence thus far that I felt I could ask no more. So, with great reluctance (but with some relief as well), I headed out of the woods toward home, knowing that I had just experienced possibly the most intimate exchange I would ever have with a wild creature, especially one so large. The fact that there were no witnesses only increases the poignancy of its memory. For an hour-and-a-half, we were each other's entire world.

Stolen moments from the author's r bear encounter.

■ **Feline vs. Canine Tracks***

	Cat Family (bobcat, lynx, mountain lion)	Dog Family (gray and red fox, coyote, wolf)
Overall shape	Round, asymmetrical	Oval, symmetrical
Heel pad	Double lobe on leading edge	Single lobe on leading edge
Area between toes and heel pad	Linear ridge	Small mound
Nails	Retractable— usually don't register in track	Usually register in track

* Exceptions exist.

create a pile referred to as a *midden*. After several years these piles can be as high as 2 feet. Middens at the base of a tree in coniferous woods are a definite sign of red squirrel activity.

Fisher—*Sign (Shelter)*
Occasionally you will find fisher tracks ending at a hole that leads to a sheltered spot under a log or rock—a temporary den, which it uses while moving around its home range. Look for signs indicating there is an inhabitant: tracks leading to, but not from, the shelter, and the formation of crystals at the opening of the hole, caused by the warmth of the body within. (Find out more about fishers on p. 29.)

A fisher hole under a log.

INSECTS & ARACHNIDS

Cattail Caterpillar—*Dormant*
The larvae of several species of moths can be found inside the seed heads of cattails during the winter months. One of the more common species is the shy cosmet (*Limnaecia phragmitella*). When you see cattails with somewhat disheveled-looking tops, and yet their seeds have not dispersed, it can be a sign that larvae reside within them. In order to have shelter and insulation, the larvae spin silk threads around the outside of cattail seed heads,

Cattail caterpillar.

and then burrow into the fluff for the duration of the winter. Up to 50 or more larvae can be found within one cattail seed head. In the spring these larvae make cocoons inside the seed head or stem of the cattail and emerge as adult moths.

European Honeybee— *Remaining Active inside Hive*
Most New England insects migrate or become inactive in the winter. Honeybees are an exception to this rule. The queen and worker bees born in the fall spend the winter as an active colony within their

hive. By clustering together and giving off heat, honeybees maintain an air temperature of about 50°F in their hive, even if it is -50°F outside. There is

constant circulation and repositioning among the bees. Those in the warm center of the cluster next to the cells feed on stored honey after which they work their way to the outside of the cluster where it is cooler. Those bees that were on the outside then make their way to the center of the hive. This movement never stops. (If there aren't enough overwintering bees to maintain this temperature, the hive fails.)

European honeybee.

When the temperature of the hive exceeds 90°F the queen lays a small number of eggs so that there will be young bees ready to work in the spring. These larvae are fed stored pollen and honey. (Read more about European honeybees on p. 219.)

Black-and-Yellow Argiope—*Sign (Egg Case)*

Silk is secreted as a liquid from a spider's spinnerets and hardens into a fiber upon contact

with the air. Because of its strength (roughly five times as strong as steel of the same density) and durability, it makes a very protective covering, or sac, for spider eggs. In the fall, the female black-and-yellow argiope spider spins a small, square, silken mat and lays 100 or more eggs on it. She then pulls in the corners of the mat and forms it into a ball, before attaching it with more silk to the stem of grasses or

Black-and-yellow argiope egg case.

weeds for the winter. When this process is complete, she dies. Inside this silken nursery the eggs soon hatch, and it is here that the young spiderlings spend the winter. During cold winter days they are dormant, but on warm days they become active and, because there are no insects, resort to eating each other. In the spring, the few spiders left exit the egg case.

PLANTS & FUNGI

Aspen.

Aspen—*Bark Photosynthesizing*

Photosynthesis does not stop in all deciduous trees after their leaves have fallen. When the temperature is above 27°F, some species of trees continue to photosynthesize, not in their leaves, but in their bark. Take a look at the bark of trembling aspen or striped maple and notice the green tint that chlorophyll gives it. From 15 to 40 percent of trembling aspen's chlorophyll is in its bark. The rate of photosynthesis, however, is less than half that of leaves, partially because of the limited ability of light to penetrate the bark.

Shelf Fungus—*Decomposing Trees*

Shelf fungi can be found on dead standing or fallen trees. These hard, woody structures are the fruiting bodies of fungi that have invaded the tree and are decomposing its remains. Inside the tree or log a mass of thread-like fungal tubes thinner than human hairs, called *hyphae*, secrete enzymes that digest organic material. Reproductive spores are produced by the shelf fungus and dispersed through the many pores on its underside. (Read more about fungi on p. 295.)

Shelf fungus.

BURLS

Occasionally you come across a swollen, warty, spherical growth on the trunk of a tree. This growth is called a *burl*. Most burls begin as galls, abnormal growths also found on herbaceous plants caused by a fungus, bacterium, or egg-laying insects (see p. 155 for more on galls). Their growth is abnormally fast—much faster than the tree on which they form. Burls do not kill trees, although they may weaken the structure of the trunk. They are much sought after by woodworkers because of the unique beauty of the grain of the wood inside them.

Burl.

■ New England Conifers

Family: Pine *(Pinaceae)*	Species	Genus Characteristics
Pines	Eastern white pine, red pine, scots pine, pitch pine, jack pine	• 41 species native to North America • Relatively long needles in bundles of two to five • Woody cones with scales thickened at tip
Larches	American larch	• Three species native to North America • Soft needles in bunches at ends of short shoots • Needles deciduous • Cones small and upright
Hemlocks	Eastern hemlock	• Four species native to North America • Needles very short and flattened • Twigs slender and rough • Cones small, pendent
Spruces	Red spruce, black spruce, white spruce, blue spruce, Norway spruce	• Seven species native to North America • Needles short, stiff, often prickly • Twigs rough • Cones pendent, scales papery
True Firs	Balsam fir	• 11 species native to North America • Needles short, blunt-tipped • Twigs smooth • Cones upright

Family: Yew *(Taxaceae)*		
Yews	Canada yew	• Two species native to North America • Short, soft, blunt-tipped leaves • Cone resembles fleshy berry; seed is poisonous

Family: Cypress *(Cupressaceae)*		
Junipers	Eastern redcedar	• 13 species native to North America • Tiny, scale-like leaves • Cone resembles berry
Arborvitae	Northern white-cedar, atlantic white cedar	• Two species native to North America • Small, upright cones with scales opened slightly • Flat, fan-shaped sprays of leaves

a closer look

Some creatures, including most **insects** (p. 394), are out of sight this time of year, tucked away under bark, in rotting logs, leaf litter, and rock crevices. Others, including many **small mammals** (pp. 377 and 379), are active, but hidden under the **snow** (p. 392) in the *subnivian layer* (the thin air layer between the covering snow and the ground surface). The **black bear** (see below) doesn't qualify as a small mammal, yet it, too, is concealed, often beneath a fallen tree or in a cavity covered with snow, giving birth to its young. While we don't regularly see all the animals that remain active during the winter, they do leave signs of their presence in the form of **scat** (p. 382), **tracks** (p. 385), and in the case of white-tailed bucks, dropped **antlers** (p. 389). The intricacy and beauty of the persistent fruiting parts of some flowering plants justifies referring to them as **winter wildflowers** (p. 397).

American Black Bear Birth—
New Life Midwinter

When American black bears go into their dens in late fall or early winter, they do so primarily because of the dwindling food supply, not in order to escape the cold weather. Most dens are not a great deal warmer than their surroundings, for they commonly are located under the roots of fallen trees, in brush piles, occasionally hollow trees, or even on the ground, but rarely in the protective caves that story books would have us believe. Bears usually curl up on their bed of leaves, grass, and twigs, leaving only their back and sides, which are covered with dense fur, exposed to the cold.

Hibernation can last up to seven months and during this entire time bears do not eat, drink, exercise, defecate, or urinate. They cut their metabolic rate in half. Sleeping heart rates drop from 60 to 90 beats per minute to 8 to 40, and breathing slows to

American black bears den in brush, fallen tree roots, and occasionally a hollow tree—but rarely a cave as many people believe.

one breath every 45 seconds. However, unlike smaller hibernating mammals—such as woodchucks and jumping mice, whose temperature hovers a few degrees above freezing—the body temperature of

During the months of January, February, and March while denning, a black bear mother is awake and caring for her young when they are active, she sleeps when they sleep.

black bears drops only a few degrees, 14 at most. Bears can maintain a high body temperature because of their thick fur, low surface-to-mass ratio, and a reduced blood supply to their limbs—only the trunk of their body and their head remain at a high temperature, in part to allow the bear to maintain brain function in order to tend newborn cubs.

Whether or not to classify an animal as a "true hibernator" has been controversial over the years. Scientists used to define hibernation strictly in terms of temperature reduction, and because the black bear's temperature doesn't drop dramatically, it was not considered a hibernator. Due to the redefinition of the state of hibernation, which now includes not only temperature drop but other metabolic rates as well, black bears are now classified as true hibernators.

Birth Month
Most black bears begin their life this month, inside dens. Weighing less than a pound, cubs have only a light covering of fur, closed eyelids, no teeth, and can barely crawl. Immediately after she gives birth,

■ A Year in the Life of an American Black Bear Mother and Her Cubs

January	Cubs are born, weighing less than a pound and measuring 7½ inches in length.
February	Mother wakes to care for nursing cubs and sleeps when they sleep.
March	Cubs' eyes open somewhere between a month and six weeks of age.
April	Mother and cubs emerge from den. Well-fed cubs weigh about 10 pounds.
May	Cubs start to taste grasses and other food mother eats, but primary diet is milk.
June	Mating season (during cubs' second year)*. Mother bear experiences delayed implantation. Young cubs begin eating solid food; 17-month-old cubs begin to disperse.
July	Cubs' blue eyes turn brown. End of mating season. Berries (raspberry, blueberry, serviceberry) ripen and become staple foods.
August	Cubs nurse and consume berries and nuts, particularly hazlenuts.
September	Cubs are usually weaned. Acorns ripen. Lethargy starts to set in.
October	Early hibernators seek dens. Last winter's cubs remain with mother.
November	Most bears hibernating by December 1. Eggs fertilized in late spring or early summer implant in uterus of mother.
December	Embryos developing inside hibernating mother.

*Black bears breed every other year, which allows the cubs to remain with their mother for 17 months.

the mother eats the birth membranes, licks her off-spring, and warms them against her thinly-furred belly. Contrary to what is commonly believed—that the mother bear spends the first few months of her cubs' lives in a constant state of hibernation—she is very much awake during their birth and actively cares for them during their infancy. She wakes and moves in response to the cubs' cues, adjusting her position so that her young can nurse easily and so that she doesn't crush them. For the most part, she sleeps only when they sleep. Because her sleep is restless, she can lose up to 40 percent of her body weight over winter, as opposed to 15 to 25 percent lost by non-nursing bears.

Apparently the size of a black bear litter is not affected by the amount of food available the previous summer and fall. In both poor food years and "mast years" that produce an abundant supply of acorns, beechnuts, berries, apples, and other fruit, as well as insects and succulent greens, most bears produce two cubs.

Out on Their Own

Mother and cubs usually emerge from their den in April, a short while after male black bears emerge. At this point the cubs weigh anywhere between 4 and 10 pounds, depending on how much milk their mother produced and how large or small their litter was. Usually the cubs are weaned in September, shortly before hibernation begins again, although occasionally this doesn't occur until the family breaks up in the following spring. After spending a second winter hibernating in a den with her yearling cubs, the mother strongly encourages them to be on their way shortly before mating season begins in June. She will begin the birthing and rearing cycle all over again, but it will be at least another year before the weanling cubs are ready to mate and produce their own families.

] FAST FACTS [
American Black Bear

▶ Food availability affects when a black bear goes into hibernation. In a year of low acorn and beechnut production, bears enter into hibernation as early as mid-October, as opposed to November in years of plentiful nuts and seeds.

▶ A black bear hibernates at a relatively shallow level and keeps its body temperature quite warm—88 to 95˚F. This is thought to be an adaptation that allows the mother to care for her newborns.

▶ A black bear's ability to arouse quickly from hibernation, its relatively warm body temperature, and the fact that it gives birth during hibernation have caused scientists to question whether or not bears are "true hibernators." The length of dormancy and the fact that no energy is taken in by the bear during this period of time qualifies it as very close to if not categorically considered a state of hibernation.

▶ Most hibernating bears wake periodically and move about during warm spells. Occasionally they even switch dens midwinter. If disturbed, black bears wake quickly and are likely to move to a new den.

▶ A black bear burns mostly fat for fuel and saves its protein supplies. This enables the bear to emerge from hibernation with about the same amount of muscle that it had going into hibernation, providing it had an adequate supply of fat with which to begin.

▶ The mother black bear loses .36 to .61 pounds a day converting fat, water, and other body stores to milk and energy.

Small Mammals—*Part One:*
The Rodent Crew

Mice, voles, lemmings, moles, and shrews—we tend to lump these diminutive, furry creatures together. While these small mammals resemble one another, they have significant physical and behavioral differences—enough so that they belong to two different groups: *Rodentia* (rodents, including mice, voles, and lemmings) and *Soricomorpha* (invertebrate-eating animals, or insectivores, such as shrews and moles). Mice, voles, and lemmings comprise 11 of the 21 species of rodents in New England; there are 10 species of shrews and moles (see p. 379 for more about them).

Rodents

White-footed and North American deermice are not strictly seed eaters. Look closely and you can see the tiny mouse incisor marks in this shelf fungus.

Rodents—beavers, porcupines, woodchucks, squirrels, chipmunks, rats, mice, voles, and lemmings—come in all sizes and shapes. Some live on the ground, others live in trees; some live a majority of their life underground, and there are even semi-aquatic species. As different as their habits and appearances may be, the features that they all share are a pair of prominent incisors in the front of both upper and lower jaws, and a lack of canine teeth.

Mice, voles, and lemmings have some pretty obvious distinguishing features. Mice generally have a relatively slender build, prominent ears, large eyes, and well-developed whiskers. Voles and

lemmings are relatively thick-bodied, small-eared, snub-nosed, short-tailed, and beady-eyed. Mice are *omnivorous*, eating both animal and plant material; voles and lemmings are primarily plant eaters, or *herbivores*. Voles are more likely to construct burrows and tunnels under the ground, as well as under grass and snow. Together, mice, voles, and lemmings make up a large percentage of many predators' diets, including those of birds of prey, coyotes, foxes, weasels, and bobcats.

Mice

New England's mouse population consists of white-footed deermice, North American deermice, house mice, and meadow and woodland jumping mice. The white-footed and North American deermouse, while technically two different species, for all intents and purposes are one and the same animal. Field guides will tell you that the tail of the white-footed deermouse is slightly shorter, less than half the length of its body, while the tail of the North American deermouse is slightly longer than the length of its body. This is not only a challenging call to make in the field, but there are many exceptions to this rule—so many that it isn't really applicable. The similarities are so great that mammalogists have to take a look at enzymes in the saliva of these mice in order to positively tell one from the other. Both of these species have pointed noses, live in both woods and fields, are active year-round, cache food, are capable of swimming and climbing, and often inhabit buildings in the winter. Both white-footed and North American deermice tend to travel quite extensively on top of the snow, although they also use tunnels beneath the surface. When they travel on top of the snow, they sometimes hold their tail vertically, in which case their tail doesn't leave a drag mark.

House mice share many physical characteristics with deermice, though their tail is far less hairy and their coat is more gray than that of white-footed

White-footed and North American deermice often travel on top of the snow. Here the drag mark left by the tail is very evident, but they often hold their tail vertically, in which case the track would not show.

Note that there aren't any tracks going into or out of this ¾-inch hole in the snow. Meadow voles often make air holes leading up to the surface of the snow from their tunnels below in order to allow carbon dioxide to escape.

and North American deermice. House mice are not native to North America, but because they seek out human habitations in which to live, we are more familiar with them than with some other species. Unfortunately they can do a lot of damage inside houses, chewing almost everything they come across, including soap, glue, books, paper, leather, wood, cardboard, and most plastics (in addition to grains and other foods).

The physical differences between jumping mice and the previously mentioned species of mice are easy to spot. (See photos of both species on pp. 274 and 275.) Both meadow and woodland jumping mice have greatly elongated hind legs and very long tails that enable them to jump long distances (relative to their size). Normally they travel by walking, but when alarmed, jumping mice live up to their name. Meadow jumping mice can leap as far as 3 feet, while woodland jumping mice can jump as far as 6 feet. Their powerful hind legs propel them and their long tail provides balance. Because our two species of jumping mice look so much alike and can occupy the same habitat, the best way to tell them apart is to get a look at their tail. Only the woodland jumping mouse's tail has a white tip.

In the fall jumping mice do not store food, but eat voraciously and acquire a layer of fat to sustain them through the winter. They hibernate longer than most mammals in North America, curling up in a ball underground for roughly six months. Research shows that only about a third of jumping mice survive hibernation and emerge in the spring.

Voles

Four species of voles inhabit New England: the meadow vole, southern red-backed vole, rock vole, and woodland vole. Even though we may not see them with regularity, meadow voles—also known as field mice or meadow mice—are one of the most abundant small mammals in North America. Their population is cyclical, peaking every four years or so. Signs of this small rodent are noticeable throughout the year. Meadow voles tend to seek cover under the snow, where they dig an extensive network of tunnels. Sometimes these tunnels are so close to the surface of the snow they can be seen as raised ridges. (In the spring when the snow thaws, vole tunnels about the width of a garden hose and running along the surface of the ground, are very obvious in fields.) Every now and then you may see a hole in the snow a little less than an inch in diameter, with no tracks leading to or away from it. These holes are often the work of meadow voles and are thought to be a means of releasing carbon dioxide from the tunnel system below. In the summer you need look no further than your garden to see signs of meadow voles. Their voracious appetite for vegetables is well known to most gardeners, as is their preference for the bark of fruit trees in winter.

Bog Lemmings

Last, but not least, of our small rodents are the bog lemmings. We tend to hear about lemmings when the Canadian population crashes, as it does periodically, sending northern hawks and owls further south into New England in search of prey (see more about bird irruptions on p. 347). Bog lemmings are less common than mice and voles. There are, however, two species found in New England—the southern and northern bog lemming.

Bog lemmings strongly resemble voles (see illustration p. 380), the major differences being that lemmings have shorter tails and grooves running down the front of their incisors, which voles lack. Southern bog lemmings occur in colonies that range in size from a handful of individuals to several dozen. Both lemmings can be found in a variety of habitats, including hillsides, fields, and mixed woods. Grasses and sedges appear to be a staple food, which is why bogs are often their chief habitat. Discarded stem cuttings are frequently found in lemming runways.

Many people are not fans of small rodents. If you are a farmer, they are a serious adversary due to their fondness for vegetation—particularly grains. If you are in the health field, you may view them as disease carriers. If you are the owner of a cat that is allowed outdoors, you may have grown weary of tiny carcasses deposited on your doorstep. For much of the population, the mere sight of a mouse is unsettling. Are these feelings warranted? We have rodents to thank for much of the valuable research that has been conducted in laboratories, to say nothing of the fact that hawks, owls, and other predators owe their very survival to these furry little creatures. Perhaps it is sometimes hard to live with them, but it would truly be harder without them.

] FAST FACTS [
Small Mammals—Rodents

▶ The woodland jumping mouse is primarily nocturnal, but stays active on cloudy days.

▶ The meadow jumping mouse becomes more active when it rains.

▶ House mice frequently construct communal nests.

▶ The tunnel systems of the southern bog lemming are very extensive and have individual chambers for resting, feeding, and storing food.

▶ The southern red-back vole forages actively throughout the winter under the snow.

▶ Both white-footed and North American deermice are omnivorous; insects form a large portion of their diet.

▶ North American deermice frequently climb trees.

Small Mammals—*Part Two: The Subterranean Insect Eaters*

One cannot review small mammals in New England without taking a look at shrews and moles. Seven species of shrews and three species of moles are running around in tunnels beneath our feet day and night, all year long. They both have five-clawed toes on each foot; a long pointed snout that extends beyond their jaws; sharp, pointed teeth (great for crunching down on insect exoskeletons); minute eyes of little use; no external ears; and fur that lies equally well when brushed forward or backward—all adaptations that favor life in a tunnel (especially when travelling in reverse).

Moles

As a group, all moles possess short front limbs with large feet adapted for digging—the palms face outward. The front feet have large stout claws for this purpose, as well. Rarely do you see a mole's eyes, for they

Some of our smaller mammals (from top to bottom): North American deermouse, house mouse, woodland jumping mouse, meadow vole, southern bog lemming, northern short-tailed shrew, and hairy-tailed mole. (For more about mice, voles, and bog lemmings, see p. 377.)

which the other two moles lack (find out more about the star-nosed mole on p. 218). The main difference between the hairy-tailed mole and the eastern mole is reflected in their names: the eastern mole's tail is nearly naked, while the hairy-tailed mole's is covered with stiff, bristly hairs. The eastern mole is found only in southern New England.

Molehills (consisting of earth that has been dug during tunnel-making and pushed up) located in wet areas such as swamps, wet meadows, and muddy streams are most likely to have been made by a star-nosed mole. Day and night this insectivore searches its tunnels and the muddy bottoms of streams looking for earthworms, beetle larvae, ants, and other invertebrates with its ever-quivering, bizarre-looking, sensory snout.

Chances are that your house is situated on a relatively dry piece of land, as opposed to a swamp or wet area. Ridges in your lawn are most likely to have been made by eastern or hairy-tailed moles, as they prefer dry, sandy, or loamy soil. These 5- to 7-inch diggers spend most of their days and some of their nights foraging for earthworms and other invertebrates in a network of tunnels just under the surface of the ground. The ridges you see are the roofs of these tunnels. Both hairy-tailed and eastern moles dig two tunnel systems—the shallow tunnels you can see from aboveground and a second maze of tunnels 10 to 18 inches beneath the surface. They use these deeper tunnels primarily in the winter (and for raising young), as they are much more insulated than the tunnels that are nearer the surface. The tunnels may be used for many years by several generations of moles.

Shrews

Shrews are not just miniature moles. They have their own unique adaptations, which include two enlarged, pincer-like, upper front incisors that protrude forward—handy tools for catching insects. The teeth of all North American shrews are tipped in a reddish-brown color, whereas mole teeth are

are hidden under its fur. Its eyelids are actually fused, confirming the notion that eyesight is not crucial to many animals adapted for a dark, subterranean life.

The star-nosed mole, hairy-tailed mole, and eastern mole all reside in the Northeast. It is very easy to identify the star-nosed mole, due to the 22 fleshy pink tentacles around the tip of its nose,

You cannot see the eyes of the hairy-tailed mole as they are hidden by its fur. Its feet are built for digging, with the palms facing out.

] FAST FACTS [
Small Mammals—Subterranean Insect Eaters

- The star-nosed mole is an excellent swimmer and has been seen foraging under the ice.
- As befits their name, American water shrews are good swimmers and divers.
- Although American water shrews are found throughout New England (except for the eastern third of Massachusetts) they are rare in this range.
- Snow cover is especially important for shrews, as they spend the winter under the snow in the *subnivian layer*, where they are both hidden from predators and well insulated.

pure white. In addition, most shrews have scent glands, which give them a distinct musky odor.

All six species of shrews in New England (masked, American water, smoky, long-tailed, American pygmy, least, and northern short-tailed) are extremely active and have very high metabolisms, which require massive amounts of food. On average a shrew eats enough earthworms, insects, slugs, snails, and vegetation in a day to equal its weight, and it has been known to eat twice that amount

The northern short-tailed shrew is one of the most abundant small mammals in New England. Even though its front feet are not as specialized as a mole's, it is a powerful digger, creating tunnels 4 to 20 inches in depth. In addition to digging its own tunnels, the short-tailed shrew makes liberal use of other mole, vole, and shrew tunnels.

Perhaps because its vision is so limited (researchers think that at best they may be able to detect light), the northern short-tailed shrew has evolved a means of locating food other than by sight. Through a series of squeaks and clicks it uses *echolocation*, emitting sound waves and using the echoes to locate prey.

The northern short-tailed shrew's greatest weapon is a toxic secretion in its salivary glands. Only shrews in its genus and the European water shrew have this adaptation. The toxin, which accompanies a shrew's bite, is powerful enough to kill other small mammals, such as mice and voles. Northern short-tailed shrews also use the toxins to paralyze smaller prey, such as earthworms, beetles, and snails, so that they can be stored for later consumption.

Like their rodent cousins, moles and shrews are not the most popular of small mammals. When one person calls another a mole or a shrew, it is not exactly a compliment. The only firsthand association many people have with either group of animals is the havoc wreaked in their lawns. There's no shortage of contraptions designed to capture, alarm, or otherwise rid your yard of these determined diggers. If you stop to think about moles and shrews, and exactly why they are destroying your green space, there is a silver lining. Both of these insectivores contribute significantly to the control of insects considered harmful to plants and crops. The more molehills the fewer the grubs. An even trade, one might (or might not) say.

Masked shrew.

Scat—*The Amazing Stories Behind Digestive Remains*

Droppings, feces, excrement, dung—call it what you will, the digestive remains that all animals produce is not a common topic of conversation, except perhaps when you're talking with a tracker, naturalist, or nature photographer. In the company of these individuals it often becomes a subject of great interest and intrigue, for *scat*, as it's referred to by most biologists, can tell the un-squeamish observer as much or more than any other animal sign about the behavior and habits of wildlife.

For the four-footed producer, scat serves as an effective and quite obvious means of communication with other animals, potentially indicating the animal's age, sex, health, mating availability, and territorial boundaries. Careful analysis of scat by humans can be equally revealing. Due to the secretive nature of most animals, many of which utilize camouflage, stealth, and nocturnal habits in order to survive, we seldom set eyes on them, and much of what we know of their habits we learn through interpretation of sign that they leave, including tracks, rubbings, evidence of eating, scratch and bite marks, scrapes, and dens. Added to this list, scat contains a treasure trove of information, and if becoming intimately familiar with the secretive lives of New England fauna is paramount to you, then you may wish to become a student of it.

Location

The initial quest is to identify the animal that left the scat. Location is key. Be aware of the habitat in which you discover the scat, as it can quickly eliminate many animals and narrow down the likely ones. For instance, mink scat would be possible but unlikely in the middle of a field; porcupine scat is a real possibility in a stand of hemlocks. Having established the habitat, notice the specific location of the scat within this area. Is it positioned on top of a promi-nent object in the middle of a trail or run, such as on a rock or log (as would be left by a red or gray fox, coyote, long-tailed weasel, ermine, or fisher)? Is it located at the junction of two trails (again, a red or gray fox, or coyote), or along a natural bridge where traffic is funneled, such as a log or beaver dam (likely a North American river otter, raccoon, or mink)? Is it placed in an area that has been scraped (a bobcat or North American river otter)? Has the animal made an attempt to cover its scat (which bobcats *sometimes* do)? Is it alone or in company? Many animals create latrines, where scat is deposited over long periods of time (such as a raccoon, North American river otter, striped skunk, or common muskrat).

Appearance

What is the scat's overall appearance? Is it in the form of individual pellets (mouse, vole, squirrel, rabbit, hare, porcupine, beaver, deer, moose) or tubular (bobcat, red or gray fox, coyote, long-tailed weasel, ermine, mink, fisher, American marten, raccoon, black bear)? If pelleted, does it appear they were deposited one at a time (eastern cottontail rabbit, New England cottontail rabbit, snowshoe hare) or in piles (white-tailed deer, moose)? If tubular, is it segmented (black bear and bobcat, usually) or not (red or gray fox, coyote, or most members of the weasel family). Note that the season and therefore the diet of the animal (moist, herbaceous vegetation versus drier woody plants and/or prey) can drastically alter the appearance of an animal's scat (white-tailed deer and moose pellets are often soft and clumped in the warmer months). Is the scat smooth with blunt ends (bobcat, black bear, raccoon) or rope-like and twisted with tapered ends (long-tailed weasel, ermine, mink, fisher, American marten)? Measure the size of the individual pellets as well as the diameter of tubular scat. Is there a distinctive odor (coyote scat is mildly musky)? Warning: Raccoon scat can contain parasites, the eggs of which, if inhaled, can be harmful to humans.

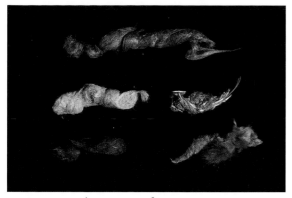

Coyote scat: The contents of a given species' scat reflect its varied diet, as is illustrated in these coyote scat samples containing the remains of (clockwise from top) deer hair, feathers, muskrat fur, porcupine quills, and snowshoe hare hair.

Red fox scat: Fox scat is twisted and cordlike (similar to coyote scat) and often deposited on prominent objects, such as stones and logs in the middle of a trail or at the junction of two trails. Wild canine scat found in New England that measures 5/8 inch or less is almost assuredly fox.

Fisher scat: Fisher scat, like that of most members of the weasel family, is often very dark, twisted, folded, and tapered at both ends. Mink scat, which is very similar in size and appearance, usually contains the fine, short hairs of small prey, whereas fisher scat is typically composed of the courser hairs of larger prey.

Content

Finally, examine the contents. (Due to possible harmful bacteria in feces, it's wise to use gloves and a stick when dissecting scat.) Is it composed primarily of vegetation such as grasses, skins of fruit, seeds, and/or insect parts (raccoon, striped skunk, American black bear) or does it consist mostly of hair and bones (coyote, long-tailed weasel, ermine, mink, fisher, American marten)? Again, consider the season, for an animal's diet can vary widely depending on the time of year (up to 50 percent of a red fox's summer and fall diet is fruit).

Habitat, shape and form, dimensions, odor, contents—together these features will not only tell you who deposited the scat, but also a great deal about the animal's daily (and nightly) habits. There are many field guides that provide scat measurements as well as the habitat and diet preferences of animals. Mark Elbroch's book *Mammal Tracks & Sign* (Stackpole Books, 2003) and Paul Rezendes' *Tracking & the Art of Seeing* (Collins Reference, 1999) are both informative and comprehensive. Armed with a guide, a tape measure, and

Porcupine scat: The individual fibrous pellets of porcupine scat are slightly curved and have a distinctive pine-like scent.

Beaver scat: Beaver pellets are composed of tiny bits of wood fiber from the bark they consume. Look for beaver scat in the water, as beavers rarely defecate on land.

Moose (left) and white-tailed deer (right) scat: The winter scat of both moose and white-tailed deer is in the form of woody, fibrous pellets. The size discrepancy easily differentiates the two.

] FAST FACTS [
Scat

▶ Many mammals have anal scent glands, which effectively turn their scat into a means of communication. The scent of an animal's scat is thought to convey its age, health, and sex, among other things.

▶ The content of a predator's scat changes as it eats its way through a large prey animal. Initially the predator eats the internal organs, which results in dark, smooth scat with very little fur or bones. By the time the last (and least nutritional) part of the prey animal is eaten, the predator's scat often consists of nothing but hair.

▶ Fishers can control the amount of scat they deposit at any one time. Infinitesimal amounts are sometimes used as markers.

▶ Some animals, such as raccoons, black bears, striped skunks, bobcats, and moles, create latrines where an individual or a species repeatedly leaves its scat.

▶ Cottontail rabbits, hares, and beavers practice *coprophagy*—eating their own droppings—in order to extract as many nutrients as possible.

▶ North American river otters often come out of the water and roll in a certain spot before defecating there. The scat typically consists of fish scales and is relatively formless.

▶ Do not handle or smell raccoon scat, as it can contain a parasitic roundworm, *Baylisascaris procyonis*, which can be fatal to humans.

a familiarity with the animals that are found in New England, all that is necessary to become a skilled scatologist is a willingness to spend as much time as possible in the woods and, perhaps, a lack of squeamishness. You can be sure that if you follow an animal's tracks long enough, you will be rewarded with the object of your desire. And the amount of information gleaned from this object directly correlates with how closely it is examined.

Animal Tracks—*Wildlife Journal Entries We Can Learn From*

How often have you set eyes on a snowshoe hare, bobcat, or a fisher? Most animals, in addition to being nocturnal, are keenly attuned to their environment, be they predator or prey, and their alertness allows them to detect our presence (and flee) long before we see them. Because of this, getting to know an individual animal's natural behavior—its travels, what it stops to investigate, where it marks its territory, what it eats, and with whom it interacts—is extremely difficult. Fortunately, there is one season of the year when we have relatively easy access to all of this information. If snow is on the ground, animals can't help but leave evidence of their activity. It can take the form of tracks, tunnels, dens, or scat (examined beginnning on p. 382). While tracks are the most ephemeral of signs, when they are fresh they reveal a tremendous amount about how an animal spends its day (or, more likely, its night).

Where to Begin

Whether you're attempting to identify a bird, wildflower, or track-maker, it all boils down to the process of elimination. Start with your geographical area. Only certain mammals are found in New England—badgers, for instance, can, for all intents and purposes, be eliminated. Then define the habitat in which you are looking. It's unlikely you'd come across fisher tracks crossing an open field, but very possible that you would find them in mixed woods. Then, focus on the tracks themselves.

Individual Tracks

Unfortunately, you rarely find a track that is even remotely as clear as those you find in a tracking field guide. The conditions that allow the kind of clarity found in guides (shallow, wet snow that isn't melting) simply don't occur very often. If you

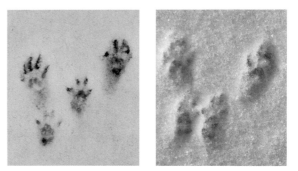

Unfortunately, you rarely find a track as clear as those in tracking field guides. Here you can see the distinct difference between eastern gray squirrel tracks in exceptional tracking conditions (left) and the same animal in typical tracking conditions (right).

are lucky, however, and snow conditions are good, tracks will be well-defined. Measure the length and width of both fore and hind feet, if possible. Notice the shape of the tracks and whether or not there are nail marks. Count the number of toes. The more details you notice, the easier the elimination process.

Track Patterns

During most of the winter, you are much more likely to encounter tracks that are without much detail due to snow conditions (dry and fluffy) or because they've been melted by the sun into a distorted size and shape. When this is the case, you are forced to use clues other than individual track dimensions. Instead, look at the pattern in the snow that the tracks make—they can be as revealing as detailed foot imprints. Certain animals, often those belonging to the same family, move in a similar manner, leaving similar track patterns. If you are familiar with the basic ways in which animals move, and you have a measuring tape, you can usually narrow down the identity of the track-maker to its family, or even its species.

In addition to a tape measure, a good track field guide is essential for positive identification

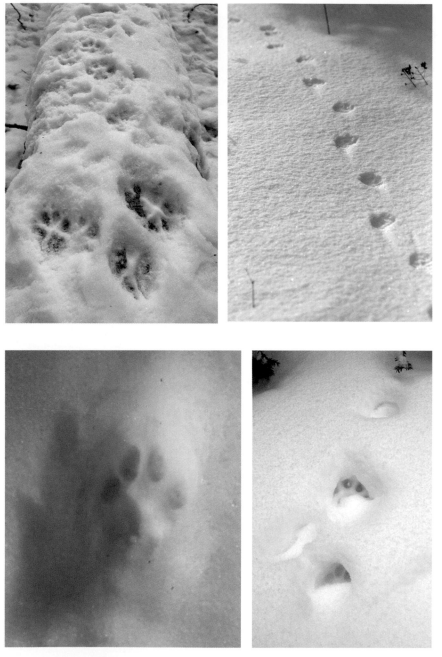

Red fox track and track pattern: Nail marks and a ridge behind the toes; the tracks are placed directly behind each other, forming a straight trail.

Bobcat track and track pattern: Lack of nail marks and a round shape; a fairly straight trail.

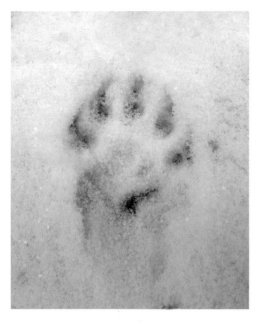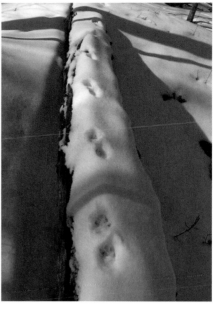

Fisher track and track pattern: Five toes (but more often four prints), and a paired, diagonal track pattern when loping.

in the field. In addition to giving individual track dimensions, field guides usually group animals by the way they move, making track patterns a key identification tool. The most common groupings tend to be *walkers and trotters; pacers; bounders;* and *lopers.*

Walkers and Trotters
The members of the cat family in New England (bobcat, lynx, and possibly mountain lion) and deer family (white-tailed deer and moose) are walkers. They all walk on their toes, with their hind feet *direct registering* (landing where the front feet were placed, making two tracks look like one).

Some field guides lump members of the dog family in New England (red fox, gray fox, coyote, and the rare wolf wandering down from Canada) in with walkers, but more often than not they trot, a faster form of walking, in which they move diagonally opposite limbs simultaneously, with the hind feet direct registering. This gait produces

a relatively straight line. Short-tailed shrews and voles are also trotters.

A sub-category of walkers and trotters are those species that are flat-footed. The North American porcupine walks on the soles of its inward-turning feet, leaving a pigeon-toed track pattern. In deep snow it leaves a trough roughly 6 to 8 inches wide (see photo on p. 337). The hind feet of the American black bear tend to land slightly in front of where its front feet were placed, which is referred to as *overstepping;* however, this can vary with the substrate. In deep snow, bears tend to direct register, but in New England bears rarely are active by the time snow is very deep. The striped skunk emerges in milder winter weather, and leaves a meandering track pattern.

Pacers
Raccoons tend to move both limbs on one side, and then both limbs on the other side. This results in paired tracks. These pacers typically have heavy

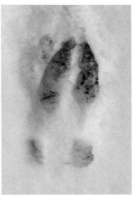

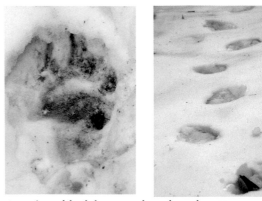

Red squirrel track pattern: Beginning and/ or ending at the base of a tree.

White-tailed deer track: A heart shape, with the pointed end in the direction of travel, and in certain conditions the deer's dew claws register.

American black bear track and track pattern: Human-shaped print and nail marks, while the track pattern is pigeon-toed.

bodies and short legs, and unlike most walkers, they are flat-footed and walk on the soles of their feet, not their toes. Front and hind feet can be differentiated, as they do not direct register.

Bounders
The two hind feet of bounding animals (mice, voles, squirrels, hares, cottontail rabbits) land simultaneously, often in front of the smaller front feet. Although there are many exceptions to this rule, the front feet of bounders that climb trees, such as squirrels, are often placed side by side, whereas those that are not tree climbers, such as hares and cottontail rabbits, are usually placed diagonally, one slightly ahead of the other.

Lopers
Most of the weasel family in New England (weasels, mink, martens, fishers, and otters) are lopers. They move much like bounders. Unlike bounding animals, however, lopers' feet each land independently and direct register, with the four feet creating a diagonally paired set of tracks.

The pattern that tracks leave is determined not only by the shape and size of the animal and the way in which it moves, but the substrate it is traveling on, as well as its gait, which can obviously vary. As tempting as it is to try and categorize tracks and track patterns, there are many ways in which a given species moves, and an equal number of track patterns that it leaves. The groupings provided here are generalities. If you wish to delve deeper into the art of tracking, there are several excellent tracking field guides (I list some at the end of this book—see p. 441), that go into the specific details of the tracks as well as patterns of North American species. These books provide the reader not only with tracking information, but interpret practically every animal sign you could possibly encounter while tracking. Pick up a field guide, grab a ruler, and head outside. Your winters will never be the same.

] FAST FACTS [
Animal Tracks

▸ Animal tracks can, under ideal conditions, reveal all or some of the following information: identity of track-maker, direction of travel, relative time when the animal passed by, gait or way the animal was moving, relative size of animal, and sex of the animal.

▸ Wild canine tracks are often found along trails, as well as in open fields.

▸ Wolves, coyotes, and foxes have five toes on their front feet and four on their hind. More often than not, only four toes register in all four foot tracks. Gray and red fox nails are semi-retractable and may or may not register.

▸ It is possible to draw an "X" in the space between the toes and pad of a coyote's or red fox's front tracks (not a gray fox's) and a "C" in bobcat and eastern mountain lion tracks.

▸ In deep snow a bobcat puts its hind foot in the exact spot where his front foot was placed (*direct register*).

▸ In deep snow the shape of the track left by a Canadian lynx resembles a cross.

▸ Several members of the weasel family (long-tailed, ermine, American mink, fisher, North American river otter, and American marten) tend to lope, leaving two tracks, one a little ahead of the other.

▸ A moose track is roughly the length of a human's hand.

▸ In deep, fluffy, snow, bounding red squirrels tend to direct register, leaving what looks like two tracks but are actually four. They often tunnel in deep snow.

▸ North American porcupine nails are large and can often be seen in their pigeon-toed tracks.

▸ Snowshoe hares and cottontail rabbits have such furry feet that their toe pads rarely register.

▸ When being chased, hares and rabbits change direction frequently, leaving a zigzag pattern.

▸ Do not bother looking for jumping mice or woodchuck tracks in the snow in mid-winter— they are hibernating.

Deer Antlers— *Their Form and Function*

There exists a living material that grows half an inch a day (it takes human hair roughly a month to achieve this much growth). This same material is so hard that it has been used to make needles, arrowheads, and harpoons. Best of all, it is a renewable resource, as long as an adequate diet is available to the animal growing it. Antler bone, the fastest-growing true bone known to science, is grown by members of the North American *Cervid* family—moose, elk, caribou, mule deer, and white-tailed deer. For eight months of the year, male white-tailed deer (or *bucks*) manufacture it on the top of their head.

What purpose could any appendage have that would be worth the inconvenience and burden that antlers pose to white-tailed bucks? Only something as crucial as producing progeny could justify the annual regrowth of these heavy (up to 9 pounds), nutrient-demanding, cumbersome structures. When bucks compete for the opportunity to breed with female white-tailed deer (*does*) they often engage in physical shoving matches. Instead of grappling with hands, they push against each other's antlers, sparring until one is the obvious victor and thus, dominant breeder. In addition to this, antlers play a major communicative role during the mating season, or *rut*.

Horns vs. Antlers
Antlers are often mistakenly referred to as "horns." The two do have similarities, but their differences are quite distinct. Horns, grown by the *Bovid* family— cows, sheep, bison, and goats, for example—are permanent, continuously-growing projections of living bone protruding from the skull. They are sheathed in a layer of *keratin*, a material similar to finger nails or horse hooves. Horns are not usually branched and are found on both males and females.

The size and number of points of a white-tailed buck's antlers are primarily controlled by nutritional intake, and to a lesser degree, age and genetics play a role.

With thousands of antlers falling to the ground each year in New England, you would think that finding one might be a common experience. Not so, for rodents such as mice, squirrels, and porcupines quickly consume this concentrated source of calcium with the help of their rugged incisors. Look for the grooves made by their teeth if you are lucky enough to happen upon a shed antler.

Antlers are also projections of bone, but they are temporary in that they are grown and shed every year. Most adult antlers are branched. They generally are found only on males (except for caribou, where both sexes possess them), the occasional white-tail doe, or rarely, moose cows with a hormone imbalance. Researchers theorize that horns may have developed as protection for the skull, whereas it's thought that antlers most likely developed as an aid in scent and visual communication during the mating season. (For a photographic comparison of horns and antlers, see p. 241.)

Growth Cycle
The seasonal growth cycle of antlers is largely determined by hormones triggered by the amount of daylight. Lengthening days stimulate antler growth in April. From this point until their growth ceases in late summer or early fall, the bony interior of antlers is covered with a soft skin called "velvet," which

supplies blood, oxygen, and nutrients to the growing bone. It is during this period of growth when injury occurring to the antlers can permanently deform them. (Interestingly, injury to a leg during this period causes abnormal growth of the antler on the opposite side of the deer's body.) In late summer diminishing daylight triggers the release of hormones responsible for a number of physical changes in bucks, including the development of stronger neck muscles, which enable the buck to carry the extra weight of the antlers, as well as the termination of the blood supply to the antlers. The bone in the antlers actually dies at this point, and the velvet dries up and falls off, or is rubbed off by the buck.

Scent Communication
Rubs are created on saplings where the buck marks its territory by rubbing his antlers as well as his face, and in so doing removes some of the bark. The highest concentration of oil and scent-producing glands on a buck's entire body is found in the velvet covering the antlers. When he rubs the shredded

velvet against a tree, he leaves his scent behind. Even after the velvet has fallen off, rubs continue to convey information regarding the buck's health and vigor. Scent glands are located on a buck's forehead, as well as below his eyes. When he rubs his antlers on a tree where he has previously rubbed these scent glands, the scent is transferred to his antlers and it is exposed to far-reaching breezes. Secretions from scent glands aren't a buck's only means of convey-ing information, however. During *rut*, or the mating season, which takes place between mid-November and mid-December, a buck's urine contains phero-mones. Bucks have been known to urinate on their own antlers in order to broadcast their availability.

"Drops"

Once mating has taken place, antlers are more of a hindrance than a help, as food must be consumed to provide energy to support their weight. During the winter food is not only scarcer, that which is avail-able isn't as nutritious, and thus it is advantageous to shed antlers. As the days shorten, testosterone levels drop and beginning in mid-December, antlers are shed or drop off, usually one at a time, separated by a few hours or days. It is not uncommon to see a one-antlered buck at this time of year. The growth cycle begins all over again in about four months.

Where Are They?

Given the large number of white-tailed bucks in New England, and the fact that each of them sheds two antlers every year, you may wonder why you aren't tripping over antlers every time you step outdoors. The explanation is a surprisingly efficient one. Antlers are a concentrated source of calcium as well as phosphorus, both of which are highly sought after by rodents such as mice, cottontail rabbits, squirrels, and porcupines, all of which possess the heavy-duty incisors necessary to carve into hard antlers. If you are lucky enough to find an antler, more often than not close examination will reveal the grooves of these

rodent teeth. (Interestingly, after rut is over and they can once again approach each other peacefully, elk have been observed eating each other's antlers.)

Antler Size

As far as antler size, extensive research has shown that while age does play a part (young bucks tend to divert a larger percent of their nutritional intake to body growth than to antlers), nutrition is definitely the key factor in determining size and number of points. The better the quality and amount of nutrition, the larger the antlers. To a lesser degree genetics and health also affect antler size. The increasing size of a buck's antlers as he ages (given an adequate diet) not only equips him with more formidable weapons, but also serves to reflect his continuing health and vigor to potential mates.

Antler Function and Growth

Antlers are very useful to their bearers. As men-tioned, they aid in scent communication, visually indicate degree of health to does (bucks in poorer health cannot afford to divert calcium and nutrients from their skeleton to their antlers, and thus have smaller racks), and promote progeny in that they serve as weapons during breeding competition. They have even been utilized as digging implements to unearth acorns when it snows early in the season.

Humans have also found many uses for antlers; due to their hardness they have been an important material for tools ever since the Paleolithic period. Archaeologists have found deer antlers sheathed in copper at prehistoric sites, indicating that they served ceremonial purposes as well. Even in the twenty-first century, antlers are utilized for everything from dietary supplements to growth hormones. More significantly, scientists feel that research on the rapid growth rate of antlers could conceivably reveal the mystery of cancer growth, which is also extremely fast (but not as fast as the growth of antlers). In addition, antler regeneration may use stem cells

] FAST FACTS [
Antlers

► The age of a white-tailed buck cannot be determined by the number of its antler tines ("points"). If conditions are good and nutrition is plentiful, each year the antlers will be greater in size and tine number. However, overcrowding and the resulting inadequate food supply can decrease the number of tines on a buck's rack.

► Under the best conditions, each antler can carry up to five tines.

► Occasionally female white-tailed does (and moose cows) with excess testosterone may produce small antlers, but they can still breed and produce young.

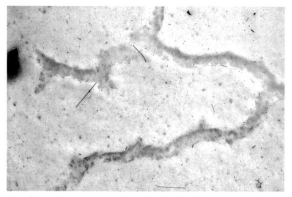

Meadow voles create a network of trails in the protected subnivian layer, the airspace between the ground and the snow. These are exposed as the snow melts in the spring.

and involves mechanisms similar to those used in limb development. It is thought that further study of these processes might possibly lead to human organ restoration. Humans are indeed fortunate—they can reap the benefits of these heavy, nutrient-demanding bony structures without having to grow or carry them on their head for two thirds of every year.

Snow—*Its Affect on Wildlife*

Peoples' reactions to a snowy winter vary from extreme pleasure to dismay; skiers celebrate, while commuters commiserate. Wildlife that remains active in winter is, if anything, affected even more than humans, in that the presence or absence of deep snow can actually make the difference between life and death.

Snowy Benefits
To understand the significance to animals of a foot or more of snow on the ground, it is helpful to understand its insulating properties—10 inches of fresh snow is approximately equal to a 6-inch layer of fiberglass insulation. This air-filled "blanket" traps the earth's heat and keeps the temperature at ground level within a degree or two of 32° F, regardless of the temperature above the surface.

Trapped heat actually melts the layer of snow right next to the earth. The water vapor rises and crystallizes on the upper layers of snow, creating a space where the snow meets the ground. This space, as well as the snow above it, is referred to as the *subnivian layer*. There are many small mammals, including mice, voles, and shrews, that could not survive the cold winters in northern New England, due to their small size and metabolism, were it not for this protective environment. Not only does the layer of snow provide them with a constant temperature often 30 or 40 degrees higher than the temperature on its surface, but it hides them from potential predators. Consequently, mice and voles spend most of the winter in the subnivian layer, where the remains of their maze of trails is evident in the spring when the snow melts to a depth of an inch or two. (Read more about mice and voles on p. 377.)

The protection a layer of snow offers is not limited to the animals living within it. Subterranean dwellers, including insectivorous moles and shrews, have an increased supply of food when snow is present. Due to the trapped heat of the earth, the frost line does not go as deep, and thus these predators can tunnel closer to the surface of the ground, where there are more insects. Although red squirrels spend most of their time on top of the snow, they regularly tunnel in it. If and when the temperature dips below -22°F, they tend to retreat to their tunnels and remain there until the air warms up.

Ruffed grouse somehow recognize the life-saving property of snow, and on extremely cold nights, when the snow is 10 inches or more deep, they will tuck their wings up and fly full speed into a snow bank, creating a kind of "snow cave" that retains the bird's body heat (see more on this, including photos, on pp. 345–346). This behavior also hides the grouse from predators, but, as an extra measure, it often burrows horizontally for a couple of feet in case its entrance hole is noticed. Often a grouse roosts in its snow cave just overnight, but if frigid temperatures persist, they have been known to spend days in them, coming out briefly at dawn and dusk to feed on buds and twigs. When making a final exit, the grouse explodes out of the snow—a startling experience for those who have witnessed it. Occasionally a crust forms on the surface of the snow, sealing the grouse into its snow cave, where it becomes easy prey for foxes, coyotes, and other predators.

Snowy Challenges

Deep snow does not always enhance survival. It presents some animals, both predators and prey, with significant challenges that are met with different strategies. Reaching food and escaping from enemies are two of these. The size (4 to 6 inches) and furry soles of the snowshoe hare's hind feet enable it to move easily and rapidly on top of the fluffiest snow. Hares create paths in the deep snow, which become so well travelled that they conserve

White-tailed deer retreat to deer yards when snow is deep, where well-trampled paths allow them to reach food with a minimum expenditure of energy.

energy they would otherwise expend breaking new trail. One benefit of a deep snow pack for hares and cottontail rabbits is that it raises them up higher so they can reach tender buds and branches that otherwise would not be accessible. (Read more about the snowshoe hare on p. 416.)

White-tailed deer have great difficulty travelling through deep snow, and because of this they are far more vulnerable to attacks from predators. They tend to gather together in *deer yards*—sheltered locations, frequently under stands of coniferous trees, on south-facing slopes. Not only are the deer protected from the wind and cold here, but the snow is not as deep, due to the conifers' branches. When it reaches a depth of 18 inches or so, the deer make trails in order to conserve energy. In very deep snow, white-tailed deer tend to remain true to these trails, even though they may be starving, in an effort to save energy. The importance of these yards is evident from the fact that they are used year after year, and that deer travel as much as 10 or 15 miles in order to find them.

Many predators also find life much more difficult when there is a lot of snow on the ground. Travel is challenging and food is often hidden

] FAST FACTS [
Snow's Affect
on Wildlife

▶ When referring to where wildlife is found in and on the snow, some scientists refer to three locations: *supranivian* (snow's surface), *intranivian* (in the snow layer), and *subnivian* (at the interface of the ground and snow).

▶ Snow is critical to the survival of many plants as well as animals. It protects against cold temperatures and drying winds, yet allows for some exchange of oxygen, carbon dioxide, light, and moisture.

▶ The melting and refreezing of the snow in the spring causes it to become denser. In this condition it transmits more light, which is detected by both plants and animals, stimulating growth and breeding, respectively.

▶ Shrews and voles can still be pursued by predators through their tunnels in the subnivian layer. The hole/tunnel of a short-tailed shrew, as well as a meadow vole, has a diameter between ¾ inch and 7/8 inch. That of a weasel's is 7/8 inch to 1¼ inches. It's a tight squeeze, but it is doable.

from view. This is less of a problem for foxes and coyotes, as they can actually hear small rodents rustling beneath the snow. Hunting consists of pouncing in the location of the sound they hear, crushing the subnivian pathways, and effectively trapping the animal. Large owls also benefit from their ability to hear mice and voles under the snow, plunging down into it to capture them.

A foot or more of snow is a mixed blessing for wildlife. From a meadow vole's vantage point, the warm, covered corridors made possible by snow are a lifesaver. For many others, such as wild turkeys trying to survive on buried acorns, life is more difficult.

Insects in Winter—
Living to Buzz Another Day

When you think about what it is like to sit outside on a summer evening, swatting mosquitoes, or how your vegetable garden can be decimated overnight by ravenous insects, you do wonder where they all disappear to come winter. While many insects die in the fall, they do so after laying eggs, which overwinter. Other species may spend the colder months as larvae, pupae, or adults.

Dormancy
Because insects are cold-blooded and cannot regulate their body temperature, they are very vulnerable to climate changes and therefore must have adapted in order to survive New England's winters. This is accomplished in part by entering a resting stage, called *diapause*, throughout the colder months, during which the insects are completely inactive. The shortening days of fall signal that it is time for insects to prepare for this resting period. If they wait until cold weather arrives they are caught short and probably perish. Fortunately, like birds, insects seem to possess an inner clock that's sensitive to light. When the hours of daylight shorten significantly, the alarm goes off, and preparation begins. Insects have further adapted to cold temperatures in one or more of the following ways.

Antifreeze
Most are able to create a kind of "antifreeze" within themselves. They do this by eliminating a considerable amount of water from their body before they become dormant. The water they retain then undergoes a chemical change, which prevents it from freezing except at very low temperatures. This inability to form ice crystals except when the temperature dips very low is key to an insect surviving in freezing temperatures, for it is the destruction of the cells by ice crystals that kills an organism.

Adult lily leaf beetles (which squeak to deter predators) spend the winter buried in the soil, and emerge in the spring to mate and lay eggs.

Migration
In addition, many insects migrate—not southward, but downward. Insects that inhabit treetops and shrubs in the summer head for the protection of leaf litter, rotting logs, and low-growing vegetation in the fall. Other insects that spend the summer months in tussocks of grass or on the forest floor go down into the soil, and insects that summer below the surface of the ground remain where they are or go deeper.

These lower habitats provide more shelter because the temperature is warmer and more stable than the air. A foot below the surface of the ground the range of the temperature is only half that of the air directly above it. Snow provides yet another layer of insulation for these creatures. If there are 6 or more inches of snow, the soil rarely fluctuates by more than 3 or 4 degrees, regardless of the air temperature.

Overwintering as Eggs

Remember those pesky black flies of early summer? Their eggs spend the winter safely submerged underwater and hatch when the ice thaws and temperatures rise. The egg cases of praying mantises, light tan in color and about an inch in length, consist not only of eggs, but of a protective, solidified foam that encases them. Look for them in overgrown fields, attached to low branches of shrubs. Once leaves have fallen off the trees you may notice shiny,

Robber flies overwinter as larvae in the soil, pupating and emerging as adults in the spring.

brown bands of eggs wrapped around black cherry branches. The moths that develop from eastern tent caterpillars laid these eggs. After depositing them, they cover the eggs with a waterproof coating resembling shellac. When the leaf buds start to open, the eggs will hatch into larvae, ready to consume the tender, young leaves. (See photo on p. 310.)

Overwintering as Larvae

Many species of insects spend the winter as larvae, curled up in a protective spot in which they avoid freezing temperatures. Beetle and firefly larvae can be found in almost any fallen log. Isabella tiger moth larvae, better known as woolly bear caterpillars, overwinter in decaying logs and leaf litter, pupating and maturing into moths in the spring. (Read more about the woolly bear on p. 293.) Larvae of June bugs, the common white beetle grubs you find in garden soil, burrow down below the frost line in the fall.

Overwintering as Pupae

Other insects that are in their larval stage in the fall, such as many moths and butterflies, will make protective silk cocoons or chrysalises within which they spend the winter as pupae, emerging in the spring as adults. The tan papery cocoon of the cecropia moth is well camouflaged among the branches of shrubs, where it is usually constructed. (See photo on p. 310.)

Overwintering as Adults

Some insect species spend the winter as adults. Most seek out protected environments that offer some shelter from the elements. Trees, especially those with loose or deeply creviced bark, are host to many adult insects, most of which are small in size and therefore able to crawl into these tiny spaces. Although most adult male mosquitoes die in the fall, fertilized female mosquitoes seek shelter under bark, as well as in cellars and eaves. One of the larger tree-dwelling residents is the mourning cloak butterfly, which spends the winter under loose tree bark and is often one of the first butterflies sighted in the spring. (See photo on p. 15.)

Queen wasps and bees, as well as flies, seek shelter in the nooks and crannies of old, wooden, weathered fences. Lady beetles can also be found congregating by the hundreds in fence holes. Even the leaves on the forest floor offer protection from winter's cold—the curled edges of dead leaves hold warm air, forming a protective blanket for life underneath the top layer. Leaf hoppers, stink bugs, and a variety of beetles and springtails are abundant in these layers. Punky, rotting logs are like multi-tiered housing projects, offering shelter for many adult insects through the winter months, including hundreds of ants gathered in tight bunches.

Out and About

Although most insects are in resting stages through the colder months, there are several species (as well as spiders) that you may run across if you are out snowshoeing or cross-country skiing in the woods. Some, such as the springtail, or snow flea,

Most grasshoppers overwinter as eggs in the soil, emerging as immature nymphs when the soil warms in the spring.

may be familiar to you—the surface of the snow, especially where tracks have been made, becomes covered with tiny, black specks that resemble pepper. A close look reveals that these specks are moving. On warm winter days snow fleas crawl up through the leaf litter and the base of tree trunks to the surface of the snow, where they are in constant motion, springing from one spot to another. (Find out more about snow fleas on p. 424.)

Not only are some adult insects active, there are even species that mate in the dead of winter. Aquatic stonefly larvae metamorphose into adults and emerge from streams in another month or so to mate and lay eggs.

There is no one hard and fast rule as to how insects overwinter. They do so in the stage and habitat that best suits their needs. A peak behind loose bark or amongst the branches of shrubbery may reward you with the discovery of such a creature, unless a hungry chickadee beats you to it.

] FAST FACTS [
Insects in Winter

▶ Grasshoppers bury several packets of eggs in the ground in a hole they dig with the tip of their abdomen in the fall. The young emerge in the spring.

▶ Luna moth larvae spend the winter on the forest floor curled up in a cocoon made out of leaves.

▶ Grubs, or larvae, of beetles such as the June beetle and Japanese beetle, migrate below the frost line in the fall and are inactive throughout the winter.

▶ Many of the house flies that are bothersome to people in the summer are descended from flies that spend the winter in a building.

▶ Some species of stoneflies—aquatic insects that live on the underside of flat rocks in clean, rapidly flowing streams—emerge in the winter to breed.

▶ The temperature of water in swift streams remains above freezing. As it moves over rocks and sprays into the air, it picks up oxygen. Because cold water can hold more dissolved gases, such as oxygen, than warm water, winter streams are very hospitable to aquatic life. Many aquatic insects remain active in the winter as a result.

A vase of winter wildflowers—in some ways as striking as its spring and summer counterparts.

them weeds because they manage to reproduce just about anywhere, out-competing other plants we might prefer to have. This remarkable adaptability is responsible for their success and is achieved through a number of strategies. Most weeds have either a long taproot or a massive root system that is successful in obtaining water in the driest of habitats, ample nectaries with which to attract pollinators, abundant production of seeds, or a diversity of seed dispersal mechanisms.

Some of these resilient plants produce flowers which are fairly inconspicuous, while others produce blossoms that stand out like beacons in fields and along roadsides. Regardless of which category they fall into, most weeds do not totally disappear after they flower, and what remains of the plant can often be found poking up through the snow throughout the winter months. Most prominent are the old flower heads, what is left of the fruiting part of the plant, which lend texture and beauty to an otherwise bleak landscape. The individual characteristics of each species' flower head make identification fairly easy with the aid of a guide such as Lauren Brown's book, *Weeds in Winter* (WW Norton & Co, Inc, 1986). Often seeds can be found inside these flower heads throughout the winter, providing a much needed source of food for a variety of birds including many sparrows, woodpeckers, finches, redpolls, and juncos.

Winter Wildflowers— *Striking Resilience*

Roadside botany in winter? An oxymoron if there ever was one. Or is it? The colorful blossoms of flowering plants that thrive on the sides of roads and in overgrown fields have come and gone, but their remnants remain. The persistent dried flower heads and seeds within them are as varied as the flowers they once were and provide ample opportunity for botanizing in winter.

Unfortunately, many of us discount the beauty and value of these wildflowers. We derogatorily call

Common mullein in the winter (left) and summer (right).

A random sampling of New England's "winter wildflowers" illustrates the uniqueness of these plants as well as their recognizability during all seasons of the year.

Common Mullein

Being a biennial (two-year life cycle), common mullein produces a circular evergreen rosette of light green leaves during its first year and the following year sends up a flower stalk. A majority of its common names (flannel-leaf, velvet-plant, blanket herb, feltwort, velvet dock) reflect the softness of its velvety leaves. Many uses have been found for these leaves, including as shoe liners and dollhouse blankets.

After the plant flowers during its second year, the rigid dead flower stalk can be seen throughout the winter months, rising up to 6 feet above the snow. The remains of the flowers are at the tip of the stalk and careful examination will reveal hundreds of two-parted seed capsules. The cavities that these capsules create were put to good use many years ago. The ends of winter flower stalks were dipped in tallow (melted animal fat), which then solidified, turning the flower stalk into a very effective torch for funeral processions and other ceremonies.

Black-Eyed Susan

With their bright yellow petals and brown, cone-like centers, black-eyed Susans are instantly recognizable in the summer. Like all members of the Composite family, the black-eyed Susan is not the single flower it appears to be, but actually hundreds of tiny, fertile, brown flowers surrounded by a ring

Black-eyed Susan in the winter (left) and summer (right).

of sterile yellow flowers at their base (which we call petals). The yellow *ray* flowers act as banners to attract the insects necessary to pollinate the central brown *disc* flowers so that they can produce seeds.

If you look closely at the button-like winter flower heads of this biennial you see the dried remains of hundreds of flowers. Shake them and out will fall many four-sided, ridged, black fruits, each no bigger than the letter "i" and each containing one seed. (Botanically speaking, "fruit" refers to the ripened ovary of a flower, which contains seeds. Unlike the fruit of an apple tree, the fruit of most weeds is small, hard, dry and often fused to the seed within it. Differentiating the fruit from the seed can be challenging.) A ring of hairy dried *bracts*, or modified leaves, encircles the base of the black-eyed Susan flower head.

Blue Vervain

Blue vervain can be found in many New England fields, where its tiny but vibrant flowers open progressively as they work their way from the bottom to the top of the flower spike. Over the years blue vervain has been thought of as a plant of magic and mystery. There are many folktales attributing all sorts of powers to it, including its ceremonial sacredness and use as an aphrodisiac, a cure for many ailments, a main component of witches'

Common yarrow in the winter (left) and summer (right).

Blue vervain in the winter (left) and summer (right).

brew, and as having the ability to ward off evil spirits and/or provide good luck.

When these flowers die, the square stalk with nearly opposite-branched spikes persists and is referred to as a "candelabra of floral stalks," for obvious reasons.

Common Yarrow

Like the black-eyed Susan, yarrow is a member of the Composite family. The leaves of yarrow are very finely divided and both their feathery appearance, as well as their camphor-like scent, are very distinctive. This plant has been used medicinally for a multitude of ailments for thousands of years.

In the winter the curled up dead leaves remain on the stem and the flower head consists of clusters of dried bracts, within which are located tiny, oblong fruits, each containing one seed. Architects often use these flower heads as trees for their models.

Rough-Fruited Cinquefoil

Rough-fruited cinquefoil (*cinquefoil* is French for "five leaves") has, in fact, leaves divided into five parts. The yellow petals of rough-fruited cinquefoil, like those of evening primrose and many other flower species, appear quite differently to the human eye than to an insect's eye, which is sensitive to ultraviolet light. While we see all-yellow petals, bees and other insects are directed to the flower's nectar by purple lines on the petals, called *nectar guides*, which radiate from the center of the flower.

Rough-fruited cinquefoil is an example of a plant that is very easily overlooked in the summer,

Rough-fruited cinquefoil in the winter (left) and summer (right).

] FAST FACTS [
Winter Wildflowers

▶ Wildflowers and grasses are herbaceous, not woody, plants. Their living parts die to the ground at the end of each growing season. If the entire plant, above and below ground, dies at the end of each summer it is called an *annual*. If the underground parts survive and new shoots are sent up in the spring it is a *perennial*. If the plant has a two-year cycle, it is a *biennial*.

▶ One curly dock plant produces up to 25,000 seeds. They are an important source of food for American goldfinches and pine siskins. The seeds that are not eaten are able to germinate after a dormancy of 50 years.

▶ St. Johnswort is a wildflower found in pastures and roadsides. Pollinated flowers become three-parted capsules, which change from green to brick red in autumn.

▶ Evening primrose is a biennial, producing a rosette of leaves on the ground the first year and a flower stalk the second spring, which persists throughout the following winter. Its seeds are eaten by many birds, especially American goldfinches.

▶ After Queen Anne's lace blooms, the tiny branches or *pedicels* that form the flower head, curve upward, closing the cluster while the fruits mature. At this time the head bears a striking resemblance to a bird's nest. After the seeds mature, the pedicels open up and spread out so that the seeds can easily be dispersed.

▶ Many people are familiar with the seeds of beggar ticks. Each seed bears two barbed prongs that point outward, allowing them to easily catch a ride on a passing animal, human or otherwise.

for it blends into the surrounding vegetation. Come winter, stalks of hairy ("rough-fruited") bracts, which once surrounded seed-filled capsules, are very noticeable in overgrown fields.

Botanists don't despair during the winter months, for even though these winter wildflowers may not be living, they are just as distinctive and identifiable as they were during the summer. What they lack in brilliancy, they more than make up for in design and texture. Both the dried flower heads as well as the seeds within them are intricate beyond imagination. Ridges along a black-eyed Susan fruit, barbs on sticktight fruit, or wispy parachutes attached to thistle fruit are revealed in all their glory through a hand lens. Spend a winter afternoon in an overgrown field or walking along a back road and you will discover a whole new world—in some of our poorest soil, some of the most beautiful and delicate designs of nature can be found. One close look at the fruit of Queen Anne's lace will convince you of this.

FEBRUARY

survival

February is a complex month—at the same time that many creatures are fighting for survival, others are bringing progeny into the world. Deep snow can mean starvation for wild turkeys, white-tailed deer, and predators such as hawks and owls. Regardless of how fierce the winter has been thus far, however, certain creatures, including snow fleas, stoneflies, American beavers, raccoons, and red foxes, mate like clockwork. North American river otters give birth while great horned owls brood their eggs. Red-winged blackbirds return to most of New England by the end of this month. The sun is stronger, the days longer. Even in northern New England the stirrings of spring have begun, albeit often under several feet of snow.

nature notes

Here's a sampling of species that are arriving from northern regions, establishing territories, nesting, hibernating, courting, breeding, and giving birth in February.

AMPHIBIANS

■ Freeze-Tolerant Frogs
Wood frog
Spring peeper
Gray treefrog

Pickerel Frog—*Hibernating*

Pickerel frogs have been hibernating in the mud at the bottom of ponds, or under stones at the bottom of rocky ravines, since October or November. They

Pickerel frog.

begin to emerge from hibernation next month, with their courtship peaking in late May.

Eastern Red-Backed Salamander—*Hibernating*

Eastern red-backed salamanders are hidden from view year-round, for they are found in the shade and

moisture of leaf litter and up to a foot deep in the soil of the forest floor. They hibernate even deeper in

Eastern red-backed salamander.

the soil, as well as under rocks and protected areas, emerging when the humidity and soil temperature rise. Groups of these salamanders have been found hibernating together, having all migrated to the same spot in the fall.

REPTILES

Red-Bellied Snake—*Hibernating*

Red-bellied snakes form mass migrations to and from their hibernation sites in the spring and fall. (Although they are solitary in the summer, they congregate when hibernating.) Anthills, abandoned rodent

Red-bellied snake.

burrows, and rotting stumps are often used as hibernation sites. DeKay's brownsnakes, common gartersnakes, and smooth greensnakes share these sites with red-bellies. In 1934 in Manitoba, Canada, a total of 257 snakes were found in a single anthill that was excavated in the fall, 101 of which were red-bellied snakes. Although a majority of northern red-bellied snakes mate in the spring, some mate in the fall. The male's sperm of those mating in the fall remains alive in the female's body throughout hibernation, and fertilization takes place in the spring.

BIRDS

Great Horned Owl—*Nesting*

Hard as it may be to believe, the great horned owl is often sitting on eggs by February. It does not

Great horned owl.

usually build its own nest; rather, it primarily seeks shelter in the unoccupied tree nests of other species of birds (and sometimes mammals). Red-tailed hawk nests are preferred, but those of crows, ravens, herons, and squirrels are also used. Any owl nesting this early in the year has to have a hardy constitution, which the great horned owl most certainly does. Research shows that they are able to incubate eggs successfully when the outside temperature dips down to as low as -27°F.

Hairy and Downy Woodpecker—*Drumming*

Woodpeckers drum against branches, as well as tree trunks, all year long, but the frequency and intensity start to build this time of year. Scientists believe drumming plays a role in establishing territory, courtship, maintaining a bond between mates, and general communication. Even though eggs won't be laid until May, this

Male hairy woodpecker.

behavior begins now and is especially noticeable on sunny, calm days. Our most common woodpeckers, the hairy and downy, have very similar drumming patterns. Some claim that there is no distinguishable difference between the two; others feel that the larger hairy woodpecker's drumming is more rapid, with longer pauses between bursts of sound.

Northern Saw-Whet Owl—*Irruptive Winter Visitor*

Northern saw-whet owls are uncommon year-round residents in New England, but winter numbers are considerably augmented as migrants move south in the fall, particularly during years of successful breeding, when numbers are high, or when prey populations are down. Mice and voles make

Northern saw-whet owl.

up a substantial part of a northern saw-whet's diet. Saw-whet owls usually consume anything over 20 grams in two meals, thus they usually only eat half

■ Owl Calls

Owl Species	Description Of Call
Eastern screech-owl	Descending whinny followed by a long, whistled trill. (Female voice slightly higher than male's.)
Barn owl	Long, hissing shriek.
Long-eared owl	Male—low, soft hoot. Female—higher, softer hoot.
Great horned owl	"Ho–hoo–hoo–hoododo–hooooo–hoo." (Female voice higher-pitched than male's.)
Barred owl	"Hoo–hoo–ho, hoo–hoo–ho–hooaw." ("Who cooks for you? Who cooks for you–all?")
Short-eared owl	Silent except in nesting season. Male—muffled "poo poo poo." Alarm call (both sexes)—high, nasal barks and wheezy notes.
Northern saw-whet owl	Repeated, low, whistled toots.

* Descriptions from David Sibley's *The Sibley Guide to Birds* (Knopf, 2000).

Barn owl.

a mouse or vole at a time, returning for the second half four or five hours later. They frequently place the uneaten half of the rodent on a branch, where, in winter, it freezes. Before consuming it, the owl thaws the remaining portion by placing it under its body, as if incubating it.

Bohemian Waxwing—*Irruptive Winter Visitor*
Only three species of waxwings exist worldwide, two of which, cedar and bohemian, occur in New England. Bohemian waxwings have white edges on their wing feathers and rusty feathers under their tail, features which distinguish them from cedar waxwings.

Bohemian waxwings are named for their nomadic tendencies in the winter. While cedar waxwings breed in New England and are present year-round, bohemian waxwings are irregular winter visitors, usually coming only as far south as northern New England, and arriving in dramatically varying numbers from one year to the next. They visit in the hopes of finding winter fruit, and when they do, a flock of waxwings can consume an entire tree's supply in very short order. They seem to have a preference for sugary fruits such as mountain ash berries, hawthorns, rose hips, and crabapples.

Bohemian waxwing.

Red-Breasted Nuthatch—*Remaining Year-Round or an Irruptive Winter Visitor*
While resident red-breasted nuthatches remain in New England through the winter, their numbers are supplemented by relatives from the north. Red-breasted nuthatches are the only species of

FEATHER STRUCTURE

A feather has a central hollow shaft and structures called *barbs* on either side (left). Smaller *barbules* extend on either side of every barb, and interlock (right). These combine to make a strong, smooth surface.

Only birds have *feathers*, structures that perform many different functions, including providing insulation, protection from rain and snow, camouflage, mate attraction, and flight. Feathers consist of only a few parts, but they are modified in different areas of a bird's plumage, and in different species they perform different functions. Looking at a wing or tail feather, you can easily see a central, hollow (less weight to carry) shaft running up the middle of the feather. On either side of this shaft are structures called *barbs*, which interlock. Taking an even closer look, perhaps through a hand lens, you can see that tiny *barbules* extend from both sides of every barb. The hooks on these barbules interlock, much like Velcro's hooks and loops interlock, creating a smooth, flat, strong surface. When you see a bird preening, it often is re-hooking the barbules of its feathers.

North American nuthatch to undergo regular irruptive movements. They usually do so every other year, as do some other boreal seed-eat-

Red-breasted nuthatch.

ing songbirds. Red-breasted nuthatches tend to move south earlier than most irruptive species, some birds beginning their flight as early as July. A shortage of winter food, primarily seeds of conifer trees, is thought to cause these movements, although northernmost birds tend to migrate south every year.

Wild Turkey—*Sign (Scat)*
Wild turkey scat frequently provides more informa-

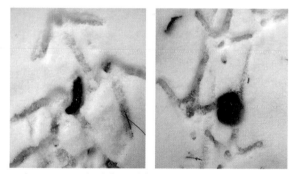

Turkey scat—male (left) and female (right).

tion than just the diet of the turkey. The shape of the scat of male and female wild turkeys reflects the differences in their intestinal tracts. "Hen" turkey scat often forms a round lump, whereas "tom" turkey scat tends to be either straight or somewhat "J"-shaped.

BIRDS KEEPING WARM

Because they are warm-blooded, or *homoiothermic*, birds that remain in the Northeast throughout the winter must adapt to the cold in order to survive. While an adequate and available food supply is essential, physical and behavioral adaptations are also necessary. One such adaptation is the creation of a "jacket" of insulating air pockets surrounding the bird and sealing in the heat of its body. As a means of combating the fierce wind and subzero temperatures, birds can adjust the position of their feathers with muscles in their skin, puffing them way out on the coldest of days, creating these air pockets. It's not your imagination—birds look much bigger on the cold winter days, because they *are*. Two other survival techniques used by birds in winter are shivering, and trying to expose as little of themselves to the wind as possible.

Northern shrike.

Blue jay.

On a subzero day, this pileated woodpecker shivered furiously for 10 minutes while it clung to white pine bark in the sun. It then turned its head toward its backside and tucked its beak and face into its feathers, leaving only the red crest on the top of its head exposed.

Common redpoll.

Dark-eyed junco.

MAMMALS

American Beaver—*Breeding*

American Beavers form permanent breeding pairs and are monogamous, even in consecutive breeding seasons. Mating, which occurs between January and March in

American beaver.

New England (peaking in February), takes place in the water (under the ice in most northern ponds) almost exclusively at night. The female is only receptive for 12 to 24 hours, so there is no time to lose. Sometime between May and July three or four kits are usually born (up to six if the weather's been mild and food is plentiful). (Read more about beavers on p. 321.)

Raccoon—*Breeding*

The peak of the raccoon mating season is in February, right after raccoons emerge from their winter rest. Raccoons are definitely not monogamous; although pair bonds are formed, both the male and female usually mate with more than one partner. During the winter the trails of raccoons in search of mates can often be seen in the snow. The

Raccoon.

male raccoon, like many carnivores, possesses a penis bone, or *baculum*, which is curved in order to assist coupling (see photo on p. 29).

Bobcat—*Breeding*

The breeding season for bobcats in New England begins in February, when they often travel a great

MUSTELIDAE OR WEASEL FAMILY

The weasel family is the largest family of carnivorous mammals, most of which share the following characteristics: short legs, long body, medium to long tail, anal scent glands, solitary, nocturnal, and active year-round. They include the:

Ermine
Long-tailed weasel
American mink
Fisher
American marten
North American river otter

Bobcat.

distance in search of mates. Bobcat courtship is described as a series of "chases, bumping behavior, and ambushes." In typical feline fashion, when the female is receptive, the male grasps her neck with his teeth and mating ensues.

North American River Otter—*Giving Birth*

North American river otters—large, aquatic members of the weasel family—give birth to anywhere from one to five young in February or March, after experiencing a 10-month gestation due to delayed implantation. Just before giving birth the female establishes a natal den. The young are born fully

North American river otter.

furred, but their eyes are closed and they lack teeth. In a little over a month they are fully active, in two months, they are foraging with their mother, and by the next winter they have dispersed and established their own territories.

Masked Shrew—*Remaining Active*

Restless, pugnacious, and voracious—these are adjectives commonly used when describing a masked (or cinereus) shrew. This little predator doesn't hibernate; it is active year-round, primarily under the snow in winter. It doesn't store any food, so it actively hunts day and night

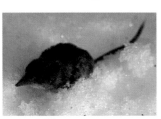

Masked shrew.

for grubs, worms, ants, slugs, snails, and spiders. Somehow it finds enough dormant insects and other creatures to keep its tiny, hyperactive body warm, though during long winters many die of starvation. (Read more about shrews on p. 379.)

Snowshoe Hare—*Sign (Scat, Urine)*

The rounded pellets of eastern cottontail, New England cottontail, and snowshoe hare scat are, for the most part, indistinguishable. These animals actually digest their food twice in order to thoroughly break down the woody plant material they consume. The first time through, their scat consists of soft, jelly-

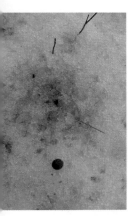

Snowshoe hare scat and urine.

TUNNEL-MAKERS AND PREDATORS

Many mammals take advantage of the cover that snow affords them and build networks of tunnels under the surface (see p. 392 for more about this). It is common to run across the openings of tunnels made by mice, voles, and squirrels that are hiding from predators beneath the snow. However, some predators, particularly members

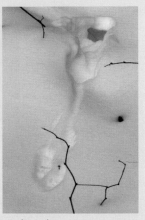

Mink tracks exiting a tunnel in the snow.

of the weasel family, are slender enough to fit in the tunnels and chase after prey. Look for weasel tunnels near stonewalls and mink near streams and wetlands.

like pellets, which are rarely seen. The rounded, fibrous pellets we are more familiar with are recycled pellets (they've been ingested and expelled again). Both hares and cottontails can have pinkish-orange urine, a characteristic thought to be connected to their diet. (For more on the snowshoe hare, see p. 416.)

North American Porcupine—*Sign (Den)*

You could almost locate a porcupine den blindfolded, as the strong scent of their urine and scat-filled hideaways is unmistakable. A good place to start looking for a porcupine den is in a large stand of eastern hemlocks. (White oak, white pine, and poplar stands are also associated with porcupines.) If there are ledges with lots of crevices or standing hollow trees, head there first. Because porcupines

North American porcupine in den.

try to conserve energy in the colder months, moving as little as necessary, they spend a great deal of time in their dens, and they don't leave to defecate. Thus, scat accumulates on the floor of their den, often to the point where it flows outside the entrance, creating a pile several feet high. (Read more about porcupines on p. 349.)

Eastern Gray Squirrel—*Sign (Nest)*

Both red and gray squirrels inhabit cavities, such as tree crevices, in the winter. In the absence of these cavities, both species construct leaf nests, or *dreys*, in trees. Red squirrel nests are often found in conifers, and gray squirrel nests in deciduous trees, but there are plenty of exceptions to this rule. Typically a gray squirrel nest is roughly between 12 and 19 inches in diameter, made of leaves and twigs, and located high up, often in the crotch of a deciduous tree. The main entrance is usually near the trunk of the tree and the inside is lined with soft, fine material, such as inner

Eastern gray squirrel nest.

bark. The material is woven together so tightly that the nest is usually fairly waterproof. Gray squirrels frequently maintain more than one nest in their home range, and several squirrels occupy a nest in the winter.

INSECTS & ARACHNIDS

Stonefly—*Breeding*

Stoneflies spend the first part of their life as immature nymphs clinging to the bottoms of rocks and sticks in fast-moving, unpolluted streams. Some species emerge as adults in February and March, others in the spring and summer. The winter-emerging stonefly nymphs molt to the adult stage in the space between the water surface and the ice. Most of the adult stoneflies

Stonefly.

you encounter (sometimes by the hundreds) walking on the snow near the edges of clear streams on warm winter days are referred to as slender winter stoneflies, one of which is the early season brown stonefly. They are very small and consume blue-green algae. Most are flightless, and they are engaged in breeding and laying eggs in the stream. These insects are a late-winter/early-spring food staple for American robins and eastern phoebes.

SNOW CREATURES

A number of invertebrates are active in the winter, both on and below the surface of the snow. Many of them climb up through the snow and mate once they've reached the surface. Some of the creatures you might encounter on a February day include spiders, snow fleas (springtails), stoneflies, harvestmen, winter crane flies, and winter scorpionflies (also called snow-born boreus). Read more about snow fleas on p. 424.

A spider on the snow.

PLANTS & FUNGI

Cattail—*Providing Micro-Habitat*

Cattails are the dominant plant in many wetlands, growing in dense stands in marshes and around the edges of ponds. There are two common species in New England—broad-leaved and narrow-leaved cattail—both of which reproduce primarily from *creeping rhizomes*, or stem-like structures growing along the ground.

Common cattail.

The male and female flowers of cattail are both located on the top spike, with male flowers positioned above the female. The hot-dog-shaped structure left on the top of a cattail in the fall consists of the remains of the pollinated female flowers that developed into 220,000 tiny seeds. As the winter progresses, most of these seeds are dispersed by the wind.

Few birds feed on the seeds of cattail for they are simply too small and too fuzzy to be appetizing. There are birds, however, including the black-capped chickadee, that have discovered larvae and their cocoons within the seed heads, and so come to feed on them.

Common Winterberry—*Fruit Persisting*

Common winterberry is also known as northern holly and swamp holly. It is at its most striking in winter, when its leaves have fallen and bright red fruits—sometimes solitary, sometimes in clusters of two or three—are visible. It is found throughout New England near swamps and in wet woods.

Common winterberry.

Birds that feed on its fruit in winter include common crows, mockingbirds, American robins, and cedar waxwings. Black bear, white-tailed deer, and white-footed deermice have been known to eat the berries, as well as browse on the twigs.

Pine Cone Willow Gall—*Providing Winter Home for Gall Gnat*

What looks remarkably like a pine cone growing on a willow tree is actually not a pine cone at all. Rather, it is a pine cone willow gall, home of the larval stage of a small mosquito-like fly, called a gall gnat. After being sheltered and fed by the gall through the winter, the gall gnat exits in the spring as a fully developed, winged adult. Galls are growths on plants, produced in response to irritation or chemicals secreted by insects laying eggs during the plant's growing season. Each species of gall insect has a specific plant host, and a characteristically-shaped gall. (Find out more about galls on p. 155.)

Pine cone willow gall.

a closer look

It is a good time of year to look for **signs of animals** (p. 420), be they the larval tunnels of **engraver beetles** (p. 423), or tracks and/or traces of active animals, such as the **snowshoe hare** (p. 416), **red fox** (p. 415), and **barred owl** (see below). Sometimes you don't have to look very far, especially if you feed birds such as the **black-capped chickadee** (p. 413). The constant movement of tiny black specks on top of the snow reveals hundreds, if not thousands, of **snow fleas** (p. 424) that have surfaced on warm, sunny days. Spend a late winter afternoon improving your identification skills by studying a tree's **bark** (p. 426) and **winter twigs** (p. 430).

Barred Owl—*Raucous Courtship*

You wake in the middle of the night to maniacal laughter outside your window. Raucous cater-wauling, one voice on top of the other, breaks the silence of the woods. After listening to this jumble of cackles, hoots, caws, and gurgles, you know it can be none other than a pair of barred owls in the passionate throes of courtship.

Barred owls can be heard every month of the year in New England but are most vocal during the months of February and March when they engage in courtship behavior prior to mating and laying eggs. As part of this ritual, the male and female often perform a dueling duet, asking each other, *"Who cooks for you? Who cooks for you-all?"* It is relatively easy to distinguish the lower-pitched male from the higher-pitched female when they call back and forth in this manner. The barred owl has a broad repertoire of calls in addition to the cater-wauling and *"Who cooks for you?"* standard. Single hoots as well as a series of ascending hoots are also given by both males and females. There is a

With its soulful brown eyes and gentle demeanor, the barred owl gives no hint of its wilder, vocal side. This seldom-seen-but-often-heard owl is aptly named for its horizontally barred throat and vertically striped breast feathers. You would never guess that underneath all those feathers is a mere pound or two of bird.

resurgence of vocalizations in late summer and fall, but it pales in comparison to the intense conversations that take place this time of year.

Bringing Death by Night
If it weren't for these calls, it would be very easy to overlook the presence of barred owls in our mature woods, for their nocturnal habits and sound-muffling feathers make them very hard to detect. The only audible hint of their presence, other

THE MECHANICS OF SILENT FLIGHT

The comb-like leading edge of an owl's first few wing feathers contributes to the silence of its flight.

An owl's feathers are designed in such a way as to allow the bird to have silent flight. Several different feather characteristics contribute to this. If you ever have the chance to pat an owl or rub a finger over one of its feathers, you will notice a distinct softness, or velvety feel to it. This quality allows the feathers to absorb high sound frequencies. In addition, if you look closely at the leading edge of the first few primary feathers of an owl's wing, you notice that they have a comb-like fringe, called *flutings*. Flutings contribute to the stability of the owl, as well as help muffle the sound of rushing air over the wing surface. Finally, the tattered, trailing feathers on the back end of an owl's wing may be even more instrumental in creating silent flight by reducing noise, as they help break up the sound waves that are generated as air flows over the top of the wings and down over the trailing edge.

At this time of year, if the barred owl isn't courting it is usually hunting for prey. The peak of its nocturnal hunting activity occurs just after sunset. Using its acute vision and hearing, the barred owl locates and consumes small mammals, such as mice, voles, squirrels, and rabbits, which comprise up to 75 percent of its diet. Birds up to the size of a grouse, amphibians, reptiles, fish, and invertebrates make up the rest, depending on the season. In addition, predators such as owls are known to occasionally eat other smaller predators. As improbable as it may seem, a dead barred owl was found in New England with the remains of a long-eared owl inside its stomach, and inside the long-eared owl's stomach were the remains of an eastern screech-owl.

Barred owls usually hunt by surveying the forest floor for signs of life while perched on a branch. When prey is spotted, the owl drops down and captures it on the ground with its sharp *talons* (nails). Barred owls have also been known to perch on a limb over open water and dive down to capture fish. Other hunting techniques that have been observed include wading into shallow water to capture crayfish and running on the ground to chase an amphibian.

A Great Big Bite
Regardless of where or how they find food, barred owls swallow small prey whole, head first. Between 8 and 12 hours after a meal the owl regurgitates the indigestible parts of the prey it has eaten in the form of an odorless, compact *pellet*. The larger the bird, the larger the pellet—barred owl pellets are approximately 3 inches in length and 1 inch in diameter. Within the pellet, fur is packed around most of the sharp objects, such as bones, nails and teeth, so as to facilitate their passage through the owl's esophagus or gullet while the pellet is being coughed up. By examining a pellet's contents you can determine the nature of the owl's diet, often right down to the species of rodent it last ate. (See photo on p. 273.)

than their calls, is the cacophony of sound when other birds—such as ravens, crows, blue jays, and songbirds—gather to harass or "mob" an owl while it perches on a limb. Making a terrible racket and repeatedly diving at the owl, these birds recognize that although birds of prey may be a threat to an individual bird, there is safety in numbers.

] FAST FACTS [
Barred Owl

▶ The belly feathers on some barred owls are pink. This coloration may be due to eating many crayfish.

▶ The larger great horned owl is one of the biggest predatory threats to the barred owl.

▶ Because the barred owl's range has extended north and westward it is now breeding and competing with the less aggressive, endangered spotted owl in the western United States.

▶ The plumage of male and female barred owls is similar; as in all owls, the female is larger in size than the male.

▶ Although considered non-migratory, when prey is scarce, barred owls may leave their territory to seek food elsewhere.

▶ Barred owls frequently nest in cavities found in deciduous trees.

▶ Young barred owls are able to climb trees using their beaks and talons.

If you're lucky, you may catch a glimpse of a barred owl gliding silently and gracefully among the branches of your woodland trees. However, these owls are definitely heard more often than they are seen. Being quite territorial and thought to mate for life (which can be as long as 18 years in the wild), barred owls tend to remain in the same area for a long time. Step outside in the middle of a February night, or sleep with your windows open—and know that what sounds like a bunch of raucous monkeys is more likely just two infatuated feathered friends.

Black-Capped Chickadee—
This Close to Domesticated

Most of us are familiar with black-capped chickadees—those inquisitive, black-and-white balls of feathers that frequent our bird feeders year-round. During the summer months, seeds and berries make up only about 10 to 20 percent of the chickadee's diet. The rest is primarily caterpillars. In the winter, their seed consumption jumps to 50 percent, with insects and spiders making up the rest. These seeds are crucial to the survival of chickadees, for they provide the fuel necessary to survive New England's long, cold winter nights.

Chickadees have evolved behavioral as well as physical traits to deal with the severity of winters in the Northeast. Not only do they seek out tree cavities and other sheltered spots to spend extremely cold nights, but they actually enter a state of "regulated hypothermia" at night, dropping their temperature about 50 degrees below their normal daytime temperature, thereby expending significantly less fuel. In addition, they cache seeds, as well as insects, behind bark, in dead leaves, in knotholes, and even in the soil in southern parts of the region. Each item is stored in a separate spot, and according to scientists, chickadees remember where they have stored food for over 28 days. They even remember cache sites that have been emptied, and when they search for cached food, they spend more time investigating sites where the highest energy food is stored.

Because of their boldness and their need for fuel, chickadees can be attracted to feeders placed near your home. With patience, they will even accept food right from your hand. First you must have an active feeder, where they come to feed on a regular basis. The rest is up to you.

Hand-Feeding Black-Capped Chickadees
When? January and February are the perfect time, as food supplies are dwindling and the temperatures

are the most severe. The necessity and relative difficulty of finding food in winter encourages birds, particularly human-friendly birds such as chickadees, to take risks that they might otherwise not.

When the temperature drops suddenly, birds tend to feed heavily, both in the morning as well as late afternoon, before settling for the night. The most opportune time is right after an ice storm, before the sun has had a chance to do its work. With tree branches coated in thick ice, chickadees do not have access to the dormant insects tucked beneath loose bark. You will probably have the best results if you start a day before and one or two days after a big snow or ice storm.

Time of day? From sunrise to mid-morning is the optimum time to attempt hand-feeding birds. They are the hungriest at this time, having burned much of their fuel supply during the night.

Procedure? Be silent and stationary! This interaction demands patience—the goal is rarely reached in a day or two. Only after several visits, during which you remain statue-like, are you likely to meet with success. The birds must become comfortable with your presence before they will dare approach you. The first three or four sessions involve standing (or sitting) very still and absolutely silent, about 15 feet from your feeder, for about 20 or 30 minutes. Once the birds resume normal feeding activity, you can, in successive visits, gradually move closer and closer to the feeder, perhaps 2 or 3 feet closer each visit. Chickadees are one of the few species of birds that will continue to feed with you closer than 8 or 10 feet (even more patience is needed with tufted titmice and nuthatches).

When the birds seem oblivious to your presence, and you are within 3 or 4 feet of the feeder, set up a step-ladder right next to the feeder. Do this at night so as to create as little disturbance as possible the next morning. In the morning empty the feeder and sit on the ladder with your hand (filled with seeds) on or near the feeder. If it is a platform

Black-capped chickadee.

feeder, place some seeds a few inches away from your hand as well as in your hand. Eventually chickadees should approach you, and when they do, they will probably snatch the seeds on the feeder first. When these seeds are gone, the only remaining seeds will be in your hand. It may take another visit or two on your part, but eventually they will land on your hand and feed from it. (Fill your feeder after each of these sessions and empty it before the next visit.) After a few successful hand-feedings, remove the feeder entirely and sit quietly with your hand extended. (Don't forget to replace the feeder when you leave.) Chances are good that your fingers will provide a perch for the hungry chickadees whose trust you have earned.

What to feed? Although chickadees may prefer pea-size bits of walnuts, pecans, and cashews, hulled sunflower seeds do just fine as a lure, at a fraction of the cost.

What if I'm impatient? Make a mock "person" (in time chickadees learn that this scarecrow is harmless) either standing or sitting near your feeder, with one "hand" extended and holding seeds. In due time, after chickadees are fearlessly feeding from this fake hand, change places with the "dummy," assuming the same position, and enjoy your feathered visitors.

] FAST FACTS [
Black-Capped Chickadee

▶ Winter flocks of black-capped chickadees consist of regular members, which spend the winter together, as well as "floaters," chickadees that move amongst several flocks. If a member of the regular flock dies, a floater may take its place and in so doing, assume the same place in the flock hierarchy as the bird it replaced.

▶ Every two years or so young chickadees make long distance movements that are referred to as irruptions (see more on this on p. 347). These flights have been correlated with poor seed production further north.

▶ In the winter, a chickadee's diet consists of 50 percent animal matter (mostly insects and spiders) and during the breeding season it rises to about 80 to 90 percent (mostly caterpillars). The rest is fruit and seeds.

▶ Adult chickadees have 15 different kinds of vocalizations.

▶ Chickadees normally fly at about 20 miles per hour.

▶ Chickadees build their cavity nests in dead snags and rotten branches, as they are not well equipped to excavate cavities in hard wood.

▶ Female chickadees build the nest, incubate the eggs, and brood the young. Both male and females feed the young.

▶ Except for occasional irruptions, chickadees remain near their initial breeding territory for their entire life.

Red Fox—*A Catlike Canine*

If your nose has been telling you for the past month or so that your woods are riddled with skunks, you may be in for a pleasant surprise. During January and February, when red foxes are breeding, their urine (particularly the males') develops a very strong musky odor that greatly resembles skunk spray. For various purposes, all manner of vegetation as well as rocks, logs, and other prominent spots are marked.

The strength of the odor of a fox's urine during these months is indicative of the important role urine plays in red fox courtship. Information as detailed as the marker's sex, age, dominance status, and breeding status is conveyed via scent posts scattered throughout the fox's territory as well as along its borders. It's no wonder a skunk-like odor pervades the winter woods of New England in February.

Like Dog, Like Cat

As we all realize from observing domestic dogs and cats, members of both the dog family, *Canidae* (dogs, foxes, coyotes, wolves), as well as members of the cat family, *Felidae* (domestic cats, bobcats, Canadian lynx, eastern mountain lions), mark with urine (as do other mammals). There are other behaviors, however, that the dog and cat family usually don't share. The hunting strategies of the dog family generally include endurance and distance running, whereas cats are built for stealth and bursts of speed. Canids approach prey openly, outpace it during a long chase, and finally pull it down, while felines stalk a prey closely and make surprise attacks.

Anyone who has had the good fortune to witness a red fox stalking and then pouncing on its prey can testify as to the similarity between its hunting traits and those of members of the cat family. In addition, the red fox possesses many of the physical adaptations that enable cats to hunt in this fashion: a good sense of balance so it can remain motionless for periods of time; retractable claws for capturing prey (red fox nails are semi-retractable, unlike coyotes and wolves, which don't retract at all); sharp dagger-like canines for dispatching prey; a vertical-slit pupil and green reflective layer in the eye, enhancing both night and day vision; and long, stiff whiskers whose sensitivity may be of assistance during nocturnal hunting.

Directed by Diet

Although it is thought that cats and dogs evolved from a common ancestral group, they have diverged into two quite separate families. The red fox has the prerequisite morphological characteristics (elongated skull, smooth tongue, four well-developed toes, semirigid elongated legs, 42 teeth) as well as behavioral traits (caching food, scavenging behavior, well-developed pair bond, and use of burrows for dens) that are typical of *Canidae*. There are, however, traits that the red fox, as well as other fox species, share with the cat family, often making them seem more catlike than doglike. The $64,000 question is "Why?" The answer may lie in the fox's diet.

A red fox can maintain itself on about a pound of meat a day in the winter. During the summer and early fall much of its diet consists of fruit and berries, supplemented with insects and small rodents. For the remainder of the year a fox's diet is almost exclusively small mammals, with the occasional bird. Small rodents can very quickly escape down tunnels or under logs, or when alerted, can remain motionless, making detection very difficult. Great cunning and stealth is needed in order to surprise and catch them. Perhaps the answer to why the red fox possesses qualities that make it a "catlike canine" is very simple and straightforward: In order to capture similar prey, foxes and cats have evolved a similar features and behaviors.

Long whiskers and vertical-split pupils are two of the physical features a red fox shares with members of the cat family.

Snowshoe Hare—
Tracking the Highly Hunted

If your objective in life is to see a snowshoe hare, there are several steps you can take to maximize your chances of success. The first is to determine when the hare population last peaked. Snowshoe hares undergo cyclic population fluctuations, with peaks every 10 to 11 years. Once you identify when the next peak year is most likely to occur, consider where and what time of day or night to look. Head for dense woods, for snowshoe hares are a forest species, and rarely stray far from wooded areas. Search between dusk and dawn, for this is when they are most active. Planning the search dur-

The snowshoe hare faces many predators, and so has developed a number of specialized adaptations to ensure species survival.

ing the winter is advantageous as their packed trails are far more obvious in the snow than on the bare ground. Lastly, notice where you see collections of their small, round droppings during the day. Unlike deer, who drop all their pellets at once, snowshoe hares drop them one at a time, so when you come upon a cluster of several pellets, you know the hare has spent a considerable amount of time in that spot—most likely because it found something edible, such as raspberry or blackberry canes—and it might well return.

Fine Dining

The pressure for snowshoe hares to adapt has been high, for not only is every predator of any significant size, including bobcats, fishers, Canadian lynx, foxes, coyotes, and great horned owls, wise enough to look for them in the right places at the right time, but hares are at the top of most predators' "fine dining" list. Being able to avoid detection by the sharp eyes of a goshawk, outrun a fisher, or simply multiply so fast that predation rates can't keep up

with productivity rates, have all proven to be effective survival techniques.

The Varying Hare's Varying Hair

Most are aware that the color of the fur of a snowshoe hare varies with the season—this is why for many years they were called "varying hares." Brown summer hairs are shed and replaced by white (only at the tips) hairs over a period of 70 to 90 days beginning in October and ending in December (see p. 291 for a photo). The reverse process takes place in the spring, turning the hare brown by the time snow has usually disappeared. Not only does the white coat camouflage the hare in the snow, but it also provides 27 percent more insulation than the brown hair. Because white is actually the absence of pigment, the cells in white hairs (as opposed to brown) are filled with air, not pigment, and thus provide additional thermal insulation.

Go Fast

Speed and agility traveling over snow have a tremendous effect on the life span of a snowshoe hare. Not only are its hind feet large and covered with dense fur, especially in the winter, but the toes can be spread as wide as 4½ inches to further increase the surface area, allowing the hare to remain on top of the snow instead of wallowing in it as many of its smaller-footed predators do. In addition, due partially to the fusion of bones in their long hind legs that gives them greater thrust, hares are able to bound up to 12 feet in a single leap, and they've been clocked running 31 miles per hour on ice.

Make Many

Even if these adaptations were to fail them, snowshoe hares have numbers on their side. Most hares reproduce at one year of age, and females breed again soon after they give birth to their litter of one to six young. (An extra advantage that hares have over many other prey animals, such as cottontail rabbits, mice, and voles, is that their young are *precocial*—born fully furred, with eyes open, able to walk, and even hop.) Gestation is a mere 37 days, allowing three or four litters per summer. Given an average of three young per litter, and three litters per year, one pair of hares, in two years, produces an average of 99 offspring (their young, plus their young's offspring). Although scientists estimate that only 15 percent of hares live long enough to reproduce (due mainly to predation), this is more than enough to maintain the species.

Snowshoe hares engage in unusual behavior during courtship. A game that resembles leap frog takes place, with one hare jumping up in the air while the other dashes under it, and then the roles are reversed. This continues for several minutes,

Snowshoe hare trails tend to be quite obvious in the snow, as they are packed down from repeated use. When alarmed, hares use them to circle through their home range of 20 to 25 square acres.

During the day the snowshoe hare sits quietly, usually in a sheltered depression under conifer branches or thickets called a *form*, which it uses throughout the year.

with the airborne hare urinating on the hare directly beneath it. This behavior may have several functions. According to scientists, it is felt that the female can detect pheromones in her mate's urine that informs her of his reproductive efficiency—a handy thing to know if you want to pass on your genes. In cottontail rabbits the "jump" is thought to help soothe the female, who is initially aggressive to a courting male. They jump each other until she calms enough for him to approach. It's very possible that this is true for snowshoe hares, as well.

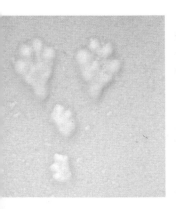

Both snowshoe hares and cottontail rabbits place their smaller front feet behind their larger hind feet when bounding. It is thought that Native Americans may have come up with the concept of snowshoes after observing the tracks of hares, whose hind feet toes can be spread as wide as 4 ½ inches in order to keep the hares on top of the snow when traveling.

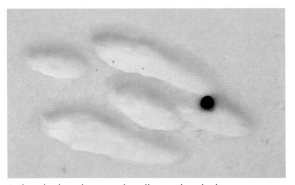

A close look at these tracks tells you that the hare was sitting (facing left), not bounding. The tracks of the hare's front feet are located in front of the tracks of its hind feet—the opposite of what occurs when the hare is moving. The single scat is typical of the snowshoe hare.

The snowshoe hare pellets we come across have been through the hare's digestive system twice. In an attempt to extract as many nutrients as possible from the twigs and buds of their winter diet (as well as their summer herbaceous diet), hares reingest their feces. Several pellets in one spot indicate that the hare that left them was stationary for a while, possibly eating, as hares drop their pellets one at a time, not all at once.

Waste Not Waste

There are also more subtle behaviors, which at first glance might not seem particularly advantageous but actually are, such as the hare's habit of reingesting its feces. This behavior is referred to as *coprophagy*, and it guarantees that the hare extracts as much nutrition as possible from the food it has eaten. One way to better break down cellulose is to lengthen the digestive tract to allow greater absorption of nutrition, and this can be done behaviorally as well as physiologically. Eating one's own scat effectively doubles the length of the digestive tract.

The first time around, the hare's soft, jelly-like pellets are eaten directly from the anus (which is why we rarely find them). It is the recycled pellets that we commonly come across on top of the snow. This practice also allows hares to eat quantities of food rapidly while exposed to the threat of predation, and then to retire to relative safety beneath a protective conifer branch or the middle of a thicket to re-ingest the food.

] FAST FACTS [
Snowshoe Hare

▶ Young hares spend the day hiding in separate spots, congregating once a day to nurse from their mother for 5 to 10 minutes.

▶ Snowshoe hares and cottontail rabbits rarely dig and generally do not use the burrows of other animals.

▶ In Canada, the snowshoe hare population peaks every 9 to 10 years. The Canadian lynx and great horned owl population, which preys heavily on snowshoe hares in this region, experiences this cycle as well.

▶ Snowshoe hare and cottontail rabbit tracks are very similar but they can easily be told from one another by measuring the width of the hind foot. Depending on the geographic area, If it is less than 1½ inches wide, it's likely to be a New England or eastern cottontail rabbit; if it is greater than 1½ inches wide, it is most likely a snowshoe hare.

Most behaviors, regardless of how odd or insignificant they may appear to us, usually play a vital part in the survival of the species exhibiting them—especially a species that is sought after by many predators. From cradle to courtship, the snowshoe hare exemplifies this.

Animal Signs—
Woodland Wildlife Calling Cards

Never forget the trail, look ever for the track in the snow; it is the priceless, unimpeachable record of the creature's life and thought, in the oldest writing known on the earth.

—ERNEST THOMPSON SETON,
NATURALIST AND AUTHOR

"Reading" the fields and woodlands is an art that anyone can master, in any season, but winter is much more of an open book than other times of the year. Many of the wildlife signs that are subtle or obscured during the warmer months are relatively obvious when snow is on the ground. Interpreting the activities of animals that stay active this time of year can add high adventure to a snowshoe walk. Following is a sampling of signs resulting from a variety of animal behaviors, including feeding signs, tracks, scat, and territorial marking. These are the kinds stories you can "read" the next time you venture out your backdoor.

Coyote-Scavenged White-Tailed Deer
Although coyotes do prey on very young, old, or weak white-tailed deer, as a rule they are not significant predators of live deer. They will, however, scavenge dead deer that they come upon. Usually they enter the deer's carcass from the rear, where

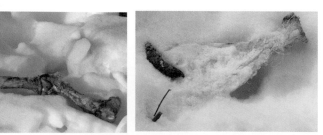

Coyote often mark carrion as a way of claiming it—here you see urine-scented deer bones (left) and coyote scat by the deer scapula (right).

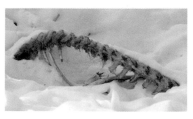

White-tailed deer carcass scavenged by coyotes. The deer's broken ribs are picked clean.

they can readily access the soft organs. Broken ribs and picked-clean bones indicate that coyotes fed on this carcass. It is common for coyotes to drag parts of a large animal, such as a deer, off, to eat in privacy. They have also been known to mark body parts with urine or scat as a way of claiming them and discouraging thievery by other predators.

White-Tailed Deer Yard
When there is little snow on the ground, white-tailed deer can easily get around and consequently eat and sleep where their search for food takes them. When the snow is deep, deer tend to congregate within a designated area called a *deer yard*. This is an area, anywhere from less than an acre to several square miles, which is often located in coniferous woods on south-facing slopes, where there tends to be less snow. All deer activity, including eating and sleeping, takes place within the yard. A network of trails is created in order to conserve energy. Often you can detect a distinct browse line where the deer have eaten the lower branches of conifers (which are within reach) in the yard. (See photo on p. 45.)

Deer beds are often located on the top of a hill within a yard, which affords them a view of the surrounding area. Often several deer will bed down in close proximity to one another, with their head facing different directions so as to not be surprised by predators. A close look often reveals indentations from the deer's "knees" at one end of the bed, created when the deer folds its front legs underneath it. A footprint can often be found in the middle of the bed, where the deer places its front foot as it stands up.

A white-tailed deer bed showing knee prints and the print where the deer placed its front foot as it stood up.

Usually deer will spend much of the day bedded down, rising shortly before dusk to eat. They often spend the night moving around, finishing feeding as the sun rises. They then bed down again, either in the same bed or a new one, for the remainder of the day. (Read more about white-tailed deer on pp. 105 and 389.)

American Black Bear Marking

Black bears mark their territory by clawing, biting, and rubbing on trees along travel routes and near bedding areas or food sources. These signs can be found year-round, although they are freshest in the spring. Often you find a combination of two of these signs, as bears frequently claw or bite the tree over their shoulder while rubbing their back on the trunk. If you should come upon claw marks or bite marks, look closely for bear hairs. They are easily caught in the bark or resin. It's thought that these markings not only indicate territorial boundaries but also communicate other information, including the state of the bear's health, its sex, and its mating status. (Read more about black bears on p. 374.)

Fisher Scent Post

Fishers are enthusiastic markers, often climbing a mound of snow, rubbing and then urinating on it. In addition, fishers commonly mark their territory by rubbing against and rolling on small saplings. If you happen upon a young tree, deciduous or coniferous, that looks rather scraggly and has a circular area packed down in the snow surrounding it, take a closer look. Often you'll find fisher scat in the vicinity and usually you can find hairs stuck to the sapling where it was rubbed. These young trees are used as marking posts by fishers over and over throughout the year. (See more about fishers on p. 29.)

This young white pine serves as a fisher scent post, marked by the animal's scat.

Red Squirrel Tunnels and Meadow Vole Hole

Unbeknownst to many, red squirrels create extensive tunnel systems under the snow between their homes and feeding sites. Many voles also travel below the surface of the snow in winter, leaving 1-inch diameter holes as the only indication of their

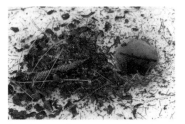

A red squirrel snow tunnel, with cone scales piled at the entrance.

American black bears mark their territory by clawing, biting, and rubbing on trees—here you see nail marks (left) and hairs caught while rubbing (right).

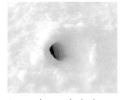

A meadow vole hole.

presence. (These may serve as escape vents for carbon dioxide that builds up in their tunnels.) These tunneling rodents are vulnerable to predators such as ermine, which have no trouble slipping right down these holes and tunnels in hot pursuit of a tasty meal. (Read more about small mammals on p. 377.)

Downy Woodpecker-Drilled Goldenrod Ball Gall
Certain galls, abnormal plant growths within which insects develop, are favored foods of specific birds. The fly larva that once inhabited this goldenrod ball gall was consumed by a downy woodpecker, which left a quarter-inch hole as evidence of its visit. (See more about goldenrod ball galls on p. 261.)

A hole in a goldenrod ball gall drilled by a downy woodpecker.

Porcupine Den
North American porcupines seek out sheltered areas in which they spend a good portion of the day. Natural cavities are usually the winter den of choice for porcupines; rock ledges, under fallen logs, and in hollow tree cavities are typical choices. Once a den is established, a porcupine often returns to it year after year. Several porcupines may occupy a den at the same time, with most individuals changing dens about every three weeks. Look for well-used trails leading to and from these dens. Quills, hairs, and urine often mark the trails, as well as muddy footprints as spring approaches and the ground thaws.

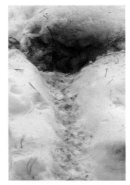

A winter porcupine den.

] FAST FACTS [
Animal Signs

▶ Red squirrels collect mushrooms and place them in the forks of branches to dry. They then collect them and cache them for later consumption.

▶ Small incisor grooves low down on shrubs and trees in the spring are often the work of voles, that eat the nutritious, living cambium layer under the bark as they tunnel through the snow in winter. Cottontail rabbits and hares, which also have a woody diet in winter, leave wider incisor marks, and often eat more than the cambium layer, thus going deeper into the inner wood than voles.

▶ Totally debarked blackberry canes can be a sign of cottontail rabbit activity.

▶ "Nip twigs"—the tender tips of tree branches that porcupines favor—contain more nitrogen, which is essential for the development of protein, than other parts of a tree. These terminal tips of hemlock branches may also be eaten because of the bad-tasting tannins in hemlock bark.

▶ Notice the height of where an animal has been feeding. Take into account the height added by packed snowfall. Moose and deer leave similar markings on a tree, but moose are considerably higher and the width of their incisors is greater. While it can be difficult to tell which species has eaten low to the ground (moose can kneel), higher scrapes indicate moose activity (deer can't jump while feeding).

▶ Red squirrels "tap" trees, leaving telltale dot-dash marks (think of a sideways exclamation point), where top incisors gripped the bark and bottom ones scraped it. (See photo on p. 11.)

▶ Red squirrels are avid markers of their territory, leaving their scent by biting and rubbing their jowls on raised surfaces of trees, such as burls. (See photo, p. 373.)

▶ Raccoons, striped skunks, and American black bears dig into the ground to reach yellowjacket and other nests. Usually some of the nest is exposed when they do so.

Engraver Beetles—*Insect Hieroglyphics*

Have you ever handled a piece of firewood and had the bark fall off to reveal elaborate patterns on the surface of the wood? This is the work of bark beetles—also known as engraver beetles, for obvious reasons.

Adult engraver beetle.

Carving Out a Home

The chewing of these tunnels isn't solely the result of a voracious appetite for wood. These hieroglyphic designs are a direct result of the beetles' procreation process. The adult male and female engraver beetles bore into the bark of a tree, leaving miniscule holes where they enter, along with small piles of wood dust. Once through the bark, they begin to mine the surface of the wood. The pair, or occasionally one male and several females, goes to work excavating a mating chamber, where breeding takes place. The female engraver beetle then creates a *brood gallery* by chewing a fairly straight tunnel away from the mating chamber, usually measuring 1 to 7 inches in length. Along the sides of this brood gallery she lays between 30 and 60 eggs at intervals in little notches.

When the eggs hatch, the small white larvae begin excavating their own individual tunnels away from and at right angles to the brood chamber. If you look closely you can often see that the further away the larval tunnel is from the brood chamber, the larger its diameter. This is due to the growth of the larva as it feeds for two to four weeks, extending the length of its tunnel. When the larva completes its growth it forms an oval cell at the end of its tunnel and pupates. About 12 days later it emerges through a round hole it eats through the bark.

Together, the brood chamber and the larval tunnels form a characteristic pattern. Different species of engraver beetles create different patterns, but they all have numerous small tunnels (larval) radiating out from a central, larger tunnel (brood gallery).

Engraver beetle brood galleries and larval tunnels.

A Dual Threat to the Trees

Some engraver beetles are important in the transmission of tree diseases. Different species of engraver beetles attack different species of trees. Some attack only recently cut trees or dead logs or branches, while other species attack living trees (mostly conifers, or cone-bearing trees). Often it is the most stressed trees, such as those lacking sufficient water, to which engraver beetles are attracted. Trees can die as a result of severe tunneling, which actually girdles the tree, preventing water and nutrients from getting to the leaves. However, most often the destruction the beetles cause is a result of their introduction of fungi. One example is Dutch elm disease, which is transmitted chiefly by the small European elm bark beetle, a species that came from Europe, along with an associated fungus that causes the disease.

Even though precautions are now taken to prevent the introduction of potentially harmful exotic species, newly introduced insects are regularly being discovered in the United States. One such engraver beetle species is the pine shoot beetle. This beetle usually lays her eggs under the bark of pine stumps, logs, or the trunks of severely weakened pines. The larvae pupate, emerge, and fly to the crowns of living pine trees where they burrow into healthy shoots. Not only does the feeding cause tremendous damage to the tree, but fungi carried by the insects also cause harm.

Not all fungi are introduced inadvertently, however. Some species of engraver beetles attack trees en masse, carrying with them a fungus that inhibits the flow of sticky pitch, thus destroying the trees' primary defense mechanism. Ambrosia beetles, close relatives of engraver beetles, go one step further in actually cultivating fungi under the bark as food for adult and larval beetles. Different species of ambrosia beetles feed on different types of fungi. They all excavate narrow tunnels in the trees. On its walls they grow fungi called ambrosia. They then must keep their larvae supplied with fresh ambrosia fungus until the larvae pupate, emerge as adults, and fly away to introduce the fungus into new galleries that they excavate. Although ambrosia beetles don't eat the wood, their tunneling can cause considerable damage to the tree.

There are many species of engraver beetles, most of which are vital members of forest ecosystems. Relatively few species have become pests, but their effect on the health of trees is significant. However, even the knowledge that engraver beetles are responsible for the great majority of insect-caused tree deaths in North American timber-producing forests doesn't diminish the beauty of the engravings that one occasionally discovers beneath the bark of a tree.

] FAST FACTS [
Engraver Beetles

▶ There are some species of engraver beetles that leave minute holes in the bark where they enter and exit. These beetles are called shothole borers. They often leave their small "worm holes" on fruit trees.

▶ Different species of engraver beetles create galleries with different patterns in different species of trees.

▶ Most adult engraver beetles measure about an eighth of an inch in length.

▶ Engraver beetles emit scents that recruit other beetles for a group attack on a tree. Resin is one defense the tree uses against such an attack.

Snow Fleas—*The Ubiquitous Neighbor*

We live among a group of insects (*Collembola*, or springtails) that number in the millions, yet many of us have never seen one. The most prominent species of springtail in New England is a snow flea, which is black in color, but has red, orange, white, green, blue, yellow, and brown relatives. Its body is covered in scales and its mouth is deeply pocketed—according to one observer it looks like "it lost its dentures and then sucked on a bunch of lemons." Some say snow fleas are the most numerous land animal on earth, after nematodes, with several hundred thousand inhabiting a cubic yard. Given their extraordinary numbers how could we possibly be unaware of these bizarre-looking creatures? For one thing, each individual measures less than a tenth of an inch, and for most of the year they live below the surface of the ground, feasting on decaying fungi and algae. Although snow fleas are present year-round, it is only on sunny, warm winter days when we are apt to notice them, for this is when they take advantage of the melted area around the bases of trees and climb up to the surface of the snow. Their dark bodies, well adapted for absorbing the sun's heat, make them stand out against the white snow.

Flight by Catapult

The name snow flea is somewhat of a misnomer, for while this particular species of springtail does appear on snow, it is not a close relative of fleas (its classification as an insect is even being questioned), nor does it bite like fleas do. However, both fleas and snow fleas share the ability to fly through the air without the benefit of wings. While a flea uses its back legs to propel itself, a snow flea has a specialized structure just for this purpose. Attached to the tip of its abdomen is a forked appendage, or *furcula*, which is nearly as long as the snow flea's body. It folds under the abdomen and is held there by a latch, or *tenaculum*. When the snow flea wishes to move, it arches its body, thereby releasing the latch and the furcula swings down, hitting the ground and catapulting the snow flea up to 20 times its own body length.

Snow fleas derive their name from their flea-like ability to leap a distance as much as 20 times their body length—a comparable leap for humans would be a third the length of a football field.

Snow fleas are most noticeable on warm winter days when they leave the leaf litter and climb up to the surface of the snow. There, they "wander," resembling a sprinkling of pepper.

Winter Overflow

Much is known about snow fleas, for they've been around for 400 million years and have been thoroughly studied by entomologists. Among other things, they prefer moist habitats, are major decomposers, exhibit elaborate courtship behavior, and are harmless to humans. But there remains one nagging question. Why do hoards of snow fleas make the arduous, energy-demanding climb up to the surface of the snow? For what purpose are they there? Theories abound: Perhaps they are mating? No, although they do mate during the winter months, females actually

pick up the little packets of sperm deposited by the males in the leaf litter, under the snow. Perhaps they are feeding? No, snow fleas graze on organic material located in the leaf litter and upper layers of soil (and in so doing stimulate a symbiotic association between fungi and certain plants, which enhances plant growth). Professor Ken Christiansen of Grinnell College in Iowa, who has studied snow fleas for the last several decades, has a relatively simple and somewhat anti-climactic explanation. He hypothesizes that due to breeding, snow flea numbers multiply at such a fast rate in the soil that by late winter they simply run out of space—and so the overflow ends up on the snow's surface. He feels the snow fleas do little more than wander around aimlessly until it's time to go back down into the upper layers of the soil as the temperatures drop later in the day. One wonders if, with additional observation, it can be proven that there is more behind this behavior than simply overcrowding.

Thanks to their internal antifreeze, *glycerol*, snow fleas are able to remain active in winter, surviving temperatures as low as -7°F. When it is very cold they are usually well below the insulating blanket of snow. However, in February you are approaching the

] FAST FACTS [
Snow Flea

▶ The order that springtails belong to, *Collembola*, means "glue piston."

▶ There are roughly 7,000 species of springtails in the world. Their defense mechanisms include their jumping ability, toxic blood that comes out of specialized pores, and a body covered with scales.

▶ A square yard of healthy soil contains tens of thousands of springtails.

▶ Underneath its abdomen a snow flea has a tube-like structure called a *collophore* or "gluepeg," which serves a multitude of purposes including water uptake, excretion, and grooming. It is also thought to help them stick to the surface of water.

▶ The act of snow fleas eating fungi and algae can stimulate interaction between fungi and certain plants, resulting in more productive plant growth in the soil.

time of year when an occasional warm day invites snow fleas to venture upward. Keep an eye out for a "sprinkling of pepper" on top of the snow. When you find it, look very closely at one speck of "pepper." If it suddenly leaps an inch or more away, you know you are looking at a very acrobatic member of the springtail family—the inimitable snow flea.

Bark Basics—
Form, Function, and Identity

As children we climb on it and carve our initials in it. As adults we spice food (cinnamon), mulch soil, treat malaria (quinine), and stop our wine bottles with it or its byproducts. Tree bark is all around us every day, but its structure remains hidden under the bark itself.

Cambium

In order to understand how bark actually forms and what role it plays in the life of a tree, you must have a basic understanding of a tree's structure and growth. Inside the bark there is a very thin layer of cells—only three or four cells thick—that runs from a tree's roots all the way out to the tips of its branches. It is called the *vascular cambium layer*, and it is the center of growth in a tree, responsible for the expanding diameter of the trunk.

Unfortunately for trees, all sorts of animals—including beavers, rabbits, and porcupines—find cambium irresistible. If the cambium layer is severed, such as when a band of bark circling the trunk is removed (a process called *girdling*), the tree will die.

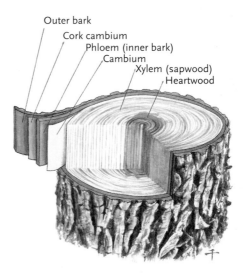

Outer bark
Cork cambium
Phloem (inner bark)
Cambium
Xylem (sapwood)
Heartwood

Tree structure.

Transport System

The cambium layer creates conducting tissue consisting of two kinds of cells, *xylem* and *phloem*, which form the transport system for the entire

American beech (light satiny gray).

White ash (finely furrowed into thin, intersecting ridges in a regular diamond pattern).

Hophornbeam (broken into short, narrow, longitudinal strips, loose at both ends).

Sugar maple (divided into long, vertical, irregular ridges that often curl outward along one side).

Black cherry—mature (separates into square-like scales curved outward at vertical edges, resembling burnt potato chips to some).

Gray birch (marked with triangular black patches or "chevrons," often below the branches).

Yellow birch (silvery-golden with thin, papery shreds ending in tight curls).

Striped maple (smooth and green with long, vertical, light-white stripes).

tree. If the cambium layer is interrupted all the way around the trunk, water and food have no way of reaching the leaves and roots. The cambium layer manufactures xylem toward the center of the tree and phloem toward the bark of the tree. Living xylem cells, also referred to as *sapwood*, form tubes through which water and dissolved minerals are carried up from the roots to the leaves. Living

phloem cells, or the *inner bark*, carry food manufactured by the leaves down to the roots and other parts of the tree.

In the spring the tree produces large-diameter, thin-walled xylem cells. In mid-summer, when growing conditions are drier and more stressful, cells produced by the cambium shrink and develop thicker cell walls. During the winter the cambium is

Red oak (unbroken vertical ridges with pinkish inner bark).

Remember, when a tree is young, its bark often bears little resemblance to a mature tree's bark of the same species. Here you see a white birch, both young (left: smooth, dark reddish-brown with conspicuous horizontal lenticels), and mature (right: white, peeling and can easily be divided into thin sheets).

dormant, but it resumes growth in the spring. It is the transition from larger spring cells (the light-colored ring in the illustration) to smaller summer cells (the darker ring in the illustration) that makes the annual *xylem ring*, which we count to tell a tree's age.

Heartwood

Xylem cell walls are filled with *lignin* and contain fibers that help form the tough, fibrous center of the tree. As they mature, these xylem cells become *heartwood*. Although no longer transporting water and minerals, the heartwood at the center of the tree provides support. A tree can live with no heartwood (we've all seen hollow, yet living, trees) but it is not as sturdy. As long as new xylem and phloem cells are being produced by the cambium layer, however, the tree goes on living.

Bark

The oldest (dead) phloem cells are toward the outside of the tree. On the outside of these cells another cambium layer forms, called the *cork cambium*. It makes cork cells to the outside, which become impregnated with a waxy waterproof substance called *suberin*. As the vascular cambium continues making new cells, adding to the tree's girth, dead phloem cells are pushed against one another, as well as against the cork cells, which crack and rip apart. This forms the fissure and ridges we see on mature bark.

Bark performs a number of functions, the foremost being protection of the inner tissue of a tree from insects, disease, storms, water loss, and temperature extremes. One way in which bark accomplishes this in certain species is by being extremely thick—as much as 2 feet in giant sequoias. The bark of some tree species contains substances such as tannins, acids, and gums that are distasteful or even poisonous to animals. This becomes evident when the bark of a tree is injured and insects suddenly appear, attracted by the smell of the inner wood and sap. Thorns, such as those on honey locust and prickly ash, discourage larger herbivores. Key to bark's ability to serve as a suit of armor for the tree is the production of a substance we are all familiar with—cork. All trees possess a certain amount of cork in their bark. Cork prevents excess water loss, helps repel insect pests and disease-carrying agents, and provides a barrier that is more or less fireproof. The bark of those trees found in locations most likely to be exposed to fire generally contains the greatest amount of cork. Often the bark on these trees also has huge ridges of corky bark, which may help to create an updraft in the case of fire, carrying the heat up and away from the trunk.

You may have noticed horizontal lines in the bark of some trees, including young black cherry or birch trees. These are loose clusters of cells called *lenticels*, which act as windows for the tree, allowing an exchange of gases between the tree's interior tissue and the air outside. A tree with bark that contains many airproof cork cells often is a candidate for lenticels.

Identifying Trees

As discussed, bark is much more than a means of identification, but it does serve that purpose as well. The way in which a species of tree responds to the pressure of an ever-increasing number of dead phloem and xylem cells can be a clue to its identity, especially useful in winter when the leaves of deciduous trees are gone. Cracks, fissures, lenticels, shedding, flaking, coloring, patterns (or the lack thereof) in a tree's bark are what allow you to recognize an ash from a maple tree with a quick glance.

Just as all the trees in a given species have similarly-shaped leaves, their bark is also similar, although there can be considerable variation. One factor affecting this variation is often the tree's age—there can be a vast difference between the appearance of the bark of a tree in its youth and when it matures, so familiarity with both the young and

] FAST FACTS [
Tree Bark

► Many trees are identifiable by the texture, color, and pattern of their bark.

► The mature bark on the lower part of the trunk of a tree often appears very different than the young bark of upper branches. The size of scales, or *furrows*, tends to become exaggerated with age.

► Cork is the bark of the cork oak. Every decade or so the outer bark of the trunk is stripped away for commercial use, leaving the cambium to grow more.

► Sticks of cinnamon are produced by cutting bark off young trees of a tree species in India. Left to dry, the bark curls up.

► The bark of the sequoia tree is practically fireproof due to its thickness, as well as the lack of resin in it.

► In the making of maple syrup, taps are drilled through the bark into the sap-conducting layer (the *sapwood*), consisting of xylem cells.

► One of the reasons canoes were made from paper birch bark is that it is extremely durable.

► Every year the cambium produces a new layer of bark, which pushes the previous year's bark outward. Thus, the oldest bark is on the outside of the tree.

► When bark is pulled off a tree, it usually separates at the cambium layer.

► The smoothness of American beech bark is due to the small amount of cork it produces.

old form of a species is advantageous. If winter tree identification is something you'd like to master, or at least become acquainted with, a very handy little pocket-size manual is *Winter Tree Finder* by May Watts (Wilderness Press, 1970). Some may prefer to wait until the buds that are now on the trees begin to swell and open. Many of them contain leaves, which, at least for this naturalist, are even easier to recognize than bark.

Winter Twigs

Identifying trees in winter? It's enough of a challenge in the summer and fall when leaves and fruits are there to assist you. In order to tell one leafless tree from another without these distinctive pieces of the puzzle, you must use information that is available this time of year. You can use bark basics (see p. 426), but the tree's silhouette—its branching pattern and the branches themselves (their buds and leaf scars)—can also provide clues to its identity. While the differences in bark and branching patterns between tree species may be more subtle than leaves or seeds or fruits, they are distinctive enough to allow you to name most trees with the aid of a basic key.

Buds

Although we tend not to notice tree buds until fall when leaves have laid branches bare, they have been present since they were formed in July or August. All buds fall into one of three categories: *leaf bud*, containing a miniature stem and leaves; *flower bud*, containing one or more undeveloped flowers (trees are flowering plants and as such bear flowers); and *mixed bud*, containing both undeveloped leaves and flowers. Sometimes flower buds are not only larger than leaf buds, but also a different shape, such as the bead-like flower bud clusters that ring red maple branches this time of year. More often, however, they are so similar you need to dissect a tree's buds to determine whether they contain leaves, flowers, or a mixture of both.

Buds of woody plants (shrubs and trees) are usually protected by several layers of overlapping scales called *bud scales*, which are modified leaves. Their appearance can vary widely. Bud scales can be quite hairy (young yellow birch), covered with a sticky substance (eastern cottonwood), or even shiny (trembling aspen). Occasionally you will find a tree or shrub, such as witch hazel or hobblebush,

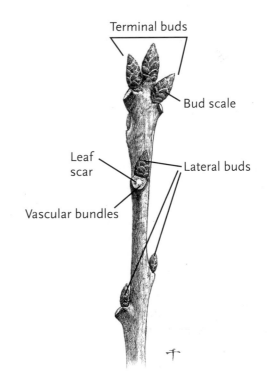

Terminal buds

Bud scale

Leaf scar

Lateral buds

Vascular bundles

Parts of a twig.

that does not have scales on its buds. These are referred to as *naked buds*. It is interesting to note that in the tropics, where there is far less need for protection from drying out or freezing, most plants have naked buds.

The bud at the end of a twig, or *terminal bud,* is often the most distinctive bud and the one most likely to lead you to the tree's identity. Most trees have a single terminal bud, but some, like the Oak family, have clusters of terminal buds. Notice not only the scales, but the size, shape, and color of the terminal bud(s). Is there a single cap-like bud scale (Willow family), two or three bud scales (speckled alder), or multiple bud scales (sugar maple)? Is the bud nearly an inch long and pointed (American beech)? Is it oval and reddish (basswood) or on a

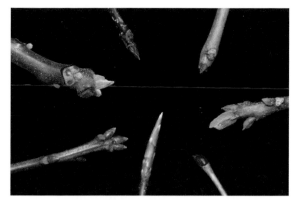

Each species of tree has its own distinctive *terminal bud*. Clockwise, starting with the red twig at the top: red maple, white ash, bitternut hickory, basswood, American beech, red oak, and black walnut.

stalk (striped maple)? Is it a bright mustard yellow color (bitternut hickory) or nearly black (black ash)?

Another important feature that can quickly narrow down the number of possible species is the arrangement of the *lateral buds*—those occurring along the branches in the leaf axils, directly above where the leaf was attached. If they are *opposite* one another, one on one side of the twig and one directly opposite on the other side of the twig, this immediately tells you that you are most likely (but not exclusively) looking at a species of maple, ash, dogwood, or viburnum, as relatively few woody plants have opposite arrangement of buds (and therefore branches). Most trees have *alternate* buds/branching, where the lateral buds are not opposite one another but are staggered along the branch, first on one side, then the other. Occasionally buds and branches are *whorled*, with three or more located around the twig at the same level, such as seen in the eastern white pine. (For a comparative illustration of these arrangements, see p. 16.)

Leaf Scars

Leaf scars—the areas where leaves were attached to the branch—provide additional clues to a tree's

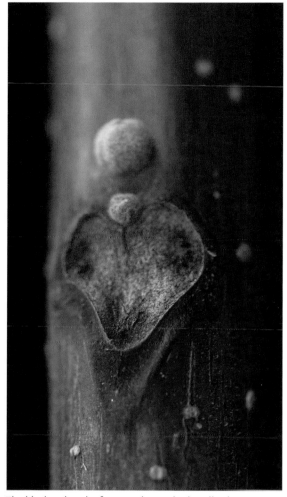

The black walnut leaf scar and vascular bundles bear a slight resemblance to the face of a monkey.

identity in winter. More than 90 percent of the water that a tree's roots take up is transpired through leaves into the air. To conserve water during winter months when it is in short supply, deciduous trees shed their leaves by forming a cork-like abscission layer of cells at the base of the leaf, allowing separation from the branch. A *leaf scar* remains on the branch where the leaf was attached. Leaf scars are like tree fingerprints—each species' is unique. They can be "U"-shaped (red maple), semicircular

(American elm), notched (white ash), or completely encircle the bud (American sycamore).

A close look at leaf scars reveals tiny dots or clusters of dots within them, otherwise known as *vascular bundles*. These are the ends of the conducting vessels that carried water and food in and out of the leaves. Just as leaf scar shapes are species-specific, so are the number and arrangement of vascular bundles within them, be they scattered, "V"-shaped or any number of other designs. One of the more amusing leaf scar/vascular bundle combinations found in New England is that of the black walnut. Notched at the top, narrow at the bottom, with appropriately placed bundles, the leaf scar has a striking resemblance to a monkey's face (see photo, p. 431). Butternut leaf scars can be distinguished from those of black walnut by the velvety strip of hairs just above the leaf scar, which black walnut lacks.

In truth, winter trees bear any number of clues to their identity. All that is needed is an observant eye and a key to the different species in your geographical area. The size, shape, color, and arrangement of a tree's buds, as well as the appearance of its leaf scars can usually enable you to determine the family, if not the exact species, of the tree in question.

] FAST FACTS [
Winter Twigs

▶ There are *terminal* (tip of branch) and *lateral* (sides of branch) buds on most trees. The terminal bud, if present, is usually larger than the lateral buds; shorter branches grow from the lateral buds than from the terminal bud.

▶ If you look closely at a twig you can determine exactly how much growth occurred each year by finding the *bud scale scars*. This is where the scales of the terminal bud fell off, leaving several lines that together encircle the twig. From the tip of the twig to the first bud scale scar is one year's growth. From the tip back to the second scar is two years' growth, and so on.

▶ *Lenticels* are the horizontal lines you see on some trees, like young cherry and birch. They serve as windows for the tree, allowing an exchange of gases.

▶ *Pith* is found in the center of the twig. Its color, as well as whether or not it is divided into separate chambers, helps identify several species of similar trees.

▶ Most oaks have clustered terminal buds. Because growth can occur in almost any direction, the clustering gives oak trees their characteristic "spreading" appearance.

▶ The American beech has been referred to as the cigar tree because of its long, pointed buds.

▶ Biological and environmental stresses can set off uncontrolled growth of buds which results in "witch's brooms," often seen in birches.

ACKNOWLEDGMENTS

a debt of gratitude

My daughter, Sadie.

Among those who have tolerated, shared, and fostered my passion for all things natural are:

Bessie Getlin, who let me climb into her bed when the whip-poor-will sang, and who introduced me to warm maple syrup, wild blueberries and the ways of the wild.

Myno and Papa, who led me along this path and provided acres to explore in my childhood.

Susan Holland, bearer of wolf scat, who has humored me and my passion for natural history her entire life.

Sadie Richards, my constant companion through forests and fields during her youth, who never fails to amaze me with her retention of bird songs, tracks, and other signs learned when she could barely walk, and who, while growing up, tolerated a freezer full of the unexpected.

Chiho Kaneko, whose friendship is as beautiful as her artwork.

Holly Lanigan, deliverer of bear scat and supporter extraordinaire.

Jenepher Lingelbach, who has shared my passion like no other.

Kay Shumway and Mary Sue Henszey, my partners-in-crime in the great outdoors.

Dick Hoefnagel and **Nardi Campion,** mentors and friends.

Lillian Marcotte, who, at 92, still sleeps outside, where the skunks steal her slippers.

Mark Humpal, who has generously given me many artifacts, most prized among them the beaver castor glands pictured in this book.

Ben Kilham, provider of a prized bear plug, also featured in this book.

Jim Andrews, provider of many herpetological facts and statistics.

Friends, too many to mention, who along the way have shared their "collectibles," as well as their enthusiasm, with special thanks to Hilary Hamilton.

Caroline Robbins, Martha Cook, and **Becca Didier** at **Trafalgar Square Books,** whose belief in my columns inspired and made this book possible.

Becca Didier, whose patient and insightful editing helped make *Naturally Curious* all that it could be.

Thornton, Asa, Josie, Hazel, Maddie, and **Emma,** loyal companions who discovered many of my best finds and patiently waited while I photographed and collected them.

Reviewers, who spent more hours than I choose to count, making sure I was on the straight and narrow: **Dan Lambert, Steve Faccio,** and **Chris Rimmer** (birds); **Paul Rezendes** (mammals and sign); **Mark Elbroch** (mammals and sign); **Mike Blust** (insects and arachnids); **Stephen Marshall** (insects); and **Peter Hope** (plants).

Photographers, who generously provided their exquisite images for use in this book alongside my own: **Jim Andrews, Nicolas Arms, Kiley Briggs, Dan Foley, Tom Wetmore, Susan Holland, J. Merrow, B. Bond, Sadie Richards,** and with special thanks to **Mary Sue Henszey**— without her bird photos, this book would not be complete.

Kay and **Peter Shumway; Roger** and **Eleanor Shepard; Sarah** and **Warren Demont**; and **Marian** and **Charles Marrin,** for so generously allowing me to roam about on their land.

COMMON AND SCIENTIFIC NAMES

for species featured in *Naturally Curious*

(Listed in alphabetical order by common name and current as of publication. Note: Species with more than one common name have been listed here by the name used foremost in this book—refer to the index and to species entries within the main text for listings of other common names.)

COMMON NAME	SCIENTIFIC NAME

Amphibians

American bullfrog	*Lithobates catesbeianus*
American toad	*Anaxyrus americanus*
Blue-spotted salamander	*Ambystoma laterale*
Eastern newt	*Notophthalmus viridescens*
Eastern red-backed salamander	*Plethodon cinereus*
Eastern spadefoot	*Scaphiopus holbrookii*
Four-toed salamander	*Hemidactylium scutatum*
Fowler's toad	*Anaxyrus fowleri*
Gray treefrog	*Hyla versicolor*
Green frog	*Lithobates clamitans*
Jefferson salamander	*Ambystoma jeffersonianum*
Marbled salamander	*Ambystoma opacum*
Mink frog	*Lithobates septentrionalis*
Mudpuppy	*Necturus maculosus*
Northern dusky salamander	*Desmognathus fuscus*
Northern leopard frog	*Lithobates pipiens*
Northern two-lined salamander	*Eurycea bislineata*
Pickerel frog	*Lithobates palustris*
Slimy salamander	*Plethodon glutinosus*
Spotted salamander	*Ambystoma maculatum*
Spring peeper	*Pseudacris crucifer*
Spring salamander	*Gyrinophilus porphyriticus*
Wood frog	*Rana sylvatica*

Reptiles

Blanding's turtle	*Emydoidea blandingii*
Bog turtle	*Clemmys muhlenbergii*
Common five-lined skink	*Plestiodon fasciatus*
Common gartersnake	*Thamnophis sirtalis*
Copperhead	*Agkistrodon contortrix*
DeKay's brownsnake	*Storeria dekayi*
Diamond-backed terrapin	*Malaclemys terrapin*
Eastern box turtle	*Terrapene Carolina*
Eastern hog-nosed snake	*Heterodon platirhinos*
Eastern musk turtle	*Sternotherus odoratus*
Eastern ratsnake	*Pantherophis alleghaniensis*
Eastern ribbonsnake	*Thamnophis sauritus*
Eastern wormsnake	*Carphophis amoenus*
Milksnake	*Lampropeltis triangulum*
North American racer	*Coluber constrictor*
Northern map turtle	*Graptemys geographica*
Northern red-bellied cooter	*Pseudemys rubriventris*
Northern watersnake	*Nerodia sipedon*
Painted turtle	*Chrysemys picta*
Red-bellied snake	*Storeria occipitomaculata*
Red-eared slider	*Trachemys scripta*
Ring-necked snake	*Diadophis punctatus*
Smooth greensnake	*Opheodrys vernalis*
Snapping turtle	*Chelydra serpentina*
Spiny softshell	*Apalone spinifera*
Spotted turtle	*Clemmys guttata*
Timber rattlesnake	*Crotalus horridus*
Wood turtle	*Glyptemys insculpta*

Birds

American bittern	*Botaurus lentiginosus*
American black duck	*Anas rubripes*
American crow	*Corvus brachyrhynchos*
American golden-plover	*Pluvialis dominica*
American goldfinch	*Carduelis tristis*
American kestrel	*Falco sparverius*
American redstart	*Setophaga ruticilla*
American robin	*Turdus migratorius*
American three-toed woodpecker	*Picoides dorsalis*
American wigeon	*Anas Americana*
American woodcock	*Scolopax minor*
Atlantic puffin	*Fratercula arctica*
Baird's sandpiper	*Calidris bairdii*
Bald eagle	*Haliaeetus leucocephalus*
Baltimore oriole	*Icterus galbula*
Bank swallow	*Riparia riparia*
Barn owl	*Tyto alba*
Barn swallow	*Hirundo rustica*
Barred owl	*Strix varia*
Bay-breasted warbler	*Dendroica castanea*
Belted kingfisher	*Megaceryle alcyon*
Black-and-white warbler	*Mniotilta varia*
Black-backed woodpecker	*Picoides arcticus*
Black-bellied plover	*Pluvialis squatarola*
Black-billed cuckoo	*Coccyzus erythrophthalmus*
Blackburnian warbler	*Dendroica fusca*

Common Name	Scientific Name	Common Name	Scientific Name
Black-capped chickadee	*Poecile atricapillus*	Great crested flycatcher	*Myiarchus crinitus*
Black-crowned night-heron	*Nycticorax nycticorax*	Great gray owl	*Strix nebulosa*
Blackpoll warbler	*Dendroica striata*	Great horned owl	*Bubo virginianus*
Black-throated blue warbler	*Dendroica caerulescens*	Greater yellowlegs	*Tringa melanoleuca*
Black-throated green warbler	*Dendroica virens*	Green heron	*Butorides virescens*
Blue jay	*Cyanocitta cristata*	Hairy woodpecker	*Picoides villosus*
Blue-winged warbler	*Vermivora pinus*	Hermit thrush	*Catharus guttatus*
Bobolink	*Dolichonyx oryzivorus*	Hooded merganser	*Lophodytes cucullatus*
Bohemian waxwing	*Bombycilla garrulus*	House sparrow	*Passer domesticus*
Boreal chickadee	*Poecile husonicus*	House wren	*Troglodytes aedon*
Boreal owl	*Aegolius funereus*	Hudsonian godwit	*Limosa haemastica*
Broad-winged hawk	*Buteo platypterus*	Indigo bunting	*Passerina cyanea*
Brown creeper	*Certhia Americana*	Killdeer	*Charadrius vociferous*
Brown thrasher	*Toxostoma rufum*	Least sandpiper	*Calidris minutilla*
Brown-headed cowbird	*Molothrus ater*	Lesser yellowlegs	*Tringa flavipes*
Buff-breasted sandpiper	*Tryngites subruficollis*	Long-billed dowitcher	*Limnodromus scolopaceus*
Canada goose	*Branta canadensis*	Long-eared owl	*Asio otus*
Canada warbler	*Wilsonia canadensis*	Louisiana waterthrush	*Seiurus motacilla*
Cape May warbler	*Dendroica tigrina*	Magnolia warbler	*Dendroica magnolia*
Carolina wren	*Thryothorus ludovicianus*	Mallard	*Anas platyrhynchos*
Cedar waxwing	*Bombycilla cedrorum*	Merlin	*Falco columbarius*
Chestnut-sided warbler	*Dendroica pensylvanica*	Mourning dove	*Zenaida macroura*
Chimney swift	*Chaetura pelagica*	Mourning warbler	*Oporornis philadelphia*
Chipping sparrow	*Spizella passerine*	Nashville warbler	*Vermivora ruficapilla*
Cliff swallow	*Petrochelidon pyrrhonota*	Northern bobwhite	*Colinus virginianus*
Common goldeneye	*Bucephala clangula*	Northern cardinal	*Cardinalis cardinalis*
Common grackle	*Quiscalus quiscula*	Northern flicker	*Colaptes auratus*
Common loon	*Gavia immer*	Northern goshawk	*Accipiter gentilis*
Common merganser	*Mergus merganser*	Northern harrier	*Circus cyaneus*
Common nighthawk	*Chordeiles minor*	Northern hawk owl	*Surnia ulula*
Common raven	*Corvus corax*	Northern mockingbird	*Mimus polyglottos*
Common redpoll	*Carduelis flammea*	Northern parula	*Parula americana*
Common yellowthroat	*Geothlypis trichas*	Northern pintail	*Anas acuta*
Connecticut warbler	*Oporornis agilis*	Northern rough-winged swallow	*Stelgidopteryx serripennis*
Cooper's hawk	*Accipiter cooperii*	Northern saw-whet owl	*Aegolius acadicus*
Dark-eyed junco	*Junco hyemalis*	Northern shrike	*Lanius excubitor*
Downy woodpecker	*Picoides pubescens*	Northern waterthrush	*Seiurus noveboracensis*
Double-crested cormorant	*Phalacrocorax auritus*	Orange-crowned warbler	*Vermivora celata*
Dunlin	*Calidris alpine*	Osprey	*Pandion haliaetus*
Eastern bluebird	*Sialia sialis*	Ovenbird	*Seiurus aurocapilla*
Eastern kingbird	*Tyrannus tyrannus*	Palm warbler	*Dendroica palmarum*
Eastern meadowlark	*Sturnella magna*	Pectoral sandpiper	*Calidris melanotos*
Eastern phoebe	*Sayornis phoebe*	Peregrine falcon	*Falco peregrinus*
Eastern screech-owl	*Megascops asio*	Pied-billed grebe	*Podilymbus podiceps*
Eastern towhee	*Pipilo erythrophthalmus*	Pileated woodpecker	*Dryocopus pileatus*
Eastern whip-poor-will	*Caprimulgus vociferus*	Pine grosbeak	*Pinicola enucleator*
Eastern wood-pewee	*Contopus virens*	Pine siskin	*Carduelis pinus*
European starling	*Sturnus vulgaris*	Pine warbler	*Dendroica pinus*
Evening grosbeak	*Coccothraustes vespertinus*	Prairie warbler	*Dendroica discolor*
Gadwall	*Anas strepera*	Purple finch	*Carpodacus purpureus*
Goshawk	*Accipiter gentilis*	Purple martin	*Progne subis*
Gray catbird	*Dumetella carolinensis*	Red crossbill	*Loxia curvirostra*
Gray jay	*Perisoreus canadensis*	Red knot	*Calidris canutus*
Great blue heron	*Ardea Herodias*	Red phalarope	*Phalaropus folic*

Red-bellied woodpecker	*Melanerpes carolinus*	Yellow-bellied sapsucker	*Sphyrapicus varius*
Red-breasted nuthatch	*Sitta canadensis*	Yellow-breasted chat	*Icteria virens*
Red-eyed vireo	*Vireo olivaceus*	Yellow-rumped warbler	*Dendroica coronata*
Red-headed woodpecker	*Melanerpes erythrocephalus*		
Red-necked phalarope	*Phalaropus lobatus*	**Mammals**	
Red-shouldered hawk	*Buteo lineatus*		
Red-tailed hawk	*Buteo jamaicensis*	American beaver	*Castor canadensis*
Red-winged blackbird	*Agelaius phoeniceus*	American black bear	*Ursus americanus*
Ring-necked duck	*Aythya collaris*	American marten	*Martes americana*
Ring-necked pheasant	*Phasianus colchicus*	American mink	*Neovison vison*
Rock pigeon	*Columba livia*	American pygmy shrew	*Sorex hoyi*
Rose-breasted grosbeak	*Pheucticus ludovicianus*	American water shrew	*Sorex palustris*
Rough-legged hawk	*Buteo lagopus*	Big brown bat	*Eptesicus fuscus*
Ruby-throated hummingbird	*Archilochus colubris*	Black rat	*Ratus ratus*
Ruddy turnstone	*Arenaria interpres*	Bobcat	*Lynx rufus*
Ruffed grouse	*Bonasa umbellus*	Brown rat	*Rattus norvegicus*
Rusty blackbird	*Euphagus carolinus*	Canadian lynx	*Lynx canadensis*
Sanderling	*Calidris alba*	Common muskrat	*Ondatra zibethicus*
Sandhill crane	*Grus Canadensis*	Coyote	*Canis latrans*
Scarlet tanager	*Piranga olivacea*	Eastern chipmunk	*Tamias striatus*
Semipalmated plover	*Charadrius semipalmatus*	Eastern cottontail rabbit	*Sylvilagus floridanus*
Semipalmated sandpiper	*Calidris pusilla*	Eastern gray squirrel	*Sciurus carolinensis*
Sharp-shinned hawk	*Accipiter striatus*	Eastern mole	*Scalopus aquaticus*
Short-billed dowitcher	*Limnodromus griseus*	Eastern mountain lion	*Puma concolor couguar*
Short-eared owl	*Asio flammeus*	Eastern pipistrelle	*Pipistrellus subflavus*
Snowy owl	*Bubo scandiacus*	Eastern red bat	*Lasiurus borealis*
Solitary sandpiper	*Tringa solitaria*	Eastern small-footed bat	*Myotis leibii*
Song sparrow	*Melospiza melodia*	Ermine	*Mustela erminea*
Spotted sandpiper	*Actitis macularius*	European hare	*Lepus europaeus*
Stilt sandpiper	*Calidris himantopus*	Fisher	*Martes pennanti*
Tennessee warbler	*Vermivora peregrina*	Gray fox	*Urocyon cinereoargenteus*
Tree swallow	*Tachycineta bicolor*	Hairy-tailed mole	*Parascalops breweri*
Tufted titmouse	*Baeolophus bicolor*	Hoary bat	*Lasiurus cinereus*
Turkey vulture	*Cathartes aura*	House mouse	*Mus musculus*
Upland sandpiper	*Bartramia longicauda*	Indiana bat	*Myotis sodalis*
Veery	*Catharus fuscescens*	Little brown bat	*Myotis lucifugus*
Western sandpiper	*Calidris mauri*	Long-tailed shrew	*Sorex dispar*
Whimbrel	*Numenius phaeopus*	Long-tailed weasel	*Mustela frenata*
White-breasted nuthatch	*Sitta carolinensis*	Masked shrew	*Sorex cinereus*
White-rumped sandpiper	*Calidris fuscicollis*	Meadow jumping mouse	*Zapus hudsonius*
White-crowned sparrow	*Zonotrichia leucophrys*	Meadow vole	*Microtus pennsylvanicus*
White-throated sparrow	*Zonotrichia albicollis*	Moose	*Alces alces americana*
White-winged crossbill	*Loxia leucoptera*	New England cottontail rabbit	*Sylvilagus transitionalis*
Wild turkey	*Meleagris gallopavo*	North American deermouse	*Peromyscus maniculatus*
Willet	*Tringa semipalmata*	North American least shrew	*Cryptotis parva*
Wilson's phalarope	*Phalaropus tricolor*	North American porcupine	*Erethizon dorsatum*
Wilson's warbler	*Wilsonia pusilla*	North American river otter	*Lontra canadensis*
Winter wren	*Troglodytes troglodytes*	Northern bog lemming	*Synaptomys borealis*
Wood duck	*Aix sponsa*	Northern flying squirrel	*Glaucomys sabrinus*
Wood thrush	*Hylocichla mustelina*	Northern long-eared bat	*Myotis septentrionalis*
Worm-eating warbler	*Helmitheros vermivorum*	Northern short-tailed shrew	*Blarina brevicauda*
Yellow-bellied cuckoo	*Coccyzus americanus*	Raccoon	*Procyon lotor*
Yellow warbler	*Dendroica petechia*	Red fox	*Vulpes vulpes*

Red squirrel	*Tamiasciurus hudsonicus*	Clouded sulphur	*Colias philodice*
Rock vole	*Microtus chrotorrhinus*	Cobweb skipper	*Hesperia metea*
Silver-haired bat	*Lasionycteris noctivagans*	Cockroach	Order: Blattaria
Smoky shrew	*Sorex fumeus*	Common antlion	Family: Myrmeleontidae
Snowshoe hare	*Lepus americanus*	Common buckeye	*Junonia coenia*
Southern bog lemming	*Synaptomys cooperi*	Common green darner	*Anax junius*
Southern flying squirrel	*Glaucomys volans*	Common pine shoot beetle	*Tomicus piniperda*
Southern red-backed vole	*Myodes gapperi*	Common sootywing	*Pholisora catullus*
Star-nosed mole	*Condylura cristata*	Common whitetail dragonfly	*Libellula lydia*
Striped skunk	*Mephitis mephitis*	Common wood nymph	*Cercyonis pegala*
Virginia opossum	*Didelphis virginiana*	Compton tortoiseshell	*Nymphalis vaualbum*
White-footed deermouse	*Peromyscus leucopus*	Crab spider	Family: Thomisidae
White-tailed deer	*Odocoileus virginianus*	Crane fly	Family: Tipulidae
Woodchuck	*Marmota monax*	Damselfly	Suborder: Zygoptera
Woodland jumping mouse	*Napaeozapus insignis*	Deer fly	*Chrysops* sp.
Woodland vole	*Microtus pinetorum*	Dogbane beetle	*Chrysochus auratus*

Arthropods (Millipedes, Insects, & Arachnids)

		Dogday cicada	*Tibicen canicularis*
		Dobsonfly	Subfamily: Corydalinae
		Dragonfly	Order: Odonata
Abbot's sphinx moth	*Sphecodina abbottii*	Dreamy duskywing	*Erynnis icelus*
American copper	*Lycaena phlaeas*	Earth-boring scarab beetle	Family: Geotrupidae
American lady	*Vanessa virginiensis*	Eastern comma	*Polygonia comma*
Ant	Family: Formicidae	Eastern pine elfin	*Callophrys niphon*
Aphid	Family: Aphididae	Eastern spruce budworm	*Choristoneura fumiferaria*
Assassin bug	Family: Reduviidae	Eastern spruce gall adelgid	*Aldelges abietis*
Bagworm moth	Family: Psychidae	Eastern tailed-blue	*Everes comyntas*
Bald-faced hornet	*Dolichovespula maculata*	Eastern tent caterpillar	*Malacosoma americanum*
Baltimore checkerspot	*Euphydryas phaeton*	Eastern tiger swallowtail	*Papilio glaucus*
Banded hairstreak	*Satyrium calanus*	Engraver beetle	Subfamily: Scolytinae
Barn spider	*Araneus cavaticus*	European elm bark beetle	*Scolytus multistriatus*
Big poplar sphinx	*Pachysphinx occidentalis*	European honeybee	*Apis mellifera*
Black-and-yellow argiope	*Argiope aurantia*	European praying mantis	*Mantis religiosa*
Black fly	Family: Simuliidae	European skipper	*Thymelicus lineola*
Black swallowtail	*Papilio polyxenes*	Fall webworm	*Hyphantria cunea*
Brown elfin	*Callophrys augustinus*	Field cricket	*Gryllus* sp.
Bumblebee	*Bombus* sp.	Firefly	Family: *Lampyridae*
Burying beetle	Family: Silphidae	Fishfly	*Nirgronia* sp.
Cabbage white	*Pieris* sp.	Flat-headed mayfly	Family: Heptageniidae
Caddisfly	Order: Trichoptera	Flea	Order: Siphonaptera
Tube-case-making caddisfly	Family: Limnephilidae	Fly	Order: Diptera
Gravel-case-making caddisfly	Family: Odontoceridae	Funnel-weaving spiders	*Agelenopsis* sp.
Square-case-making caddisfly	Family: Brachycentridae	Forest tent caterpillar	*Malacosoma disstria*
Canadian tiger swallowtail	*Papilio canadensis*	Gall adelgid (spruce pineapple gall)	*Aldelges abietis*
Carolina sphinx moth		Gall aphid (grape aphid gall)	*Viteus vitifoliae*
(tobacco hornworm)	*Manduca sexta*	Gall aphid (poplar leaf stem gall)	*Pemphigus populitransversus*
Carpenter bee	*Xylocopa virginica*	Gall gnat (pine cone willow gall)	*Rhabdophaga strobiloides*
Casebearer moth	Family: Coleophoridae	Gall wasp (oak apple gall)	*Amphibolips confluenta*
and relatives (leafminers)		Gall wasp (wool sower gall)	*Callirhytis seminator*
Cattail caterpillar	*Limnaecia phragmitta*	Giant swallowtail	*Papilio cresphontes*
Cecropia moth	*Hyalophora cecropia*	Goldenrod bunch gall midge	*Rhopalomyia solidaginis*
Cicada	Family: Cicadidae	Goldenrod gall fly	*Eurosta solidaginis*
Click beetle	Family: Elateridae	Goldenrod gall gelechiid	*Gnorimoschema*
Clouded skipper	*Lerema accius*	(elliptical gall)	*gallaesolidaginis*

Goldenrod gall tortricid	*Epiblema scudderiana*
Goldenrod spider	*Misumena vatia*
Grasshopper	Order: Orthoptera
Great golden digger wasp	*Sphex ichneumoneus*
Great spangled fritillary	*Speyeria cybele*
Ground cricket	Subfamily: Nemobiinae/ Gryllinae
Gypsy moth	*Lymantria dispar*
Hairstreak	Subfamily: Theclinae
Gray hairstreak	*Strymon melinus*
Harvestman	Order: Opiliones
Hawk moth	Family: Sphingidae
Horse fly	Family: Tabanidae
Hover fly	Family: Syrphidae
Hummingbird clearwing	*Hemaris thysbe*
Isabella tiger moth (woolly bear)	*Pyrrharctia isabella*
Japanese beetle	*Popillia japonica*
Jumping spider	Family: Salticidae
June beetle	*Phyllophaga* sp.
Juvenal's duskywing	*Erynnis juvenalis*
Katydid	Family: Tettigoniidae
Lady beetle	Family: Coccinellidae
Convergent lady beetle	*Hippodamia convergens*
Multicolored Asian lady beetle	*Harmonia axyridis*
Lacewing	Family (green): Chrysopidae
	Family (brown): Hemerobiidae
Large milkweed bug	*Oncopeltus fasciatus*
Leafcutter bee	Megachile *rotundata*
Leafhopper	Family: Cicadellidae
Long-horned beetle	Family: Cerambycidae
Luna moth	*Actias luna*
March fly	Family: Bibionidae
Meadow fritillary	*Boloria bellona*
Milkweed tussock	*Euchaetes egle*
Monarch butterfly	*Danaus plexippus*
Monkey slug	*Phobetron pithecium*
Mosquito	Family: Culicidae
Mourning cloak	*Nymphalis antiopa*
Native elm bark beetle	*Hylurgopinus rufipes*
North American millipede	*Narceus americanus*
Nursery web spider	Family: Pisauridae
Orb web spider	Family: Araneidae
Organ pipe mud dauber	*Trypoxylon politum*
Painted lady	*Vanessa cardui*
Paper wasp	*Polistes* sp.
Pearl crescent	*Phyciodes tharos*
Peck's skipper	*Polites peckius*
Pelecinid wasp	*Pelecinus polyturator*
Pine shoot beetle	*Tomicus piniperda*
Pollen wasp	Family: Vespidae
Polyphemus moth	*Antheraea polyphemus*

Potter wasp	Family: Vespidae
Praying Mantis	Family: Mantidae
Predaceious diving beetle	Family: Dytiscidae
Primrose moth	*Schinia florida*
Question mark	*Polygonia interrogationis*
Rattler round-winged katydid	*Amblycorypha rotundifolia*
Red admiral	*Vanessa atalanta*
Red-legged grasshopper	*Melanoplus femurrubrum*
Red milkweed beetle	*Tetraopes tetraophthalmus*
Robber fly	Family: Asilidae
Rosy maple moth	*Dryocampa rubicunda*
Sawfly	Suborder: Symphyta
Scale insect	Superfamily: Coccoidea
Scorpionfly	Order: Mecoptera
Silver-spotted skipper	*Epargyreus clarus*
Six-spotted tiger beetle	*Cicindela sexguttata*
Snow flea	*Hypogastrura nivicolor*
Snowy tree cricket	*Oecanthus fultoni*
Spicebush swallowtail	*Papilio troilus*
Spined soldier bug	*Picromeris maculiventris*
Spittlebug	Super family: Cercopoidea
Spring azure	*Celastrina ladon*
Squash bug	Family: Coreidae
Stink bug	Family: Pentatomidae
Stonefly	Order: Plecoptera
Tangle web spider	Family: Theridiidae
Tiger moth	Family: Arctiidae
Tree cricket	Subfamily: Oecathinae
True bug	Order: *Hemiptera*
Twelve-spotted skimmer dragonfly	*Libellula pulchella*
Twelve-spotted tiger beetle	*Cicindela duodecimguttata*
Walking stick	Order: Phasmatodea
Water boatman	Family: Corixidae
Water strider	Family: Corixidae
Western conifer seed bug	*Leptoglossus occidentalis*
Whirligig beetle	Family: Gyrinidae
White admiral	*Limenitis arthemis*
White-marked tussock moth	*Orgyla leucostigma*
Whitefly	Family: Aleyrodidae
Widow skimmer	*Libellula luctuosa*
Wolf spider	Family: Lycosidae
Viceroy butterfly	*Limenitis archippus*
Yellowjacket	*Vespula* sp. *(Dolichovespula* sp.)

Plants & Fungi

American beech	*Fagus americana*
American Caesar's mushroom	*Amanita caesarea*
American elm	*Ulmus americana*
American highbush cranberry	*Viburnum trilobum*
American holly	*Ilex opaca*
American hornbeam	*Carpinus caroliniana*
American sycamore	*Platanus occidentalis*

Balsam fir	*Abies balsamea*	Common burdock	*Arctium minus*
Balsam poplar	*Populus balsamifera*	Common buttercup	*Ranunculus acrus*
Basswood	*Tilia americana*	Common cattail	*Typha latifolia*
Beaked hazelnut	*Corylus cornuta*	Common dandelion	*Taraxicum officinale*
Bedstraw	*Galium* sp.	Common evening primrose	*Oenothera biennis*
Beechdrop	*Epifagus virginiana*	Common hazel	*Corylus avellana*
Beggar tick	*Bidens cernua*	Common milkweed	*Asclepias syriaca*
Bigtooth aspen	*Populus grandidentata*	Common mullein	*Verbascum thapsus*
Bird's foot trefoil	*Lotus corniculatus*	Common polypody	*Polypodium virginianum*
Bird's nest fungus	*Cyathus* sp.	Common ragweed	*Ambrosia artemisiifolia*
Bitternut hickory	*Carya cordiformis*	Common winterberry	*Ilex verticilatta*
Black ash	*Fraxinus nigra*	Common yarrow	*Achillea millefolium*
Black birch	*Betula lenta*	Coral fungus	Family: Clavariaceae
Black cherry	*Prunus serotina*	Cork oak	*Quercus suber*
Black locust	*Robinia psuedoacacia*	Corkscrew plant	*Genlisea* sp.
Black raspberry	*Rubus occidentalis*	Cow vetch	*Vicia cracca*
Black spruce	*Picea mariana*	Curly dock	*Rumex crispus*
Black walnut	*Juglans nigra*	Cut-leaved grape fern	*Botrychium dissectum*
Black willow	*Salix nigra*	Cut-leaved toothwort	*Cardamine concatenata*
Black-eyed Susan	*Rubeckia hirta*	Dutchman's breeches	*Dicentra cucullaria*
Blackgum	*Nyssa sylvatica*	Dwarf huckleberry	*Gaylussacia dumosa*
Bloodroot	*Sanguinaria canadensis*	Early saxifrage	*Saxifraga virginiensis*
Blue cohosh	*Caulophyllum thalictroides*	Earthstar	*Geastrum* sp.
Blue vervain	*Verbena hastata*	Eastern cottonwood	*Populus deltoides*
Blue-eyed grass	*Sysyrinchium montanum*	Eastern hemlock	*Tsuga canadensis*
Blueberry	*Vaccinium angustifolium*	Eastern larch	*Larix laricina*
Bottle gentian	*Gentiana clausa*	Eastern redcedar	*Juniperus virginiana*
Boxelder	*Acer negundo*	Eastern white pine	*Pinus strobus*
Bracken fern	*Pteridium aquilinum*	Eyelash cup	*Scutellinia scutellata*
Bristly clubmoss	*Spinulum annotinum*	False hellebore	*Veratrum viride*
British soldier	*Claytonia cristatella*	False morel	*Gyromitra* sp.
British soldier alga	*Trebouxia erici*	False Solomon's seal	*Maianthemum racemosum*
British soldier fungus	*Cladonia cristatella*	Field horsetail	*Equisetum arvense*
Broad-leaved helleborine	*Epipactis helleborine*	Field thistle	*Cirsium discolor*
Bull-head lily	*Nuphar lutea*	Flowering dogwood	*Cornus florida*
Bunchberry	*Cornus canadensis*	Giant goldenrod	*Solidago gigantean*
Butternut	*Juglans cinerea*	Giant puffball	*Calvatia gigantean*
Canada goldenrod	*Solidago canadensis*	Goldthread	*Coptis trifolia*
Canada thistle	*Cirsium arvense*	Granular puffball	*Arachnion album*
Cardinal flower	*Lobelia cardinalis*	Grape ferns	*Botrychium* sp.
Chanterelle	Family: Cantharellaceae	Gray birch	*Betula populifolia*
Chicken of the woods	*Laetiporus sulphureus*	Greater yellow lady's slipper	*Cypripedium paarviflorum*
Chicory	*Cichorium intybus*		var. *pubescens*
Christmas fern	*Polystichum acrostichoides*	Greenbriar	*Smilax* sp.
Cinnamon fern	*Osmunda cinnamomea*	Hay-scented fern	*Dennstaedtia punctilobula*
Clintonia	*Clintonia borealis*	Helleborine	*Epipactis helleborine*
Coconut palm	*Cocos nucifera*	Hepatica	*Hepatica nobilis*
Coltsfoot	*Tusilago farfara*	Hobblebush	*Viburnum lantanoides*
Combtooth fungus	*Hericium ramosum*	Honey fungus	*Armillaria lutea*
Common apple	*Malus pumila*	Honey locust	*Gleditsia triacanthos*
Common blackberry	*Rubus fruticosus*	Hophornbeam	*Ostrya virginiana*
Common bladderwort	*Utricularia vulgaris*	Horned bladderwort	*Utricularia cornuta*
Common blue violet	*Viola sororia*	Indian cucumber root	*Mediola virginiana*

Indian pipe	*Monotropa uniflora*	Sequoia	*Sequoia sempervirens*
Intermediate wood fern	*Dryopteris intermedia*	Sessile-leaved bellwort	*Uvularia sessilifolia*
Interrupted fern	*Osmunda claytoniana*	Shadbush	*Amelanchier arborea*
Jack-in-the-pulpit	*Arisaema tryphyllum*	Shagbark hickory	*Carya ovata*
Jelly fungus	Order: Tremellales	Sharp-lobed hepatica	*Hepatica nobilis var. acuta*
Jewelweed	*Impatiens capensis*	Shelf fungus	Family: Polyporaceae
Lesser yellow lady's slipper	*Cypripedium parviflorum var. parviflorum*	Showy lady's slipper	*Cypripedium reginae*
		Skunk cabbage	*Symplocarpus foetidus*
Maidenhair fern	*Adiantum pedatum*	Silver maple	*Acer saccharinum*
Marginal wood fern	*Dryopteris marginalis*	Slippery elm	*Ulmus rubra*
Marsh marigold	*Caltha palustris*	Smooth-stalked helvella	*Helvella* sp.
Miterwort	*Mitella diphylla*	Southern ground cedar	*Diphasiastrum digitatum*
Mountain laurel	*Kalmia latifolia*	Spadderdock	*Nuphar varigatum*
Narrow beech fern	*Phegopteris connectilis*	Speckled alder	*Alnus incana*
Narrow-leaved cattail	*Typha angustifolia*	Spicebush	*Lindera benzoin*
New England aster	*Symphyotrichum movae-angliae*	Spreading dogbane	*Apocynum androsaemifolium*
Northern red oak	*Quercus rubra*	Spring beauty	*Claytonia virginica*
Northern white-cedar	*Thuja occidentalis*	St. Johnswort	*Hypericum perforatum*
Orange cedar rust gall	*Gymnosporangium juniperi-virginianae*	Staghorn sumac	*Rhus typhina*
		Stinkhorn	Order: Phallales
Ostrich fern	*Matteuccia struthiopteris var. pensylvanica*	Striped maple	*Acer pensylvanicum*
		Sugar maple	*Acer saccharum*
Oxeye daisy	*Leucanthemum vulgare*	Sweet-scented water lily	*Nymphaea odorata*
Painted trillium	*Trillium undulatum*	Thread-leaved sundew	*Drosera filiformis*
Partridgeberry	*Mitchella repens*	Trailing arbutus	*Epigaea repens*
Pinesap	*Monotropa hypopithys*	Trout lily	*Erythronium americanum*
Pink lady's slipper	*Cypripedium acaule*	True morel	*Morchella esculenta*
Poison hemlock	*Conium maculatum*	Turtlehead	*Chelone glabra*
Poison ivy	*Toxicodendron radicans*	Velvety earth tongue	*Trichoglossum hirsutum*
Pokeweed	*Phytolacca americana*	Venus fly trap	*Dionaea muscipula*
Princess pine	*Dendrolycopodium obscurum*	Virgin's bower	*Clematis virginiana*
		Virginia creeper	*Parthenocissus quinquefolia*
Purple pitcher plant	*Sarracenia purpurea*	Water hemlock	*Cicuta maculata*
Purple-flowering raspberry	*Rubus odoratus*	White ash	*Fraxinus americana*
Quaking aspen	*Populus tremuloides*	White baneberry	*Actaea pachypoda*
Queene Anne's lace	*Daucus carota*	White birch	*Betula papyrifera*
Red ash	*Fraxinus pennsylvanica*	White campion	*Silene latifolia*
Red baneberry	*Actaea rubra*	White oak	*Quercus alba*
Red clover	*Trifolium pratense*	White spruce	*Picea glauca*
Red hawkweed	*Hieracium aurantiacum*	Wild red columbine	*Aquilegia canadensis*
Red maple	*Acer rubrum*	Wild cucumber	*Echinocystis lobata*
Red pine	*Pinus resinosa*	Wild ginger	*Asarum canadense*
Red trillium	*Trillium erectum*	Wild grape	*Vitis vinifera*
Red-osier dogwood	*Cornus sericea*	Willow	*Salix* sp.
Rough-fruited cinquefoil	*Potentilla recta*	Wintergreen	*Gaultheria procumbens*
Round-lobed hepatica	*Hepatica nobilis var. obtusa*	Witch hazel	*Hamamelis virginiana*
Round-leaved sundew	*Drosera rotundifolia*	Wood anemone	*Anemone quinquefolia*
Running clubmoss	*Lycopodium clavatum*	Yellow birch	*Betula alleghaniensis*
Sassafras	*Sassafras albidum*	Yellow goatsbeard	*Tragopogon pratensis*
Scarlet cup fungus	*Sarcoscpha coccinea*	Yellow hawkweed	*Hieracium caespitosum*
Sensitive fern	*Onoclea sensibilis*	Yellow lady's slipper	*Cypripedium parviflorum*
		Yew	*Taxus canadensis*

Mary Holland recommends the following book & audio resources

AMPHIBIANS

Books

Bishop, Sherman. *Handbook of Salamanders*. Ithaca and New York: Comstock Publishing Co., Inc. 1943.

Conant, Roger & Collins, Joseph. *A Field Guide to Reptiles and Amphibians, 3rd Edition—Peterson Field Guides*. Boston and New York: Houghton Mifflin Company, 1998.

Tyning, Tom. *A Guide to Amphibians and Reptiles—Stokes Nature Guides*. Boston, Toronto, London: Little, Brown and Company, 1990.

Audio

Elliott, Lang. *The Calls of Frogs and Toads*. (Book & CD) Stackpole Books, 2004.

Elliott, Lang. *The Frogs and Toads of North America: A Comprehensive Guide to Their Identification, Behavior, and Calls*. (Book & CD) Mariner Books, 2009.

Cornell Laboratory of Ornithology. *Voices of the Night: The Calls of the Frogs and Toads of Eastern North America*. (CD). MacAulay Library (www.macaulaylibrary.org).

ANIMAL SIGNS

Elbroch, Mark. *Bird Tracks & Sign*. Mechanicsburg, PA: Stackpole Books, 2001.

Elbroch, Mark. *Mammal Tracks & Sign*. Mechanicsburg, PA: Stackpole Books, 2003.

Rezendes, Paul. *Tracking & the Art of Seeing: How to Read Animal Tracks and Sign*. New York, NY: HarperCollins Publishers, Inc., 1999.

BIRDS

Field Guides

Brinkley, Edward; Tufts, Craig. *National Wildlife Federation Field Guide to Birds of North America*. New York and London: Sterling Publishing, 2007.

Dunn, Joh and Alderfer, Jonathan. National Geographic Field Guide to the Birds of North America, 5th Edition. National Geographic, 2006.

Kaufman, Ken. *Kaufman Field Guide to Birds of North America*. New York: Houghton Mifflin, 2000.

Pasquier, Roger. *Watching Birds: An Introduction to Ornithology*. Boston: Houghton Mifflin Co., 1977.

Peterson, Roger Tory. *A Field Guide to the Birds of Eastern and Central North America*, 5th Edition, 2002. New York: Houghton Mifflin.

Sibley, David. *The Sibley Field Guide to Birds of Eastern North America*. New York: Alfred A. Knopf, 2003.

Terres, John K. *The Audubon Society Encyclopedia of North American Birds*. New York, NY: Alfred A. Knopf, Inc., 1980.

AUDIO RESOURCES

Borror, Donald. *Common Bird Songs*. Dover Publications, 2003.

Cornell Laboratory of Ornithology. *Guide to Bird Sounds*. Cornell Laboratory of Ornithology, 1985.

Elliott, Lang; Read, Marie. *Common Birds and Their Songs*. (Book & CD) Boston & New York: Houghton Mifflin Company, 1998.

Elliott, Lang. *Music of the Birds—A Celebration of Bird Song*. (Book & CD) Boston & New York: Houghton Mifflin Company, 1999.

Kroodsma, Donald. *The Singing Life of Birds*. (Book & CD) Boston & New York: Houghton Mifflin Co, 2005.

Lawson, Robert; Walton, Richard *Birding by Ear: Guide to Bird Song Identification*. (Booklet & CD) Boston & New York: Houghton Mifflin Harcourt, 2002.

Lawson, Robert; Walton, Richard. *More Birding by Ear: Eastern and Central*. (Booklet & CD) Boston & New York: Houghton Mifflin Harcourt, 2000.

Peterson, Roger Tory, Ed. *A Field Guide to Bird Songs: Eastern and Central North America*. Boston & New York: Houghton Mifflin Harcourt, 1999.

Stokes, Donald. *Stokes Field Guide to Bird Song* (*Eastern*). Hatchet Audio, 1997.

BIRD NESTS

Harrison, Hal. *A Field Guide to Birds' Nests*. The Peterson Field Guide Series. Boston & New York: Houghton Mifflin Company, 1975.

Headstrom, Richard. *A Complete Field Guide to Nests in the United States*. New York, NY: Ives Washburn, Inc., 1970.

BUTTERFLIES

Brock, Jim P. & Kaufman, Kenn. *Butterflies of North America*. Kaufman Focus Guides. New York, NY: Houghton Mifflin Company, 2003.

Glassberg, Jeffrey. *Butterflies Through Binoculars*. New York, NY: Oxford University Press, 1993.

CATERPILLARS

Allen, Thomas; Brock, Jim; Glassberg, Jeffrey. *Caterpillars in the Field and Garden. A Field Guide to the Butterfly Caterpillars of North America*. Oxford and New York: Oxford University Press, 2005.

Wagner, David. *Caterpillars of Eastern North America*. Princeton and Oxford: Princeton University Press, 2005.

DRAGONFLIES AND DAMSELFLIES

Lam, Ed. *Damselflies of the Northeast*. Forest Hills, New York: Biodiversity Books, 2004.

Nikula, Blair; Loose, Jennifer; Burne, Matthew. *A Field Guide to the Dragonflies and Damselflies of Massachusetts*. Massachusetts Division of Fisheries & Wildlife, Natural Heritage & Endangered Species Program, 2003.

FERNS

Cobb, Boughton; Farnsworth, Elizabeth; Lowe, Cheryl. *A Field Guide to Ferns and Their Related Families*. Boston and New York: Houghton, Mifflin and Harcourt, 2005.

Moran, Robbin C. and Tryon, Alice F. *The Ferns and Allied Plants of New England*. Lincoln, MA: Massachusetts Audubon Society, 1997.

FLOWERING PLANTS

Newcomb, Lawrence. *Newcomb's Wildflower Guide*. Boston, New York, Toronto, London: Little, Brown and Co., 1977.

Sanders, Jack. *The Secrets of Wildflowers*. Guilford, Connecticut: The Globe Pequot Press, 2003.

FRESHWATER INVERTEBRATES

Voshell, J. Reese. *A Guide to Common Freshwater Invertebrates of North America*. Blacksburg, Virginia: The McDonald & Woodward Publishing Company, 2002.

FUNGI

Lincoff, Gary. *National Aububon Society Field Guide to North American Mushrooms*. New York: Alfred A. Knopf, 1981.

Pacioni, Giovanni. *Simon & Schuster's Guide to Mushrooms*. New York, London and Toronto: 1981.

HABITAT

Benyus, Janine. *The Field Guide to Wildlife Habitats of the Eastern United States*. New York and London: Simon-Schuster, 1989.

Thompson, Elizabeth; Sorenson, Eric. *Wetland, Woodland, Wildland—A Guide to the Natural Communities of Vermont*. Vermont Department of Fish and Wildlife and the Nature Conservancy, 2000.

INSECTS

Borror, Donald; White, Richard. *A Field Guide to Insects: American North of Mexico (Peterson Field Guides)*. Boston & New York: Houghton Mifflin Harcourt, 1998.

Elliott, Lang; Hershberger, Wil. *The Songs of Insects*. Boston & New York: Houghton Mifflin Harcourt, 2007.

Kaufman, Kenn. *Kaufman Field Guide to Insects of North America*. Boston & New York: Houghton Mifflin Harcourt, 2007.

Marshall, Stephen. *Insects—Their Natural History and Diversity*. Buffalo, New York: Firefly Books, 2006.

National Audubon Society. *Field Guide to North American Insects and Spiders*. New York: Alfred A. Knopf, 1980.

White, Richard; Peterson, Roger Tory. *Beetles: A Field Guide to Beetles of North America (Peterson Field Guides)*. Boston & New York: Houghton Mifflin Harcourt, 1998.

MAMMALS

Feldhamer, George; Thompson, Bruce; Chapman, Joseph, Editors. *Wild Mammals of North America*. Baltimore and London: The Johns Hopkins University Press, 2003.

Godin, Alfred J. *Wild Mammals of New England*. Baltimore and London: The Johns Hopkins University Press, 1977.

Hamilton, Wilham; Whitaker, John. *Mammals of the Eastern United States*. Ithaca and London: Comstock Publishing Associates, Cornell University Press, 1998.

Reid, Fiona. *Peterson Field Guide to Mammals of North America: Fourth Edition*. Boston: Houghton Mifflin Harcourt, 2006.

MOTHS

Covel, Charles. *A Field Guide to Moths of Eastern North America*. Martinville, Virginia: Virginia Museum of Natural History, 2001.

Himmelman, John. *Discovering Moths. Nighttie Jewels in Your Own Backyard*. Camden, Maine: Down East Books, 2002.

NATURAL HISTORY INTERPRETATION

Eastman, John. *The Book of Forest and Thicket. The Book of Field and Roadside. The Book of Swamp and Bog. Birds of Field and Shore. Birds of Forest, Yard, & Thicket. Birds of Lake, Pond and Marsh*. Mechanicsburg, PA: Stackpole Books.

Elliott, Lang. *A Guide to Night Songs: The Nighttime Sounds of 60 Mammals, Birds, Amphibians and Insects*. Stackpole Books, 2004.

Heinrich, Bernd. *Winter World. Summer World*. New York, NY: HarperCollins.

Wessels, Tom. *Reading the Forested Landscape: A Natural History of New England*. Woodstock, VT: The Countryman Press, 2005.

NEW ENGLAND NATURAL HISTORY

DeGraaf, Richard M.; Yamasaki, Mariko. *New England Wildlife: Habitat, Natural History, and Distribution*. Hanover and London: University Press of New England, 2001.

REPTILES

Conant, Roger & Collins, Joseph. *A Field Guide to Reptiles and Amphibians of Eastern & Central North America (Peterson Field Guide Series)*. Boston and New York: Houghton Mifflin Company, 1988.

Klemens, Michael. *Amphibians and Reptiles of Connecticut and Adjacent Regions*. State Geological and Natural History Survey of Connecticut, Bulletin 112.

Krulikowski, Linda. *Snakes of New England*. Old Lyme, CT: LuvLife Publishing, 2004.

SKULLS AND BONES

Elbroch, Mark. *Animal Skulls—A Guide to North American Species*. Mechanicsburg, PA: Stackpole Books, 2006.

Wolniewicz, Richard. *Field Guide to Skulls and Bones of Mammals of the Northeastern United States. Vol. 1 and 2*. Magnolia, Massachusetts: Richard Wolniewicz, 2001.

SPIDERS

Foelix, Rainer. *Biology of Spiders*. New York and Oxford: Oxford University Press, 1996.

Ubick, D.; Paquin, P.; Cusing, P.E. and Roth, V. Ed. *Spiders of North America: An Identification Manual*. American Arachnological Society, 2005.

TREES

Farrar, John Laird. *Trees of the Northern United States and Canada*. Ames, Iowa: Iowa State Press, 1995.

Sibley, David. *The Sibley Guide to Trees*. New York: Alfred K. Knopf, 2009.

Tudge, Colin. *The Tree*. New York: Crown Publishers, 2005.

VERNAL POOLS

Colburn, Elizabeth. *Vernal Pools*. Blacksburg, VA: The McDonald & Woodward Publishing Co., 2004.

Kenney, Leo and Burne, Matthew. *A Field Guide to the Animals of Vernal Pools*. Westborough, MA: Massachusetts Division of Fisheries & Wildlife, Natural Heritage & Endangered Species Program, 2000.

Flowering sessile-leaved bellwort and a visiting pollinator.

"The 1752 Calendar Change." Connecticut State Library. 2010. Web.

Ackerman, Diane. *A Natural History of the Senses*. New York: Random House, Inc., 1990.

Alexander, Richard. *Singing Insects*. Chicago: Rand McNally & Co., 1967.

"All About Birds." The Cornell Lab of Ornithology. 2009. Web.

Allen, Thomas; Brock, Jim; Glassberg, Jeffrey. *Caterpillars in the Field and Garden*. A Field Guide to the Butterfly Caterpillars of North America. Oxford and New York: Oxford University Press, 2005.

"American Birding Association Checklist." American Birding Association. 2008. Web.

"The American Robin." *The Auk*. 117(1):274-276. 2000. Web.

Angier, Bradford. *Field Guide to Edible Wild Plants*. Harrisburg, Pennsylvania: Stackpole Books, 1974.

"Attracting Wildlife with Dead Trees." National Wildlife Federation. 2010. Web. 30 September 2008.

Austing, G. Ronald. *The World of the Red-tailed Hawk*. Philadelphia and New York: J.B. Lippincott Co., 1964.

Austing, G. Ronald; Holt, John. *The World of the Great Horned Owl*. Philadelphia and New York: J.B.Lippincott, 1966.

Babcock, Harold. *Turtles of the Northeastern United States*. New York: Dover Publications, 1971.

Beck, B.; Muhlenberg, E. & Fiedler, K. "Mud-puddling behavior in tropical butterflies: In search of proteins or minerals?" *Oecologia*. 119(1): 140–148, 1999.

Beebe, William. *The Log of the Sun—A Chronicle of Nature's Year*. Garden City and New York: Garden City Publishing Co., Inc., 1927.

Bent, Arthur C. Life Histories Series. New York: Dover Publications.

Benyus, Janine. *The Field Guide to Wildlife Habitats of the Eastern United States*. New York and London: Simon-Schuster, 1989.

Berenbaum, May. *Ninety-nine Gnats, Nits, and Nibblers*. Urbana and Chicago: University of Illinois Press, 1989.

Berenbaum, May. *Ninety-nine more Maggots, Mites, and Munchers*. Urbana and Chicago: University of Illinois Press, 1993.

"Bird Check Lists by State and Province." Thayer Birding Software. 2010. Web.

"Birding Resources." Peterson Field Guide. Web. 25 August 2008.

The Birds of North America Online. 2010. Web.

Bishop, S.C. *The Salamanders of New York*. New York State Museum Bulletin, 324:1-365.

Bishop, Sherman. *Born in the Spring: a collection of spring wildflowers*. Athens, Ohio: Ohio University Press, 1976.

Bishop, Sherman. *Handbook of Salamanders*. Ithaca and New York: Comstock Publishing Co., Inc. 1943.

Blakeslee, Albert; Jarvis, Chester. *Northeastern Trees in Winter*. New York: Dover Publications, Inc., 1972.

Borland, Hal. *Hal Borland's Book of Days*. New York: Alfred A. Knopf, 1976.

Borror, Donald & DeLong, Dwight. *An Introduction to the Study of Insects*. New York, Chicago, San Francisco, Atlanta, Dallas, Montreal, Toronto, London, Sydney: Holt, Rinehart and Winston, 1971.

Borror, Donald & White, Richard. *A Field Guide to the Insects*. Boston: Houghton Mifflin Company, 1970.

"Box elder tree." All Allergy. 1998. Web.

Brands, S. J. "Antheraea polyphemus" *Systema Naturae*. 1 September 2008.

Brett, James. *Feathers in the Wind*. Kempton, Pennsylvania: Hawk Mountain Sanctuary Association, 1976.

Brock, Jim P. & Kaufman, Kenn. *Butterflies of North America*. Kaufman Focus Guides. New York, NY: Houghton Mifflin Company, 2003.

Brockman, C.Frank. *A Guide to Field Identification: Trees of North America*. New York, NY: Golden Press, 1968.

Brockman, C.Frank. *Trees of North America*. Racine, WI: Western Publishing Co., 1968.

Brodo, Irwin. *Lichens of North America*. New Haven: Yale University Press, 2001.

Brown, Lauren. *Grasses—An Identification Guide*. Boston, New York, London: Houghton Mifflin Co., 1979.

Brown, Lauren. *Weeds in Winter*. New York, NY: W.W.Norton & Company, Inc., 1976.

Brown, Vinson. *Reading the Outdoors at Night*. Harrisburg, PA: Stackpole Books, 1972.

Buck, Margaret. *Where They Go In Winter*. New York & Nashville: Abingdon Press, 1968.

Burnie, David. *Tree*. (Eyewitness Books) New York, NY: Alfred A. Knopf, 1988.

Burt, William. *A Field Guide to the Mammals.* Peterson Field Guide Series. Boston: Houghton Mifflin Company, 1964.

Caduto, Michael. *Pond and Brook—A Guide to Nature Study in Freshwater Environments.* Englewood Cliffs, NJ: Prentice-Hall, 1985.

Capinera, John; Scott, Ralph; Walker, Thomas. *Field Guide to Grasshoppers, Katydids and Crickets of the United States.* Ithaca and London: Cornell University Press, 2004.

"Carnivorous Plants/Insectivorous Plants." Botanical Society of America. Web. 25 June 2008.

Carroll, David. *Swampwalker's Journal: A Wetlands Year.* Boston and New York: Houghton Mifflin Company, 1999.

Carroll, David. *The Year of the Turtle.* Charlotte, Vermont: Camden House Publishing, Inc., 1991.

Carter, Kate. *Wildflowers of Vermont.* Waterbury Center, Vermont: Cotton Brook Publications, 2001.

Chapman, Frank. *Bird-Life.* New York: D. Appleton and Co., 1897.

Chapman, Frank. *What Bird is That?* New York, London: D. Appleton-Century Co., Inc., 1943.

Choiniere, Joe. *Butterfly Atlas .* Massachusetts Audubon Society.

"Climate change and the demographic demise of a hoarding bird living on the edge." The Royal Society. 2006. Web.

"Climates of the States, Climatography of the United States No. 60." NOAA Satellite and Information Service. 2005. Web.

"Club Moss, Lycopodium clavatum." Herbs2000.com. Web. 11 November 2007.

Cobb, Boughton; Farnsworth, Elizabeth; Lowe, Cheryl. *A Field Guide to Ferns and their related families.* Boston and New York: Houghton Mifflin Harcourt, 2005.

Colburn, Elizabeth. *Vernal Pools.* Blacksburg, VA: The McDonald & Woodward Publishing Co., 2004.

Colby, C.B. *The First Book of Animal Signs.* New York: Franklin Watts, Inc. 1966.

Comstock, Anna. *Handbook of Nature Study.* Ithaca: Cornell University Press, 1967.

Conant, Roger & Collins, Joseph. *A Field Guide to Reptiles and Amphibians—Peterson Field Guides.* Boston and New York: Houghton Mifflin Company, 1988.

"Connecticut Ferns." Connecticut Botanical Society: 2005. Web.

Cooper, Gale. *Inside Animals.* San Diego: Atlantic-Little, 1978.

Costello, David. *The World of the Porcupine.* Philadelphia and New York: J.B. Lippincott Co., 1966.

Covel, Charles. *A Field Guide to Moths of Eastern North America.* Martinville, Virginia: Virginia Museum of Natural History, 2001.

Crompton, John. *The Spider.* New York: Nick Lyons Books, 1950.

Dally, Joanna; Clayton, Nicola; Emery, Nathan. "The Behaviour and Evolution of Cache Protection and Pilferage." *Animal Behaviour.* Vol. 72, Issue 1, 2006: 12 -23.

Dana, W. *How to Know the Wild Flowers.* New York: Dover Publications, Inc., 1963.

DeBruyn, Terry. *Walking with Bears.* New York: The Lyons Press, 1999.

DeGraaf, Richard M. Yamasaki, Mariko. *New England Wildlife: Habitat, Natural History, and Distribution.* Hanover and London: University Press of New England, 2001.

DeGraaf, Richard; Sendak, Paul. *Native and Naturalized Trees of New England and Adjacent Canada.* Hanover and London: University Press of New England, 2006.

DeGraaf, Richard; Witman, Gretchin. *Trees, Shrubs and Vines for Attracting Birds.* Amherst, MA: University of Massachusetts Press, 1979.

Dennis, John. *A Complete Guide to Bird Feeding.* New York: Alfred A. Knopf, 1975.

Densmore, Frances. *How Indians Use Wild Plants for Food, Medicine and Crafts.* New York: Dover Publications, Inc., 1974.

"The Diet of American Robins: An Analysis of US Biological Survey Records." Web. *The Auk.* 103: 710-725. October, 1986.

Ditmars, Raymond. *Reptiles of the World.* New York: The MacMillan Co., 1933.

Dowden, Anne. *Look at a Flower.* New York: Thomas Y. Crowell Co., 1963.

Dunn, Erica and Tessaglia-Hymes. *Birds at Your Feeder.* New York and London: W.W.Norton & Co., 1999.

Dunn, Jon and Garrett, Kimball. *A Field Guide to Warblers of North America.* Peterson Field Guide Series. Boston, New York: Houghton Mifflin Co., 1997.

Dunn, Joh and Alderfer, Jonathan. *National Geographic Field Guide to the Birds of North America, 5th Edition.* National Geographic, 2006.

Dunne, Pete. *Essential Field Guide Companion.* Boston, New York: Houghton Mifflin Harcourt, 2006.

Dunne, Pete. *Pete Dunne on Bird Watching.* Boston and New York: Houghton Mifflin Harcourt, 2003.

Durand, Herbert. *Field Book of Common Ferns.* New York and London: G.P.Putnam's Sons, 1949.

Earley, Chris. *Hawks & Owls of the Great Lake Region and Eastern North America.* Buffalo: Firefly Books, 2004.

Earley, Chris. *Sparrows & Finches.* Buffalo: Firefly Books, 2003.

Earley, Chris. *Waterfowl of Eastern North America.* Buffalo: Firefly Books, 2005.

Eastman, John. *The Book of Forest and Thicket.* Mechanicsburg, PA: Stackpole Books, 2000.

Eastman, John. *Birds of Field and Shore.* Mechanicsburg, PA: Stackpole Books, 2000.

Eastman, John. *Birds of Forest, Yard, & Thicket.* Mechanicsburg, PA: Stackpole Books, 1997.

Eastman, John. *Birds of Lake, Pond and Marsh*. Mechanicsburg, PA: Stackpole Books, 1999.

Eastman, John. *The Book of Field and Roadside*. Mechanicsburg, PA: Stackpole Books, 2003.

Eastman, John. *The Book of Swamp and Bog*. Mechanicsburg, PA: Stackpole Books, 1995.

Eaton, Eric; Kaufman, Ken. *Field Guide to Insects of North America*. New York: Houghton Mifflin Harcourt, 2007.

Eberhardt, L. S. 1994. "Sap-feeding and its consequences for reproductive success and communication in Yellow-bellied Sapsuckers" (*Sphyrapicus varius*). Ph.D. diss., Univ. of Florida, Gainesville.

"Echinocystis lobata." USDA Germplasm Resources Information Network. 2003. Web.

Eckert, Allan. *The Owls of North America*. Garden City, NY: Doubleday & Co., Inc., 1974.

Ehrlich, Paul; Dobkin, David; Wheye, Darryl. *The Birder's Handbook: A Field Guide to the Natural History of North American Birds*. New York, London, Toronto: Simon & Schuster, Fireside, 1988.

Eisner, Thomas. *For Love of Insects*. Cambridge, Massachusetts and London: The Belknap Press of Harvard University Press, 2003.

Elbroch, Mark. *Animal Skulls—A Guide to North American Species*. Mechanicsburg, PA: Stackpole Books, 2006.

Elbroch, Mark. *Bird Tracks & Sign*. Mechanicsburg, PA: Stackpole Books, 2001.

Elbroch, Mark. *Mammal Tracks & Sign*. Mechanicsburg, PA: Stackpole Books, 2003.

Elliott, Lang and Hershberger, Wil. *The Songs of Insects*. Boston and New York: Houghton Mifflin Company, 2007.

Elliott, Lang. *Music of the Birds*. Boston and New York: Houghton Mifflin Harcourt, 1999.

Elpel, Thomas. *Botany in a Day*. Poz, Montana. HOPS Press, 2001.

Elphick, Jonathan, Ed. *Atlas of Bird Migration*. Buffalo: Firefly Books, 2007.

"Endangered Bats." US Fish & Wildlife Service. Web.

Epple, Anne. *The Amphibians of New England*. Camden, Maine: Down East Books, 1983.

Erhardt, A. and Ruterholz, H. "Do Peacock butterflies (*Inachis io*) detect and prefer nectar amino acids and other nitrogenous compounds?" *Oecologia* 117(4): 536-542, 1998.

Eshleman, Alan. *Poisonous Plants*. Boston: Houghton Mifflin Harcourt, 1977.

Farrar, John Laird. *Trees of the Northern United States and Canada*. Ames, Iowa: Iowa State Press, 1995.

Feldhamer, George; Thompson, Bruce; Chapman, Joseph. *Wild Mammals of North America: Biology, Management, and Conservation*. Baltimore: The Johns Hopkins University Press, 2003.

Felt, Ephraim. *Plant Galls and Gall Makers*. New York: Hafner Press, 1965.

Fischer-Nagel, Heiderose and Andreas. *Life of the Honeybee*. Minneapolis: Carolrhoda Books, Inc., 1982.

Foelix, Rainer. *Biology of Spiders*. New York and Oxford: Oxford University Press, 1996.

Forrest, Louise. *A Field Guide to Tracking Animals in the Snow*. Harrisburg, Pennsylvania: Stackpole Books, 1988.

Foster, Steven; Caras, Roger. *Venomous Animals and Poisonous Plants*. Peterson Field Guide. Boston and New York: Houghton Mifflin Harcourt, 1994.

Gertsch, Willis. *American Spiders*. Princeton, New Jersey, Toronto, London and Melbourne: DiVan Nostrand Co., Inc., 1949.

Gibbons, Diane. *Mammal Tracks and Sign of the Northeast*. Hanover and London: University Press of New England, 2003.

Gibson, William. *Secrets Out of Doors*. New York and London: Harper and Brothers Publishers, 1913.

Glassberg, Jeffrey. *Butterflies Through Binoculars*. A Field Guide to Butterflies in the Boston—New York—Washington Region. New York and Oxford: Oxford University Press, 1993.

Glob, P.V. *The Bog People—Iron Age Man Preserved*. New York: Ballantine Books, 1965.

Godin, Alfred J. *Wild Mammals of New England*. Baltimore and London: The Johns Hopkins University Press, 1977.

Griggs, Robert. *Grigg's Key to the Families of Flowering Plants— Wild or Cultivated in the Northeastern United States*. Hanover, New Hampshire: Dept. of Biological Sciences, Pub. No. 3, 1962.

Halfpenny, James; Ozanne, Roy. *Winter—An Ecological Handbook*. Boulder, Colorado: Johnson Books, 1989.

Halfpenny, James. *A Field Guide to Mammal Tracking in North America*. Boulder, Colorado: Johnson Printing Co., 1986.

Halfpenny, James; Ozanne, Roy. *Winter: an ecological handbook*. Boulder, CO. Johnson Publishing Co., 1989.

Hallowell, Anne and Barbara. *Fern Finder*. Rochester, New York: Nature Study Guild Publishers, 2001.

Hamilton, Wilham; Whitaker, John. *Mammals of the Eastern United States*. Ithaca and London: Comstock Publishing Associates, Cornell University Press, 1979.

Hammerson, Geoffrey. *Connecticut Wildlife: Biodiversity, Natural History and Conservation*. Hanover and London: University Press of New England, 2004.

Harding, Judith. *An Animal Damage Identification Guide for Massachusetts*. Amherst, Massachusetts: Massachusetts Cooperative Extension Service, 1979.

Harlow, William. *Trees of the Eastern and Central United States and Canada*. New York, NY: Dover Publications, Inc., 1957.

"Harris' Checkerspot." Mass Audubon. 2010. Web.

Harris, James and Melinda. *Plant Identification Terminology—An Illustrated Glossary*. Spring Lake, Utah: Spring Lake Publishing, 2001.

Harrison, Colin. A Field Guide to the Nests, Eggs and Nestlings of North American Birds. Cleveland, New York, Toronto, London: William Collins Sons & Co., Ltd., 1978.

Harrison, Hal. *A Field Guide to Birds' Nests*. The Peterson Field Guide Series. Boston: Houghton Mifflin Company, 1975.

Harrison, Hal. *The World of the Snake*. Philadelphia and New York: J.B. Lippincott Co., 1971.

Headstrom, Richard. *A Complete Field Guide to Nests in the United States*. New York, NY: Ives Washburn, Inc., 1970.

Headstrom, Richard. *Adventures with a Hand Lens*. New York and Philadelphia: J.B.Lippincott Company, 1962.

Headstrom, Richard. *Adventures with a Microscope*. Philadelphia and New York: J.P. Lippincott Company, 1941.

Headstrom, Richard. *Families of Flowering Plants*. South Brunswick and New York: A.S. Barnes and Co., 1978.

Headstrom, Richard. *Nature in Miniature*. New York. Alfred A. Knopf, 1968.

Headstrom, Richard. *Spiders of the United States*. South Brunswick, New York and London: A.S. Barnes and Co., 1973.

Headstrom, Richard. *The Beetles of America*. South Brunswick and New York: A.S. Barnes and Co., 1977.

Headstrom, Richard. *Whose Track Is It? An Introductory Field Book to Animal Tracks Found in the United States East of the Mississippi*. New York: Ives Washburn, Inc., 1971.

Heinrich, Bernd. *The Trees In My Forest*. New York, NY: HarperCollins, 1997.

Heinrich, Bernd. *Winter World*. New York, NY: HarperCollins, 2003.

Heinrich, Bernd. *Summer World*. New York, NY: HarperCollins, 2009.

Heintzelman, Donald. *A Guide to Eastern Hawk Watching*. University Park, Pennsylvania and London: The Pennsylvania State University Press, 1976.

Heintzelman, Donald. *Hawks and Owls of Eastern North America*. New Brunswick, New Jersey and London: Rutgers University Press, 2004.

Henry, J. *Red Fox—TheCatlike Canine*. Washington, D.C. and London: Smithsonian Institution Press, 1996.

Herberstein, M.; Craig, C.; Coddington, J.; Elgar, M. 2000. "The functional significance of silk decorations of orb-web spiders: a critical review of the empirical evidence." *Biological Reviews*. 75: 649-669. Cambridge University Press.

Hill, John and Smith, James. *Bats—A Natural History*. Austin, TX: University of Texas Press, 1984.

Hillyard, Paul. *The Private Life of Spiders*. Princeton and Oxford: Princeton University Press, 2007.

Himmelman, John. *Discovering Moths—Nighttime Jewels in Your Own Backyard*. Camden, Maine: Down East Books, 2002.

Hitchcock, C.; Sherry, D. "Long-term Memory for Cache Sites in the Black-capped Chickadee." *Animal Behavior*, 40, 701-712, 1990.

Hopkins, Hilary. *Never Say It's Just a Dandelion*. Cambridge: Jewelweed Books, 2001.

Hosie, R.C. *Native Trees of Canada*. Ottawa: Canadian Forestry Service, Dept. of the Environment, 1973.

Hunter, Malcom; Calhoun, Aram; McCollough, Mark. Ed. *Maine Amphibians and Reptiles*. Orono, Maine: The University of Maine Press, 1999.

Hutchins, Ross. *Galls and Gall Insects*. New York: Dodd, Mead and Co., 1969.

Hutchins, Ross. *Grasshoppers and Their Kin*. New York: Dodd, Mead and Co., 1972.

Hutchins, Ross. *Paper Hornets*. Reading, Massachusetts: Addison-Wesley Publishing Co., 1973.

Hutchins, Ross. *The Bug Clan*. New York: Dodd, Mead and Co., 1973.

Hutchins, Ross. *The Carpenter Bee*. Reading, Massachusetts: Addison-Wesley Publishing Co., 1972.

Hutchins, Ross. *The Cicada*. Reading, Massachusetts: Addison-Wesley Publishing Co., 1971.

Hutchins, Ross. *The world of Dragonflies and Damselflies*. New York: Dodd, Mead and Co., 1969.

Hutchins, Ross. *This is a Leaf*. New York, NY: Dodd, Mead & Company, 1962.

Hutchins, Ross. *This is a Tree*. New York, NY: Dodd, Mead & Company, 1964.

Hutchins, Ross. *Caddis Insects*. New York: Dodd, Mead and Co., 1966.

Hutchins, Ross. *Insects*. Englewood Cliffs, New Jersey: Prentice-Hall, 1966.

Hutchins, Ross. *The Mayfly*. Reading, Massachusetts: Addison-Wesley Publishing Co., 1970.

Hyland, Fay; Hoisington, Barbara. *The Woody Plants of Sphagnous Bogs of Northern New England and Adjacent Canada*. Orono, Maine: University of Maine at Orono Press, 1981.

Ibid. (same author) *Fruit Key & Twig Key to Trees & Shrubs*. New York, NY: Dover Publications, Inc., 1946.

"Influences of species, latitudes and methodologies on estimates of phenological response to global warming." Wiley Interscience. 2007. Web.

International Carnivorous Plant Society. Web. 24 June 2008.

Jaegar, Edmund. *Desert Wildlife*. Chicago: Stanford University Press, 1961.

Jaegar, Ellsworth. *Tracks and Trailcraft*. London: The MacMillan Co., 1948.

James, Wilma. *Know Your Poisonous Plants*. Healdsburg, California: Naturegraph Publishers, 1973.

Jardine, Ernie. *Bird Song Identification Made Easy*. Toronto: Natural Heritage/Natural History Inc., 1996.

Johnsgard, Paul. *Waterfowl of North America*. Bloomington, Indiana and London: Indiana University Press, 1975.

Johnson, A. and Smith, H. *Plant Names Simplified: Their Pronunciation, Derivation & Meaning*. Herefordshire, England: Landsmans Bookshop Ltd., 1931.

Johnson, Charles. *Bogs of the Northeast*. Hanover, New Hampshire: University Press of New England, 1985.

Johnson, Charles; Estrin, Nona. *In Season—A Natural History of the New England Year*. Hanover and London: University Press of New England, 2002.

Johnson, Gaylord. *Nature's Program*. Nelson Doubleday, Inc., 1926.

Johnson, Sylvia. *The World of Bats*. A Lerner Natural Science Book. Minneapolis: Lerner Publications Company, 1985.

Johnson, W. C. and C. S. Adkisson. Dispersal of beech nuts by Blue Jays in fragmented landscapes. Am. Midl. Nat. 113: 319–324, 1985.

Jorgensen, Neil. *A Sierra Club Naturalist's Guide-Southern New England*. San Francisco: Sierra Club Books, 1978.

Journey North—A Global Study of Wildlife Migration and Seasonal Change. 2010. Web. 28 August 2008.

Judd, Walter; Campbell, Christopher; Kellogg, Elizabeth; Stevens, Peter; Donoghue, Michael. *Plant Systematics—A Phylogenetic Approach*. Sunderland, Massachusetts: Sinauer Associates, Inc., 2002.

Kaufman, Ken. *Advanced Birding*. Boston and New York: Houghton Mifflin Harcourt, 1990.

Kaufman, Ken. *Birds of North America* —Kaufman Focus Guide. New York and Boston: Houghton Mifflin Co., 2000.

Kaufman, Ken. *Lives of North American Birds*. Boston, New York: Houghton Mifflin Harcourt, 1996.

Kays, Roland; Wilson, Don. *Mammals of North America*. Princeton and Oxford: Princeton University press, 2002.

Kenney, Leo and Burne, Matthew. *A Field Guide to the Animals of Vernal Pools*. Westborough, MA: Massachusetts Division of Fisheries & Wildlife, Natural Heritage & Endangered Species Program, 2000.

Ketchum, Richard. *The Secret Life of the Forest*. New York: American Heritage Press, 1970.

Kiel, Warren. *The Butterflies of the White Mountains of New Hampshire*. Guilford, Connecticut and Helena, Montana: Globe Pequot Press, 2003.

Kingsbury, John. *Deadly Harvest—A Guide to Common Poisonous Plants*. New York, Chicago, San Francisco: Holt, Rinehart and Winston, 1965.

Klemens, Michael. *Amphibians and Reptiles of Connecticut and Adjacent Regions*. State Geological and Natural History Survey of Connecticut, Bulletin 112, 1993.

Klimas, John; Cunningham, James. *Wildflowers of Eastern America*. New York: Alfred A. Knopf, 1974.

Klots, Alexander and Elsie. *Insects of North America*. New York: Doubleday and Co., Inc., 1972.

Klots, Alexander. *A Field Guide to the Butterflies*. Peterson Field Guide Series. Boston: Houghton Mifflin Harcourt, 1951.

Klots, Elsie. *The New Field Book of Freshwater Life*. New York: G. P. Putnam's Sons, 1966.

Kricher, John; Morrison, Gordon. *Eastern Forest—A Field Guide to Birds, Mammals, Trees, Flowers and* More. Boston and New York: Houghton Mifflin Harcourt, 1998.

Krochmal, Arnold and Connie. *A Guide to the Medicinal Plants of the United States*. New York: Quadrangle/The New York Times Book Co., 1973.

Kroodsma, Donald. *The Singing Life of Birds*. Boston and New York: Houghton Mifflin Harcourt, 2005.

Krulikowski, Linda. *Snakes of New England*. Old Lyme, CT: LuvLife Publishing, 2004.

Labaree, E.E. *Breeding and Reproduction in Fur Bearing Animals*. Toronto, Canada: Fur Trade Journal of Canada, 1953.

Lam, Ed. *Damselflies of the Northeast*. Forest Hills, New York: Biodiversity Books, 2004.

Lauber, Patricia. *Seeds! Pop! Stick! Glide!* New York: Crown Publishers, 1981.

Laughlin, Sarah and Kibbe, Douglas, Ed. *The Atlas of Breeding Birds of Vermont*. Hanover and London: University Press of New England, 1985.

Lazell, James. *Reptiles & Amphibians in Massachusetts*. Lincoln, Massachusetts: Massachusetts Audubon Society, 1972.

Leahy, Chirstopher; Mitchell, John; Conuel,Thomas. *The Nature of Massachusetts*. Massachusetts Audubon Society. Reading, Massachusetts: Addison-Wesley Publishing Co., Inc., 1996.

Lee, D. and Funderburg, J. *Wild Mammals of North America,* "Marmots Marmota monax and allies." Baltimore: Johns Hopkins University Press, 1982.

Levine, Carol. *A Guide to Wildflowers in Winter*. New Haven and London: Yale University Press, 1995.

Lincoff, Gary. *National Aububon Society Field Guide to North American Mushrooms*. New York: Alfred A. Knopf, 1981.

Llutz, Frank. *Field Book of Insects*. New York and London: G.P. Putnam's Sons, 1918.

Long, Tom. *New England Nature Watch*. Beverly, Massachusetts: Commonwealth Editions, 2003.

Long, Steven, ed. *Northern Woodlands Magazine*. Decenber, 2006.

Long, William. *How Animals Talk*. Rochester, Vermont: Bear & Co., 2005.

Lynch, Wayne. *Owls of the United States and Canada: A Complete Guide to Their Biology and Behavior*. Baltimore: The Johns Hopkins University Press, 2007.

"Mammals of Vermont." Vermont Fish & Wildlife Department—Nongame and Natural Heritage Program. 2008. Web.

Marchand, M.N. and Litvaitis, J.A. "Effects of landscape composition, habitat features, and nest distribution on predation rates of simulated turtle nests." *Biological Conservation*. Volume 117, Issue 3, pages 243-251, May 2004.

Marchand, Peter. *North Woods—An Inside Look at the Nature of Forests in the Northeast*. Boston: Appalachian Moutain Club, 1981.

Marshall, Stephen A. *Insects: Their Natural History and Diversity*. Buffalo: Firefly Books Ltd, 2006.

Martin, Alexander; Zim, Herbert; Nelson, Arnold. *American Wildlife & Plants: A Guide to Wildlife Food Habits*. New York, NY: Dover Publications, Inc., 1951.

Martin, Laura. *Wildflower Folklore*. New York, Boston, Charlotte: East Woods Press, 1984.

Martin, Laura. *Wildlife Folklore*. Old Saybrook, Connecticut: The Globe Pequot Press, 1994.

Mason, George. *Animal Feet*. New York: William Morrow & Co., 1970.

Mason, George. *Animal Tails*. New York: William Morrow & Company, 1958.

Mason, George. *Animal Teeth*. New York: William Morrow and Co., 1965.

Mason, George. *Animal tools*. New York: William Morrow & Company, 1951.

Mason, George. *Animal Weapons*. New York: William Morrow & Co., 1949.

Mathews, F. Schuyler. *Field Book of Wild Birds and Their Music*. New York and London: G.P.Putnam's Sons, 1921.

Mattison, Chris. *Snake*. New York: DK Publishing, Inc., 1999.

McDougall, Len. *The Complete Tracker: Tracks, Signs and Habits of North American Wildlife*. Guilford, Connecticut: The Globe Pequot Press, 1997.

McGavin. *Essential Entomology*. An Order-by-Order Introduction. Oxford: Oxford University Press, 2001.

Menninger, Edwin. *Fantastic Trees*. New York: The Viking Press, 1967.

"Migration of Birds: Influence of Weather." USGS—Northern Prairie Wildlife Research Center. 2006. Web.

Mikula, Rick. *Garden Butterflies of North America*. A Gallery of Garden Butterflies & How to Attract Them. Minocqua, Wisconsin: Willow Creek Press, 1997.

Miller, Orson. *Mushrooms of North America*. New York: E.P.Dutton, 1977.

Miller-Rushing et al. "Bird migration times, climate change, and changing population sizes." *Global Change Biology*, 2008.

Mitchell, John. *A Field Guide to Your Own Back Yard*. Woodstock, VT: Countryman Press, 1999.

"Monarch Butterfly Ecology." Karen Oberhauser, Dept. of Fisheries, Wildlife and Conservation Biology, University of Minnesota, St. Paul, MN. Ecology info. Web.

Monarch Larva Monitoring Project—Monarchs in the Classroom, University of Minnesota. 2010. Web. August 2008.

"The Monarch of Migration." World Wildlife Fund. 2010. Web. 28 August 2008.

Monarch Watch. Web. 28 August 2008.

"Monotropa uniflora." Tom Volk's Fungi. Dept. of Biology, University of Wisconsin-La Crosse. 2002. Web. 18 August 2008.

Montgomery, Sy. *The Wild Outside Your Window*. Camden, Maine: Down East Books, 2002.

Montgomery, Sy. *The Curious Naturalist*. Camden, Maine: Down East Books, 1993.

Montgomery, Sy. *Seasons of the Wild*. Shelburne, VT: Chapters Publishing, Ltd., 1995.

"Moose." New Hampshire Fish & Wildlife. Web. 24 June 2008.

Moran, Robbin C. and Tryon, Alice F. *The Ferns and Allied Plants of New England*. Lincoln, MA: Massachusetts Audubon Society, 1997.

Moran, Robbin. *A Natural History of Ferns*. Portland, Oregon: Timber Press, Inc., 2004

Morgan, Ann. *Field Book of Animals in Winter*. New York: G.P. Putnam's Sons, 1939.

Morgan, Ann. *Field Book of Ponds and Streams*. New York and London: G.P.Putnam's Sons, 1930.

Morse, Susan. Personal conversation.

Muenscher, W. *Weeds*. New York: The MacMillan Co., 1949.

Muller-Schwarze, Dietland; Sun, Lixing. *The Beaver*. Ithaca and London: Cornell University Press, 2003.

Murie, Olaus. *A Field Guide to Animal Tracks*. The Peterson Field Guide Series. Boston: Houghton Mifflin Harcourt, 1954.

Murie, Olaus; Elbroch, Mark. *Animal Tracks*. Peterson Field Guide. Boston and New York: Houghton Mifflin Harcourt, 2005.

"National Climatic Data Center." NOAA Satellite and Information Service. 2010. Web.

National Geographic Society. *The Curious Naturalist*. Washington, D.C.: National Geographic Society, 1991.

"Native Plant Database." Ladybird Johnson Wildflower Center, Native Plant Information Network, University of Texas. 2010. Web.

"Native Snakes of Rhode Island." Rhode Island Department of Environmental Management—Fish & Wildlife Department. Web. 25 August 2008.

NatureServe. 2009. Web.

Naval Oceanography Portal. 2010. Web.

Nearing, Helen and Scott. *The Maple Sugar Book*. New York: Galahad Books, 1970.

Newcomb, Lawrence. *Newcomb's Wildflower Guide*. Boston, New York, Toronto, London: Little, Brown and Co., 1977.

Nikula, Blair; Loose, Jennifer; Burne, Matthew. *A Field Guide to the Dragonflies and Damselflies of Massachusetts*. Massachusetts Division of Fisheries & Wildlife, Natural Heritage & Endangered Species Program, 2003.

Nikula, Blair; Sones, Jackie; Stokes, Donald and Lillian. *Beginner's Guide to Dragonflies*. New York, Boston and London: Little, Brown and Co., 2002.

Norman, Richard. "The Oak and the Jay." *Northern Woodlands*. Autumn, 2007.

"Notophthalmus viridesces." (Amphibiaweb). Web.

O'Brien, Michael; Crossley, Richard; Karlson, Kevin. *The Shorebird Guide*. Boston, New York: Houghton Mifflin Company, 2006.

Oberhauser, Karen and Solensky, Michelle, editors. *The Monarch Butterfly: Biology and Conservation*. Ithaca & London: Cornell University Press, 2004.

"Orb-web Spiders: a critical review of the empirical evidence." *Biol. Rev.* 75, pp. 649±669, 2000.

Outwater, Alice. *Water: A Natural History*. New York, NY: Basic Books, 1996.

Pacioni, Giovanni. *Simon & Schuster's Guide to Mushrooms*. New York, London and Toronto: 1981.

Palmer, E. Laurence. *Fieldbook of Natural History*. New York: McGraw-Hill Book Company, 1971.

Palmer, E. Laurence. *The Nature Almanac*. American Nature Association. Philadelphia: J. P. Lippincott Co., 1927.

"Plants and Animals, Partners in Pollination." Smithsonian Education. 2010. Web.

Park, Ed. *The World of the* Otter. Philadelphia and New York: J.B. Lippincott Co., 1971.

Parker, Gerry. *Eastern Coyote: The Story of Its Success*. Halifax, N. S.: Nimbus Publishing Ltd, 1995.

Parmasan, Camille. "Influences of species, latitudes and methodologies on estimates of phenological response to global warming." *Change Biology*. Volume 13, Issue 9, pp. 1860–1872, 2008. National Climatic Data Center.

Pasquier, Roger. *Watching Birds: An Introduction to Ornithology*. Boston: Houghton Mifflin Harcourt, 1977.

Patent, Dorothy. *Spider Magic*. New York: Holiday House, 1982.

Peattie, Donald Culross. *A Natural History of Trees*. New York, NY: Bonanza Books, 1963.

Peng, X-J., Tso, I-M, S.-Q. "Five New and Four Newly Recorded Species of Jumping Spiders from Taiwan (Araneae: Salticidae)." *Zoological Studies*. 41(1): 1-12, 2002.

Peterson, Lee. *A Field Guide to Edible Wild Plants*. Peterson Field Guide Series. Boston: Houghton Mifflin Harcourt, 1978.

Peterson, Roger and Marie. *A Field Guide to the Birds of Eastern and Central North America*. Boston, New York: Houghton Mifflin Harcourt, 2002.

Peterson, Roger Tory and McKenny. *A Field Guide to Wildflowers*. Peterson Field Guide Series. Boston: Houghton Mifflin Company, 1968.

Petokas, P.J., and M.M. Alexander. "The nesting of Chelydra serpentine in northern New York." *J. Herp.* 14(3):239-244, 1980.

Petrides, George. *A Field Guide to Trees and Shrubs*. Peterson Field Guide Series. Boston: Houghton Mifflin Harcourt, 1958.

Pettingill, O. Sewell. *Ornithology in Laboratory and Field*. Minneapolis: Burgess Publishing Co., 1970.

Phillips, Roger. *Mushrooms and Other Fungi of North America*. Buffalo, NY: Firefly Books Ltd., 2005.

Pivnik, K. and McNeil, J. "Puddling in butterflies: sodium affects reproductive success in *Thymelicus lineola*." *Physiological Entomology* 12(4): 461–472, 1987.

"Pollination Ecology in the Classroom." Yale-New Haven Teachers Institute. 2010. Web.

Porter, George. *The World of the Frog and the Toad*. Philadelphia and New York: J.B.Lippincott Co., 1967.

Powell, Roger. *The Fisher—Life History, Ecology and Behavior*. Minneapolis and London: University of Minnesota Press, 1993.

Prance, Ghillean. *Wildflowers for All Seasons*. New York: Crown Publishers, Inc., 1989.

Proctor, Noble S.; Lynch, Patrick J. *Manual of Ornithology—Avian Structure & Function*. New Haven and London: Yale University Press, 1993.

Project FeederWatch—Cornell Laboratory of Ornithology. 2009. Web.

Projects of the University of Minnesota Monarch Lab. University of Minnesota. 2008. Web. August 2008.

Pyle, Robert. *Handbook for Butterfly Watchers*. Houghton Mifflin Harcourt, 1992.

Rea, Ba; Oberhauser, Karen; Quinn, Micael. *Milkweed, Monarchs and More—A Field Guide to the Invertebrate Community in the Milkweed Patch*. Glenshaw, Pennsylvania: Bas Relief Publishing Group, 2003.

Reid, Fiona. *Peterson Field Guide to Mammals of North America: Fourth Edition*. Peterson Field Guide Series. Boston: Houghton Mifflin Harcourt, 2006.

Rezendes, Paul. *Tracking & the Art of Seeing: How to Read Animal Tracks and Sign*. New York, NY: HarperCollins Publishers, Inc., 1999.

Rezendes, Paul; Roy, Paulette. *Wetlands—The Web of Life*. Burlington, VT: Verve Editions, 1996.

Rickett, Harold. *Wildflowers of the United States*, Volume 1 and 2. New York: McGraw-Hill Book Co., (The New York Botanical Garden), 1966.

Rinehart, Kurt. *Naturalist's Guide to Observing Nature.* Mechanicsburg, Pennsylvania: Stackpole Books, 2006.

Robbins, Chandler; Bruun, Bertel and Zim, Herbert. *Birds of North America—A Guide to Field Identificaton.* New York: Golden Press. 1966

Roberts, June. *Season of Promise: Wild Plants in Winter, Northeastern United States.* Athens, OH: Ohio University Press, 1993.

Roever, J.M. *Snake Secrets.* New York: Walker & Co., 1979.

Rogers, Walter. *Tree Flowers of Forest, Park and Street.* New York: Dover Publications, Inc., 1965.

Roze, Uldis. *The North American Porcupine.* Washington, D.C. and London: Smithsonian Institution Press, 1989.

Rue, Leonard Lee. *Game Birds of North America.* New York, Evanston, San Francisco, London: Harper and Row, 1973.

Rue, Leonard Lee. *The World of the Beaver.* Philadelphia and New York: J.B. Lippincott Co., 1964.

Rue, Leonard Lee. *The World of the Raccoon.* Philadelphia and New York: J.B. Lippincott Co., 1964.

Rue, Leonard Lee. *The World of the Red Fox.* Philadelphia and New York: J.B. Lippincott Co., 1969.

Rue, Leonard Lee. *The World of the Red Fox.* Philadelphia and New York: J.B.Lippincott Company, 1969.

Rue, Leonard Lee. *The World of the White-tailed Deer.* Philadelphia and New York: J.B. Lippincott Co., 1962.

Rue, Leonard Lee. *Game Birds of North America.* New York Evanston, San Francisco, London: Harper & Row, 1973.

Russell, Franklin. *Watchers at the Pond.* New York: Alfred A. Knopf, 1973.

Russell, Helen. *Winter Search Party.* New York & Camden: Thomas Nelson, Inc., 1971.

Russell, Sharman. *An Obsession with Butterflies.* Cambridge, Massachusetts: Perseus Publishing, 2003.

Ryden, Hope. *Lily Pond.* New York: Lyons and Burford, Publishers, 1997.

Sanders, Jack. *The Secrets of Wildflowers.* Guilford, Connecticut: The Globe Pequot Press, 2003.

Schneider, J., Roos, J., Lubin, Y. and Henschel, J. "Dispersal of *Stegodyphus dumicola* (Araneae, Eresidae): They do balloon after all!" *The Journal of Arachnology.* **29**: 114–116, 2001.

Schnieper, Claudia. *Amazing Spiders.* Minneapolis: Carolrhoda Books, Inc., 1989.

Schorre, Barth. *The Warblers.* Austin, Texas: University of Texas Press, 1998.

Schwartz, Randall. *Carnivorous Plants.* New York: Avon Books, 1975.

Scott, James. *The Butterflies of North America.* Stanford, California: Stanford University Press, 1986.

Scott, Virgil et al. "Cavity-Nesting Birds of North American Forests." *Agriculture Handbook.* No. 511. Washington, D.C.: Forest Service, U.S. Dept. of Agriculture, 1977.

Searfoss, Glenn. *Skulls and Bones: A Guide to the Skeletal Structures and Behavior of North American Mammals.* Mechanicsburg, PA: Stackpole Books, 1995.

Selsan, Millicent. *Bulbs, Corms and Such.* New York: William Morrow and Co., 1974.

Serrao, John. *Nature's Events: A Notebook of the Unfolding Seasons.* Harrisburg, PA: Stackpole Books, 1992.

Shedd, Warner. *Owls Aren't Wise & Bats Aren't Blind.* New York, NY: Three Rivers Press, 2000.

Sheldon, Ian; Hartson, Tamara; Elbroch, Mark. *Animal Tracks of New England.* Renton, Washington and Edmonton, California: Lone Pine Publishing, 2000.

Sibley, David. *Birding Basics.* New York: Alfred A. Knopf, 2002.

Sibley, David. *The Sibley Guide to Birds.* (National Audubon Society) New York, NY: Alfred A. Knopf, 2000.

Sibley, David. *Sibley Guide to Bird Life and Behavior.* (National Audubon Society) New York, NY: Alfred A. Knopf, 2001.

Siegler, Hilbert. *New Hampshire Nature News.* Orford, New Hampshire: Equity Publishing Corporation, 1962.

Silver, Helenette. *A History of New Hampshire Game and Furbearers.* Concord, New Hampshire: New Hampshire Fish and Game Dept., Survey Report No. 6, 1957.

Smith, Helen. *Winter Wildflowers.* Michigan Botanical Club, Inc., 1973.

Smith, Hobart. *Amphibians of North America.* Racine, Wisconsin: Western Publishing Co., Inc., 1978.

Smith, Howard. *A Naturalist's Guide to the Year.* New York: E.P.Dutton, iInc., 1985.

Smith, Richard. *Animal Tracks and Signs of North American.* Harrisburg, Pennsylvania: Stackpole Books, 1982.

Snedigar, Robert. *Our Small Native Animals: Their Habits and Care.* New York: Dover Publications, Inc., 1963.

Sprunt, Alexander. *North American Birds of Prey.* New York: Harper and Brothers, National Audubon Society, 1955.

Stager, Curt. *Field Notes from the Northern Forest.* Syracuse: Syracuse University Press, 1998.

Stewart, P. A. "Migration of Blue Jays in eastern North America." *N. Am. Bird Bander.* 7: 107–112, 1982.

Stokes, Donald and Lillian. *A Guide to Animal Tracking and Behavior.* Boston and Toronto: Little, Brown and Co., 1986.

Stokes, Donald and Lillian. *A Guide to Bird Behavior, Volumes 1, 11, 111.* Boston, New York, Toronto, London: Little Brown and Co., 1979, 1983, 1989.

Stokes, Donald and Lillian. *Bird Gardening Book*. Boston, New York, Toronto: Little, Brown and Co., 1998.

Stokes, Donald and Lillian. *Complete Birdhouse Book*. Boston, New York, Toronto: Little, Brown and Co., 1990.

Stokes, Donald and Lillian. *The Birdfeeder Book*. Boston, New York, Toronto: Little, Brown and Co., 1987.

Stokes, Donald and Lillian. *The Bluebird Book*. Boston, New York, Toronto: Little, Brown and Co., 1991.

Stokes, Donald and Lillian. *Stokes Field Guide to Warblers*. Boston, New York, London: Little, Brown and Co., 2004.

Stokes, Donald and Lillian; Williams, Ernest. *The Butterfly Book*. An Easy Guide to Butterfly Gardening, Identification and Behavior. Boston, New York, Toronto, London: Little, Brown and Co., 1991.

Stokes, Donald. *A Guide to Nature in Winter*. Boston and Toronto: Little, Brown and Company, 1976

Stokes, Donald W. *A Guide to Observing Insect Lives*. Stokes Nature Guides. Boston and Toronto: Little, Brown and Company, 1983.

Stokes, Donald. *The Natural History of Wild Shrubs and Vines*. New York: Harper and Row, Publishers, 1981.

Swan, Lester; Papp, Charles. *The Common Insects of North America*. New York, Evanston, San Francisco and London: Harper and Row, Publishers.

Symonds, George. *The Tree Identification Book*. New York: William Morrow & Company, Inc., 1958.

Symonds, George. *The Shrub Identification Book*. New York: William Morrow & Company, Inc., 1963.

Tallamy, Douglas. *Bringing Nature Home—How Native Plants Sustain Wildlife in Our Gardens*. Portland, Oregon and London: Timber Press, Inc. 2007.

Tate, J., Jr. "Methods and annual sequence of foraging by the sapsucker." *The Auk*. 90: 840–856, 1973.

Taylor, G. *The Amphibians and Reptiles of New Hampshire*. Concord, NH: New Hampshire Fish and Game Department, 1993.

Taylor, James; Lee, Thomas; McCarthy, Laura. Ed. *New Hampshire's Living Legacy—The Biodiversity of the Granite State*. New Hampshire Fish and Game Dept., Nongame and Endangered Wildlife Program, 1996.

Terres, John K. *The Audubon Society Encyclopedia of North American Birds*. New York, NY: Alfred A. Knopf, Inc., 1980.

The Burroughs Nature Club. *The Burroughs Nature Club Course of Study*. Boston and New York: Houghton Mifflin Harcourt, 1917.

Thomas, William. *Field Book of Common Mushrooms*. New York & London: G.P.Putnam's Sons, 1928.

Thompson, Bill, et al. *Identify Yourself*. Boston and New York: Houghton Mifflin Harcourt, 2005.

Thompson, Elizabeth; Sorenson, Eric. *Wetland, Woodland, Wildland—A Guide to the Natural Communities of Vermont*. Vermont Dept. of Fish and Wildlife and the Nature Conservancy, 2000.

Tudge, Colin. *The Tree*. New York: Crown Publishers, 2005.

Tuttle, Merlin D. *America's Neighborhood Bats*. Austin, TX: University of Texas Press, 1988.

Tyning, Tom. *A Guide to Amphibians and Reptiles—Stokes Nature Guides*. Boston, Toronto, London: Little, Brown and Company, 1990.

Ubick, D.; Paquin, P.; Cusing, P.E. and Roth, V. Ed. *Spiders of North America: An Identification Manual*. American Arachnological Society, 2005.

University of Michigan Herbarium. Web.

Urquhart, Fred. *The Monarch Butterfly: International Traveler*. Chicago: Nelson-Hall, 1987.

US Dept. of Agriculture. "Cavity-Nesting Birds of North American Forests." *Agriculture Handbook*. No. 511, 1977.

US Dept. of Agriculture. *Common Weeds of the United States*. Agricultural Research Service. New York: Dover Publications, 1971.

USDA Natural Resources Conservation Service—Plants Profile: *Echinocystis lobata*. 2010. Web.

Uva, Richard; Neal, Joseph; DiTomaso, Joseph. *Weeds of the Northeast*. Ithaca and London: Cornell University Press, 1997

Van Wormer, Joe. *The World of the Black Bear*. Philadelphia and New York: J.B. Lippincott Co., 1966.

Van Wormer, Joe. *The World of the Bobcat*. Philadelphia and New York: J.B.Lippincott, 1964.

Van Wormer, Joe. *The World of the Coyote*. Philadelphia and New York: J.B. Lippincott Co., 1964.

Veit, Richard and Petersen, Wayne. *Birds of Massachusetts*. Massachusetts: Massachusetts Audubon Society, 1993.

Vermont Institute of Natural Science. *Vermont Daily Field Card*, 2002.

The Vermont Reptile and Amphibian Atlas. 2005. Web.

Von Frisch, Karl. *Animal Architecture*. New York and London: Harcourt Brace Jovanovich, Inc., 1974.

Von Frisch, Karl. *The Dancing Bees—An Account of the Life and Senses of the Honey Bee*. New York and London: Harcourt Brace Jovanovich, 1953.

Voshell, J. Reese. *A Guide to Common Freshwater Invertebrates of North America*. Blacksburg, Virginia: The McDonald & Woodward Publishing Company, 2002.

Vuilleumier, Francois, ed. *Birds of North America* (American Museum of Natural History). DK Publishing, 2003.

Wagner, David. *Caterpillars of Eastern North America*. Princeton and Oxford: Princeton University Press, 2005.

Wagner, David; Giles, Valene; Reardon, Richard; McManus, Michael. *Caterpillars of Eastern Forests*. Morgantown, West Virginia: Forest Health Technology Enterprise Team, USDA, FHTET-96034, November, 1997.

Waldbauer, Gilbert. *A Walk Around the Pond: Insects In and Over the Water*. Cambridge, Massachusetts and London: Harvard University Press, 2006.

Walker, Lewis. *The Book of Owls*. New York: Alfred A. Knopf, 1974.

Walters, Michael. *Birds' Eggs*. Eyewitness Handbooks. London, New York, Stuttgart: Dorling Kindersley, 1994.

Watts, May and Tom. *Winter Tree Finder: A Manual for Identifying Deciduous Trees in Winter*. (Nature Study Guides) Berkeley, CA: Nature Study Guild Publishers, 1970.

Watts, May. *Tree Finder: A Manual for the Identification of Trees by Their Leaves* (Nature Study Guides) Berkeley, CA: Nature Study Guild Publishers, 1963.

Weeks, Harmon P. Jr. 1989. "Mast Importance, Production, and Management. " In: Clark, F. Bryan, tech. ed.; Hutchinson, Jay G., ed. Central Hardwood Notes. St. Paul, MN: U.S. Department of Agriculture, Forest Service, North Central Forest Experiment Station.: Note 9.12.

Wells, Diana. *100 Flowers and How They Got Their Names*. Chapel Hill, NC: Algonquin Books of Chapel Hill, 1997.

Wells, Kentwood. *The Ecology and Behavior of Amphibians*. Chicago: University of Chicago Press, 2007.

Wessels, Tom. *Reading the Forested Landscape: A Natural History of New England*. Woodstock, VT: The Countryman Press, 2005.

Western Hemisphere Shorebird Reserve Network. 2009. Web.

Wheeler, Brian. *Raptors of Eastern North America*. Princeton, New Jersey. Princeton University Press, 2003.

Wherry, Edgar. *The Fern Guide*. Doubleday & Co., Inc., 1961.

Whitaker, John O. Jr. and Hamilton, William J. Jr. *Mammals of the Eastern United States*. Ithaca: Cornell University Press, 1998.

Whitfield, Philip. *The Hunters*. New York: Simon & Schuster, 1978.

Wildlife Management Institute. *Ecology and Management of the North American Moose*. Washington, D.C., 1997.

Wildman, Edward. *This Week Out of Doors—A Nature Calendar*. Narbeth, Pennsylvania: Livingston Publishing Co., 1955.

Williams, Ernest. *The Nature Handbook*. Oxford, New York: Oxford University Press, 2005.

Wilson, Don. *Bats In Question*. The Smithsonian Answer Book. Washington and London: Smithsonian Institution Press, 1997.

Wilson, Lars. *My Beaver Colony*. Garden City, New York: Doubleday and Co., Inc., 1964.

"Winter Shrub and Tree Identification." 2000. Web. Ontario trees and shrubs.

Wishner, Lawrence. *Eastern Chipmunks: Secrets of Their Solitary Lives*. Washington, D.C.: Smithsonian Institution Press, 1982.

Wolniewicz, Richard. *Field Guide to Skulls and Bones of Mammals of the Northeastern United States. Vol. 1 and 2*. Magnolia, Massachusetts: Richard Wolniewicz, 2001.

Zimmer, Carl. *New York Times*, Science Times, "Blink Twice If You Like Me," 6/30/2009.

Zomlefer, Wendy. *Flowering Plant Families*. London and Chapel Hill: The University of North Carolina Press, 1994.

Red fox kits.

For species discussed extensively, page numbers in *italics* indicate representative illustrations.

Left: Black-and-yellow argiope.

Fruit
    in bird diet, 25
    defined, 398
    seed dispersal and, 301, 302
    baneberry, 246
    basswood, 208
    blackberry, 208–209
    bunchberry, 136, 174, 246
    common winterberry, 410
    false Solomon's seal, 246
    flowers and, 15
    gray birch, 248
    high-bush cranberry, 247
    honeysuckle, 199
    Indian cucumber root, 133–134
    partridgeberry, 172
    raspberries, 135
    shadbush, 51
    Virginia creeper, 247
    virgin's bower, 248
    wintergreen, 173
    witch hazel, 299
    See also Mast
Fungi
    consumers of, 422
    lists of, 280–281, 438–440
    mycorrhizal, 231, 296
    plant symbiosis, 150, 208, 295–297
    in tree disease, 423–424
    White Nose Syndrome and, 178–179
    See also Lichens; Mushrooms
Fur. See Hair coat

Gadwall, 6
Gall gnat, 410
Galls
    about, 155–156
    burls and, 373
    goldenrod ball, 261–263
    hosts of, 244
    on jewelweed, 265
    orange cedar rust, 90
Gartersnake. See Common gartersnake
Gender determination
    green frog, 116
    Jack-in-the-pulpit, 112–113
    snapping turtle, 140
    See also Sexual dimorphism
Genetically engineered plants, 192
Geomyces destructans, 179
Giant goldenrod, 261–262
Giant predacious diving beetle, 277
Gilled agaric, 281

Girdling, of trees, 217, 426–427
Gizzards, of birds, 333, 345
Glands, 84, 185. See also Scent marking
Gliding, by flying squirrels, 127. See also
    Soaring, by birds
Global warming, effects of, xvii–xix, 9, 82,
    255, 264–265, 334
Glowworms, 131, 185–186, 187
Glucose, 344
Glycerol production, 262–263, 364,
    425–426
Goldenrod ball gall, 261–263
Goldenrod crab spider, 189–190, 244
Goldenrod gall ball, 422
Goldenrod gall fly, 262–263, 277
Goldfinch. See American goldfinch
Goldthread, 91
Goshawk, 238, 345
Grackle. See Common grackle
Grains, 174, 215
Grape aphid, 156
Grape fern, 279
Grasses, 172, 174
Grasshoppers, 169, 226–227, 242, 277,
    395, 396
Gray birch, 50, 248, 427
Gray catbird, 123, 319
Gray fox, 13, 13, 309, 338, 355, 382
Gray jay, 6
Gray squirrel, 309, 338, 357, 385, 409
Gray treefrog
    call, 37, 117
    cryptic coloration, 327
    eggs, 118
    hibernation, 364
    tadpoles, 196
    winter adaptations, 344
Great Backyard Bird Count, 348
Great blue heron, 199
    fledglings, 199
    migration, 6
    nesting/young of, 75–76, 125, 126
    scat, 306
    tracks, 199
Great crested flycatcher, 81, 81, 313, 320
Great golden digger wasp, 171
Great gray owl, 348, 367
Great horned owl, 403
    call of, 404
    diet, 345, 349–350, 413
    nesting/young of, 81, 126, 313, 320,
        321, 403
    range, 367

Great spangled fritillary butterfly, 194, 277
Greater yellow lady's slipper, 89–90, 92,
    150–151
Greater yellowlegs, 198
Green frog, 37, 116, 116, 118, 196
Green heron, 200
Green-winged teal, 6
Ground cricket, 226
Group chorus, of coyotes, 201–202
Grouse. See Ruffed grouse
A Guide to Amphibians and Reptiles
    (Tyning), 118, 196
Gymnosperms, 15, 360
Gypsy moth, 277

Habitat loss, effects of, 225, 271
Hackmatack, 278–279, 282
Hag moth caterpillar, 183
Hair coat
    insulating properties, 292, 356, 395,
        417
    porcupine adaptations, 349
    seasonal color changes, 290–291,
        309, 323, 417, 419
Hairstreak butterfly, 49
Hairy woodpecker, 81
    drumming, 403
    habitat, 313
    nesting/young of, 42–43, 81, 161
    winter adaptations, 333
Hairy-tailed mole, 380, 381
Halloween ladybug, 292–293
Hand-feeding, of birds, 413–414
Hares, 352–354, 357, 422. See also
    Snowshoe hare
Harrier, Northern, 6
Harrison, Hal, 320
Harvestmen, 242, 409
Hatching muscle, 77
Hawk moths, 49, 129, 206–207, 277
Hawks. See Raptors
Hawk-watch sites, 238, 251
Hay-scented fern, 279
Headstream, Richard, 320
Hearing
    in crickets, 226, 227
    in mammals, 275
    See also Sound
Heartwood, 428
Hedgehog caterpillar. See Woolly bear
    caterpillar
Hellgrammites, 87, 167
Hemlock, 173

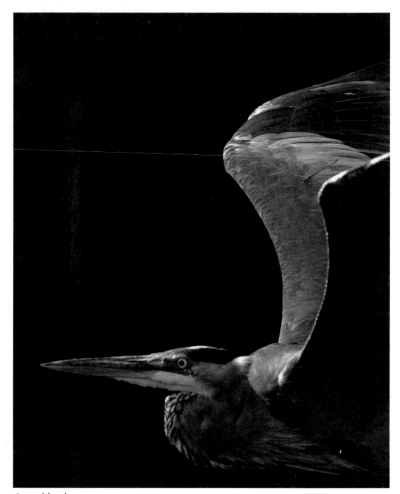

Great blue heron.

A common loon chick swallows dinner.